GREEK THINKERS

GREEK THINKERS

A HISTORY OF ANCIENT PHILOSOPHY

By THEODOR GOMPERZ

PROFESSOR AT THE UNIVERSITY OF VIENNA, AND MEMBER OF
THE IMPERIAL ACADEMY; HON. LL.D., DUBLIN;
HON. PH.D., KÖNIGSBERG

AUTHORIZED EDITION

VOLUME I

TRANSLATED BY

LAURIE MAGNUS, M.A.

MAGDALEN COLLEGE, OXFORD

LONDON
JOHN MURRAY, ALBEMARLE STREET, W.

First Edition   . .   *January; 1901*
Reprinted . . . . . *March, 1906*
Reprinted . . . . . *April, 1920*
Reprinted . . . . . *April, 1939*
Reprinted . . . . *January, 1949*

PRINTED IN GREAT BRITAIN BY
WILLIAM CLOWES AND SONS LIMITED, LONDON AND BECCLES

To the

MEMORY OF HIS MOTHER

DEC. 19, 1792 : APRIL 30, 1881

THE AUTHOR

DEDICATES THIS VOLUME

TRANSLATOR'S PREFACE.

THE present version of the first volume of *Griechische Denker* has been rendered directly from the German edition of 1896, published by Veit & Company of Leipsic, which was placed in my hands in June, 1899. In the later stages of my work I have incurred a considerable obligation to the author, whose masterly knowledge of English has helped to purge the proof-sheets of my translation from the errors into which I had been betrayed. The confidence with which I now present it to English readers is largely due to the fact that every doubtful point has been thoroughly discussed in proof and revise between Professor Gomperz and myself. In no single instance has he failed to make his meaning clear to me, and I must take the sole responsibility for any errors that may remain. I welcome this opportunity, too, of expressing my cordial thanks to Frau Professor Gomperz, whose interest in the book and complete command of its subject have been of the utmost service to me throughout the course of my labours.

It would be a work of supererogation on my part, though it would add considerably to my pleasure, to introduce this book to English scholars ; but I may at least express the hope that I have not been entirely unsuccessful in conveying in the English language something of the brilliance and charm of style which the author's German readers recognize and admire in his own. In many of the passages quoted by Professor Gomperz from Plato and Thucydides I have availed myself of the renderings by the late Dr. Jowett, now the property of Balliol College, Oxford, and I am glad to acknowledge the benefit which my work has derived from them.

The second volume of " Greek Thinkers," dealing mainly with Socrates and Plato, will, it is hoped, be published in the course of this year ; and since, to my regret, I am not at leisure to continue the work myself, steps have already been taken to find a competent translator. The third volume of the German edition will include the author's indexes, but I have thought it advisable to supply the present instalment of the work with a provisional index of subjects and names. I should add that, in translating the notes and additions to this volume, I have, with the author's sanction, introduced sundry technical changes, chiefly in reference to English books or to foreign works in English editions. In the instance of Zeller's *Philosophie der Griechen*, I have made an exception to this practice. Professor Gomperz quotes uniformly from the last German edition of that work, which has been considerably modified and enlarged since the English rendering was effected.

L. M.

LONDON,
    Jan. 1, 1901.

AUTHOR'S PREFACE.

— ◦✦◦ —

MY design in the present undertaking is to compose a comprehensive picture of the department of knowledge in which, during several decades past, I have been at pains to increase the material and to sift the problems. The work, which summarizes the labours of a lifetime, will be complete in three volumes, and will, it is hoped, be accessible to wide circles of cultivated readers. The point of view from which I have written is not that of any one-sided and exclusive school. I endeavour to do equal justice to the different tendencies of ancient thought, every one of which has contributed its part to the complete structure of modern intellectual civilization, to consider them all impartially, and to judge them fairly. The historical relief in which the narrative is set will not be unduly contracted, and its subjective features will be confined to emphasizing what is essential as sharply as possible, and to sundering as thoroughly as possible what is enduring and significant from what is indifferent and transient. Portions of the story of religion, of literature, and of the special sciences, indispensable to an understanding of the speculative movement, its causes and effects, will be incorporated in the work. The boundaries dividing these provinces appear to me in all cases to be floating. The ideal I have in view could only completely be realized in an exhaustive universal history of the mind of antiquity. When so monumental an undertaking has been successfully effected I shall be the first to admit that the present far more modest attempt is superseded and antiquated.

The second volume and the third or concluding volume will comprise the remaining six books, entitled respectively, (4) "Socrates and the Socratics," (5) "Plato and the Academy," (6) "Aristotle and his Successors," (7) "The Older Stoa," (8) "The Garden of Epicurus," and (9) "Mystics, Sceptics, and Syncretists." In order not unduly to increase the compass of the work, the evidence of authorities has had to be reduced to the smallest dimensions, and, with regard to references to the later literature of the subject, economy has had to be practised in all cases excepting those where my own exposition may claim the greatest originality and those, again, where it can claim the least. In the latter instance the obligation has arisen of acknowledging my close dependence on predecessors, and, in the former, of advancing grounds for my radical divergence from traditional views.

Finally, I may be permitted, not to palliate, but to apologize for, the shortcomings of my work in the phrase employed in a letter of Gustave Flaubert to Georges Sand: "Je fais tout ce que je peux continuellement pour élargir ma cervelle, et je travaille dans la sincérité de mon cœur; le reste ne dépend pas de moi."

TH. GOMPERZ.

VIENNA.

CONTENTS.

BOOK I.

THE BEGINNINGS.

INTRODUCTION.

CHAPTER I.

OLD IONIAN NATURE-PHILOSOPHERS.

CHAPTER II.

ORPHIC SYSTEMS OF COSMOGONY.

CHAPTER III

PYTHAGORAS AND HIS DISCIPLES.

CHAPTER IV.

THE DEVELOPMENT OF THE PYTHAGOREAN DOCTRINE.

CHAPTER V.

ORPHIC AND PYTHAGOREAN DOCTRINES OF THE SOUL.

BOOK II.

FROM METAPHYSICS TO POSITIVE SCIENCE.

CHAPTER I.

XENOPHANES

CHAPTER II.

PARMENIDES.

CHAPTER III.

THE DISCIPLES OF PARMENIDES.

CHAPTER IV.

ANAXAGORAS.

CHAPTER V.

EMPEDOCLES.

CHAPTER VI.

THE HISTORIANS.

BOOK III.

THE AGE OF ENLIGHTENMENT.

CHAPTER I.

THE PHYSICIANS.

CONTENTS.

CHAPTER II.

THE ATOMISTS.

CHAPTER III.

THE ECLECTIC PHILOSOPHERS OF NATURE.

CHAPTER IV.

THE BEGINNINGS OF MENTAL AND MORAL SCIENCE.

CHAPTER V.

THE SOPHISTS.

CHAPTER VI.

PROTAGORAS OF ABDERA.

CHAPTER VII.

GORGIAS OF LEONTINI.

CHAPTER VIII.

THE ADVANCE OF HISTORICAL SCIENCE.

BOOK I.

THE BEGINNINGS.

" To one small people . . . it was given to create the principle of Progress. That people was the Greek. Except the blind forces of Nature, nothing moves in this world which is not Greek in its origin."—SIR HENRY SUMNER MAINE.

GREEK THINKERS.

INTRODUCTION.

ALL beginnings are obscure, whether owing to their minuteness or their apparent insignificance. Where they do not escape perception, they are liable to elude observation. The sources of history, too, can only be tracked at a foot-pace. They must be followed to their fount, like the current of a stream which springs in a mountain fastness. Such steps or paces are called inferences. They are of two kinds, according as they proceed from causes or from effects. In the second case, we try to infer the existence and the nature of causes from the existence and the nature of effects. Inferences of that type are indispensable, but frequently fallacious. For though every cause, taken by itself, produces the same invariable effect, yet the converse proposition does not by any means hold good. Each effect is not invariably the product of one and the same cause. The condition known as "plurality of causes" plays an important part in the intellectual no less than in the physical universe. The contrary process yields more trustworthy results. It starts from the causes, from the series of great and tangible factors, plainly manifest or readily to be found, which must have influenced the events to be accounted for, and in which the degree of such influence is the sole object of doubt. In the present instance, where we are dealing with the higher intellectual life of a nation, the first place is claimed by its geographical conditions and the peculiar character of its homes.

Hellas is a sea-girt mountain-land. The poverty of her soil corresponds to the narrowness of her river-valleys. And here we find the first clue to some of the essential features of Hellenic evolution proper. It is clear, for instance, that a permanent home and a steady and manifold care and attention were offered to any seeds of civilization which might be deposited in her soil. Her mountain-barriers served her in the office of stone walls, breaking the force of the storm of conquest which sweeps unchecked across the plains. Each hilly canton was a potential seat of culture. Each could develop a separate type of that strongly marked individualism, which was ultimately to prove so favourable to the rich and many-sided civilization of Greece, so fatal to the political concentration of her powers. The country was full of piquant contrasts. Her Arcadia—an inland canton, sunk in torpid provincialism—vas matched at the opposite extreme by the extent and curvature of the coast. Her sea-board was larger than Spain's, her mainland smaller than Portugal's. Other conditions, too, fostered this variety of natural gifts. The most diverse trades and professions were practised in the closest proximity. Seamen and shepherds, hunters and husbandmen, flourished side by side, and the fusion of their families produced in ater generations a sum of talents and aptitudes complementary to each other. Again, the good fairies who presided at the birth of Greece could have laid no more salutary blessing in her cradle than the "poverty which was ever her familiar friend." It worked powerfully in three ways for the advancement of her civilization. It acted as a spur to compel her to exert all her powers ; it served as a further defence against invasion, for the comparatively poor country must have seemed but indifferent booty—a fact noted in connection with Attica by the most philosophical historian of antiquity ; and last, and chiefly, it lent a forcible impulse to commerce, navigation, emigration, and the foundation of colonies.

The bays that offer the best harbourage on the Greek

peninsula open towards the east, and the islands and islets, with which that region is thickly sown, afford, as it were, a series of stepping-stones to the ancient seats of Asiatic civilization. Greece may be said to look east and south. Her back is turned to the north and west, with their semi-barbaric conditions. Another circumstance of quite exceptional good fortune may be ranged with these natural advantages. There was Greece in her infancy on the one side, and the immemorial civilizations on the other: who was to ply between them? The link was found—as it were by deliberate selection—in those hardy adventurers of the sea, the merchant-people of Phœnicia, a nation politically of no account, but full of daring and eager for gain. Thus it happened that the Greeks acquired the elements of culture from Babylon and Egypt without paying the forfeit of independence. The benefits of this ordinance are obvious. The favoured country enjoyed a steadier rate of progress, a more unbroken evolution, a comparative immunity from the sacrifice of her national resources. And if further proof be required, take the fate of the Celts and Germans, whom Rome enslaved at the moment that she civilized; or take the sad lot of the savage tribes of to-day, who receive the blessing of civilization at the hands of almighty Europe, and wear it too often as a curse.

Still, the determining influence in the intellectual life of Greece must be sought in her colonial system. Colonies were founded at all times, and under every form of government. The Monarchy, a period of perpetual conflict, frequently witnessed the spectacle of settled inhabitants giving way to immigrating tribes, and seeking a new home beyond the seas. The Oligarchy, which rested entirely on the permanent alliance between noble birth and territorial possession, was often constrained to expel the "pauvre gentilhomme," the type and symbol of disorder, and to furnish him with fresh estates in foreign parts, whither he would speedily be followed by further victims of the incessant party strife Meantime, the growth of the maritime trade of Greece, the flourishing condition of her industries, and her increasing population, soon made it necessary to establish fixed commercial stations, an uninterrupted supply of raw material, and safe channels for the importation of food. The same outlets were utilized, chiefly under the Democracy, to relieve the indigent poor and to draft off the surplus population. Thus, at an early period, there arose that vast circle of Greek plantations which stretched from the homes of the Cossacks on the Don to the oases of the Sahara, and from the eastern shore of the Black Sea to the coast-line of Spain. Great Greece and Greater Greece,—if the first name belong to the Hellenic portion of Southern Italy, the second might well be given to the sum of these settlements outside. The mere number and diversity of the colonies practically ensured the prospect that any seeds of civilization would happen on suitable soil, and this prospect was widened and brightened to an incalculable degree by the nature of the settlements and the manner of their foundation. Their sites were selected at those points of the coast which offered the best facilities for successful commercial enterprise. The emigrants themselves were chiefly young men of a hardy and courageous disposition, who would bequeath their superior qualities to their numerous issue. Men of duller parts, who lived by rule and rote, were not likely to turn their backs on their homes except under stress of necessity. Again, though a single city-state took the lead in the foundation of each colony, it would frequently be reinforced by a considerable foreign contingent, and this cross-breeding of Hellenic tribes would be further extended by an admixture of non-Hellenic blood, owing to the preponderance of the men over the women among the original emigrants. Thus, every colony served the purpose of experiment. Greek and non-Greek racial elements were mixed in varying proportions, and the test was applied to their resulting powers of resistance and endurance. Local customs, tribal superstitions, and national prejudices swiftly disappeared before the better sense of the settlers. Contact with foreign civilizations, however imperfectly developed, could not but enlarge their mental horizon to a very appreciable degree. The average of capacity rose by leaps and bounds, and the average of intellect was heightened by its constant engagement in new and difficult tasks. Merit counted for more than descent. A man there was a man; good work could command a good wage, and poor work meant a hard bed and indifferent protection. The whole system of economic, political, and social life cried out to be reorganized and reformed, and in these circumstances the force of mere tradition and the reign of unintelligent routine were involved in rapid decline. True, some of the settlements succumbed to the attacks of hostile residents; others, again, were so far outnumbered by the natives that their individuality was gradually absorbed. But from first to last the communication of the colonies with their mother-city and mother-country—a communication fostered by religious ties and frequently strengthened by later arrivals —was sufficiently intimate to preserve in all its parts the reciprocal benefits which proved so eminently fruitful. Greece found in her colonies the great playground of her intellect. There she proved her talents in every variety of circumstances, and there she was able to train them to the height of their latent powers. Her colonial life retained for centuries its fresh and buoyant spirit. The daughter-cities in most respects outstripped their mother in the race. To them can be traced nearly all the great innovations, and the time was to come when they would steep themselves in intellectual pursuits as well, when the riddles of the world and of human life were to find a permanent home and enduring curiosity in their midst.

2. There is a period in Greek history which bears a most striking resemblance to the close of our own Middle Ages, when the repetition of similar causes produced similar effects.

On the threshold of modern Europe stands the era of the great discoverers, and the geographical limits of the Greek horizon at this time were likewise wonderfully extended. On the far east and west of the world, as it was then known, the outline emerged from the mist.

Precise and definite knowledge replaced the obscurity of legend. Shortly after 800 B.C., the eastern shore of the Black Sea began to be colonized by Milesians; Sinope was founded in 785, and Trapezunt about thirty years later. Soon after the middle of the same century, Eubœa and Corinth sent out the first Greek settlers to Sicily, where Syracuse was founded in 734 B.C., and before the century's end the ambition and enterprise of Miletus had taken fast foothold at the mouths of the Nile. Three conclusions are involved in the fact of this impulse to expansion. It points to a rapid growth of population on the Greek peninsula and in the older colonies. It presumes a considerable development of Greek industry and commerce; and, finally, it serves to measure the progress in ship-building and in kindred arts. Take navigation, for instance. Where vessels formerly had hugged the shore, and had not ventured in deep waters, now they boldly crossed the sea. The mercantile marine was protected by men-of-war. Seaworthy battleships came into use with raised decks and three rows of oars, the first of them being built for the Samians in 705 B.C. Naval engagements were fought as early as 664 B.C., so that the sea acquired the utmost significance in the civilization of Hellas for the commerce of peace and war. At the same time, the progress of industry was fostered by a notable innovation. A current coinage was created. The "bullocks" of hoary antiquity and the copper "kettles" and "tripods" of a later date successively passed into desuetude, and the precious metals replaced these rougher makeshifts as measures of value and tokens of exchange. Babylonian and Egyptian merchants had long since familiarized the market with silver and gold in the form of bars and rings, and the Babylonians had even introduced the official stamp as a guarantee of standard and weight. A convenient shape was now added to the qualities of worth and durability which make gold and silver the most practical symbols of exchange, and the metals were coined for current use. This invention, borrowed from Lydia about 700 B.C. by the Phocæans of Ionia, conferred remarkable benefits on commerce. It facilitated intercourse and extended its bounds, and its effects may be compared with those of the bill of exchange, introduced in Europe by Jewish and Lombardy merchants at the close of the Middle Ages. Similar, if not greater, in effect was the change in the methods of warfare. The old exclusive service of the cavalry, which had flourished in the dearth of pastoral and corn-land as the privilege of wealthy landowners, was now reinforced by the hoplites, or heavy-armed infantry, who far exceeded the cavalry in numbers. The change was analogous—and its consequences were equal in importance —to that which enabled the armed peasantry of Switzerland to disperse the chivalry of Burgundy and Austria. New orders of the population achieved prosperity and culture, and were filled with a strong sense of self-esteem. A sturdy middle class asserted itself by the side of the old squirearchy, and bore with increasing impatience the yoke of the masterful nobles. But here, as elsewhere, the contradiction between actual conditions of strength and legal dues of prerogative became the cause of civil strife. A battle of classes broke out. It spread to the peasants, where persistent ill-usage and by no means infrequent serfdom had sown the seeds of revolt, and out of the rents and ruins of society there was hatched a brood of usurpers, who partly destroyed and partly set aside the existing order of things. They constructed in its place a form of government which, though commonly short-lived, was not without notable results. The Orthagorides, the Cypselides, the Pisistratides, a Polycrates, and many another, may be compared with the Italian tyrants of the late Middle Ages—the Medici, the Sforza, or the Visconti —precisely as the party feuds of the one epoch recall in the other the conflict between the lords and the guilds. The obscure origin and questionable title of these newly founded dynasties were discreetly veiled in the glitter of warlike undertakings, of alliances with foreign potentates, public works on a lavish scale, splendid buildings, and munificent benefactions, combined with an enhanced regard for the safety of the national sanctuaries and for the

encouragement of the fine arts. But we must look deeper for
the most lasting result of this *entr'acte* in history. It tran-
quillized party feeling ; it overthrew the rule of the nobles
without breaking the foundations of social welfare ; it
poured new wine in the old vessels, revealing unsuspected
possibilities in the extant forms of the constitution. The
"tyranny" served as a bridge to the system of democracy,
first in a moderate, and at last in its fully developed shape.

Meantime, the stream of intellectual culture found
broader and deeper channels. The ballads of the heroes,
which had been sung for centuries in the halls of Ionian
nobles to the accompaniment of the lyre, slowly fell into
desuetude. New forms of poetry began to emerge, and
with them, in some instances, the poet's personality emerged
from the material of his song. Subjective poetry came
into existence, as was bound to happen, when, as now,
men escaped in ever-increasing numbers from the groove
of hereditary conventions. The State was involved in
change and vicissitude, society was governed by uncertain
conditions, and individual life accordingly acquired a more
adventurous complexion. Men's talents would be more
sharply defined, their independent activity stimulated, their
self-reliance encouraged. In civic and party business a
man would play his own part, advising and blaming as
counsellor or critic, and boldly giving vent among his fellows
to his sentiments of expectation or disappointment, his joy,
his sorrow, his anger, and his scorn. He became a unit
in society, self-made for the most part, and entirely self-
dependent, and would deem his private concerns of
sufficient importance to display them in the light of
publicity. He poured out his heart to his fellow-citizens,
making them the arbiters in his love-suits and law-suits,
and appealing to their sympathy in the injuries he suffered,
the successes he achieved, the pleasures he enjoyed. A
new spirit, too, was breathed in the older poetical forms.
Myth and legend were refashioned by the masters of choric
song in differing, if not in contradictory, modes. The
didactic poets still aimed at system, order, and harmony
in their treatment of the material, but side by side with

those endeavours a manifold diversity was to be remarked,
and a licence in criticism, expressing itself in a prejudice
or preference in respect to this or that hero or heroine of
holy tradition. Thus, the neutral tints of the background
were ever more and more relieved by strong, self-conscious
figures standing out from the uniform mass. Habits of
free-will and feeling were created, and with them there
grew the faculty of independent thought, which was
constantly engaged and exercised in wider fields of
speculation.

3. The Greeks were naturally keen-sighted. The faithful representation of sensible objects and occurrences constitutes one of the chief charms of the Homeric poems, and
the imitation of figures and gestures by a hand that
waxed in cunning now began to succeed to the arts of
language and speech. Greece became the apprentice of
older civilized countries, turning to Egypt above all for
the paramount example of artistic instinct, natural joy, and
engaging humour. But even in the limited sphere of the
observation of men's ways and manners, fresh material
was constantly collected. As travelling grew easier, its
occasions would be multiplied. Not merely the merchant,
ever intent on new gain, but the fugitive murderer, the
exiled loser in the civil strife, the restless emigrant wandering on the face of the earth, the adventurer whose spear
was at the service of the highest bidder, who would eat
the bread of an Assyrian monarch to-day and to-morrow
would pour down his burning throat the barley-water of
Egypt, who was equally at home in the fruit-laden valley
of the Euphrates and in the sands of the Nubian desert,—
all of these would add to the sum of knowledge about
places, peoples, and mankind. The frequent meeting or
regular congregation in certain centres of Greeks of all
cities and tribes served the purpose of huge reservoirs, in
which the observations of individuals and the reports they
made to their fellow-townsmen were collected and stored.
The shrine of the oracle at Delphi was a chief example
of the first, while the second condition was fulfilled by the
recurring festivals of the Games, among which those at

Olympia held the foremost rank.   The sanctuary at Delphi, sacred to Pythian Apollo, was situated in the shadow of steep, beetling crags.   Thither would come, and there would meet, an endless line of pilgrims from all parts of Greece and her colonies—private citizens, representatives of whole states, and, since the middle of the seventh century at least, occasional envoys from foreign courts. They all came to consult the god ; but the answers they received were mostly the result of the priest's ingenious manipulation of the stock of useful knowledge deposited by former clients.   And few indeed can have departed from that romantic mountain glen without finding their imagination quickened and their experience augmented by contact with their companions on the road.   The Games which we have mentioned were celebrated in the broad river-valley of the Alpheius, and the attractiveness of that brilliant spectacle increased with each generation.   The programme was constantly extended by the inclusion of new kinds of competitions, and the spectators, who at first were drawn merely from the surrounding country, gradually began to arrive—as is shown by the winners' lists, extant since 776 B.C.—from all points in the circumference of the wide Hellenic world.   Nor would their intercourse be confined to the exchange of news and information.   Men would take one another's measure ; opinions would be freely canvassed ; the merits of the different institutions in that land of many subdivisions—their customs, habits, and beliefs—would form topics of general discussion. Comparison engendered judgment, and judgment brought reflection in its train to bear on the causes of the differences and on the permanent element in change.   It induced, that is to say, an inquiry for the common canons which obtained in the commerce and dogma of daily life. The observation of common things, growing keener and richer by experience, led to comparative discussion and estimation, and, finally, to reflective criticism.   Many a proud stream was nourished by that source.   To it we refer sententious poetry, the invention of types of human character, and the proverbial wisdom which thoughtful citizens and philosophic statesmen have sown broadcast in the world.

The art of writing, the main vehicle for the exchange of thought, helped to distribute the fresh acquisitions of knowledge. Writing, it is true, was no novelty in Greece. When we read in the Homeric poems of the intimate intercourse with Phœnicia, we readily conceive that the sharp-witted Greek would have borrowed that wonderful aid to the preservation and communication of thought from the Canaanitish dealers, for the customer must often have surprised the merchant making entries in his account-book. Nay, the art of writing would appear to have been familiar, to some of the Greeks at least, even before that date. It is no more possible that the syllabic writing on the recently discovered Cypric monuments, with its awkward and clumsy devices, could have been later than the use of the simple Semitic letters, than that the invention of the battle-axe could have followed that of the musket. All that was wanted was a convenient and easily fashioned material. The want took some time to supply. The remedy was not found till soon after 660 B.C., when Greek trade with Egypt under Psammetich I. received a notable impulse. Then a writing-material of a kind which can hardly be improved was afforded by the pulp of the papyrus shrub, split into slender and flexible strips. From city to city, from land to land, from century to century, the sheets of written symbols now began to fly. The circulation of thought was accelerated, the commerce of intellect enlarged, and the continuity of culture guaranteed, in a degree which can well-nigh be compared with that which marked the invention of the printing-press at the dawn of modern history. To the oral delivery of poems, designed to captivate the hearer, there was presently to be added their silent appeal to the solitary enjoyment of the reader, who could weigh, compare, and discriminate to the top of his critical bent. Yet a little while, and literary communication was to break the last of its bonds, and the beginnings of prose composition were to supersede the era of metric language.

4. The west coast of Asia Minor is the cradle of the intellectual civilization of Greece. Its line stretches from north to south, but the heart of the movement must be sought in the country enclosing the centre of the line, and in the adjacent islands. There nature poured her gifts with lavish profusion, and those on whom they fell belonged to the Ionian tribe, at all times the most talented among Hellenes. The birthplace of the Ionians is obscure. We know that their blood was mixed with elements from central Greece, if, indeed, they were not a mere product of such fusion, and their diverse origin is doubtless mainly accountable for the complexity of their natural gifts. At least, it was not till they were settled in their new Asiatic home that their individuality reached its full powers. As bold seafarers and energetic traders, they enjoyed every benefit of the keen and fertilizing influence to be derived from intercourse with foreign nations in a more advanced state of civilization. They had the further advantage of intermarrying with other fine races, such as the Carians and Phœnicians, a fact which indisputably increased their original diversity of talent. The Ionians were the furthest removed of all Greeks from that fatal stagnation to which dwellers in isolated countries succumb so readily. It must be added that they lacked the sense of security which friendly mountain-barriers and an infertile soil bestow. The proximity of civilized nations, highly developed and united in a State, was as prejudicial to the political independence of the Ionians as it was beneficial to their intellectual progress. The yoke of foreign dominion which was laid on one part of the people, the compulsory exile in which another part was driven, the slow but sure corrosion of its manhood by the inroad of Oriental luxury,—these were among the consequences of the devastating attacks by barbarians from Cimmeria, followed by the victories of the Lydians and Persians. The nett result of this cross-series of good influences and bad was the rapid rise and swift decline of a period of prosperity. The ripe fruit fell all too soon, and the seeds it dropped were borne by fugitives from the foreigner's

yoke, who would return now and again to the safe protection of Attica's fertile soil.

The evolution we have been describing took its course in but a few centuries; its splendid results included the full bloom of heroic minstrelsy, the triumph of the new forms of verse we have mentioned as the heirs of epic poetry, and, lastly, the rise of scientific pursuits and philosophical speculation. New answers were given to the eternal question of mankind—What is the meaning of self, God, and the world? and these new answers gradually replaced or reshaped the former acceptations of religious belief.

5. Greek religion is a vessel which has been replenished from the treasury of enlightened minds. Poets and artists have combined to idealize its gods as types of perfect beauty. Still, its ultimate springs are those from which mankind has derived an infinite variety of figures and forms, partly beautiful and wholesome, partly hurtful and ugly.

Human thought follows twin channels. It obeys the law of likeness, and it obeys the law of contiguity. While similar ideas suggest one another, yet the same result is evolved by ideas which occur simultaneously or in immediate succession. An absent friend, for instance, may be recalled to our thoughts not merely by the sight of his portrait; the rooms in which he dwelt, the tools which he handled, serve the purpose just as well. These laws are summarily known as the laws of the association of ideas, and the conception of natural phenomena, which may be called the personification of nature, is directly and inevitably due to their action. Whenever the savage perceives a motion or some other effect, which, whether by its rarity or by its intimate connection with his interests, strikes his mind strongly enough to set his associative faculties at work, he will infallibly conclude that the occurrence is the outcome of an exercise of will. The reason is extremely simple. A savage or civilized man perceives the connection of will-power with movement—or, indeed, with effects of any kind—every day and hour of his life;

and no other combination whatever enters in his direct experience.

Observation of other living beings continually strengthens the association which springs from this inner experience. Indeed, effects of all kinds and the deliberate exercise of will-power are connected so frequently in our mind that where one of the two is found we confidently look for the other. This expectation has been gradually confined to narrower limits by the operation of experiences of a different order, chief of which may be mentioned the gradual dominion which man has usurped over nature. But in instances where the associative force of ideas is strengthened by powerful passions, or where it is insufficiently checked by experience of an opposite tendency, or, again, where it is reinforced by the second principle of association, which would here be expressed by a likeness between an unintentional and an intentional event, in such instances our expectation breaks all bounds, and reduces the civilized man, for moments at least, to the level of the primitive savage. These are cases in which we are enabled to test the truth of that explanation by a kind of experiment. Take the view of the savage, for example. A watch, or a gun, or any other unfamiliar mechanism, he regards as a living being. But in our own instance, we are not thrown back on such primitive conceptions. We do not unconditionally refer lightning and thunder, plague and volcano, to the activity of such beings. Nevertheless, there are moments when even a scientific man admits the thought of outside purpose and power, even though he be unable to assign a definite form to the power whose intervention he believes in. Among such occasions may be counted any exceptional windfall, or any unparalleled misfortune, especially when the obvious causes of the event happen not to be in adequate proportion to the effect that is produced. Even a trivial effect may afford an illustration of our argument when the conditions of its origin—as in the dispensations of the gambling-table— defy all human calculation. Such inarticulate thoughts stand wholly apart from the religious beliefs held at this date by civilized mankind. It is not merely that the unbeliever is affected by them; the man of orthodox creed is frequently quite unable to bring the suggestions that flash across his mind into harmony with the dogmas that he has formed for himself or accepted from others as to the government of the world and the nature of its ruler. This Puck of superstition, from whose visitation no man is completely exempt, is the wan and spectral image of that mighty and universal generating power whence is derived an endless host of phantoms of all shapes and colours.

A second step towards the formation of religion follows imperceptibly on the first. We have marked the assumption that an effect is due to an exercise of will. Next comes the observation that a series of frequently recurring effects is to be referred to one and the same natural object. Thus natural objects would be regarded as the animate and volitional authors of such processes, and human instinct and inclination, human passion and design, were ascribed to them in their capacity of exercising an effective will-power after the human pattern. Wonder and admiration were paid to them, and according as their operations were useful and wholesome, or the reverse, they were regarded with love or fear. The great objects of nature exert a very considerable influence over human life, and it was chiefly in such cases that man would feel himself impelled to win their favour, to confirm their good will, and to turn their possible hostility to an auspicious disposition. He would endeavour to persuade the heaven to send fertilizing rain on earth instead of destructive storm; he would try to induce the sun to impart a gentle warmth instead of a scorching heat; he would implore the flood not to sweep away his dwelling, but to bear his frail craft uninjured on its mighty stream. He would seek to mollify the powers that govern his existence by petitions, thanksgivings, and offerings—means he found so efficacious in the instance of his earthly masters. He would invoke their gracious protection, he would thank them for their benefactions in the past, and he would supplicate for their forgiveness when he feared to have incurred their displeasure. In a word, he would employ both prayer and sacrifice in the forms suggested by his limited experience. He would possess a religion and a cult.

Hosts of spirits and demons, not wholly disembodied, and yet not wholly material, speedily range themselves in line with these objects of worship, which we may call natural fetishes. Savage man, unacquainted as he was with the finer distinctions of scientific thought, was led to believe in these beings by a triple set of inferences. The first was drawn from real or apparent observations of the outer world; the second from the inner or moral life; and the third depended on observations taken at the transition from life to death in the human and animal creation.

The smell of a flower teaches the primitive man that there are objects not the less real because they evade his sight and touch. The wind, whose material nature he can but partially understand, makes him acquainted with objects that can be felt, but not seen. Shadows, that contain the outline of an object without its material resistance, and still more the coloured images reflected in a sheet of water, bring astonishment and confusion to the mind of primitive man. In both instances he is aware of something precisely resembling the material object, which yet mocks his endeavour to seize it and touch it. Dream-pictures serve but to increase his confusion. He perceived them, he thought, with all his senses at once; they stood in bodily shape before his eyes, and still in the morning the doors of his hut were as firmly closed as overnight. Men and beasts, plants, stones, and tools of all kinds, stood indisputably before him, plainly perceptible to sight, hearing, and touch, and yet in many instances there could actually have been no room for them in the limited accommodation of his dwelling. Thus he is driven to the conclusion that, like perfumes and winds, shadows and reflections, they were the souls of things. Occasionally it happens that the visions of sleep require and demand a different sort of explanation. The dreamer is not always receiving visits from the souls of other persons or things. Frequently he believes himself to be traversing long distances, and conversing with his friends in far-off homes. Hence he concludes that something—his own soul or one of his souls, the belief in a plurality of souls being both natural and common,—has temporarily left his body. He is subject to the same experiences with the same train of inferences in the state which we have learnt to call hallucination. The irregular life led by primitive man, with its long fastings and sudden excesses, rendered him as liable to such attacks as to heavy and exciting dreams. Those souls or essences of things must be taken as standing in the closest relation with the things themselves, which are affected by whatever affects their souls. In popular belief it is still a bad omen to tread on a man's shadow, and in one of the tribes of South Africa the crocodile is believed to get a man in its power if it merely snaps at the reflection of the man which is thrown on the water from the bank. So the doings and sufferings of persons in dreams is of the gravest import to the living originals.

But popular belief endows the soul with far greater power and with practical independence by a second series of considerations, depending, not on the observations of sense, but on those of the processes of will. So long as the inner life of primitive man moves in a uniform and even groove, he has little cause to reflect on the seat and origin of his will and endeavour. It is when the blood begins to surge in his veins, when he glows and thrills with emotion, that his beating heart teaches him of its own accord how that region of his body is the theatre of occurrences which he is impelled to explain to himself by the light of his own perception and of the analogies already at his disposal. Hitherto he has been accustomed to connect each particular effect with a particular Being; and the more violent and sudden the change, the less he will be able to rid himself of the impression that some Being of the kind is stirring and ruling in his own breast. There are moments when he is seized by an overpowering passion. Rage, for instance, fills his heart and drives him to a deed of bloodshed that he may presently bitterly repent. Or, again, in the very act of committing it, a sudden impulse makes him hold his hand ; and it is in moments such as these that he is overcome by an irresistible belief in one or more Beings, within him or without him, who drive him to action or restrain him from the act. Man's belief in the soul reaches its most effective point in the circumstances which accompany the extinction of the individual life. It is once more the cases of sudden change which make the deepest impression on the observer, and give the lead to his reflection. If dying were always a gradual decay and a final folding of the hands to sleep, or if the dead man were always changed beyond recognition, the inferences drawn from the cessation of life might have taken a different form. Frequently, however, no outward changes disturb the features of the dead. Death comes as a sudden transition from complete vigour to complete silence, and the spectator asks himself to what causes is due this dread and terrifying transformation. Something, he says in answer to himself, has departed from the dead man that lent him life and movement. A cessation of powers and qualities which a moment ago were in evidence is taken literally as a departure and as a separation in space. The warm breath, so mysterious in its origin, which the living body always exhaled, has been extinguished, and the reflection is obvious that the source of the arrested processes of life has perished simultaneously with the breath. Violent deaths, when life seems to leave the body with the blood pouring from the wound, awaken sometimes a belief that life itself is borne on that crimson stream. A second theory is to be remarked among some other peoples. The reflection in the pupil of the eye which vanishes at the approach of death is there regarded as the source of the processes of life and animation. But these attributes, after all, are most commonly ascribed to the warm breath or steam which proceeds from within the living organism, and by far the most of the words which are used in different languages to signify "soul" and "spirit" express that primary meaning. We saw in both explanations of the visions of sleep that the soul was supposed to be separable from the body. Their temporary separation accounts for states of unconsciousness, catalepsy, and ecstasy, just as the explanation of pathological conditions of all kinds, such as madness, convulsions, and the like, may best be sought in the entry of a foreign soul into the body. The instance of demonic possession is a case in point. The difference is that the separation of the two elements in death is regarded as enduring and final.

We see, then, that the breath is regarded as an independent being, but there is no ground to assume that when it has left the body it must perish as well. On the contrary, the picture of the beloved dead is an unfading possession ; his soul, in other words, hovers round us. And how—so primitive man asked himself—should it be otherwise ? The soul is plainly impelled to haunt as long as it can the old familiar places, and to linger about the objects which it cared for and loved. The last doubt on this question is dispelled by the frequent visitation of the image of the departed in the dreams of survivors in the night-time.

Two results ensue from the assumption of independent souls or spirits outliving their connection with the human and maybe the animal body. In the first place, it gave rise to a second class of objects of worship parallel to the natural fetishes. Secondly, it supplied a pattern on which imagination could mould a series of other Beings, which either existed independently or temporarily occupied a visible habitation. There was no lack of urgent motives for the adoption of this creed, and for such operations of the fancy on the part of primitive man. He was governed by outward circumstances in a hardly conceivable degree. His desire to enlighten the darkness that surrounded him at every step was only matched by his inability to give it practical satisfaction. Sickness and health, famine and plenty, success and failure in the chase, in sport, and in war, followed one another in bewildering succession. Savage man naturally wished to recognize the agents of his fortune,

and to influence them on his own behalf, but his power-
lessness to fulfil that longing in any rational manner was
stronger than the wish itself. A maximum of curiosity in
each individual was combined with a minimum of collective knowledge. Fancy was set in motion on every side
with hardly a noticeable exception in order to span that
gulf, and it is difficult to form an approximate conception
of the amount of imagination at play. For the protective
roof which civilization has built over man is at the same
time a party-wall interposed between him and nature.
The objects of natural worship were indefinitely extended.
Forest and field, bush and fountain, were filled with them.
But the needs of primitive man outgrew their rate of
increase ; he could not but observe that his weal and woe,
his success and misfortune, were not invariably connected
with objects perceptible to sense. He observed a sudden
scarcity where game had formerly been abundant ; he
found himself all at once no match for the foe he had
frequently routed ; he felt a paralysis creep through his
limbs, or a mist obstruct his consciousness, and in none
of these instances could he blame any visible being.
He seized on any outward circumstance which gave a
momentary direction to his bewildered thought as an
infallible guide. He would assume a close and definite
connection between occurrences that happened in fortuitous
coincidence or succession. If an unknown animal, for
instance, were suddenly to burst from the thicket at a
time when a pestilence was raging, he would straightway
worship it and implore its good graces as the author of
the plague ; and through all this uncertainty primitive
man never ceased anxiously to look for the agents of his
good luck and ill. His longing for help and salvation remained insatiable throughout. Presently he turned for aid
to those who had watched over him in life, and addressed
his prayers to the spirits of his departed kinsfolk, parents,
and forefathers. The worship of ancestors was started,
and with it went the supplication of spirits not confined
to natural objects, but associated in thought with the
ordinances and occurrences of life. Spirits were assumed

with powers of protection and mischief. We are thus presented with three classes of objects of worship, overlapping one another at various points. They began to react on one another, and to pass into one another's spheres.

The legendary figure of some remote ancestor, the forefather of a whole tribe or race, would be ranked on a footing of equality with the great natural fetishes. It might happen, indeed, that just as a nation or an illustrious tribe would regard and worship the sun or the sky as the author of its existence, so this legendary forefather would be identified with one of those fetishes. Nor need it arouse our surprise that objects of nature or art should come to be looked on as the homes of ancestral or other spirits, and as such should receive a form of worship and be ranked as secondary fetishes. They would owe these honours not so much to any palpable influence they exercised as to their strangeness, their unaccustomed shape or colour, or their accidental connection with the memory of some important event. Finally, it is obvious that spirits or demons, originally confined to no fixed abode, would be confused at times with a natural fetish through their similarity in name or qualities, and would at last be merged with it in a single being. It is wholly illegitimate to infer from occurrences of this more or less isolated character that any of the three great classes of objects of worship, natural fetishes or independent spirits, for example, is foreign to the original belief of the people, or of later and adventitious derivation. As well might one conclude from the proved worship of animals, as such, or from the deification of men, which has been frequently observed, and which still obtains through the great Hindoo civilization, that these are the sole or even the chief sources of religious belief. It is always difficult and often hopeless to attempt to follow the details of such a process of transformation, and to sift the nucleus of a religion from its gradual accretions. But the fact that such transformation took place, and that the course of religious development was thereby deeply affected, is a truth which may be stated without reserve. At this point, however, it will be well to return to the more modest path from which we have digressed.

6. The gods of Greece assembled in Olympus round the throne of Zeus, hearkening the song of Apollo and the Muses, sipping nectar from golden goblets, involved in adventures of war and love—we cannot but perceive how little they resemble the earliest and roughest products of religious imagination. They are severed by a yawning gulf which it would seem to be impossible to bridge over. Nevertheless, the appearance is fallacious. The exact observer will remark a vast number of links and stepping-stones, till he will hardly venture to distinguish between the beginning of the one series of beings and the end of the other ; above all, between the end of the natural fetish and the beginning of the anthropomorphic god. Comparative philology tells us that Zeus, the chief of the gods of Olympus, was originally no other than the sky itself. Hence he was said to rain, to hurl the lightnings, and to gather the clouds. Homer himself still entitles the Earth-goddess "broad-bosomed" or "broad-wayed" indifferently, and thus shifts, like the colours of the chameleon, between two quite contrary conceptions. When Earth is represented by an old theological poet as giving birth to high mountains and to the starry heaven that it may wholly encompass her, or when Earth as the bride of Heaven is represented as the mother of deep-eddying Ocean, and Ocean again with Tethys as engendering the rivers, we are plainly standing with both feet in the realm of the pure worship of nature. Presently, however, we are confronted with a different set of stories. Fair-flowing Xanthus is represented by Homer as subject to a wrathful mood ; Achilles fills his bed with dead men ; he is sorely pressed by the flames ignited by Hephæstus, smith of the gods ; he is in danger of defeat ; he stays his course in order to escape from the conflagration ; and he implores Hera the white-armed, the woman-like consort of the king of the gods, to help him to resist the savage onslaught of her son. In all these instances we are surely conscious of two fundamentally different kinds of religious

imagination, of two strata, as it were, which a volcanic eruption has thrown into hopeless confusion.

The following reply may be attempted to the question why Greek religion, like that of countless other peoples, has undergone this transformation. It was an intrinsic tendency of the associative faculty, which led to the personification of nature, to lend more and more of a human character to the objects of worship. First came the connection in thought between movements or effects and the impulses of the human will. Next volition was connected with the whole range of human emotion; and, finally, the range of human emotion was associated in thought with the external form of man and the sum of the conditions of human life. This development took a slow course. It was delayed by man himself, who, on the confines of savagery, knowing no law but that of need, and harassed as he was by real and imaginary dangers, was not yet sufficiently in conceit with himself to form these supreme powers in his own mean and ignoble image. Still, the gradual beginnings of civilization tended to level the differences and to reduce the distance between the heights and the depths. No people, we may conjecture, ever yet came to regard the great powers of nature as savages living on roots and berries in a state of semi-starvation. But a tribe with an abundance of rich hunting-grounds might conceive a heavenly huntsman such as the Germanic Wotan, or, like the farmers of ancient India, would figure the god of heaven and his clouds as a shepherd with his flock. And this tendency was notably strengthened by the auspicious circumstances of external life, which awoke the desire for clearness, distinctness, and a logical sequence of ideas. It is now the exception, and no longer the rule, to meet with such vague, indefinite, and contradictory conceptions as that of a sensitive stream, or of a river brought to birth by generation. We may not be able to assert conclusively whether the worship of ancestors or of fetishes was the earlier in time, but we can assert that, old as demonism may have been, it must have been extended by the division

of labour and the growing diversity of life. Fresh demons
had to be created to meet the multiplicity of human
business and experience. But these independent spirits
offer less opposition to the personifying faculty than objects
of natural worship, and they presently formed the model
on which the last-named were moulded. Demons, like
souls, were conceived as entering human bodies. Our
remarks about demonic possession will recur in this connection, and the process which nothing prevented and
many conditions assisted was speedily adapted to the case
of natural fetishes. Spirits and gods whose habitation is
confined to external things, which they use as their instruments, now replace or accompany the volitional and conscious objects of nature. Thus the god and the external
thing are no longer completely identified. They merely
stand in the relation of tenant and abode. The god
becomes more independent of the destiny of the object
he inhabits ; his sphere of activity is no longer confined to
it, but he obtains an allowance of free action.

The graceful feminine figures which the Greeks worshipped as nymphs afford an instructive example of this
transformation. Homer's hymn to Aphrodite takes cog-
nizance of dryads who share in the dance of the Immortals
and sport with Hermes and the fauns under the shadows
of the rocks. But the pines and the high-branching oaks
they inhabit are something more than their mere dwelling-
place. These beings are but half divine ; they are born,
they grow, and they die together with the abodes they
haunt. Other nymphs are exempt from that fate. They
dwell in water-brooks, meadows, and groves, but they are
numbered with the Immortals, and they are not missing
from the great council of the gods when Zeus gathers
them in his gleaming halls. We may draw the following
conclusion. There was a time when the tree itself was
personified and worshipped. Next came a period when
the spirit of its life was regarded as an independent being,
separable from it, but closely bound up with its destiny.
Finally, this last bond was severed as well ; the divine
being was liberated, as it were, and hovered indestructibly

over the perishable object of its care. This final and decisive step put polytheism in the place of fetishism. Traces of the era of fetishes linger about but a few of the great unique objects of nature, such as the earth, the stars, and the legendary Oceanus. And even in these instances fresh figures were created under the influence of the new thought to accompany the older deities, barely touched as they were by the finger of anthropomorphism. A further development may here be remarked. These natural spirits, released from their external objects, were set an appointed task just as certain independent deities presided over whole categories of occupation. They were appointed to wood or garden, to the fountain, the wind, and so forth, and became what has appropriately been termed " class-gods." This transformation was assisted, apart from the influence of demonism, by the progressive perception of the intrinsic likeness in whole series of beings. Man's generalizing powers found here their earliest satisfaction, and his artistic and inventive faculties were provided with inexhaustible material in the contemplation of the free action of the gods.

The Greeks were furnished in a pre-eminent degree with the conditions requisite for the progress of personification, and for the idealization of the divine powers which depended on it. The demand for clearness and distinctness may have been a birthright of the Greeks ; it was obviously strengthened by the bright air and brilliant sky enjoyed through the greater part of Hellas, by the sharp outline of its hills, by its wide and yet circumscribed horizon. The Greek sense of beauty was constantly fed on landscapes combining in the smallest compass all the loveliest elements of nature. Green pastures and snowy peaks, dusky pine-woods and smiling meadows, wide prospects over land and sea, fascinated the eye at every turn. And the inventive spirit which was later to display itself in the rich and teeming inheritance of Greek poetry and art must surely have seized on the first material at its disposal, and therein have spent the powers which were denied expression elsewhere.

It is difficult to follow the course of this evolution in detail, and our difficulty is enhanced by the character of the literary monuments that have reached us. It was a cherished belief of former generations that Homer's poems were produced in the infancy of Greece. Schliemann's spade has destroyed this illusion. A notable degree of material civilization clearly distinguished the eastern portions of Greece—the islands, and the shore of Asia Minor—soon after 1500 B.C. The conditions of human life depicted by the Homeric poems are the result of a comparatively long development contaminated by Egypt and the East. When we recall the splendid banqueting-halls, with their plates of beaten metals, their blue glazed friezes on a gleaming alabaster ground, their ceilings artistically carved, and their drinking-cups of embossed gold, we look in vain for traces of primitive man in the princes and nobles whose Round Table was the theme of the Homeric poems. Their passions, it is true, were still uncontrolled. Otherwise the insatiable wrath of Achilles or Meleager would never have become a favourite subject for poetic description. We recall the period in which the Niebelungenlied was composed, when the original and untamed force of passionate sensibility fell on an era of foreign manners and imported refinement of taste. But we find no trace in these heroes of the timidity and awe with which the almighty forces of nature were regarded by primitive man. The gods were fashioned by the nobles after the pattern of their own existence, as they acquired more and more self-esteem, more and more security, in the stress of life. Olympus became a mirror of heroic experience, and its gorgeous and frequently tumultuous features were faithfully reproduced. Gods and men approached each other with a familiarity never since repeated. Men wore no little of divine dignity ; the gods took no mean share of human weakness. The virtues ascribed to the gods were the virtues dearest to those warriors—qualities of valour and pride, and steadfastness in friendship and hate. Gods, like men, were affected by strong individual motives ; the obligation of duty was almost always a matter of personal loyalty, and in the Iliad at least they but rarely appear as the champions of abstract justice. To their worshippers who lavished precious gifts on them, to the cities that dedicated splendid temples to them, to the tribes and races which traditionally enjoyed their favour, they lent their faithful protection with a loyalty as resolute as it was untiring. They were but little restrained by any scruples of morality ; nay, their special favourites were endowed by them with talents for perjury and theft. They seldom paused to consider the rights or wrongs of the matter to which they devoted their assistance, else how could some of the gods have been found on the side of the Greeks, while others with equal interest and trouble supported the Trojan cause ? How, again, could Poseidon in the Odyssey have persecuted patient Ulysses with inexhaustible hate, while Athene proved herself in every danger his trusty counsellor and shield ? Their obedience was solely due to the god of heaven, chief of the gods, and more often than not they obeyed him with reluctance, and used every artifice of deceit and guile to evade the obligation of his command. Moreover, the heavenly overlord resembled his earthly prototype in that his power did not rest on the immovable foundation of law. He found himself frequently obliged to extort the fulfilment of his orders by the employment of threats, and even by violent maltreatment. There was a single peremptory exception to the chaos induced by the acts and passions of the Immortals. Moira, or Fate, was supreme over gods and men alike, and in her worship we recognize the faint and earliest perception of the operation of law throughout the range of experience. Thus the oldest monuments of the Greek intellect that have reached us show us the gods in as human a form as is compatible with reverent worship, and instances indeed could be found where that last limit was transgressed. Take, for example, the love-story of Ares and Aphrodite ; it stirred the Phæacians to ribald mirth, and it evinces a worldliness in religious conception which, like the exclusive cult of beauty of the

Cinquecento, could hardly have spread over wide classes of the population without seriously affecting the heart of religious belief. The majesty of the ancient Greek religion is not to be found in the confines of the courtly epic, where the joys of the world and the flesh and the frank deliciousness of life disperse the gloomier aspects of belief, and clothe them, so to speak, with their brilliance. The exceptional occurrences that seem to contradict this view will be found to be its clearest illustration.

Homeric man believed himself to be constantly and universally surrounded by gods and dependent on them. He attributed his good luck and ill, his successful spear-thrust or his enemy's escape, to the friendship or hostility of a demon. Every cunning plan, every sound device, was credited to divine inspiration, and every act of in-fatuated blindness was ascribed to the same cause. It was the aim of all his endeavours to win the favour of the Immortals and to avert their wrath. But despite this de-pendence, and despite the occurrence, in the Iliad especially, with its shifting battle-scenes, of situations fraught with dire peril, it is to be noted that man himself, the costliest of human possessions, is never offered as a sacrifice to the gods. The religion of the Greeks, like that of most other peoples, was familiar with human sacrifices ; but though it survives till the full light of historic times, it is completely missing from the picture of civilization displayed by the Homeric poems. Or rather, the abominable custom is mentioned therein on one single occasion, as the exception which proves the rule. At the splendid obsequies devised by Achilles in honour of Patroclus, the well-beloved, we are told that, besides innumerable sheep and oxen, besides four horses and two favourite hounds, twelve Trojan youths were first slaughtered and then burnt with the body of his dead friend. This complete consumption of the offering by fire is proved by more recent ritual evidence to have been the ceremony in vogue among worshippers of the infernal deities. The blood of the slaughtered beasts and men is first suffered to trickle over the corpse, and the soul is supposed to be present and to be refreshed and honoured by the gifts it receives. Achilles performs by this act a solemn obligation to the dead, and narrates it to the soul, when it appears to him by night, and again at the funeral itself. But, strangely enough, the description of this revolting deed has none of that sensuous breadth and detail which we correctly call the epic style, and find so characteristic of Homer. Rather the poet glides, as it were, with deliberate haste over the horrible story. He and his audience seem to shrink from it ; it is the legacy of a world of thought and feeling from which the vitality has departed, and this impression is strengthened by other and kindred observations. Except for this single instance, hardly any trace whatsoever is found in the Homeric poems of the whole series of rites connected with and dependent on the belief in the protracted existence of powerful beings rising with spectral influence from the grave, and constantly demanding fresh tokens of propitiation. There are no sacrifices to the dead, whether bloody or bloodless, there is no purification for homicide, no worship of souls or ancestors. The souls, it is true, survive the bodies, but they are well-nigh exclusively confined to the far infernal realms of death, where they wander as "powerless heads," vagrant shadows, and bloodless ghosts, of no efficacy and of little account. It was quite different in later times, and, as we learn from trustworthy discoveries and equally trustworthy conclusions, in earlier times too. We may appropriately dwell on this point, which is of great importance to the history of the belief in souls and to religious history in general.

7. The sacrifice of prisoners or slaves is a funeral custom of remote antiquity, and one which is widely spread in our own times. The Scythians, when they buried their king, used to strangle one of his concubines and five of his slaves—the cook, the cup-bearer, the chamberlain, the groom, and the doorkeeper—and these, together with his favourite horses, and with a quantity of costly vessels, of golden goblets and so forth, would be committed to the royal grave. After the lapse of a year, fifty more chosen slaves were strangled, set upon as many

slaughtered horses, and stationed round the tomb like a guard of honour.

Many pages and chapters might be filled with the enumeration of similar customs, from which the Hindoo suttee is also derived. Naturally they show a long course of gradations, varying from the savage and barbarous to the tender and refined. Human sacrifices were followed by animal sacrifices, and these in their turn by drink sacrifices and other bloodless offerings. Æschylus and Sophocles represent Agamemnon's tomb in Mycenæ as the recipient of libations of milk, locks of hair, and garlands of flowers. But newly discovered tombs of the kings in that city, dating from hoary antiquity, show traces of sacrificial offerings of a far more substantial kind. Bones of animals, and human remains too, were found there, besides innumerable most costly weapons, drinking-cups, and other vessels. Taking these objects in connection with the altars discovered in the vaulted tomb at Orchomenus in Bœotia, we may infer that the souls of the dead enjoyed adoration and worship in the proper sense of the word. The cult of ancestors and souls has been in almost universal vogue. It is still as widely spread among the most debased savages in all regions of the earth as among the highly civilized Chinese, in whose state-religion it plays the most important part. It takes precedence, too, in the beliefs of nations of Aryan descent. The Romans observed it no less than the Greeks, and the "Manes" of ancient Rome were the "pitaras" of the Hindoos. The extinction of a family at Athens was regarded as ominous, inasmuch as its ancestors would be deprived of the honours that were due to them. The whole population of Greece, and the communities of which it was composed in a series, as it were, of concentric circles, addressed their prayers to real or imaginary forefathers. And so imperious was this need that professional brotherhoods or guilds would invent a common ancestor, should they otherwise not possess one. The custom was bound up with the origins of state and society, which were originally ranked as merely extended family groups. But our immediate interest is confined to the deepest root of this custom—the belief in the protracted existence of the soul as a powerful being with enduring influence on the success and failure of its living descendants. We have already discussed the source of this belief, and we shall later be occupied with the changes that it underwent. At present we have to dispel a misunderstanding which might darken our historical insight.

The souls depicted by Homer have dwindled to pale and ineffectual shadows. Their worship, and the customs that arise from it, are practically obsolete in his poems, but it would be erroneous to conclude from these facts that the evidence from comparative ethnology should be neglected, or that the oldest form of this part of the Greek religion is preserved in epic poetry. The discoveries dating from the period of civilization which is now called the Mycenæan have shattered the last foundation of every possible doubt. The causes that induced this change in religious ideas can only be arrived at by conjecture. It plainly depended, not merely on temporal, but also on local conditions, and at first, at least, it was probably confined to certain classes of the population. At the period of which we are speaking the custom of burning the dead body prevailed, and the consequent belief obtained, and was clearly expressed by Homer, that the consuming flames finally severed body from soul, and consigned the soul to the realm of shadows. In connection with the development of Greek religion, considerable influence has been attached to this custom and its results. Of hardly secondary account may be reckoned the local separation of colonists from their ancestral tombs, and from the seats of worship appertaining to them in the mother-country. But of greater importance than all was the joy in life and the world, so repellent to melancholy and gloom, which pervades the Homeric poems. It shrank from the sinister and the spectral with the same invincible optimism that banished the ugly and the grotesque from its purview. Nor was it only the shades of the dead that had to recede into the background. Spectral godheads such as Hecate, horrible spirits such as the Titans with their hundred arms

and fifty heads, coarse and revolting myths such as that
of the emasculation of Uranus, were similarly compelled
to give way to the instinct of joy ; and monsters of the
type of the round-eyed Cyclops were treated in a more
playful humour. Two alternative inferences present themselves. We may either regard the gradual growth of the
sense of beauty and the rise in the standard of life
dependent on the progress of material civilization as the
chief factor of development ; or we may ascribe to the
people who invented philosophy and natural science the
possession, even in those early times, of the elements of
rationalistic enlightenment. In other words, is the change in
the soul-idea which confronts us in Homer to be attributed
in the first instance to the lightness or to the brightness
of the Ionian genius ? This question does not yet admit
of a definite answer. We owe the possibility of its discussion to the brilliant intellectual and analytical powers
of a contemporary student in these fields.

8. The personification of Nature must, then, primarily
be thanked for the inexhaustible material it supplied to
the play, first of imagination and next of imagination
heightened to art. But it must further be recognized as
having been the earliest to satisfy the curiosity of man,
and his craving for light in the deep darkness in the
midst of which we live and breathe. The "why" and
"wherefore" of sensible phenomena are questions that
cannot be avoided, and the spontaneous presumption that
everything which happens is due to the impulse of volitional beings—a presumption springing from the unlimited
dominion of the association of ideas—affords, it must be
admitted, a sort of answer in itself. It is a kind of philosophy of nature, capable of infinite extension in proportion
to the increase of the number of phenomena observed, and
to the more and more clearly defined shapes of the powers
of nature, regarded as living beings. Primitive man is not
merely a poet, believing in the truth of his inventions ; he
is, in his way, a kind of investigator as well. The mass of
answers which he gives to the questions continually pressing
on him is gradually composed to an all-embracing weft,

and the threads thereof are myths. As evidence of this, we may instance the popular legends of all times and countries with their remarkable points of likeness and their no less striking points of difference. The two greatest heavenly bodies figure in almost every nation as a related pair, whether in the relation of husband and wife or of sister and brother. Numberless myths represent the phases of the moon as the wandering of the lunar goddess, and the occasional eclipses of sun and moon as the consequences, partly of domestic strife, partly of the hostile attacks of dragons and monsters. The Semite, for example, explained the weakness of the sun in winter by the story of Samson's —the sun-god's—bewitchment by the seductive goddess of the night, who robbed him of his shining hair; as soon as his long locks, the sunbeams, in which his strength resided, were cut off, it was an easy task to blind him. The ancient Indian regarded the clouds as cows—as soon as they were milked the fruitful rain poured down ; if the quickening moisture were long delayed, the drought was ascribed to evil spirits who had stolen the herds and hidden them in rocky caves, and Indra, the god of heaven, had to descend on the storm-wind to free them from their bondage, and rescue them from the robbers. The dreadful spectacle afforded to the gaze of primitive man by a mountain emitting flames would forthwith seem to him the work of a demon dwelling in the bowels of the earth. Many tribes would content themselves with this explanation, but one or another would presently ask why it was that so mighty a spirit should be confined in infernal darkness. The answer would suggest itself spontaneously, that he had been vanquished in conflict with a yet more powerful being. Thus Typhon and Enceladus were looked on by the Greeks as the vanquished opponents of the great god of heaven, bearing the heavy penalty of their crime. Or take the instance of the earth, from whose womb came forth a constant procession of fruits. How natural it was to represent her as a woman impregnated by the heaven above her, who sent down his life-giving rain. This world-wide myth has been turned to various forms. The Maoris

and Chinese, the Phœnicians and Greeks, would ask why
husband and wife were kept so far apart from each other,
instead of dwelling in the intimate relations of a conjugal
pair.   The inhabitants of New Zealand replied with the
story that the offspring of Rangi (heaven) and Papa (earth)
had no room to live as long as their parents were united.
So at last they made' up their minds to relieve themselves
from the pressure and the darkness, and one of them—the
mighty god and father of the forests—succeeded, after
many vain attempts on the part of his brethren, in sundering their parents by force.   But the love of heaven and
earth survived their separation.   Passionate sighs, which
men call mist, still rise to heaven from the breast of mother-
earth, and tears still trickle from the eyes of the sad god
of heaven, and are called by men drops of dew.   This
ingenious and highly poetical myth of the Maoris gives
the key to a similar but far coarser legend which obtained
in Greece, and of which merely fragments have come down
to us.   Hesiod tells us that the earth was cramped and
oppressed by her teeming burden of children, of which
heaven was the father.   But heaven, adds the poet, would
not suffer them to come to birth, but thrust them back
in their mother's womb.   Panting from her labours, she
devises a cunning scheme, and confides its execution to
one of her sons.   Cronos whets his sickle and mutilates
Uranus his father, so that he is debarred from further procreation, and Gaia is released thenceforward from her
husband's embraces, and is enabled, we may add, to find
room for the offspring with whom she is teeming.

We may mark at this point the following conclusion.
The process of personification was not confined to mere
objects, but was extended to forces, states, and qualities.
Night, darkness, death, sleep, love, appetite, infatuation,
were all looked on by the Greeks as individual beings
more or less successfully personified.   Some are completely
embodied, others stand out from the background of their
content as imperfectly as a bas-relief.   The relations
existing between these forces or states are explained by
analogies from human or animal life.   Likeness, for

instance, figures as relationship, death and sleep are twin brothers ; consecution figures as generation, so that day is the offspring of night, or night of day indifferently. All groups of like nature appear as tribes, kindred, or families, and traces of this process of thought are to be found in our language to this day. Finally, the habit of explaining an enduring condition or the recurring incidents of the world by mythical fictions led to the attempt to solve the great riddles of human life and fate in a similar manner. The Greek in his dark hour of pessimism would ask why the evils of life were so much in excess of its blessings, and the question immediately suggested a second one— Who and what brought evil in the world ? And his answer mainly resembles that of the modern Frenchman, the sum of whose researches into the source of innumerable trans- gressions was contained in the words " cherchez la femme." But the ancient Greek cast his indictment of the weaker and fairer sex in the form of a single charge. He relates that Zeus, with the help of the rest of the gods, in order to punish Prometheus for his theft of fire and the conse- quent arrogance of mankind, created a woman adorned with all the graces as the mother of the female race, and sent her down to the earth. At another time the Greek, still groping for enlightenment on this subject, accused curiosity or the thirst for knowledge as the root of all evil. If the gods, he said, had endowed us with every blessing, and had locked up all evils in a box, and had straightly warned us not to open it, human—and chiefly woman's— curiosity would have set at nought the divine prohibition. Both myths are merged in one : Pandora, the woman, as her name implies, adorned with every seductive gift, is the woman, stung by curiosity, who lifts the lid of the fateful box and lets its perilous contents escape. Once more we are astounded at the similarity of mythical invention obtaining among the most diverse peoples, and one almost involuntarily recalls the allied Hebraic story of Eve—the mother of all life—and the ominous conse- quences of her sinful curiosity.

9. The multiplicity of myths and the crowd of deities

must at last have proved a weariness and a stumbling-block to the orthodox Greek. Legends clustered like weeds in a pathless and primeval forest, obstructed by ever-fresh undergrowth. The thinning axe was wanted, and a hand was presently found to wield it with thew and sinew. A peasant's vigour and a peasant's shrewdness accomplished the arduous task, and we reach in him the earliest didactic poet of the Occident. Hesiod of Ascra, in Bœotia, flourished in the eighth century B.C. He sprang from a soil where the air was less bright than in the rest of Greece, and man's heart was less light in his breast. His intellect was clear but clumsy; he was versed in the management of house and field, and was not a stranger to lawsuits. His imaginative powers were of comparatively restricted range, and his disposition was yet more unyielding. A Roman among Greeks, the author of "Works and Days" was distinguished by sober sensibilities, by a strict love of order, and by the parsimonious thrift of a good business man trained in the manufacture of smooth account-books, averse from any hint of contradiction, and shy of all superfluity. It is in this spirit, so to speak, that he took an inventory of Olympus, fitting each of the Immortals in the framework of his system by the genealogical clamps. He pruned the luxuriance of epic poetry, reviving the immemorial but dimly understood traditions extant among the lower orders of Greece without respect to their claims to beauty. Thus his theogony comprised a complete and comprehensive picture, with but rare gleams of true poetry and hardly a breath of the genuine joy of life. The names of Homer and Hesiod were coupled in remote antiquity as the twin authors of Greek religion. But they stand, in point of fact, in strong contrast. The unchecked imagination of Ionian poets, which made light of the contradictions and diversities of legend, differed as widely from the home-keeping, methodical wisdom of the Bœotian peasant as the brilliant *insouciance* of their noble audience from the gloomy spirit of the meek hinds and farmers for whom Hesiod's poems were composed.

The "Theogony" is at once a cosmogony; the "Origin of the Gods" included the origin of the world. We are chiefly concerned with the last named of these pairs, and may let the poet speak for himself. At the beginning, he tells us, there was Chaos: then come Gaia, the broad-bosomed earth, and next, Eros, loveliest of the gods, who compels the senses of mortals and immortals alike, and melts the strength of their limbs. Chaos engendered Darkness and Black Night, and Air and Day—Æther and Hemera—sprang from their union. Gaia first created of her own accord the starry heaven, the high mountains, and Pontus, the sea; then, as the bride of Uranus, she brought forth Oceanus, the stream that encompasses the earth, and a long series of children, some of them mighty monsters, and others of an almost allegorical description, besides the gods of the lightning called Cyclopes, and Tethys, the great goddess of the sea. From the marriage of Ocean and Tethys sprang fountains and the streams. The sun-god, the moon-goddess, and the Dawn were born to two other children of Heaven and Earth. Dawn is united to her cousin Astræus, god of the stars, and the Winds, the Morning-star, and the rest of the luminaries were born of that marriage.

Part of this exposition is so puerile in its simplicity, that hardly a word of comment is required. "The greater is the author of the less:" hence the mountains were born of the Earth; mighty Oceanus and the smaller streams and rivers stood in the relation of father and sons; the little Morning-star was the son of the wide-spreading Dawn, and the rest of the stars were clearly to be set down as his brothers. It is less obvious why the Day should have sprung from the Night, for the opposite theory would have been equally admissible, and an old Indian hymn-writer actually poses the question whether Day or Night was created first. Still, Hesiod's opinion may perhaps be called the more natural. Darkness appears to us as a permanent state requiring no explanation; light, at each manifestation, is due to a special event, whether it be the rise of the sun, the lightning of the storm-cloud, or the ignition of a flame by human hand. So far, then, we have merely had to deal with the earliest reflections of thoughtful and bewildered man. These tell their own story, but a more attentive examination is required when we come to the most important part of Hesiod's work, where he discusses the origin of the world.

The brief and arid character of this exposition is the first point that we notice, and it arouses our astonishment. The stage-bell rings, as it were, and Chaos, Gaia, and Eros appear as the curtain rises. No hint is vouchsafed as to the reason of their appearance. A bare "but then" connects the origin of Earth with the origin of Chaos. Not a single syllable of explanation is given of the When and How of this process, whether Earth was born of Chaos or not, and what were the aids to birth ; and the same unbroken silence is preserved on the promotion of the Love-god to the prominent part which he fills. Of course one may say, the principle of love or generation must have entered the world before any procreation could take place. But why should the didactic poet drop it without a word, why should he never refer to that function of Eros at all, and why should he rather disguise it, as we plainly perceive to be the fact ? Various epithets are here predicated of the Love-god, and in a later passage he is given a place next to Himeros—craving—in the train of Aphrodite. But none of these allusions recalls in the remotest degree the mighty, vitalizing creative Being who alone is appropriate in this connection, and whom we shall meet later on in other cosmogonic experiments, where the origin and function of Eros come to adequate expression. One thing is as clear as noonday. A wide gulf is fixed between the summary and superficial methods of Hesiod's inquiry into origins and the devotion of those who applied the whole force of their immature philosophy to the solution of the great enigma. Hesiod's system is a mere husk of thought which must once have been filled with life. It has survived the loss of its contents, just as the shell survives the shell-fish. We seem to be gazing at a *hortus siccus* of conceptions, the growth and development of which we are no longer able to watch. Inference has to take the place of direct observation, and a start must be made at the terms the poet used, presumably with but partial comprehension. These terms will help us to construct the process of thought of which they are the dead deposit. We shall be assisted herein by the consideration of kindred phenomena, not merely in Greece, but in other countries as well. We have already briefly described the nature of Eros, and may now proceed to discuss the meaning of Chaos.

Chaos resembles empty space as closely as the inexact thought of primitive man approximates to the speculative conceptions of advanced philosophers. Primitive man endeavours to imagine the primordial condition of things, in all its striking contrast to the world as he knows it. The earth, and all that is therein, and the dome of the sky were not extant. All that remained was a something stretching from the topmost heights to the uttermost depths, and continuing immeasurably on either side the hollow emptiness interposed between the Heaven and the Earth. The Babylonians called it *apsu*, "the abyss," or *tiamat*, "the deep." The Scandinavians knew it as *ginnunga gap*, "the yawning gap," a term of which the first word belongs to the same root as the Greek *Chaos*. This gaping void, this abysmal deep, was conceived as obscure and dark simply because—in accordance with the principles of this system—none of the sources of light had as yet been put in action. For the same reason, the observer confined his imagination to the depths rather than the heights of Chaos, height and light being hardly distinguishable in his mind. Chaos filled the whole space known to or even suspected by primitive man. Earth and her complement—the dome of heaven with its luminaries —sufficed for his knowledge and his thought; even his vague and aspiring curiosity was content to flutter in those limits. His intellect stopped short at the idea of the distance between heaven and earth stretching into the infinite. The two other dimensions of space troubled him scarcely at all, and whether he believed in their finite or infinite extension it would be equally futile to inquire.

Thus Hesiod's inventory included not merely the simple popular legends but also the oldest attempts at speculation. These last, indeed, are presented in so rough and incomplete a guise that his sparse allusions can only acquaint us with the existence of such attempts at his time, and with their barest and most general outline. We shall have to trust to later accounts to discover their contents more accurately, though our knowledge at the best can only be approximate. Then, too, we shall have occasion to examine the standard of thought to which such experiments belong. Meantime, our survey of Hesiod would be incomplete without a reference to one side of his scheme which also bears a more speculative character Many of the beings he presents to us, and interweaves in his genealogies, show little or nothing of the vivid personification which marks the figures of simple popular belief. "Lying Speeches," for instances, would hardly impress any one at first sight as individual personages. Yet they are found with "Toilsome Labour," "Tearful Pains," "Battles," and "Carnage" in the enumeration of the offspring of Eris, or Strife. The experience is repeated in the instance of the children of Night. These do not merely include mythical figures of a comparatively life-like kind, such as Eris herself, Sleep, Death, the Moiræ, or goddesses of Fate, and so forth, but also blank, spectral personifications, such as "Deceit" and "Ruinous Old Age." "Deceit's" title to that place would appear to rest on its habit of avoiding the light ; Old Age is promoted to it on no other ground than that every untoward and unwelcome event seems appropriate to the region of darkness and gloom, very much in the same way as we ourselves speak of "gloomy thoughts" and "black cares." No one can exactly determine Hesiod's debt to his predecessors either here or elsewhere ; but it is fair to believe that in such purely speculative excursions he was trusting to his own imagination.

CHAPTER 1.

THE OLD IONIAN NATURE-PHILOSOPHERS.

BEFORE speculation could flourish, a considerable mass of detailed knowledge had to be collected. In this respect the Greeks were exceptionally lucky in their inheritance. The cause of Greek science was unconsciously served by the ancient Chaldæans and Egyptians. The Chaldæans laid the foundations of astronomy, when they computed the empiric laws of eclipses in their observation of the courses of the stars in the crystal sky of Mesopotamia. The Egyptians invented an art which comprised the elements of geometry, when they measured the ploughland, alternately wasted and fertilized by the Nile, in order to determine the amount of taxes it should yield. The Greeks were ever the favourites of fortune, and here again must be recorded what is perhaps the chief instance of their good luck. So far as the evidence of history extends, an organized caste of priests and scholars, combining the necessary leisure with the equally necessary continuity of tradition, was at all times indispensable to the beginnings of scientific research. But its beginning and its end in such cases were only too likely to coincide, for when scientific doctrines are mixed up with religious tenets, the same lifeless dogmatism will commonly benumb them both. The child's indispensable leading-strings become an intolerable chain when the child has grown to manhood. Thus we may account it a double blessing for the free progress of thought among the Greeks that their predecessors in civilization possessed an organized priesthood, and that they themselves lacked it. The pioneers

of human knowledge had all the advantages without any
of the disadvantages derived from the existence of a
learned priesthood in their midst.   Supported on the
shoulders of Egypt and Babylon, the genius of Greece
could take wing without check or restraint, and could
venture on a flight that was to lead it to the highest
attainable goals.   The relation between the Greeks and
their forebears in the work of civilization, between the
authors of true generalizing science and the purveyors
and preparers of the necessary raw material, recalls
Goethe's picture of himself as a citizen of the world,
between a prophet on the right hand and a prophet on
the left.

Two series of effects are to be traced from the extension
of natural science and of human dominion over nature
acquired by the Greeks in these centuries.   Take the
religious sphere first.   The conception of the universe as
a playground of innumerable capricious and counteracting
manifestations of Will was more and more undermined.
The subordination of the many separate deities to the
supreme will of a single arbiter of destiny was here the
expression of the steady growth of man's insight into
the regularity of natural phenomena.   Polytheism inclined
more and more to monotheism, and we shall later have to
deal with the gradual phases of this transformation.   But
the better knowledge and closer observation of the processes of nature led at the same time to speculations on
the constitution of material factors ; the eye of the student
of nature was no longer exclusively occupied with the
world of gods, spirits, and demons.   Cosmogony began to
free itself from theogony, and the problem of matter
emerged into the foreground of men's thoughts.   They
began to wonder if matter existed in as many separate
kinds as the difference of material things suggested to
their senses, or if, on the contrary, it were possible that
this endless variety could be reduced to a smaller, perhaps
a very small, number, if not to unity itself.   They observed
that the plants, which depend for their nourishment on
earth, air, and water, serve animals for nourishment in

their turn ; they observed that animal excretions helped to nourish the plants, and that both are finally resolved into earth, air, and water once more. So they would ask if these beings in their steady circular course were really of alien nature, or if they were not rather mere variations of originally homogeneous substances—nay, it might be of a single substance. The world, they would go on to conjecture, instead of springing from chaos, might have come from some such single substance and might return to it again, and they would look for a general rule by which to characterize the series of the variations of form that they observed. Such were the questions which began to occupy the mind of the more profound thinkers familiar with the beginnings of positive science. Even the Homeric poems are not absolutely free from traces of similar speculation. Take the passages, for instance, where earth and water are mentioned as the elements into which the human body is dissolved ; or, better still, take the references to Oceanus as the source of all things, and to the derivation of all the gods from the marriage of Oceanus with Tethys, goddess of the seas. The last strains of immemorial fetishism and the overture of positive philosophy are combined in those passages. Now, however, a stricter method supervenes. The veil of mythology was rent and the ideas were pressed with .ruthless consistency to their utmost logical content. Two of the corner-stones of modern chemistry—the existence of elements, and the indestructibility of matter—now come into sight: each is important in itself, and their importance is doubled in combination. A twofold series of considerations led to the belief in the indestructibility of matter. Matter was seen to emerge unhurt from the manifold phases of the course of organic life, and it was by no means a long step to the conjecture that matter could not be destroyed, and that its annihilation was never more than apparent. Moreover, a keener observation refuted the theory of absolute destruction, in the sense of a reduction to nothing, in instances which afforded the strongest presumption in its favour. When boiling water dried up, or when solid bodies were burnt, there was seen to remain a residue of steam, smoke, or ashes. Here, then, we find that genius anticipated science. The full truth of these doctrines was not finally established till the great era of chemistry in the eighteenth century, led by Lavoisier with the balance in his hand. At another point the "physiologists" of Ionia actually outstripped the results of modern knowledge. The bold flight of their imagination did not stop at the assumption of a plurality of indestructible elements ; it never rested till it reached the conception of a single fundamental or primordial matter as the source of material diversity. Here it may almost be said that inexperience was the mother of wisdom. The impulse to simplification, when it had once been aroused, was like a stone set in motion which rolls continuously till it is checked by an obstacle. It advanced from infinity to plurality, from plurality to unity ; no inconvenient facts could place impediments in its path, nor could call a peremptory halt. Thus the impetuous uninstructed sense of that early epoch attained an intuition which is just beginning to dawn through countless doubts and difficulties on our own mature and enlightened knowledge. Once more the belief is breaking on the most illustrious of modern philosophers that the seventy-odd elements reckoned by chemistry to-day are not the ultimate destination in the journey of that science, but are merely a stage in its progress towards the final decomposition of matter.

2. Thales of Miletus is regarded as the forefather of this whole line of philosophers. This remarkable man was the product of a mixture of races ; Greek, Carian, and Phœnician blood flowed in his veins. He was accordingly a type of the peculiar many-sidedness of Ionian descent, and his image flashes on our eyes in the most varied colours of tradition. Now he appears as the embodiment of the remote and contemplative sage, who tumbles headlong in the well while gazing at the stars of heaven ; now he is represented as turning his knowledge to his private advantage ; and in a third version we see him offering his fellow-countrymen, the Ionians of Asia Minor, counsels of extraordinary political

acumen directed to the creation of a federal state—a
conception absolutely novel to the Greeks of that age.
Indisputably he combined the *rôles* of merchant, statesman, engineer, mathematician, and astronomer.   He owed
his rich intellectual training to travel in distant parts.   He
had been as far as Egypt, where he devoted himself, among
other problems, to that of the rise of the Nile.   He was the
first to raise the clumsy methods of land-surveying current
among the Egyptians, and directed merely to the requirements of single cases, into a deductive science of geometry
resting on general principles, and his name is still given
to one of the most elementary geometrical demonstrations.
We may readily credit the tradition that Thales supplied
his Egyptian masters with the method they had sought in
vain of computing the height of the towering pyramids which
are the wonders of their home.   He pointed out to them
that at the time of day when a man's shadow—or that of
any other object presenting no difficulty to mensuration—
is exactly equal to the size of the original, then, too, the
shadow of the pyramid can neither be longer nor shorter
than its actual height.   He had probably familiarized
himself in Sardis with the elements of Babylonian wisdom,
and he borrowed from it the law of the periodicity of
eclipses, which enabled him to foretell the total eclipse of
the sun on May 28, 585 B.C., to the utmost astonishment
of his fellow-countrymen. /It is impossible that he could
have reached this insight on theoretical lines, for he was
still dominated by the old childish conception of the earth
as a flat disc resting on the water./ His weather prognos-
tications were probably derived from the same source.   He
turned them to commercial uses, and would hire a number
of oil-presses in order to exploit his advantage if he
happened to foresee an exceptional harvest in the olive
gardens.   The knowledge of astronomy he acquired was
put at the disposal of the seafarers, for his fellow-countrymen practised commerce and navigation more extensively
than any of their contemporaries.   He directed their
attention to the Little Bear as the constellation which
most precisely marks the north.   It is doubtful if he wrote

books, but his doctrine of primary matter can hardly have been published by that means. Aristotle, at least, though acquainted with it, is plainly at a loss to know how Thales supported it, and approaches his reasons from a conjectural point of view. The food of the animal and vegetable world being damp, organic warmth has its origin in dampness ; further, the same quality is displayed by vegetable and animal seeds. | On this account, according to Aristotle, Thales would have regarded water, the principle of all dampness, as the primary element.| But whether or not Thales was actually influenced by such considerations, whether or not he was affected by older speculations, both native and foreign, and to what extent, if at all, he was dependent on them, is as much a riddle to us, at the present date at least, as his attitude towards things theological.

/The doctrine of primary matter admitted and required extension on three several lines. First, the rank assigned by Thales to water in the precedence of matter could not remain unassailed. Air as the most volatile, and fire as the most powerful, of the widest-spread elements, would inevitably find advocates to contest the prominence to which the fluid element was promoted. Secondly, it would occur to some reflective and far-sighted genius that it was vain to look for the primordial form of matter in the circle of its present and visible manifestations, but that it was necessary to go behind and beyond them. Lastly, the theory of a primary element contained a germ of scepticism which was destined sooner or later to come to maturity of growth. (Thales might be content to conclude that all things proceed from water and return to it again, but his doctrine was obviously liable to be expanded in course of time into the contention that the primary form of matter was its only true and real shape, and that the rest were mere delusions. And if it were once believed that wood and iron, for example, were not wood and iron, but water or air, there was not the remotest reason why the suspicion of the evidence of sense should make a pause at that point.

3. Anaximander, who was born in 610 B.C., followed the second of these lines of thought. He was the son of

Praxiades, and, like Thales, a native of Miletus, and may well have been his friend and disciple. We may fairly look on Anaximander as the author of the natural philosophy of Greece, and consequently of the Occident. He was the first to attempt to introduce a scientific method in answering the vast questions as to the origin of the universe, the earth, and its inhabitants. He had an extraordinary sense for identity, a remarkable faculty for recognizing elusive analogies, and an impressive talent for inferring the imperceptible from the perceptible. Childish as some of his endeavours were to grope out the way of nature, yet his merits as a pioneer and a path-finder command our awe and respect. Unfortunately, we have frequently to depend on scanty, detached, and partly contradictory reports for our knowledge of his ideas. His work on "Nature" is the first account of scientific doctrines which we know of in Greek prose, and this monument of a life devoted to deep reflection and occupied partly with affairs of state, suffered untimely loss. Anaximander did not decide to publish it till shortly before his death at the age of sixty-three. Manifold and eminently meritorious were the preliminary labours which were crowned by this latest production, of which but a few lines have reached us, with no sentence entire. Anaximander first gave the Greeks a map of the earth and a globe of the sky. Though his name was not illustrious in the annals of travel, yet his map comprised the researches of all the travellers who returned from their voyages over land and sea to his Ionian home, which enjoyed exceptional advantages as the centre of the tourists' world. Ancient Egypt had not been ignorant of the art of map-making, but the practice had been confined to the graphic reproduction of separate districts. The dwellers in the valley of the Nile had never conceived the thought of a general map of the world, nor indeed were their unfamiliarity with the sea and their lack of distant colonies adapted to the collection of the necessary material. We are told that a characteristic feature of Anaximander's chart of the world was the assumption of a sea-basin surrounded by land, and again of an outer sea encircling the earth with a girdle. Doubtless the father of scientific geography was acquainted with the Babylonian invention of the gnomon, or pointer, as a means to mathematical and astronomical mensuration. The pointer rested on a horizontal basis, and the length of its shadow, varying with the hours and seasons, served to determine the true meridian of any given locality, and to discover the four cardinal points and the winter and summer solstices. Anaximander, or his successor Anaximenes—the tradition halts between their names—is said to have set up a gnomon of this kind in Sparta. The history of science does not recognize our philosopher as the author of new mathematical doctrines, though it credits him with a systematic exposition of geometry. But at least he cannot be written down as lacking mathematical training; his accounts of the size of the heavenly bodies, though hardly intelligible at this date, afford good evidence to the contrary. As an astronomer, our Milesian was the first to make a well-nigh complete breach with the puerile conceptions of antiquity. If he still failed to conceive the earth as a globe, he was equally far from imagining it as a flat disc, resting on a basis and covered by the bell-like vault of heaven. He did not represent the sun as sinking every night into Oceanus that flowed round the earth, nor yet as following in its channel from the west to the east. If some steady and regular movement was to account for the fact that the sun and the rest of the stars, after they had set in the west, rose once more in the east, Anaximander was compelled to suppose that they continued underground the revolving movement which we watch above the horizon. His supposition was supported by the observation that the constellations next to the pole never set, but describe a revolution. Hence the heavenly hemisphere that we see must actually form a half of a complete sphere. The dome of heaven stretched above our heads was perfected by a complementary dome beneath our feet. Earth was deprived of the basis stretching to unfathomed depths on which she should have been supported, and was left free to float in space. The pancake theory was abandoned in favour of a columnar or cylindrical earth, with its equilibrium guaranteed by the condition of a base-diameter longer than the measure of its height. The proportion of three to one, which fulfilled that condition, probably commended itself to the ancient philosopher by its simplicity. But he employed a remarkable argument to explain the equipoise of the drum-shaped earth, ascribing its undistracted condition to the equal distance it maintained from all parts of the heavenly vault. This doctrine commits the Milesian philosopher to two opinions: on the one hand, gravity cannot have been identified by him with a downward tendency; on the other hand, he is obviously a precursor of that school of metaphysicians who preferred to base the law of inertia on *à priori* grounds rather than on experience. It has been said that a body at rest could not begin to move except by the impulse of some outside cause, for if it did it would have to move either up or down, or forwards or backwards. But as there was no reason why it should do the one rather than the other, therefore it did not move at all. Thus Aristotle, who called the argument of this ancient philosopher a brilliant mistake, compared Anaximander's earth at rest to a hungry man who would have to starve because he had no reason to stretch his hand to the right rather than to the left, in front of him rather than behind him, in order to reach the food disposed at equal distances all round. For the present, however, we must turn our attention to Anaximander's attempts at cosmogony.

Hesiod's theogony has already made us acquainted with the immemorial conception of the universe beginning in chaos. We saw that the idea of chaos was produced by the endless extension of the void yawning between heaven and earth. We saw, too, that those early philosophers took account of one only of the three dimensions of space— height or depth — without respect to its relation with length and breadth. This conception, logically followed out, put space, unbounded in all directions, in the place of the gaping chasm, and such space, filled with matter, was what Anaximander's theory started from. But the question arose, What was this primary matter extended in infinite space? We can state at once that it was no matter with which we are acquainted. Such forms of matter, with their constant fusion and re-emergence, were regarded by Anaximander as factors of equal value and rights, and he would certainly not have promoted any one of them to be the author or progenitor of the rest. And of all the unsuitable candidates for that post the elemental water of Thales must have appeared to him to be the worst. Its very existence required the presumption of warmth which, according to the philosophy of that age, was caloric matter, or fire. For solids are changed to fluids by melting, that is, by the application of heat or caloric matter. Similarly air-substances, such as steam, are produced by the action of fire on fluids. Thus the solid and the fiery seemed to be solely qualified to lead off the line of individual conceptions. And the very contrast between the two caused them to be looked on as a united pair, the complementary members of which had come simultaneously to existence. Thus they actually figure in Anaximander as "the cold" and "the warm," and he set them down to a process of "differentiation" from the original primary matter which comprised all material variations. But we are not acquainted with his further ideas on the origin of the endless series of separate substances. We can merely conjecture that a progressive "differentiation" from the fundamental forms of matter was supposed to continue the process just described. But however that may have been, the substances were at least arranged about and above one another in the order of their weight and density. The earth was the innermost kernel; its surface was covered by water; next came a layer of air; and the whole was enclosed by a ring of fire, as "the tree by its bark." At this point a twofold problem obtruded itself on the orderly mind of Anaximander. He saw that the earth still formed the kernel of the structure, with the air as its outer raiment, but there was no longer a uniform covering of water, and fire was merely visible at separate points of the sky, though these indeed were innumerable. So he began to ask whence arose this disturbance of the primordial uniform programme for the distribution of matter. His answer took shape as follows: The existing sea was merely a residue of the original roof of water, the content of the sea having been reduced in course of time by the evaporating action of the sun. His assumption was supported by the evidence of geology, which plainly showed that the sea had retreated at many points of the Mediterranean basin. Whether he relied on the formation of deltas or on the discovery of sea-shells on dry land, Anaximander drew the most far-reaching conclusions in support of his doctrine from phenomena of that kind. As to the ring of fire, he believed that it burst at some time, doubtless by the violent dislocation of masses on the principle of the sling-stone, a theory which reminds us of the doctrine of Kant and Laplace. Our philosopher would obviously have been acquainted with the operation of centrifugal force, by watching the games of children and the use of sling-stones in war. He would have noticed that the centrifugal force operated with greater intensity in proportion to the larger size of the stone slung at the end of the line. Hence he seems to have concluded that, taking the earth as the centre of the world, the great mass of the sun had been flung to the furthest distance; next, at a lesser distance, the smaller mass of the moon; and, nearest of all, the little stars in their order, planets and fixed stars alike. But Anaximander's imagination did not stop at this point. He thought that masses of air were torn away by the same force, that they became congealed in the process, and closed on the masses of fire. These husks of air, so to speak, with their fiery contents inside, he conceived in the appearance of wheels, provided with openings like the mouth of a bellows, from which a constant stream of fire issued. One wonders how he reached this conception, and a conjectural answer may be given as follows: sun, moon, and stars revolved round the earth, but while there was no known analogy for the regular revolution in space of masses of fire, the rotation of wheels was a matter of daily observation. Thus, concrete objects took the place of abstract orbits, and the difficulty of the problem was very considerably reduced. As long as the wheels existed, and their motory impulse lasted, the rotation of the stars was assured. Finally, Anaximander explained the eclipses of the sun and moon by temporary obstructions in the orifices of the sun-wheel and the moon-wheel.

The ingenuity of the philosopher of Miletus was like-wise devoted to the problem of organic creation. He conceived the first animals to have sprung from sea-slime, presumably because the animal body is composed of solid and fluid elements. Hence, as we saw in the Homeric poems, water and earth were supposed to be its elements. But the presumption may have been strengthened by the wealth of all kinds of life contained in the sea, not to mention the discovery of the remains of pre-historic marine monsters. Further, Anaximander attributed to those primeval animals a bristly integument, which they cast at the transition from sea to land ; it is likely enough that the analogous change sustained by some insect larvæ may have led him to this hypothesis. We can hardly doubt that he traced the forefathers of terrestrial fauna from the descendants of these marine animals, thus obtaining a first vague glimpse of the modern theory of evolution. His statements on the origin of human species were more definite. Mythology represented the earliest men as having sprung directly from the earth, but Anaxi-mander found the following objection to the adoption of that theory. The helpless human infant, who requires more lasting attention than any other species of being, could never have kept himself alive—at least, by natural means. So our philosopher looked for analogies to facilitate the reading of this riddle. He found his best counsellor in the shark, who was popularly believed to swallow her young when they crept out of their shell, to vomit them forth and swallow them again, and go on repeating the process till the young animal was strong enough to support an independent existence. Similarly, he supposed that the ancestors of the human race had their origin in the bellies of fish, and did not quit that habitation till they had reached full vigour. Possibly Anaximander was influenced in this belief by the old Babylonian theory of a primeval race of fish-men, but that, at least, we cannot assert with confidence.

But, whatever his views of the origin of separate worlds, separate forms of matter, and separate beings and substances may have been, one point, at any rate, does not admit of the least doubt. He was quite clear that every created thing is doomed to destruction. Primary matter alone, the source and destination of all life, he regarded as "without beginning and without end." And his conviction afforded him a satisfaction which we may characterize as a moral or religious sentiment. Each separate existence he regarded as an iniquity, a usurpation, for which the clashing and mutually exterminating forms of life would "suffer atonement and penalty in the ordinance of time." All single substances were destructible, all forms of life decomposed and died, and Anaximander extended these material processes to a comprehensive natural order which transformed itself in his mind to a comprehensive order of justice. He might have cried with Mephistopheles that "all that hath existence is worthy to decay." Nothing seemed to him "divine" but Matter, the repository of force, dateless, "eternal and unaging." Divine, too, in his conception were the separate worlds or heavens, but their divinity was limited by the fact that, having been created, they were liable to decay, and they ranked as gods of an inferior order, as it were, who could count on a protracted life in succession to, if not in co-existence with, one another, but whose life at the best was but temporal. We are not told by what processes they returned again and again to the womb of primary matter, but we may conjecture that such processes were connected with the principle of differentiation. We saw that "differentiation" was responsible for the origin of the worlds, and their separate existence was doubtless put an end to in the course of long cosmic periods by fresh admixtures and combinations of their elements. Everything would be gradually brought back to the undivided unity of the original universal Being, which would thus prove its inexhaustible vital force by ever-fresh transmutations, and would realize its invincible supremacy in ever-fresh acts of destruction.

4. Anaximenes, son of Eurystratos, the third great citizen of Miletus, who died between 528 and 524 B.C., walked in the footsteps of Thales. He substituted air for water as the primary principle which engendered " all that was, that is, and that shall be." So completely did air succeed to the inheritance of the discredited element that Anaximenes conceived it as the basis of the earth, which figured once again as a flat disc. Nor is it hard to explain the preference shown to air. Its greater mobility and its greater extension doubtless prompted its choice instead of the fluid element. The first of these qualities was expressly mentioned by Anaximenes himself in the sole fragment of his work that we possess, composed, we are told, in " simple unadorned " prose. Matter, we remember, in the doctrine of all these philosophers—the so-called Ionian physiologists—was commonly supposed to contain in itself the cause of its own motion, and nothing could be more natural than that precedence should be given to its more mobile form, the form that ranks in organic life as the vehicle of vital and psychic force, in which connection it is useful to recall that " psyche," or soul, signifies " breath." Anaximenes himself compared the breath of life with the air. The one, as he believed, held together human and animal life, and the other composed the world to unity. When he came to the question of its extension, he had merely to imagine earth, water, and fire as islands in an ocean of air which spread about them on all sides, penetrating all the pores and interstices of the rest of material substances, and bathing their smallest particles. Like his predecessor, Anaximenes ascribed to the primary matter unlimited diffusion and incessant motion. But the process by which he derived from it other material substances rested in his argument, not on speculative imagination, but on actual observation. He was the first to proclaim as the ultimate reason of all material transformation

a "true cause," a *vera causa* in Newton's sense of the words, and thereon rests his title to immortality. He did not follow Anaximander in deriving "the warm" and "the cold" from primary matter by the enigmatic process of "differentiation," but he ascribed the separation of material substances to Condensation and Rarefaction, or differences of proximity and distance in the particles. When most evenly diffused—in its normal state, so to speak—air is invisible ; when most finely diffused it becomes fire, and in its progress towards condensation it becomes liquid, and finally solid. All substances—we may read into the text of the fragment from Anaximenes—are in themselves capable of assuming each of the three forms of aggregation, whether or not we have hitherto succeeded in effecting the transformation. The importance of this philosophic discovery will be obvious to every one, if he remembers that it was not till a hundred years ago that it became the common property of the most advanced thinkers, and even then not without a struggle. Moreover, to read between the lines of Anaximenes' meditations, if our senses were fine enough, we should recognize through all these transformations the identical particles of matter now drawing nearer to one another, and now withdrawing to a greater distance. Thus his doctrine affords a foretaste of the atomic theory, a conception of the material world which, whether or not it pronounces the last word on the subject, has at least proved down to contemporary times an invaluable aid to philosophy. It detracts but little from his claim to immortality that Anaximenes took the trouble to support his teaching by miserably misunderstood experiments. One of these may be mentioned in illustration : he urged as a serious argument on behalf of his doctrine that the air of the whistle is cold, and the air of the yawn is warm.

The doctrine of matter, as we have seen, made immense strides under the comprehensive induction of Anaximenes, and one might fairly expect that similar progress would be recorded in the instance of astronomy. Unfortunately, such expectation will be disappointed. Now for the first time we are presented with a spectacle which the history of the sciences brings again and again before our eyes. We need not entirely defer to Mr. Buckle's plausible view of the essential opposition between the inductive and the deductive methods ; but we may fairly admit that the representatives of either seldom or never exhibit a talent for both. Turning from the general to the particular, it is hardly surprising to find that Anaximander's temerity of thought left many errors of fact for his more pedestrian successor to fasten on. Anaximenes, the successor in question, was keen-sighted enough to repudiate the puerile explanation of eclipses by temporary obstructions in the sun-wheel and moon-wheel ; unluckily, he was not far-sighted enough to recognize the merits and extend the conclusions of the clever anticipation of the theory of attraction designed to justify the equipoise of the earth. Thus his critical intellect and smaller endowment of imagination united their qualities and defects, and Anaximenes descended a few paces from the height reached by his predecessor. We have already mentioned his return to the disc-and-basis conception of the earth. Consequently the sun could not move under the earth at night, but only sideways round it. Thus, in order to account for its invisibility at night, he was reduced to suppose that it was hidden behind high mountains in the north, or that it receded further from the earth than during the day. We need not dwell on the details of his somewhat crude astronomy. It was partly redeemed by the statement that the luminaries are accompanied by dark earth-like bodies, and Anaximenes doubtless made this statement in order to account for eclipses on the theory—correct enough in principle—of occultation. We are occasionally astounded at the happiness, sometimes at the correctness, of his guesses at the nature of meteorological and other natural phenomena. He dealt with the lightning, the rainbow, earthquakes, saline phosphorescence, hail, and snow, the last two with especial success, and even where his explanation was totally wrong, it was extremely ingenious and significant in principle.

The reasoning on which he based his views of saline phosphorescence may, for example, be reconstructed as follows. Air in its finest state of diffusion turns to fire, and accordingly burns and shines; but these qualities do not spontaneously arise from that state of diffusion, but are indigenous to air, and in favourable circumstances may be recognizable even in another state. Now, an exceptionally dark background, such as the sea by night, will give visibility to the most dimly luminous body. Thus set in relief, the particles of air which enter the hollows where the waves are parted by the oar, become bright and shining. Here we meet the earliest gleams of the thought that the qualities of bodies are not liable to abrupt changes. It is a thought which will reappear as the qualitative constancy of matter, and which we shall find maintained by the later nature-philosophers with uncompromising vigour. Finally, Anaximenes agrees with Anaximander in his theory of cosmic periods and of quasi-secondary gods, or of gods derived from the "divine" primary substance, and therefore intrinsically perishable.

5. Far from the streaming life of the market and the roaring docks of Miletus, the teachings of Heraclitus were matured in the shadow of a sanctuary. Heraclitus was the first of the philosophers of Greece whom we are passing in review by whom the counting-board, the measuring-tape, and the drawing-block were alike eschewed. Without using his hands in any way, he devoted himself entirely to speculation, and the really remarkable fertility of his mind is still a source of instruction and refreshment. At the same time he was a mere philosopher, in the less complimentary sense of the term. He was a man, that is to say, who, though master in no trade, sat in judgment over the masters in all. We have still many fragments of his work, composed in language somewhat florid in style and not devoid of artificial touches; and these, with a few important details of his life, bring the imposing figure of "the obscure or dark" man nearer to us than that of any of his predecessors or contemporaries.

Moreover, legend was early employed in spinning its threads about the head of the "weeping" philosopher. The years of his birth and death are unknown to us ; his "floruit" was placed about the sixty-ninth Olympiad (504–501 B.C.), presumably on the ground of some occurrence with a specific date in which he took a part. He was a descendant of the city-kings of Ephesus, with claims of his own to the joint hierarchic and monarchical office ; and though he yielded these claims to his brother, there is no doubt that he frequently intervened in the politics of his birth-place, and he is even said to have induced the ruling prince, Melancomas, to resign his usurped authority. But the date of the completion of his work, on account of its political references, cannot be placed before 478 B.C.

Solitude and the beauty of nature were the muses of Heraclitus. He was a man of abounding pride and self-confidence, and he sat at no master's feet. If we seek the first springs at which he satisfied his thirst for know-ledge, and caught the intimations of universal life and of the laws that rule it, we must go back to his pensive boyhood, when he roamed in the enchanting hills, with their well-nigh tropical luxuriance, that surrounded his native city. The great poets of his country fed his childish fancy, and filled it with gorgeous images, but they afforded no lasting satisfaction to his mature intellect. For, chiefly owing to the influence of Xenophanes, men began to doubt the reality of the myths, and the Homeric gods, with their human lusts and passions, began to be replaced in sensitive souls by the products of a higher ideal. The poet who, according to Herodotus, was associated with Hesiod in the invention of Greek religion would not have been honoured by Heraclitus, but "banished from public recitations and scourged with rods." For Heraclitus was equally opposed to all objects of popular belief. He contemned the worship of images, which was as if "a man should chatter to a stone wall ;" he despised the system of sin-offerings which expiated one stain by another, "just as if a man who had stepped into mud were to wash himself clean with mud ;" and he

inveighed against the "abominable" rites of the Bacchanalia as strongly as against the "unhallowed observance"
of the Mysteries. Hesiod "the polymath, whom most
men follow as their master," Pythagoras the philosophizing
mathematician, Xenophanes the philosophic rhapsodist,
Hecatæus the historian and geographer, were all tarred
with the same brush. He learnt from them all, but he
owned the mastery of none. For Bias alone, with his simple
practical counsels of wisdom, he reserved a word of warm
praise, and he acknowledges his debt to Anaximander,
whose influence is real and lasting, by omitting him, with
Thales and Anaximenes, from the list of the proscribed
masters of polymathy "which does not instruct the mind."
The best in himself he believed that he owed to himself, for
"of all whose opinions" he was acquainted with "none had
attained true insight." And if his attitude towards poets
and thinkers was distinguished by sullenness or mistrust,
we can conceive the contempt he must have felt for the
mass of the people. His invectives fall on them like
hailstones; "they fill their bellies like cattle," and "ten
thousand do not turn the scale against a single man of
worth." We can hardly expect that a man who held the
mob in such light esteem should have cared to court
its favour, or should even have troubled himself to make
his meaning understanded of the people. His enigmatic
philosophy is addressed to the fit and few, without regard
to the multitude "baying like curs at a stranger," or to
"the ass that preferred the bundle of hay to the nugget
of gold." Heraclitus was aware of the adverse criticism
which would attach to the oracular form and melancholy
contents of his work, but he met it by an appeal to the
most illustrious examples. The Pythian god "expresses
naught and conceals naught, but merely hints at his
meaning;" and "the voice of the Sibyl rings through the
centuries by the power of the god that speaks through her
and proclaims its joyless message to mankind, naked and unadorned." Nor was Heraclitus troubled by the postponement
of his reward; "one thing," says a fragment, "worthy men
choose in preference to all others—renown incorruptible."

The political and moral condition of Ephesus served to feed the contempt which Heraclitus felt for his fellow-men. The stranger's yoke had oppressed the Greeks of Asia Minor for half a century or more. Oppressive though it was, its immediate harshness was frequently relieved by the fact that indigenous dynasties interposed between the subject states and the loosely knit feudal empire of Persia. Still, it would have been nothing less than a miracle, if the loss of national independence had not brought in its train a depression of public spirit and an excessive growth of private interests. Indeed, the soil for such symptoms of decay had been long since prepared. The heightened standard of luxury and the refinement of the East had partly sapped the vigour, while it corrected the savagery, of ancient Greece. Given these conditions, and given the gall and venom of Heraclitus, we are not surprised that his criticism fastened unfavourably on his fellow-countrymen, and that he found them little suited to wield the sceptre at the time that democracy arose from the wreck of the Persian sway. Be this as it may, he was found in the party-feuds of that epoch on the side of the aristocrats, whose cause he espoused with a zeal proportionate to the contempt he cherished for his antagonists. The climax of his hate was reached in the following embittered utterance :—

" The Ephesians would do well to hang themselves man by man, and to deliver their city to their infant sons, seeing that they expelled Hermodorus, saying, ' No worthy man shall be among us ; if there arise such a man, let him dwell elsewhere and with another people.' "

The exile who is the subject of this eulogy found a new and honourable field for his activity in a distant home. His juristic advice was consulted by the authors of the Roman laws of the Twelve Tables, and a monument was erected to his memory which was seen as recently as by Pliny. But the veteran friend of Hermodorus was weary of the yoke of popular rule. He withdrew to the solitude of the mountains, where he ended his days, having first deposited in the temple of Artemis a roll of manuscript containing the result of his life's work as an inheritance for generations to come.

The full enjoyment of this precious book was denied even to the ancients. It was so heterogeneous and self-contradictory that Theophrastus could find no other explanation than that its author had been subject to occasional mental aberrations. Aristotle complained of its bewildering grammatical difficulties, and a host of commentators—some of them of the best repute—have endeavoured to illumine the dark places in which the work abounds. The broken fragments that have reached us defy all attempts to restore them to their original consecution, or to attribute them with certainty to the three sections—physics, ethics, and politics—in which the work was divided.

Heraclitus' great claim to originality does not rest on his theory of matter, nor yet on his theory of nature. It is rather to be discovered in the fact that he was the first to build bridges, which have never since been destroyed, between the natural and the spiritual life, and that he constructed comprehensive generalizations comprising both realms of human knowledge, as it were, with a mighty bow. In principle he is most closely allied with Anaximander. Both were equally impressed by the transitoriness of all single objects, the ceaseless mutation and transformation of things, and the aspect of the order of nature as an order in law. But Heraclitus parted from his greatest predecessor in the restlessness of his temperament, so averse from all patient research, in the more poetic trend of his imagination, and in his demand for conceptions of a richer and more sculpturesque kind. The primary matter of Anaximander, devoid of all qualitative distinction, and the colourless, invisible First Substance of Anaximenes, were alike alien to his taste. The form of matter which seemed to Heraclitus best to correspond to the process of the world, and therefore the most dignified, was fire. It never bore the remotest appearance of rest or even of minimal movement ; it was the principle of vital heat in beings of higher organism, and thus it appeared as the element of animation engendering and consuming all things. "This one order of all things," he exclaims, "was created by none of the gods, nor yet by any of mankind, but it ever was, and is, and shall be—eternal fire—ignited by measure, and extinguished by measure." He represents primary fire as sinking to the other and lower forms of matter in a minor and a major circle, and as rising again through the same gradations to its original form, for "the up-road and the down-road are one." Fire changes to water, and as water half of it returns directly to heaven as "fire-steam," half of it changes to earth, which becomes water again, and thus is finally changed back to fire. Evaporation, melting, and freezing may be regarded as the processes which operate in this circular system. We must remember, too, that the extinction of a burning substance by water would have counted in the primitive physics of Heraclitus as a transformation of fire to water. The first principle of our poet-philosopher is not merely the ceaseless spring of birth and decay; it is not merely divine, as it was to his predecessors. Heraclitus regarded it as the source of the world's intelligence, as the conscious regulative principle of all existence which "will not be called Zeus," since it is not a personal being with individuality of its own, and yet "will be called Zeus," since it is the supreme principle of the world, and accordingly the highest principle of life. In this connection it should be remembered that the Greek "zên" means "to live," and the corresponding forms of the name Zeus may well be kept in recollection. Still, we should not regard this primary being as a divinity acting with a fixed purpose, and selecting the means appropriate to his end. We are rather taught to regard him as a "boy at play," amusing himself with counters, and building castles on the sea-shore for the sake of throwing them down again. Construction and destruction, destruction and construction—this is the principle which regulates all the circles of natural life, from the smallest to the greatest. Cosmos itself, which sprang from primary fire, is bound to return to it again by a double process which, however protracted its duration, operates in fixed periods, and will constantly repeat its operation.

The speculations of Heraclitus in this respect were assisted by the geological observations of Xenophanes and Anaximander. He seems to have followed the last-named thinker in concluding, from the obvious evidence of the Mediterranean Sea, that the extension of the water had been greater in past time than it was in the present ; and we can quite well understand that he should push his physical doctrines to the further inference that, as land proceeded from water, so water proceeded from fire. Thus he reached a point of departure when nothing but fire existed. But seeing that he was pledged to Anaximander's belief in a circular order of occurrences, he could not regard that process of evolution as a single and unique event. All other material substances sprang from fire, and into fire they were bound to return, in order that the process of differentiation might begin anew and again reach the same end. In breadth of view Heraclitus is here akin to the greatest of modern philosophers, and, whether by chance or by genius, he is in agreement with them at least in respect to the solar system, even in the details of his conception of the cyclical system of the world. To him as to them a ball of fire marks the starting-point and the goal of each cosmic period.

So much, perhaps, for the broad lines of Heraclitus' doctrine. Unluckily he found himself in occasional contradiction, not merely with the nature of things, but with the principles of his own teaching, and it is hard to say how far he was conscious of these objections, and how he reconciled them in his own mind. When we read his axiom that "fire feeds on vapours which rise from the damp," we are impelled to wonder if the gradual diminution and final extinction of the fluid element would not involve the destruction of the source of the food of fire. And again, if space were already full, what room could be found there for Matter when its volume was increased by heat? The Stoics who followed Heraclitus found a way out of his difficulty by putting a vast expanse of empty space at his disposal for that purpose. We can assert with complete confidence, however, that Heraclitus was innocent of this expedient. The assumption of an empty space would have stamped him as a precursor of Leucippus, and our authorities would never have failed to acquaint us with that fact.

Heraclitus, then, ascribed to matter an unceasing transmutation of forms and qualities. We have next to note that he regarded it as constantly moving in space. Matter, moreover, was alive to him, and its life was life not merely in the sense in which his immediate predecessors were correctly entitled "hylozoists" or animators of substance. In as far as they placed the cause of movement in matter itself, and not in an outside agent, they were followed by the Ephesian philosopher. But his "everlasting fire" was not merely alive in that sense. He watched the circulation of matter, as visible in the animal and vegetable kingdoms, and the fact impressed him so strongly that he used its analogy as the leading principle of all his reflections on material processes. All life was involved in continual decomposition and renewal; and if matter was regarded as alive in the first-named meaning of that word, it is by no means surprising that by the association of ideas it should eventually be regarded as organically alive in the secondary meaning of the term. Hence was derived Heraclitus' doctrine of the flux of things. It was a mere optical delusion if we looked on anything as stationary: the thing was actually subject to incessant transformation. And if it were objected that the transformation did not lead to the destruction of the object, Heraclitus explained that as the particles of matter were detached from it they were constantly replaced and reunited in uninterrupted succession. His favourite simile was that of the flowing stream. "We cannot step into the same river twice, for fresh and ever fresh waters are constantly pouring into it." And since the river regarded as an enduring mass of water was the same, but regarded as a combination of particles was not the same, this reflection was pointed to the paradox that " we step into the same river, and we do not step into it ; we are, and we are not."

The half-truths of Heraclitus' analogy were interwoven with correct observations and far-reaching inferences. Among the inferences may be mentioned the supposition that our impressions of smell and of sight—the inclusion of sight was natural to the belief of those times—were produced by particles of matter continually detaching themselves from their respective objects. But be that as it may, his reasoning terminated in a theory of nature which displays quite remarkable points of likeness with the doctrines of modern physics. The agreement is so exact that a comprehensive summary of those doctrines corresponds almost verbatim to an ancient account of the teaching of Heraclitus. Aristotle, in a passage which plainly refers to the Ephesian and his disciples, states that " it is held by certain people that it is not the fact that some objects move while others do not, but that all objects are always moving, though their movements elude our observation." And a natural philosopher of our own times remarks that " modern science takes it for granted that the molecules of matter are always vibrating or in movement, . . . though these movements may be imperceptible." In these circumstances, it is astonishing to recall the conditions of scientific knowledge at the date when Heraclitus was writing. It was an age which was equally ignorant of our theories of heat, light, and sound, which had no more reached the conception of waves of air and ether than it had perceived that a molecular movement underlies the sensation of heat even in solid bodies ; which had not the faintest acquaintance with chemical and cellular processes ; and which, finally, was without the microscope whereby our astonished gaze is made familiar with movements in places where the naked eye can only see blank rest, and whereby we are irresistibly persuaded that the rule of motion extends infinitely further than our feeble observation can pursue it. Taking all these considerations in account, we are struck with the greatest admiration for the genius and insight of Heraclitus, and perhaps one is most astonished that his brilliant anticipations produced so poor a crop of detailed knowledge of nature. But our disappointment should not diminish the renown of the Ephesian philosopher. His mere recognition of the fact that imperceptible motions exist served to break down the wall between the secrets of nature and their investigators. In order to render his discovery really useful and fertile, a second departure was required. The assumption had to be made of similarly invisible, indestructible, and unchangeable particles which enter into the composition of all material substances and emerge unhurt from all their vicissitudes of form ; and this was the great contribution of the Atomists to the evolution of thought. Heraclitus himself was not to inaugurate the mechanical explanation of nature. For that task he was disqualified by the poetic bias of his mind. But he succeeded in drawing conclusions from his principle which served to illuminate some other departments of knowledge.

The succession in qualitative mutations found its exact counterpart in co-existent diversity. Here too the attentive observer is confronted by a multiplicity which seems to threaten the unity of an object and of its constituent properties. The action of an object may vary, even to the point of contradiction, with the varieties of the object on which it acts. " Sea-water is the purest and most disgusting ; it is drinkable and wholesome for fishes, undrinkable and noxious for men." Every one who is acquainted with the fragments extant of Heraclitus' work will be aware that he was not recording an isolated observation in that sentence. Rather he was announcing for the first time the principle of the relativity of qualities which he pushed forthwith, as his manner was, to its extreme consequences, in the words "good and bad are the same," reminding us of his former paradox, "We are and we are not." And in point of fact the Ephesian's doctrine of flux and his doctrine of relativity lead to the same result ; the successive states of an object, as well as its simultaneous qualities frequently both bear the stamp of a far-reaching diversity which amounts at times to complete contradiction. Our

philosopher believed that he had rid himself of all definiteness and fixity in being ; he revelled in phrases that set
common sense at naught, and he forgot or neglected the
reservations by which, and by which alone, such statements
become comprehensible and acceptable.   In one sense the
river remains the same, in another sense it becomes a
different river ; in one aspect X is "good," in another
aspect it is "bad."   Such distinctions troubled Heraclitus
but little ; the inexperience of his thought played into
the hands of its arrogance ; the more unfamiliar the results
he reached, the more they satisfied his delight in paradox,
his predilection for enigmatic oracles, and the light esteem
in which he held all plain and obvious truths.   Henceforward he regarded it as proven, as a fundamental law
in the natural as well as in the spiritual world that contraries were not mutually exclusive, but rather presupposed
and conditioned, or were even identical with, each other.
It would be purblind folly to bear him a grudge for this, for
in the case of mistaken or neglected truths, and especially
in the instance of such truths as naturally lend themselves
to mistake or neglect, the thing of supreme and primary
importance is that they should be discovered at all.   The
exaggerations into which their discoverer is betrayed are
as pardonable as they are intelligible, and in the long
run they may be found to do more good than harm.   The
logician with his rod is not likely to keep them waiting
very long ; and sooner or later the shears which are to
clip the luxuriance of thought will do their remorseless
work.   Meantime the extravagance and assertiveness with
which these elusive truths were originally invested will
have set them in such brilliant relief that they can never
again be overlooked.   Above all, the point of their paradox
will have penetrated the mind of their inventor, who will
keep them in constant readiness as an inalienable possession.   Therefore the "speculative" revels of Heraclitus
may be regarded by us as the source of the most precious
contribution with which he has enriched the treasury of
human knowledge.   For verily the pen of the historian might
hesitate where to begin or end if he endeavoured to write

an adequate account of the inexhaustible range of fundamental truths contained in the exaggerated statements of
Heraclitus. His theory of relativity, for example, contained
like a folded flower the correct doctrine of sense-perception
with its recognition of the subjective factor ; and it taught
Greek thinkers the lesson they were bound to acquire if
they were to be saved from a bottomless scepticism, that
one and the same object in the outside world acts differently on different objects and individuals, and may even
exercise varying effects on the varying states of the same
individual. Nay, it brought the deeper and the more indispensable admission that opinions, laws, and institutions
appropriate and wholesome for one phase of human development become inadequate and unwholesome when another
stage has been reached. " Reason becomes nonsense, the
blessing is turned to a curse "—simply because, as time
changes and as constituent elements vary, the same
object may come to exercise a very different and even
a contradictory effect. Relativism is the spur which
pricks the side of a sluggish conservatism in all departments of life—taste and morals, politics and society—and
it is the absence of relativism in the present as in the past
which lends the cry of " it has always been thus " its force
in opposition to reform. And it serves not merely the
cause of progress, but the cause of sound conservatism as
well ; without a sense of relativity no sufficient explanation
can be given, no satisfactory estimate made, of the changes,
vicissitudes, and contradictions between the good and evil
of yesterday and to-day Without it, every actual alteration
in existing institutions, every barest observation that the
same laws are not always and universally valid, gives rise
to a far-reaching and incurable scepticism as to the justification of all institutions whatever. Human life fulfils itself
in many ways, and human nature adapts itself to its conditions of time and place, so that an adequate philosophy
of life must be amenable to these Protean transformations,
and no philosophy of life will be adequate which finds its
salvation in a frigid rigidity and identifies every evolutionary
change with the arbitrary dominion of chance.

And now at last we reach the doctrine of the coexistence of contraries. Our poet-philosopher is never weary of its statement and illustration. He tells us that "the dissonant is in harmony with itself;" he assures us that "the invisible harmony which springs from contraries is better than the visible;" and he states that "sickness has made health desirable, satiety hunger, and weariness rest." Now with oracular brevity, now with the clearness and breadth of sunlight, Heraclitus pointed his lesson that the law of contrast is supreme in nature no less than in human life, and that "it would not be better for mankind if they were given their desires;" if, that is to say, all contraries were dissolved in an unalloyed harmony. Homer himself is blamed by Heraclitus as much for wishing to expel "all the evils of life" as for desiring to be rid of "strife from the circle of gods and men," and thus promoting "the downfall of the universe." The pithy dicta we have quoted require or admit of countless explanations. They express implicitly or explicitly a long series of modern conceptions. They contain all that we denominate in the widest sense of the word "polarity" in the realm of natural forces; they contain the necessity of change for the operation of sensation, and especially of pleasurable sensations; they include the condition of the opposite evil in every conception of good; they include the indispensability of competition and of what we have learnt to call the "struggle for existence," if human powers are to develop and increase; and among much else they comprise the necessity of the coexistence of antagonistic elements in state and society. And our philosopher's eye is ever glancing from the inanimate to the animate, from animate to inanimate creation. Or rather, the distinction was nonexistent for him. To his eye the whole world was eternally living fire, and the soul, the vehicle of life, nay, the godhead itself, were fire and nothing but fire.

The hardest point in our inquiry is to credit Heraclitus with the sociological insight to which allusion was just now made; but precisely in this regard the wording of one of his dicta is absolutely unequivocal. He entitles war

"the father and king" of all things or beings. Now, if
the fragment had broken off here, no one would think of
understanding it in any but its purely physical and cosmological sense. On all sides the eye of the philosopher of
Ephesus discovered the play of opposite forces and qualities,
which reciprocally promoted and conditioned one another.
He conceived a law of polarity encompassing the whole of
life and comprising all separate laws in itself. Rest
without struggle led in his conception to universal sleep,
coma, and destruction; "the mixture," he wrote, "which
is not shaken becomes decomposed." The principle of
struggle and strife is at the bottom of that incessant motion
which is the source and preservative of life; and its
qualities as progenitor, ruler, and guardian are characterized
by the titles "father and king." Formerly one might
have stopped at this point, but now we are enabled
to go further, since a lucky discovery made about forty
years ago has put us in possession of the continuation of
the fragment. "Some," it goes on, "war has proved to
be gods, others to be men; some he has made slaves,
others he has made freemen." The slaves are the prisoners
of war and their descendants; their conquerors and rulers
are the freemen. Thus it is clear, from the drift of
Heraclitus' argument, that he conceived war as testing and
preserving the qualities of mankind, as making a distinction
between the competent and the incompetent, as founding
the state and organizing society. He praises war for
bringing this differential value to full expression, and we
perceive what significance he attached to it by his co-ordi-
nation of gods and men with the categories of slaves and
freemen. For war too effected the division between the
human and divine: the man become god stood to the
average man in the same relation as the freeman to the
slave, and Heraclitus imagined that there were chosen
spirits exalted from earthly life to divine being, besides
the crowd of common souls hidden in the under-world and
limited in that region of damp and misery to the single
sense of smell in the place of the higher perceptions. He
conceived a ladder of beings with different rungs of rank,

different merits, different abilities, different excellences. He referred the succession of rank to a gradation of merit, and then inquired into its causes. These he discovered in the friction of forces which sometimes manifested itself as war in the strictest sense of that term, and sometimes as a kind of more or less metaphorical warfare. Such shades of meaning provided the requisite links between the cosmological and sociological significance of the phrase. Still, too much stress ought not to be laid on the use of metaphorical language. We have to allow for the degeneracy of his Ionian kinsfolk, whom Xenophanes was already castigating for their effeminate luxury; we have to reckon with the indolence of his fellow-citizens, against which Callinus was protesting, and with the heavy misfortunes which his country was suffering, before we can fully appreciate his estimation of the virtues of war. " The fallen in war," he exclaims, "are honoured by gods and men, and the greater the fall the louder the pæan " of honour and admiration. But for the thinker whose strength lay in his genius for generalization, the most painful experiences were merely a spur to the pursuit of his track of thought. Its goal in this instance was no meaner object than the triumphant realization of the truth that struggle and resistance are a fundamental condition of the preservation of human power on its road to progressive perfection.

However deep and numerous the truths may be which Heraclitus has taught us hitherto, the greatest surprise is yet in store for us. He pursued his observations of nature and human life through the series of single rules which he noted to one all-embracing rule. His eye perceived a universal law in strict unexceptional operation. And his recognition and proclamation of the universal rule of law, of the dominion of unexceptional causality, marks a distinct turning-point in the intellectual development of mankind. We may quote in this connection the following dicta of Heraclitus :—

" The sun will not transgress his measures : were he to do so, the Erinyes, abettors of Justice, would overtake him,

" He who speaks with understanding must take his foothold on what is common to all, even more firmly than the city stands on the foothold of law ; for all human laws are nourished by divine law.

" Though this logos—this fundamental law—existeth from all time, yet mankind are unaware of it, both ere they hear it and in the moment that they hear it."

If we were asked how Heraclitus succeeded in climbing to these heights of knowledge, a provisional answer might be given that he was here summarizing tendencies which pervaded the spirit of his age. It was an age when man's acquaintance with nature had been extended, and his moral aspirations enlarged to a degree which could not rest satisfied with an explanation of the world based on the capricious and arbitrary interference of supernatural beings. The progressive exaltation of the supreme god— the god of heaven—kept pace with his moral refinement ; the attempt was constantly renewed to derive the many-coloured multiplicity of objects from a single material source, and in these phenomena we may mark the growing belief in the uniformity of the universe and in the unity of its rule. The road was open for the pursuit of all-comprehensive laws, and its pilgrims submitted to more and more stringent conditions. The astronomers had been the first to lay the foundations of exact natural science, and these had speedily been followed by the mathematical physicists, among whom Pythagoras takes the foremost place. We can hardly conceive the impression that must have been produced when Pythagoras announced the results of his experiments in acoustics. Sound, the most volatile of phenomena, had been imprisoned by number and measure, and had passed under their yoke ; and what, men asked themselves, would in future be able to resist those tyrants ? The cry spread from Lower Italy through Greece, " number is the essence of things." It is perfectly plain that the Ephesian philosopher did not shut himself off from these influences. The ideas of harmony, of contrast, and especially of measure, are prominent features in his speculations, a large part of which may indisputably be referred to Pythagoras, and a minor part to the influence of Anaximander. Heraclitus was not cast for the *rôle* of an exact investigator ; his passions were too free, he lacked the requisite soberness, and he was too prone to seek satiety in a debauch of metaphors ; but he was admirably suited to be the herald of the new philosophy. In this respect, as well as in his frequent injustice towards the actual promoters of science, he may fairly be compared with Francis Bacon, between whom and himself less convincing points of likeness have recently been remarked. But the power of Heraclitus was not confined to his force of language and his talent for plastic expression. The explanations he vouchsafed in single instances may have been childish to a degree ; he may have written that "the drunken man is led by a beardless boy and stumbles because his soul is wet," or that "a dry soul is the wisest and best ;" but he was marked in an extraordinary degree by a genius for identity, for distinguishing likenesses under the most illusory disguises. He possessed an almost unparalleled faculty for pursuing views that he had obtained in a limited and special field through the whole perspective of life and through the twofold vista of the natural and spiritual worlds. We have already seen that he had no need of constructing a bridge between nature and spirit ; for him and his immediate predecessors the gulf no longer existed. And in this respect he was considerably assisted by his choice of a primary matter. This world was built of fire, or "soul-stuff," and starting from this assumption he was completely at liberty to extend his generalizations from any and every department of nature to the phenomena of soul and the political and social phenomena that proceed from them. To this we owe his comprehensive collection of generalizations, the pinnacle of which was reached in the recognition of universal law at the root of all mundane occurrences.

We have now to remark the particular impulse depending on Heraclitus' theory of flux, together with his very imperfect theory of matter, which impelled him to climb that summit and to proclaim with all the emphasis at his disposal that the highest goal of knowledge was the one law regulating all events. Otherwise he must have apprehended that no object of trustworthy knowledge would have been left extant, and the reproach unjustly levelled at him by Aristotle would have appeared to be thoroughly merited. But this was now out of court. Universal law stood unmoved and unshaken through all the changes of individual objects and all the vicissitudes of material forms, in defiance of the destruction on which the cosmic system hastened at regular intervals, and from which it was reconstructed anew; and under the vague mystic description of universal reason or universal godhead it took its place by the side of primary matter, endowing it with reason and soul, as the one thing permanent in the cyclic stream of occurrences, without beginning and without end. To recognize universal law or reason was the highest function of intellect; to bow to it and to obey it was the ultimate test of conduct. Obstinacy and self-will were the embodiments of falsehood and evil, which were fundamentally one. "Self-conceit" was compared with "epilepsy," one of the most terrible diseases that can befall mankind, and one which throughout antiquity was looked on as sent by demons. "Insolence," again, "must be extinguished like a conflagration." "Wisdom consists in this alone, to understand reason (or universal intelligence), which steers all things through all." It was by no means easy to satisfy this condition, for truth was paradoxical. "Nature," wrote the philosopher, "loves to hide herself, and escapes detection by her incredibility." But the patient inquirer must use his best efforts, must keep his cheerful courage at the sticking-place, and be constantly equal to surprises, for "if ye expect not the unexpected, ye shall not find truth, seeing that it is hard to discern and not readily accessible." Again, we read that "we must not speculate about the highest things in lightness of heart," we must not be governed by caprice, for "punishment will overtake the lie-smith and the false witness." Human institutions were limited in duration and extent by their agreement with divine law, which "ruleth as far as it listeth, sufficeth for all, and overcometh all things." But within those limits the law shall prevail, which "the people shall defend like a rampart." But law was by no means the arbitrary whim of the many-headed unreasoning mob; it was rather the insight and frequently "the counsel of one man," to whom "obedience was due" on account of his superior wisdom.

Heraclitus exerted on posterity a curiously two-edged influence, and as an historical factor he reveals the same double aspect which is shown by natural objects in his theory. He became the head and fount, not merely of religious and conservative tendencies, but also of scepticism and revolution. If we may echo his own cry, he was and he was not a bulwark of conservatism, he was and he was not the champion of revolt. Still it was in accordance with his idiosyncrasy that the weight of his influence should have leaned to the side of defence. Within the school of the Stoics, his tendency was precisely opposed to the radical tendency of the Cynics. His views on the subordination of all occurrences to fixed laws were responsible for the strict and implacable determinism of the Stoics, which was liable in all but the clearest brains to pass into fatalism. From those views were derived the quality of resignation, not to say of quietism, which we meet as early as Cleanthes, and the willing submission to the dispensations of destiny of which Epictetus and Marcus Aurelius were the apostles. Heraclitus, too, is the first to introduce us to the Stoic manner of moulding and adapting philosophy to the requirements of popular belief. Similarly we may recall Hegel, his disciple in modern times, the author of the "philosophy of restoration," of the metaphysical glorification of tradition in church and state, and of the famous dictum, "the real is reasonable, and the reasonable is real." Yet the Neo-Hegelian radicalism, too, as is shown by the example of Lassalle, is also closely akin to Heraclitus. And for the most striking parallel, the exactest counterpart to the Ephesian which modern philosophy has produced, we must refer to the great revolutionary spirit of Proudhon. In separate and highly characteristic doctrines they are as alike as two peas, and Proudhon's mental habits and his consequent love of paradox remind us most vividly of Heraclitus.

The key to the contradiction is not far to seek. The innermost essence of Heraclitism was its insight into the many-sidedness of things, and the breadth of its intellectual horizon as opposed to every kind of narrow-mindedness. The habit and capacity of broad views tend to reconcile us to the imperfectness of nature and the hardship of history. Frequently they help us to perceive the remedy beside the disease, the antidote beside the poison. They teach us to discern the deep inner harmony in apparent conflict, and to discover in what is ugly and hurtful inevitable bridges and stepping-stones to the beautiful and wholesome. Thus they lead to an indulgent judgment of the universe in its natural and historical aspects, and pave the way for "theodicies" and for attempts to redeem the character of single individuals as well as of entire epochs. They foster the historical sense, and are akin to movements of religious optimism. Such tendencies, indeed, were actually strengthened by the revival of Heraclitism that took place in the age of Romance. But the same capacity and habit of mind produce a contrary effect. They are inimical to authority in that they forbid the formation of one-sided judgments. Dogmatism in laws and institutions is entirely incompatible with a high-strung versatility and flexibility of thought. A moment's reflection will make this clear. Heraclitus assumed a state of universal flux. Each single phenomenon in his theory was a link in the chain of causality, a transitory phase of evolution, and it would obviously have been impossible for him to bend the knee to an isolated product of the incessant series of transformations, as though it were eternal and immune.

We may justly assert that Heraclitism is conservative, since it discerns the positive side in things negative ; it is revolutionary, since it descries the negative side in things positive. It recognizes nothing absolute either in good or in evil; therefore there is nothing that it unconditionally rejects, nothing, too, that it unconditionally accepts. This habit of relative judgments brings historical justice in its train, but it prevents the acquiescence in any state of things as final. The doctrines of Heraclitus have been fruitful even till our own times, but from these recent manifestations of his influence we must revert to its sources. The names of Pythagoras and Xenophanes have occurred more than once in our mention of the men who exerted an influence on Heraclitus, and Pythagoras and Xenophanes themselves were not without their precursors. The vivid intellectual life of these centuries flowed in so many streams parallel or partly identical with one another, that it is hardly possible to keep our eyes fixed on one without temporarily losing sight of others which are of no less importance. Hence we may fitly sound a retreat at this point, and pick up what we may have neglected too long.

CHAPTER II.

ORPHIC SYSTEMS OF COSMOGONY.

1. MUST it be said that the courtly epic poetry, with its enlightened traits, with its delight—at times its frivolous delight—in the pleasures of this world, brought about a kind of reaction, or was it merely that, as the lower classes rose to power and prosperity, their views of life—the views of the bourgeois and the peasant—usurped the determining place? Be that as it may, the religion and morality of post-Homeric Greece wear a thoroughly altered aspect. Solemn, gloomy, and dismal features begin to predominate. We hear for the first time of the expiation of murder, the worship of souls, and the sacrifices to the dead, or where such customs were formerly the exception they now become the rule. The many essential points of likeness between these observances and opinions and those which obtained among kindred peoples, especially among the nations of Italy, as the most closely allied to the Greeks, show us that we are not dealing with wholly new ideas, but rather, to a considerable extent at least, with the revival or the first visible appearance of an immemorial tradition. There is one reservation to be made. The doctrine of immortality undoubtedly underwent a progressive transformation, and its serious influence on the development of Greek speculation compels us to discuss it at greater length.

Men's thoughts have always been busy with images of the next world, though the shapes and colours it assumes vary with national moods and circumstances. At

first the future would be conceived as the mere continuation of the present. The happy looked forward to it with
joy, the heavily-laden with fear. Princes and nobles
viewed the next world as a kind of limitless vista of the
pleasures of the chase and the table; serfs and slaves
discerned in it an unending chain of hard and exacting
duties. Still, the uncertainty which is inseparable from
the future, left an ample field for the tremors of anxiety
as well as for the flights of hope. For, if the wish is
father to the thought, care may be called its mother, and
their offspring show in varying proportions the features
of both their parents. If a man's lot on earth has been
running over with pleasure, he will readily conceive the
future as a pale and shadowy reflection of his mortal
experience; if such experience has left him a wide
margin for wishes and longings, then fancy will dip her
brush in the rosy colours of hope; finally, excess of
suffering, and the habit of sufferance it engenders, blunt
the edge of hope as well as that of desire, and imagination is left to exercise its skill on purely joyless pictures
of the future. And to outward conditions must be
added the differences of national temperament. But,
speaking generally, and confining our attention to the
factors already enumerated, the conception of the future
may be taken as resembling the actual present; its
lights and shades will be distributed according to the
idiosyncrasies we have mentioned. Nevertheless, it is not
hard to conjecture at what points in the course of time
imagination will have burst those bonds. The key to the
departure is to be sought in that theory of the next world
which may be described in one word as the retributive. It
is a doctrine which rested in the first instance on the fact
of common observation that a man's moral and mental
qualities determine to a great extent his lot. Power and
fortune in this life are apt to favour the brave, the strong,
the circumspect, the resolute; and hence, by an obvious
inference, or by the mere association of ideas, he expects
the same fate to attend him in the life to come. Another
factor must be looked for in the likes and dislikes of the

gods. Clearly the favourites of the gods, and especially their descendants, must preserve in the next world the advantages gained in this over persons bound by no such tie to the rulers of human destiny. And if prayer and sacrifice can win the good-will of heaven, there is plainly no reason to suppose that the liking thus bestowed will lose its efficacy under the conditions of future existence. This, then, is the sum of the matter. As state and society grow, the mighty forces of nature acquire a moral significance ; they are ranged with the family gods as the guardians and defenders of human laws and institutions, and this process gives rise to the thought—though it ripens but late and slowly—that the sceptre of heavenly justice is bound by no earthly confines, but that even beyond the limits of this life it is strong to pursue and overtake with the reward of righteousness and the punishment of wrongdoing.

In reviewing the development of Greece we are confronted with some of these phases. An age or a sphere of life drowned in immoderate passions and drenched in incessant conflicts, affording ample employment for the complete scale of human sensibility, is as ill-adapted for dreaming of futurity as for repining at the days that are no more. The active and actual hour absorbs the distant future no less than the distant past, and Homer's heroes, in their rare intervals of repose when war and fighting were laid aside, would beguile their leisure by descriptions of battles and adventures—their own, their ancestors', or their gods', whom they conceived so completely in their own likeness. No one envied the inhabitants of Hades their nerveless, noiseless existence. The warrior of Troy asked nothing better than to walk in the light of the sun. Achilles would rather endure a poor journeyman's humble lot on earth than reign as a monarch among the shades. Even if one of the warriors should be exalted by the gods to a share in heavenly bliss, such a distinction was a purely personal affair ; it was not the reward of glorious action, nor was its recipient therefore superior to any of his less-favoured fellows. The instance of Menelaus is a case in point. It was otherwise in Hesiod's time, or rather in the classes of people to whom his writings were addressed. These were confronted with a gloomy present, and imagination was bound to supply the missing happiness and brightness by embellishing the past as well as the future. They fondly looked back at a long-vanished " Golden Age ; " the gradual deterioration of man's lot on earth was stated by them as a fact, and it became a problem whose solution was a constant puzzle to the thoughtful. The state of the souls after death was frequently taken as glorified. The dead were often promoted to spirits who watched over the destinies of the living. The " Elysian Fields " and the " Fortunate Islands " began to fill with inhabitants. But with all this there was no dogmatic precision ; the whole range of these ideas was vague, vacillating, misty, and it remained so for some time. Homer, it is true, shows traces of a germ of the retributive doctrine, in the torments of hell that overtook certain irrepressible wrongdoers and " enemies of the gods ; " but many centuries were still to elapse before the seed came to flower. Tantalus and Sisyphus in agony are succeeded by Ixion and Thamyras ; but apart from the penalties exacted in Tartarus for exceptional insolence against the gods, the average lot of humanity in the next world was still regarded as completely independent of moral feelings and deserts. And above all, though the radiance of eternity might be stained by many shafts of colour, yet the state religion as the final expression of the conscience of the ruling classes, took but slight account of the belief in immortality. Antiquity—so far, at least, as its public religious systems are a guide to its thoughts and desires—was intent on this side of the grave.

We have been speaking of the main current of religious life. It should not be forgotten, however, that cross-currents and under-currents were at work which gradually gained in strength, though liable to temporary shallows, till they grew to a mighty stream hollowing its greedy course through the very heart of Hellenic religion.

One feature was common to all. The worshippers of the Mysteries and the disciples of Orphic Pythagoreanism were moved alike by a heightened interest in the future of the soul, based in the first instance on their disdain for earthly life, and resting ultimately on the gloomy view which they took of it.

2. The Orphic doctrines—called after Orpheus, the legendary minstrel of Thrace, whose name was attributed to all the sacred books of those sects—have come down to us in various recensions widely differing in parts from one another. Our fullest source of information dates from the evening of antiquity when Plato's latest heirs, the so-called Neo-Platonists, were delighted to revert to teachings so acceptable and congenial to their own. They introduced in their writings frequent references to the Orphic poems, and quoted directly from them. Now, when we remember that the Orphic doctrine is not a homogeneous whole, but is the compilation of diverse hands in various epochs of history, it is not surprising that the evidence of these late witnesses should have been received with suspicious scrutiny. It would appear at first sight a sound principle of criticism to discredit all evidence of this kind except for the age of its origin. But some of the most recent discoveries have afforded a striking proof of the will-o'-the-wisp character of such critical lights. In the tombs of Lower Italy, for example, dating from the third century B.C., which have lately been opened, gold plates have been found inscribed with Orphic verses formerly known to us merely by a reference in Proclus, a Neo-Platonist of the fifth century A.D. Thus seven hundred years were added at a stroke to their presumptive antiquity. Similarly Phanes, one of the most important figures of Orphic worship, was vouched for by no writer earlier than the Augustan historian Diodorus, till we found his name invoked on another of these tablets of Thurii. Criticism has thus been exposed as hypercriticism in these instances, and the excess of cautious foresight as a defect of sound insight. It is wiser on the whole to allow a fair margin for errors in

detail than to shut out the view into the inter-connection of these doctrines by the obstructive use of the principle —not wholly unreasonable in itself—which would limit the validity of each piece of evidence to the age to which it indubitably belongs. The new criticism, too, has tried to compensate for the absence of direct testimony by carefully sorting and comparing such hints and allusions as occur.

Let us first try to focus the intellectual endowment of the men whom Aristotle calls the "theologians," and whom we may perhaps describe as the right wing of the oldest group of Greek thinkers. Their mind was less scientific than that of the "physiologists." They made a far keener demand for a vivid representation of the origin and development of the world. The common mythology of the Hellenes did not fully satisfy them, partly because it was at variance with their standard of morality, partly because it answered the questions of cause and descent in too vague or too crude a fashion. Still, their original speculations were quite rudimentary. But they could not remain so. The demand for mythological completeness was still too strong to be neglected. The blank spaces had to be filled up, and they were filled up by traditions from other sources. There was an eager hunt for such adjuncts, and where were they more likely to be found than in isolated local legends, in the records of foreign peoples, and especially in those of nations with a halo of immemorial civilization? These three elements—original cosmogonic speculation, the local legends of Greece, and the complementary traditions of foreign people—would constitute the threads on which the new learning was strung. That such was really the fact may be gathered from a glance at the contents, and above all at the character, of the Orphic and allied doctrines. The admixture is clearly seen in the theory of origin propounded by Pherecydes of Syros. We place him at the head, not by any means because he is the oldest, but because he is the first representative of this movement whose date can be fixed with well-nigh absolute certainty. About the middle of the sixth century B.C., he published a prose composition under the title of Pentemychos, out of which some verbatim quotations have come down to our times. He was influenced by older co-religionists, one of whom, the poet Onomacritus, is known to us by name. He lived at the court of Pisistratus, tyrant of Athens, where he founded an Orphic community, though how far he was the disciple and prophet of the Orphic doctrines we are hardly able to say. Pherecydes was further devoted to astronomical research. He probably borrowed the principles of the science from Babylon, and his observatory was for a long time one of the sights which were shown to visitors to Syros. As a philosopher, then, he recognized three primordial beings—Chronos, or the Time-principle; Zeus, whom he called Zas; and Chthonie, the goddess of earth. The variant "Zas" was doubtless connected with that signification of the name which we have already met in Heraclitus, and which sought to represent the chief of the gods as the highest principle of life. From the seed of Chronos sprang "Fire, Air, and Water," and from these again "many generations of the gods." In later and therefore possibly contaminated traditions we come across two more elements under the names of "Smoke" and "Darkness;" and thus the quintett of first principles alluded to in the title of Pherecydes' work is completed. Each was originally supposed to inhabit a separate region of the world. But a battle of the gods broke out in which Ophioneus, the serpent-god, and his followers attacked Chronos and his attendant deities. The struggle closed with the disappearance of one set of combatants in the sea, which figures in Pherecydes as "Ogenos," presumably a Babylonian name corresponding to the Greek Okeanos. Some further features of his cosmology may be noted. Zas, or Zeus, is transformed as the creator of the world into the Love-god Eros; next he fashions "a mighty and beautiful garment wherein are inwrought the pictures of Earth and Ogenos and his habitations," and this garment he spreads over "the winged oak;" lastly, "beneath the Earth is the region of Tartarus guarded by the Harpies and Thyella, the daughters of Boreas, whither a god who sins by overweening pride is ever hurled by Zas." Add to this that Chthonie changes her name to Ge "after Zas had given her the earth as her portion," and that Rhea the mother of the gods is called Rhe, perhaps to counterbalance Ge, and our account of Pherecydes' teachings about the gods and the world is complete as far as we know it.

It is a wonderful mixture of a little science, a bit of allegory, and a lump of mythology. Let us try to find our bearings in the maze of speculation. Our thinker is at one with the "physiologists" in his recognition of first principles dating from eternity, and in his endeavour to derive the manifold forms of the material world from a few fundamental elements. Another and very characteristic point of agreement is this, that he represents the bulk of the minor gods as proceeding from those material elements. But he parts company from them in the following details : He does not go as far as the "physiologists" in the reduction of matter, so as to recognize a single fundamental element. If we understand him correctly, he does not even refer to air as an independent element. But, above all, his elements are not primeval. Primary beings take their place in that respect, and are not conceived as coarsely material. From them the material elements are supposed to spring. This mode of origin is specified merely of the three elements operating in the upper world. Still, the parallelism in his account seems to warrant the assumption that the two materials belonging to the region of Darkness—our acquaintance with which is solely due to chance references in S. Augustine—are likewise to be traced to the serpent-god presiding in the under-world. It is tempting to speak in this connection of the middle place taken by our "theologian" between Hesiod on the one side and the nature-philosophers on the other. But this would not be an exhaustive account of the matter. The chief parts in the "Theogony"—apart from certain divine principles—are sustained by natural agents conceived as possessing souls, such as the "broad-bosomed Earth," the "wide heaven," and many others.

In the instance of Pherecydes, it is no longer legitimate to speak of natural fetishes. Zas and Chronos appear rather as spiritual beings, and Chthonie is expressly distinguished from "Earth," whose name the goddess does not bear till she has received the material earth from the hands of Zas. We may imagine Pherecydes stating, "The earth-spirit precedes the earth and is joined later with the earth as the soul is with the body." Here there is foreshadowed a mode of thought which has no little bearing on the conception of body and soul, characteristic of the Orphics, strictly so called, as well as of Pherecydes himself.

We have noted the statement that a battle of the gods preceded the final disposition of the world, and we meet it so frequently in Greek and non-Greek mythologies alike, that it is not surprising to find it again in Pherecydes. A twofold consideration probably lies at the root of this widespread belief, and its obvious connection with the thought of primitive man makes it not unworthy of mention. He could hardly have looked on the rule of law as an immemorial fact, for he ascribed to the powers whom he postulated behind the visible world a will and passions as strong and as unbridled as belonged to the superior members of human society—the sole society which he knew, and which was far removed from discipline and law. And if, thus, primitive man must have held that the regularity which he observed in natural phenomena was the arbitrary law imposed by the victors on the vanquished, this presumption would be strengthened by the fact that the most powerful factors in nature are, comparatively speaking, but seldom in the exercise of their full force. Earthquakes, tempests, and active volcanoes form but rare and short interruptions of the prevalent peace of nature. This state of things, men would argue, could not have dated from everlasting. The terrible powers inimical to man must at one time have reigned unmolested. Yet mightier powers must then have engaged them in conflict, and their ultimate defeat in that struggle would account for the restricted limits of their sway. The more closely we examine the features of the battle of the gods according to the version of Pherecydes, the more we are reminded in many details of Babylonian cosmology. Eminent scholars, indeed, incline to the theory of plagiarism. Further, when Zas transforms himself into the god of love to assist his creation of the world, we have not far to look to discover the source of this legend. Hesiod has already familiarized us with the thought borrowed from organic life and extended by a process of generalization, that it is the procreative instinct alone which unites congenial elements and warrants the continuity of existing orders and races. And the Hesiodic account is set in such rigid lines that we perceive that the theory must have flourished long before he adopted it. We must probably look to the worship of the love-god in some ancient sanctuaries—that of Thespiæ in Bœotia, for instance—for the home of the mythical speculation touching the "love that built the world." And, finally, we may fairly conjecture that the garment spread by Zas over the winged oak was merely a pictorial expression of the belief that the kernel or framework of earth was adorned by this first principle of life with the beauty that it now wears. Moreover, there is considerable plausibility in the recent conjecture that Pherecydes attributed wings to the framework of earth because he had rejected the disc-and-basin theory of earth which Thales maintained in favour of Anaximander's conception of the earth floating freely in space. Lastly, it is not so much the detailed doctrines of the "theologian" of Syros that vex our understanding as the habit of mind from which they directly sprang, and which wavered so strangely between science and myth. We have no reason to question the earnest enthusiasm by which Pherecydes was inspired, nor is his memory sullied by any trace of miracle-mongery. Accordingly, the problem he presents is difficult to solve. He offers a minute description of the origin of the gods and the world, and yet he was no poet; he assumes the confidence of the orthodox believer, and yet he was a stranger to the "fine frenzy" of inspiration in which the secrets of the universe are revealed. We at least can suggest no other solution of the riddle than that alluded to above. Pherecydes may have owed some features of his doctrine, especially in his theory of the elements, to his own speculative thought; some other features, as we have seen, he borrowed from the researches of his predecessors; but the brilliant picture as a whole cannot have been composed by either of these methods. It was indebted to native and foreign traditions alike. The philosopher believed them because they agreed in principle with his own conclusions, and on that account he turned, changed, and fused them with a licence which he himself failed to realize. Nothing is at once so difficult and so indispensable to our task as to frame a conception of the imperfect state of criticism at that day. Many separate legends it did away with altogether. Others which rested on precisely the same foundation it adopted with complete faith, so that its attitude towards tradition in general, so far from being systematic, was of the kind which naively expected to discover a key to the deepest secrets of the universe in the names and fables of individual gods. Pherecydes, then, may be regarded as one of the earliest representatives of that half-critical, half-credulous eclecticism which serves to typify so many thinkers of other peoples and times.

3. The life and teaching of the founder of the Orphic sect were subject to the same disadvantage which we meet in other religious communities. Diverse and contradictory reports accompanied or succeeded one another. In our opinion it would be wholly as illegitimate to speak of "forgery" or "apocryphal" writings in this connection as in that of the second covenant of Moses in the Old Testament, or of the doctrine of the Logos in the New. Thus the Orphic theory of cosmogony appears in various recensions whose consecution in time it is impossible to fix with certainty. And we may even assume that several of them were current at the same time without supposing that their readers were more repelled by the contradictions they contained than the students of other holy writings. Four such versions or fragments of them have come down to our time. (1) We owe one of these versions to Eudemus,

the historian of science and disciple of Aristotle. Unfortunately, his account has dwindled down to little more than the bare mention that Night in Pherecydes was the supreme primary being. The conception is interesting as reminding us of the Homeric verse which relates how Zeus was refrained from acting contrary to Night, where we see the faint gleam of the belief that Night was superior even to the father of the gods. The Maoris, too, recognize "a first mother, Night," and the doctrine comes to frequent expression in the cosmogony of the Greeks themselves. It plays the chief part in the legendary Musæus no less than in Epimenides the seer, in Acusilaus the fabulist, as well as in a fourth writer whose name is unknown. (2) We need hardly mention the second version, which consists of a dozen verses describing the origin of the world put by Apollonius, the Alexandrian poet, in his "Argonautica" into the mouth of Orpheus. For while it makes no claim to historical value, its contents would wholly disqualify it from making good such a claim. The principle of "Discord," which here divides the four elements, is taken, with the elements themselves, from the young nature-philosopher Empedocles. Next the battle of the gods is described in partial agreement with Pherecydes, and the slight departures that are made do not create an impression of any greater faithfulness to tradition. Pherecydes, for instance, makes Ophioneus and Chronos fight for the mastery and gives the upper world to the victor and the under world to the vanquished as their habitation and empire. In Apollonius, however, we find Ophioneus in possession of Olympus, and as serpent-beings belong by nature and accordingly by myth to the region of earth, we cannot but recognize here a further divagation from the original form of the legend, and an artificial continuation of it. (3) Nor need the third version delay us long. It is expressly stated by its authorities to be opposed to the current Orphic doctrine, and its distinctive features, which rest on the evidence of Hieronymus and Hellanicus, witnesses of doubtful date and personality, are by no means such as to warrant a respectable antiquity. (4) It is completely otherwise with the fourth and last version of

Orphic theogony and cosmogony, which was formerly contained in the so-called "Rhapsodies." Modern scholarship,
following the masterly lead of Christian August Lobeck, has
found clear evidence that it was known to the poets and
thinkers of the sixth century B.C., and was employed by them;
and the arguments hitherto and still levelled against this
claim to antiquity have been shown to be completely invalid. This controversy involves some important questions
of principle, and we cannot altogether avoid it. First, however, we should enumerate the chief contents of this theory
of cosmogony. As in Pherecydes, Chronos or the Time-
principle stands once more at its head. It existed from
eternity, whereas Light-stuff or Fire-stuff, under the name
of Æther, and the "huge gulf" under the name of Chaos,
came next into existence. Then "mighty Chronos" formed
"a silver egg" out of Æther and Chaos with its contents
of "dark mist." From the "egg" sprang the first-born
of the gods, who is variously known as Phanes the shining
one, Eros the love-god, Metis or counsel, and Ericapæus,
a name which has not yet been interpreted. As the repository of all the seeds of being, Phanes was at once male and
female, and produced spontaneously Night and Echidna, a
horrible serpent-deity, and with Night Uranus and Gaia,
heaven and earth, the progenitors of the "secondary race"
of the gods. We shall not dwell on the Titans, Giants,
Moiræ, and the Hecatonchires, for the account given of
them in the Orphic theogony differs hardly at all from
that of Hesiod. Further, Chronos and Rhea belong to the
secondary generation of gods. But their son "Zeus, at
once head and centre and author of all things," "Zeus the
cause of the earth and of the star-sown heaven," swallows
Phanes, and thus becomes the universal progenitor in his
turn, and the father of the third and youngest race of the
gods and of the whole visible world.

We have now to try to master the fundamental principle
of this theory, to acquaint ourselves with its peculiar
characteristics, to discover as far as possible its historical
sources, and thus to contribute our share to the solution of the problem mentioned above. The impression

forces itself on our belief that the separate parts of this cosmogony are not fully homogeneous, but have been gradually fused into a complete whole. For it seems, if not in actual contradiction, at least alien to the nature of myths that Æther, the element of light and fire, should appear at an earlier stage of the cosmic process than Phanes, whose name signifies "shining," and who is represented as the first-born of the gods. Mythology always aims at strong effects, and has no taste for anti-climax. We are thus led to imagine that two streams of speculative myth-making have here mingled their waters; the one would display more naturalistic features, and the other would allow for the creative activity of proper god-like beings. If we look for the actual thought which found its mythical expression in the first part of that cosmogony, we should cast it somewhat in this form : As a plant unfolds and grows under the animating rays of the sun, so "the world was formed in course of time out of the matter floating darkly in space under the influence of light and heat." A second and essentially different thought may be expressed as follows : "A divine being of light sprang, in order to create the world, out of the original shapeless darkness." In the passages of Orphic poetry where Phanes is designated as "the son of resplendent Æther" we find a link between these two views. Similarly, the fable of the world-egg would seem no longer to confront us in its original form. It must obviously have been first invented by some such argument as this : The world is alive, and it must have had a beginning. Its origin, continued the argument, must be like that of a living being ; and then the round vault of heaven reminded the authors of this argument of the shape of an egg. Such an egg, they inferred, would once have existed, and when it burst, its upper portion went to form the dome of the sky, the lower part engendered the earth and all that is therein. We are by no means committed to the belief that the transformation of the fable of the world-egg took place on the soil of Greece. It is, indeed, a world-wide myth. It is found not merely among the Greeks, the Persians, and the Indians, but these share it in common with Phœnicia, Babylon, and with Egypt, where, indeed, it appears in precisely the same form as in the Orphic cosmogony. We may quote, for instance, the following Egyptian account of the creation of the world :—

" In the beginning was neither heaven nor earth. The universe was surrounded by thick darkness, and was filled with boundless water [known to the Egyptians as Nun] which carried in its lap the germs of male and female, or the beginnings of the future world. The divine First Spirit, inseparable from the watery First Matter, felt an impulse to create activity, and his word called the world into life. . . . The first act of creation began with the formation of an egg out of the elemental waters, and from the egg went forth Râ the Daylight, the direct source of earthly life."

In another version—and it may not be useless to notice the variations of the legend in the valley of the Nile-- it was the "god Ptah who, according to his worshippers, turned the egg, from which the world issued, like a potter on his wheel." It will not have escaped the attentive reader that in the male and female germs mentioned in the Egyptian fable a parallel is found to the Light-god of the Orphic legend who creates the world and whose nature combines both male and female attributes. We are yet more strongly reminded by the twofold nature of Phanes of the epicene godheads who occur by no means infrequently in the Babylonian Pantheon. Add to this that, according to the unimpeachable testimony of Eudemus, the Phœnician cosmogony reproduces the Time-principle that stands at the head of our cosmogony, not to speak of the Persian Avesta, where it appears as Zrvan Akarana or boundless time, and our readers will have been sufficiently familiarized with the thought that foreign traditions exercised no inconsiderable influence on the origin of the Orphic doctrine. The centre from which these lights radiated may almost certainly be identified with the country which was not merely one of the oldest homes, but practically the cradle of human civilization ; it was the country ruled by

Babylon and situated between the Euphrates and the Tigris. In stating this conviction, we are prepared to encounter opposition. We shall draw on our heads the bitter contempt of many worthy antiquarians who would regard it as derogatory to the Greeks to send them to school among older civilized nations, and to assume them to have borrowed thence the sources of their knowledge and belief. But the narrow-minded obstinacy which would rigidly isolate the Greeks and withdraw them from the influence of other and older civilizations, cannot possibly be maintained in the face of the evidence which is constantly presented with stronger and clearer force. To-day hardly any one attempts to deny that the Greeks owe to the Orient the elements of material civilization as well as the beginnings of their art, though a score of years ago this proposition was disputed with equal confidence and vehemence. The same views would be valid in the spheres of science and religion if their acceptation had not been checked by the hasty, partial, and unsystematic efforts of previous generations. But here, too, the opposition must finally be vanquished. Though it is led by men as illustrious as Lobeck, whom we have mentioned above, yet it must ultimately yield to the unprejudiced and universal appreciation of historical facts. At this point a question might be asked as to the means by which religious and speculative views were transferred from the older nations to Greece, and the problem recalls a striking parallel from the literary history of mediæval Europe. Practically the entire fairy-lore of the Occident is derived from India. No one disputes this assertion to-day, but no one as yet can give a completely clear account of the ways and means by which its journey was accomplished. The Greeks, as we have seen, came at an early time into frequent and intimate contact with foreign peoples as soldiers and merchants, as adventurous seamen and warlike settlers. They would meet in the camp, at the bazaar, and in the caravanserai. They would exchange ideas on the starlit decks of merchant vessels or in the intimate darkness of the nuptial chamber when a Greek settler took a native as his bride, and it is likely enough

that their confidences on such occasions would have ranged
from earth to heaven. Other circumstances, too, contributed
to the welcome extended to foreign doctrines of religion.
From them the Greek had already borrowed several of his
gods and heroes, such as the Semitic Astoreth (Afthoret or
Aphrodite), and Adonis her lover, and later the Thracian
Bendis and the Phrygian Cybele ; and as his ancient native
traditions failed more and more to satisfy his increasing
curiosity and thirst for knowledge, foreign sources would be
drawn on more freely in an age of acute intellectual vigour
and progress. Moreover, national pride was no great op-
posing force. The Greeks were always ready to recognize
their own gods in those of other nations, and to reconcile
contradictions between native and foreign traditions by their
nimble and pliant genius for adaptation. This process,
which was developed to a remarkable degree, is admirably
illustrated by many amusing instances in Herodotus. To
revert to Babylon and its central and important position
in the history of religion, the striking results of modern
research may be summarized quite briefly. A few years
ago the present writer was desirous of establishing the
possibility of the transference of religious doctrines from
Mesopotamia to Egypt. To that end he was at pains to
collect a mass of evidence directed to prove the early and
active intercourse of the inhabitants of both countries.
This evidence may now be cheerfully committed to the
waste-paper basket, since it has been more than confirmed
by the splendid discoveries of a yet later date. I refer to
the cuneiform archive found at El-Amarna in Egypt, which
contains a diplomatic correspondence between the monarchs
of both empires written about fifteen hundred years B.C.
Nor is its interest exhausted by its contents. In conjunction with the latest finds at Lachish in Palestine, it shows
us that the language and writing of Babylon were a current
means of intercourse in wide regions of Western Asia ; that
they found exact scholars in Egypt itself ; that, finally, to
the confusion of the incredulous, the Egyptians took sufficient interest in the religious traditions of Babylon, to
transcribe some of them from the brick libraries of

Mesopotamian sanctuaries, where they had lain since hoary antiquity. Further, to prove that India was likewise not unaffected by the influence of that centre of civilization, we may cite a single significant word which was borrowed from Babylon. The term "Mine" as a token of weight occurs in the hymns of the Rig-Veda. The lands of the Euphrates and Tigris, and those of the Indus and Ganges, stood of old in reciprocal relations of culture, and the addition of important evidence to this effect will, we trust, be presently published by an eminent authority.

But after this necessary digression, let us revert to our subject. The swallowing of Phanes by Zeus is fashioned on older precedents. Chronos, for instance, swallowed his children, and Zeus again swallowed Metis, and Athene, with whom she was pregnant, then sprang from his head. But the use of this crude motive would appear to have been governed by a desire to unite a congeries of myths into a harmonious whole. At the root of it there obviously lies an older pantheistic conception of the supreme god bearing within him all "the force and seeds of life." But now that the new cosmogony ascribed the generative part to Phanes, or the god of light, some means had to be found of rescuing that dignity from "the first-born of the gods" on whom mythology had hastily bestowed it, and of conferring it in turn on the last ruler of the world as the final link in the long chain of the races of gods. A doubt, entirely baseless in our opinion, has been thrown on the antiquity of the Orphic doctrine on account of this pantheistic current. If we recall the uncompromisingly pantheistic trend of the oldest nature-philosophers, or if we remember that before the middle of the fifth century Æschylus ventured from the stage to address the assembled people of Athens in verses like the following:—

> "Zeus is the heaven, Zeus the earth, Zeus the air,
> Zeus is the universe and all besides,"

we shall not hesitate to believe that this comparatively tame pantheism flourished in the sixth or even in the seventh century in the restricted circle of the Orphic conventicles. Considerable points of agreement no less than of divergence result from a comparison of this theory as a whole with that of Pherecydes. Chronos, Æther, and Chaos correspond to Pherecydes' trinity of primary Beings— Chronos, Zas, and Chthonie. Hesiod has already acquainted us with Chaos and Æther, but their present place and constitution have in some respects been changed. The Hesiodic Æther is but one of several beings of light ; it ranks by no means as a favourite. Chaos, too, has altered its nature. It is no longer merely the symbol of the gulf yawning between the highest height and the lowest depth ; it represents a " dark mist," a mass of unorganized matter floating in that gulf. The Orphic Æther, or the light- and fire-stuff, is probably the animating or vivifying element— as opposed to the inanimate mass—which was refined and clarified by Pherecydes to Zas, the divine principle of life. Doubtless the same relation exists between Chaos and Chthonie, the spirit or godhead of the earth. So far as a definite statement can be made on so difficult a question, it may be said that the doctrine which stands philosophically halfway between Hesiod and Pherecydes belongs to an intermediate date. This view is supported by the observation that the Orphic theogony agrees with Hesiod in attributing a temporal origin to Æther and Chaos, whereas the thinker of Syros, in rare and almost unique conformity with the "physiologists," ascribes eternal existence to his three world-principles indifferently. But the Orphic attempts at cosmology were at the best but the work of children. Of far greater moment and consequence were their psychological speculations. These are connected with an entirely new conception of life. They parted company with the old Hellenism, undermining the beauty and harmony of the Greek view of life, and preparing the way for its final overthrow. But at this point the threads of the Orphic doctrine are so closely interwoven with the threads of another and deeper intellectual movement, that we cannot continue till we have considered this course of evolution and its great author.

CHAPTER III.

PYTHAGORAS AND HIS DISCIPLES.

" PYTHAGORAS, son of Mnesarchus, has practised research and inquiry more than all other men, and has made up his wisdom out of polymathy and out of bad arts." This invective of Heraclitus and another quoted by us above, comprise almost the sole contemporary testimony to the life-work of a man whom an endless train of disciples has lauded and admired to the utmost, and whom posterity has honoured like a demi-god. Pythagoras was born at Samos, an island famous at that time for its navigation, its industry and commerce, between 580 and 570 B.C. The son of Mnesarchus a stonecutter, he was one of the most original figures in Greece, and indeed in all the world. As a mathematician of brilliant parts, as the founder of acoustics and the guide in untrodden paths of astronomy, as the author of a religious sect and of a brotherhood which admits comparison with the orders of mediæval chivalry, as a man of science, a theologian, and a moral reformer, Pythagoras commanded a kingdom of talents of the most composite and sometimes of the least compatible kinds. It is hard to rescue the prototype from the flood of tradition which increases in volume the further it is removed from the source. No line from his own pen has been preserved, and it seems well-nigh certain that he did not avail himself of written communication, but relied for his influence on his disciples on the power of the spoken word and the speaking example.

According to one tradition, which is not completely

vouched for, Pythagoras was the pupil of Pherecydes. It appears to be beyond doubt that he was engaged in distant journeys which late antiquity has exaggerated into a kind of Odyssey, and the various elements of culture which he collected in his travels formed the stones of his brilliant house of learning. By no other means, we may be confident, could he ever have satisfied his thirst for knowledge in an age comparatively poor in literary monuments, and in no other way could he have deserved the eulogy implied in the gibe of the sage of Ephesus. It would have been almost miraculous if the adept at mathematics had failed to visit Egypt, the cradle of that science, whither a century or two later a Democritus, a Plato, and a Eudoxus turned their steps for the same purpose. Moreover, it can scarcely be doubted that he borrowed from the priesthood of Egypt all kinds of practices that have ranked as distinctive features of his foundation. Herodotus the historian, a trustworthy witness in this instance, does not hesitate to speak of the " Orphics and Bacchics " as " Pythagoreans and Egyptians," and he hints emphatically enough at the like origin of another corner-stone of Pythagoreanism—the belief in the transmigration of souls. Whether or not Pythagoras saw the golden spires of Babylon, who shall say ? It is at least probable that the curious Greek would have visited this seat of immemorial civilization, and have dipped in its treasury of native and foreign traditions. When Samos was ruled by the tyrant Polycrates, Pythagoras, arrived at man's estate, left his island home and found in Southern Italy a ripe soil for his experiments in reform. His chief field of activity was Croton, famous at that time for its wholesome situation, excellent physicians, and powerful athletes, but fallen now into decay, with its once proud name transferred to the miserable fishing-village of Cortona. This Achæan colony had just been worsted in battle by luxurious Sybaris, its ancient rival ; and the humiliating defeat had prepared men's minds for moral, religious, and political innovations. The new settler took advantage of this receptive mood for the promotion of

his schemes of reform. He forthwith founded his community, which admitted both men and women in its
fold, and recognized distinct degrees of membership ; and
the ingenious system by which the rigours of the order
were graduated extended its influence over wide classes
of candidates. The fruit of the reform was a revival in
the public spirit, manifested by a strong aristocratic
government within the walls of the city, and by success in
arms abroad ; and this result was not long confined to
Croton, but extended itself to other cities in Magna
Græcia, such as Tarentum, Metapontum, and Caulonia.
A reaction was bound to ensue. The cohesion of the
aristocrats in a religious and social community with beliefs
and observances of its own which set them apart from the
mass of the citizens as a kind of *populus in populo* and
rendered them haughtier and less accessible than ever,
could not but increase the bitterness of the existing battle
of the classes. The clamour for further political rights
rose to a higher pitch ; the outcry against the foreign
intruder and his new-fangled notions grew louder, and to
these manifestations was added the personal resentment
of unsuccessful candidates for admittance to the brotherhood. So the Pythagorean community in Croton was
doomed. A catastrophe as horrible as that which destroyed
the Knights Templar overtook it about 500 B.C., when its
members were burnt alive, presumably in their place of
assembly. The accounts are too vague to enable us to
decide whether Pythagoras himself was a victim, or whether
he had died at an earlier date. A similar fate overtook
the branches of the order. True, there were always
disciples of Pythagorism, but the Pythagoreans as a
community were destroyed. In Greece itself the last
adherents of the school lingered on in Bœotia, where the
great Epaminondas received instruction from its members.
Others again went to Athens and began the fusion of
Pythagorean doctrines with those of other schools of
philosophy, among which that of Socrates was the foremost.
Finally, Pythagorism dissolved into those constituent elements compressed by the force of one great genius

into the limits of a system which was anything but homogeneous. The positive science of the doctrine and its mathematical and physical methods fell to the care of specialists, while its religious and superstitious maxims and practices were preserved in Orphic circles.

2. The claim to immortality which this school may advance rests on its contributions to science. We reverently do homage to the genius of the men who first showed the way to a thorough comprehension of the forces of nature and to their final mastery. And here we must pause to make a remark of more universal import. The ancients and moderns have both, with partial correctness, reproached the Pythagoreans with a want of sobriety and a caprice of imagination. But it is a pleasure to be able to point out that this play of fancy and emotion, and the corresponding delight in what is beautiful and harmonious, though they occasionally obstructed the path of scientific research, yet in many decisive instances smoothed the obstacles away and lent wings to inquiry. Pythagoras was always passionately devoted to music, an art to which his disciples ever gave the chief place among the means for exciting and appeasing the emotions. And without this kind of artistic delight he would certainly never have attained his insight into the dependence of the pitch of sound on the length of the vibrating chord, which ranks as his greatest and most important discovery. The monochord which he used for his experiments in the physics of sound, "consisted of a string stretched over a resounding-board with a moveable bridge, by means of which it was possible to divide the string into different lengths, and thus to produce the various high and low notes on one and the same string." Great was the surprise of the inquirer, well versed as he was both in mathematics and music, when this simple experiment revealed at a single stroke the most wonderful operations of law in a field hitherto completely closed to scientific investigation. He was still unable to determine the vibrations on which the separate sounds depended, but inasmuch as he could now measure the vibrating chord which was the material cause that produced the sound,

rule and law and spatial quantity were thus imposed on
something that had hitherto been wholly intangible, unde-
finable, and almost of another world. The history of
science contains no luckier hit than this. In other
departments of nature, such as those of dynamics, the
underlying laws are hidden away from the eye of the
spectator, and can only be reached by extremely artificial
contrivances. Here, however, the simplest conceivable
experiment sufficed to bring to light a great regulative
principle embracing a wide domain of nature. The
intervals between the sounds—the fourth, the fifth, the
octave, and so forth—which had hitherto solely been perceptible to the fine ear of the professional musician, but
which could neither be communicated to others nor referred
to comprehensible causes, were now reduced to clear and
fixed numerical relations. And as soon as the foundations
had been laid for the mechanics of sound, all other systems
of mechanics might seem to be open to investigation.
Great was the delight aroused by this wonderful discovery,
and we can hardly be surprised if the further speculations
of the Pythagoreans transgressed the bounds of moderation.
The brilliance and obscurity of their doctrine lie within a
step of one another, and we reach at once the Pythagorean
mysticism of number, which strikes us at first sight as
opposed to reason and understanding. Sound, one of the
most volatile of phenomena, had been shown to be measur-
able in space. But number is the measure of all space ;
it is the expression of the regularity so suddenly observed
to pervade every department of nature, and it was an easy
inference to regard it as the heart and essence of things.
It reminds us of the Ionian "physiologists" with their
contradictory and therefore fruitless attempts to discover
the single primary matter which underlay and survived all
change. The theories of Thales and Anaximander could not
give lasting satisfaction, but their common desire to discover
the fixed pole in the flight of phenomena could not but
survive the failure of their several experiments. Then
came Pythagoras and his disciples. Their astonished eyes
were suddenly opened to the suggestive spectacle of a

universal uniformity ruling nature and dependent on numbers. What wonder if the material principle was temporarily eclipsed by the formal, masquerading as quasi-material? The question of a primary principle was dropped for a time, or rather it appeared in another shape. Fire and Air, and Anaximander's "infinite," comprising all material contraries, were deposed as the Principle of the world, and the vacant throne was taken by Number as the expression of universal law. We have just now marked the historical explanation of this view, which, in defiance of the natural order of things, regarded Number as their most intimate essence, and not merely as the expression of relations and proportions. We may now reach the same goal from another point of departure. In the researches undertaken by this school the quality of matter is of considerably less account than the forms which it wears in space. But here the growing habit of abstract thought led the philosopher to regard a conception as more primordial and valuable, according as it was more refined and further removed from concrete reality. We possess the faculty of dissociating in our minds the body itself from the planes in which it lies, and the planes from the lines that bound them ; or, to put it more accurately, we can temporarily make abstraction of the corporeal and superficial areas, and regard the planes and lines as things existing by themselves. These abstractions, as Aristotle expressly tells us, were accorded by the Pythagoreans, not merely complete reality, but actually a higher reality than the concrete objects from which they were derived. The planes, they argued, are conditional to the existence of the bodies, but can themselves exist without them. And they passed a similar judgment on the lines in relation to the planes ; and, finally, on the points of which the line is composed. Points are the smallest units of space. We abstract from them not merely thickness and breadth, but length likewise, thus completing their abstraction from spatial extension. It is an abstraction which is of use where the limits of extension are concerned rather than extension as such. Now these points were identified by the Pythagoreans with Unity—that is, with the element of Number. Number, then, appeared to them as a kind of fundamental principle, in which the objective world was not merely dissolved by thought, but from which it proceeded. It was, as it were, composed and built up of Number, so that the line which consisted of two points would represent duality, the plane would represent the conception of three, and the body the conception of four. This delusion was supported by an idiosyncrasy of Greek language and thought as innocent in its origin as it was perilous in its consequences. The analogy between numbers and spatial relations led to the description of qualities of the former by epithets which are strictly appropriate to the latter alone. Nor are we wholly free from the influence of our masters, the Greeks. If we no longer speak of oblong or cyclic numbers, we still have square and cubic numbers ; but all that we mean by these phrases is that the products stand to their factors in the same proportion as the spatial-content of a plane or body to the key-numbers of the lines containing its superficial area or corporeal volume. We shall hardly be accused of exaggeration if we say that this kind of linguistic artifice is expressly calculated to confuse a mind unversed in the practice of abstraction. The parallelism between the two series of phenomena would inevitably rank as identity ; the spatial form or figure would appear as substantially the same as the number indicating the mass of spatial-units it contained ; number would, or could at least, be regarded as a principle, or, as we still say, a " root " of the plane and consequently of the body too ; the expression "raising a number to its cube " would lead to the illusion that a body or object grew out of Number as an object is composed out of its elements ; and in these misleading terms are we not justified in perceiving the origin of the whole, or at least of more than the half, of the Pythagorean doctrine of number ?

More than half at least, for one branch of the doctrine and that by no means the least important, seems at first not to be covered by this explanation. Number was the ultimate basis of the spiritual no less than of the material world. Seven, for instance, was identified witn health ; eight with Love and Friendship, as a harmony best expressed by the octave ; Justice figured as a square number, doubtless because the " eye for eye " theory of retribution recalled the composition of a number out of two like factors. And in instances where we are no longer able to perceive the association between numbers and ideas, the same principle obviously operated. But what was the purpose of this game of thought played in quite sober earnest ? And how, we wonder, are we to account for the Pythagorean numerical explanation of the essence of all things in the moral and spiritual world ? The true answer would probably take this shape : As soon as Number had once been exalted to the type of reality in the physical universe, other realities too would inevitably have been co-ordinated with the same type, and in that age and long afterwards our abstractions were their realities. It is hard for us to conceive the dilemma in which they were placed. They had to choose between two alternatives : either they must deny the existence of health, virtue, love, friendship, and so forth, or they must discern their inmost essence in Number, the root of all other reality. Further, we must bear in mind the fascination exercised by numbers on the senses of mankind. They do not merely fill the multitude with intellectual delusions, as is shown in the history of religions, but strong men of rare and subtle powers are sometimes liable to their sway. We ought to realize the intoxicating force of these all-comprehensive abstractions, working as they did on minds at home only in the thin air of those intellectual heights, or at least debarred from the counterpoise afforded by gifts and occupations of a widely differing kind. The sacredness of the number three meets us as early as Homer, where a trinity of gods, Zeus, Athene, and Apollo, are addressed in a single supplication. Three, again, and its square play the most prominent part in the rites of the Greeks and Romans and of the Eastern branches of the Aryans. We find it in ancestor worship, where the father, grand-father, and great-grandfather are selected out of the whole

lineage as Tritopatores or paternal triad. We find it again
in the number of the expiatory sacrifices, of the dedicatory
offerings, of the funeral festivals, of the Graces, the Fates,
the Muses, and so forth, and we need merely mention the
Indian Trimurti—Brahma, Vishnu, and Siva—and kindred
religious conceptions, and the trinity of primary beings of
Pherecydes and the Orphics generally. The Pythagoreans sought to establish the sacred character of this
number by claiming that it contained a beginning, a
middle, and an end, an argument which was not entirely
without effect on the highly cultivated mind of Aristotle.
It is not without surprise that we are strongly reminded
of the Pythagorean doctrine of numbers in the speculations
of Giordano Bruno and Auguste Comte. The importance
assigned to the numbers three, four, and ten in the Comtist
philosophy is replaced in the master's later and religious
phase by the significance he attaches to the prime numbers.
Finally, Lawrence Oken, a leader of the modern school
of "nature-philosophy," did not hesitate to incorporate the
following sentence among his aphorisms : " Everything
that is real, posited, finite, has become this out of numbers,
or, more strictly speaking, every Real is absolutely nothing
else than a number." After that no one can be astonished
at the curious teachings which issued from the Pythagoreans. We read there without surprise that Unity, or
the Monad, contains the two fundamental contraries—the
Unlimited and the Limited—which form the basis of the
universe ; we are told that their harmonious mixture
engendered the numbers on which all being depends, and
is thus accountable for the origin of the world ; the odd
numbers correspond to the Limited, and the even to the
Unlimited. Further, this doctrine informs us that the
number ten, as the sum of the first four numbers, $1 + 2
+ 3 + 4$, is the most perfect of all, and so forth, and so
forth. Nor need we be astonished at the "table of contraries" which reached the Pythagoreans from Babylon,
and was eagerly adopted and highly honoured by them.
According to that table, the original opposites of the
Limited and the Unlimited brought forth a series of nine

other pairs—the Odd and Even, the One and Many, the Right and Left, the Male and Female, the Straight and Crooked, the Light and Dark, the Good and Evil, the Square and the Oblong. At this point there presently arose a mist which obscured the brilliance of Plato's theory of ideas in the mind of its ageing author, and threw its shadow over many of the movements of more recent speculation. Towards the beginning of the Christian era antiquity, which was falling in a decline, gathered the multiplicity of positive systems into one collective whole. It was a period of decadence, when the palate of thought required more stimulating diet, and the last appetizing touch was added to the philosophic brew by the mysticism of the Neo-Pythagoreans.

We can imagine our astonished readers inquiring if the pioneers of exact science were at the same time the pioneers and the most influential prophets of mysticism. The fact is undoubted, but the astonishment seems to us to argue an insufficient acquaintance with the peculiarities of the mathematical temperament. It is true that inductive reasoning, lighted by the steady torch of the sciences of space and number, leads to a brightness and clearness of perception which may even fringe on a one-sided disregard for the dark riddles of the universe. Experiment and observation, however, played a comparatively restricted part in Pythagorean practice ; first, the art of experimentation was still in its infancy, and, secondly, the knowledge of mathematics was still too little advanced to be applied on an extensive scale in the cause of physical research. With the sole exception of the fundamental experiment in acoustics mentioned above, we are acquainted with no other similar contribution on the part of the founder of the school, though when we remember the proposition in geometry which is called after his name, and his doctrine of proportion, we see that Pythagoras was of indisputable service to the cause of the mathematical sciences. But a one-sided mathematical genius shows very different features. The mere mathematician tends inevitably to dogmatic judgments, a tendency which is doubtless due to the fact that his proofs must either be valid or must fail. He is a complete stranger to the nuances of thought, to the delicate intellectual refinement, and the open-minded pliability which characterize the historian. This contrast may be illustrated by the polar examples of Heraclitus, the father of relativism, and the absolutism of the " mathematicians." The mathematician's attitude, when he is confronted with mere probabilities and plausibilities incapable of demonstration, will depend in a remarkable degree on the accidents of temperament and training. In religion and folklore as a whole he will be completely at a loss. At one time he will reject them root and branch with the impatience of reason towards nonsense ; at another time he will willingly bow his neck under the yoke of tradition. Finally, the proud structure of these sciences is composed of a series of deductions. The foundation of experience which is at the bottom of the building is lost under the towering superstructure, and its loss is the less remarkable in that its area was small and was familiar at so early a stage that its empirical origin is likely to be overlooked. Thus it happens that those who cultivate these branches of knowledge are but too frequently apt to mistake the firm concatenation of a doctrine as an adequate substitute for its defects on the side of outward proof. The rigour of deduction is often compatible in their minds with an arbitrary and subjective looseness in the premises. Other facts, too, should be remembered if we are to grasp the key to the mystery. In the first place, the school was founded in an era of overweening credulity. Secondly, Pythagoras himself was as much a man of religious temperament as of scientific training. His personality, too, was imposing, and he had the further advantage of having successfully inaugurated new doctrines and customs which had invested him with a kind of halo. The old Pythagoreans, with their defective criticism and their proneness to superstition, were mocked at as men of clumsy and ungainly intellect. More than the disciples of any other school, they swore to the words of their master. " Ipse dixit " was their favourite cry ; it was the magic shield which warded off every doubt and repelled every hostile attack.

Nor have they been spared the reproach of having adapted the facts of nature to suit their preconceived opinions, and of having filled up by fictions the lacunæ in their system. They lived and moved in the science of numbers, and Aristotle tells us that—

"they collected and fitted together any points of agreement they could discover between the numbers and harmonies on the one side, and the conditions and parts of heaven and the universe on the other. And where there was a slight misfit, some gentle pressure would be applied for the sake of rendering their theory a homogeneous whole. I mean, for instance," he continues, " that since they regard the number ten as a perfect whole comprising the rest of the numbers, therefore they assert that the moving luminaries of heaven are also ten in number. Now, as a matter of fact, merely nine are visible, so they invented the counter-earth as a tenth."

The same authority condemns their malpractice yet more sharply as follows :—

" Further, they construct a second earth in opposition to our own, which they call the counter-earth, and therein they do not look for theories and explanations, but corrupt the facts in reference to certain theories and favourite opinions, and thus, it may be said, they display themselves as co-operators in the creation of the universe."

3. The justice of Aristotle's indictment cannot accurately be estimated till we have briefly examined the Pythagorean astronomy. The qualities and defects of their method are displayed most clearly in that field, and their combination is at times so close as to produce an inextricable confusion. Anaximander, we remember, has already delivered the earth from its supposititious basis, and had let it float freely in space as the centre of the world. Neither Pythagoras nor the train of his immediate successors seems to have questioned the equilibrium or the central position of the earth. But whereas Anaximander had merely departed from the primeval conception of a flat disc-like earth, so far as to give it the shape of a drum, Pythagoras now went further. He recognized

and stated that the earth is spherical. There are three
possible ways by which Pythagoras may have reached this
original discovery. He may have based it on the right
interpretation of phenomena, above all on the round
shadow cast by the earth in the eclipses of the moon.
Or he may have extended the groundless assumption of
a spherical sky to the separate luminaries of heaven. Or,
finally, he may have been prepossessed in favour of a
ball-shape by his view of it as the "most perfect" of
corporeal forms. But whichever alternative we adopt, it
was in all circumstances a grand and new step in the
direction of the true, the Copernican view of the universe.
For not merely was the earth now indued with spherical
shape, but the moon, whose phases had perhaps been the
chief contribution to the right theory, and the sun, and
the planets were also looked on as globular, so that the
exceptional privileges of our own luminary were repealed.
It became a star among the stars. And the spherical
shape was best suited to its progressive movement in
space. The vessel, we might say, was constructed in the
shape most convenient for its voyage ; the moorings were
cut, and nothing but an urgent motive-force was wanted
to launch it from the harbour where it lay. The motive
was supplied by the stress of the greater accuracy
attained in the observation of facts, combined with the
principles of the Pythagorean school, and a system of
astronomy was built up which has frequently been mocked
and ridiculed, but which is seen, in the clear light of
modern impartial research, to have been one of the most
original and brilliant creations of the Greek intellect.

CHAPTER IV.

THE DEVELOPMENT OF THE PYTHAGOREAN DOCTRINE.

1. VOLTAIRE called the later Pythagorean astronomy, connected with the name of Philolaus, a "Gallimathias," and Sir George Cornewall Lewis indicts it as "wild and fanciful." But the great French writer with his frequently over-hasty judgments and the Englishman with his excess of conscientiousness have fallen into the same mistake. It is true that the doctrine in question is a tissue of truth and invention, but its features of truth were its vital and fundamental parts, whereas the fictitious portions were merely a superficial covering which was soon to dissolve like smoke-wreaths. But if we are to understand the motives which inspired the cosmology of Philolaus, we must pause a moment at the commonest phenomena of the heavens.

Each day the sun runs his course from east to west. Simultaneously he climbs higher up the sky to sink at the end of a few months from the height he has reached. The combination of his daily and annual movements has the effect of the windings of a screw or spiral—something like the shell of a snail—and like it, too, the intervals between the circles contract as the zenith is approached. This view was hardly likely to satisfy inquirers who had approached the question of celestial motion in the confident belief that it was "simple, steady, and regular." It may be permissible to blame this belief as a prejudice; but though it was in part a preconceived opinion, yet the closer observation of facts tended generally to confirm it. And even where such confirmation was wanting, the belief was of excellent use as a principle of research, just like the kindred assumption of a teleological purpose in the structure of organisms. It was possible to get rid of the confusing irregularity. For a complex movement may be irregular while the partial movements that compose it are regular. What was needed was an act of mental separation. And the clue was found by separating the daily movement of the sun from its annual movement. At this point our early philosophers had a brilliant flash of inspiration. They conceived the daily movement of the sun and moon, and indeed of all the whole starry heaven, as not real at all, but merely apparent. Their supposition that the earth was moving from west to east enabled them to dispense with the assumption that the sun, moon, planets, and fixed stars were moving in an opposite direction. The question suggests itself here, Did these Pythagoreans recognize and teach the rotation of the earth round its axis? Our answer is: They did not do that, but they did recognize and teach the existence of a movement which operated in a precisely similar manner. It was, so to say, the rotation round its axis of an earth-ball with a considerably enlarged circumference. They represented the earth as circulating in twenty-four hours round a central point, the nature of which will presently occupy us. Here, however, the reader should familiarize himself with a simple feature of this doctrine. A moment's reflection will show him that, for any given point in the earth's surface, and for its shifting relations with the sun, moon, and stars, it makes not the remotest difference whether the ball on which it is situated revolves on its axis in the course of a day, or describes a circular course, while facing the same directions, which brings it back to its starting-point in the same limit of time. We can hardly exaggerate the importance of this discovery. The revelation that there were apparent heavenly motions broke the barrier that obstructed the path to further progress. The central position of the earth and its immobility had both been given up, and the way was open for the Copernican doctrine which followed after an interval the extraordinary brevity of which is hardly sufficiently recognized. Nor need we be at all surprised that an equivalent for the theory of rotation was adopted instead of the theory. For though we never actually see a luminary turning on its axis, yet changes in its position are matters of daily and hourly observation. Nothing, then, could be more natural than that scientific imagination, which had just succeeded by a mighty effort in freeing itself from the delusions of sense, should have been content to replace the apparent immobility of the earth by a movement moulded on familiar models, and not by one unique in its kind and entirely without a parallel.

The centre round which the earth was now admitted to move served equally as the centre of the rest of the luminaries, which had formerly been supposed to revolve round the earth. The moon accomplished its course once a month; the sun once a year; the five planets visible to the naked eye required various periods, which, with the exception of Mercury and Venus, were considerably longer; finally, the firmament of fixed stars, whose daily rotation had been recognized as apparent, was similarly equipped with a circular movement of its own, though of a very much slower order—a conception which may either have been due to the mere desire for conformity, but which is far more probably to be ascribed to that change of position already observed and taken in account which we call the precession of the equinoxes. The daily movement of the sun—or rather, according to this theory, of the earth—took place in a plane which was now recognized to incline towards the plane in which the annual movements of the sun, moon, and planets were situated; in other words, the obliquity, whether of the equator or of the ecliptic, had been recognized, and the new conception was thus completely adequate to explain the changes of the seasons.

We come now to the problem of the central point round

which the heavenly bodies were to move in concentric circles. It was no ideal centre, but rather an actual body, consisting of universal or central fire. The enemies of Philolaus call it "a dreary and fantastic fiction," but those who try to throw themselves with temperate judgment into the modes of thought obtaining in the dawn of science will rather call it "the product of analogical inferences, the force of which must have been well-nigh irresistible." The assumption that the heavenly bodies described circles was not merely approximately true, but apart from the circular segments traversed by the sun and moon on the firmament, it appeared that no other conclusion could be derived from the circular courses described before our eyes by the circumpolar fixed stars that never set ; and though that movement, like the movement of the whole firmament of fixed stars, had now been recognized as purely apparent, yet the daily motion of the earth that took its place was bound to have the same circular character. Here, accordingly, the type was given, conformably with which all the heavenly bodies had to move. But human experience supplies no example of circular movements without an actual centre. A wheel turns on its axis ; a stone, attached to a string for the purpose of slinging, turns round the hand which holds it and which sets it in motion ; and, finally, when divine worship invited Greek men and women to the dance, the altar of the god formed the centre of their solemn and rhythmic paces. It may be asked, however, what need there was of inventing a central fire, when it actually existed and was visible to every man's eye. What was wanted was a centre of motion and a source of vigour and life But instead of accrediting the universal light of the sun with the rank that belonged to it, a luminous body was invented whose rays no mortal eye had seen, and, considering that the habitable side of the earth was turned away from the central fire, no mortal eye would ever see. It was an hypothesis removed by a perverse ingenuity from every chance of verification, and one wonders why its mistaken authors did not rather jump straight away at the heliocentric doctrine, and rest satisfied therewith.

Three sufficiently valid solutions may be suggested for this problem. Remembering that the delusions of sense are only abandoned by degrees, and that the human mind habitually follows the path of least resistance, we have first to note that the heliocentric theory was bound to be later than that of rotation round an axis. It was obviously impossible to let the earth revolve round the sun in a daily and yearly course simultaneously, and we have already learned to justify the precedence of the Pythagorean equivalent over the rotation theory. A second considerable obstacle to the prompt admission of a heliocentric or Copernican astronomy lay, we conceive, in the exact similarity between the sun and moon. The great luminary of day and his more modest sister of the night were visible to men as two heavenly bodies regularly relieving each other and combining to measure time by their revolutions, and it was plainly impossible that, except by a process of elimination, shutting out every other issue, men would ever be brought to believe that luminaries so closely connected differed in the fundamental point that the moon was condemned to ceaseless wandering while the sun was vowed to eternal rest. But, thirdly and chiefly, universal fire was more satisfactory as the centre of the world than the sun. Our sun is the central point of a system of luminaries by the side of which countless other systems exist without visible design or recognizable order. Human intelligence resists this belief, as it resists every other call to renunciation, till the compulsion of fact leaves it no second alternative. But first it demands a uniform picture of the world instead of a fragmentary view of this kind, and the demand springs from the natural impulse towards lightening and simplifying the intellectual complexus—an impulse assisted in the present instance, indeed, by highly developed æsthetic and religious wants.

It will be readily admitted that this picture of the universe owed no little to the contribution of the emotions and the fancy. The circular course of the divine luminaries which had been raised by the fictitious counter-earth to the sacred number ten was described as a "dance." The rhythm of this starry dance was set to the sounds arising from the motion itself, and making unceasing music, which was recognized and known as the "harmony of the spheres." Next, the universal fire, which was the central point of the celestial procession, was known by many names. It was called the "mother of the gods," the "citadel of Zeus," and so forth, but two of its titles may be mentioned as especially characteristic. These were the "altar" and the "hearth of the universe." The stars revolved round the sacred source of all life and motion like worshippers round an altar, and the universal hearth was the centre of the world or cosmos as a man's domestic hearth was honoured as the sacred centre of his home, or as the flame that burned and was never extinguished in the civic hearth of the Prytaneum formed the holy rallying-point of every Greek community. Hence streamed the rays of light and heat, hence the sun derived his beams and communicated them again to both earths and to the moon, just as the mother of the bride lighted at a Greek wedding the fire of the new home from the parental hearth, or as a new colony would borrow its fire from the hearth of the mother-city. All the threads of the Greek view of life are combined here. We see the exalted joy in existence, the loving awe for the universe ruled by divine forces, the sublime sense of beauty, symmetry, and harmony, and not least the comfortable affection for civic and domestic peace. Those, then, who held these views, and whose universe was surrounded by the fire-circle of Olympus as by a strong wall, found in it their home, their sanctuary, and the type of their art. Nowhere else do we find a picture of the universe at once so genial and so sublime.

2. The emotional faculties, then, were satisfied in a truly wonderful degree, though at the cost of the intellect. We have now to estimate the price which reason had to pay, and which will be found to have been by no means exorbitant. Even the "dreams of the Pythagoreans" contained a modicum of truth ; or, where that modicum was wanting, there was at least an indication given of the road which would ultimately lead to truth. At first sight, for

instance, no doctrine could appear more arbitrary than that of the harmony of the spheres. It obviously sprang in the last resort from an æsthetic demand which was formulated as follows: Our eyes are filled with the grandest sights; how is it, then, that the twin sense of our ears should go empty? But the premise on which the answer rested was not wholly unreasonable. For unless the space in which the stars revolve is completely void, the matter that fills it must undergo vibrations which in themselves are capable of being heard. Even in recent times, no meaner philosopher than Karl Ernst von Baer, the great founder of embryology, has asked if there is not "perhaps a murmur in universal space, a harmony of the spheres, audible to quite other ears than ours." Now, it was objected to the Pythagoreans that we do not actually hear such sounds; but they deprecated the astonishment of the cavillers by the following happy analogy. A blacksmith, they said, is deaf to the continuous, regular beat of the hammers in his workshop; and herein they anticipated the teaching of Thomas Hobbes, who argued that the operation of the senses depends on a change in the stimuli; the stimulation must be interrupted, or altered in degree or kind. There was nothing fanciful in the Pythagorean doctrine except only the belief that the differences of velocity in the movements of the stars were capable of producing a harmonious orchestration and not merely sounds of varying pitch. At this point their artistic imagination had a freer rein, inasmuch as they were completely unable to determine the relative distances of the planets and the absolute velocities that ensued from them, though they could arrive, approximately at least, at the circular segments which the planets described in a given time—in other words, at the angular velocities of their movements.

But here, too, we shall presently find ourselves ready to mitigate our judgment. We have to remember that the premise of law and order, as pervading the universe, could hardly have been applied by the Pythagoreans to any other relations than those of geometry, arithmetic, and music—the last named because of the importance of acoustics in their natural philosophy. Simplicity, symmetry, and harmony were ascribed indifferently to all three. They neither knew nor divined anything of the forces which produce celestial movements, so that, even had they been acquainted with the elliptic orbits of the planets, that knowledge, we may remark, would never have satisfied their demand for order. They would not have recognized the curve as the resultant of two rectilinear forces. Their heaven, says Aristotle, "is all number and harmony," and we may add that a correct intuition of the highest significance was still clothed in unsuitable shape. The seekers were incapable of discovering law where it was really in operation, and it was anyhow better to look for it where it did not exist than not to look for it at all. Further, the assumption that the sun shines with borrowed light may be traced in the main to the parallelism between the sun and the moon which we mentioned just now. Moreover, the homogeneous conception of the universe might conceivably have suffered if a second independent source of light had been assumed so near the centre of the world. But since they could not altogether dispense with such an assumption, they found it in the Olympus alluded to above as the girdle of the universe, containing all the elements in their unsullied beauty. The firmament of fixed stars, and possibly the planets, derived all their light from Olympus, and the sun borrowed a part of his from the same source, to make amends, we presume, for his otherwise too frequent obscurations. The porous and glass-like qualities of the sun, which enabled it to collect the rays of light and to emit them again, should be noted in this connection. Next we come to the second great fiction of the Pythagoreans—that of the counter-earth. We may readily follow Aristotle in believing that the sacredness of the number ten played a part in this conception. But the introduction of a new luminary and its insertion between the earth and the central fire had many important consequences, and there is no reason to doubt that this fiction of the counter-earth was recommended to its inventors as

much for the sake of its results as for the reason alleged
by the Stagirite. The lacunæ in the information at our
disposal do not permit us to pass definite judgment ; but
Boeckh's opinion that the counter-earth was to act as a
screen of the central fire, so as to explain its invisibility,
is certainly defective. For the supposition that the un-
inhabited western hemisphere of the earth was turned
towards the fire was a quite sufficient explanation. It is
more probable that the counter-earth was invented partly
as an ostensible cause for the eclipses of the moon which
occurred so frequently as to seem to require the shadow
of the counter-earth in addition to the shadow of the earth.

The facts of history, however, are more eloquent than
all the arguments. Historically considered, the theory
of central fire promoted and did not retard the progress
of scientific research. In less than a century and a half it
engendered the heliocentric doctrine. The fantastic excrescences of the Philolaic system fell away piece by piece.
The counter-earth was the first to go : the death-blow was
struck at this fiction by the extension of the geographical
horizon. The foundations of the hypothetical structure
built by the Pythagoreans began to give way in the fourth
century at latest. At that time exacter news reached
Greece of discoveries in the west and in the east. Hanno,
the Carthaginian, had made his great voyage of discovery,
and had passed the barrier of the Pillars of Hercules,
where the Straits of Gibraltar now are, which had ranked
till then as the furthest limit of the Western world ; and
shortly afterwards the outline of the East was more
clearly defined by Alexander's march in India. A coign
of observation had been reached from which the counter-
earth should have been visible, and since neither the
counter-earth nor the central fire, thus robbed of its last
protection, came in view at that point, this portion of
the Pythagorean cosmology was spontaneously shattered.
Nor was this all : the daily circular movement of the earth
disappeared with the fictitious centre that conditioned it,
and the doctrine of rotation took the place of the theory
we have described as its equivalent. Ecphantus, one of

the youngest of the Pythagoreans, taught that the earth turned on its own axis. The second step on the road to the heliocentric doctrine followed swiftly on the first. The marked increase in luminosity which the planets occasionally display was first noticed in Mercury and Venus, and the true cause of the phenomenon suggested itself inevitably as the occasional closer propinquity of these wandering stars to the earth. Thus it was clearly impossible that they could revolve concentrically round the earth. These two nearest neighbours of the sun had plainly confessed their dependence on that luminary by the revolution they respectively accomplished in the course of a solar year. Accordingly they were the first of the planets whose movements were combined with the sun's. This was the masterly discovery of Heraclides of Heraclia on the Black Sea, a man whose powerful genius, contained in a misshapen body, was familiar with the most diverse regions of science and literature, who had visited the schools of Plato and Aristotle, and had kept up a lively intercourse with the latest Pythagoreans. But here, again, there was no finality. Mars likewise displayed a conspicuous change in his degree of brightness even to the incomplete observation which obtained in that age, and thus a link was forged to unite the two inner planets with one at least of the outer ones. Philosophy was approaching the point of view reached in later times by Tycho de Brahe, who represented all the planets with the exception of the earth as revolving round the sun, while the sun with his train of planets revolved round the earth. The last and final step was taken by Aristarchus of Samos, the Copernicus of antiquity, about 280 B.C., who completed what the astronomer from the Pontus, to whom allusion has just been made, had less definitely begun. Eudoxus had given the clue to this great intellectual achievement by his discovery that the size of the sun is considerably greater than the earth's. Aristarchus computed their relative proportion at seven to one ; and inadequate as this estimate was in comparison with the actual fact, it was sufficient to expose the absurdity of setting the great ball of fire to revolve like a satellite round the small world that we inhabit. The earth had to lay down the sceptre which had recently been restored to it ; heliocentricity superseded geocentricity, and the goal was reached for which Pythagoras and his disciples had smoothed and pointed the way. As things turned out, however, it was soon to be abandoned again, and its place to be taken for another long series of centuries by the immemorial delusions fostered in the name of religion.

But it is time to return from this historical forecast to its starting-point at the old Pythagorean doctrines, and there is now nothing to prevent our resuming the thread of the inquiry which we dropped at the close of the last chapter but one.

CHAPTER V.

ORPHIC AND PYTHAGOREAN DOCTRINES OF THE SOUL.

1. ORPHICISM and Pythagorism might be called the male and female forms of the same conception. In the one there is a surplus of visionary and fantastic elements ; in the other, of rational and scientific method. The one answers to the need for personal salvation ; the other to the requirements of state and society. The one is dominated by a love of purity and by a fear of contamination ; the other promotes the cause of morality and civil order. The one is wanting in vigorous self-confidence, and tends to a contrite asceticism ; the other exhibits the resolute discipline of an ethical culture, nourished on the arts and on self-examination. Among the Orphics it is a religious brotherhood which unites the members of the community, whereas the union of the Pythagoreans takes the form of a semi-political knightly order. Orphicism takes no account of mathematical or astronomical research ; Pythagorism holds aloof from the speculations of cosmogony and theogony. But despite every difference in degree, and in the midst of these distinctions, there is yet a most striking concordance, strong enough at many points to fuse the two sects in one, and to make it almost impossible to say which gives to or takes from the other.

In one respect, however, the difference may be stated with comparative clearness. The two sects may be distinguished by that important part of their doctrine which refers to metempsychosis, or the transmigration of souls.

Aristotle tells us that, "according to the Pythagorean myths, any soul goes into any body," and, to say nothing of the evidence of countless authorities of a later date, Xenophanes, a younger contemporary of Pythagoras, relates a story which illustrates this point. His verses on the subject are still extant. He tells us that Pythagoras, seeing a dog being maltreated, and hearing him howl, cried out in pitying tones, "Leave off beating the dog, for I recognize in his tones the voice of the soul of a friend." An anecdote of this kind—and its anecdotal character is vouched for by the words "it is related," with which Xenophanes introduces the story—could hardly have been invented, unless the incident had been typical of the man of whom it was told. As a matter of fact, Pythagoras—as we see from Empedocles, for instance—had many wonderful tales to tell of the previous existence of his own soul. It will be instructive to pause for a moment at this strange doctrine. We call it strange, but if we remember how widely it was spread we shall perhaps revise the epithet. It is shared by the Gallic Druids and the Druses of the Middle Ages ; it is maintained to-day by the Zulus and the Greenlanders, by the Indians of North America and the Dayaks of Borneo, by the Karens of Burma and the inhabitants of Guinea ; it counts among its adherents the worshippers of Brahma and Buddha, and it attracted the sympathetic assent of a Spinoza and a Lessing. The wide extension of this theory in space and time is sufficient evidence of its deep roots in human thought and sentiment. It must be noted as a preliminary condition that the doctrine of the transmigration of human souls into animals and plants and conversely, which, it may be added, is not admitted in all the instances we have cited, was incompatible with the pride of species, which would place impassable barriers between these natural kingdoms. In this connection we may trace the following development of thought. In the first place, from the phenomena of dreams, ecstasy, and obsession was derived the right of free movement, one might almost say the right of free domicile, which the soul enjoyed ; and, this being granted, there was

no reason why, when its temporary abode broke up, the
soul should not seek and choose a new dwelling-place for
itself. There was no more reason why the soul should not
change its body than why a man should not change his
clothes. Next, it would be asked whence all the souls
were derived which inhabit and animate men, animals, and
plants for a brief period of time ; and, further, if they were
as numerous as the short-lived beings with whom they
were temporarily joined. Take the child, for example, who
dies at a tender age : was his soul created for that span
of time, or had it been waiting since the beginning of the
universe for its little term of incarnation ? And what was
to happen to it afterwards ? Was the spiritual being,
with its power of animating a human or an animal body,
to exercise that capacity for a few weeks, or days, or
hours, or moments alone, and then to return to the eternal
silence ? And even apart from this exceptional instance, it
was surely more natural to regard these imperishable or
hardly perishable higher beings as more limited in number
than the swiftly falling material beings, constantly vanishing
and constantly replaced, over which the souls preside. The
officers of an army, we remember, are less numerous than
the soldiers they command. And finally, as soon as thought
began to assume a stricter logical precision, the analogical
inferences here concerned must likewise have become more
rigid. The survival of the body by the soul was and is, almost
without exception, a universal belief of mankind. And as
there was no reason to contemplate the later extinction of
the soul, its survival became more and more unlimited, till,
with the doctrine of eternity, it was promoted to eternal
existence. And as everything that is created is demonstrably perishable, the thought was bound to occur with
irresistible force that the imperishable was also the un-
created, that the eternity of after-existence was the guarantee of an eternity of pre-existence. In periods of more
advanced civilization a further conclusion was drawn. It
was seen that even in the material world things were not
actually created and destroyed, but were rather involved
in constant change and circulation ; and, transferring this

observation to the spiritual universe, a similar circulation was postulated, in pursuance of which one and the same being changed its earthly form innumerable times, and, after an incalculable series of transformations, returned at last to an earlier or even to its earliest shape.

The Greeks, equally with other nations, might have derived their belief in metempsychosis from these and kindred speculations. Nevertheless, this does not seem to have been the case. No one tells us anything of the kind, and if the belief had been established in Hellas from of old, it would not have escaped the notice of Xenophanes, who had travelled so much and was well versed in such topics. It would hardly have occurred to him to mention this doctrine as peculiarly characteristic of Pythagoras, and to have ridiculed him on that account. Our opinion is supported by a consideration of a more general kind. Though kindness to animals was the foundation on which the doctrine rested, yet the temperament of the Greek people was never especially friendly to animals. With a few quite isolated exceptions, there were no sacred animals in Greece, as there were in India and Egypt. Finally, it is *à priori* in the highest degree improbable that Pythagoras invented a belief which was already firmly seated in many popular creeds. The general problem, then, is reduced to the particular question, From what people or creed did the sage who was famous above all for his far-reaching "inquiry" borrow the doctrine of metempsychosis? Herodotus replies by a reference to Egypt, whence men, whose names he knew, but was reluctant to mention, had transplanted the doctrine to Greek soil. Unfortunately, the direct evidence which we now possess of the Egyptian theory of the soul prevents our complete acquiescence in that account. The "Book of the Dead" recognizes the privilege of good souls to assume various shapes of animals and plants; it may "appear one day as a heron, another as a cockchafer, and yet another as a lotus-flower on the water;" it may display itself as the winged phœnix, as a goose, a swallow, a plover, a crane, or a viper. And the wicked soul, too,

the restless vagabond between heaven and eartn, seeks a
human body in which to pitch its tent, in order to torment
it with sickness, and to harry it to bloodshed and madness.
But when Herodotus goes on to speak of the regular course
pursued by the soul of the dead, "through all departments
of life, on land, in the sea, and in the air, till after the
expiry of three thousand years it returns to a human body
again," we note that he is exceeding his Egyptian text, at
least as far as it has hitherto been deciphered. Whether
or not the last word has been said by the antiquarians on
a subject so constantly changing and so rife with contradictions, for the present at any rate we are unable to
accept the statement of Herodotus. There is a far closer
agreement between Pythagorism and the Indian doctrine,
not merely in their general features, but even in certain
details, such as vegetarianism ; and it may be added that
the formulæ which summarize the whole creed of the "circle
and wheel" of births are likewise the same in both. It
is almost impossible for us to refer this identity to mere
chance. It is true that no account would be acceptable
which would require Pythagoras to have sat at the feet of
Indian priests or to have been even indirectly influenced
by the newly hatched Buddhistic religion. But we may
dispense alike with both of these wild assumptions. The
Indian doctrine of metempsychosis is older than the
Buddhists, and it is not too much to assume that the
curious Greek who was the contemporary of Buddha, and
it may have been of Zarathustra too, would have acquired
a more or less exact knowledge of the religious speculations of the East, in that age of intellectual fermentation,
through the medium of Persia. It must be remembered
in this connection that the Asiatic Greeks, at the time
when Pythagoras still dwelt in his Ionian home, were
united with a part of the Indian nation under the single
sway of Cyrus, the founder of the Persian empire. Still,
be the origin of the belief what it may, it was fused at an
early date with Orphic doctrines. These were originally
severed from Pythagorism, though we now know them
better in combination ; and, in attempting to explain these

common theories, we must dwell, above all, on their fundamental doctrine, of which metempsychosis was only a part,
though a part of considerable magnitude.

2. This common doctrine may be epitomized in a single
significant phrase as the "fall of the soul by sin." The soul
was of divine origin, and its earthly existence was unworthy
of it. Its body was a fetter, a prison, a grave. Nothing
but its own guilt could degrade it from heavenly excellence
to the impurity of earthly life. Its sin involved it in peni-
tential punishment, for through atonement and purification
alone would it be able to return to the divine home whence
it came. This process of purification and atonement was
accomplished in two ways—by the penalties of Hades, and
by the cycle of births. We can hardly believe that two
such different means for the attainment of a single end
should have been combined from the beginning. For this
reason and others, we may conjecture that the penalties of
Hades were a later accretion to the Pythagorean doctrine
of metempsychosis, derived from the Orphics, and fused
with it through their influence.

We have hitherto been acquainted with the Orphics
merely as the founders of an original doctrine of cosmogony,
and in that connection have obtained a purely casual insight
into their methods of thought. To distinguish these more
accurately, we must glance at the myth which took a central
position in their creed. It is known as the legend of
Dionysus Zagreus. As the son of Zeus and Persephone,
Dionysus was still a child when his heavenly father entrusted him with the empery of the world. He was persecuted by the Titans, who had formerly been worsted in
their struggle with Uranus. The divine boy escaped from
their wily attacks in divers shapes and forms, till he was
finally caught by them in the form of a bull, whom they
tore to pieces and devoured. His heart alone was rescued
by Athene, and Zeus presently swallowed it in order to
create from it "the new Dionysus." To punish the Titans
for their crime, Zeus struck them with his thunderbolt. Out
of their ashes rose the race of mankind, whose nature
contained both elements—the Titanic and the Dionysic,

springing from the blood of Zagreus. The Titans were the embodiment of the principle of evil, Dionysus of the principle of good, and in their fusion were contained the seeds of that conflict between the godlike and the ungodlike which occurs but too frequently in the human breast. Thus this strange legend, the other characteristics of which do not concern us here, abuts in an elucidatory myth to explain the duality of human nature, and to account for the inward conflict which rends it and bends it continually.

This conflict went deep. The glaring contrast between earthly suffering and earthly imperfection on the one part, and heavenly bliss and heavenly purity on the other, lies at the heart and core of the philosophy of the Orphics and Pythagoreans. Hence came their longing for purification, for atonement and final redemption. The goal they aimed at was hard to attain ; a single earthly existence was not enough to cleanse the soul from its original sin and to redeem it from the defilement with which later misdeeds had sullied it. A long series of palingeneses formed a kind of continuous pilgrimage, extending through thousands of years, and interrupted and embittered by the penalties suffered by the soul in the "pool of mire." Late, if at all, the soul was freed from its labours, and returned to the starting-point of its journey. As a pure spirit once more, it re-entered its home and rejoined the brotherhood of the gods. The three gold tablets committed to the tombs of dead men during the fourth and third centuries B.C. in the neighbourhood of ancient Thurii *—a district formerly hospitable to Pythagoreans—contain some illustrative references in this connection. "I escaped from the burdensome circle of lamentation "—this was the cry of hope raised by the purified soul which had "fully atoned for its works of iniquity," and which approached "holy Persephone, Queen of the Shades," in the guise of "a suppliant for protection," proud to belong to the "blissful race" of that goddess and her peers in the under-world. They would send it "to the seats of the innocent," and would utter the redeeming word in its expectant ears—"a

* *Vide* Ch. II. § 2.

god shalt thou be instead of a mortal." These series of
verses are clearly the variant recensions of a common and
an older text. They combine with several other fragments,
partly belonging to the same age and to neighbouring
localities, partly to the island of Crete and the later Roman
epoch, to form the scanty remains of what we might
conveniently call the Orphic "Book of the Dead." In
them we can trace the journey of the soul in the under-
world; their different recensions display an exact correspondence with one another as well as with the tablets of
Thurii, and recent experience warrants the good hope
that our information may presently be more complete.

3. We have here to reckon with a possible fact. The
"fall of the soul by sin" is as completely unknown to the
texts we have just discussed as it is to the writings of
Pindar the poet and Empedocles the philosopher, who
are our most ancient authorities on the teachings of the
Orphics. Both instances may be due to pure chance, for
our information in either case is of a fragmentary character.
But another explanation may be offered. It is conceivable
that that central doctrine of the Orphics has undergone
a further development, and the allegation of a cause for the
fall of the soul—"this evil, too, is the expiation of a crime"
—may have been a later accretion. Taking this assumption,
three elements are left as native to that doctrine. First,
we have the melancholy view of life which depreciated
earthly existence and the goods of this world; secondly,
an assured confidence in the justice of the gods, who
punished every misdeed and rewarded every merit; and,
thirdly, the fixed belief in the divine nature and the
divine origin of the soul. At present we have merely to
note that pessimistic view of life which contrasted so
grimly with the brilliant *insouciance* of the Homeric age.
We may postpone the explanation, though we marked the
beginnings of the change as early as Hesiod. It will be
readily conceded that Hesiod and Homer were dealing with
different orders of the population, and stern indeed must
have been the experience of war and peace which prepared
the Greek mind for such gloomy views of life. A man who

believed in the retributive justice of Heaven must have based
his belief on a recognition of the dominion of the principle
at least of right and law; for it is obvious that as long as
personal favour, or personal loyalty at best, was the governing factor in State and society, the confidence of reasonable
expectation could have had no leg to stand on. We have
already referred to the nature of the belief in retribution,
but it will assist us to understand its details if we recall
the image of the Erinyes, for instance, who were originally conceived as the souls of the murdered men, wrath-
fully seeking their own revenge. The private vengeance
of the individual and the family formed the basis of the
penal code in earthly states, and the blood-code of the
gods in the courts of the after-world was due to a similar
extension. We may quote as evidence for this conclusion
those pictures of the infernal regions where we see the
evil-doer persecuted by the soul or avenging spirit of his
victim. Next, it is to be noted that the direction to the
future life given to the belief in retribution would have
gained most ground in pessimistic times and climes. An
Aeschylus, for instance, who held this belief more stoutly
than any other Greek poet, hardly glances beyond the
confines of earthly existence. The hero of Marathon was
content with the grand spectacle of divine justice of which
he had been the witness and abettor. Here, however, if
we are to gain a clear understanding of the divine descent
of the soul, we must arm ourselves against misleading
analogies.

The conception of the soul of the dead fully partici-
pating in the bliss of the gods, joining their table, sharing
their carouses, and abandoning itself to all kinds of sensual
enjoyment, was common to the ancient Indians and
Germans, as well as to the Indians of Central America,
and probably to the Thracians too. It should be clearly
stated that it had next to nothing in common with
the main lines of the Orphic doctrine, and it is equally
illegitimate to refer that belief in the higher nature of the
soul to the mere evidence of spiritual phenomena which
are the property of the mystics of all countries and times.

The goals at which the religious mystic aims have everywhere and always been the same. By direct intercourse and gradual assimilation, he strives after a final identification with his god. But though the aim be uniform, the ways which lead to it are many. Some have accompanied their progress by the beating of drums, the tinkling of cymbals, and the shrilling of flutes. Others approach their deity through the sensuous mazes of the dance, and others, again, seek his presence by an absorption in monotonous contemplation or by the hypnotic trance engendered by continuous gazing at some gleaming object. By this means the Maenad of Greece, the Brahman ascetic, the Mohammedan dervish, and the Buddhistic monk were exalted to ecstasy, were relieved of the burden of self-consciousness, and were admitted to the freedom of the godhead or of the source of light. In wide circles of the people, as soon as the storm of a spiritual epidemic of that kind had blown over, the nervous frenzy or stupefaction would be succeeded by the "mysterion," or "sacramentum," which gave the true believer the feeling of identity with the godhead and freed him for awhile from the burdensome coil of individual existence. Those acts and excitements, by which man lost his manhood and felt himself a god—we need but mention the Bacchants and Sabazians, the Rās and Osirises of Egypt, and the like— were superseded by symbolic ceremonies, by the bearing of holy vessels, the tasting of sacred food and drink, and occasionally by symbolic sexual unions, all of which ceremonies helped to create the illusion of an identity with the gods, wherein we meet the essence of the Greek mysteries, connected with Bacchus, Eleusis, and so forth. Religion was here, as elsewhere, wholly divorced from morality. Since the ecstasy loosened each and every restraint, it tended to immorality rather than its converse, and the enthusiasm of the Bacchanalia has always formed a striking contrast with the strict propriety of respectable conduct. It is a contrast which renders it superfluous to speak of certain hole-in-a-corner mysteries, the excesses of which were a disgrace to Greece no less than to other countries. But in tracing the development of human altruism, which was at first confined to the circle of family sentiments, we see that the gods were exalted from their original non-moral attributes to the rank of guardians and protectors of all that State and society held dear ; and the refinement of the new ideals which was shed on the objects of worship reacted in turn on the worshippers. Thus the mystic rites of Greek religion, with the important mysteries of Eleusis sacred to the infernal deities at their head, became by no means wholly indifferent to the claims of morality. Evildoers were excluded from the rites which gave their participants a foretaste of eternal bliss, and the prohibition was probably not confined to the class of murderers alone. The Orphics too possessed a mystic cult, of which we know little more than that it embodied the chief myth of that sect, though this embodiment fell behind the Eleusinian representation of the myth of Demeter in its sensuous and brilliant qualities. But the grand feature which distinguishes the Orphic branch of Greek religion from the rest of the mysteries was the consistent energetic force of its morality, the sole approximation to which was found in the religion of Apollo with its centre at Delphi. In the emphasis which was laid on the ethical consciousness we are justified in recognizing the essential portion of the third, the most significant and the most characteristic part of the Orphic doctrine of the soul.

A parallel will help to make our meaning clearer. In chapter cxxv. of the Egyptian "Book of the Dead," there is contained a negative confession of sin which reads like a long-drawn-out version of what is epitomized in a few words on the gold tablets of Lower Italy to which allusion has so frequently been made. In both, the soul of the dead man emphatically calls itself "pure," and it is solely on the ground of this purity that it bases its claim to everlasting bliss. But here a distinction is to be noted. The soul of the Orphic worshipper contends that it has done atonement for its "works of iniquity," and therefore is conscious of its freedom from their consequent pollution. The soul of the Egyptian, on the contrary, recounts the full tale of the iniquities which it avoided in its earthly pilgrimage. There are not many facts in the history of religion and morality which are so well calculated to arouse our astonishment as the archives of this ancient confessional. Sins against the ceremonial law are mentioned in it, but not in any great number. And by the side of the precepts of civil morality common to all ethical codes we find traces there of a refinement of moral feeling in an uncommon and partly in a surprising degree. The following quotations will illustrate this point :—

" I have not oppressed the widow.

" I have not withdrawn the milk from the mouth of the suckling.

" I have not made the poor man poorer.

" I have not made the journeyman work beyond his contracted time.

" I was not negligent ; I was not idle.

" I have not traduced the slave to his employer.

" I have not made any man's tears to flow."

Moreover, the ethical teaching which shines between the lines of this confession enjoined acts of positive benevolence as well as the avoidance of wrongdoing. The soul of the departed cries out, "I have spread the canopy of joy everywhere ; I have fed the hungry, given drink to the thirsty, clothed the naked. I have provided a boat for the retarded voyager," and so forth. Finally, the righteous soul, its long discipline over, attains to the chorus of the gods. "My impurity is cleansed," it cries, with exultation, " and the sin that lay on me is cast off. I reach this land of the blessed, and ye who stand before me "—the gods mentioned just now—" reach me your hands : I am become one of you."

It is impossible for us to decide whether the parallel which confronts us here is a mere accidental likeness, or the result of historical causation. But we should remember in this context that the development of the Orphic doctrine ensued—and ensued by no means remotely—on the beginnings of an intimate intercourse between Egypt and Greece.

The Greeks, too, it will be noted, looked up to the monuments of Egyptian architecture and sculpture with reverent sentiments of awe. To borrow Plato's expression, they with their young civilization felt themselves mere "children," when they contemplated the hoary institutions of Egypt. It would not, accordingly, be surprising if they had borrowed from that source religious and ethical features of far-reaching significance. We must leave to the investigators of the future the task of deciding this question by a final and impartial judgment. For our purposes, the example drawn from Egypt is sufficient to show the connection in other countries too between a deeper conception of morality and the belief in the divine nature of the soul. And if we mark the discrepancy between the exalted demands which a man of fine ethical ideals makes on his will and sentiment and the brutish instincts which so frequently oppose the satisfaction of those demands, we shall see that nothing could be more natural. This discrepancy would obviously contribute to the belief that a deep gulf was fixed between the two parts of human nature, and that they could by no means have sprung from the same source. This view of human nature, dividing it in its elements into alien and hostile halves, must have reacted favourably on the development of the conscience and on its struggle against impulses inimical to good and human deeds. But all light has its shadow, and the shadow in this instance was the duality of self, the disturbance of man's mental harmony, the hostility to nature, and the ascetic abnegation of its harmless and even of its wholesome demands. All these features are combined in this ancient system of Puritanism which brought in its train a long series of unprofitable customs and unlovely versions of mythology. The movement in itself was a great one, dimmed though its greatness has been by these tributary accretions.

We shall gain a better knowledge of the origin of the movement if we take in consideration the historical conditions under which it arose. The religious crisis was clearly a reflex of the social crisis. It was the accompaniment of the battle of the classes which filled the seventh century and a part of the sixth. Distress, as ever, was the mother of prayer ; and the first to gaze with longing eyes at a more blissful future, and to look to the gods to redress the inequalities of earth, were doubtless the victims of conquest and of the harsh rule of the oligarchs. At least it may be stated with certainty that Orphicism took its rise among the middle classes, and not among the nobles. A prominent tenet in the creed of its adherents was their horror of bloodshed, and this moral idea points to a class of society which neither yearned for warlike renown nor was famous for its prowess in arms. Further, Justice and Law, which occupy as Dike and Nomos a high place in the Orphic pantheon, have always been mentioned in the prayers of the weak and oppressed rather than of the strong and mighty. It is almost legitimate in this connection to speak of a conscious opposition to the life and ideals of tne ruling classes no less than of an open rebellion against the ruling religion. To this last factor it is due that the Thracian god Dionysus, who was a comparatively late arrival in the Hellenic heaven, took so prominent a place in the system of the Orphics. It is important, moreover, to note that when the new religion proceeded to build up its mythical structure it took no account of heroic deeds, such as those of Hercules, the heavenly aristocrat, but it exalted the unmerited "sufferings" of a popular god like Dionysus. Take the story of the wicked Titans and of the helpless child Dionysus, and we perceive that it reflects as in a mirror the insolence of the violent oppressor whom the vengeance of heaven will overtake at the last, and the impotence of the blameless sufferer whose confidence in Justice will be crowned with ultimate victory. It must be acknowledged that this was not the original meaning of the legend. It was rather intended to explain, as has been conjectured with reasonable certainty, a rude orgy of sacrificial rites in which live animals were torn to pieces and devoured. But in this instance, as in others religious imagination transformed the material at its disposal, invested it with a new meaning, and turned it to the purpose of new ideas. There were two factors at work to promote the opposition to the nobles, who were at once the trustees of the State religion and the guardians of the national traditions: first, the courts of the tyrants, and, secondly, the conventicles of the Orphics. If the view we have taken be correct, Orphics and tyrants alike were the representatives of the same classes of the people—of the citizens, that is to say, who were devoid of rights, and of the peasants who had bowed their neck.* The parallel works out with remarkable closeness. Take the case of Clisthenes, for example. It was he who broke up the oligarchy in Sicyon, and substituted grossly abusive epithets for the grand old titles of the Doric tribes ; and it was he, again, who forbade the recital of the Homeric poems, who deprived Adrastus, the national hero and demigod, of his honours, and tacked them on to Dionysus. The resemblance may further be traced in the political habits of those dynasties. They were eager to form alliances with foreign potentates, and some of their members—the instance of Corinth occurs to us—even went so far as to adopt outlandish names from Phrygia or Egypt such as Gordius and Psammetich. In precisely the same way the Orphic worshippers introduced gods from Thrace and Phœnicia—the Kabiroi—by the side of the Hellenic deities, and were not averse, as we have been at pains to show, from adapting their cosmogony to the teachings of Egypt and Babylon.† Taking all these points into consideration, it was plainly something more than mere chance that Onomacritus, the founder of the Orphic community at Athens, enjoyed the protection of the Pisistratides, and dwelt as a guest at their court.

In the course of our inquiry, we shall frequently have occasion to cross the path of Orphicism. We shall become acquainted with the fruits of its harvest, and mark the misgrowths that disfigured it. We shall see the influence that it exercised on Plato, and through him on posterity. And here we shall hardly fail to note that the psychical dualism which divided body and soul was

* *Vide* Introd., § 2.   † *Vide* Ch. II. § 3.

extended and expanded at this point to a real dualism between the world and the Deity. This consequence was implicit in the fundamental principles of Orphicism, though the Orphics never drew it themselves. They acquiesced in an enlightened Pantheism, in which the chief stress was laid on the unity of universal life. Finally, we shall watch the descent of the mighty stream in the clear light of the wonderful discoveries of modern times, and especially of the restoration of the "Apocalypse of St. Peter." The sources of that stream are still shrouded in obscurity, but the sun has risen on the era of early Christianity to which it flows, and on the wide reaches of that movement in which its current can be traced.

4. The origin of Orphicism is obscure to this day, but it may be stated without hesitation that it was crossed at an early date by the beginnings of Pythagorism. There is internal evidence in support of this view, and there is, further, the authority of trustworthy traditions. The names of men are mentioned in antiquity as the authors of Orphic poems who are partly known to us as members of the Pythagorean circle, and partly as dwellers in precisely those regions — Lower Italy and Sicily — where the doctrines of Pythagoras were first and most widely sown. We have, accordingly, to resign all attempts to draw a clear line of demarcation, but in the region which more particularly concerns us we are able to point to tenets which, on traditional grounds and by internal testimony, we may describe as Pythagorean rather than as Orphic. The Orphics, for instance, were satisfied to locate the soul between one incarnation and another in the reformatories of Hades, but the Pythagoreans, with their more scientific tendencies, went on to ask how it happened that there was always a soul at hand and ready to enter a body whenever and wherever a new being came into existence. In this respect, as they perceived, it was immaterial whether they took the moment of conception, or the moment of birth, or some period of time between the two. Having posed this question, they went on to answer it themselves. They pointed to the example of the particles of dust in

the sunlight. There they were provided with corpuscles which surround us on all sides, and which we inhale with every breath we draw, but which stand on the border-line of perceptibility, and are not visible till the sunlight falls on them. It is true, indeed, that the continuous vibration of those sensitive particles of dust, even when the air was apparently quite still, reminded the observer of the cease-less motion which was ascribed to the soul, and thus assisted the identifying process; but even without this adventitious aid the theory was intelligible, and from its author's point of view was an eminently reasonable one. It was customary at that epoch to regard the soul, not as an immaterial being, but as one so finely composed of matter as to be invisible or hardly visible. Thus the question and its answer were alike completely justified. Modern science, it may be added, has reached a well-founded conclusion on precisely the same lines. It has observed that certain lower organisms are spontaneously engendered wherever the conditions are favourable to their development, and hence it has inferred that the air is full of invisible germs of that kind.

We are far less completely acquainted with the theology of the Pythagoreans. There is no evidence to show that their theology stood in any kind of sharp contrast with the popular religion. It exhibits an apparent leaning to monotheism, or, according to other accounts, to a sort of dualism. In this connection we are reminded of the fantastic theory of numbers, which identified unity, as the principle of good, with the godhead, and duality, as the principle of evil, with the material world. But such speculations, in so far as they are credible at all, clearly belong to later phases in the development of the Pythagorean doctrine. It is otherwise, as it seems, with the dogmas of the exhalation of the world, which makes it appear as an animate being, and of the origin of the world, which was supposed to have started from one point and to have been continued and completed by the attraction of that point on its nearest surround-ings and on ever-wider portions of space. But tenets of this kind bear the unmistakable mark of the childhood of science. Of far greater importance is a doctrine of equal antiquity for which we depend on the authority of a very striking remark by Eudemus. Eudemus was a pupil of Aristotle whose careful study of the history of astronomy and geometry must have given him an exact insight into Pythagorism, and in one of his lectures on the conception of time and of temporal identity he uttered the following words: "If we are to believe the Pythagoreans, I shall once more gossip among you with this little staff in my hand, and again as now will ye be sitting before me, and likewise will it be with all the rest." The excellent Eudemus merits our hearty thanks for having let slip this allusion in the heat of his discourse, and we shall be hardly less grateful to his industrious disciples who preserved the remark in their note-books for the benefit of posterity. The delightful picture is conjured up vividly before our eyes: the master sitting on his marble chair, smiling at his humorous fancy and playing with the badge of his office; the pupils facing him in long rows of seats, and listening half puzzled, half amused. But the thoughts that are contained in this brief piece of information are virtually inexhaustible, and, it may be said at once, they redound to the greatest credit of the Pythagoreans. For the pregnant little sentence is neither more nor less than an unconditional surrender to the theory of universal law. It is an inference derived with strict logical precision from the union of that theory with the belief in cyclical succession. Anaximander and Heraclitus have already familiarized us with this belief, and since we shall presently meet it again in Empedocles and in far later authors, it will be well to consider more closely the question of its origin.

To this end we must revert to the motives of cosmogonic speculation as such. The problem of the origin of the world was first and chiefly obtruded on men's minds by their daily experience of the rise and decay of fresh visible objects. For what was found to be true of single objects was believed to be true of their totality, the world. At a later stage an impulse was added by all the real and supposed evidences of order and regularity in the world, especially by the existence of Air, Earth, and Sea, the three vast agglomerations of homogeneous matter, which never quite came to be regarded as primordial. Further and finally, the process was assisted by the changes that close observation revealed on the surface of the globe, such as the formation of deltas, the shifting of land and sea, and so forth. The earlier experiments in cosmogony had commonly been confined to the presumption and description of a beginning of the existing order; they had rarely gone on to ask what preceded that beginning, and whether or not the existing order would endure till eternity. Thus a second problem awaited the more mature development of thought, and when the philosophers approached it they were confronted with the alternative supposition of an absolute beginning and an absolute end, or of a cosmic process without beginning or end in the proper sense of those terms. The Greek thinkers, who were apt at seizing analogies serious, as a rule, though not always well-interpreted, adopted at once and with practical unanimity the second alternative of a ceaseless process of transformation without a proper beginning and without a proper end. And here, too, there was a parting of the ways. Geometrically speaking, the cosmic process might be compared either with a trajectory or with a cycle. As the one it would be a journey to an unknown goal, as the other it would be a circular course of phenomena always returning to its starting-point. And with these alternatives before him the Greek thinker could not hesitate which to choose. There was no decisive analogy to impel him to adopt the first. In favour of the cyclical theory he could quote the spectacle of decay and resurrection which constantly renewed itself in the life of plants, and it was further supported by the circulation of matter, the recognition of which may have been the original motive of the doctrine of primary matter, and which Heraclitus, at least, presents with complete clearness of expression. And to this uniformity of natural life there was but a single exception ; the souls of the dead, whether they were regarded as shadows in Hades or were exalted to the seats of the blessed, broke the law of cyclical succession. At the same time the doctrine of metempsychosis, which itself depended to some extent on the more general analogy, was calculated to redress the harmony which this single exception disturbed. Furthermore, the circulation of the seasons must have been of paramount significance. We can conceive nothing more convincing than the regular return of the great gleaming luminaries with the beneficent powers that they exercised on natural and human life, and the consequent veneration they enjoyed as beings of a godlike order. We may parenthetically note at this point the greatest boon which astronomy conferred on mankind. It was the first science which combined the notions of God and law. It spread the halo of divinity over the conceptions of order and rule, and, more than that, it preserved the conception of divine dominion from the risk of ultimate and inseparable confusion with that of arbitrary power.

Thus, then, the belief was reached in the cyclical succession of phenomena. It acquired a more rigid shape by its adaptation to the doctrine of the "world-year" or "great year" due to the astronomical researches of the Babylonians or perhaps of still older civilized peoples which had extended over thousands of years. From such observations and their consequences men came to recognize or guess at immense tracts of time. The solar year, for example, stood to the world-year of Babylon in the relation of a second to a day—a second equal to two of our own seconds, since the Babylonians divided the day into twelve instead of twenty-four hours. And the great year of this computation was itself but a day in the life of the universe. If we look for the motive of these gigantic units of time, we shall doubtless find it in the belief that the rest of the heavenly luminaries, whose changes of position had become discernible by observations extending over a series of centuries, were governed by the same laws as the sun, moon, and stars, which returned after regular intervals to the positions they had originally occupied. The framework of astronomy thus devised in the East was filled up by the cyclical doctrines of Hellenic as well as of Indian philosophers. Our readers are already acquainted with Heraclitus's belief in the periodical consumption of the world by fire.* The Babylonians had likewise assumed periodical conflagrations and floods. But while we render all honour to the wide intellectual horizon of the authors of this conception, we cannot but characterize its details as fantastic in the extreme. Their conflagration was fixed for the time when all the planets should be congregated in the sign of Cancer, and their flood for the date of their meeting in Capricorn. It is perfectly clear that this rested on the fact that the division of the zodiac which the sun reaches at the period of the summer solstice is associated with burning heat, whereas that of the winter solstice is associated with pouring deluge. The Pythagoreans apparently kept free from this wild play of associated ideas, though their theory of a "double destruction" by the fall of heavenly fire and of the lunar water would appear to have been influenced by the Babylonian doctrine. But the remarkable theory which Eudemus reports to us cannot otherwise be explained than by the presumption of a cyclical dissolution of existing cosmic or earthly conditions. We cannot admit that it is directly derivable from the theory of the world-year by the intermediate maxim, "when the stars resume their former places, all occurrences will repeat themselves as before." Such an admission would ascribe to the Chaldean astrology a quite unwarranted influence on Pythagorism, no trace of which is elsewhere perceptible. On the contrary, Theophrastus himself, a fellow-pupil of Eudemus, expresses the greatest astonishment at the sham-science of Babylon which then became known in Greece. And it is equally inadmissible, in our opinion, to drag in the transmigration of souls to account for this doctrine. In the first place, it was eagerly adopted by the later school of the Stoics, who did not believe in metempsychosis ; secondly, the soul, as we shall presently

* *Vide* Ch. I. § 5 (p. 64).

have reason to show, was not conceived in the whole course of this period as the sum of the intellectual or moral qualities by which the individual is constituted, and apart altogether from these objections, the doctrine of the transmigration of souls does not explain what needs explanation. The theory we are dealing with requires the simultaneous resurrection of innumerable men in the identical shapes of body as well as of soul. Furthermore, if Eudemus was to come to life again with the same corporal and psychical disposition which clothed him at that moment, his physical progenitors and their ancestors in turn, no less than the whole series of his intellectual forebears, Aristotle his master, and his masters Plato, Socrates, and so forth, must previously have returned to existence. Again, if the staff which he was then swinging was to be placed in his hands once more, the tree from which it was cut must have grown afresh, it must have sprung from the same seed and taken root in the same soil as aforetime. But we need not elaborate these details; we are doubtless correct in assuming that Eudemus was merely exemplifying for his own disciples and contemporaries a universal law which he deemed valid for all other generations and events. Briefly stated, each several recurrence of all existing persons, things, and phenomena can solely be accomplished by the fresh unwinding of a finished web of causation. And here we believe we are confronted, not with a contingent circumstance, but with the central essence of the doctrine. It embraces two conditions: First, the belief in the strict causal concatenation of everything that happens; secondly, the belief in a fresh and absolutely similar starting-point for this series of causation. It is with no sense of surprise that we discover the first condition in Pythagorism. We have already met it in Heraclitus in passages which we correctly interpreted as the echo of the fundamental innovations introduced by Pythagoras into physics. And the theory of numbers itself is at bottom nothing but a belief in the rule of universal law embracing all occurrences. In this connection we note that Heraclitus drew no sharp line of demarcation between psychical and physical processes, and we have no reason to be surprised at what we may call the natural and naive determinism of an age when the problem of will had not yet been formulated. We reach now the second premiss of the Pythagorean doctrine contained in the remark of Eudemus. It is merely the assertion of the principle with almost mathematical precision of the cyclical recurrence of an original condition of the world. The presumption of the same natural factors in equal number and like distribution, and pervaded by the same powers, is itself the presumption of a source from which the stream of causation, flowing a second time, will reproduce its occurrences with faithful and detailed exactitude. Now, is it legitimate, we may ask, for those of our own philosophers who expect that the solar system at least will return to its starting-point, to draw the same conclusions which the Pythagoreans drew? The resisting medium with which space is presumably filled is to effect a gradual decay of the original impulse of planetary motion; it is to bring about the prevalence of the central attraction, which is constantly renewed, and it is finally to cause the precipitation of the planets into the sun, which will be followed by the production of an immense amount of heat and by the transformation of the whole system into that nebulous mass from which it first proceeded. Starting from these premises, must we not reach the conclusion of a universal and minute repetition of all earthly processes? The conclusion is unavoidable, we reply, provided that the region which is occupied by the sun, the planets, and their satellites be enclosed in a kind of ring-fence, shut in and shut out on all sides. But there is no district of the universe which can be compared with Fichte's "close community." Not to speak of the enormous quantities of heat which in the course of millions of years have been radiated into space and have never returned, every meteorite and every meteoric particle which has wandered into our system from another sphere of attraction, or from ours into another, every ray of light that has passed from Sirius to the sun or from the sun to Sirius—all have contributed to shift the balance of matter and force in our system in a degree which prevents the possibility of its exact reproduction from the beginning. The "universal formula," to adapt a well-known reflection of Laplace, from which a mind adequate to the task could deduce the whole sequence of development down to its smallest details could not conceivably be the same in both cases. It may be argued, however, that the whole of the universe, and not any part of it, should be taken as the field in which this process of identical causation is enacted. To this we reply that spectrum analysis has revealed to us growing worlds by the side of decaying worlds, so that various phases of development are simultaneously exhibited in different parts of the universe. But neither the one nor the other of these objections could have occurred to the philosophers of antiquity. Once more they were saved by the comparative narrowness of their science, which permitted them, undistracted by the limitations or the misgivings of detailed knowledge, to hold fast to thoughts true in their essence and pregnant with great results. Thus they were able to think their thoughts out to the end, and to express them in splendid pictures which seize the imagination of mankind.

The theory of cosmic uniformity spinning itself out without beginning or end might conceivably be pillorized as a joyless and comfortless doctrine. The greater, then, is the honour due to the author who proved himself completely free from the weakness of condemning a thesis as false, if it does not flatter the wishes of our heart. In searching for this author, the name of Hippasus of Metapontum occurs to us. He was counted among the Pythagoreans, but in common with Heraclitus, he regarded the primary matter as fire, and taught the doctrine of the destruction and reconstruction of the world in definite periods. As a thinker who followed in Heraclitus' footsteps, he would obviously emphasize the reign of universal law in natural and human life. The Stoics, too, who looked up to Heraclitus with reverent awe, would not refuse to accept a theory which played a considerable part in their own system from the hands of a Pythagorean who was at the same time half a Heraclitean. But we must resign the hope of complete certainty. In all discussions of this school of thought it is always difficult and generally purposeless to attempt to draw distinctions of that kind. The very piety of the Pythagoreans towards the Master, on whose head they heaped all the honours without regard to their personal claims, is an obstacle in the path of this inquiry. No field of literature is more crowded with apocryphal monuments, and it is on these that we have chiefly to depend for the record of the work of individuals. Many names have reached us of the earlier adherents of the school, but they are little more than names. The men and women they conceal—for women too took an eager part in the semi-religious movement inaugurated by Pythagoras—were united in a close community. Their loyalty to one another, the communistic solidarity of their interests, and the altruistic friendship they displayed, are features as characteristic of the brotherhood as their earnest endeavour to moderate and control their passions. For the ideas of harmony and measure which prevailed in their philosophy were likewise the ideals of their life. One man only, of marked individuality, is in clear relief against this background. His astronomy shows us that the influence of the early Ionians was stronger than that of Pythagoras, but his intimate connection with some members at least of the Pythagorean community is obvious from the dedication of his work.

5. "Alcmæon of Croton, son of Pirithous, to Brontinus, Leon, and Bathyllus, saith "—thus runs the beginning of the book, which unfortunately survives but in a few fragments. "The gods alone," it continues, "possess full certainty touching the invisible things, but, in order to draw contingent conclusions after the fashion of mankind"— here, unhappily, the sentence is interrupted like a broken sign-post on the road to truth. The physician of Croton, a younger contemporary of Pythagoras, was fully conscious of the limits of human knowledge. In departments where the evidence of the senses was excluded he confined himself to conjectural utterances, and to the drawing of

inferences in which we confidently expect to see traces of careful observation and of some regard for circumspect reasoning. The sentence we have quoted just now raises hopes of a series of detached tenets and not of a complete system embracing all things human and divine. It promises more because it pledges itself to less.

Alcmæon's chief work was accomplished in the fields of anatomy and physiology. His claim to immortality rests on the fact that he was the first to recognize the brain as the central organ of intellectual activity. A trustworthy tradition relates that he used the evidence of animal dissection, and his own references seem to support this account. By this means he discovered the chief nerves of sense, which he agrees with Aristotle in calling "conduits," or "canals," and traced them to their termination in the brain. Modern science reinforces the functional significance of such anatomical facts by observations taken during illnesses or lesions, and Alcmæon followed the same method. We know for certain that he employed in this way the disturbances of the senses which result from concussion of the brain. He explained them in a rational though somewhat one-sided fashion by what we should call an interruption of the conducting lines. Deafness and blindness, according to Alcmæon, were caused by the shifting of the brain out of its normal position, and by the consequent closing of the roads by which impressions of sight and hearing commonly reached it. The widespread belief that the sperma originates in the spinal marrow he refuted by the direct evidence of animals killed immediately after coition and showing no diminution of the marrow contained in the vertebræ. It will readily be understood that Alcmæon's positive contributions to the theories of procreation and embryology could have had no particular value. Of more importance was his doctrine concerning sickness and health, which was not without influence on succeeding philosophers. Health he represented as maintained by the equilibrium or "isonomy" of the material qualities existing in the body. A surplusage of one of those qualities would be the cause of illness, and the cure would be effected by the restoration of the disturbed equilibrium, whether by natural or by artificial means. As "the majority of human things," including the qualities aforesaid, occur at once as contraries and pairs, the remedy was obviously easier. An excess of cold would be cured or corrected by an increase of heat, too much dryness by an antidote of moisture, and so forth. This theory enjoyed a long life. We meet it as late as in the writings of Geber, the master of the Arabian alchemists. But it was contracted and petrified, as it were, by the Hippocratic pathology of the humours, in which the causes of sickness were referred to the excess and undue diminution of the chief fluids of the body.

Alcmæon submitted the several senses to a searching investigation, with the exception of the sense of touch. This omission redounds to his credit, inasmuch as he apparently disdained to fill up by arbitrary guesswork the blanks that could not but occur here in his scanty empirical knowledge. In each instance his starting-point was the anatomical constitution of the respective organs of sense. The air-hole in the ear, for example, he regarded as a resounding-board, and he explained the capacity of the tongue to reduce solid bodies to fluids, as a preliminary to the sensation of taste, by the moisture, softness, and flexibility of that member, and by its fulness of blood, which he called heat. Furthermore, Alcmæon was the first to turn his attention to the subjective impressions of sense, thus opening the path which was ultimately to lead to a deeper insight into the nature of the act of perception and of the process of cognition in general. Plainly, however, he merely took the first step. His curiosity was aroused by the photopsy in an eye which has received a heavy blow, and this phenomenon stimulated his powers of scientific imagination. It forms, we conceive, no mean evidence of Alcmæon's genius for science that he realized the significance of this rare and abnormal phenomenon, and regarded it as the key to the normal act of vision. It was inevitable that his explanation should be crude and childish in character. He seized on a purely material factor, where we speak of the specific energy of the nerve of sense. He postulated fire in the eye ; and in the fire which it does not contain and the water which it does he found his two indispensable vehicles of visual perception—a light-giving and a transparent element.

The rudiments of physiology led to the rudiments of psychology. In this field Alcmæon's contemporaries confounded well-nigh indiscriminately the functions of the intellect, and his endeavours were directed to imposing order on the chaos. He derived memory from sense-perception, and ideation or opinion (Doxa) from memory. From memory and Doxa combined he derived the reason or insight which distinguished human-kind alone from the lower orders of being. The soul, as he taught, was immortal, and he based his conviction on an argument which sounds strangely in our ears. The immortality of the soul was due to its likeness to the immortals, and that likeness consisted in the incessant motion which it displayed in common with the gods, for sun, moon, stars, and the whole firmament were conceived as never at rest. It is obvious that no one who held this belief could regard the soul as wholly immaterial ; otherwise he would hardly have compared it with the luminaries which, despite their divine and indestructible attributes, yet possess a body and dimension. Still less would he have based its claim to immortality on its resemblance to those luminaries in respect, not to their divinity, but to their ceaseless motion in space. When we come to ask what led Alcmæon to attribute constant motion to the soul, we see that he could not have derived it from the uninterrupted psychical processes of ideation, emotion, and volition. For even if he left the possibility of an absolutely dreamless sleep wholly out of account, he must have perceived that body and soul stood precisely on a level in this respect. Pulsation, respiration, and so forth, which are processes of the body, are incessant movements too. It is clear, then, that Alcmæon conceived "psyche" in some wider sense, which included the source of all spontaneous bodily processes—in one word, as the vital force. He must actually have regarded it as a well-spring of force, a conception fully confirmed by Plato, who transformed and extended the doctrine, and spoke of the soul in precisely this connection as the "source and spring" of movement. At the present date, it must be added, the whole argument is very irrelevant. We no longer regard the stars as truly imperishable, and we have ceased to look elsewhere than to the chemical processes attendant on respiration and nutrition for the springs of vital force. But, to revert to Alcmæon, our philosophic physician undertook the further task of proving the perishability of the body. "Men perish," he wrote—and his dictum may be extended to animals—"because they are unable to join their beginning to their end." The words sound enigmatic, but they are fully illuminated by the context in which Aristotle, our authority, employs them. Alcmæon's meaning is simply this : If old age were not merely figuratively but literally a second childhood, men (and animals) would be able to live for ever, since a cycle would be created which could be constantly renewed. But the series of changes suffered at the various periods of human (and animal) life follow a progressive, and not a cyclical line. It is quite conceivable, therefore, that the progress should lead to an ultimate goal. There was nothing to prompt Alcmæon to adopt a third hypothesis lying outside of these alternatives, that the aforesaid series of changes resemble a straight or a crooked line continued to infinity. The natural processes, by the analogy of which he was led, suggested but those alternatives ; and, parenthetically remarked, it is greatly to his credit that he used the analogical method, and did not acquiesce in the *à priori* assumption, "All that is created must necessarily decay." It is an assumption which has frequently been repeated from antiquity down to the most recent times, despite the fact that it is untenable in itself, and that, as we now know, it is refuted by the example of the simplest organic formation, the protoplasm. Modern science, we may add, has not made much progress with this problem since the date of the " Father of Physiology." It recognizes changes due to old age which, apart from the countless injuries by which the complicated human organism is constantly threatened, tend of themselves to its final decay. But when it comes to the question of the causes governing these changes, the mists are as thick to-day as they were four and twenty centuries ago.

It would be interesting to inquire more deeply into the intellectual life of the sage of Croton, to discover, if we could, his thoughts about the Deity, about primary matter, and the origin of the human race. But our authorities are dumb. And this conspiracy of silence is plainly not accidental. Alcmæon differed from his predecessors in not proposing a solution for every problem that confronted him. And his reticence reminds us that we are no longer watching the " beginnings " of Greek science. It reminds us that we have already crossed the threshold of the era in which the spirit of criticism and scepticism takes loftier flights than heretofore.

BOOK II.

FROM METAPHYSICS TO POSITIVE SCIENCE.

" Ein metaphysischer Schluss ist entweder ein Trugschluss oder ein versteckter Erfahrungsschluss."—H. VON HELMHOLTZ.

BOOK II.

UPON LITERATURE IN PRACTICAL LIFE.

CHAPTER I.

XENOPHANES.

1. MANY whose wanderings led them through the provinces of Greece about 500 B.C. would have met an aged minstrel sturdily stepping along, and followed by a slave who carried his guitar and his slender household utensils. In the public squares and market-places he would be thronged by crowds of the populace, and he would offer the gaping multitude the commonest wares that he bore, stories of heroes and of the foundation of cities, of his own or alien manufacture. For his more trusted customers, however, he would dive in the recesses of his memory for stores of a more select kind, which his happy art would successfully press on the reluctant acceptation of his audience. The poor rhapsodist, who regarded a palatable meal as the fit reward for artistic fame, was the greatest and the most influential innovator of his age. This minstrel's calling was by no means remunerative, but it served to screen the perilous activity of the religious and philosophic missionary. The wrinkled and white-haired veteran had fought in the hey-day of youth against the national foe. At the age of five and twenty years, when victory crowned the standard of the conqueror, and Ionia became a Persian province,* Xeno-phanes ranged himself with the Phocæans, the most hot-blooded of his countrymen, to found a new home in the far West in the Italian townstead of Elea. The old name still belongs to a single soaring tower overhanging a deep-receding bay at the gorge of a wide valley divided by a

* 545 B.C.

double range of hills into three narrower chasms, with the snows of the Calabrian mountains in the background. Here Xenophanes made his home, and here, at more than ninety-two years old, he closed his tired eyes, bequeathing his work to disciples, who revered him as the master of a powerful and influential school. Oblivion has fallen on the epic poems that he wrote, describing in thousands of verses the foundation of piny Colophon, his mother-city, and the settlement in Elea. But many a precious fragment remains of his didactic poem with its philosophic depth of thought, as well as of his fascinating elegies, pointing to so much genuine wit and genial warmth in their author, whom one cannot but love and honour as a man of fearless mind and unimpeachable intentions. True, he poured the vials of his scorn over much that was dear to the heart of his people; the figures of the epic gods were especially reserved for his indignation on account of the example they supplied. Homer and Hesiod, he maintained, taught men no better lessons than "theft, adultery, and mutual deceit." And, generally, the anthropomorphic conception of the divine aroused his most vehement opposition. If bulls, horses, and lions, he argued, had hands to paint pictures or mould statues, they would represent the gods as lions, horses, and bulls, just as men represent them in their own image. And Xenophanes stood equally aloof from other departments of national life, which he regarded with no less hostility. In his view it was the height of absurdity to crown the victor in the boxing match or wrestling bout, in the foot-race or chariot-race, with the highest honours. And it seemed to increase the humiliating aspect of his own fortune in life when he saw the brilliant reception accorded by the mass of the people to the brute strength of the prize-fighter. "It is ill done," wrote Xenophanes, "to cherish the strength of the body higher than beneficent wisdom," and "better is our wisdom than the strength of horses and men." Thus, one after another, he attacked the institutions sacred to Greek tradition. He had no more respect for the high, heavenly images of earthly existence than for the worship of the powers of the human body and of the beauty of man. It is impossible to pursue this inquiry without asking how it happened that Xenophanes broke away so suddenly from the habits of his own people, and whence he derived this reaction from the national standards of sensibility and thought—a reaction which opened and pointed the way to the boldest innovations of later times.

The answer is found in the ominous decree of history, of which Xenophanes was a witness in the impressionable days of youth. He saw Ionia fall before the sceptre of the Great King. He saw its inhabitants bow with hardly a show of resistance to the yoke of the stranger. Phocæa and Teos alone chose freedom in exile before bondage at home, and the rising generation which watched these stirring events could not but feel their influence in its views on life and the world. Self-knowledge and reform have at all times been the message which great minds have received from the downfall of their country and the loss of national independence. When Napoleon had triumphed over Germany, and Jena and Auerstädt had been fought and lost, national sentiment and historical Romanticism began to succeed to the reign of Rationalism and cosmopolitan ideas, and a no less far-reaching change took place after the victories of Cyrus over the Greeks of Asia Minor. That crushing defeat could not satisfactorily be accounted for by blaming the luxury and effeminacy of Oriental life. Xenophanes did not fail to accuse the upper "thousand" of his fellow-citizens who had "previously learnt useless splendour from the Lydians, and had walked across the market-place clothed in purple and dripping with unguents." But his penetrating wisdom did not stop at this point. He subjected to a searching examination the moral standards and the ideals of the people, their masters and their sources; and it is not to be wondered at that a man of penetrating intellect and character should have denounced as the root of the evil the materialized religion of the Greeks, and the epic poetry, its mouthpiece, with which the rhapsodist would be but too well acquainted.

Though his heart bled at the necessity, yet he tore himself away from the traditions of his nation ; he turned his back, not merely on his dishonoured country but on the ideals that it cherished.   The iconoclastic criticism that he practised was eminently favoured by his long period of vagabondage, which he himself computed at no less than sixty-seven years, with the exceptional breadth of his horizon in the world of space and time.   Nor was his withering sarcasm confined to the contradictions, the absurdities, and the degrading features of the legends of the gods and heroes.   He scrutinized the workshop of anthropomorphism with all the discrepancies and con-trarieties of its various religious products.   Xenophanes knew that the negro represented his gods as snub-nosed and black, whereas the gods of the Thracians displayed blue eyes and red hair ; and the philosopher could conceive no reason why the Greeks should be right, but the Thracians and negroes wrong.   His acquaintance with the Phœnician lament for Adonis did not exclude an acquaintance with the Egyptian lament for Osiris, and his ban fell on both alike and on the allied rites of the Greeks.   When they wept for their dead gods, he scorn-fully bade them take their choice ; let them mourn such beings as mortal men or worship them as immortal gods. Thus Xenophanes was the first to use the methods of indirect attack and of mutual demolition which rest on comparison and parallelism—methods which proved such effective weapons in the war against positve tenets and dogmas when wielded by a Voltaire or a Montesquieu.

2. But the sage of Colophon, like the sage of Ferney, was not a mere mocker at religion.   Xenophanes too worshipped " a Supreme Being," for—

> " There is a greatest god among gods as well as among men,
>   Nor is he mortal in form, nor is his thought as a mortal's."

This god is not the creator of the universe : he is neither outside the world nor above it ; but though never ex-pressly so called, he is, virtually, the soul or spirit of the universe.   In a passage of Aristotle, which is plainly a transcript and not deductive in character, we are told that " Xenophanes looked at the whole structure of heaven, and declared this One to be the Deity." And Timon the Phliasian,* who composed a satiric poem ridiculing the teachings of philosophy, puts the following words in the mouth of Xenophanes : " Wherever I turn my mind, everything resolves itself in a single Unity." Our thinker himself says of his supreme god that "he governs everything by the power of his mind," and we should be inclined to discover a dualistic tendency in that phrase if it were not corrected by expressions that meet us at the same time. The god is denied the possession of human members and organs when he is said by Xenophanes " to see and hear and think as a Whole," but he is not therefore regarded as outside the conditions of space. And when we further read of him that " he clings undisturbed to the same place, and is averse from every movement," this description expressly shows that he is extended in space, as the universe, we may add, is immovable and changeless as a whole, though this cannot be predicated of its parts. At this point we cannot help smiling at the sight of the stout assailant of anthropomorphism made the victim of an anthropomorphic attack. The changeless rest of the Supreme Deity is justified on the ground that " it does not beseem him to wander hither and thither." It is a striking phrase but it obviously means nothing more than that the chief of the gods must not hurry officiously to and fro like an obsequious serving-man ; he must cultivate the majestic inactivity of a king on his throne. But the conception of the Highest Being hovering between mind and matter may be proved with certainty on other grounds as well. Dualistic theism is as alien to the predecessors of Xenophanes as to his contemporaries and followers, and the philosopher's " God-Nature " is not a jot more remarkable than the Primary Being of Anaximander, which was at once material and divine, or the thought-endowed Fire of Heraclitus. The system of the disciples of Xenophanes did not afford any room for a creator of the world, or for the

---

* Born *circa* 300 B.C.

deliberate methods of a master-craftsman, still less for a heavenly father manifesting his anxiety by single acts of interference, or for a judge dispensing punishments and rewards. Yet who would ever have thought of regarding the Eleatic metaphysicians as the disciples of Xenophanes if they had differed from him, who was theologian far more than metaphysician, in respect to his fundamental theory of the godhead ? And when we come to the question of Xenophanes as a Pantheist, we see that there was nothing so terribly novel in his views. They fall into their place in the development of the popular religion, depending on the growing conviction of the uniformity of nature and on the heightened standard of the moral conscious-ness. At the root of the popular religion there lay the bias to nature-worship, and in so far it might be more correct to speak of reaction than of innovation. The reformer in this instance was in no slight degree a restorer as well. Beneath the ruins of the temple which he destroyed he discovered another and an older sanctuary. He removed the anthropomorphic stratum of religion, which was the exclusive contribution of the Greeks embodied in the poems of Homer and Hesiod, and laid bare the earlier stratum which was common to the Aryans, and which had been preserved intact by the Indians and especially by the Persians as the religion of nature. At this point we are confronted by the contentious problem whether or not Xenophanes admitted individual gods by the side of his universal Being. Literary authorities, whose evidence is now recognized as worthless, have denied it ; but an affirmative answer is given by utter-ances of the philosopher himself, the authenticity of which is beyond dispute. We refer especially to an explanation of the relation of the lower gods to the supreme god, which is vouched for as genuine by an imitation in Euripides. That relation was not intended to recall the attitude of an overlord to his serfs. The rule of law is precisely the contrary of the rule of might, and it is the recognition of universal order and uniformity which meets our eyes in that utterance. Nor is there the remotest reason to withhold our acceptance from this solution. It is obvious that the sage of Colophon would never have addressed his prayers to the children of Leto and the white-armed consort of Zeus. He regarded it as a delusion, which it was his duty to combat to the utmost, that "the gods, as mortals believed, were born and possessed the sensibility, the voice, and the form of mortal men." At the same time, his philosophy was quite as reluctant as that of his contemporaries and predecessors to admit a conception of nature at once soulless and godless. The Orphics had emphasized the uniformity of cosmos, but had in no wise denied the multiplicity of divine beings ; Heraclitus had tolerated subordinate deities by the side of his thought-endowed First Fire ; Plato and Aristotle themselves had shrunk from immolating the star-gods to their supreme Deity ; and pure monotheism in its strict exclusiveness was always regarded by Greek minds as a sacrilege. This, then, being the rule, it would have been hardly less than a miracle if Xenophanes, a man of deep religious feeling and of essentially Greek modes of thought, had formed an exception to the rule at so early a date. There is much to foster the belief, and nothing at all to gainsay it, that Xenophanes paid divine homage to the great factors of nature. The master of the Eleatics was not the pioneer of monotheism ; he was rather the herald of a pantheism corresponding to the natural bent of his countrymen, and saturated in the civilization of his age.

3. The account of the genius of Xenophanes is not exhausted by this survey. The poet and thinker was likewise a student and scholar of the first rank, and in this capacity he was praised or blamed by his younger contemporary Heraclitus.* The surprise that we might have experienced at the multifarious activity of the sage has already been discounted, for it was plainly his search for knowledge that put the pilgrim's staff in his hand, and "drove his musing mind to and fro in Greece" for many restless decades. He would have sought rather than avoided the farthest boundaries of the wide colonial area, for it was

* Bk. I. Ch. I. § 5 (p. 65).

precisely at these outposts of Hellenic culture, among the
Egyptians of Naucratis or the Scythians of Olbia, that the
wayfarer would have been most welcome.   Like a modern
lecturer from a European country in St. Louis or New York,
he brought a message from the seat of national learning.
Thus in an age in which personal inquiry was far more
important than book-knowledge, Xenophanes had ample opportunity of gathering and utilizing the richest intellectual
harvest.   Geology was the chief of the separate sciences
which counted him among its oldest experts.   So far as we
know, he was the first to draw correct and far-reaching inferences from the fossilized remains of animals and plants.
He found impressions of fishes, and probably of seaweeds,
in the younger Tertiary strata of the celebrated quarries of
Syracuse, and he discovered all kinds of marine shells in
the older Tertiary stratum of Malta.   Hence he deduced
certain changes which the surface of the earth had undergone in remote periods, and as an anticatastrophist, to
follow Sir Charles Lyell's definition, he regarded these
changes, not as the result of immense separate crises, but
as the outcome of steady and imperceptibly minute processes gradually consummated to effects of colossal dimensions.   He assumed a slow graduated periodical change of
land and sea, and the assumption reminds us of the cyclical
doctrine which we met in our consideration of his nominal
teacher, Anaximander.   Xenophanes combined it with a
similar theory in respect to the regular and natural development of human civilization—

"Never the gods showed mortals everything from the beginning,
   But they search for themselves until they discover the better."

Here a note of strict scientific reason is unmistakably
struck, and it invests the picture of the sage of Colophon
with a new and by no means insignificant feature.

Let us review once more the successive stages in the
lifework of this extraordinary man.   The poignant sufferings which he experienced in early youth aroused in his
mind a spirit of scepticism towards the worth and
tenability of the popular traditions, especially where they

dealt with religion. Nearly seventy years of wandering deepened and confirmed this scepticism by the wide acquaintance which he obtained with the beliefs and habits and customs of many peoples and tribes. They placed in his ready hands the most effective engines of iconoclasm. The religious reformer was now fully equipped to enter on the road which he had opened. He did not reject the influence of his own moral ideals, of impulses which might be described as inherited or atavistic, and of the results of the scientific culture of his age. His mind, a storehouse of refined humanity and justice, was naturally averse from the employment of rude force, and led him to make a clean sweep of all the elements of popular belief which were hostile to his higher standard. The worship of nature was imbibed by the Greeks with their mothers' milk, and it came to more exalted expression through the poetical and religious personality of Xenophanes, who united with it the belief in the rule of universal law which he shared with his more enlightened contemporaries. Thus he attained to a conception of the supreme godhead as a uniform and all-pervading power, governing the universe as the soul governs the body, endowing it with motion and animation, but inseparably bound up in it. The picture we are drawing is not complete without the mention of yet another impulse. Xenophanes was distinguished by a deep-seated instinct for truth which was fostered and cherished by his criticism of the myths. It led him to condemn the conventional theology, not merely on account of its ethical inadequacy, but by reason of its defective justification in fact. The accepted tenets, he would have us understand, do not only tell us what, in respect to the most exalted topics, we should not believe, but they tell us what we cannot believe. Some of the statements repel him by their worthlessness, others by their arbitrariness as well. He brought his hand down sharply on conceptions morally innocuous, but monstrous and adventurous, describing, for instance, as an "invention of the ancients" the belief in "giants, Titans, and centaurs." Further, the teaching of Xenophanes did not merely differ from that of his theological forebears, but he taught less than they did. He was content to dwell on a few fundamental conceptions without investing them with fuller and more exact form. In the words of Aristotle's grumble, " Xenophanes has expressed himself with broad distinctness on no subject." And his reticence went yet further. In ever-memorable verses he disputed dogmatic certainty in general with an implied reflection on his own teaching, and thus it may be said that he repudiated before-hand all responsibility for the excesses of dogmatizing disciples. " No one," he exclaims, " has attained complete certainty in respect to the gods and to that which I call universal nature, nor will any one ever attain it. Nay, even if a man happened to light on the truth, he would not know that he did so, for appearance is spread over all things." We shall meet this immortal maxim more than once in the course of our labours. First, in the work of an eminent champion of sound methods of natural philosophy, the friend of Hippocrates, if not Hippocrates himself, in the monograph " On Ancient Medicine," the determined attack on the arbitrariness of the nature-philosophers which this pamphlet contains is led by the motto we have quoted from Xenophanes. But to this we shall revert later on. At present we may close our delineation with the remark that Xenophanes, like all genuinely great men, was an amalgam of contrary qualities whose apparent in-compatibility went deep. He united in his own person the inspiration of a god-intoxicated enthusiast and the sober perception of a critic acquainted with the limits of human knowledge. He was at once sower and reaper. With one hand he sowed the seed from which a stately tree was to rise in the forest of Greek speculation ; with the other hand he sharpened the axe which was to fell, not that tree alone, but many another mighty trunk.

CHAPTER II.

PARMENIDES.

1. POLYBUS, son-in-law of Hippocrates, the founder of scientific medicine, opened his treatise "on the nature of man" with a lively polemic. He attacked physicians and *litterati* who represented the human body as composed of a single substance. Some declared this "All-in-one" to be air, others fire, and others again water, and each of them, according to Polybus, "supported his doctrine by evidence and proofs which in reality mean nothing." The truth of the assertion, declared its author, becomes as clear as daylight if one watches the dialectic tourneys devised for the entertainment of the public. For while he who is in possession of the truth makes it triumph always and everywhere, here victory falls to the chance possessor of the most persuasive tongue. And this memorable polemic concludes by saying, "So far as I can see, these people throw one another successfully by means of their speeches, and by their imprudence they help the thesis of Melissus on its legs." Now, arguments which help a doctrine on its legs, which support it and strengthen it, that is to say, may fairly be supposed to have prepared the way for it and to have contributed to its first appearance. We shall, therefore, be well advised not to lose sight of this incisive remark, but to bear it in mind, when we are looking for the principle of the Eleatic doctrine. Its fullest expression is associated with Melissus, a Samian noble, whose date is definitely fixed by the naval victory which he won over the Athenians in 441 B.C. Above

all, we shall have to fix our attention on two important aspects of this inquiry. We shall have to determine what relation was borne by Polybus to the nature-philosophers whom he attacked with such uncompromising vigour, as well as to the metaphysician of Samos, whom we may fairly include as a member of the Eleatic school. Polybus is severed from his adversaries by wide differences of opinion, but the worst reproach that he levels at them is that they assisted the victory of Melissus. This sounds like the admonition of a good patriot to whom party conflicts and differences are immaterial when a worse enemy is knocking at the door. And such was actually the case. The sharpest contrast with the physicists and natural philosophers, of all kinds and schools, was formed by those whom the biting wit of their contemporaries stigmatized as "unnatural philosophers" or " stoppers-of-the-universe." The "thesis" of Melissus meant nothing else, to use his own words, than that " we neither see nor know what is." The brilliant world by which we are surrounded, and of which our senses bring us tidings, is a mere semblance and deception. All change, all motion, all growth, and all occurrences, everything that provides matter for natural science and speculation is a dream, a shadow, and nothing more. The one reality behind this phantasmagoric illusion is—what ? The two pioneers of this school of thought part company here. In the destructive part of their doctrines they agree, but they are not completely at one in the positive solutions that succeed it. It will be well, then, to consider the doubts and negations which they shared in common, having previously acquainted ourselves with the older and more important representative of the doctrines.

2. The senior of Melissus was Parmenides, the veritable founder of the famous doctrine of unity. He was born at Elea as the son of prosperous and respected parents, whose position would naturally have entitled him to take part in political life. He is said to have drawn up a code of laws for Elea, and the well-authenticated reference which fixes his *floruit* in the 69th Olympiad (504–501 B.C.) may be taken as the date of some public act of this kind.

Xenophanes, whose death must have occurred after 478 B.C., survived that Olympiad by a quarter of a century, and the two great men had undoubtedly been intimately acquainted. But we shall do well to beware of regarding Parmenides as the pupil of Xenophanes, for the brief sojourn of the wandering rhapsodist in the home of his adoption precluded him from working as a teacher. On the other hand, we are acquainted with the names of two Pythagoreans, one of whom, Aminias, is said to have given Parmenides an impulse to philosophic inquiry, while to the other, Diochaites, he felt himself so much indebted that he dedicated a "heroön," or memorial chapel, to the memory of his master. We shall presently see that, as a matter of fact, the philosophic system of Parmenides owed as much to Pythagoras as to Xenophanes. The disciple of Pythagoras was ready to build up his pantheistic doctrine in the forms of strict evidence borrowed from the science of mathematics, but the peculiar direction of thought which he gave to it shows beyond dispute that Pythagorism did not fully satisfy him. And if his thought was founded on the pantheism of Xenophanes, and its lines were determined by the mathematics of Pythagoras, it set its compass by yet a third system, namely, that of Heraclitus. For it was the doctrine of flux, first formulated by the sage of Ephesus, which made the deepest impression on the mind of Parmenides. It sounded the bottom of his scepticism, and impelled him, as it impelled his successors, to adopt conclusions of the kind in which the characteristic speculation of the Eleatics found its most powerful expression. The younger representative of the school may perhaps be taken as the mouthpiece of this scepticism. His lucid and flowing prose will at least be more refreshing in our ears than the didactic poetry of his master, with its closely-packed arguments and crowded sentences. Melissus' account runs as follows :—

"If earth, water, air, and fire, likewise iron and gold, *are;* if the one be living and the other dead, if this be white and that be black, and so on through the whole range of things of which men say that they really *are;* if these things *are*, and we see and hear aright, then each and every object would have to be as it seemed to us at first, and not change and become an object of a different form, but it would ever be whatever it is. Furthermore, we claim to see and to hear and to recognize aright; but what is hot seems to us to become cold, and what is cold to become hot, and the hard thing soft, and the soft thing hard, and the living to die and to be engendered from the not-living, and all these changes to take place, and what a thing *was* and what it now *is* to be in no wise alike. Rather doth iron, which is hard, seem to become rubbed away by the finger that it encircles [as a ring]; and gold and precious stones, and all else that we regarded as strong, suffer the same change, and earth and stones seem to be engendered by water. Wherefore it ensueth," concludes the thesis of Melissus, "that we neither see nor know what *is*."

Two conditions are accordingly required in the things of sense: the inviolable stability of their existence, and the inviolable stability of their qualities. In respect to each of these demands, they are weighed in the balance and found wanting. They are reproached at once for their perishability and for their mutability. And if the two demands, and respectively the two conclusions, appear as if they were one, the fault lies in the ambiguity, which had not yet been recognized, of the verb "to be" in its two-fold sense, (1) of "existence," as "the sun is," and (2) of a mere copula, as "the sun is a luminary." Nor shall we discuss the question whether or not Melissus was justified in dismissing the perishable and mutable to the realm of visionary appearance. But we can very well conceive that the search for a sound, we might say a robust, object of cognition was not successful in the province of sensible things in an age when the science of matter was in so rudimentary a stage. The leaf which is full of sap and verdant to-day is sere and yellow to-morrow, and brown and shrivelled the day after. Where, then, are we to seize the Thing itself; how recognize and grasp its permanent element? Heraclitus compendiously summarized these everyday experiences, and extended them beyond the confines of

actual observation, clothing his resultant scepticism with
a paradoxical garb which challenged the common
sense of mankind.   Thus, supposing the impulse to
knowledge could not rest satisfied in the view of the bare
uniform succession of phenomena, not merely was it now
deprived of its foothold, but the natural desire for a
harmony of thought, wholly free from contradictions, was
disturbed and impelled to protestation.   It was unsatisfactory enough to have to acquiesce in the view that "the
things of the sensible world are involved in incessant
transformation," but sound reason rose in revolt against
the further principle that "things are and they are not,"
and the spirit of rebellion was strongest among men of
most disciplined minds.   No wonder, then, that those who
had enjoyed the benefits of a Pythagorean or mathematical training were most strongly affected by this reaction, and it is not surprising that Parmenides, with his
Pythagorean traditions, should have stigmatized as "the
twin roads of error" the common philosophy that basked
in the reality of the sensible world, and, secondly, the
doctrine of Heraclitus.   He assailed that doctrine with the
most poisoned shafts of his invective.   Those "to whom
being and not-being are at once the same and not the same"
he denounces as "deaf and blind, helplessly staring, a
confused herd ; " "double-headed" he calls them on account
of the double aspect of their Janus-like theory of things; and
the fate which his satire reserves for them is to fall into their
own stream of flux and be carried away on its flood ;
"know-nothings" he calls them, and "retrograde is their
path," like the metamorphoses of their primary matter.

Characteristic as these outbreaks are for the spirit of
the Eleatic philosopher and his relation to the doctrine of
Heraclitus, his quarrel with his second and more important
adversary, the general opinion of mankind, is yet more
fascinating and instructive.   The excitement by which he
was moved can be felt in his panting sentences and
verses ; with breathless energy he struck at the popular
conception of the world, and the ringing strokes of his
scepticism fell like the blows of an axe.   His iconoclastic

method was applied to the reality of sensible objects, to birth and death, and every motion and change. We may quote the following phrases from the negative part of his work :—

" How should the thing that is ever be unmade ; how should it ever have come into being ? If it came into being, there must have been a time when it was not, and the same holds good if its beginning is still in the future. . . .

" Where wilt thou seek for the origin of the thing that is ; how and whence did it grow ? I shall not permit thee to say or think that it came forth from the thing that is not, for the not-being is unspeakable and unthinkable. And what need, moreover, would have driven it to existence at one time rather than another ? . . .

" Furthermore, the power of insight will prevent thee from believing that out of the thing that is another can become by its side."

And next to these negatives we may put the following affirmative utterances. The thing that *is* is not merely " not-become and imperishable," and accordingly " without beginning and end ;" not merely are " changes of place and shiftings of hue unknown to it," but it is a limited and thinking being, an " indivisible whole, uniform, continuous, similar in all its parts, not being less here and greater there, but resembling the bulk of a well-rounded and equably weighted ball." At these words the reader experiences somewhat the same kind of shock as when he is startled from a dream. A moment ago we were soaring beyond the aerial stars, and now the confines of reality are closing in on us again. Parmenides, too, it would appear, essayed a flight on the wings of Icarus above the region of experience into the ethereal domains of pure being. But his strength betrayed him halfway ; he sank, and fell to the familiar plains of corporeal existence. The truth is, his theory of Being prepared the way for the kindred conceptions of later ontologists without being identical with those theories. It was still of the earth earthy ; it brings us to the forecourt, but not to the fane, of metaphysics.

3. At this point we shall do well to revert to the dictum

of Polybus, from which we started. The philosophic
physician recognized that the self-contradictory statements
of the physicists lent force to the scepticism of Elea.
He would doubtless have had us understand that those
who declared all things to be air denied, with but a single
reservation, the trustworthiness of the evidence of the
senses ; that the same held good, with merely a change
in the reservation, of those who replaced air by water
or fire. Representatives of this doctrine must have played
into the hands of thinkers, if they did not actually engender
them, who would lump together the concordant negatives
and strike out the contradictory affirmatives ; these would
cancel one another, like the items on a balance-sheet, and the
thinkers would merely have to add the separate negations
of the "physicists" to one grand total negation.* No one
who follows out this thought will cherish a moment's hesitation as to the source of Parmenides' theory of Being. It
is a kind of dividend, the residue or deposit of the spontaneous disintegration of the doctrine of primary matter.
The various forms in which that doctrine had clothed
itself in turn were full of implicit contradictions which
presently disproved one another, and the greater then was
the influence on mankind of the common truth that underlay them when the clash of opinions had cleared away.
In Aristotle's words, it is "the common doctrine of the
physicists," by whom he meant the nature-philosophers
from Thales downwards, that matter is neither generated
nor destroyed. This doctrine was domiciled in the mind
of the cultivated Greek for the full span of a century ; and
considering how often it changed its form, and how
brilliantly it survived those transformations, it is not
surprising that it should ultimately have ranked as unimpeachable, and have been invested with well-nigh axiomatic
force. To quote Aristotle once more, this "ancient and
undisputed tenet" derived point and pith from the reaction
against the doctrine of Heraclitus, and at the same
time it was extended by other contributions into the
source of which we have now to inquire.

* Cp. Bk. I. Ch. I. § 2.

We are already acquainted with the first and most important of these contributions. Unchangeability was added to eternity as an attribute of the universal being, filling all space, in the system of Parmenides. It differed from the primary beings of Thales, Anaximander, Anaximenes, and Heraclitus in escaping the liability to manifold modification, transformation, and rehabilitation. It is to-day in nature and condition the same as it ever was and as it ever will be. Nay, one of Parmenides' expressions even seems to cast doubt on the passage of time itself; and, seeing that nothing happened in time, that reality was denied to each and every temporal process, there was actually nothing left for the time-conception to denote. Parmenides' power of abstraction reached its zenith at this point, but his mind did not dwell there for long, and he reverted with increased impressiveness to the unchangeableness of his spatial being. He added the condition of qualitative constancy to that of quantitative constancy, the germ of which, at least, had been contained in the doctrine of primary matter from the very beginning, and had gradually come to clearer expression through the influence of Anaximenes in particular. The constitution of matter was to remain unaltered at the same time that its mass was to be exempt from increase and diminution. This extension of the doctrine was entirely native to its spirit, as we hope to show by a brief digression lying a little outside the chronological limits of our immediate inquiry. Anaxagoras, whose name will occupy us presently, was, so far as we know, in no wise influenced by the teaching of Parmenides. Still, the common foundations of their theories were surmounted by the same superstructure, and a telling fragment from his work which has only recently been discovered, will best illustrate the method by which he and many others arrived at this extension of the doctrine of primary matter. " How," he asks, " should hair have come from not-hair and flesh from not-flesh ? " and herein he fancies he has disproved a sheer impossibility. In order to follow Anaxagoras, we must remember the fascination exercised by language on the minds even of the deepest philosophers. Matter is eternal, and out of nothing there can never come something; this, as we saw just now, had already passed into a commonplace. The transition thence to the new axiom was easy and imperceptible. If a being never comes from a not-being, why should such-and-such a being ever come from not-such-and-such a being? Both postulates would be covered by a single formula : no being can come from a not-being, no white from a not-white, and so forth. We have already had occasion to remark the equivocal use of the word "to-be," and its vacillation between the meaning of "existence" and its employment as a copula to join the subject to the predicate. But though the new postulate may and must have arisen in this way, though the association of ideas and the ambiguity of language may have helped to call it in existence, yet its value and significance are not therefore condemned. The belief in causation was likewise born in darkness, as the child of the associative faculty, but the obscurity of its origin would not reconcile us to abandoning its lead, now that experience is ever confirming the ample promise it contained, and now that the scion of the inductive canon has been grafted on the wild stock. Nay, supposing the impossible were to happen; supposing the staff which guided the steps of our forebears on this planet through myriads of years were to break asunder in our hand; supposing water were suddenly to cease to quench our thirst, and oxygen to feed the process of combustion; even on this wild hypothesis we should yet have had no alternative, we should yet be unrepentant of having held the belief that the future would resemble the past; we should yet not regret having followed the only path open to us through the maze and wilderness of natural phenomena.

The case is similar, though not quite the same, when we come to the twofold postulates for the stability or constancy of matter. Not quite the same, because the world would still not necessarily be reduced to chaos ; purposeful action would not be an impossibility, provided there existed phenomenal processes, held together by the bond of causal uniformities, even without any permanent substratum. But no good purpose is served by fantastic suppositions of this kind. Presupposing the existence of material bodies, and presupposing likewise the series of experiences on which, as we have seen, the doctrine of primary matter depended for its source and strength, the progress of science was then indeed bound up with the growing belief in the permanence, quantitatively and qualitatively, of the contents of space. This was the sole condition for comprehending the universe and for inferring the future from the past ; and the demand for this condition must have powerfully fostered the popularity of the new belief, if it did not actually engender it. But there are still, even at this date, considerable distinctions to be drawn between the two branches of the doctrine. We believe to-day that nothing comes from nothing, and nothing passes into nothing. The opposite opinion has been proved to be nugatory time after time, especially in departments of thought where modern science has made most progress ; we possess, too, the additional negative proof that no single trustworthy instance has ever been adduced to the contrary. Still, the statement that nothing *can* come from nothing, and that nothing *can* pass into nothing, is one that we have no right to concede either to Parmenides himself or to his countless anti-empirical successors. Its apparent philosophic necessity is the merest delusion. The method was to introduce new elements in a conception—in this instance, the conception of being— and then, when they had coalesced among themselves and with their verbal husk, to mistake the artificial product for a natural, if not for a supernatural, product. Eternal permanence was first given the name of "being," and subsequently it was clearly demonstrated that such a being could neither arise nor decay, inasmuch as in that case it would not be a being at all. It is otherwise with the second of these twin postulates, which is still the almost exclusive property of the strict scientist of to-day. Its opposition to the evidence of sense is considerably greater than that of the older twin. It is far more a guiding star for the investigators than a goal which they have reached and maintained by means of experience. Briefly stated, as developed by modern science, the postulate amounts to simply this: In all natural phenomena there is a central string of occurrences which radiates in countless branches. That central string is composed of nothing but processes of motion, and we may call the objects in which these movements or changes of position occur with approximate accuracy bodies devoid of quality. The branches or radii are the sensuous impressions which produce the appearance of a change of quality. We may illustrate this theorem by a few examples. There is the wave of air, and the impression of sound which corresponds to it; there is the wave of ether, and the corresponding impression of light; and there is a chemical process denoting in the ultimate resort a separation, conjunction, or shifting of particles of matter, with the corresponding impression of taste or smell. We are already acquainted with the processes of motion in the realm of optics and acoustics, corresponding with the qualitative impressions which they radiate. When we come to chemistry, however, our information is by no means so complete. It was only the other day that a distinguished physiologist described as the task of the future "Newton of chemistry"—

"The reduction of the simplest chemical processes to terms of mathematical mechanics. Chemistry," he continued, "will never become a science in the highest sense of the word till we have succeeded in comprehending the energies, the velocities, the stable and unstable equilibria of particles as thoroughly as the motions of the stars."

And the same author declares, touching the beginnings of this ideal science, that he is not aware of

"any more wonderful production of the mind of man than structural chemistry. It was hardly more difficult to build up the mechanics of the planetary system out of the movements of luminous points than to develop step by step such a doctrine as that of the isomeric relations of the carburetted hydrogens out of the apparent quality and transformation of matter as revealed to the five naked senses."

4. Our digression has led us a long way from Parmenides, but we felt it due to the curiosity of our readers and to the memory of the old philosopher to hint at the fruits folded in his doctrine of the unchangeability of matter like the flower in the bud. Moreover, it will have helped us to understand and to appreciate the most paradoxical portions of his teaching. We perceive without overmuch surprise that, granting the postulate or assertion of material unchangeability, with the nourishment it derived, by means not unfamiliar to us, from correct conjecture and delusive association, the reverse side of the theory was the rejection of the evidence of the senses. Their testimony contradicted the postulate, and their trustworthiness was accordingly denied. There is a gap, however, in the logical consistency of this argument, for no other witness than that of touch, or rather of muscular resistance, could be conclusively quoted for the belief in the existence of the contents of space, and even of space itself. Still, Parmenides was plainly quite honest in his conviction that he had expelled from his universe everything dependent on the perception of the senses. He erred in this conviction. He shared with Immanuel Kant, to mention but one out of many, his mistake of the sensuous origin of the idea of space, but he cannot fairly be blamed for it. It is more astonishing that, while he left space and its corporeal contents undisturbed, he dismissed to the limbo of appearance that movement in space which depends on the same evidence. The contradiction cannot be evaded, and we may perhaps explain it as follows. The fact most incredible to Parmenides was the change of quality. Now, if we remember how much is comprised in the conceptions of organic structure, growth, development, and decay ; if we reflect that in wide tracts of natural life these changes of quality go hand-in-hand with movement in space, including changes of volume ; if we further add that the essential connection of both series of facts came to exalted expression in Heraclitus' doctrine

of flux, which coupled incessant changes of place with incessant changes of quality, we shall see that it was perfectly natural that the sworn foe of that doctrine should never have succeeded in dividing the halves so intimately bound together, but should rather have included them both in a common condemnation. This tendency, so strong in itself, was considerably strengthened by an outside influence. Parmenides contested in unequivocal language, which however has but seldom been rightly understood, the existence of a vacuum. His argument, we may remark in parenthesis, is of considerable historical importance as affording the sole evidence of the presence of the opinion at that date. Nor was it present in a mere rudimentary form. It had already assumed that developed shape which distinguished and comprised the conceptions of continuous space void of corporeal contents, and of interstices existing in the bodies themselves and separating their particles from one another. As to the origin of this theory, it is merely a conjecture, but a safe one, that, designed as it was to explain the fact of motion, it sprang from the circle of the Pythagoreans, who were unique at that time in devoting serious attention to the problems of mechanics. Parmenides and those who thought with him would have seen in the acknowledgment of a vacuum a being or existence of the not-being. He was accordingly impelled to dispute the emptiness of space, and thus the fact of movement itself would appear to him inexplicable and, therefore, impossible. In this way the universe of Parmenides rises visibly before our eyes, or perhaps it would be more correct to say that it visibly grows less and less. We have watched the disappearance of all differences in sensuous objects and their various states ; we have watched the vanishing of all changes of place from the universe which was not denied spatial extension and contents, and what, we may ask, is now left? Nothing but a bare uniform homogeneous mass, a lump of matter without form or contour,—nothing else would have been left to the mind of any one but a Greek, with his instinct for form and beauty, who was at once a poet and a disciple of Pythagoras. It was solely due, in our opinion, to this combination of qualities that the infinite became finite, and the formless became beautiful in the shape of that "well-rounded ball" with which we have already made acquaintance. For there is no possible doubt that, consistently with the premises of the system of Parmenides, we should have expected an infinite rather than a finite extension of the spatial Being. Every boundary is a barrier ; and how, one might ask, could it come to pass that the only genuine all-inclusive Being, suffering nothing, not even nothingness, to exist beside itself, was at once bounded and barred ? Proofs of this kind would doubtless have been adduced to fill up any lacuna in the doctrine of Parmenides, and a considerable degree of inner credibility would have attached to them. But, as a matter of fact, there is no such lacuna at all. Parmenides tells us the precise contrary in quite unequivocal language ; and though, owing to the loss or irremediable mutilation of that portion of his work, we shall never know his logical defence of it, yet we can hazard a very fair guess at its psychological foundation. We have already anticipated one part of this inquiry. Parmenides was a Greek, which is equivalent to saying that his mind was imaginative and poetical, and was thus protected from the logical consequences of his premises. Add to this that in the Pythagorean tables of contraries the unlimited was ranged with the imperfect. Moreover, ludicrous as it sounds, it can hardly be denied that the sworn foe of sensuous appearances fell a victim at this point to a grave optical delusion. For did not in truth the apparent globe of heaven, which is stretched as a vault above our heads, give rise to the Parmenidean conception of the globular form of the only true Being ? There is yet another question to be considered. Was the universal Being of Parmenides merely matter, merely corporeal and extended ? And did its author, who valued rigour of thought above all things, relegate thought and consciousness to the outer darkness of appearance ? This seems well-nigh incredible ; the supposition is rather forced on us that for Parmenides, as Spinoza might have said, thought and extension were the two attributes of one substance, and the real was at once the thinking and the extended. We cannot support this opinion by any fragment of his teaching that has come down to us. There are but two sentences which could possibly be interpreted in that sense—"thinking and being are the same," and "thinking, and that of which it is the thought, are the same;" but the context in each instance forbids it. They mean nothing more than that the genuine thing that *is* is the only object of thought, and that thinking can never be directed to the thing that is-not. But, in default of direct statement and unimpeachable testimony, the fact may be determined by internal evidence. The doctrine of Parmenides supplied dogmatic materialism with some of its most powerful weapons, but the master himself was never a consistent materialist. As such he could not have been reputed a disciple of Xenophanes. As such his place would have been untenable within the Eleatic school between the pantheists Xenophanes and Melissus. As such Plato, the bitter enemy of materialists and atheists, would never have addressed him as "the great," and would never have rendered him a degree of homage which he withheld from the rest of his predecessors in philosophy. And if the supposition be simply incredible on these grounds, the last traces of hesitation are removed by the example of Spinoza, which we have quoted already, and the parallelism in the Vedanta philosophers of India. The material Being of Parmenides was incontestably a spiritual Being as well. It is universal matter and universal spirit at once, but the matter is sterile because capable of no expansion, and the spirit powerless because capable of no action.

5. Parmenides built a lofty system of philosophy, but it strikes cold on the senses with a dismal feeling of monotony. One almost wonders if the architect entirely escaped that impression. Hardly, it would seem ; for he did not rest satisfied with the formulation of his "Words of Truth," but he followed them up—on phenomenal lines, as we should now say —by his "Words of Opinion." Many

previous workers in this field have been unable to contain their astonishment that Parmenides should have taken this step; to our own thinking, it would have been more remarkable if he had omitted it. He was a man deeply immersed in the science of his age; his mind was exceptionally inventive and exceptionally agile, and he was not likely to content himself with the reiterated repetition of a few meagre principles, important enough in their consequences, but mostly of a negative tendency. He found himself prevailed on, or, as Aristotle put it, "impelled to trace—or account for—phenomena." And in this there was nothing inconsistent; for, though he rejected sense-perception as illusory, yet it had not therefore vanished from the world. Trees still grew green before his eyes, the brook still whispered in his ears, flowers were still fragrant, and fruits still palatable to his taste. And if this held good in his instance, it held good of the rest of mankind, yesterday as to-day, there as here, whenever and wherever they existed. Nor was he in any wise precluded from transgressing these limits of time and space. He was free to speak of the rise of the human race, the origin of the earth, or the mutations of the universe, for he merely implied that "such-and-such phenomena would have presented themselves to me and to those like me, if we had been alive then and there." Though Kant's "General History and Theory of the Heavens" actually preceded his "Critique of Pure Reason," yet their order might as well have been reversed: the sage of Königsberg's belief that only the "thing in itself" possessed objective reality need no more have prevented his derivation of the solar system from a primeval nebula than the sage of Elea's ontology need have stood in the way of his cosmogony. This was the point of view which Parmenides maintained in the composition of Part II. of his didactic poem; or rather, he would have maintained it with complete consciousness if the distinctions of "subjective and objective," "absolute and relative," and the like, had been clearly and logically grasped by him, and had been fixed, with their corresponding terminology, as part of the furniture of his mind. But this, as we know, was not the case. His own expressions betray him, chiefly the Greek word δόξα, which we have to render by "opinion," but which really conveys several finer shades of meaning. It signifies the sense-perception—the thing that appears to men ; and it signifies equally the idea, or view, or opinion—the thing that appears to men to be true. Thus Parmenides was precluded, by the habits of thought and speech prevailing in his times, from treating and approaching with any degree of confidence what we designate subjective or relative truth. What he offered were "the Opinions of Mortals ; " and this description did not merely cover other people's opinions. It included his own as well, as far as they were not confined to the unassailable ground of an apparent philosophic necessity. He laid them before his reader with the specific warning not to yield them unquestioning credence ; he spoke of the "misleading structure" of his theory, and called its exposition "plausible" or acceptable in contrast with the "convincing force of truth" which belongs to ideal reason. As he wrote in his dithyrambic introduction, both parts of his didactic poem were put in his mouth by a goddess. The second half contains some of his most original dogmas, which were taken in earnest and widely esteemed in antiquity, and cannot therefore have been intended to act merely as a foil for the brilliance of his "Doctrine of Truth." Doubtless he was also glad of the opportunity of displaying the amount of his learning in this form, for he straightly wrote that the reader of his work would be "second to no mortal in knowledge" or insight. Further, besides satisfying the desire of his own heart, he enjoyed the welcome chance of finding himself in no too great opposition to the religious traditions and sentiment of his age. He adopted the same method in this instance as in that of his doctrine of phenomena, ranging himself, that is to say, with the popular belief modified by Orphic influences, and introducing deities such as the "all-controlling goddess" enthroned in the centre of the universe, and "Eros the first-created." Meantime it is doubtful how far such godheads were mere personifications of natural forces and factors. We shall hardly be wrong if we presume that the mind of the philosophic poet was torn by as deep a misgiving as that which quite recently gave us Fechner's "Day and Night Views" by the side of his "Atomic Theory."

The cosmogony of Parmenides starts from the assumption of two primary matters. They bear a striking resemblance to the first differentiation of the primary Being of Anaximander, with the thin, the bright, and the light on the one side, and the thick, the dark, the heavy on the other. Parmenides conceived the origin of the world as inexplicable, except by the co-operation of both factors, which were sometimes called light and darkness. He explicitly condemns the assumption of a single primary matter and the rejection of the second—a condemnation which was intended to apply to the theories of Thales, Anaximenes, and Heraclitus, but which fell chiefly on the last-named of the three, who was the principal opponent of the Eleatic philosopher. In verses which have not come down to us, Parmenides described the creation of "the earth, the sun, the moon with its borrowed light, the common ether, the heavenly milk, the outermost Olympus," already known to us, "and the warm force of the stars." We can credit him with a knowledge of the globular shape of the earth without any hesitation. He is said to have been the first to give literary form to the theory, and to follow the older Pythagoreans in not disputing the central position of the earth-ball in the universe. Moreover, he developed the doctrine of the different zones ; and, misled apparently by false analogies drawn from the heavenly zones, which he transferred to the central earth, he considerably exaggerated the size of that strip of the earth which is rendered uninhabitable by its heat. The different regions of the heaven were known to him as "wreaths." He represented them as enclosing one another in concentric circles composed partly of "unmixed fire," and partly of fire mixed with the dark or earthy matter. As a natural philosopher he followed both Anaximander and Pythagoras, and we have already shown cause to believe that he was influenced by the "table of contraries." That influence becomes clearer when we pass to Parmenides' theory of generation. He referred the difference of sex in the embyro to its local position, so that the contrast of male and female corresponded with that of right and left. In the same theory we mark the tendency, so characteristic of a Pythagorean or mathematical training, to derive distinctions of quality from differences of quantity. He followed Alcmæon in using the hypothetical proportions of the male and female generative elements to account for idiosyncrasies of character, and above all for the peculiar sexual inclinations of the male and female products. In precisely the same way he referred the intellectual differences of individuals and their mental condition with its temporary variations to the greater or smaller share of the two primary matters which their bodies contained. Empedocles, as we shall presently see, repeated this mode of thought, which led him to an important and genuinely scientific modification of the doctrine of elements. These two philosophers, Parmenides and Empedocles, display other points of contact, to which we shall return later on. At present we have merely to pass in review the younger representatives of the Eleatic school before we say a last word on the work of Parmenides as a whole.

CHAPTER III.

THE DISCIPLES OF PARMENIDES.

1. MELISSUS is the *enfant terrible* of metaphysics. The childish clumsiness of his false conclusions betrays many a secret which the finer art of his successors was careful to preserve. In this way we may explain the striking change in their attitude towards him which constantly surprises us. At one time they shun his intimacy and deny their uncouth predecessor much in the same way as a man's family will turn his back on him in order to avoid disgrace. At another time they are delighted to find that their own views were shared by so early a representative of their school; they pat their awkward champion encouragingly on the back, and exert themselves to explain away the worst blemishes that sully the serviceable philosophy of Melissus. Thus the thinker is alternately called clumsy and clever, crude and creditable, and these epithets succeed one another in pictorial succession from the times of Aristotle till the present day.

We are already acquainted with the starting-point of the doctrine of Melissus, and, further, with its goal—so far, at least, as it coincided with that of Parmenides. So far as we are aware, they diverged from each other at three places. Melissus kept extension as an attribute of being, but purged it of everything that was grossly material. He added infinity in space to infinity in time, and finally he ascribed an emotional life to being—a life that was innocent of "grief and pain," and which we must therefore call a condition of undisturbed bliss. Thus we see that considerable progress had been made in the process of abstraction inaugurated by Parmenides. So successful has been the decomposition of the material picture of the universe, that its features are liable to vanish altogether and to make room for a blissful being. In this respect Melissus must be numbered with the mystics, but in one particular, at least, he was distinguished from the great majority of them, whether in the East or in the West. He endeavoured, with what success he might, to support his conclusions on logical grounds, and not on mere inward light or intuition. It will be well to gain acquaintance with his logical processes, though it seems hardly possible to give a fair and simple account of them without submitting them to a critical examination. The first words which Melissus placed at the head of his work were the following: "If nothing is, how should we come to speak of something as being?" We are grateful to him for having admitted the possibility that the starting-point of his discussion could be illusory, and for having attempted to clear it up by an argument. Nor shall we linger to ask if the argument was tenable, or if one might not have replied that the conception of being, in the strict sense in which alone it can bear the consequences which are here tacked on to it, may possibly have rested on an illusion of the human mind, which Melissus himself believed to be liable to so many illusions. But without pausing at this point, we may continue our quotation from Melissus:

"What is," he went on, "was from everlasting and will be to everlasting; for, if it had become, before it became it must have been nothing; and if it was nothing, then we ought to say that something can never arise out of nothing. But if it has not become, and yet it is, then it was from everlasting and will be to everlasting. It possesses no beginning and no end, but it is infinite. For if it had become, it would possess a beginning (for it would have begun, if it had become); and an end (for it would at some time have ended if it had become). But if it has neither begun nor ended, and always was, and always shall be, then it possesses no beginning and no end. Furthermore, it is impossible that anything be everlasting which does not comprise everything in itself."

To avoid the possibility of a mistake, we must quote at this point two more brief fragments :

"As Being is for ever, it must also be infinite for ever in size."
"That which possesses beginning and end, is neither everlasting nor infinite."

Every one must perceive the desperate leap from temporal to spatial infinity which Melissus hazarded at this point. Aristotle remarked on it justly and emphatically enough, but the most surprising and memorable feature in the argument is the following. Whatever really requires demonstration is taken as self-evident, or at the best the proof is left to be read between the lines ; the really tautological and therefore self-evident proposition is clothed in the forms of a wide-spun and tedious argumentation. As an example of the first class we may quote the thesis, "that which has arisen must decay," to which the parenthetic little sentence, "for if it had become it would at some time have ended," is added by way of assertion rather than of proof. Moreover, the proposition, which is neither more nor less than a fully intelligible generalization from actual experience, could not have been proved, in the strict sense of that term. It is precisely the same with another thesis, similarly derived from the facts of experience : "Only that which has nothing outside of it whereby it could be injured or destroyed can be everlasting." This is a thought which must have been present to the mind of Melissus, since it is the sole possible justification of his statement that the universe alone is eternal. Not a jot more proof is adduced in support of the thesis on which the whole argument is based, that "something can never come from nothing." Here the metaphysician was borrowing from the physicists ; he took from them the chief principle of their doctrine of primary matter, which had first been based on actual evidence, which had been confirmed by the progress of observation, but which could never have been deduced from any necessity of thought. Melissus, on the contrary, used the strict forms of logical demonstration, drawing consequences and conclusions where nothing was proved or concluded, but where the statement actually rested on a mere verbal change : " that which begins has a beginning ; that which ends has an end ; that which neither begins nor ends has no beginning and no end ; that which has no beginning and no end is infinite." It would be erroneous to conclude that this apparent series of demonstration was entirely devoid of a progress in thought, but it was due to the help of equivocation or of the ambiguity of language, which imperceptibly replaced the temporal beginning and end with the corresponding spatial conceptions, that it moved forward at all and broke the spell of tautology. On the whole we may call it a model and masterpiece of *à priori* reasoning which renounces every appeal to experience. By this act of renunciation the philosopher starts without any provision for his journey. We can hardly wonder, accordingly, that he should pick up whatever he encounters on his way —substantial products of experience no less than threads of fantastic dreams—concealing his sleight of hand by a glib equivocation which clothes with fresh and ever-rich meaning the old husks of language. And by the time he reaches his goal, our eyes are dazzled with the borrowed gaudy colours in which his proud *à priori* truths conceal their contraband origin, or we fail to mark the tacit presumptions and slippery parentheses by which the concealment is effected.

The belief in the spatial infinity of being having thus been obtained, its unity was deduced from it. "For if," wrote Melissus, "there were two beings, then being would be bounded by another being." In other words, the thing which is unlimited in space can neither be bounded nor limited by another being in space. The principle is as unimpeachable as it is unproductive, nor was it made productive till the apparatus of equivocation was set to work again, and the quantitative conception was changed into a qualitative one. Unity was transformed without delay into uniformity and homogeneity. And these ideas were employed to draw conclusions touching the character of being, which were just as appropriate as if one said that a die ceases to be *one* as soon as all its six sides cease to display the same colour. But let us listen to Melissus in his own defence:

"Thus," he declared, "being is everlasting, and infinite, and one, and wholly homogeneous. It is incapable of decay or increase, nor can it suffer a cosmic change. It is equally insensible to pain or grief, for if it could experience any of these, it would no longer be one."

These principles were defended by their author in detail, but we shall merely have occasion to draw attention to a few points. In the first place, we may note the argument which led to the denial of every change. Melissus maintained that a change of being, since it prevents its remaining homogeneous, would destroy what had been, and would bring what had not been into existence. So the impossibility of rise and decay was not confined to the existence of being, but was extended to its nature, and thus it came about that the attribute of homogeneity was extended from the simultaneous to the successive states of being. Our previous inquiry has prepared us for this transition from the "What" to the "How," but the argument by which the loss of former qualities and the acquisition of fresh ones are made coincident with the decay of what had been and the rise of what had not been is a new feature in the reasoning. The following reflection is calculated to excite our surprise: "If the Universe were to change in ten thousand years by as much as a hair's breadth, it would be destroyed in the course of all time." We are delighted here at the wide perspective which is in such striking contrast to the narrow horizon of older philosophers with their childish cosmogonic and mythological speculations. It is greatly to the credit of Melissus that he should have learnt to cast up minute processes to a total of incalculable effects—a lesson which was chiefly due to the geological researches of Xenophanes. But creditable as this was to the elasticity of his mind, it was bound to injure the logical accuracy of his thought: inferences drawn from empirical facts had no business in his system, which was openly at war with experience. We are confronted with the same employment of the results of experience and with a similar illicit generalization therefrom in the argument intended to confirm the exemption of being from pain and grief:

"It is sensitive to no pain," wrote Melissus, "for it is impossible that it could be wholly filled with pain, seeing that a thing filled with pain cannot exist for ever. But the thing that suffers is not of the same nature as the thing that is sound, wherefore, if it suffered (partial) pain, it would no more be homogeneous. Further, it would suffer pain only by some loss or accretion, and would then—for this reason too—not be homogeneous. Further, it is impossible that a sound thing should feel pain, for then would the sound thing that *is* be destroyed, and the thing that is-not would arise. And in respect to grief there is the same proof as in respect to pain."

The reader is already familiar with some of the fallacies contained in this exposition, and they call for no special mention. There is a striking instance of the naïve employment of experience in the argument from the empiric fact that pain is an accompaniment of inward disturbance, and that the inward disturbance is frequently at least the precursor of dissolution. It was an observation transferred from the animal organism to the conception of being, which resembled it in well-nigh no respect. Our philosopher appears to have forgotten one of the commonest causes of physical pain, which lies in functional disturbances. His eye was fixed on its most obvious causes, in the loss of a limb or in the formation of malignant growths. We are quite unable to determine how he would have modified his argument in order to prove the second part of his contention, which denied all suffering of the spirit or soul. It may almost be conjectured that he shrank from the difficulties of the task. Melissus' campaign against the possibility of the movement of being was fought with the well-known weapons of Parmenides. There could be no movement—thus much the physicists had shown—without a vacuum ; emptiness is nothing, and nothingness cannot exist. Further, the admitted homogeneity of Being was employed to deny it any different degrees of density.

Here we reach the last and the most difficult portion of the doctrine of the philosopher of Samos. He granted, as we have been told with wearisome iteration, the spatial extension of being ; how did this agree with his contention that it possessed no corporeity—that, in his own words, "since it is one, it cannot have a body ; for if it had thickness, it would have parts, and then it would no longer be one"? It is true that Parmenides had expressly stated of his primary being that it was "not divisible." But we are by no means obliged to credit him with the absurdity of giving it a globular shape and denying it the possession of parts. We shall doubtless be correct in taking his negation to imply, not the impossibility of ideal partition, but of actual separation into parts. The indivisibility of being in this sense is only a special case of its general incapacity to move as maintained by Parmenides. In the instance of Melissus, this loophole of escape is closed against us, since he expressly denies not the separability, but the existence of parts. No one will seriously contend that in denying the thickness of being Melissus was merely denying its third dimension, and declaring it a being in two dimensions or a mere plane. Such a conception would be foreign to the whole of antiquity, and it further contradicts the actual statement of Melissus that all space was filled by his primary being. We are reduced, then, to the belief that Melissus did not identify the filling of space with corporeity, but was anxious to free his omnipresent and completely blissful universal being from every trace of gross materialism. The conception is too indistinct to admit of precise formulation, but it does not lack parallels even of the most recent date, among which will be remembered the newly revived identification of space with the Deity. It would have been more comprehensible, or at least more consistent, if Melissus had used the arguments

we have cited to relieve his being of the categories of
space and time altogether. For absolute unity is incompatible with all coexistence and succession. Numerical
ideas, including the idea of unity, are known to us purely
as relative ; the tree is singular in relation to its fellows in
the forest, but plural in relation to its branches ; the
branches are singular to one another, but plural to their
leaves, and so forth. Now, if we agree to forget this, and
to take our conception of unity in earnest, we shall be
entering a path which will lead us to no minor goal than
the complete " emptification," not merely of material existence, but of spiritual existence as well, inasmuch as our
states of consciousness describe a temporal succession. At
this point unity, dispossessed of all its contents, passes
into naked nothingness. Later, we shall have to consider
the history of a revolution of this kind, by which nihilism
or the doctrine of nothingness proceeded from the Eleatic
ontology or doctrine of being.

2. We feel that in parting from Melissus we have not
been over-lenient towards him, but, blameworthy though
he may have been in much of his methods and results, no
one can desire to deprive him of one title to fame. The
gallant admiral was a thinker of undiminished fearlessness.
He followed up his line of thought with entire indifference
to the reception, whether favourable or otherwise, which
might be awaiting him at the end. Grave fallacies must
be laid to his charge, but there is not the least ground to
impute to him any deliberate imposture or any deception
save the deception of himself. This brave and honest
philosophic courage was the best inheritance bequeathed
by Xenophanes to the school, and it likewise characterized
the great champion of criticism with whom we have
now to occupy ourselves. The champion was Zeno of
Elea. He was a tall man of distinguished presence, who
enjoyed the intimacy of Parmenides, and shared his interest
in political life, though his junior by five and twenty years.
He died the death of a martyr owing to the part he took
in a conspiracy aimed at the overthrow of a usurper, and
the unexampled endurance with which he bore his torments

has been a theme of admiration to this day. He was a born fighter and a born master of dialectic, and an early call to self-defence provided a use for that talent. Parmenides' doctrine of unity had set a peal of laughter ringing through the whole of Greece, and this outburst of mirth and ridicule, as noisy as that which less than two centuries ago greeted Bishop Berkeley's denial of matter, summoned Zeno to the lists. He was burning to retaliate, and he promptly seized his opportunity. He paid the scoffers, as Plato tells us, "with their own coin in full, and added something in the bargain."

He challenged them somewhat in this wise : "You laugh at us because we reject all movement as absurd and impossible ; you rail at us for fools because we rail at the senses for liars ; because we see in the plurality of objects nothing but idle delusion, therefore you throw stones at us. See to it that you are not yourselves living in a glass house !" And then he began to empty the quiver of his polemic, teeming with pointed barbs. Like a row of pearls, he strung the silken thread of his dialectic with the chain of subtle arguments which have puzzled the heads of generations of readers, and have proved insurmountable obstacles to more than one powerful intellect, of whom we need but mention Peter Bayle.

We take a grain of millet and let it fall to the ground. It sinks noiselessly to the earth. The same thing happens with a second and a third, and with every one in turn of the ten thousand grains which the bushel in front of us contained. Now we collect the grains and pour them back into the bushel and turn it over. The fall of the grains is accompanied this time by a great noise, and Zeno asked how it could happen that the combination of ten thousand noiseless processes should result in one full of noise. He deemed it inexplicable that the sum of ten thousand noughts, instead of being nought, should make a sensible, and a very clearly sensible, magnitude. Zeno's difficulty is our own difficulty too, nor can it be solved till we have looked a little closer at the nature of this puzzling process. This deeper insight was not possible in the age when Zeno lived, and his paradox or "apory" possesses the great merit of having brought the impossibility home to every thinking person. It gave a voice to the cry for a psychology of sense-perception. There was no way out of the difficulty as long as the sensible qualities were regarded as the pure objective possessions of the objects, but a way is found at the moment that we take hold of the act of perception and recognize the essentially complicated character of the process which seems so simple. Such complication is always present, and its ramifications are at times very many. And, likewise, we must first admit the possibility that here, as elsewhere, an expenditure of force without palpable effect need not therefore be lost, nor its value equivalent to *nil*. A single instance will help us to comprehend both truths. Take a child's hand pulling at a bell-rope. It sets the bell in no perceptible motion. Now add a few more children to pull, and their combined effort will succeed in swinging the bell with its clapper. With twice or three times the number of little hands they may be able to set the clapper beating on the rim of the bell, but the stroke may still perhaps not be strong enough, and the concussion of air too weak to produce the physical changes in our auditory apparatus indispensable for the effect of sound. And an exertion of force sufficient for that purpose may still be inadequate to the amount requisite for the physiological process which we call a stimulation of the auditory nerve. Further, such stimulation may ensue, but its degree of intensity may be inferior to that required to produce the decisive process in the brain depending on the nerve-stimulus. And, finally, this process too may be effected, and yet its strength may be too little to raise the corresponding psychical impression over the threshold of consciousness. Our own psychical condition at the time must also be taken in account. If our senses are subdued by sleep, or if our attention is concentrated elsewhere, the resistance to be overcome will be greater than under other and more favourable conditions. The failure of the ultimate end is no proof whatever that any one of the mediate processes, whose number we have certainly underestimated, did less than its own share in contributing to the final success. Even the first and apparently ineffectual effort of a single child's hand performed its due part in the whole ; it assisted in lessening the resistance which would only be fully overpowered when the number of hands had been multiplied. But the demand that each unit of force exerted at the beginning of the process should produce a hundredth part of the success finally attained by a hundred such units is wholly unjustified in such cases. A cog-wheel may measure one inch or ninety-nine inches in diameter, but it will not be able to catch the next cog-wheel till its diameter has been increased to a hundred inches if that be the distance to be covered. Then, and then only, will the whole series of consequences ensue which depend on the revolution of the second wheel, and the relations of the second to the third, of the third to the fourth, and so on, are determined by the same conditions. The ultimate working of the machine depends for its success or failure on the presence or absence of the hundredth inch. Zeno's paradox which we have discussed so minutely gave an impulse to speculations of this kind, and may claim its share in the progress of the doctrine of sense-perception. It was about this time that sense-perception was recognized, not as a mere reflection of objective qualities, but as the result of the influence of an object on a subject derived through a long chain of causal processes. And the light kindled at Zeno's torch began to spread in all directions.

3. We reach now the famous paradoxes respecting movement in space. Zeno began by submitting the conception of space itself to a not very searching criticism. He argued that if every being, every real thing or object, is discovered in space, space itself, unless it lacks reality, must be in space—in a second space, that is to say—and this secondary space must be in a tertiary space, and so on *ad infinitum*. We are accordingly left with the alternative of saying ditto to this absurd reasoning, or of denying the reality of space. It would be paying Zeno an undeserved compliment to refer here to the criticism which Kant

and other modern philosophers have brought to bear on the conception of space. The word τόπος, which was used in Greek, might equally well be translated "place" without the least injury to the argument. Every object lies in a place, and that place, if it is something real, must be situated in a second place, and so forth. Moreover, the paradox which Zeno applied to the juxtaposition of objects might have been extended to their existence. Every real or existent thing possesses existence ; such existence, unless it be chimerical, must possess a second existence, and so forth. In short, we are merely dealing with the deep-rooted tendency of language arising from the use of substantives as the names of abstractions of every kind—of forces, qualities, conditions, and relations—to measure every such conception by the standard of concrete things. A conception of that kind had to pass the thing-test, as it were, or it failed to qualify for existence. According as it passed or failed, or, rather, according as its existence was regarded as indispensable or otherwise, it would be relegated to the realm of fancy, or, far more frequently, it would be conceived as a kind of thing, as the spectre of an object. The value of the paradox consists in setting clearly before our eyes this fatal tendency of the human mind, to which we may trace the worst and most obstinate errors and delusions, and the absurdities which it engendered serve to warn us from its influence.

When we reach the puzzles to which Zeno himself gave expression in respect to the problems of motion, we are on far less primitive ground. Every one knows "Achilles and the Tortoise." The type of swiftness and one of the slowest of creatures agree to run a race, and, strangely enough, we are hardly able to understand how the first is to overtake and pass the second. Achilles, according to the terms of the competition, gives the tortoise a start and runs ten times as fast. Taking the start to be a metre in length, as soon as Achilles has completed the metre, the tortoise is a decimetre in advance ; when Achilles has run that decimetre, the tortoise has crawled on another centimetre ; by the time he has covered that centimetre, his opponent is a millimetre further on, and so on *ad infinitum.* Thus we see the two coming nearer and nearer to each other, but we cannot perceive how the minimum interval which finally divides them is ever to be completely bridged over, and accordingly the conclusion is that Achilles will never overtake the tortoise. The tyro at mathematics is greatly astonished to learn that this exposition, apart from its conclusion, is wholly vouched for by mathematical experts. The swift-footed son of Thetis will actually never reach his clumsy adversary at any of the points here mentioned or alluded to, not at the tenth, nor at the hundredth, nor at the thousandth, ten-thousandth, hundred-thousandth, nor millionth of the second metre of its creeping progress. But simple arithmetic will show us that Achilles will reach the tortoise at the moment it has completed the ninth part of this journey, for he runs ten-ninths of a metre, or one metre and a ninth, in the time that the tortoise crawls one-ninth, and the whole endless series $\frac{1}{10} + \frac{1}{100} + \frac{1}{1000} + \frac{1}{10000} + \frac{1}{100000} + \frac{1}{1000000} + \ldots$ does not exceed the amount of $\frac{1}{9}$. Let us put the problem and its solution in a more universal form. If the two velocities stand in the proportion of $1 : n$, the overtaking will not occur at any point in the series $\frac{1}{n} + \frac{1}{n^2} + \frac{1}{n^3} + \frac{1}{n^4} + \frac{1}{n^5} + \frac{1}{n^6} \ldots$; but this infinite series is included in the finite quantity $\frac{1}{n-1}$. So far all is in order. A quantity may be divisible into infinite parts, but it does not therefore cease to be a finite quantity. Infinite divisibility and infinite quantity are two very different conceptions, though the danger of confusing them be great. Further, it is easy to account for the apparent permanence of the distance which divides the two competitors in our mental sight. Our capacity to realize minute fractions of space is strictly limited. We soon reach a barrier which imagination cannot transgress. We may go on diminishing by words the smallest unit of space which we are able to conceive, we may go on talking of the hundred-thousandth or millionth part of a metre or foot, but the same smallest unit of space which our imagination can grasp is in reality ever before us. It emerges again and again after each attempt at division, and it defies our endeavour to bring it nearer to nothingness. But though we may admit all this, it is still legitimate to ask if we have completely and finally solved the difficulty so clearly perceived and so brilliantly expounded by Zeno. The great master of dialectic has helped us to answer this question by recasting his paradox in a simpler and less insinuating form. How, he asks, can we ever traverse a portion of space? For before we attain the end we must first have completed half our journey, and then a half of the remaining half, a quarter of the whole, that is to say; and then a half of the last quarter, or an eighth of the whole; and then a sixteenth, a thirty-second, a sixty-fourth part, and so on *ad infinitum*. The answer generally given is that, in order to traverse an infinitely divisible space, the time requisite for that purpose must likewise be infinitely divisible; and, as far as it goes, this is correct. But it does not go very far, for the crux of this problem too lies in the relation of an infinite series to a finite quantity. It is true that mathematicians assure us and prove that the series reached here by division by two no more exceeds a finite quantity than the former series in tens. Just as $\frac{1}{10} + \frac{1}{100} + \frac{1}{1000} + \ldots$ do not exceed $\frac{1}{9}$, so $\frac{1}{2} + \frac{1}{4} + \frac{1}{8} + \ldots$ do not exceed 1. And this presents no great difficulty. But what startles us is their further assurance, which alone is valid for our purpose, that each of these infinite series actually reaches the respective finite quantities of $\frac{1}{9}$ and 1. We cross at one step a certain length of space, and experience no shock if we are told that that length is divisible in infinite parts. But now, working backwards, let us take the synthetic instead of the analytic road, and endeavour to build up the finite quantity out of the given infinitude of parts. Will there not always be a remainder, a fragmentary part, however small, wanting to complete the structure? Is it possible to exhaust the inexhaustible? If we take counsel with the mathematicians, we shall be advised to neglect the infinitesimally small or vanishing quantity at the end of a series, just as they proceed in converting a recurring decimal fraction to a vulgar fraction. Such artifices are quite legitimate and of eminent service to the purposes of natural science, but they seem to contain the confession that it is impracticable to deal in full earnest with the conception of infinity, and this, we believe, rather than the empirical conception of motion, was the true objective of the paradoxes we have discussed, however contrary it may have been to the intention of their author.

It is with a positive sense of relief that we turn from the perplexities of thought with which we have just been exercised to the two last paradoxes of Zeno concerning the problem of motion. The third paradox has not come down to us in a very distinct form, but it may be stated approximately as follows : An arrow is sped from its bow ; it measures one foot in length, and traverses ten feet a second ; is it not accordingly legitimate to say that the dart occupies a space equal to its length in every tenth part of that period of time ? Now, to occupy a space and to rest are the same ; and the paradox consists in asking how ten states of rest can result in one state of motion. The question can be put in a yet more captious form : Does an object move in the space in which it is, or in the space in which it is not ? Neither alternative is defensible, for to be in a space and to occupy it are equivalent to resting there, whereas in the space in which an object is not, it can neither act nor be acted on. This is the paradox, and its solution is simple enough. We have only to reply that the premise is as false as it is insidious. A body in continuous motion does not occupy a space even in the smallest conceivable fraction of time. On the contrary, it is always engaged in passing from one portion of space to another. But the paradox is valuable inasmuch as it compels us to form a clear idea of continuousness and to hold fast by it. The difficulty arose from the vagueness of the outline of this idea ; from the confusion, that is to say, between the notion of steadiness or continuousness and that of discontinuous units—a contrast which we shall presently meet in another shape.

The fourth and last of the paradoxes of motion relates to a problem of velocity. We shall perhaps be able to explain it best if we modernize the ancient "arena" in the following fashion. Three railway trains of equal length are on three parallel pairs of rails. The first train (A) is in motion ; the second (B) is at rest ; the third (C) is moving at the same rate as A, but in the opposite direction. Now, it is clear to every one that A will reach the end of B in twice the time that it requires to reach the end of C, though C and B are of equal length. Hence, if we are asked to state the velocity with which A moved, we must give different answers according as we measure it by the standard of C, which was moving at an equal rate, or by that of B, which was at rest. The objection will probably be raised that the last-named standard is the normal one. We use it in the considerable majority of cases, and we are compelled to use it in all cases where the thing to be determined is the expenditure of force underlying the velocity. But this objection carried no weight with Zeno. He would have replied that truth and error are not determined by a plebiscite of instances. It is enough, he would have said, to be able to point to examples such as the one given above, in which it may correctly be contended that the moving body completed the same distance in the whole time and half the time at once. If the standard of movement in time is relative, how, he would have asked, can movement itself be something absolute and objective, and thus be something real ?

4. The plurality of objects guaranteed by the evidence of the senses was supposed to be annulled by the following double argument. It was represented as leading to two contradictory conclusions, under which the many objects would be at once without magnitude and infinitely great. They would be without magnitude because there would not be a plurality of objects unless each of the objects was a unit. But a veritable unit cannot be divisible, whereas an object remains divisible as long as it possesses parts. Now, it possesses parts when it is extended, so that if it is to be a veritable unit it must be without

extension and consequently without magnitude. On the other hand, the many objects would at the same time be infinitely great, for each object, if existence is to be ascribed to it at all, must possess a magnitude. Its possession of a magnitude implies that it consists of parts with a magnitude belonging to each part. Further, if those parts are to be different, they must be separate from one another, and they could only be separate from one another if other parts were situated between them. This process goes on *ad infinitum*, for the intermediary parts would always have to be separated from one another by another set of parts endowed with a certain magnitude. Thus every body would comprise an endless number of parts each of which would possess a certain magnitude; in other words, it would be infinitely great.

The premises of this reasoning are not quite as arbitrary as they appear at first sight. For one thing, it must be remembered that the conceptions of unity and plurality are not used here in the relative sense in which we commonly meet them. We have already proved to our satisfaction that a unity which is always and everywhere to remain a unity can actually possess no parts, and that it is, accordingly, not to be found either in the world of co-existence or of succession. A unity of this kind is absolute, not relative, and it is therefore quite true to say that it is incompatible with the idea of spatial extension and magnitude. Considered in this light, the first part of the argument is really irrefutable. And this character of absoluteness belongs equally to the premise of plurality which underlies the second part of the argument. If two parts of a body are never and nowhere to be regarded as a unity, there must at least be a sharp line of demarcation, and the reservation implied by our "at least" goes to show that we consider the present argument as less powerful than its counterpart. The line or boundary must be real; accordingly, if an object without magnitude is to be accounted unreal, this boundary in question must possess magnitude or bodily extension. But an extended object consists once more of parts, and therefore the line of

demarcation is characterized by precisely the same conditions as have just been proved of the parts of the body
which it holds asunder. And this reasoning may be
pressed *ad infinitum.* Each argument may be summarized
by a single convenient formula as follows :—

If each of the objects is really one, it must therefore
be indivisible ; that is to say, it must be unextended and
without magnitude.

Secondly, If objects are multiple, then each pair
of them must be separated by an intercalary object
possessing extension and therefore parts, which in their
turn must be similarly separated, and so on *ad infinitum.*

The double argument thus stated does not appear to
us to be entirely valueless for the progress of knowledge.
Unity and plurality are not absolute conceptions, but
purely relative. If I have an apple before me, it will
depend entirely on my point of view, on the purpose by
which I am directed, whether I regard it as a unit, as a part
of a collection of apples, or as a plurality, as the aggregate
of its constituent parts. Unity and plurality cannot be
treated as absolutes. We cannot talk of units which in
no circumstances could become plural objects, nor yet
of plural objects which in no circumstances could become
units, without assuming premises as wild and grotesque
in character as those which we have just followed to
their suicidal conclusions.

We stumble here against the roots of many other
actual and possible paradoxes, for our inquiry first brings
to light the essential opposition between unity and
plurality, and their common hostility to the conception of
reality. A real object, according to the tenets of this school,
is an object which possesses magnitude, which, accordingly,
is extended, divisible, and plural. But a plural object
requires preliminary units of which it is the aggregate.
Such units, however, as true and absolute units, must be
indivisible and unextended. They must be conceived
to be without magnitude, and therefore without reality.
Thus we see that the conception of being or reality was

full of flaws, and was burdened with contradictions from the start. Every real object was an aggregate composed of units, but the units were devoid of reality, and the Colossus of the Real rested on the clay feet of the Unreal. Nor should we be attended by better fortune if we made the endeavour to liberate reality from its delusive foundation and to set it on a firmer basis. It would still crumble to pieces by internal decay. For if the plural object remains an aggregate, and the parts of which it must be composed in order to possess extension, magnitude, and consequently reality, are not reducible to units, it will lack all tenable or untenable foundation ; it will be infinitely divisible ; it will fall to pieces more and more till it is completely annihilated. Thus we may take it as proved that neither together nor apart are the notions of " unity " and " plurality " suitable vehicles for the notion of reality or being. The " one " is unreal at the start ; the " many " becomes unreal whether it is left to rot on its own foundation or whether it is rebuilt on the sands of the " one " till they go to pieces together.

We should wrong the memory of Zeno if we looked on the reflections which we have freely rendered here as a mere puppet-show of idle abstractions. They contain a criticism of the conception of matter, partly prevalent to this day, as serious in intention as it was successful in execution. The infinite divisibility alleged of matter was threatening it with extinction when the thought arose, probably in the Pythagorean circle, that this divisibility would not transgress a limit which, though distant, was definite. Certain minute nuclei, which might be compared with pin-points or motes in the sun, would set a limit to its further division. It is Zeno's indisputable merit to have pointed out the contradictions implied in this view. Either those nuclei possessed magnitude and extension, in which case they would be subject to.the law of divisibility, or they did not possess those attributes, in which case they could not have been employed to build up the structure of the material world. For one object without magnitude added to another does not make a magnitude ; we may pile up a mountain of nothings, and the result will still be nothing.

But here our agreement must pause, and even within these limits it requires a considerable reservation. The authors of the theory which Zeno vanquished so valiantly worked with a contradictory premise, but they were not on the wrong road. We shall presently become acquainted with a doctrine of matter which followed the same path without falling into the same contradiction ; it is the path which has led the natural science of recent times from one triumph to another. The point is that, though a whole must possess parts if it is to fall asunder, yet its possession of parts need not imply their disintegration in the near, the remote, or even the remotest future. There is undoubtedly a connection in thought between ideal divisibility and actual separability, but they need not therefore be connected in fact. The assumption of such material nuclei not devoid of extension in space, but actually indestructible, may or may not be a final truth ; at least it contains a considerable element of truth, or, more strictly speaking, its logical consequences agree so well with actual phenomena that they become an engine of unparalleled force in the hands of physical research. Except for the blasphemy of the thought, we are almost tempted to exclaim that perhaps the Creator of the world was not quite as clever as Zeno. At any rate, His sublime wisdom did not require to be as much on the alert for victories of logic and logomachy as the wit of the pugnacious Eleatic. More seriously stated, Zeno's rigour of thought is not always of true weight and measure. His arguments frequently contain traces of two points of view, each of which is defensible on its merits, but is completely incompatible with the other. Zeno would play off the one against the other ; he would couple the conception of the finite with that of the infinite, of continuous space with discreet units of time, of continuous time with discreet units of space.

We return at last to our guiding principle, which is the historical point of view. Did Zeno remain till the end, as he started at the beginning of his task, a faithful acolyte of Parmenides? The answer is frequently given in the affirmative, but it does not appear to be tenable. True, he wielded a stout club to punish the anti-Eleatics, but we should hesitate to say that the Eleatic philosophers enjoyed the fruits of their victory. We should even venture to doubt if the "continuous one" of Parmenides —his globular universal Being—emerged unscathed from the fray. The artifices of interpretation would have to be put to quite illegitimate uses in order to make the assertion. No; an impartial witness will admit that the fundamental conceptions of the Eleatics, unity, extension, and reality itself, were shaken or, rather, crushed by this criticism. In the immediate circle of the school and its adherents no doubt was entertained on that point. Plato makes Zeno say that his work was the production of his untamed youth when the blood ran hot in his veins; it was purloined without his knowledge, and published without his consent. Readers of Plato will know how to interpret these remarks. His admiration of the "great" Parmenides made him keenly alive to the fact that Zeno, the disciple of Parmenides, wielded a two-edged weapon with only too much dexterity. The "inventor of dialectic" was invested with a halo, but its rays were not equally to illumine all portions of his work. As a matter of fact, his genius took the bit between its teeth, and Zeno was carried far beyond the goal he originally had in view. As an ontologist, he entered the field as an ardent believer in the doctrine of unity; he left it as a sceptic, or, rather, as a nihilist. We have repeatedly had occasion to refer to the spontaneous decomposition of the theory of primary matter; in Zeno's lifework we are presented with the spontaneous decomposition of the Eleatic theory of being.

It is far cry from Xenophanes to Zeno, yet the beginning and the end stand in close relationship. At the one extreme the soluble character of the great problems of life is disputed on principle;* at the other, the knife is ruthlessly applied to existing attempts at their solution. The history of the school is the history of the gradual

* *Vide* Bk. II. Ch. I. § 3 *fin.*

growth and enfranchisement of the spirit of criticism. Hercules begins by strangling two serpents in his cradle. It is fair to expect some further feats of strength when the infant reaches maturity. Criticism first laid sacrilegious hands on the brilliant tissue of mythology. Next, it rent the brilliant tissue of the sensible world, till finally it exposed the inherent contradictions in that part of the conception of the world which had eluded its previous attacks. The development followed a straight line. The three chief representatives of the Eleatic school form a group of that class of intellectual firebrands, whose business it is to rouse mankind from indolence of thought and the disposition to dogmatic slumber. These pioneers of criticism were as confident as they were bold. It was their firm conviction that the designs which they conceived as reasonable must be stamped on the face of the universe. But as excess of fire and a sensibility impatient of control are not inexcusable in youth, so the overweening self-dependence which marked the early years of scientific thought may fairly claim the same privilege. Thus much we concede. It is rather the middle period of the movement which causes misgivings in the spectator. The results attained are neither complete nor coherent. An unwarrantable quantity of dogmatism is left over, which is not merely a deposit from former conceptions of the universe, but is the less acceptable, inasmuch as it is due to an arbitrary process of transformation and malformation, as unsatisfactory to the natural instinct as to the trained intelligence. The unfavourable impression is relieved if we take a comprehensive view, and join the baseless affirmation with the negation that succeeds to it. For it is this consecutive progress of criticism which gives the Eleatic movement its true value and historical significance. It was the first considerable trial of strength, the first school in which Western philosophy was tempered and steeled till it became conscious of its powers.

A proof of this progress is the clear distinction, hinted at in Xenophanes but now defined by Parmenides, between Knowledge and Belief—Reason and Opinion. The

distinction gains in importance if we recall the hopeless
confusion of these elements in the contemporary teaching
of the Pythagorean School. We are standing here at the
parting of the currents. Two streams flow from one fount,
and take different directions. Nor are their waters
destined to meet again till they mingle in the flood of
decadence.

"Double-headed" was the reproach of the Eleatic,
levelled at the disciples of the Ephesian. The epithet
recoils on himself. For, like Iocaste, his doctrine is pregnant with twin brothers at strife. Consistent Materialism
and consistent Spiritualism are diametrically opposed to
each other in the realm of metaphysics. Yet they grew on
one stem. They trace their descent in common from that
strict conception of Substance which, though it did not
originate at Elea, was most clearly extracted—not to say
isolated—by the Eleatics from the doctrines of Primary
Matter. Abstraction having ventured thus far securely,
its next step brought the inevitable bias, first towards
Anti-Materialism, and then towards Spiritualism proper.
The evidence of the muscular sense—the sense of resistance—was sent the way of the rest, and nothing was left
save the bare conception of Substance, the complexus,
that is to say, of the attributes of eternal persistence and
eternal immutability. Once more there was a parting of
the ways. New metaphysical entities had been created
which might or might not be treated as the vehicles of
force and consciousness. The choice was determined in
each instance by the requirements of the individual thinker,
and on occasions, as we shall see in Plato, it varied with the
taste of the chooser. Eleaticism worked here by indirect
rather than by direct means. For the precedent set by
Melissus found no successor worth mentioning. Except
in the Megaric School, the least important of the Socratics,
we hear no echo of his efforts. If we had to discover an
exact parallel to the blissful Primary Being of Melissus,
with its total lack of initiative and influence, we should
have to turn to India. In the lore of the Vedanta philosophers the world is similarly represented as mere delusive

appearance with a central Being whose sole attributes are : Essence, Thought, and Bliss (*sat, cit,* and *ânanda*). The second alternative, which substituted innumerable material substances for the extended One, is of infinitely greater importance in the history of science. We shall meet it presently in the beginnings of Atomism, a theory which agrees with Parmenides in his strict conception of Substance, but parts company with him in his negative attitude towards the plurality of objects, the *vacuum* dividing them, and the movement in space depending on it. Here, too, an historical connection is at least not improbable. The next question that suggests itself is far less easily dismissed : Was such an intervening link between the old forms of the doctrine of Primary Matter and this, its latest and maturest presentation, necessary at all ? and, if so, to what extent ? The answer will be found in the consideration of two thinkers, connected so closely by likeness and contrast as not to admit of separate treatment.

CHAPTER IV.

ANAXAGORAS.

1. Two contemporaries stand before us : their minds were directed to the same problems, their methods were based on similar assumptions, and their results showed signs of a very striking consentaneity. And yet the contrast is most remarkable. The one was a poet, the other a geometer. The one was gifted with glowing imagination, the other with cool and sober judgment. The one was swollen with vainglory and self-esteem, the other completely disappeared behind his work. The one was all flowers and flourishes of expression, the other a model of language unadorned. The one was so malleable and versatile that his joints seemed positively liquid, the other so rigidly consistent as at times to appear grotesque. The best qualities of each were more or less the defects of the other. Empedocles excelled in the wit and brilliance of his *aperçus ;* his elder contemporary was distinguished by the coherence and uniformity of his majestic system of thought.

Anaxagoras brought philosophy and natural science from Ionia to Attica. The son of aristocratic parents, he was born at Clazomenæ, in the immediate neighbourhood of Smyrna, in or about 500 B.C. He is said to have neglected his patrimony and to have devoted himself at an early age to the exclusive pursuit of wisdom. We have no record of the schools he visited nor of the places where he acquired his knowledge. He shows frequent signs of contact with the doctrines of Anaximander and Anaximenes, but the tradition which makes him a disciple of Anaximenes is refuted by the evidence of dates. About his fortieth year he migrated to Athens, where the great statesman, whose ideal Athens was to be the literary no less than the political centre of Greece, honoured the philosopher with his friendship. For full thirty years Anaxagoras adorned the select circle with which Pericles had surrounded himself. He was fated, too, to be drawn into the whirlpool of party politics. In the dawn of the Peloponnesian war, when the star of Pericles, the leading statesman, first began to wane, his philosopher friend, like the charming and accomplished companion of his life, was arraigned on a charge of impiety. The sentence of exile brought him back to his home in Asia Minor, and there in Lampsacus he died, surrounded by faithful disciples, in the seventy-third year of his blameless life. Considerable fragments survive of his work, complete in several volumes, and written in unaffected but not ungraceful prose. It was published by the author at some date subsequent to 467 B.C., the year of a great fall of meteorites which was mentioned in the work, and it is interesting to add that it was the first book illustrated with diagrams which Greek literature possessed.

He resembled his older Ionian fellow-countrymen in his preoccupation with the problem of matter, but the solution which he offered was entirely original. It completely distinguished him from all previous thinkers, and it showed that the new criticism inaugurated by the Eleatics had not affected him in the least. He may have been acquainted with the didactic poem of Parmenides, but its contents had failed to exercise any influence on his mind. We need look no further than at the doubts which Parmenides voiced so emphatically as to the value of the evidence of the senses and as to the plurality of objects, in both of which crucial instances Anaxagoras neither accepted nor opposed his teachings. There is no reference to them in any of the fragments which have come down to us, nor in any of the supplementary testimony of antiquity. The precise contrary is the case. His system was based on the unconditional belief in the testimony of the senses, and its cornerstone was not merely a bare plurality of objects, but an inexhaustible crowd of fundamentally different entities existing from the beginning of things. For a moment at least we are accordingly the more surprised to find Anaxagoras in complete agreement with Parmenides with respect to the double postulate which we have already sufficiently discussed. His system recognized no beginning and no perishing, nor any change in the qualities of things. "The Greeks," he wrote, "err in speaking of a beginning and a perishing of things, for no object begins, neither does it perish, but it is composed by a mixture of existing objects, and it is decomposed into them by separation. Thus it would be better to call the beginning a mixture, and the perishing a separation." We have already learnt to recognize how the second and later of these propositions —the dawn of which we saw in Anaximenes—sprang from the earlier postulate, which was described, in the pregnant phrase of Aristotle, as "the old common undisputed doctrine of the physicists." Nor are we reduced to conjecture in order to explain the actual process of development in the mind of Anaxagoras himself. A brief fragment of his work, the claims of which, as we saw,[*] were overlooked for so long, has thrown a clear light on this process. The doctrine of matter which is emblazoned with the name of Anaxagoras, was based on the following trinity of postulates : The nature of objects is such as the senses perceive ; they have not become and they are not destructible ; and as it is with the objects so it is with their qualities. His doctrine bears the traces of the rigid consistency of his thought, and it is equally conspicuous by its lack of the philosopher's indispensable instinct to reject the guidance of logic when it deviates from the highway of truth. In brief, this theory of Anaxagoras was almost the exact opposite of what science has taught us about matter and its constitution. His fundamental or elemental matter was sought in organic combinations which are really the most complicated, and materials which, if not exactly simple, are at

* Bk. II. Ch. II. § 3.

least far less complicated, such as water and atmospheric air, ranked in his system as the most composite combinations. If ever a man of powerful intellect chose a wrong path and maintained it with imperturbable perseverance, Anaxagoras did so in his doctrine of matter. It bore the same relation to the results of chemistry as the reverse of a carpet bears to its face. The following argument may be framed to illustrate his method of reasoning. A loaf of bread lies before us. It is composed of vegetable matters, and helps to nourish our body. But the constituent parts of the human or animal body are multiple : it has skin, flesh, blood, veins, sinews, cartilages, bones, hair, etc. Each of these parts is distinguished from the rest by its light or dark hue, its softness or hardness, its elasticity or the contrary, and so forth. How, then, could it happen, Anaxagoras asked himself, that the uniformly constituted bread should produce this rich multiplicity of objects ? A change of qualities was incredible, so that the sole remaining hypothesis was that the bread which nourishes us already contained the countless forms of matter, as such, which the human body displays. Their minuteness of size would withdraw them from our perception. For the defect or "weakness" of the senses is the narrowness of their receptive area. These elusive particles are rendered visible and tangible by the process of nutrition which combines them. What was true of the bread was likewise true of the corn. Hence Anaxagoras was led to ask how the variegated medley of particles could have entered in the corn if it had not already been present in the sources of its nourishment, earth, water, air, and solar fire. Moreover, such particles would be discoverable there in the greatest number and variety, corresponding to the countless different beings which derived their nourishment from those sources ; so that earth, water, fire, and air, which were apparently the simplest of all bodies, were in reality shown to be the most composite. They were full of " seeds" or elements of matter of every conceivable kind, and were little more than mere collections or storehouses. And, as it was with the characteristics of the parts of the human body so it was, according to Anaxagoras, with the fragrance of every roseleaf, the hardness of the sting of every bee, the blended colours in every eye of the peacock's tail. The primary particles were, in all these and innumerable other cases, extant from all eternity, but in a state of extreme dispersion, awaiting the circumstances favourable to their congregation which alone could render them perceptible. The elements of primary matter must have been as inexhaustible in number as the differences, down to their least perceptible shades, which our senses record, and as the combinations, in the utmost possible variety, which a single and simple material object could display. No one can fail to perceive that the contents of this doctrine stand in the most glaring contradiction with the actual results of modern science, but the point to be noticed is this: that the methods and motives of both display the most striking concordance. Anaxagoras, too, was concerned to render the processes going on in the universe thoroughly intelligible. He reduced chemistry to mechanics, and he stripped physiology of every taint of mysticism till it was likewise brought within the purview of mechanics. He used combinations and separations— changes of site, that is to say—to explain all the most secret alterations and transformations. The theory of matter taught by the sage of Clazomenæ was an experiment, rough and immature though it may have been, to conceive all material occurrences as effects of mechanical motion. We are for the most part ignorant of the manner in which the details of the theory were worked out. We cannot say, for instance, how Anaxagoras dealt with the alterations in the aspect and character of objects which accompany the change in their state of aggregation. In this connection we have to rely on a single saying of the master which is itself not a little enigmatic in meaning. He contended that snow must be as dark as the water from which it comes, and that to no one who knew this would it ever again appear white. We appreciate the difficulty which confronted his theory at this point. It consisted in the problem of the change of colour which ensues when the particles of

water are brought in closer contact by cold. The appeal
to the "weakness" of our sense-perception had no force
in this instance. Anaxagoras' fixed conviction that the
particles of water were necessarily dark-coloured in all
circumstances rendered the philosopher, we would venture
to believe, a victim to a gross delusion of senses. We
conceive that in his desire to see clearly, he gazed at the
white quilt stretched across the landscape and gleaming in
the wintry sun, till his dazzled sight began to see everything black, and he was misled into reading in that
optical delusion the confirmation of his preconceived
opinion. If we recall the hardly less crude misinterpretation of facts which we marked in the reasoning of Anaximenes,* the crudity of the mistake will be mitigated.
And when the representatives of the old doctrine of
primary matter lifted up their voices against his theory,
their criticism was robbed of half its force by Anaxagoras'
appeal to the invisible particles of matter and their invisible movements, which Heraclitus had been the first to
defend. They asked him how objects fundamentally
different could be actively and passively related with one
another, and he answered that each contained a portion of
each ; "the objects in this one world," cried Anaxagoras,
"are not completely divided nor hewn asunder as with an
axe"—a phrase, we may remark in parenthesis, containing
the sole metaphorical expression in all the fragments of
his work. Each several object was described, according to
this theory, by the kind of matter which prevailed in it, and
therefore took precedence of the rest. And to minimize
the disbelief in the reality of the Invisible in general, he
quoted the example of the invisible air imprisoned in an
inflated bag, and the resistance it offers to our endeavours
to compress it.

2. The cosmogony of Anaxagoras moves up to a
certain point in the lines laid down by Anaximander and
seldom deserted by his successors to any serious extent.
Here too there is a kind of Chaos at the beginning. But
the place of the single primary matter extended without

* Bk. I. Ch. I. § 4.

bounds is taken by an untold number of primary matters in the same boundless extension. "All things were together;" the infinitesimal primary particles in their indiscriminate confusion formed an original composite medley, and their indistinguishable quality corresponded to the still absent difference of quality in the one universal Being of Anaximander. The "seeds" or elements were primarily endowed with material characteristics, and a mechanical separation took the place of the old dynamic "differentiation." Anaxagoras did not feel himself impelled to arrive at the necessary physical process by mere inferences nor to construct it on familiar analogies. He presumed that he saw it in the apparent revolution of the firmament—a phenomenon that is still enacted before our eyes every day and every hour. This revolution was not merely supposed to have brought the first material separation to pass in the beginning of time, but the same cause was supposed to produce still and now the same effect in other parts of universal space. This attempt to connect the most distant past with the immediate present, and the present again with the most distant future, bespeaks a firmness of conviction which arouses our keenest surprise. Anaxagoras' belief in the uniformity of the forces that govern the universe and in the regularity of its phenomena was in striking contrast with the mythical mode of thought prevailing in former ages. The question arises how the revolution of the firmament could have operated in the manner alleged of it, and the answer he gave took about the following form. At one point of the universe a rotatory movement first took place which described ever wider and wider circles, and will continue so to describe them. The north pole may be regarded with some probability as the starting-point of this movement, which would obviously be continued in circular lines due in each instance to the shock or pressure exercised by each particle of matter on its environment. By this means alone could the first shock, the origin of which will presently occupy our attention, bring to pass in a natural way the extraordinary effects which Anaxagoras ascribed to it. The inconceivable "violence and velocity" of this rotatory motion, we may interpret Anaxagoras as thinking, produced such a jarring and clashing that the former cohesion of the mass was relaxed, the friction of the particles was overcome, and they were enabled to follow the bias of their specific gravity. Then for the first time masses of uniform matter were enabled and obliged to form themselves together and to inhabit various regions of the universe. At its centre, "where the earth is now, was the meeting-place of the Thick, the Fluid, the Cold, and the Dark, but the Thin, the Warm, and the Dry escaped far away into the ether." The primary process which began with a rotation in a limited area of space, engendered, it will be perceived, an endless chain of consequences. But the process itself required a causal explanation, and in this instance physical analogies no longer served our philosopher. He was reduced to what we may half correctly call a supernatural expedient. Half correctly, we say, because the agent which he summoned to his help was neither wholly material nor wholly immaterial. It was neither composed of a common element, nor was it completely divine ; moreover, though it was described as "boundless and self-governing," yet its force was so rarely, nay, so exceptionally employed that its actual dominion over nature might be called a sovereignty in principle, but never a sovereignty in fact. It was the Nous which was supposed to have given that first shock, and we prefer to leave this word in the original Greek, since every translation, whether we render it by "mind" or by "thought-element," introduces something foreign to its nature. According to Anaxagoras' own account, it was "the finest and purest of all things ;" it was "alone free from admixture with any other thing, for had it been so mixed it would have participated with all other things"—it will be remembered that the segregation of elements was incomplete— "and its admixture would have prevented it from exercising the same force over any single object" as its pure condition enables it to do. Further explanations describe the Nous as possessing "all knowledge

about everything, past, present, and future," and endow
it with "supreme power." But the temptation to rank it
with the highest godhead is opposed by other considerations no less essential to its character. We read of a
"more and less of" Nous ; it is described as divisible and
as "inhabiting some things," by which all living beings are
to be understood.

This doctrine can be traced to two quite distinct
motives which mutually kept each other in check. The
universe is full of indications of order and beauty ; its
factors are linked together in the guise of means to an end,
and this spectacle suggests the thought of conscious
government and deliberate operation. In fact, the
design-argument is still the strongest weapon in the
armoury of philosophic Theism. Later thinkers have
entrusted this exalted task to a Being purged from every
material element, but Anaxagoras believed that its requirements would be satisfied by a kind of fluid or ether.
In this he was following the precedent of Anaximenes and
Heraclitus, whose Air and Fire, though they did not set
definite ends before them, were yet honoured as the vehicles
of universal intellect, and he agreed likewise with nine-
tenths of the ancient philosophers in so far as they regarded
the individual "soul" as a substance not immaterial, but of
an extremely refined and mobile materiality. With this
theory the teleological problem entered on the field for the
first time, never again to disappear, and it involved a serious
danger to the progress of science. But happily Anaxagoras, who so frequently drove his logic to excess, was
content to be illogical in this instance. Plato and Aristotle both blamed him for his lack of consistency. They
were delighted at the introduction of the new agent, but
their pleasure was considerably tempered by its use as a
stop-gap or makeshift. They complained that Anaxagoras
employed the Nous as the *deus ex machinâ* of the dramatists,
whose function it was to descend from heaven and cut the
tragic knot when no milder means could be found of dis-
entangling its confusion. For all minor details Anaxagoras
had recourse to "air, and ether, and water, and other

eccentricities," to anything, in short, in preference to his curious reasoning fluid. Of course he might have acted otherwise ; he might have satisfied Plato's condition, and have made his whole inquiry from the point of view of " the better ; " at every separate phenomenon he might have asked why and to what end it occurred instead of how and under what conditions it came to pass, but in such circumstances his contribution to human knowledge would have been yet far more modest than ' was actually the case. Our own limited horizon and the consequent impossibility of guessing the intentions of the Being who governs the world would make this road a path of error and delusion, which Anaxagoras was fortunate to avoid. He was not merely half a theologian, but he was a full-grown natural philosopher as well, though his endowment was extremely one-sided. To his own contemporaries he appeared a very type of that kind, the more so as the new theology, by which the Nous doctrine may be described, had completely released him from the old mythological fetters. The great objects of nature were no longer divine in his eyes : they were masses of matter, obedient to the same natural laws as all other material aggregates whether great or small. It was a constant topic of adverse criticism among his own contemporaries that he looked on the sun, for instance, no longer as Helios the god, but as nothing more or less than "an ignited stone." There was only a single point in his theory of the formation of the firmament and the universe in which he deserted his mechanical and physical principles to assume an outside intervention. That first shock which set in motion the process of the universe that had hitherto been in repose reminds us in a most striking fashion of the first impulse which the Deity is supposed by some modern astronomers to have given to the stars. Or rather, it would be more correct to say that both ideas are practically identical. They were intended to fill up the same lacuna in our knowledge ; they sprang from the same desire to introduce in the mechanism of heaven a second force of unknown origin to take its place by the side of gravity.

We would not by any means be understood to credit the sage of Clazomenæ with an anticipation of Newton's law of gravitation or with a knowledge of the parallelogram of forces, and of the twofold composition of the orbits described by the stars, consisting of gravity on the one part, and on the other of a tangential force harking back to that one original shock. But a brief consideration will show how nearly his thought was allied with the principles of modern astronomy. In the course of his cosmogony he taught that the sun, moon, and stars had been torn away from the common centre of the earth by the violence of the cosmic revolution. Thus he assumed a series of projections or "hurlings-off" in precisely the same kind as the theory of Kant and Laplace assumes for the formation of the solar system. They were caused, according to Anaxagoras, by a force which could only effect that result after the cosmic revolution had begun and had attained considerable strength and velocity. This force we call the centrifugal. Next Anaxagoras turned his attention to the gigantic meteorite of Ægospotami which we mentioned above, and which was compared to a millstone. He argued that as this stone had fallen from the sun, so all the starry masses would fall down on the earth as soon as the force of rotation relaxed and no longer kept them in their courses. Thus, from the most diverse coigns of observation his eye was led back to the same starting-point, at what we may venture to call the primeval secret of mechanics. The force of gravity did not appear to him to be adequate. His conception of it, parenthetically remarked, was imperfect, including as it did a belief in the absolute lightness of certain substances. He could not employ it to explain the separation of the masses of matter nor the origin, duration, and motion of the luminaries and firmament. He concluded that an opposite force was at work. Its operation was at once direct and indirect, and in the latter category was chiefly comprised the opportunity that it gave to the action of centrifugal force. In both categories it released an immeasurable series of effects indispensable to the comprehension of universal phenomena. The origin of this force was hidden in outer darkness. Anaxagoras referred it back to an impulse which was intended to complete the operation of gravity in precisely the same way as the shock in which the predecessors of Laplace had affected to discover the starting-point of tangential force.

3. The cosmogony of Anaxagoras was distinguished by the spirit of true science. It was especially displayed in his acceptation of bold hypotheses where the facts left him no alternative, while he brought to bear on such hypotheses an extraordinary degree of ingenuity, thus enabling them to fulfil a large number of requirements at once, like the best examples of the legislative art. A minimum of hypothesis, that is to say, was to cover a maximum of explanation. We have already sufficiently shown in what admirable stead this talent stood him in the single instance of quasi-supernatural intervention. We have next to mention the remarkable attempt which sprang from the same mental tendency to explain the intellectual superiority of man. Anaxagoras referred it to the possession of the single organ of the hand, and compared it, in all probability, with the corresponding part of the body in the animal structures that stand next to us. The theory reminds us of Benjamin Franklin's phrase about the "tool-making animal." We are not acquainted with the details of his argumentation, and we readily admit that it may have substituted the part for the whole. But it bore witness to that deep-rooted objection to piling specific differences on one another and multiplying inexplicable final facts, which is perhaps the chief feature by which the genuine philosopher may be distinguished from his counterfeit.

The rest of the astronomy of Anaxagoras was little more than an heirloom of Miletus. The great man might almost be said to have inherited the self-satisfaction of the Ionians of the Twelve Cities whom Herodotus satirized so bitterly. He was quite unamenable to any influence which did not proceed from his own country. He ignored or rejected as incredible the globular shape of the earth which Parmenides had promulgated. He agreed with

Anaximenes in regarding the earth as flat, and in the explanation of its state of rest. At this point, however, we are met by a difficulty which has still to be realized and explained. According to Aristotle's account, Anaxagoras conceived the earth as closing the centre of Cosmos like a lid and resting, as it were, on an air-cushion, from which the air underneath was unable to escape. But, according to other equally trustworthy accounts, his theory admitted that the stars moved under the earth as well as above it, and it is impossible to reconcile these two versions. We must note, by the way, that in the beginning of time the stars moved sideways round the earth, and thus never sank below the horizon, so that the second proposition of Anaxagoras had not always held good in his theory. He would not accept the inclination of the earth's axis as a primeval fact, evidently because it failed to satisfy his strong bias to uniformity. So he believed it to have taken place at a later date, by what means we are not told. It was dated after the beginning of organic life, doubtless because that extraordinary event required a complete revision of existing cosmological conditions, and was perhaps better compatible with a permanent spring than with the changes of the seasons. In other respects the views of Anaxagoras were childish enough. His notions of the size of the heavenly bodies may be illustrated by his statement that the sun was greater than the Peloponnesus. He could suggest no more fortunate explanation for the solstice than that the density of the air compelled the sun to turn round. And the moon with its milder heat was supposed to be less capable of resisting the dense air, and therefore to be obliged to turn more frequently. Still, if we may trust the reports, despite all these blemishes on his astronomy, Anaxagoras can point to one important achievement. He may claim to have been the first to have elaborated the correct theory of the phases of the moon and of eclipses. In the last-named instance, it must be acknowledged that he detracted from his own merits by adding the non-luminous stars of Anaximenes to the shadows of the earth and moon as the causes of an eclipse.

Another part of the doctrine of Anaxagoras is extremely instructive for the weaknesses as well as the strong points of the spirit he brought to his inquiries. He made an attempt to explain the accumulated clusters of stars in the Milky Way by which he dismissed them as merely apparent and due to the strong contrast in that region of the sky between the light of the stars and the shadow of the earth. We may suppose him to have reasoned as follows. The daylight prevents us altogether from seeing the stars in the sky, which only become visible in the darkness of night. Additional darkness, therefore, will be accompanied by additional visibility, and the greatest visible number of stars will merely afford evidence that the darkness in that region had been the greatest. And he had no other explanation to offer of this maximum of darkness save the one mentioned above. At the best the theory was at variance with the facts of common observation. It illustrates afresh the one-sided deductive bias of the mind of Anaxagoras and his indifference to the justification of his hypotheses. If his explanation were correct, the Milky Way would have to coincide with the ecliptic, whereas it is actually inclined to it, and an eclipse of the moon would be bound to occur whenever it passed over the Milky Way. Nevertheless we must recognize his argument as exceptionally ingenious, and must admit that the problem he approached was no idle intellectual riddle. Anaxagoras was probably a little exorbitant in his demands on the symmetry of cosmic phenomena. We have already had occasion to mark this tendency, which is by no means surprising in the author of the doctrine of Nous. But the sage of Clazomenæ may claim some points of contact with the astronomers of to-day. They too are not content to explain the Milky Way as due to an original irregularity in the distribution of cosmic matter. And they likewise seek for a mere optical delusion behind that huge exception, and they find it in the crowded condition which the stars assume in our eyes owing to the presumed lenticular shape of the Milky Way system to which the earth belongs.

In the meteorology of Anaxagoras his correct explanation of the winds as due to changes of temperature and atmospheric density is worthy of mention ; and in his geography
we may instance the account given of the rise of the Nile as
the result of the melted snows in the mountains of Central
Africa—an account which antiquity pursued with ridicule,
but which is at least partially correct. Anaxagoras followed
in Anaximander's footsteps with respect to the beginnings
of organic life, but he struck out a path of his own in his
doctrine that the first vegetable germs had fallen on the
earth with the rain out of the air, which was filled with
"seeds" of all kinds. This doctrine is probably to be
connected with the great significance attached by the sage
to the operation of air in organic life. Plants, for instance,
in his theory were represented as breathing after a fashion,
though the statement could have rested on no exact observations, and he was the first to discover that fishes breathed
through their gills. In other respects, too, Anaxagoras did
not recognize any impassable gulf between the animal and
the vegetable creations. Plants were supposed to participate
at least in feelings of pleasure and pain, the pleasure
being the accompaniment of the growth of trees, and pain
of the loss of their leaves. Similarly, though no hint of the
doctrine of evolution was compatible with his theory of
matter, he refused to regard the various orders of the
animal kingdom—to transfer his expression from another
context—as "hewn asunder with an axe." It is difficult to overpraise his tendency, which we have already
had occasion to notice with approval, not needlessly to
pile up specific differences on one another, and it saved
him in this instance too from the mistakes of some later
thinkers. In intellectual endowment he recognized only
differences of degree, and his Nous was located by him in
all animals without exception, the great and the small,
the high and the low, with no other difference except
that of quantity.

4. Anaxagoras' theory of the senses need not detain us
long. We should note, however, that it did not admit the
principle of relativity except where the facts were quite

unequivocal. In the feeling of temperature he was ready to allow that an object such as water will make a warmer impression on the sense, the colder the hand that tries it. But in general it may be said that he regarded the evidence of the senses as truthful, but weak. He affected to build up on it a completely true conception of the outer world, and our readers are already well acquainted with the doctrine of matter which the sage of Clazomenæ based on that foundation. Still, it will not be out of place to recall its features once more. There were two original premises, the first of which stated that "there is no change of qualities," and the second of which asserted that "objects really possess the qualities which the senses reveal to us." From these premises the inevitable conclusion was deduced that "every difference of sensible qualities is fundamental, original, and inalienable." There is, therefore, not one primary matter, or a few of them, but absolutely countless primary matters. Or, more precisely stated, nothing was left but the distinction between homogeneous accumulations (homoiomeries) and heterogeneous mixtures, thus involving the disappearance of that between original and derivative forms of matter. Anaxagoras had reverted to the crude conception of nature held by primitive man ; he had abandoned the doctrine of primary matter which previous philosophers had taught, and he had even gone back on those early endeavours towards the simplification of the material world which are found in Homer, in the Avesta, or in the book of Genesis. The arguments underlying that doctrine were nevertheless not shaken. Their irresistible force still overwhelmed the inquirer with a conviction of the interdependence of the countless elements of matter, so that it might almost be said that postulates of equal cogency stood in irreconcilable opposition. The problem of matter, in a word, had been stranded on the shallows. It was a *cul-de-sac* from which there was but one possible outlet. The premises of the theory of primary matter had been completely refuted by the conclusions derived from them—conclusions thoroughly false, as we now know, and incredible in themselves, as

Anaxagoras' own contemporaries had not failed to perceive. But the premises were not therefore necessarily wrong ; they might merely have been incomplete, and if so, it would have been enough to supplement them without altogether rejecting them. The stumbling-block was rolled out of the way, and the belief in the qualitative constancy of matter, which we have learnt to call the second postulate of matter, could be permanently maintained as soon as one condition was fulfilled. This condition was to recognize a part only of sensuous qualities as truly objective, and not their totality. The new doctrine of cognition came to the rescue of the old doctrine of matter. A distinction arose between objective and subjective, primary and secondary qualities of things, and this was the great intellectual feat which was alone calculated to reconcile the hitherto irreconcilable demands, and which actually effected their reconciliation. A fresh tier was added—a higher one, though surely not the highest—to the rising mansion of science, and the name of Leucippus must always be mentioned with honour in connection with this great service to philosophy. The vessel which had grounded on the sands was floated once more through his handiwork. And Anaxagoras deserves a hardly less honourable meed. It was his supreme merit, in our opinion, to have made visible to the weakest sight the necessity of thus supplementing the theory of matter, for the undeviating logic of his arguments had not even shrunk from absurdities.

As often happens, the renown which Anaxagoras enjoyed in antiquity was due as much to the defects as to the qualities of his mind. His teaching was marked by a patriarchal dogmatism. His method of thought, and doubtless his manner as well, were stiff and hard ; the doctrines with which he frequently did violence to the common sense of mankind were promulgated with oracular conviction, and we can hardly doubt that by this he succeeded in exercising a fascinating influence far and wide. For his characteristics would have contrasted as sharply as possible with the vague uncertainty of his times. It was an age

of excessive mental suppleness, when thought was as full of
the germs of scepticism as the air or water in the doctrine
of Anaxagoras with the "seeds" of things. Nor can we
altogether escape the record of a second impression. There
was bound to be a little curling of the lips among the contemporaries of Anaxagoras when their esteemed teacher
paraded so intimate an acquaintance with all the secrets
of the universe, as if he had personally assisted at the
origin of the world; when he proclaimed the wildest
paradoxes—his doctrine of matter, for instance—in tones
of the calmest infallibility; and when, with the confidence
of revelation, he told stories of other worlds, worlds which
repeated in detail the procession of earthly phenomena,
worlds inhabited by a race of men who built their homesteads and ploughed their fields and carried their produce
to the market—and all this with the reiterated assurance,
occurring like the burden of a song, "just as it is with us."
Yes, it is quite comprehensible that Xenophon should have
been expressing not merely his personal conviction, but
a current opinion of his age, when he stated that the
great philosopher was "a little off his head." The times
in which he lived were seething with scepticism, but he
stood apart from it in all respects except his attitude of
disdain towards the popular religion. For the rest, he
clung to the evidence of senses as it were to a rock,
reminding us by his unquestioning faith of the least philosophic of modern followers of natural research; he betrayed
no taste or understanding for dialectic discussion, and
probably neglected if he did not despise the subtle doubts
and arguments of Zeno; like a greater thinker—

> "for ever
> Voyaging through strange seas of thought alone,"

he pursued his course with the unsuspecting temerity of
a sleep-walker unconscious of obstacles, undisturbed by
doubts, and undistracted by the difficulties of the way;
his arid teachings were unillumined by a spark of poetry
or humour; and the solitary author of these apodictic
and venturesome doctrines cannot always have cut the

best figure among the great men of his age with their versatile gifts and their almost excessive pliability. Many people were greatly impressed by his fine air of calm and his confident self-esteem ; others execrated his bold-ness for looking too deeply into the secrets of the gods ; others, again, and these by no means the least numerous, must at least have regarded him as a little "twisted," if not as absolutely awry. To our thinking, Anaxagoras was a man of great deductive powers, of exceptional inventive-ness, and with a strongly developed sense of causation : but these advantages were counteracted by a striking want of sound intuition, and by a virtual indifference to the justification by fact of his finely wrought hypotheses.

CHAPTER V.

EMPEDOCLES.

THE modern traveller who visits Girgenti is reminded at every step of Empedocles, for the beautiful piety of the Italians, fostered by the continuity of their civilization, takes no count of chronological barriers. What Virgil is to his Mantuans, Stesichorus to the inhabitants of Catania, and the great Archimedes to his fellow-citizens of Syracuse, so dear and so beloved is the memory of their great fellow-countryman Empedocles, the philosopher and the leader of the people, to the inhabitants of Girgenti.* He is worshipped as a democrat by the disciples of Mazzini and Garibaldi, because he overthrew the rule of the nobles who had oppressed Acragas for three years, and refused the royal crown for his own head. This tradition, which is credible in itself, is in unison with all that we know of the circumstances of his life and of the condition of his native city. Moreover, similar stirring scenes were enacted about that time in other Sicilian communities. The family of Empedocles was one of the most aristocratic in the country. It was at the height of its wealth and splendour at the date of his own birth—between 500 and 480 B.C. In the year 496 B.C. another Empedocles, his grandfather, had taken the prize at Olympia in the four-horse chariot race. A quarter of a century later, in 470 B.C., Meto, the father of the philosopher, had taken an active and prominent part among the citizens of Acragas in overthrowing the tyranny of Thrasidæus. We are, therefore, not overmuch

* Agrigentum, Acragas.

surprised to learn that the road to royal power stood open
for his high-spirited and high-born son. Nor need we
ascribe it to the motive of pure love for the people that
Empedocles resigned the chance of solitary rule as well as
a participation in the oligarchic government. His decision
may well have been due to the force of shrewd common
sense. As one of the founders of rhetoric, he was an
orator as well as a thinker, and he may conceivably have
hoped to play a more distinguished part under democratic
institutions than in the narrow circle of his peers. Furthermore, it is no mean title to fame to have refused a crown ;
the crown that has not been worn is innocent of blood
and mud, but the throne that has arisen from the troubled
waters of revolution may lightly sink back into them.
Empedocles lived in an age of ferment, when the princely
dignity itself was not exempt from the changes of popular
favour. But as a private man he was safe at least from
the vengeful steel of the republican fanatic. If the wayward
mob grew tired of his leadership it could drive him into
exile, and this would appear to be the fate which actually
overtook Empedocles. At the age of threescore years he
succumbed to an accident in the Peloponnese, and died a
stranger in a strange land. Antiquity deemed this end
unworthy of the wonderful man, and, according to one fable,
he perished in consequence of a leap into the crater of Ætna,
while another account sent him straight to heaven in a
cloud of flame.

But the strenuous ambition of Empedocles soared
higher than all princely thrones. A shining palace on
the bank of "the yellow Acragas" might be tempting
enough, but the dominion over 800,000 subjects is insignificant in comparison with the mastery exercised over
countless souls bound by no temporal or local conditions,
by the sage, the seer, the miracle-worker. A king is
inferior to a god, and no meaner boast did Empedocles
make to his elect—"I am an immortal god unto you ;
look on me no more as a mortal." In purple vestments,
with a golden girdle, with the priestly laurel bound in
the long hair that framed his melancholy features, and

surrounded by the hosts of men and women who worshipped him, Empedocles made his progress through the Sicilian land. He was acclaimed by thousands and tens of thousands of the populace, who clung at his feet and implored him to direct them to a prosperous future, as well as to heal in the present their sickness and sores of all kinds. He claimed the sceptre of the winds, the key of the burning sunbeams and destructive falls of rain. And he could point to examples of his might. It was he who had freed the city of Selinus from its deadly pestilence by draining its soil; it was he who had bored through a rock and opened a road for the north wind to give his native city a wholesome climate. His achievements as an engineer were matched by his achievements or promises as a physician. He had wakened from catalepsy a victim who had lain thirty days like a dead woman "without pulse or breath," and Gorgias, his disciple, had seen him "perform magic feats," a piece of evidence which cannot fairly be interpreted as referring to hypnotic or other cures due to the power of the imagination.

It is difficult to form a just estimate of a mind and character in which the true gold of genuine merit was mixed with so strange an alloy of tawdry and showy tinsel. It is an excuse, though hardly a justification, to recall the peculiarities of the fellow-countrymen, and perhaps fellow-citizens, of Empedocles. The inhabitants of the island which proved the cradle of rhetoric, were always disposed to ostentation and pretence. The very ruins of the temples which crown the heights of Girgenti create a disagreeable impression of an exaggerated desire for effect. It is yet more difficult to trace the doctrines of our philosopher to their fountain-head, for they appear, at first sight at least, to be deficient in the virtue of strict consistency, and have not escaped the reproach of a vicious eclecticism.

2. The physician, the hierophant, the orator, the politician, the author of works for the common good, whatever their secondary tastes, are united by their prime interest in man. We shall therefore expect to find that

Empedocles the philosopher was an anthropologist as well as a cosmologist, and that his investigation of nature led him to the regions of physiology, chemistry, and physics, rather than to those of astronomy and mathematics. And the facts justify our expectation. The sage of Acragas never concerned himself with the science of space and numbers, and he was but an indifferent student of the science of the stars. In biological research, on the contrary, he introduced some fresh contributions which proved by no means unfertile; but the crowning point of his work was attained in his doctrine of matter. It is hardly an exaggeration to say that Empedocles takes us at a bound into the heart of modern chemistry. We are confronted for the first time with three fundamental conceptions of that science: the assumption of a plurality, and of a limited plurality, of primary elements; the premise of combination in which such elements enter; and, finally, the recognition of numerous quantitative differences or proportional variations of the said combinations.

It is not improbable in this connection that the practical physician led the footsteps of the speculative chemist. Alcmæon, who preceded Empedocles by about half a century, has already familiarized us with the theory that illnesses are caused by the conflict or disproportion of the heterogeneous elements contained in the animal body. It was a doctrine which had taken firm hold in medical circles at least, and which was used, according to Polybus, in a passage quoted above,* as a chief weapon against material monism. But apart from the attack from this quarter, that doctrine was obviously not well suited to give an exact account of the phenomena. No one can fail to perceive that with the progress of the study of nature the vague process of generalization was bound to defer more and more to detailed investigation and research. The old Ionian philosophers, with the honourable exception of Anaximenes, had acquiesced in an indefinite "transformism" which rested neither on well ascertained facts nor yet on precise reflection; and when its defects had been exposed,

* Bk. II. Ch. II. *init.*

no second alternative remained but to refer the plurality of phenomena to an original plurality of material substances. Anaxagoras, the older contemporary and intellectual congener of Empedocles, approached the new task of philosophy in a spirit of defiance. He threw away the wine with the lees, rejecting at a single stroke all differences between the elements and the substances derived from them, thus returning for the nonce to the infancy of human thought. But Empedocles took a less violent method. In rejecting the single element he did not throw overboard the whole theory of elements. He may have learnt to appreciate the value of compromise in the school of practical politics, and this experience may have saved him from the error of the rigid "this or that"—either one primary element or nothing but primary elements. The problem was to secure a plurality of fundamental elements, and in order to gain this end it was sufficient to join together the doctrines of Thales, Anaximenes, and Heraclitus ; or, to speak more precisely, it was sufficient to take a comprehensive view of the popular system of physics which lay at the root of the teaching of those philosophers, and in accordance with its tenets, to combine the Earth with Air, Fire, and Water. The "four elements" which compose and preserve the world, now surviving merely in folklore and poetry, have a long and glorious history. Aristotle embodied them in his theory of nature, and his authority sped them over the stream of the centuries, and impressed on the doctrine the stamp of unimpeachability. Nevertheless it was devoid from the start of all intrinsic justification. It obviously rests on the crudest possible confusion, for we shall hardly be asked to prove that it reverts in the last instance to the distinction of the three states of aggregation—the solid, fluid, and gaseous—and that the fourth element which was added to these fundamental states was the mere accessory of a process, and was nothing but the phenomenon, so dazzling to the senses, which accompanies combustion. The mistake was to regard the fundamental forms of substance as homogeneous kinds and as the only fundamental kinds of substance.

Despite these objections, the merit of the doctrine was incalculable. The value of a doctrine in the history of science is not always commensurate with its degree of objective truth. A theory may be wholly true, and yet the unpreparedness of human understanding may make it useless and abortive, whereas a second theory, though wholly untrue, may render abundant service to the progress of knowledge precisely on account of that stage of intellectual development. In the age with which we are dealing, and far beyond its confines, the doctrine of a single primary matter belongs to the first-named category of ineffectual theories ; in the same era and in those immediately succeeding to it the doctrine of the four elements belongs to the second of our categories. We may make as many deductions from the truth of the doctrine as we choose ; we may explain that no one of the elements was a genuine element ; that Water, which had the best claim to that title, was a compound combination ; that Earth and Air, on the contrary, were each but a single name for countless material substances partly simple and partly complex, each respectively in but one of its phenomenal shapes ; and we may discreetly pass over the nonentity of the element of Fire : still, this pseudo-science was, as it were, the bud from which the true flower of science was to unfold. A model was given which represented the fundamental conceptions of chemistry, and from which alone those conceptions could be derived. If philosophy had waited to form the conceptions of elements and combinations till it had become familiar with real elements and real combinations of the same, it might have waited for ever. For the goal of the theory of matter, like that of astronomy itself, was only to be reached by paths of error.* The reflections of Empedocles in this connection were as correct as their application was misleading. He was as reluctant as any of his predecessors to recognize an absolute beginning and end, and, moreover, he surpassed his predecessors in the clear grasp which he obtained of the positive counterpart of those negations. To him, as to Anaxagoras, each

* Bk. I. Ch. IV. § 1 (pp. 114, 115).

apparent beginning was really "only a mixture," each apparent end a mere separation of the mixture. But he leaves Anaxagoras behind in his perception and statement of the fact that the sensible qualities of a compound depend on the manner in which it is composed. His first hint of this perception is contained in a remarkably significant simile. To illustrate the endless multiplicity of qualities which objects offer to our senses, he recalled the process that is constantly at work on the artist's palette. He compared his four primary substances with the four primary colours used by the artists of his day, from the mixed proportions of which were derived the countless shades and gradations of hue. It may be urged that this is a mere simile, and not an explanation, but it is a simile which at least contains some of the elements of an explanation. It brings one important fact very clearly to light, that a merely quantitative difference in a compound of two or more elements causes a qualitative difference in its sensible qualities. It is not a mere matter of inference that Empedocles was master of this fact ; it may be directly proved by the testimony of his own writings. For with a venturesomeness which reacted on the details of the experiment, he attempted to reduce the qualitative differences in the parts of the human body to quantitative differences of composition. Thus flesh and blood were supposed to contain equal parts of the four elements— equal in weight, and not in volume—whereas the bones were composed of $\frac{1}{2}$ Fire to $\frac{1}{4}$ Earth and $\frac{1}{4}$ Water. It cannot be disputed that he was obliged to employ this aid to explanation in the most comprehensive fashion, otherwise he could never have maintained with such emphasis the dependence of sensible qualities on the mode of composition as in the simile mentioned just now. The four elements in themselves could give but a very small number of possible combinations, viz. one four, four threes, and six twos. But as soon as the principle of proportional combination was admitted the possible number was infinitely extended, and the doctrine of Empedocles rose to the height of its intention, and was able to account for a really inexhaustible variety of substances. And here let us pause to remark that we are confronted with one of the most striking anticipations of the results of modern science. The chemistry of our century from Dalton downwards is dominated by the theory of proportions or equivalents. In the realm of organic chemistry in especial, where the four primary elements C, H, O, N completely justify the comparison with the four primary colours borrowed from ancient painting, its value is most significant, and in recent times we owe to it the discovery that the number of atoms in albuminoids, for instance, can be counted by their hundreds.

3. Empedocles is at one with the modern chemist in his recognition of the changeless condition of the primary elements side by side with the Protean variation of their compounds. But of all the intermediate links in this chain of thought one alone, so far as we are aware, was fully grasped by Empedocles, namely, the significance mentioned above of proportional quantities in combination. He may have perceived, but he never clearly expressed his knowledge or acceptance of the second and more important fact that the qualities of a compound are affected by its structure, by the conditions of its parts in respect to situation and movement, and that a body which is distinguished from another body by these conditions will exercise a different influence on other bodies and on our organs of sense. Yet we fancy that Empedocles must have guessed at this fact, else he must have been content to forego every explanation of the circumstance that the elements in their combination "traverse each other," to use his own words, "and show a different face." And we miss something else in Empedocles. We look in vain in this connection for the full recognition and appreciation of the part which is played by the subjective factor in our sense-perceptions, though he comes much nearer to it than any of his predecessors except one. The exception is Alcmæon, the independent thinker and observer included in the Pythagorean circle, with whom time has dealt a little hardly. Alcmæon gives us the first hint of subjective sensible

phenomena, and Empedocles, as may be abundantly testified, followed in his footsteps. Alcmæon was the first and
Empedocles was the second, and there was no intermediary
thinker, who represented the interior of the eye as consisting
almost entirely of Fire and Water. Hereon was based
the comparison of the structure of the eye with the making
of a lantern. The transparent plates to protect the flame
from the wind which might extinguish it correspond in the
eye to the thin films covering the contents of the orbit,
which are partly of a fiery and partly of a watery nature.
Next came the principle, probably derived from the
analogy of the sense of touch and resistance, that like is
recognized by like, and in accordance therewith the fiery
parts of the eye were to recognize external fire, and the
watery parts external water, those two elements being taken
as the types of light and darkness. The act of perception
was accomplished as follows. At the approach of fiery or
watery effluvia from the substances, fiery or watery particles went out to meet them from the funnel-shaped pores
of the eye. The meeting was caused by the mutual attraction of similar materials, and the perception was brought
about by the contact of the particles entering the pores
from without with those quitting them from within at a
point outside the eye, though presumably close to its
surface. Thus sight was assimilated to touch, light being
touched by light and dark by dark, and it depended on
which of the two elements was less strongly represented,
and therefore more susceptible of its complement, in the
eyes of the respective kind of animals or individuals whether
they were better adapted to receive colour-impressions
and to see clearly by daylight or by dusk. This view
of the mechanism and the process of the act of sight
is crude and fanciful enough. It does not even explain
what it professes to explain, and countless questions arise
to which it does not pretend to give an answer. Still it
possesses one undisputed merit. It was an attempt, however inadequate, to explain perception by intermediate
processes.* It was an attempt, moreover, which admitted,

* Cp. Bk. II. Ch. III. § 2.

however reluctantly, the subjective factor, thus completing one stage of the journey whose ultimate goal it is to recognize that our sense-perceptions are anything rather than the mere reflections of exterior objective qualities of things. Further, this theory of Empedocles did not wholly reject the principle of relativity. We saw that the increased mass of the fiery or watery matter contained in different eyes was to explain the differences of perception, and we may add that the shape and size of the pores were here, as in other instances of sensation, to permit or prevent the entry of the " effluvia." Such effluvia alone as corresponded with the pores were regarded as perceptible. Thus error once more was justified of its offspring, and this erroneous theory smoothed the way for a true insight into the nature of sense-perception. The old stumbling-block which left the human intelligence no choice save between a blind acceptance and an equally blind rejection of the evidence of sense receded further and further in the distance. That evidence was more carefully guarded against the objections arising from individual or temporary differences of impression, and thus the knowledge derived from this source was at once restricted to narrower limits and more firmly secured within them.

4. Empedocles displays in the rest of his allied doctrines the same merits and defects as in his physiology of sense. They exhibit a common tendency to reduce the physical and psychical phenomena of the human, animal, and vegetable worlds to universal natural processes. The barriers between the organic and inorganic, between the conscious and unconscious, were to be destroyed ; better still, they were never to be erected or completed. It was at once the strength and weakness of our philosopher that he looked so deeply into the unity of all natural and spiritual life. It was his weakness because his comprehensive generalizations rested rather on a neglect of differences than on the evidence of likeness in difference, and because the experiment is fully as crude and premature as the kindred attempt of Anaxagoras.* The

* Cp. Bk. II. Ch. IV. § 1.

perception that made the deepest impression on the mind
of Empedocles was that of the mutual attraction of like
by like. This doctrine applied equally to the masses
of homogeneous matter, earth, air, clouds, and sea, as to
the parallel observation, taken from social life and raised
to the dignity of a proverb, "like to like." On the other
hand, the attraction depending on the difference of sex was
but little taken in account, and the natural phenomena
with which we have been familiarized by the doctrine
of electricity, and which contradict this principle of
attraction, were unknown at that time. Thus there
was nothing to prevent the constant and general application of this so-called universal law. At one time it
was used to explain the growth of plants ; at another the
origin of the human race, and in both cases the fire in
the interior of the earth was supposed to yearn towards
the external fire, and thus impel to the surface and beyond
it the various forms of vegetable life and the yet un-
formed human "lumps" consisting of earth and water.
Another illustration may be taken from the phenomenon
of breath. Respiration was due, according to the doctrine
of Empedocles, to the fire in the living organism which
was impelled by the same force to drive out the air
contained therein, and thus to bring about expiration.
A further point to be noticed is that the dwelling-place
of the various kinds of animals is determined, no less
than the rest of their qualities, by the same fundamental
principle of the predominance of a single element in each.
Animals full of air seek the air, those full of water make
for the water, and those with a preponderance of earth
in their composition have a natural bias to the earth.
The perception of like by like ranks as a universal rule
applicable not merely to the region of sense-perception,
as we have already seen, but to the realm of thought
itself. In the theory of sight which we have just
examined we saw that like required to be completed
by like, and the same principle was taken to govern all
manifestations of desire, such as that of hunger, for
instance, and to account no less for the sensation of

pleasure in the satisfaction of desire than for that of pain in its non-satisfaction. Such doctrines, of course, were one-sided and partly fanciful, but we cannot escape the impression of grandeur which they create, recalling to our memory the breadth of the Heraclitean philosophy. Still, there is something refreshing in the occasional interruption of these monotonous elucidatory endeavours by a genuine observation of nature, however imperfectly it may have been applied. We come across an observation of this kind, or, to speak more correctly, across a truth ascertained by experiment, in the account of the breathing, or exhalation, which takes place through the skin. Empedocles employed in this connection a very apt illustration. He took the case of a bottle held mouth downwards in a basin of water with a finger closely pressed against the opening, and remarked that even after the removal of the finger the bottle would not fill with water, though in other circumstances it would be flooded forthwith ; and he was quite clear on the point that it was the air which had been prevented from escaping from the bottle that kept the water from entering. In the same way, so he argued, external air could only enter the body when the blood had receded from the surface and had welled back to the inner organs. The regular consecution of this tidal process of the blood accounted, according to his doctrine, for the exhalation through the pores of the skin. We see that Empedocles ascribed very considerable influence to this pretended universal law of the attraction of like by like. At the same time he could not possibly have regarded it as the only regulating principle. He must have sought some explanation of the origin and self-preservation of organic beings, each of which he perceived to contain more than one of the four elements or all the four at once. Hence he conceived, in the tendency of like to separate from like and of unlike to combine with unlike, a second principle precisely contrary to the first to check and control its operations. The existing order of things represented a kind of compromise between the two

natural causes. The origin of each individual was due
to the operation of the second tendency ; its nourishment,
especially in the Empedoclean sense which we noticed just
now, and its dissolution of earth to earth, air to air, and so
forth, were due unmistakably to the first. At this point
we must revert for a moment to the teaching of Anaximander
and Anaxagoras about the differentiation of matter and
the separation of the elements. Those philosophers had
taught that such processes were not primeval, but that they
were preceded in time by a condition of complete homogeneity of matter in which the individual substances were
either not yet differentiated or were thoroughly mixed and
combined. Now, by adopting this belief, whether at the
hands of his predecessors or by his own investigations,
Empedocles reached a point in time at which one of the
two fundamental tendencies in all natural life would
have reigned in solitary splendour. That was the time
when the attraction of like by like was entirely out-
weighed by the rival principle of the attraction of unlikes.
Having reached that point, the symmetry of thought
would have rendered it practically necessary to provide a
similar period of solitary reign for the first and more
powerful principle. Finally, Empedocles, following in the
footsteps of Anaximander, Heraclitus, and at least a
proportion of the Pythagoreans,* and regarding all
phenomena as cyclical in character, would not have considered the succession of these two epochs of the world
as having taken place once for all, but as a constantly
recurring alternation of such periods. This, in fact, was
his teaching, and he selected as its vehicles a couple
of forces, working in consecutive epochs of temporary
superiority. These powers dominated matter under
the names of "Friendship" and "Discord." It was the
part of the first to combine and unite substances
of different natures, whereas Discord, as soon as its
turn arrived, broke those bonds of union and left the
elements free to obey their natural tendency of like to
like. It was not supposed that each of the two powers

* Bk. I. Ch. V. § 4.

vanquished the other suddenly or at one blow. The steady conflict went on during each of the successive periods, and one by one they obtained the mastery, till the weaker in each instance was gradually supplanted, and then devoted itself again to recuperative efforts with a view to reversing the victory. Thus Empedocles distinguished in the ebb and flow of this movement between two eras of rise and decay, first, the triumph of Friendship and the ensuing growth of Discord; next, the triumph of Discord and the growth of Friendship. We have tried to give a correct account of the nature of this conception, but there is still one feature which calls for further remark. There is something eminently characteristic of the deep insight into nature which distinguished Empedocles in the gradual method of transition by which he conceived the supremacy to pass from one power to the other. It manifests his incredulous attitude towards sudden and immediate changes and his view of their continuity as a fundamental law of the universe. Taking the successive periods as the zenith and the nadir, then the first, when Friendship is at its height, will correspond to a condition of things which we may compare with the primeval "confusion" of Anaxagoras and its analogue in Anaximander. An immense sphere contains the elements, which are molten and mingled in indiscriminate chaos. The zenith of Discord presents us with quite a contrary picture. The four fundamental types of matter will be almost completely sundered from one another, and will be gathered separately in a conglomerate mass before our eyes. But the attention of Empedocles was chiefly directed to the problem of organic life, and this can neither begin nor prosper at one or the other culminating point of the successive periods. For each organism is composed of several elements combined with one another in varying proportions. Such elements exist, in the external world from which the organism derives its nourishment, in a state of at least partial separation— or rather easily separable—but at the same time they must be capable of combining with one another. At neither of the two culminating points are both conditions present at once ; the first is wanting when Friendship has the upper hand, and the second in the reign of Discord. They are never found in conjunction except in the two transitional stages which divide the extremes of cosmic evolution. Thus organic life can only originate and flourish at the two focal points where the streams of tendency cross each other ; and as soon as one or other of the upward movements reaches its goal or zenith, organic life will always be annihilated.

5. We have now briefly to advert to the details of the Empedoclean cosmology. Neither by its virtues nor by its faults has its influence been considerable, and our information in this respect is, moreover, defective. We can but suggest a conjectural answer to the question whether our philosopher regarded the earth as round or cylindrical in shape. He agreed with Anaxagoras in supposing that the quality of order or "cosmos" had hitherto been acquired by a part only of primeval matter. At the period when friendship was at its zenith, the communion and comminglement of the elements lent it the shape of a motionless ball which was invested with the attributes of personality and bliss under the name of Sphairos. Material separation began, according to a verse of Empedocles, with a severance of "the heavy" and "the light," • and it is legitimate to conjecture that the mechanical agent was a kind of whirlwind which collected the heavier matter, consisting of mixed earth and water, in the central spot which is now our own place of habitation. One point remains obscure. We are unable to identify the original motive in this process, which made it possible for "all the limbs of the god to move in turn." Fire first, and a portion of the air, escaped upwards. The air was supposed to have been fastened to the crystalline vault of heaven under the influence of fire, and to have acquired a kind of glaze. The remaining central mass soon came to a standstill, but the regions round the earth continued their rotatory movement, and their pressure squeezed the water out of the quiescent mass. Meantime the heavenly

fire drew the air that still remained for some unknown
reason in this sea or "sweat of the earth" by the process
of evaporation. The problem suggests itself why the earth
should have stood still, and why it should not have sunk
downwards, and Empedocles met his questioners by an
argument from analogy which, if it failed to do anything
else, would at least excite our admiration for the vivid and
mobile genius by which he united the most discrepant
conceptions. While he was groping about to explain the
apparent quiescence of the earth, he remembered by a
happy inspiration a trick as familiar in the fairs of
antiquity as in those of this day. Several goblets are
filled with water or with some other fluid, and are then
tied to a hoop with their open mouths pointing inwards.
The hoop is then set in swift rotation, and the essence of
the trick is that the water does not escape. Empedocles
seized on this mountebank's exploit for the solution of his
problem. Set the goblets revolving quickly, and their
contents will not escape ; set the firmament revolving
quickly, and the earth at its centre will not slip. Empedocles was content with this analogy, though it provokes
a smile to-day and is hardly intelligible at first sight. We
know that the fluid is constantly impelled to the bottom
of the goblet, and its attempts to escape are counteracted
by centrifugal force. But that force could never have been
brought into play if the fluid itself had not been made to
rotate together with the goblet that contained it, and we
ask with surprise how any one could have come to
compare the relative quiescence of the fluid with the
presumptive absolute quiescence of the earth. But Empedocles was not in possession of that causal insight.
In both cases he regarded the smaller force and velocity
of the downward tendency as overcome by the "quicker"
rotatory movement. Empedocles, we must remember, was
a warm-blooded Sicilian, whose brilliant intellect was distinguished by breadth rather than by depth of thought.
He had a keen scent for analogies, and the mistake he
made in this instance was characteristic of his hasty conclusions. He explained the alternation of day and night

by the revolution of the firmament, which consisted in his theory of two hemispheres, the one light and the other dark. Furthermore, the sun was not conceived as shining by its own light, but as a kind of glass-like body absorbing and reflecting the light of ether. In this doctrine Empedocles may have given a lead to the younger Pythagoreans.* He agreed with Anaxagoras in supposing that the light of the moon was borrowed from the sun, and, further, in his correct explanation of the eclipses of the two luminaries. He agreed with Alcmæon in distinguishing between the fixed stars, literally fixed in heaven, and the freely moving planets. At this point, however, we may leave his meteorological speculations. They were partly correct and generally ingenious, but we may return more profitably to his theories about organic life and its origin.

6. Two modes were suggested for the beginnings of organic being. On the one which rests on the progress of the separation of the elements our information is incomplete ; we have already made acquaintance with the shapeless lumps from which mankind was later to be formed, and which constitute the sole reference to this aspect of the question. When we come to the gradual and continuous perfection of the forms of animal and vegetable life under the sign of "Friendship," our authority is fuller. The vegetable world was supposed to have preceded the animal, and to have belonged to a period anterior to the present inclination of the axis of the earth —a detail which once more reminds us of Anaxagoras. The belief that the less perfect preceded the more perfect is the guiding thought of his zoogony, which, fanciful as it was, was yet not wholly devoid of scientific significance. First of all, single limbs were supposed to have sprung from the earth—"heads," for instance, "without neck and trunk," "arms without shoulders," and "eyes without a face." Some of these fragmentary creatures were bound together by Friendship, others were driven to and fro in a solitary condition, unable to effect a landing and gain a

* Cp. Bk. I. Ch. IV. § 2.

foothold on the "shore of life." Whenever such combinations took place, all kinds of monsters would be created, "double-headed and double-breasted beings," "human forms with heads of bulls," "bodies of bulls with human heads," and so forth. These grotesque shapes disappeared as quickly as the original separate limbs, and only such combinations as exhibited an inner harmony evinced themselves as fit for life, maintained a permanent place, and finally multiplied by procreation. It is impossible not to be reminded here of the Darwinian survival of the fittest. There is nothing to prevent and everything to favour the belief that we are confronted with an attempt, as crude as it could be, but yet not entirely unworthy of respect, to explain in a natural way the problem of design in the organic world. Empedocles used the processes of vegetable and animal life as the favourite playground of his genius for research. Gleams of inspiration are crossed by glimpses of childish impertinence in which the philosopher fondly expects to rob nature of her veil before he has learnt the A B C of renunciation. Among the inspired utterances we may quote the saying that "hair and foliage and the thick plumage of birds are one." It is a thought which makes Empedocles a predecessor of Goethe in the realm of comparative morphology, and though its author hardly used it, it was yet a fresh contribution towards the theory of descent. The child in Empedocles must answer for the fantastic attempts to explain the deepest secrets of procreation—the birth of male or female offspring, their resemblance to the father or the mother, the production of twins or triplets, the shocks sustained by pregnant women and their supposed relation to birthmarks, the origin of monstrosities, and the sterility of mules. Less fanciful was his conception of sleep as a partial, and of death as a total, chilling of the blood.

We have already directed attention to the links by which the Empedoclean theory of matter is closely united with his theory of cognition. We have made acquaintance with his maxim that like is recognized by like, "earth by earth, water by water, divine ether by ether, destructive fire by fire," and the conjecture lay ready to hand that Empedocles regarded matter itself as endowed with consciousness, and that he drew no strict distinction between the animate and the inanimate worlds. The conjecture is justified by the facts. Empedocles did not merely follow Anaxagoras in ascribing sensibility to plants, but he taught that, without exception, "everything possesses the power of thought and a share in understanding." Attempts have been made to divide Empedocles from his predecessors, the Hylozoists, and even to represent him as opposed to them in principle, on account of his doctrine of the two immaterial forces causing the succession of universal periods. That doctrine, it must be admitted, introduced a dualistic germ in his system, but it never took root nor made any growth, and we are now in a position to see how completely erroneous these attempts were. For beside the two alternately ruling powers, and superior to them, there was, as our readers are aware, a single natural force of truly universal sway inherent to matter itself—the attraction of like to like. Next, there is the extraordinary power of thought which he ascribed to matter, and the universal extension of the franchise of consciousness. The doctrine of Empedocles might be called Hylozoism *in excelsis.* It gave to matter not merely life, but a soul. And there is a second point to be mentioned in contravention of the view that Empedocles regarded matter as something dreary and dead, responsive to outside impulses alone, but not as the seat of motion in itself. If this had been his opinion by no conceivable right could he have given to his four elements the names of gods, and of gods, moreover, who, like Hera and Zeus, occupied the highest places in the Greek Pantheon. It has been urged that this was nothing but a poetic licence without any serious meaning. But we are not convinced by that argument. The author of a new theory, in our opinion, is commonly fully aware of the innovation he is making, and of its contrast with older doctrines; he tends rather to emphasize those features than to weaken and destroy their force by clothing them in antiquated forms. Further, it may be noticed that Aristotle at least took those names as signifying something more than mere rhetorical devices. He expressly states of the Empedoclean elements that "these, too, are gods to him." But without enumerating these more or less secondary arguments, we need but refer to the verse quoted above, in which the problem whether its author was or was not a champion of the theory of universal animation is decided once and for all. And if any shadow of doubt should yet remain, it will be allayed by the following consideration. We remember that the recurring triumph of " Friendship " which united the aggregate of matter to indivisible unity raised it each time to the highest divine honours under the name of Sphairos ; and we are unable to believe that the mere fact of combination could have endowed with consciousness, filled with force, and exalted to divine bliss substances which in their separate condition were dead, powerless, inert, and responsive merely to impulses from without. And our belief is the less constrained since the Sicilian philosopher was here a strict logician, and maintained his fundamental theory in its ultimate consequences. Thus, though he would doubtless have been inclined to ascribe every kind of cognition to this "most blessed god," yet the divinity was found wanting in one respect. He lacked the knowledge of " Discord," inasmuch as Discord was foreign to the pious peace of his universe. For not merely was each element perceived and recognized by that same element, but " Friendship" was recognized "by Friendship," and " Discord by horrid Discord."

7. We have eulogized Empedocles on account of his consistency, but when we come to his psychological teaching it would seem that our praise must be recalled. It was dualistic in character. It comprised on the one side what is practically his physics of the soul. Turning to this first, we see that he reduced the psychical to the material without exception and without intervention. He did not even postulate an intermediate soul-substance, but he based all differences of psychical properties and

functions on corresponding material differences, as well in the species of beings as in individual beings, and in the varying states of the individual—

" E'en as the matter at hand, so man increaseth in wisdom ; "

and—

" Ever as men do change, there cometh in constant succession
One thought after another."

Every preferential endowment was traced by Empedocles to the wealth of material composition and the success of the admixture. Thus he explained the superiority of organic beings to the inorganic creation containing but a few elements or one only. Thus, too, he explained the superiority of individual gifts, such as the pre-eminent tongue of the orator and the master-hand of the sculptor. And hence, further, he derived the adaptation of the blood, as that part of the body in which the combination was most complete, to be the agent of the highest functions of the soul. Empedocles conceived the blood welling forth from its source in a pure and untroubled stream as displaying the four elements in their most equable proportions. And in this belief he wrote that "the blood of the heart is thought."

The other side of the dualism we have mentioned is found, if the expression be permissible, in the Empedoclean theology of the soul. Every soul is a " demon " which has been thrust out of its heavenly home to " the unamiable fields," " the joyless place," the valley of lamentation. There it assumes the most diverse shapes. Empedocles himself claimed to have passed through the metamorphoses of a boy, a girl, a bush, a bird, and a fish. The soul is bound to that habitation by its native guilt, especially of bloodshed or perjury, and the "vagrant fugitive" cannot return to its original home, if at all, till after the lapse of 30,000 ὧραι, or 10,000 years. We have already made acquaintance with this doctrine. It is a reproduction of the Orphic-Pythagorean psychology depicted in glowing colours and adorned with all the magic of an inspired and fervid eloquence ; and, appropriately enough, we find

Empedocles extending a meed of eulogy and honour to the "mighty mind" of Pythagoras. He describes in moving verse the fatal mistakes to which orthodoxy itself may impel those who are uninitiated in metempsychosis. There was the blinded father, for example, who was fain to offer an acceptable sacrifice to the gods and slew unwittingly the son of his own loins, thus preparing a fatal meal for himself with the very words of prayer on his lips. Similarly, sons devoured their mother, and not till too late did the guilty appeal to Death, who might have saved them from the execution of their horrible misdeed. The road of purification was a long road, and its steps were marked by centuries; nor could sinful men regain their lost divinity till they had climbed the topmost rungs of the ladder of earthly existence as seers or poets or physicians or princes. Side by side with the process of moral perfection went a series of outward ceremonies, initiations, and libations, to which Empedocles devoted an entire poem which was called the book of "Purifications." Its remnants combine with the fragments of his three books "On Nature" to form his literary bequest.

Here, then, we have the two parts of the Empedoclean psychology, and it may reasonably be asked how two such different doctrines, which practically exclude each other, could have found a common resting-place in one mind. It is little or no explanation to utter the word Eclecticism. We have seen that, apparently, at least, a great gulf was fixed between the spiritualistic doctrine on the one side and the materialistic on the other, and if this gulf really existed there are but two conclusions we can draw. Either the philosopher himself must have been lacking in reason and judgment or he must have counted on finding those defects in his readers, to whom he offered this contradictory dualism as the expression of his serious conviction. But in point of fact there is no need for any such desperate resort. The apparent contradiction was partly non-existent, and was partly by no means limited to Empedocles. His "soul-demon," like the "soul" or psyche of most of his predecessors, was not

the vehicle of psychical qualities denoting an individual or
a kind of beings.* In proof of this we may quote his own
express statements in the passages that refer to his
previous existence ; for the bush, the bird, or the fish,
which he claimed to have been, obviously bore no remotest
resemblance to the richly dowered human personality
which he felt himself at the time. It was the same
with the popular belief which the Homeric poems had
already embodied. The psyche of Homer played precisely the same idle part in the existence of man on
earth as the "soul-demon" in Empedocles. The fact
may arouse our surprise, but it is beyond dispute. Psyche's
sole *raison d'être* would appear to be her separation from
the body at death and her survival in the underworld.
Not a single instance can be quoted in which she
appears as the agent of human thought, will, or emotion.
We may go further than this. Those functions, so far
from being performed by the Homeric psyche, actually
belonged to a being of quite a different formation—to
a perishable being which dissolved in air at the death
of animals and men. To that extent it is even legitimate to speak of a two-soul theory in Homer, and
this second mortal soul went by the name of Thymos.
The word is identical with the Latin *fumus*, or smoke,
with the Sanskrit *dhumas*, the Old Slavonic *dymu*, and so
forth. We were ignorant of the nature of this smoke-soul
till it was illustrated by a remark of Alfred von Kremer,
who in the course of his inquiries into Oriental peoples
and civilizations, stated that "the steam ascending from
the warm and freshly-shed blood" was regarded as the
psychic agent. The smoke-soul is older in origin than
the exclusively Greek psyche. Its antiquity is proved
by the existence of the word with partially the same
meaning in the allied languages, and traces of its original
signification still linger in some isolated references in
Homer, as when, in awaking from unconsciousness, Thymos,
who was nearly scattered, is collected in the breast or
diaphragm. Thus when the breath-soul came in the field,

* Cp. Bk. I. Ch. V. § 4 (p. 144).

the ground was already occupied by the smoke-soul or blood-soul, and the later comer had to be content with a more modest though nobler part. The situation remained unchanged for many centuries. The poet Pindar, for instance, wrote that " Psyche, who alone is descended from the gods, slumbers as long as the limbs are in motion," and the popular religion agreed with him in ascribing no activity to Psyche except in dreams. It was not till science began to extend itself to the phenomena of the soul that the old process of thought, dating from centuries before, was repeated afresh. Thymos had long since lost its original meaning, and was therefore altogether inadequate to the demand for a material principle of explanation ; so that Empedocles, in placing the seat of psychic activity in the blood of the heart, may be said to have invented the blood-soul for the second time in its history. And if he still retained a belief in the immortal soul, he was not, therefore, more inconsistent than the poets of the Homeric age, or even than his immediate predecessor Parmenides. For Parmenides too reduced to material causes not merely the moral qualities, but the temporary psychic states of men.* Moreover, he ascribed a partial perception of darkness and cold and silence even to dead human bodies, and in his theory no beings whatsoever, not even the objects that at no stage of their existence were connected with a psyche, were without some kind of perception. Nevertheless, his doctrine did not exclude a belief in the soul and its immortality. Under Orphic influence, no doubt, he represented the souls as descending into Hades, and as reascending thence to the upper world. Philolaus, a younger Pythagorean, proved himself in this respect an apt follower of Parmenides. The elder master had derived the "mind of man" from the composition and elemental mixture of his bodily parts, and Philolaus called the soul itself a "mixture and harmony" of such parts, though this in no wise prevented him from assuming the existence of a substantial soul, and from believing, in accordance with the teaching of "old divines

* Cp. Bk. II. Ch. II. *fin.*

and soothsayers," that it was exiled to the body as the penalty of guilt.

And this is the conclusion of the whole matter. The belief in an immortal psyche might very well have been dispensed with, but Empedocles was no more inclined to reject it than were the representatives of the popular religion or his own philosophical forebears and contemporaries. In other words, he was liable to the same religious as well as scientific motives as was the rest of the world. We next come to the question of his self-contradiction. He made the fate of the soul dependent on the acts of the men whose bodies it temporarily inhabited ; at the same time he reduced the mental disposition of those men—the source of their conduct, that is to say—to the material composition of their bodies. Such is the charge, and it is admittedly proven. But he shares the responsibility for the contradiction, not merely with the Orphics, whose psyche certainly meant nothing more than that of a Pindar or a Parmenides, but its germ can clearly be traced back to the Homeric poems themselves. For even there the contradiction is glaring. Some souls at least, such as those of Tityus, Tantalus, and Sisyphus, are paying, in the eleventh book of the Odyssey, the penalty for crimes which the immortal souls cannot be held to have committed, according to the doctrine prevailing in the totality of the poems even down to their latest additions. The history of religion in all ages is rife with similar anomalies. We need hardly refer to the conflict between predestination and retribution in the ecclesiastical canons of mediævalism, or to the Buddhistic doctrine, so completely parallel to the Orphic, of the retributive reincarnation of the dead, who were at the same time denied the possession of a substantial soul. It is difficult, if not impossible, to explain away this contradiction from the central tenets of the widest-spread of all religions ; and the "Questions of King Milinda," with their extraordinary endowment of ingenious subtlety, are sufficient testimony to that fact. The spirit of science was as strong in Empedocles as the sway of religious emotion, so that both conflicting tendencies were intensified in his instance. That was the characteristic of Empedocles, and it stamps him with a grotesque trait. He appears at one and the same time as an orthodox member of the Orphic community, filled with pious faith, and as an eager champion of scientific natural research, as the heir of venerable mystics and priests, and as the immediate precursor of the atomic physicists. This duality may have interrupted the consistency and uniformity of his system, so rigidly maintained up to a certain point, but it affords a shining testimony to the universality of his sympathies and to the wealth of his natural endowments.

8. Curiously enough, in the theology of Empedocles, where it would seem most likely that his dualism would have displayed itself, there is scarcely a trace of it to be found. Here he succeeded in welding the two halves of his system of thought in a practically undisturbed harmony. On the top of his conception of matter as endowed with force and consciousness there was obviously no room for an extra-mundane deity controlling, ordering, or even creating the world. But there was no obstacle to his belief in divine beings of the kind which we met with in the other Hylozoists and designated gods of the second rank. We are already aware that the four divinely conceived elements of Empedocles disappear at the time of their union in Sphairos, and lose their separate existence ; and we now have to add that the same fate, presumably in the same moment of the restoration of the original universal unity, likewise overtook the rest of the gods to whom Empedocles expressly denied immortality, calling them long-lived, but not eternal. The universal periods by which their longevity was limited presumably served to measure the fate of the soul-"demons" as well. Thus his theology and psychology were linked by a common bond ; one and the same term was set to all the separate existences which might disturb the perfect unity of being. Except in a single instance, no details are forthcoming anent these secondary gods, but in some memorable verses about Apollo, Empedocles describes him as not possessed of human limbs, and calls him "a spiritual being (Phren), holy, ineffable, hastening

with swift thoughts through the world." To our thinking it is as inadmissible to identify this "demon" with Sphairos—the animate universe or universal godhead—as to subordinate Sphairos, in whom all things are comprised, to this deity.

There is, therefore, no serious reason to reproach Empedocles with eclecticism or with borrowing other men's thoughts without taking overmuch trouble to see that they were suitable. But a certain weight is lent to the charge by a defect of the philosopher's mind which was intimately blended with its qualities. He was a thinker of restless activity, constantly engaged in the pursuit of fresh problems and standing in the closest communion with nature, and thus his spirit lacked the patience which is absolutely necessary for the prosecution of every thought to its goal. At the same time, despite the wealth of his teeming imagination, he failed to exhibit that sovereign self-security which would have enabled him to neglect the bounds of empirical knowledge, and which enabled Anaxagoras, for instance, to raise his pseudo-chemistry to a system as deficient in outward proof as it was internally homogeneous. The best illustration of this habit of his mind will be found in his relation with the Eleatics. We may safely assume that Empedocles was acquainted with the didactic poem of Xenophanes ; indeed, the fact is vouched for by the occasional attitude of hostility which he assumed towards it, and we may fairly trace the influence of the sage of Colophon in the pantheistic doctrine of Empedocles, culminating in the conception of Sphairos, and in his dislike for the anthropomorphism of the popular religion, which in one instance at least, as we have just now seen, came to unequivocal utterance. Further, his acquaintance with a second Eleatic philosopher is proved by his frequent imitation of verses by Parmenides, with whose poems he must have been familiar. An enduring impression was made on his mind by the teachings of his predecessor contained in the "Words of Opinion," and relating to physics in the widest sense of that term. The same is true in a less degree of the metaphysics of Parmenides. Empedocles adopted in an almost literal form his *à priori* demonstration of the impossibility of birth and decay. But we have to go back to Anaxagoras to find a clearer and more precise statement than is to be found in Empedocles of what we have called the second postulate of matter. Empedocles, it is true, was convinced of the general stability of the elements, but what we miss is an accurate application of that principle. His optics were based on the presumption that every element had a fixed and original property of colour, but we look in vain for a clear explanation of the endless multiplicity of coloured substances proceeding from these primary colours. Anaxagoras's theory of matter was capable of explaining how the four elements "traversing one another showed a different face." His account, though contradicted by the facts, was consistent with itself and with the postulate of qualitative constancy. But Empedocles failed in both particulars. And as it is impossible to believe that Anaxagoras was acquainted with or appreciated even the outline of the didactic poems of Parmenides, our conviction is strengthened that both postulates of matter—the second no less than the first—were necessarily evolved from the theories of Ionian physiologists, and that they owed to the Eleatics, not their invention, but merely their stricter formulation.* At the close of an earlier chapter † we left it doubtful whether and to what extent an intermediary link was required to connect the older forms of the theory of primary matter with the later stages of its development That doubt, we venture to think, has now been satisfactorily resolved.

* Bk. II. Ch. II. § 3.   † Cp. Bk. II. Ch. III. *fin.*

CHAPTER VI.

THE HISTORIANS.

1. THE intellectual enfranchisement of the Greeks did not exclusively follow the lines of natural research. The conditions of time as well as of space by which their horizon was contracted were responsible for the endurance of mythological modes of thought. We have already been occupied by occasional attempts to widen the spatial bounds, and the limits of both were extended simultaneously and permanently by the rise of twin-sciences which were soon united in the same hands.

Greek historiography began with the civic chronicles, the lists of priests, and the records of victors in the national games. Mercenaries, freebooters, merchants, and colonists were the pioneers of Greek geography, and the powerful independent intellect of Hecatæus was the first to combine in one grand sweep both these regions of knowledge. His wide travels and his still wider inquiries had supplied him with a treasury of information which he was able to put at the disposal of his Ionian countrymen in their insurrection against the Persian rule (502–496 B.C.) in his capacity as a master of statecraft and an accomplished diplomatist. The results of his investigation were contained in two works of which we possess merely fragmentary remains. The first was entitled " A Description of the Earth," and its three books were called after the names of the continents, Europe, Asia, and Libya, and the second was comprised in his four volumes of " Genealogies." This historical work was prefaced by a motto which, in its intellectual pride and the cold clarity of its reason, sounds in our ears to-day like the blare of trumpets at dawn. "Thus speaketh," it runs, "Hecatæus of Miletus. I have written everything down as it appeared to me to be true ; for manifold and laughable are the sayings of the Hellenes, as they seem to me." Once more, then, we find ourselves at the cradle of criticism. The same light that Xenophanes had poured on the natural universe Hecatæus was now to pour on the universe of human affairs. The cause and method of his doing so are practically revealed in the very wording of his audacious prelude. He was obliged to exercise his selective faculty in the contradictions of historical tradition, and we see that the spirit of rationalism had already taken hold of him in the courage he displayed in applying the knife of criticism to the historical absurdities incompatible with his standards of credibility and possibility. Nor was he content to accept one tradition and to reject another. He felt himself justified to revise those legends and to extract the kernel of truth from its legendary husk. His object was to relate the facts as they appeared to him to be true. He had no archives or evidences at his disposal whose age and origin and mutual dependence he might have sifted, for the practice of recording contemporary events in a trustworthy manner was of late growth in Greece. The myths and the poets who related them were the vehicles of by far the greater part of historical material, though prose authors began to range themselves by the side of the poets somewhile after 600 B.C. Hecatæus was accordingly precluded from questioning witnesses and authorities, and from testing their degree of credibility. His faculty of judgment was confined to the use of inner criteria. He had to abandon criticism or to practise subjective criticism alone. His method was one which has been called the semi-historical—an expression we prefer to that of "the rationalistic," which is liable to abuse. Meanwhile we have still to mention a factor of decisive importance. The wide view of foreign legends and histories did not merely contribute its considerable share to the distrust of national traditions ; it also pointed the way which would have to be followed unless the investigator was determined with undiscriminating iconoclasm to throw the whole mythology overboard. One experience that occurred to Hecatæus may be related here as typical of the impressions which he and his like had frequently to derive from their contact with older civilizations. He was talking to the priests in Egyptian Thebes, and he had shown them, doubtless with a certain complacency, his genealogical tree, which began with a divine ancestor separated from Hecatæus only by fifteen generations. Thereupon the priests led him into a hall where the statues of the high priests of Thebes were placed. They numbered no less than three hundred and forty-five, and Hecatæus was assured by his close-shaven guides that each of the statues had been erected during the lifetime of its original, that the priestly dignity was hereditary, and that the high office had descended uninterruptedly throughout the series before him from father to son; that all its incumbents had been mortal men, and not one of them a god or even a demigod; and they added for his information that at an earlier date there had been gods on earth, but that from the time of the first high priest downwards history had been the history of mankind alone, fully authenticated by documentary evidence. It is difficult to describe the impression, at once astounding and convincing, which this priestly rebuke made on the traveller from Greece. He must have felt as if the roof of the hall in which he stood had been lifted high above his head, and had narrowed the dome of heaven. The region of human history stretched before him in infinite, and the field of divine intervention was diminished in proportion. Gods and heroes, he perceived, could not possibly have taken part in such events as the Trojan war or the expedition of the Argonauts, to which indisputable authority assigned a comparatively recent date. Things must have occurred in those circumstances much as they occur at present. The canons of the possible, the natural, and therefore of the credible, had to be applied to the events of an age which had formerly been the playground of supernaturalism and miracles. Hecatæus rose to the occasion, and applied those canons to the myths. He rejected the conventional story of Hercules, who drove the cattle he had stolen from Geryon out of the fabulous Erythea, situated presumably in the neighbourhood of Spain, to Mycenæ in Greece. In his revised version Geryon appeared as the ruler of territories in Epirus, in the north-west of Hellas, whose cattle were renowned for their beauty and strength. The country seemed to deserve the name of Erythea, or the Red Land, from the colour of its soil. Similar nominal resemblances, and the boundless resources of etymology, played in the main a considerable part in Hecatæus' reconstruction of the myths. In the same way he applied the historizing method —and we shall see it repeated in Herodotus—to the events connected with the Trojan war. Further, our critic displayed from his judgment-stool no mercy to a fabulous monster such as Cerberus, the three-headed watch-dog of hell. Hecatæus identified it, on grounds that we cannot now verify, with a mighty serpent which had once inhabited the Laconian promontory of Tænarum. But, not to multiply these details, we have quoted enough to show how the spirit of criticism and scepticism effected its first entry in the historical studies of the Greeks, and we have illustrated the shapes which by an inner necessity it began to assume and to maintain. For when Hecatæus, the Milesian historian, makes room for his greater successor, we shall see that he too followed in the same lines of reform.

2. That greater successor was Herodotus of Halicarnassus. The date of his birth falls not long before 480 B.C., and as the author of the most perfect masterpiece of the historical art, which will delight the heart of man till the end of all time, Herodotus too was a thinker in his kind. We lack the requisite material for comparison in order to fix the precise degree of his originality, but it is the more necessary to consider his work at some length inasmuch as he does not speak to us merely with his own voice, but with the voices of several of his contemporaries whose writings have not come down to us. And indeed we can conceive no more delightful labour than to return again and again to the refreshing fountain of his histories. The very beginning

of his work is full of instructive merits, displaying as it does his consummate art of combining or rather of coalescing historical with geographical science, and of uniting in a uniform perspective of narration the stories of the most diverse peoples. He searched for the origin of the ancient strife between the Orient and the Occident which reached its zenith in the Persian wars, the goal and summit of the histories of Herodotus. He went back to the Trojan war, and the abduction of Helen that led to it, before he approached King Crœsus of Lydia, the first conqueror of Greek cities in Asia ; and he led up to the tragedy of Troy by the narratives akin to it in his conception of the fate of Io, Europa, and Medea. The figures and events so familiar to us in Greek mythology and legend were transformed by the art of Herodotus to new, nay, to modern shapes. It was no longer the jealousy of Hera which drove Io to wander in distant lands, Io the favourite of Zeus metamorphosed in a cow ; it was no longer the Father of Heaven who ravished Europa in the form of a bull ; Medea the sorceress, the granddaughter of the Sun-god, disappeared, and with her went her share in the capture of the Golden Fleece. Colourless princesses replaced the brilliant heroines of antiquity, and Phœnician merchants, pirates from Crete, and freebooters from Hellas did the work of the supreme god and of Jason, the godlike hero. The second abduction was represented as the atonement of the first, and the third of the second. Heralds and envoys protested against the violation of international law, and might only took the office of right on the principle of "like for like" when the evildoers refused to make restitution. Here once more we observe the traces of the semi-historical method formerly practised by Hecatæus, but its range had now been enlarged to include a causal connection between the so-called authentic events. Herodotus appealed to the evidence of Phœnicians and Persians, who alleged that the Greeks had intensified the existing racial strife. The Greeks, they said, had been the first seriously to undertake to avenge the abduction of a woman, to build a powerful fleet, to besiege Ilion and destroy it for one woman's sake alone. Similar attempts

were made by the Phœnicians to exculpate themselves.
They contended that Io had not been carried on the ship
by force, but rather that her illicit relations with the
master of the vessel had made her ready to flee from the
anger of her parents before they discovered the traces of
her guilt. If we look for the key to this petty historical
method and to the decline of the greatness of the heroes
of mythology, we shall find it in the last resort in the
motive we marked in Hecatæus, in his desire, that is
to say, to widen the historical horizon and to contract
the limits of the supernatural. The exalted figures
of the legends drenched in the colours of poetry were
degraded by those means to the level of the natural
and credible till they verily sank to the plane of triviality.
Herodotus himself was shrewd enough to reserve his
judgment on the historical value of the accounts he reproduced. But between the lines of his narrative it may
clearly be read that in his own mind too the credulous
faith of earlier generations had been damaged and shaken
by these combinations of foreign scholars or "the learned"
who maintained a cold and alien attitude towards the
mythology of Hellas. He betrayed his alienation yet
more distinctly in his own treatment of the legend of
Troy. He followed Hecatæus in the statement that during
the siege of Ilion Helen was residing in Egypt, and not in
the beleaguered city. Adverse winds had driven Paris to
Egypt, where the high-minded King Proteus detained the
wife of Menelaus in order to restore her to her lawful and
injured lord. We need not concern ourselves here with
the questions how this belief arose in Egypt itself, how
its way was made smooth by the poet Stesichorus, nor how
Herodotus tried to support it by quotations from the Iliad.
But it was extremely characteristic of the new method of
thought that Herodotus should have been at pains to
establish this pseudo-historical version as intrinsically the
one possible and true account. He argued that the sole
reason why the Trojans did not put a stop to the long
miseries of war by the surrender of Helen was that she
was not in Troy, "for surely Priam could not have been

so infatuated, nor the others his relatives, as to be willing
to expose their own persons, their children, and the city
to danger, in order that Paris might cohabit with Helen." *
Their refusal might have been conceivable at the beginning of the siege, but not after the loss of so large a
number of citizens, and when at least two or three of the
sons of Priam were numbered among the victims ; there
was also the consideration that Hector, the heir to the
throne, was the elder and more capable prince, and not
Paris, the younger brother. We turn to a second
example of the semi-historical method. The priestesses
at Dodona had given the historian the following account
of the origin of the oracle. A black dove had flown thither
from Thebes in Egypt, and, speaking with a human voice,
had ordained from her perch on a tree the foundation of
an oracular shrine. But "how," so Herodotus objects, in
almost querulous tones, "could a dove speak with a human
voice ? " And when the priestesses went on to tell him
that a second black dove had flown to Libya, where she
had founded the oracle of Ammon, the historian rushed to
the conclusion that that legend was an echo of another
which he had himself heard at Thebes. According to that
account, two women employed in the temple had been
carried away by the Phœnicians and sold as slaves, the one
into Libya, and the other into Greece, where they had respectively established those two famous shrines. This plump
invention, due to the arrogance of the Egyptians, aroused in
Herodotus a transient emotion of scepticism which found
vent in the question " how they knew this for a certainty,"
but he presently accepted it as a fact, for the consentaneity
of the whole thing was so complete. The inhabitants of
Dodona had regarded the strange woman as a bird, because
her barbarous language had reminded them rather of the
chattering of birds than of human speech. Further, in
saying that the dove was black they showed that she had the
dark skin of an Egyptian. After a time she acquired the
language of the country, and this was the meaning of the
report that the dove had spoken after the fashion of men.

* Herod., ii. 120 : trans. Cary.

Finally, news reached her of the fate of her sister who had been taken to Libya, and she disseminated it in Dodona. We smile at this strange medley of childish simplicity and subtle sophistication, but the smile dies on our lips, and we cease to be annoyed at the unlovely transformation of the naïve popular mythology when we reflect on the significant part played in the intellectual progress of mankind by the historizing process of interpretation. The poesy of legend had claimed the dignity of reality, and it was hardly surprising that the reality in turn should have broken the bounds of poesy. In the existing state of the methods of research, it was not even approximately possible strictly to distinguish the frontier-line. Nay, the ancient territorial dispute is not yet completely settled to this day. If the "Father of History" was inclined to admit the historical claim of every legendary tradition which might possibly have its origin in historical truth, it is the opposite tendency which has obtained the upper hand at the present time.

3. We have seen that this transformation of the myths was due to two causes. There was first the extension of the horizon of space and time, and secondly the exchange of thought with critics of native traditions whose foreign nationality excluded them from sympathy with Greek mythology. But we have still to mention a third factor, which was perhaps the most efficacious of all. It was to be found in the painful conflict between the ancient faith and the new science, which were seeking reconciliation. The increased store of empirical knowledge, and the growing mastery of nature by man, had visibly strengthened the belief in the stability of the phenomenal universe. Thus the problem was to avoid as far as possible a sudden and irreparable breach with the hallowed traditions of antiquity. The historizing interpretation of the myths sacrificed a part in order to save the rest. It was one of those half-measures or compromises which are due to promptings of instinct, and which, despite unintelligent ridicule, are really of the highest value. They may be compared to the "fictions" of the law which formed at a certain stage of human development the foundation of all true and enduring progress. Another

instance of these beneficent compromises related to the activity of the gods themselves. Herodotus tells us that the Thessalians explained the deep gulf that formed the river-bed of the Peneius as the work of Poseidon :

"and their story is probable," he adds ; "for whoever thinks that Neptune shakes the earth, and that rents occasioned by earthquakes are the works of this god, on seeing this would say that Neptune formed it. For it appears evident to me that the separation of these mountains is the effect of an earthquake." *

The conclusion suggests itself that Herodotus entirely and deliberately rejected the intervention of supernatural agents ; that he regarded every god merely as the president of a department of nature or life regulated by fixed forces. Such a conclusion, however, would be in the highest degree unjust to the double thread of positive science and traditional religion which traversed the mind of the historian of Halicarnassus with equal force and strength. He had noted the changes on the surface of the earth, and had paid them the compliment of systematic reflection ; he had reduced the single phenomena back to general causes, and might therefore presume to dispense in that connection with the theory of direct divine interposition. To that extent at least he was a pupil of Anaximander or Xenophanes, his predecessors, and of Xanthus, the historian of Lydia, whose work was composed in Greek ; and he was no less the pupil, without injury to himself on this occasion, of his Egyptian masters. By their example he was enabled to explain the origin of the Nile delta in a manner as rational as it was correct, and we hardly know whether to be more surprised at the keenness of his natural observation or at the confidence with which he dealt with immense periods of time ; he estimated the present age of the earth at no less than twenty thousand years. Other instances might be quoted in which Herodotus expressed his doubt as to the direct intervention of the gods. The Persian magi had charmed a severe storm by sacrifices and incantations, but Herodotus,

* Herod., vii. 129 : trans. Cary.

in reporting this account, added the sceptical remark, " or perhaps it abated of its own accord." Moreover, he refused to decide the question whether this storm, which had been so destructive to the Persian fleet, had or had not been caused by the prayers of the Athenians to Boreas and the sacrifices they had likewise offered. His doubts may have been aroused by the proximity of similar appeals uttered by Greeks and Barbarians ; but in instances where such a corrective was wanting, or where the passion of the circumstances thrust his sober doubts in the rear, our historian surpassed himself in his narratives of miraculous divine apparitions, of heaven-sent dreams which he contrasted with those due to natural causes, of significant presages, and of the wonders of the soothsayers' art. In this respect there is a striking difference between various parts of his work, and some short-sighted critics have hastened to the conclusion that the several books were composed at long intervals of time corresponding to changes in Herodotus' speculative views. But hypotheses of this kind are at once uncalled-for by the circumstances, and without any secure foundation. They would, further, be quite inadequate to expunge the elements of contradiction from the historian's theology. His conception of the affairs of the gods is essentially vacillating and parti-coloured. He might be claimed as an opponent, not merely of anthropomorphism, but of polytheism itself, when we recall his eager endeavours to trace back no few of the Greek divinities and ceremonials to Egyptian prototypes and influences, and when we read his audacious declaration that—

Hesiod and Homer lived four hundred years before my time, and not more ; and these were they who framed a theogony for the Greeks, and gave names to the gods and assigned to them honours and arts, and declared their several forms." *

In this connection it is to be noted that he expressly contrasted the nature-worship of the Persians with the anthropomorphism of the Greeks, relating, not without a trace of inner agreement, that they offered sacrifices to the

* Herod., ii. 53 : trans. Cary.

great forces of nature, sun, moon, earth, fire, water, and winds, and conceived Zeus as merely the "complete firmament." It can, indeed, hardly be disputed that Herodotus was liable to similar fits of scepticism through the influence, perhaps, of Xenophanes and other philosophers. But the doubts had not taken root in his soul. We could prove this in many ways, but we may refer especially to the anxious humility with which he concluded a scathing criticism of a Greek heroic legend with an appeal for the forgiveness of the gods and heroes whom he might have offended. It is in the same passage, too, that he reserved the epithet of "the truest" for the Greek doctrine of a double Hercules, one more ancient and veritably divine, the other of later date and merely a hero or deified mortal, distinct from each other and worshipped at separate shrines. The doctrine, we may add in parenthesis, affords us the earliest example of an artifice of criticism, more popular in later times, by which the contradictions in legendary traditions were obviated. The outcome of the scepticism of Herodotus was probably chiefly his conviction that human knowledge at the best is but a poor standard by which to measure divine things, and that, looking at these through the descriptions of the poets, we see them through a glass darkly. The reservation made by Herodotus on one particular occasion—"if we may otherwise trust the epic poets"—has a deep and wide-reaching significance, and there is a bitter earnest in his complaint that "all men know equally much," that is, equally little, "about the gods."

We can well understand how some critics have mistaken Herodotus for a monotheist in disguise. The description is erroneous, but it is none the less surprising that in places where he discusses questions of religion from an independent point of view he does not speak of Apollo or Athene, or of Hermes, or of Aphrodite, but almost exclusively of "the god" and of "the divine." Still, our astonishment is diminished when we remark that in all those passages the reference is to general laws regulating the course of nature and of human life. Homer speaks in such cases of "the gods" and "Zeus" almost without discrimination, and even in immediate proximity. In the magnificent verses, for instance, in which the frailty of the human lot is incomparably brought before our eyes, we read—

"Lo, he thinks that he shall never suffer evil in time to come, while the gods give him happiness, and his limbs move lightly. But when, again, the blessed gods have wrought for him sorrow, even so he bears it, as he must, with a steadfast heart, for the spirit of men upon the earth is even as their day, that comes upon them from the father of gods and men." *

And everywhere, in brief, where the point to be emphasized is not the separate endeavours of the gods, but the common action resulting from their uniform will, they tend to be regarded either as executing the decree of the highest god or as the vehicles of a uniform principle shared by all alike. This at least was the view of Herodotus, and it would be illegitimate on that account to attribute to him a negative attitude towards the individual deities, uncertain though his knowledge about them may have been, and serious though his objections undoubtedly were to the coarser forms of anthropomorphism. There are three distinct points at which his method of thought may be contrasted with that of Homer. In the first instance, long and earnest reflection on the order of nature and on the lot of mankind united with the increased comprehension, to which we have so often referred, of the uniformity of the universe, to give more frequent occasion for the discussion of the general laws that govern it. Secondly, the diminished confidence in the literal truth of the myths robbed the figure of the supreme god of many a human trait which had formerly attached to him. And, finally, the philosophers who had long since discovered the source of all existence in an impersonal principle superior to the separate deities had not failed to leave traces of their

* "Odyssey," xviii. 139 : trans. Butcher and Lang.

influence. That ruler of the universe was supreme over
the destiny of mankind and over the will of the gods,
but he possessed at present no strictly personal character,
or rather a character deficient in individual marks. He
could accordingly be termed, without too great a sacrifice
of consistency, "the god" or "divine" indifferently. We
reach now another instance of the self-contradiction of
Herodotus, and one which may be termed the most
important of all. It is connected with this primary
Principle itself, which vacillated so indecisively between
the personal and the impersonal. Sometimes we see it
as a tender and intrinsically benevolent being, sometimes
as mischievous and intrinsically malevolent ; nor have any
attempts succeeded in explaining away or even in reducing the differences. "Divine Providence, in its wisdom,"
is represented as having bestowed a rich gift of fertility
on weak and timorous animals, while restraining the
reproductive powers of strong and noxious animals.
Thus far, then, the Divinity was concerned for the
preservation and the prosperity of creation. Frequently,
too, it fostered the acts and happiness of mankind by
favourable decrees and dispensations ; but there were
occasions, on the other hand, when it took delight in overthrowing "all the proud" and "mutilating all the pre-
eminent" just as the "lightning discharges itself on high
buildings and trees." In a speech, then, that Herodotus
put in the mouth of the wise Solon, he said that the
divinity was "always jealous and delights in confusion."
And the supreme deity who is here identified with the idea
of destiny is conceived as dispensing at once, not merely
the tenderness of a father, the envy of a jealous god, but
likewise the justice of a bitter avenger of the guilt of
mankind. These contradictory features were not wholly
unknown to ancient mythology, but men's reflections on
the idea of purpose in the world had been extended
by this time ; their pessimism had increased, and their
ethical consciousness had been deepened by sudden
changes of fortune and great historical revolutions ;
and thus the differences in the self-contradictory theories

of earthly phenomena had been intensified. Nor are we concerned with a mere distinction of degree. The conflict of tendencies and intentions, in passing from a variety of separate beings into the keeping of one supreme god, had passed into another and more glaring condition of discord.

With regard to the judicial office of the godhead alluded to above, we are struck by a very remarkable distinction. At one time it is represented as a part of what might almost be called the automatic order of things ; at another time the divine judge appears as a purposeful power artfully selecting the means for the accomplishment of his ends, deriding all human intentions, and compelling them to serve his own purpose. Take, for instance, the story of the heralds sent by Darius to the cities of Greece in order to demand their submission. In Athens, as well as in Sparta, the time-honoured requirements of international law had been set at nought by the execution of those envoys. "What calamity befell the Athenians," as a retribution of this misdeed, says Herodotus, "I cannot say, except that their territory and city were ravaged. But I do not think," he adds, "that happened in consequence of that crime." On the Spartans, however, his story continues, there alighted the anger of the semi-divine ancestor of the Spartan heralds' guild of the Talthybiadæ. He was incensed against his countrymen on account of the murder of the Persian heralds. For years the sacrifices to the gods were accompanied by unfavourable omens; then two of the noblest sons of the Lacedæmonians, Bulis and Sperthies, resolved to free their native city from its pollution by going as a free-will offering to Susa and surrendering to the successor of Darius. The Persian monarch did not accept the sacrifice, but the mere offer sufficed temporarily to abate the wrath of Talthybius. After a long interval, however, in the first years of the Peloponnesian war, his anger was again aroused, and the sons of Bulis and Sperthies, who had been sent as ambassadors to Asia, were captured by a Thracian king, and, being carried to Attica, were put to death by the

Athenians. That event was regarded by Herodotus as a signal instance of the direct intervention of the deity.

"For that the wrath of Talthybius," he writes, "alighted on messengers, and did not cease until it was satisfied, this was but right (and natural); but that it should fall on the sons of the men who went up to the king on account of that wrath . . . this does seem to me to be plainly the doing of the godhead." *

In other words, Herodotus recognized that the hand of deity had interposed.

4. Apart from deviations due to his religious sensibility, the judgment of Herodotus displays in other places too a remarkable vacillation between the critical and the uncritical methods. Antiquity ridiculed his credulity and blamed him as a mere "story-teller," but for our own part we are hardly less surprised at his occasional display of hypercriticism. He is frequently credulous where he should be sceptical, but, on the contrary, he is frequently sceptical where belief would be better in place. He had only heard a vague account, for example, of the long polar nights; but, instead of availing himself of the means at his disposal and applying the method of concomitant variation to the legendary tale— the higher the latitude the longer the night—he preferred to commit it to the limbo of fable by his emphatic declaration that "men are found who sleep six months at a time, but this I do not at all admit." † Similarly, he was quite well aware that the Greeks depended on the north of Europe for their tin no less than for their amber; he refused, however, to permit them to locate the home of that metal in the group of islands of Great Britain, which the Greeks entitled the "Isles of Tin" precisely on account of that important product. The reason he alleges is that no trouble on his part had availed to discover an authority who could vouch for the existence of the sea as the boundary of Northern Europe by the evidence of his own eyes. Again, he was acquainted with the tendency of

---

* Herod., vii. 137 : trans. author.
† Herod., iv. 25 : trans. Cary.

the human mind to expect in the products of nature rather more than a common degree of regularity and symmetry, and accordingly he was not unjustly disposed to ridicule his predecessors who had drawn their map of the earth with Europe and Asia as continents of an equal circumference. But he went on to "smile" at the further description of the geographers—the reference is to Hecatæus in especial —who represented the earth as "made circular as if by a lathe." * It is abundantly clear that Herodotus was not prepared to accept the doctrine published by Parmenides of the globular shape of the earth. But in this connection the most remarkable fact is that Herodotus himself fell a victim on one occasion to the same misleading tendency. Even where his predecessors had happened on the right path, he suspected them of adopting fictitious proofs of regularity, and this was precisely his own method in the parallelism which he affected to discover between the streams of the Nile and the Danube as the two greatest rivers of his acquaintance. It was at all times an extremely difficult task to pronounce with any degree of certainty on the limits of possible variations in the organic world. We could, therefore, forgive Herodotus for not rejecting as incredible in itself the existence of winged serpents in Arabia, but we cannot avoid an expression of surprise that the alleged gigantic gold-digging ants of the Indian desert, which were "larger than foxes, but smaller than dogs," should not have been dismissed as fabulous; for this at least was the fate of the one-eyed Arimaspians, of whom our historian explicitly declared, " neither do I believe this that men are born with one eye, and yet in other respects resemble the rest of mankind.".†

We shall conclude this discussion by accompanying Herodotus to the extreme point which he reached in his advance of scientific thought. Among all the various attempts to explain the flood of the Nile there was none which he treated with such contemptuous disdain as the attempt to connect that enigmatic phenomenon, in a

* Herod., iv. 36 : trans. Cary.
† Herod., iii. 116: trans. Cary.

manner difficult for us to follow, with the stream of Ocean that flowed round the earth. Herodotus indicted this mode of explanation as the second of two ways which were "scarcely worth mentioning;" he wrote of it that "it shows still less judgment than the first, but, if I may say so, is more marvellous," and he went on to say in regard to this phenomenon, that "the person who speaks about the Ocean, since he has transported the question to the domain of the inscrutable, does not admit of refutation." But it must not, therefore, be supposed that he reserved his judgment in this instance, or that he held the question of the correctness of the theory to be intrinsically insoluble. The precise contrary was the case. The undisguised contempt of the passage we have quoted above is supported by the ridicule of the words that immediately follow : "for I do not know any river called the Ocean, but suppose that Homer or some other ancient poet, having invented the name, introduced it into poetry." His meaning practically amounts to this: A supposition so entirely remote from the region of fact and sense-perception as not even to provide a handle for refutation, is *ipso facto* convicted. In other words, an hypothesis with claims on our respect, and therefore on our discussion, must in the last resort be capable of verification. Herodotus stood for the nonce on purely positive, not to say positivist, ground. He recognized a gulf that could not be filled up between the inquirer in search of scientific facts and the poet creating amiable fictions. For once, though doubtless for once only, Herodotus is revealed in a brilliant flashlight as a modern of the moderns. Inspired by the heat of conflict, and moved by a passionate desire to outstrip his predecessors and rivals, a fundamental truth of methodology, namely, that those hypotheses only are legitimate which can be wholly or partly verified, became as clear to him as noonday, and he would doubtless have been the first to take alarm at his own boldness if he had perceived the full meaning of his thought. But there was no such risk. Batteux's shrewd maxim applies here as elsewhere : that " the ancients must never be credited with the consequences

of their principles or with the principles of their consequences "— least of all, we may add, ancients like Herodotus and Hecatæus, whose activity fell in the midst of a
great period of transition.   Of that period we have now
to take leave, though we may have occasion to return to it
in detached references in the future.

BOOK III.

THE AGE OF ENLIGHTENMENT.

" Ce furent les Grecs qui . . . fondèrent . . la science rationelle dépouillée de mystère et de magie, telle que nous la pratiquons maintenant."—MARCELLIN BERTHELOT.

" Vielleicht wird die atomistische Hypothese einmal durch eine andere verdrängt ; vielleicht, aber nicht wahrscheinlich."—LUDWIG BOLTZMANN.

" τὸν μὲν βίον
ἡ φύσις ἔδωκε, τὸ δὲ καλῶς ζῆν ἡ τέχνη."
UNKNOWN DRAMATIC POET

BOOK III

THE AGE OF ENLIGHTENMENT

CHAPTER I.

THE PHYSICIANS.

1. MORE than one title to fame is the inheritance of Greece. The men of genius to whom she gave birth dreamed the brightest speculative dreams. To them it was given to create incomparable works in likeness and in speech, but there was one creation of the Greek intellect which was not merely incomparable—the positive or rational science of Greece was no less than unique.

We boast of our extensive dominion over nature, and of our insight into nature, on which that dominion depends. Our eye sees deeper every day—not indeed into the essence of things, but into the sequences of phenomena. The adepts of the mental sciences, following in the footsteps of natural research, have begun to recognize the causal laws that govern even human affairs. They have slowly but surely trans-figured tradition, till we see them building a rational system of the order of life corresponding to the relation of means to ends. In all these triumphs of the intellect our humble acknowledgment is due to the founders of science in Greece. The threads that bind antiquity with modern times lie open to view, and our present inquiry will have to take them in account. Inevitably we ask, On what did it rest—this prerogative of the Greek intellect ? We may confidently reply that it was no peculiar privilege vouchsafed to the inhabitants of Hellas and denied to all other nations. Scientific thought is no magician's wand, efficacious in the hands of Greeks alone to conjure the gold of wisdom out of the mine of facts. Other peoples too might advance a just claim for genuine contributions to science. The chronology of the Egyptians, and the phonetics of the old Indian grammarians, need not fear comparison with the products of the Hellenic mind. To explain the supremacy of the last-named, we may recall a saying of Herodotus, who ascribed the good luck of Hellas to the fact that she "enjoys by far the best-tempered climate." * Here, as elsewhere, the secret of success lay in the combination and inter-communion of opposites. We can trace the springs of Greek success achieved and maintained by the great men of Hellas on the field of scientific inquiry to a remarkable conjunction of natural gifts and conditions. There was the teeming wealth of constructive imagination united with the sleepless critical spirit which shrank from no test of audacity; there was the most powerful impulse to generalization coupled with the sharpest faculty for descrying and distinguishing the finest shades of phenomenal peculiarity; there was the religion of Hellas, which afforded complete satisfaction to the requirements of sentiment, and yet left the intelligence free to perform its destructive work; there were the political conditions of a number of rival centres of intellect, of a friction of forces, excluding the possibility of stagnation, and, finally, of an order of state and society strict enough to curb the excesses of "children crying for the moon," and elastic enough not to hamper the soaring flight of superior minds. At the point of development to which we have now attained it was chiefly the critical faculty which advanced with great strides, and which stood in need of ever-new reinforcement. We have already made acquaintance with two of the sources from which the spirit of criticism derived its nourishment—the metaphysical and dialectical discussions practised by the Eleatic philosophers, and the semi-historical method which was applied to the myths by Hecatæus and Herodotus. A third source is to be traced to the schools of the physicians. These aimed at eliminating the arbitrary element from the view and knowledge of nature, the beginnings of which were bound up with it in a greater or less degree, though practically

* Herod., iii. 106 : trans. Cary.

without exception and by the force of an inner necessity. A knowledge of medicine was destined to correct that defect, and we shall mark the growth of its most precious fruits in the increased power of observation and the counterpoise it offered to hasty generalizations, as well as in the confidence which learnt to reject untenable fictions, whether produced by luxuriant imagination or by *à priori* speculations, on the similar ground of self-reliant sense-perception. But before we turn to the consideration of medicine and to its influence on the thought of the age, we must first acquaint ourselves with the authors and representatives of that branch of human knowledge, and take its rudiments in account.

"One man practised in medicine verily outweigheth many other men"—this compliment greets the medical profession at the rise of Greek literature, and posterity would not recall it. The art of healing in its earliest stages, springing as it does from crude superstitions and hardly less crude and frequently misinterpreted experience, is a wilderness of magical customs and of practices partly efficacious, though dependent on unanalyzed observation, and partly thoroughly nonsensical. The medicine-man among savage tribes is more than half a conjuror and less than half a custodian of old guild-secrets reposing on genuine or apparent experience. The science of healing among the original Indo-Europeans had scarcely advanced beyond this stage. A monument of it still survives in a formula of blessing, of which the Germanic and Indian versions are so precisely in agreement that their identical origin is beyond dispute. There is a fascinating picture, too, of the earliest practice of medicine in India in the extant "Song of a Physician." We see him making his jovial journey through the land with his fig-wood chest of drugs, and wishing for the sick recovery and for himself a rich reward, seeing that he lacks "cob, cow, and coat." His "herbs overthrow everything that afflicteth the body," and "disease flyeth before them as before the bailiff's grasp." But he does not merely claim to be an "expeller of sickness," but a "slayer of demons" too ; for in India, as elsewhere, all illness was

looked on partly as a heaven-sent punishment, partly as
the work of hostile demons, and partly, too, as the consequence of human imprecation and black arts. The wrath
of the offended deity might be appeased by prayer and
sacrifice ; the mischievous spirit might be mollified by soft
speeches or exorcised by spells ; and, similarly, the noxious
effects might be averted by counter-charms, and where
possible they would be made to recoil on their author
Besides the formulæ of spells, amulets, and symbolic
acts, herbs and salves had also their uses, and it might
happen that one and the same means of healing would
be applied to quite different cases. In the Indian art of
medicine, as revealed to us principally in the Atharva-
Veda, and in that of all other primitive peoples, the foregoing remarks hold good. Nor will they be found less
applicable to the popular medical notions of the Middle
Ages and of modern or even of recent times. The fact
that the selection of the means of healing was determined
as much, if not more, by the force of the association of
ideas as by specific experience, left ample room for the play
of the element of fancy. In this way the plant eye-bright
was prescribed as a cure for diseases of the eye, because a
black speck which is contained in the flower suggested the
idea of the pupil. Similarly, the red colour of the blood-
stone, or hæmatite, formed its pretended qualification to
stop a hæmorrhage. An Egyptian belief maintained that
the blood of black animals could prevent the whitening of
the hair, and modern Styria reproduces the ancient Indian
doctrine that jaundice may be expelled into yellow birds.
As was only natural, the art of surgery through all its
stages was the least affected by any kind of superstition,
and we are positively astonished at its high degree of
cultivation among the nations of antiquity, and even in
prehistoric times, as well as among the savages of to-day.
They did not even shrink from operations of so bold a
character as trepanning or the Cæsarian section.

Turning now to the earliest evidences of Greek civilization, it is a somewhat striking fact that there is no
mention in the Iliad of medical incantations. Weapons

are drawn out of the bodies of wounded heroes, the flowing blood is staunched, and the wounds are smeared with ointments; exhausted warriors are restored with wine, pure or mixed, but there is not a single word about any kind of superstitious customs or spells. It is a fact which perplexed the ancient commentators on Homer, and it agrees with other indications which point to the dawn of an era of enlightenment. When we come to Hesiod and the later literature in general, in which incantations and amulets and beneficial dreams play an important part, we see that such enlightenment was confined to the circle of nobles. Even in the Odyssey, which describes the beginnings of civic life, and the hero of which was rather the ideal of enter-prising merchants and intrepid seamen than of noble warriors, there is at least one passage—the episode of the boar-hunt on Parnassus—in which the incantation or epode is used as a means for the curative treatment of a wound. And in the same younger Epic poem we hear for the first time of professional medical practitioners, who, like the physician in the Rig-Veda, take their way through the land, and are summoned into men's homes like the carpenter, the minstrel, or the soothsayer, in order to sell their services to those who have a use for them.

2. The physician's profession was amply recognized in Hellas at an early date. Its oldest and most famous seats were the lovely island of Cos and the neighbouring peninsula of Cnidus, in the southern portion of the west coast of Asia Minor, Croton, in the toe of Italy, and Cyrene, far away in Africa, where grew the umbelliferous plant Silphion, so highly valued on account of its medicinal virtues that it formed a royal monopoly. Cities and princes competed with one another for the services of eminent physicians. Democedes of Croton, for instance, was retained one year by the city of Athens, and in the next year by the commonwealth of Ægina, and the third year by the tyrant of Samos. His annual salary reached a sum of which the mere quotation of the figures—8,200, 10,000, and 16,400 drachmæ, or francs—is hardly an adequate expression in view of the greatly diminished purchasing-

power of money. After the fall of Polycrates, Democedes was taken as a captive from Samos to Susa, where we presently meet him at the royal table and as confidential adviser to King Darius (521–485 B.C.). Indeed, so admirably had he treated the king and his consort Atossa that the Egyptian body-physicians who had hitherto enjoyed the royal favour fell swiftly in disgrace, and were in actual danger of their lives. Again, about the middle of the fifth century, we find the Cypriot physician Onasilus and his brothers, who had rendered medical service in the field during the siege of Edalion by the Persians, enjoying the highest honours and equipped in a princely style with ample crown property. It is to be noted in this connection that the esteem in which physicians were held corresponded to the moral demands that were made on them. A guild, the members of which were rewarded so richly and honoured so highly, was not likely to lack its charlatans and ignorant swindlers. But the conscience of the profession, which was composed for the most part of honourable and capable physicians, suppressed, if it did not expel, those parasites on the noble tree.

At this point we have to mention a document of which the antiquity is not its sole claim to veneration. "The Physician's Oath" is a monument of the highest rank in the history of civilization, and it is full of interest for the study of the internal constitution of the guild as well as for that of the ethical standard to which physicians were required to conform. We can trace therein the transition from a close professional caste to the free and general exercise of an art. The apprentice promised to honour his master as his parents, to assist him in all his necessities, and to impart gratuitous instruction to his offspring should they choose the same vocation, but to no one else save only to his own sons and to pupils bound by contract and by oath. He swore that he would help the sick "according to his knowledge and power;" that he would rigidly abstain from every evil and criminal abuse of the means and instruments of his art; that he would not give poison even to those who asked for it; that he would supply no woman with means to procure abortion; that he would not perform castration—the abomination of Greek sentiment—even where it appeared to be medically advisable; and, finally, he bound himself to avoid every abuse, erotic or otherwise, of his position towards his patients of both sexes, whether free or slaves, and to keep an inviolable silence about all the secrets which he learnt in the exercise of his calling or even outside of it. This oath brings the memorable document to a close, with repeated solemn adjurations to the gods, and it adds considerably to the significance of the record that, in the complete absence of State control, it formed the one public set of regulations for the practice of the art of medicine. It is supplemented by numerous passages in the medical writings of those times, in which the same pungent satire is directed at the arrogance of ignorance as at the humbug of quackery. Physicians who are such "in name, but not in fact" are compared with the "mute persons" or supernumeraries of the stage. The courage of wisdom is contrasted with the foolhardiness of ignorance. Touting for fees is deprecated, and a conference with other physicians in cases of doubt or hesitation is urgently enjoined. We quote here a fine remark: "Where there is love of humanity there will be love of the profession." If two or more ways of medical treatment were possible, the physician was recommended to choose the least imposing or sensational; it was an act of "deceit" to dazzle the patient's eye by brilliant exhibitions of skill which might very well be dispensed with. The practice of holding public lectures in order to increase his reputation was discouraged in the physician, and he was especially warned against lectures tricked out with quotations from the poets. Physicians who pretended to infallibility in detecting even the minutest departure from their prescriptions were laughed at; and, finally, there were precise byelaws to regulate the personal behaviour of the physician. He was enjoined to observe the most scrupulous cleanliness, and was advised to cultivate an elegance removed from all signs of luxury, even down to the detail that he might use perfumes, but not in an immoderate degree.

3. We have entered imperceptibly that region of literature in which " the father of medicine " reigns supreme. Hippocrates the Great, as Aristotle is the first to entitle him, was born in 460 B.C. in the island of Cos, and was recognized by all antiquity as the type of the perfect physician and author of medical treatises. His fame eclipsed that of all his professional brethren, and a large collection of writings have been ascribed to his pen which bear unmistakable traces of a diversity of authorship and sometimes of a feud of schools. The ancients were fully aware of this fact, though the attempts of their scholars to adjudicate the authorship were hardly more successful than those of modern or recent critics. This problem is one of the most delicate in the history of literature, and we shall not attempt to arrive at a solution in this place. The names of the authors of the books must remain hidden from us, and the same is true in most cases of the dates of their composition. We must be content with expressing the conviction that no portion of the so-called *corpus Hippocraticum*, with a few inconsiderable exceptions, is later than the close of the fifth century B.C. Those treatises, accordingly, may be accepted as affording ample testimony for the intellectual movement of the age that we are now considering. An irrefutable proof of the correctness of this view is contained in the special subject with which we are immediately concerned, for the names of two philosophers only—Melissus * and Empedocles—are contained in this multifarious mass of literature. Other thinkers whose influence may be traced in it are Xenophanes, Parmenides, Heraclitus, Alcmæon, Anaxagoras, and Diogenes of Apollonia, whose acquaintance we have not yet made. But the treatises contain not the faintest indication whatever to lead us outside of the chronological limit we have set to them. This in itself is evidence of the existence of that limit, for it would surely be astounding if, in an age of the most rapid intellectual development and of the most facile circulation of ideas, the authors of medical works had in their *pros* and *cons* confined themselves exclusively to

* Cp. Bk. II. Ch. II. *init.*

systems which were either already antiquated or were swiftly becoming so. Nor does the spectacle of a few belated stragglers, if in reality there were any, affect the certainty of our view of the reciprocal influence of medical and philosophical thought.

Those mutual relations existed, though they have often been sought in the wrong place and at an insufficient depth below the surface. We find external points of resemblance, for instance, such as the Hippocratic parallel to the four elements of Empedocles in his view of the quadruple nature of the humours of the body—blood, phlegm, yellow and black bile—determining health and disease. Or we find mere verbal analogies, which do not always point to the fact of a loan, nor even, when the language has been borrowed, to the borrowing of the doctrines as well. We must look deeper for the features of genuine resemblance in the spirit and method of the two sciences. Another glance backward will assist us in this search. Doubtless there had been a time when the treasury of a Greek practitioner, like that of his brother in Egypt, had contained little else than magical spells and prescriptions. The elimination of the superstitious elements from therapeutics went hand-in-hand with the release of the nations of antiquity from their general burden of primitive superstition. In some orders of society it occurred at a remarkably early period, in others comparatively late, but it was never complete. The system of popular medicine in which the chief part was played by amulets and charms was never completely expelled. But the lapse of time may be recognized by one very distinct mark. As superstition grew old it preferred to cover its nakedness with more and more meretricious finery ; it glittered with foreign authorities, such as the physicians of Thrace, the Getic and Hyperborean miracle-mongers Zalmoxis and Abaris, and the magicians of Persia, till the overflowing stream of Chaldean and Egyptian pseudo-science swept up these rags and tags of superstition and bore them down on its flood. Moreover, the healing arts of the priests always asserted their place by the side of worldly or lay therapeutics. We need but mention in this connection the cure by sleeping in a temple, and the beneficial dreams which commonly occurred in the sanctuaries of Asclepius. Though advanced thinkers poured their contempt * on these superstitious practices sanctioned by the national religion, yet they were held in undiminished respect by wide classes of the populace, and their efficacy was occasionally proclaimed in the ravings of learned but foolish men, such as Aristides, the rhetorician of Imperial Rome. By these means they survived the era of Paganism. Indeed, the seats in which they were located owed a part of the virtual permanence of their attraction to their combination with rational methods of treatment, and another part to their salubrious situation and surroundings. Epidaurus, for example, the most famous of these priestly health resorts, was situated in hilly country in the heart of beautiful pine-woods at no great distance from the sea. It was sheltered on the north by a range of mountains, and with its precious springs of water it fulfilled all the requirements of a modern sanatorial establishment. Nor was the public at that watering-place deprived of the means of recreation and enjoyment. It possessed a racecourse and a theatre, the stately ruins of which we are still able to admire. It was contended in antiquity that lay medicine derived considerable benefit from the comments on the treatment and course of diseases made by the priestly physicians. We find it difficult, however, to place credence in that statement. We have lately come in possession of a long series of such notes discovered in Epidaurus itself, and we are bound to confess that they would be adapted to any other purpose better than to that of the study of medicine. It would not be inappropriate, for instance, to find them a home in the fables of the " Arabian Nights." Among other tales which we owe to the inscriptions on those stones, there is a story of a broken goblet which was made whole again without human intervention ; and another of a head severed from its trunk, which the inferior demons who had cut it off were unable to replace till Asclepius had hastened in person to accomplish

* Cp. Aristophanes, " Plutus."

the miracle. In these accounts of the priestly cures, as in other annals of wonder-working, the dietetic and therapeutic factors, which had been genuinely efficacious, were either overlooked by the scribes or were purposely omitted. Progress was made in the lay art of medicine because the material for observation was constantly accumulating, and successive generations benefited by their dower of centuries of experience, and because the physicians of Greece shared with her poets and sculptors the same splendid faculties of keen sight and of faithful reproduction of the thing seen. Still, all this accumulation and sifting of the raw material sufficed to provide little more than a foundation-stone for a scientific system of medicine. The complete structure was yet in the dim perspective. Other preliminaries, other powerful incentives, were required for its realization, and these may be claimed as the contribution of that impulse towards generalization which grew and flourished more than elsewhere in the Greek schools of philosophy.

We need hardly remind our readers of Alcmæon, the philosopher-physician, and of the important discoveries connected with his name. The various parts for which Empedocles was cast included the character of the physician, and among other figures in which the physician was concealed by the philosopher there were—as a recent discovery has shown—Philolaus, Hippo, and Diogenes of Apollonia, who has been mentioned just above. But the ideal union of these two sciences is of far more importance than the fact that both were occasionally practised by one and the same person, and it was fostered by the conviction which gradually grew out of the culture of those times, and which may be formulated as follows :—

The human being is a part of the whole of nature, and cannot be understood without it. What is wanted is a satisfactory general view of the process of the universe. Possessing this, we shall find the key in our hand which will open the most secret recesses of the art of medicine.

A number of the alleged treatises of Hippocrates take the attitude therein defined displaying a common leaning to the systems of the nature-philosophy, and a common eclecticism, though in varying degrees, in employing them; the majority, too, are marked by their connection with the medical teachings of the school founded at Cnidus, though it is impossible at this date to determine with certainty whether such connection was mainly accidental or depended on the peculiar character of the doctrines of the school. In support of the last-named alternative, we may instance the fact that the Cnidian physicians preferred with Empedocles * the more physical method of viewing the phenomena of life. Accordingly we have to distinguish between two great groups of medical treatises, those, namely, that were dominated by this standard of thought, and those that were opposed to it. We place them in this order, not because we can assert with certainty that each number in the first group is older than each number in the second, but rather because their principles and chief examples are related in that way. The philosophy of nature gained an influence on medicine and began to transform it. Then came the reaction against its influence, and the attempt to hark-back to the older and more empiric art of medicine. In the ensuing pages we shall describe this conflict and its issue, but in accordance with the proportions of our undertaking, we shall be content to illustrate the doctrines and methods most characteristic of both movements.

4. The author of the work in four books entitled " On Diet " opened with a discussion of principles.

" I contend "—so runs the conclusion of his preface—" that he who will write correctly on the subject of human diet must first of all know and understand the nature of man. He must know the parts of that nature out of which it is originally composed, and he must understand which of those parts predominates in its government. For if he be ignorant of its original composition, he will be unable to know what effects it produces; and if he do not understand what part is supreme in the body, he will not be enabled to recommend to man what is beneficial to him."

* Cp. Bk. II. Ch. V. § 3.

Among other demands which the author brought forward were a knowledge of the constitution of all food-stuffs and drinks, and a comprehension of the far-reaching contrast between work and nutrition. "For the performances of work," he wrote, "are directed to the consumption of what exists, and food and drink are intended to replenish the void thus created." The fundamental condition of health is a correct proportion between work and nutrition in view of the constitution of the individual and of the differences of age, season, climate, and so forth. Except for the one factor of the individual constitution which previous to illness was unknown to the physician, good health, in the opinion of our author, could be preserved from all disturbance. Next he turned to the elements of the animal and human body, which he described as two in number, and it will not be fanciful to trace the influence of Parmenides in a writer who is otherwise strongly influenced by Heraclitus when we discover that he defined those two elements as fire and water. Fire he recognized as the universal principle of movement, and water as the universal principle of nutrition. In a passage which unmistakably refers to the movement of the luminaries we read that—

"when fire reaches the outermost boundary of water it begins to lack nourishment, so it turns round and reverts to the sources of its nourishment; when water reaches the outermost boundary of fire it begins to lack movement, so stands still and becomes . . . the prey of the fire in want of nourishment."

The condition of the permanence of the universe in its existing state is that neither of the two elements shall gain dominion over the other, and the connecting link between the physiological and material doctrines is the idea, borrowed perhaps from Alcmæon, of an equilibrium between the performance of work and nourishment on the one part, and between the cosmic agents of those functions on the other.

Here for the moment we may call a halt. Enough has been said to enable the attentive reader to acquaint himself, approximately at least, with the character of this work in its weakness as well as in its strength. We are confronted with a reflection, the greatness of which is not diminished because its significance was exaggerated by its author. Its effect is : The integrity of the organic economy rests on the equilibrium of its income and expenditure. We chose the method of verbal quotation above in order to avoid the suspicion of crediting even unconsciously an old and old-fashioned author with modern habits of thought. We shall gain a clearer conception of his great generalization if we remember that similar though less far-reaching reflections were made by other medical writers of presumably an earlier date. Euryphon, the head of the Cnidian school and an older contemporary of Hippocrates, conjectured that the causes of illness lay in a surplus of food ; and Herodicus, another Cnidian, approached even more closely to the dictum of the author of "On Diet" in his statement that "men fall ill when they indulge in food on insufficient exercise." At the same time our author may claim the merit of having been the first to give expression to a fundamental truth in its full capacity, while he is no more affected by the reproach that he discovered in a single condition the sole operative cause of health than were his less far-sighted predecessors. It is one thing to discover new significant truths, it is another thing to realize the limits of their capacity ; it is one thing to give the reins to the generalizing instinct, it is another thing to know when to check it, and it would be foolish to ask an early pioneer of science to display both qualities at once. The value of that performance was more seriously affected by the attempt, laudable in itself, but unattainable by the methods then—and even since—at the disposal of science, to build physiology on a cosmological foundation. Some mischief was bound to be wrought by the purely speculative doctrine of matter and the strangely primitive, not to say anthropomorphic, astronomy which were used in this connection. Similarly, the thought that man was a model of the universe, a microcosm by the side of a macrocosm, was bound to lead to fanciful interpretations. It was a grand idea in itself, but even in more advanced ages it was found to darken rather than to illumine the path of natural research, and it contains features which remind us of the philosophy of Schelling and Oken, such as, for example, the comparison between "the sea" and "the belly," as the universal "storeroom which provides for all and receives from all." Nor does the ambitious start of our dietetic author come to grief merely at these objective obstacles. His mind was like a stream which runs deep but not clear. He was well-nigh intoxicated by the enigmatic wisdom of Heraclitus, and the quiet and orderly disposition of his subject-matter was disturbed by his constant desire to illustrate the teachings of his master by ever fresh examples taken from the most various departments of life. Nor did he disdain to imitate and surpass the Ephesian in the use which he made of the rights of paradox and self-contradiction. At one time he spoke in the manner and the very words of Heraclitus of the steady ceaseless "transformation" of matter; at another time he agreed with Anaxagoras and Empedocles in reducing all "birth and decay" to "combinations and separations," and apologized for the use of those expressions as a convenience of popular usage. In other respects, too, much that he borrowed from Empedocles is not even verbally harmonized with his Heraclitean principles. Thus it happened that the great principle originally promulgated failed to perform all that it promised. It remained the leading point of view for a large number of dietetic precepts, especially in questions of nourishment and gymnastic exercises, elaborated with a wealth of instructive detail. But even these most important parts of his undertaking were injured by the vain attempts, repeated with wearisome iteration, to derive the differences of physical and even psychical conditions from the proportion of the two fictitious primary substances, though many actual experiences were turned to good account in this connection, and at least one original experiment was made, namely, that of artificial vomiting in order to test the respective digestible qualities of food-stuffs simultaneously consumed.

And now for the concluding book. It is entitled "On Dreams," and we might say of it, after Horace, that it formed a fish-like tail of a lovely figure of a woman. It begins with the distinction, already familiar to us from Herodotus, between supernatural and natural visions. The first kind was left to the interpretation of soothsayers who were quite gravely alleged—and we regret the absence of irony—to possess "an exact knowledge" on the subject. Dreams which sprang from natural causes, however, were used as the basis of inferences as to the constitution of the body, and we may readily agree that certain dreams can be traced back to over-feeding, and treated by an aperient. But in his desire to exploit the inquiry to some purpose, our author speedily transgressed the limits which at least preserved him from absurdity. He set full sail on the flood of child-like superstition, and by reasonings in the style of Artemidorus he attained to goals of childishness to which we are indisposed to follow him.

Mention must be made of a further treatise "On the Muscles," which we perceive, from its references to a foregoing and a succeeding book, to have been but a brief section of a comprehensive work "On the Science of Medicine," and which exhibits the same characteristics of attractive self-contradiction. The author is here revealed as a practitioner of ripe experience who has seen much and observed keenly, as long, at least, as his faculties of sight and observation were not obstructed by preconceived opinions. He was the first to recognize that the so-called spinal marrow is entirely distinct from the common marrow of the bones, that it possesses membranes, and is related with the brain. Thus he came considerably nearer than his predecessors to a correct appreciation of its nature and meaning. Again, he had seen suicides who had attempted to cut their throats, and who had been robbed of their speech by the knife penetrating the trachea ; speech had been restored to them by the closing of the scission, and thence he drew the correct conclusion that it had been the air escaping through the wound which had made it impossible for them to speak, and he used his observation to confirm his true theory of the formation of vocal sounds. Nor was he content with mere observations of this kind and the occasional experiment of a lesion and its surgical treatment. He undertook deliberate experiments of his own, though on a modest basis. He was aware, for example, of the coagulation of blood drawn from the body, but he had prevented the formation of a clot by shaking the blood. Again, in order to distinguish the composition of the various tissues he subjected them to the process of boiling, and drew conclusions as to their constitution from the relative ease and difficulty with which they could be boiled. We cannot conceal our admiration of these accurate observations, methodical experiments, and logical conclusions, which were accompanied, nevertheless, by misobservations and arbitrary assumptions to an almost incredible extent. Thus his belief in the efficacy of the number seven in all processes of natural and human life practically blinded him to the evidence of facts. He was bold enough to declare that no eight-months child ever remained alive. Besides the normal term of pregnancy—nine months and ten days, or 40×7 days—he would only admit a prospect of preservation for a seven-months child. On the other hand, he asserted that he had seen embryos of seven days old in which all the parts of the body were plainly discernible. He was equally prepared to prove that abstention from food and drink could not last longer than seven days without causing death, whether within that period, or—as he naïvely added —at a later date. Even people who, after the expiry of seven days, desisted from this kind of suicide—by no means rare in antiquity—were likewise irretrievably lost, for their body, he stated, proved incapable of assimilating nourishment.

The rigour of our author's thought did not save him from the spell of number, and in other directions too he succumbed to the wiles of imagination. But their victim may well be pardoned, for it is difficult to see how questions which defy the resources, not of that age merely, but of this, could have been answered save by fancy. Nay, more. His attempts at solution were predestined to sterility, and the questions themselves have been prohibited by modern science. For our author was engaged with no smaller task than the problem of organic creation. No hint of the doctrine of evolution had crossed his mind. Accordingly he did not search, as the boldest of our own contemporaries have hitherto searched in vain, for the possible mode of the origin of the simplest organisms on earth, but he sought to derive man himself, the crown of earthly existence, directly from material substances. And from what substances! The single tissues and their combinations were to be derived by putrefaction and coagulation, by condensation and rarefaction, by melting and boiling, from the warm and the cold, the moist and the dry, and the fat and the gelatinous. It was only by way of exception, too, that an element of doubt or reservation was introduced by an occasional "it seems to me" in the dogmatic and self-confident argumentation. "Thus came the lungs into existence," "thus was the liver formed," "the spleen was composed as follows," "the joints were composed in this manner," "thus the teeth grew"—one paragraph after another with wearisome uniformity opens with some such phrase. We need not trouble about their contents, but our interest is aroused by the level of thought attained by these premature attempts to penetrate the most intimate secrets of natural life. An important distinction must here be drawn. We have to get rid of the first disagreeable impression, difficult though it may be, with which we are filled by the temerity of the undertaking. By that means alone shall we be able to reach the sound kernel of the work which is concealed under the adventurous exterior. It brings a thought to light which would not be belied even by the science of our own times. We yield assent to the statement that the art of healing must be based on a knowledge of pathological processes, and that this must in turn be founded on an acquaintance with life in health. The science of corporeal functions presupposes an acquaintance with the organs by which they are conditioned, nor can that acquaintance be gained without understanding their elementary constituent parts and the substances and forces which are at work in them and on them. Finally, in Aristotle's words, "he who sees things grow from the beginning will have the finest view of them." In other words, therapeutics must be founded on pathology, pathology on physiology and anatomy, physiology and anatomy on histology, chemistry, and physics. The theory of evolution shows us the road which leads from the lowest or simplest organisms to the highest or most complicated, and the goal of the long journey is faintly seen in the perspective in the revelation of the causes of the development of the organic from the inorganic world. In the experiment with which we are dealing the intermediate links are omitted or are sketched in the faintest colours, and the end of the long series is connected directly with the beginning. Our author's work is characterized accordingly by an extraordinary audacity which we shall better understand if we are content to regard it as an indication of the self-confidence of youth. To the bright hopes of the childhood of the ages which no failure had yet availed to dim, the ultimate goals of science may well have appeared so near as to be within arm's length. The author of the book "On the Muscles" is just such a disciple of nature-philosophy. Countless details of his doctrine, not to speak of the spirit which inspired him, show him plainly as a man who had learned from Heraclitus, Empedocles, and Anaxagoras, and had written in an era when the eclectic fusion of their doctrines had already begun. At the very introduction of his treatise he referred to the "common teachings" of predecessors to whose work he has contributed his part, and he felt himself bound to premise as much "about heavenly things" as was necessary to show "what man and the other animals are, how they originated and arose, what is the soul, what health, what sickness, what evil and good in man, and whence death comes to him." As the primary principle he selected "the warm, which is immortal, which sees, hears, and understands all things, and is cognizant of the present and the future." Its bulk had disappeared into the heights of celestial space in consequence of that "concussion" of the universe which he agreed with Anaxagoras and Empedocles in describing as the starting-point of cosmic phenomena, and that warm he states to be what the ancients had called Æther. When we have added that the "rotation" of cosmos also appeared to him as a consequence of that concussion, we shall have carried sufficiently far our investigation into the details of his fundamental doctrine.

The book "On Muscles," with its somewhat unfortunate title, had its sequel in the work "On the Number Seven." This treatise, the bulk of which has only been preserved in an Arabic and a Latin translation, need not delay us very long. It marks the most flourishing epoch in the popular belief in the wonderful efficacy of that number. Once more we are told that "the embryo takes shape after seven days, and proves itself a human being." Once more, as in the books "On Diet," we are introduced to the "seven vowels" or rather the seven vocal signs of the Greek language, among which ē and ō are included, while ā and ī and y are absent, because in the Greek alphabet they happen to have no distinctive symbols. No less a man than Solon had already considered the dominion of the number seven in the demarcation of the ages of man, but now the whole world, the winds, the seasons, the human soul, the human body, the functions of the head, each and all were to be stamped with the hall-mark of seven. Another ruling thought in this treatise has likewise been made familiar to us by our discussion of the work "On Diet." It consists in the comparison between the individual and the universe, the analogy between the microcosm and the macrocosm. We may quote at this point our author's own words—

"Animals and plants on earth have a constitution which resembles that of the universe. Wherefore, since the whole agrees, its parts must likewise show the same composition as the parts of the world. . . . The earth, being firm and immovable, resembles the bones in its stony and solid parts. . . . That which surrounds them is like the soluble flesh of man. . . . The water in the rivers resembles the blood that flows in the veins,"

and so forth. Both thoughts are combined in the almost ludicrous comparison of the earth with the human body, in which seven parts of the body and seven parts of the earth are arbitrarily selected and ranged with one another. A parallel, for instance, is discovered between the Peloponnesus as "the seat of high-minded men " and the "head and face," between Ionia and the diaphragm, between Egypt with its sea and the belly. These and similar excesses of an unbridled imagination were calculated to produce a reaction. There is nothing like them in history, except perhaps the alchemy of the Arabs with their seven metals, seven stones, seven volatile bodies, seven natural and seven artificial salts, seven kinds of alum, seven chief chemical operations, etc. The reaction that ensued marks the first dawn of the true science of Greece and the Western world.

5. Without soaring aspiration and without daring deed there is no science, no knowledge of nature. The conquest of a new region of knowledge resembles in many respects the occupation of virgin territory. First come the roadmakers, who unite a number of isolated points ; then come the bridge-makers, who span many a yawning chasm ; and last come the temporary shelters, which must ultimately be replaced by statelier buildings on deeper foundations and composed of more durable materials. These processes correspond respectively to the preliminary generalizations restrained by no manner of obstacles, to the bold arguments from analogy, and to the first construction of hypotheses. But woe to the settlement where the hand of its founders has been guided by blind enthusiasm rather than by shrewd calculation. Traffic will retire from the deserted streets, palaces will fall in ruins, and the homesteads will remain untenanted. That fate threatened the intellectual achievements of the epoch with which we are dealing. The apprentice-years of the mere collection of facts were followed by the *Wanderjahre* of vague, restless speculation.

These had now lasted long enough, and it was time for the *Meisterjahre* of quiet, methodical research to succeed if science was to acquire steady and sedentary habits instead of losing itself in a maze of phantasies, revolving in idle circles. It is the undying glory of the medical school of Cos that it introduced this innovation in the domain of its art, and thus exercised the most beneficial influence on the whole intellectual life of mankind. " Fiction to the right ! Reality to the left ! " was the battle-cry of this school in the war they were the first to wage against the excesses and defects of the nature-philosophy. Nor could it have found any more suitable champions, for the serious and noble calling of the physician, which brings him every day and every hour in close communion with nature, in the exercise of which mistakes in theory engender the most fatal practical consequences, has served in all ages as a nursery of the most genuine and incorruptible sense of truth. The best physicians must be the best observers, but the man who sees keenly, who hears clearly, and whose senses, powerful at the start, are sharpened and refined by constant exercise, will only in exceptional instances be a visionary or a dreamer. The line of demarcation dividing reality from the fictions of the imagination is dug more deeply in his instance, as it were, till it becomes an impassable gulf. He can never be absent from his post in the campaign against the encroachments of fancy on the domain of reason. Even in our own century we have to thank the physicians for our liberation from the tyranny of the nature-philosophy. The bitterest denunciations of that error and of the mischief that it works still proceed from the lips of men who have sat at the feet of Johannes Müller, the great physiologist and anatomist. It is no valid argument to reply that there is merely a nominal and external likeness between the nature-philosophy of Schelling and that of Heraclitus or Empedocles. The point to be remembered is that the defective logic which was a common characteristic both of the modern and of the ancient schools was far more pardonable and comprehensible in the earlier than in the latter growth. The signs of degeneracy, of reaction, and of senile decay in the one are but the natural accompaniment in the other of the slow emancipation of science from the mythological traditions of the childhood of the world. But whether the light was newly kindled, or whether it had long been burning with a steady flame, the shadows that threatened to darken it had to be dispelled in either instance.

The author of the treatise " On Old Medicine " was the first to open the campaign along the whole line of battle. With a deep sense of the dignity of his calling, and with a keen appreciation of its significance for the welfare and prosperity of mankind, he refused to be indifferent to a movement which tended to degrade its worth, to annul the distinction between good physicians and bad, and—what was most important—to undermine the structure of the science itself. His attack was not directed at isolated details in the system of his adversaries ; he went to the root of the evil. He condemned the method of the " new-fangled " art of healing, without respect and without reserve. The science, he urged, was not to be founded on hypothesis, though this was the primrose path. It was taking things too easily to assume—

" a single primary cause for illnesses and for death, and the same cause in every instance, and to postulate as that cause one or two factors, whether the warm or the cold, the damp or the dry, or any-thing else that occurred. . . . But the healing art "—which was no pseudo-science, and had, moreover, to deal with sensible objects— " possesses all things from of old, a principle, and a beaten track along which in the course of ages many splendid discoveries have been made, and along which the science will be perfected, if men of adequate talent, equipped with the knowledge of the discoveries made hitherto, take these as their starting-point, and set out thence on further inquiries. He who rejects and despises all this, however, and undertakes his investigations on another road and in other forms and claims to have discovered something, he is deceived and deceives himself, for it is impossible."

At first we might seem to be listening to the voice of some old crusted Tory who held aloof from every kind of

innovation. But such a judgment would be wholly unjustified. Our author was fully capable of defending his
exclusive preference for the old empiric—we do not say
inductive—method. He began by pointing to its merits,
placing them in the clearest light by extending the
conventional bounds covered by the art of healing. Nor
was it merely dietetics, in the full sense of that term,
which he regarded as a constituent branch of the art. He
included in his inquiry the transition from the coarse
nourishment, which, as he pertinently remarked, men originally shared with the brute creation, to the refined *cuisine*
of civilized peoples. This transition, which we take as a
matter of course, he characterized as "a great invention,
elaborated and perfected in the course of centuries with no
mean display of intelligence and imagination." Precisely
parallel to the experiments by which the indigestible quality
of that primitive diet had been proved of old were the fresh
experiments which enabled the physician to vary the
nourishment appropriate to a healthy man with that fit
and wholesome for an invalid. In the instance of the
treatment of health, every one was more or less an expert,
and it is not surprising that it was separated from the
treatment of disease which demanded professional knowledge. Nevertheless, the science was uniform, and its process
in both cases was precisely the same. In the one as in the
other, it was advisable to correct the foods which the human
body could not assimilate by mixing them, mitigating
them, or diluting them, so that the healthy organism in
the one case and the diseased organism in the other could
master them and derive benefit from them. Our author
next turned to individual differences in matters of diet,
which he illustrated by many examples. He found that
they rested partly on original distinctions of constitution and
partly on distinctions of habit. They were not reducible to
any one common principle, but could only be discerned and
taken in account by the most careful and unremitting observation. It was an obvious consequence of this need of strict
individual treatment that precise accuracy could not always
be guaranteed. Another and no less fruitful source of error

was the fact that there are dangers of a precisely opposite kind. The physician was bound to be on his guard against excess as well as against defect, against a too strong as well as against a too weak quality of the means of nourishment. At this point we are first confronted by the conception of an "exact" science—of a science, that is to say, admitting determination by quantities. In its present stage it was purely an ideal, the attainment of which in the realm of dietetics and medicine had to be abandoned on the spot. "One must aim at a standard," we read, "but a standard, weight, or number which shall serve thee as a sure guide thou shalt not find, seeing that there is no other than the sensibility of the body." And precisely because this was merely an approximate standard without strict exactitude, slight divagations to the right or the left of the mean were practically inevitable. The highest praise was due to that physician who committed merely trivial blunders ; the majority were like those steersmen who repeatedly err with impunity in a quiet sea and under a cloudless sky, but whose mistakes are fraught with fatal consequences if a storm arise.

The new medicine was swiftly exposed to another reproach of more incisive importance. Its premises and precepts were alleged not to cover the actual many-sidedness of objects. The new-fangled teaching—an epithet which applied to the doctrine of Alcmæon as well as to that of the books "On Diet"—recommended the application of " the cold against the warm, the warm against the cold ; the moist against the dry, the dry against the moist." Every time that—

"one of these factors had wrought mischief, it was to be corrected by the application of the opposite factor. . . . But those physicians, so far as I know," continued our author, " have hitherto discovered or invented no warm, or cold, or dry, or moist which is so in itself, unalloyed with any other quality. It is rather my opinion that they are acquainted with no other foods and drinks than those which we all employ. It is impossible, then, for them to order the invalid to feed on a 'warm,' for he would instantly ask, On what kind of a 'warm'? And thereupon they would have recourse either to empty verbiage or to one of the substances with which we are familiar."

It would make considerable difference, too, whether the "warm" were an astringent or aperient, or which of the other natural qualities it possessed ; and this difference in effect would not merely apply to men, but to wood and leather, and many other objects by no means as sensitive as the human body.

We reach now the most important part of the book, in which the fundamental principles of our author came to their clearest expression.

"Some people say," he wrote, "physicians as well as sophists" —by whom, as we conceive, he merely meant philosophers—"that it is not possible to understand the medical art except by learning what man is. He who would treat men in the right way must first understand this. This saying of theirs is directed at philosophy as it has been practised by Empedocles and others who have written about nature and have discussed the origin of man, how he came into existence, and how his parts were joined together. But I believe," he continued, "that all that sophists or physicians have said or written about nature belongs less to the art of medicine than to that of painting. It is my opinion, on the contrary, that certain knowledge about nature can be gained from no other point of view than from that of medical science. This is attainable, however, by any one who chooses to approach that study in a proper fashion, and with regard to the fulness of its extent. But it seems to me that there is a long road still to be travelled before that degree of erudition is reached which shall know what man is, by what cause he was created, and all else to the least detail."

We may pause here, not unprofitably, in order to explain some points. Our readers will note the almost verbal resemblance of the above introductory words with the passage quoted just now, at the beginning of section 4, from the work "On Diet," where the proposition that is here so energetically disputed is vindicated with equal energy. We can hardly fail to recognize a direct polemical intention, and it affords a glaring instance of the so-called uniformity of the Hippocratic canon. The mention of painting in this connection gives us a momentary shock, but a brief consideration will show that the author could hardly have chosen a more appropriate expression for his thought. He obviously wanted to say that descriptions of the origin of animals and men, of the kind attempted by Empedocles, might be attractive, fascinating, and seductive, but they were not science. Now, the contrary of science, which aims at truth rather than at pleasure, is found in such cases in the region of the fine arts, inasmuch as the imagination can deal freely therein with the shapes and colours that it invents. The type which we should obviously select is that of poetry, but it would have been out of place for the present purpose of inveighing at the contents of the work of Empedocles on account of the poetic form in which that work was composed. The sharp and almost harsh manner in which our author contrasted fiction and fact, and dismissed the first from the realm of serious attention, reminds us of the contempt expressed by Herodotus about the stream of ocean, and quoted by us at the close of the last book. We should be glad to see the hint that medicine, practised in a proper fashion and in its full capacity, is the beginning of all true knowledge of nature developed more fully to its conclusions. For we may almost detect in the saying the insight, or at least the conjecture, that all our knowledge about nature is relative, and that the true goal of human inquiry is not what nature is in herself, but what she is in her relation to man's perceptive faculties. This at least is the trend of the sequel of this important passage, with which we hasten to acquaint our readers :

" For to me too," continues our author, " it seems necessary that every physician should possess knowledge about nature, and that he should give himself the utmost pains in that respect if he wishes to be equal to his task. He must know the relation of man to the food and drink that he consumes, and to all else that he does and practises. He must know what effect each thing exercises on each man. Nor is it enough to be of opinion that cheese is a bad food because it inconveniences him who is satiated with it. The physician must know what kind of inconvenience it produces, and what is its cause, and with what part of the human body it fails to conform. For there are many other foods and drinks which are naturally injurious, which yet do not affect men in the same way. Let me select the instance of wine, which, if enjoyed unmixed and in large quantities, will affect men in a certain way. And observation shows to all that this is the work and the effect of wine. We know, too, through what parts of the body it chiefly produces that result, and I could wish that equal clarity should be shed over all the other instances."

These remarks too require a word of explanation. The first point to be noticed is the incisive and doubtless deliberate contrast between our author's everyday language and his homely example and the high-flown matter and no less aspiring manner of Empedocles and those who thought like him. We can conceive the anti-philosopher addressing his adversaries in this wise: "I too am striving after a comprehensive knowledge of nature, the threads of whose most intimate secrets ye think ye have already unravelled and proclaim your triumph in gorgeous phrases. But how modest are my immediate ends, how far I remain behind the proud flight of your thought, how verily I creep along the ground of trivial occurrences and everyday questions which have yet been solved but in the smallest proportion." Yes, our excellent author deemed himself as free as possible from the taint of temerity and the disease of scholar's pride, and yet fate overtook him precisely at that point. The bitter contempt that he poured from a full horn over his predecessors was avenged by fate on his own person, and in view of the evidence we have collected as to the soundness of his knowledge we are well-nigh tempted to exclaim, his modesty was rooted in immodesty, and his was the pride that vainly aped humility. The modicum of certain knowledge to which he laid claim and which he considered as self-evident truth was but the semblance of knowledge. For since he was entirely ignorant of the chemistry of digestion no less than of the physiology of the brain, the heart, and the blood-vessels, his explanations of the indigestibleness of cheese and of the intoxication produced by wine, whatever forms they may have taken, were certainly built on a false foundation.

We are startled and almost confused at the result of the preceding investigation. The question rises to our lips, Was it all in vain—this reaction on the part of the clear-sighted physician against the arbitrary methods, his enthusiastic return to the genuine evidence of facts, and his unremitting polemic against those of his predecessors who had "misled the art of medicine from its ancient track and started it on the road of hypothesis"? For he too had fallen unwittingly into the toils of hypothetical research, nor was his relapse confined to a few false observations more or less, nor to the misinterpretation of isolated facts; it involved complete explanatory attempts proceeding wholly from the region of a physiology based on hypothesis. Let us guard against the risk of misunderstanding. We would not, therefore, depreciate or condemn our author's achievements, still less would we brand his polemic as altogether vain and ineffectual. In order to frame an adequate judgment, we must make a further slight digression; and, in choosing the longer road, we may hope to attain to a height from which we shall be able to form a truer and more comprehensive appreciation of the two conflicting tendencies of thought.

6. An hypothesis is an assumption or a supposition. Where and as long as full certainty of knowledge eludes us, it is necessary to set up mere assumptions. That necessity is twofold. It is indispensable to the matter discussed and inevitable to the man discussing. Humanly inevitable, because the mind has not yet been created which can receive and retain a long series of details without encircling them and connecting them by a common bond. Memory craves relief, and in the realm of the co-existence of phenomena that craving is satisfied by classification, whereas in the realm of causal succession the aid of hypothesis has to be invoked. And if the demands of reason and of the causal sense possess sufficient strength in the investigator's mind, they cannot remain idle even at the beginning of his task. Tentatively at least, hypotheses must be formed in the earlier stages of an inquiry which shall serve as the rungs of

the ladder to ascend to the ultimate goal. It has been acutely remarked that every approved theory of to-day was at one time an hypothesis. It is subjectively impossible, in dealing with the countless details of which a comprehensive theory is ultimately to be composed, to keep them during its construction in their original segregation and to preserve their psychical isolation ; and a similar objective impossibility would attend the endeavour to descry, gather, and sift the elements of experience, or even to create them by the artificial means provided in natural science, unless the light of a preliminary hypothesis were shed over the path of the investigator to guide his footsteps to his end. Precisely the same process is set in motion when the end in view is not the attainment of general truths, but the ascertainment of single occurrences. Before a judge comes to consider his verdict he will generally have begun by considering the grounds of suspicion, and every such ground of suspicion is expressed in a supposition or hypothesis. Moreover, if his mind be awake through the trial, the depositions of witnesses and the other evidence collected on the basis of such an early hypothesis will give rise in the course of the proceedings to ever-fresh hypotheses, and, supposing him to have a logical as well as a wakeful mind, to ever-fresh and more exact approximations to the ultimate verdict or truth. Two causes alone can affect the value of the preliminary assumption as a stage on the victorious road to truth. The first is due to a subjective error to be traced to the mind of the inquirer, and the second to an objective defect attaching to the means of inquiry. The hypothesis will obstruct and hinder, instead of facilitating, the attainment of a final solution, if the inquirer's mind be lacking in the requisite pliability and adaptability. He will then overlook the provisional character of his assumptions ; he will disband the forces of his intellect at too early a date, and will mistake a portion of his journey, and a very short portion perhaps, for the completion of his task. And the hypothesis will be devoid of scientific value, or at least of the highest scientific value, if it be intrinsically incapable of emerging from a provisional

and assumptive truth into an ultimate and definitive one
—in other words, if it offer not the least handle for the
purpose of verification. It would be idle to expect
complete clearness on this and on kindred questions of
method from the earliest author who offers us any discussion whatsoever on the value of hypothetical investigations, and who, indeed, as far as any record has come
down to us, is the first to have used the word "hypothesis"
in its technical sense. The greater is the credit that
redounds to him that he was by no means unfamiliar with
the most far-reaching of the distinctions that are here
to be considered. It must be conceded that he used the
word "hypothesis" in a somewhat loose fashion, without
expressly distinguishing between verifiable and non-
verifiable assumptions; but the brunt of his attack fell on
the second of these classes, which was more or less the
object of all his invectives against hypothetical investigation. For when he argued against the application of that
new method to medicine, he supported his cause by the
following significant remarks: that science needed no
"empty hypotheses," he wrote, as did—

"the invisible and unfathomable things. Any one who should
attempt a description of such things would have to avail himself
of hypothesis. Thus with regard to things in heaven or to those
under the earth. And even though he knew and said what was
correct about them, yet neither he nor his hearers would be aware
if it were the truth or not, for he has no standard which he can
apply in order to attain full certainty."

The term "empty" in this connection is a jewel in the
crown of science. It is meant to stigmatize hypotheses,
in themselves incapable of proof, and likened to idle
fictions which are refused admittance across the threshold
of genuine science. Let us renew our recollection of two
similar treasures before we attempt to estimate its worth.
There was first the passage from Xenophanes * which
emphasized, in language closely similar to our present
quotation, and still more so to the Greek original, the

* Bk. II. Ch. I. § 3, *fin.*

significance of verification ; and there was, secondly, the
similarly inspired utterance of the historian Herodotus, to
which we have already had occasion to refer.* Taking
these in account, and remembering that our author's feud
against hypothetical investigation was essentially directed
at a special kind of hypotheses, we see that there was
nothing to prevent him from using hypotheses on his own
account without incurring the charge of inconsistency. It
was inevitable that he should have formed hypothetical
conceptions about the nature of the digestive process and
the causes of drunkenness ; they were as natural to the
childhood of physiology and its sister sciences as was
their subsequent correction when the sciences matured.
But it is one thing to make an erroneous hypothesis, it is
quite another thing to make an unscientific hypothesis
which is entirely or partially incapable of verification. It
may be urged that every hypothesis is not clearly
brand-marked as unverifiable or the contrary, as doomed
to remain a hypothesis for ever, or as possessing the
power to develop its own means of proving, approximately at least, its truth or falsehood. But though this
is generally the case, it is not universally so. These retorts
and counter retorts, however, need not occupy us long, for
" the hot " and " the cold," " the dry " and " the moist,"
as the fundamental constituent parts of the human
organism, or even as the chief factors that affect it, were,
to speak precisely, even less than mere hypotheses—they
were fictions, or rather abstractions disguised as realities.
Certain qualities were segregated from the complex of
attributes with which they were really indissolubly connected, and were moreover invested with a supremacy
that did not reasonably belong to them ; for these variations of temperature and of the state of aggregation, which
were there brought into play, do not always bring in their
train a decisive change in all the rest of the attributes. It
was one of the great positive merits of the treatise which
we are discussing, that it emphasized this consideration and
hinted at the comparatively greater significance of the

* Bk. II. Ch. VI. § 4, *fin.*

chemical qualities of bodies, throwing at the same time a side glance at the influences these exercised on substances not belonging to the living organism. Our author was therefore justified in describing heat and cold as qualities which possess a comparatively very small power over the body, and in recalling such phenomena of reaction as the effect of inward heat produced by taking a cold bath.

But it is time to abandon these details. The question whether this or that hypothesis was more or less scientific in character, whether a greater or a less degree of legitimacy attached to it, is not as important to our purpose as the broad conflict of methods with which our readers should by this time be familiar, and which presents no very great difficulties. The rule of sound common sense, " to start from the known or the sensible and thence to infer the unknown," was as obvious to Herodotus and Euripides as at a later date to Epicurus, and we have here to remark that it was violated quite openly and crudely by the physicians who planted their footsteps in the lines of nature-philosophy. Problems, such as that of the origin of organic life or of the human race, which modern science still regards as insoluble, were placed at the head of their programme, and medical precepts were founded on attempts to solve them which bore not merely a hypothetical, but a fantastic character. We cannot affect to be surprised that a reaction should have set in, nor should we attempt to deny that such a reaction was wholesome. Still, we must be on our guard against one-sided and exaggerated views. The new way was a necessary way, and it would be false to describe it as wholly and solely a misleading way. It was inevitable that the doctrines of nature-philosophy should penetrate the several sciences and begin to transform their methods. We have already seen reason to believe that the arbitrary element which clung to most of those theories was bound to be expelled, but its elimination did not necessarily destroy all the effects of its influence ; some of them, and those not the least beneficial, might survive. Above all, an ideal that has once been erected, however pitiable, however grotesque its subsequent failure may be, is not lost to posterity, and the attempt to rescue the science of medicine from the isolation which threatened to swallow it, and to regard it as a single branch on the great tree of universal science, was at any rate an ideal. At first, it must be conceded, and for long afterwards, this ambitious undertaking failed for want of the requisite foundations, and thus a return became necessary which was almost equivalent to a retreat to the older methods of research and to the narrow limits in which they had been confined. But here too we must guard against misunderstanding. It is not enough to summarize the relation between the two conflicting tendencies in the conventional formula : the false deductive method was buried in the ruins of the philosophical theory of medicine, and the correct inductive method was borne in on the triumph of Hippocrates. For in dealing with highly complicated phenomena, with aggregate processes composed of innumerable details, no other method is recommended to investigators than that which builds up the whole out of its parts, and refers the so-called empiric or derivative laws to the simple or ultimate causal laws from which they spring. The secret of the former and even of the present employment of cruder and less suitable methods is not to be found in the intrinsic falsehood of the deductive method. It is rather a sign that that method can only be applied with success in an infinitely more advanced stage in the development of science, and an indication that pathology was then found wanting in its anatomical and physiological basis, and that physiology then, as partly even now, rested on an insecure foundation of cellular-physiology, of physics, and of chemistry. We are dealing here with the beginnings of a period of transition which has continued down to our own times, for it is only to-day that the most advanced portions of organic science admit at least a partial use of deduction, and have thus begun to enter the last and highest stage of scientific treatment. The type of deduction is calculation, and calculation is most fully employed at this date in the business of the oculist, so far as it is founded on optics. But there are other branches of therapeutics in a high degree of development which rest on a deductive basis. Take, for instance, the anti-septic treatment of wounds, the object of which is the destruction of micro-organisms which have been recognized with complete certainty as the agents of disease—an object which is attained by the use of substances the chemical qualities of which hold out with equal certainty a prospect of the desired result. This method offers the completest contrast with the proceeding in cases where there is no clear evidence of causation, and where the defect cannot be supplied either by direct, unequivocal, and drastic cures —the genuine experimental method,—nor yet by the decisively favourable results of observations taken in such numbers as to eliminate the element of chance—in other words, by the statistical method. Those are the medica-ments of which it is correctly said that they are "re-commended to-day, eulogized to-morrow, and forgotten two years hence." The undying glory of the school of Cos does not rest on their selection and use of methods of re-search better in themselves or nearer to ideal perfection. Their chief title to esteem is rather the insight they displayed in perceiving that the premises for the applica-tion of the deductive method were not yet extant, that they had not even come in view, and that fantastic con-ceptions were taking the place of the requisite and valid inductions. The pioneer virtues which distinguished the Coic masters from their opponents were a self-abnegation, and a timely renunciation of ambitions, fascinating enough and even exalted in themselves, but at that era and long afterwards out of reach, and these virtues entitle them to our ungrudging admiration at this day. We recognize their supreme merit in having developed, with tireless powers of observation and extraordinary faculties of clear sight and strong sense, those branches of the art of healing which were capable of extension without digging their foundations more deeply. Above all, we may specify their contributions to symptomatology which, by their endless supply of nice distinctions and acute observations, are a source of pleasure and instruction to modern students of that branch of learning.

Unfortunately, however, they could not wholly renounce the construction of comprehensive theories. They too dabbled in hypotheses which, as far as they went, were as fruitful of errors as those of their predecessors, and were only less fruitful because they did not go as far. Their humoural pathology, for instance, which is the hall-mark of the Hippocratic school, and which referred all internal diseases to the constitution and proportion of the four presumable cardinal humours, possesses, in the judgment of modern science, not a jot more truth than the anthropogony of the book " On Muscles " or the fictitious theory of matter which was combated in the treatise " On Old Medicine."

7. This, then, at least must be conceded. The genius of the physicians of Cos was fertile in generalizations of all kinds, whether true or false, and their motive-power may most probably be traced to the speculations of the nature-philosophers. This " old medicine " of the alleged reaction was no more the real old medicine than the France of the Restoration was the France of the Ancien Régime. The goal and trend of the movement were determined henceforth by the critical sense and sceptical genius of the Hippocratic school. At an early date it assumed as definite an attitude towards the supernatural theology as it had already assumed towards the fantastic excesses of some doctrines of the nature-philosophy, and towards those metaphysical theories which transgressed all bounds of experience.* Here, as elsewhere, we are struck by the contrast between Cos and Cnidus. The treatise " On the Nature of Women," which is as full of the influence of Cnidus as the larger work " On the Diseases of Women," to which it went back, exalts "the divine" and "divine things" to a place of differential superiority over and above all other factors. "The divine" is mentioned at the opening of the Hippocratic " Prognosticon " as an agent of occasional efficacy, so little removed from the operations of natural law, that physicians are expressly enjoined to take account of its activity in their "foresight." But in two productions of the Hippocratic school war was declared

* Bk. II. Ch. I. § 3, *fin.*

against all supernaturalism with extraordinary energy. The first of these passages is to be found in the book "On Water, Air, and Sites," which forms one of the most remarkable pieces of the Hippocratic collection. We are there listening to a man who had trodden the soil of South Russia as well as the valley of the Nile, whose critical eye had surveyed all sorts and conditions of circumstances, and whose thoughtful mind had endeavoured to weave the countless details to a uniform and consistent design. But his many valuable observations, his many partly premature conjectures about the connection between climate and health, between the succession of the seasons and the course of diseases, these were all surpassed by the undying honour that attached to the first attempt to establish a causal bond between the characters of nations and their physical conditions. We may call the writer of this treatise the precursor of Montesquieu, and the founder of national psychology. He it was who, in discussing the so-called "feminine disease" of the Scythians, uttered an energetic protest against the assertion that this or any other illness was the effect of a particular divine visitation, and in almost precisely the same words the notion was combated afresh in the treatise "On the Sacred Disease," by which name epilepsy was designated in popular superstition on account of its supposed divine origin. In both cases alike the denial of supernatural intervention was accompanied by an expression of belief in the strict compatibility of a uniform obedience to law in all natural phenomena with the religious faith in a divine fountain-head as the ultimate source of those phenomena. "Everything is divine and everything is human," thus ran the wonderfully suggestive formula invented by the author of the work "On the Sacred Disease;" and he added that it meant nothing more than that it is unreasonable to call one illness more divine than another. All alike were caused by the great natural agents of heat and cold, and sun and winds, all of which were divine in their nature, but no one of which in itself was "unfathomable and untractable" or removed from human insight and human influence. And a yet wider generalization was promulgated in the maxim, "The nature and cause of this illness arise from precisely the same divine from which all else proceeds"—a maxim reproduced by the writer of the book "On Water, Air, and Sites" in his statement of belief that "to me, too, these complaints appear divine, and all others likewise, since no one is more divine or more human than another. Each of them possesses nature [*i.e.* a natural cause], and no one of them originates without it." The more pugnacious author of the work on epilepsy gave vent to discursive and scornful attacks on the "windbags and street-corner prophets" who undertook to cure diseases by their superstitious practices of "purifications and incantations," who "sought to conceal their own ignorance and impotence under the mantle of the divine," and who might be shown in the clear light of day to disbelieve in the truth of their own teaching. This last was the sharpest barb in our author's quiver of invectives :

" For if these sufferings," he wrote, "could be cured by the purifications and the rest of the treatment they recommend, what should prevent their creation for the infliction of mankind by other similar contrivances? But then their cause would no longer be divine, but human, for the physician who is able to expel a disease by magical and purificatory means could introduce it by setting other means at work, and then there would be an end of the divine and of its efficacy."

The same argument was applied to the whole gamut of proceedings, which rested collectively, as he asserted, on the supposition that there were no gods, or that they were devoid of power :

" For if it were true," he wrote, "that a man could fetch down the moon and make the sun disappear, could summon the storm, and recall fair weather by sacrifices and the black arts, I should hold that there were nothing divine in all that, but that it were all human, for in such cases the power of the divinity would be subdued to the yoke of human intellect."

This treatise too, we may remark in parenthesis, is extremely notable for its reaffirmation of the significance of the brain in the physical and especially in the psychical life. The discovery had been made by Alcmæon,[*] but it was used here in its widest extension and with increased emphasis. As a physician our author, with his eclectic tendencies in philosophy, was not a pure Hippocratic, and he was led to this important digression by his discovery, which modern science has confirmed, that epilepsy springs from a disease of the central organ.

We might close the present section at this point. Nothing is lacking to the proof of the contention from which we set out—that the study of medicine was the source of the third great wave of criticism which poured its fertilizing stream over the fields of Greek learning. The authors of the book " On Old Medicine " and the two treatises we have just discussed were as free from every taint of mythical thought as Hecatæus or Xenophanes— as free, or actually freer. Nor were these heralds of the dawn content with banishing from their minds every appeal to primitive modes of thought. They differed from their predecessors, who had opened the epoch of transition, in not stopping at mere negation. They unlocked the doors of their reflection to positive methods of scientific research, and took as their guiding star the inspired maxim of Epicharmus, the philosophic playwright of Syracuse:

> " A sober sense of honest doubt
> Keeps human reason hale and stout."

Nor was this the limit of their achievement. By their theory of the gods, which was compatible with the untrammelled progress of knowledge, they paved the way for every conceivable advance ; but they further endeavoured to assist the advance themselves by their not inconsiderable successes in their special region of inquiry. The proportions of the present work do not, unfortunately, permit us to bring forward the evidence for this view, but we are reluctant to part from the precious collection of the Hippocratic writings, which are still so little known and appreciated, without offering a few more proofs of

[*] Cp. Bk. I. Ch. V. § 5, *init.*

the sound scientific spirit which penetrates a considerable portion of them. One of the most generous marks of that spirit is a respect and appreciation for great thoughts which derive their descent from an opposite or hostile school, and thus we find the valuable doctrine of the necessary equilibrium between exercise and nourishment, which was taught by the physicians of Cnidus, reappearing in the work "On Diet in Acute Illnesses," though it opened with a bitter polemic against the *chef d'œuvre* of that school, "The Cnidian Sentences." The author in that instance was as innocent of vain pretensions to originality as he was free from the vulgar eagerness for cheap and superficial triumphs. He displayed a genuine spirit of research in his endeavour to strengthen the doctrine which he was combating by fresh and weighty arguments, as when he wrote in one place, "my opponent's view will be assisted by the following consideration." No less sturdy and incorruptible was the instinct for the truth evinced by the author of the work "On the Joints," which Littré characterized as "the great surgical monument of antiquity and a model for all future ages." The writer, a physician of noble mind and lofty thought, did not shrink from recording his own failures for the information of his fellow-investigators. In the immortal language in which one such passage was composed, we read, "I have written this down deliberately, for it is valuable to learn of unsuccessful experiments, and to know the causes of their non-success." In that instance he was obviously anxious to withhold no means to knowledge from the service of those who came after him ; and in another he exceeded the wonted limits of didactic writing on account of his desire to protect the patient from any burden that could possibly be avoided :

"It may be urged," he wrote, "that such questions lie outside the precincts of medicine, for what profit is there in a further study of cases that have already become incurable ? Such arguments, I answer, are very wide of the mark. In curable cases all pains must be used to prevent their becoming incurable ; but incurable cases must be recognized as such, in order to save the sick man from useless maltreatment."

Nor was he otherwise disposed to spare his own exertions. He had the joy of work which is a true mark of genius. In this way he extended anatomical research from the human to the animal creation ; he compared the structure of the human skeleton with that of other vertebrate animals, and two passages in his work speak so eloquently of the grandeur of this attempt that we do not hesitate to entitle him an early if not the earliest pioneer of comparative anatomy. But we conclude by citing an important generalization due to the same powerful intellect, the brilliancy of which is testified by the wide range that it described, by the evidence, constantly increasing, of the truth of its contents, and by the deep significance of its consequences. We refer to the maxim touching the necessity of function for the preservation of health in an organ.

"All parts of the body," he wrote, "which are designed for a definite use are kept in health, and in the enjoyment of fair growth and of long youth, by the fulfilment of that use, and by their appropriate exercise in the employment to which they are accustomed. But when they are disused they grow ill and stunted, and become prematurely old."

CHAPTER II.

THE ATOMISTS.

1. AT an early date rumour was busily engaged in spinning threads of intercourse between "the father of medicine" and the man whom we may call the father of physics. The worthy citizens of Abdera had been alarmed by the strange conduct of their great countryman Democritus, so they summoned the master of the art of healing to examine his mental condition. The master came, convinced them of their error, and enjoyed an instructive intercourse with the sage, which was presently continued by letter. Their correspondence formed a romance in letters, which the Hippocratic collection has preserved to us, and which may to a certain extent be the mirror of genuine facts. It is at least in the highest degree probable that two philosophers born in the same year—460 B.C.—and both of them great travellers, should have been brought into personal contact. It is clear, too, that Hippocrates was actually at one time in Abdera. We are still able to accompany him on his round of professional visits that took him by turns to the Thracian Gate, the Sacred Way, and the High Street. And thus there may be an element of truth in the legendary picture of the house and garden in the shadow of a tower of the city wall, with the umbrageous plane-tree beneath whose spreading foliage the great sage of Abdera used to sit and write with his knee for a table, surrounded by his scrolls and by the anatomical specimens at which he was at work.

The wealthy commercial colony of Abdera had been

founded by Ionians. It was situated opposite the island of Thasos, in the neighbourhood of lucrative gold-mines on the borders of Thrace and Macedonia, and it played a short but exceptionally brilliant part in the history of Greek learning. It is associated with the name of Leucippus, the friend and teacher of Democritus, who was older than his pupil by a score or so of years. For, though the master was probably born at Miletus, and enjoyed instruction, according to trustworthy evidence, at Elea, under the sharp-witted Zeno, yet he certainly died in the city of Abdera, and founded there the school to which his disciple Democritus lent imperishable fame. The figure of the teacher has been dwarfed by the giant proportions of the pupil, and his few literary remains were included in the comprehensive collection of the works of Democritus. Even in antiquity, his personality and the more intimate circumstances of his life were so little known, that doubts were even expressed as to his historical reality. Still, we may assert, on the evidence of few witnesses but fit, that Leucippus devised the plan of the building which Democritus completed, adorning it with an inexhaustible wealth of facts based on experience, and composing it with a literary art which made him a master of Greek prose. To Leucippus we owe the sentence in which the universal rule of causation was proclaimed in unequivocal language: "Nothing happens without a cause, but everything with a cause and by necessity." His book, "On the Order of the Universe," which, to distinguish it from the smaller compendium on the same subject by Democritus, was known as "The Great Order of the Universe," contained the essence of atomic physics, and his treatise "On the Mind," doubtless supplied the outline of the psychology of the school. Time has robbed us of the privilege of considering apart the intellectual legacies of these two men. We are therefore compelled to renounce such distinctions, and to discuss the atomic theory as a whole. But we may pause at the outset, to glance at the personal characteristics of its younger and far more famous representative.

We possess some valuable material for this purpose, and our first evidence may be taken down at the lips of Democritus himself.

"I am the most travelled," he wrote, "of all my contemporaries; I have extended my field of inquiry wider than any one else; I have seen more countries and climes, and have heard more speeches of learned men. No one has surpassed me in the composition of lines accompanied by demonstration, not even the Egyptian knotters of ropes, or geometers."

The emphasis that was laid here on the mere scope of his culture and achievements is in full accord with our conception of the man in whom we recognize less of the initiative faculty of invention than of the erudition that continues and expands it. Nor should we be repelled by the boastful tone that is taken. Lessing said, with a very slight exaggeration, that "politeness was a thing unknown to the ancients," and his saying might be transferred to modesty with even better right. Besides the example before us, the instance of Empedocles will be fresh in our readers' memory, and there is, further, the case of Thucydides, whose cooler judgment weighed his words more carefully, and who yet did not hesitate to entitle his history "a possession for all time." Moreover, Plato himself, who eclipses himself in his Dialogues so completely behind Socrates his master, felt no constraint in quoting a verse in which he and his brothers were described as "the god-like issue of a glorious father." Another circumstance, too, should be taken in account in considering the self-praise of Democritus. He appears as long as he lived to have enjoyed a purely local reputation. "I came to Athens, and no one knew me," so runs a second fragment of autobiography, and it may well have been his resentment at finding himself still unknown in the capital of the Greek intellect, despite his enormous exertions and achievements, that induced him to blow his own trumpet. Be that as it may, his fame was at least well earned. He had trodden with equal vigour all the paths of learning, from mathematics and physics to ethics and poetics. His writings were almost innumerable, and we may quote the testimony of Aristotle to the intellectual value of their contents. That most competent and impartial critic did not hesitate to declare of Democritus that no one before him had " dealt with growth and change except in the most superficial way." In this connection he spoke of him as a man who seemed " to have thought about everything." And not his piety towards his master Plato, not the deep gulf of dissent that divided him from the atomists, prevented him from crowning Democritus and Leucippus at the expense of Plato with an incomparable crown of eulogy. Their theory of nature, too—such is the drift of his remarks—was marred by great defects, but it was based on an hypothesis ripe with valuable conclusions. The following was the difference to be noted. The habit of natural observation induced the faculty of building hypotheses to connect long series of facts with one another. That faculty was diminished by predominant intercourse with mere concepts which alienates us from reality, contracts our vision on a narrow circle of facts, and leads us through such straits of observation to the formation of inadequate theories.

2. With that "hypothesis" we are now concerned. Its non-hypothetical basis, however, must be our first consideration. It belongs to the theory of knowledge and to the attempt to solve the problem of matter. We left that problem in a parlous condition in the hands of Anaxagoras, and have lost sight of it since then. It was torn asunder by claims of equal weight which were at once unreconciled and irreconcilable.* One of two courses was open to it—to renounce either qualitative constancy or the internal inter-dependence of substances. The alternative left was between one or very few elements of desultorily changing qualities and numberless primary substances foreign to one another and with no kind of bond of relationship, nor was there any other choice. We have already remarked by anticipation that the school of Abdera came to the rescue here, and put an end to that fatal dilemma.* The glory of the act, as

* Cp. Bk. II. Ch. IV. § 4.

Aristotle leads us to believe, belongs to the mind of Leu-cippus, but we know the epoch-making theory only in the form in which it was clothed by Democritus. " According to convention," he said, " there are a sweet and a bitter, a hot and a cold, and according to convention there is colour. In truth there are atoms and a void." Let us first leave the atoms and the vacuum out of account, and then turn to the significant negative portion of the passage. We say "the negative portion," because the stress laid on what exists in truth can imply nothing else than that the first-named qualities, temperature, colour, and taste, and, let us add, smell and sound, are denied objective truth. In this connection the expression "according to conven-tion " requires a few words to make it clear. The contrast between nature and convention was familiar to the intel-lectual life of that age. Men's conventions—their habits, customs, and laws—changing and varying from city to city, from country to country, and from generation to generation, were then a favourite type of contrast with the unchangeableness of nature. Thus convention became as it were the symbol of the changeable, the arbitrary, and the accidental. With respect to the perceptions of the senses, there were numerous observations at the disposal of Demo-critus to convince him of their dependence on the respective constitutions of individuals, on the variations in the conditions of the same individual, and, finally, on the multifarious forms assumed by the same particles of matter. Thus a jaundiced subject feels a bitter taste in honey, the degree of cold or heat in air or water is determined by whether or not we ourselves are warm, many minerals display different colours before and after pulverization, and so forth through countless examples. We who command the resources of a modern vocabulary have learnt to express these differences in more appropriate language. We distinguish between relative and absolute qualities, between subjective and objective truth. Our analysis has struck deeper roots. It has discovered at least a subjective element in the so-called objective or primary qualities of things, and, on the other hand, it has left us no shadow of doubt that the production of the infinite varieties of subjective impressions is not an anarchical process, but is indissolubly bound by strict laws of causation. The discovery of that subjective element in the objective qualities of things will occupy us at a later period, when we reach the so-called Cyrenaic philosophers, of whom Berkeley and Hume were the intellectual heirs, and we shall presently see that Democritus, no less than his modern successors, Thomas Hobbes or John Locke, was familiar with the second of these discoveries. Nay, even the indefeasible validity of the law of causation as taught by Leucippus admitted no exception whatsoever. On the present occasion, however, Democritus was merely concerned to give utterance as emphatically and unreservedly as possible to a novel truth of fundamental importance. A striking parallel is supplied by the manner in which another and perhaps yet greater thinker seized and expressed the same fundamental principle. The following words, in which it might be erroneous to trace the influence of Democritus, occur in the polemic entitled, "The Assayer," and written * by Galileo Galilei :—

"If I represent a material or bodily substance to myself, I cannot but represent it as bounded by limits and as possessed of this or that shape, ... situated in this or that spot, ... as at rest or in motion, as touched or not touched by another body," and so forth. At the same time he was equally convinced "that those tastes, smells, colours, etc., in relation to the object in which they appear to reside are nothing but mere names (*non sieno altro che puri nomi*)."

Across the twenty-two centuries that stretched between these giants of thought Democritus and Galilei were both fully aware that the so-called secondary qualities of things were more than mere arbitrary assumptions, conventional opinions, or appellations. Still, their agreement was not confined to the promulgation of that highly important distinction. They agreed, too, in proclaiming it in a manner

* 1623 A.D.

which was eminently liable to produce a false and misleading impression, so far, at least, as it was not corrected
by other of their own utterances. And seldom or never,
we may add, have new fundamental truths made their
entry in the world, or even in the minds of their inventors,
in a less objectionable form.

But it is full time to pass from the outward shape of
the doctrine to the more interesting consideration of its
intrinsic meaning. Its appearance meant the disappearance of the stumbling-block at which investigation had
halted so long. The maturity of research had arrived,
and it was no longer a matter of vexation that the leaf
which was green to-day should be yellow to-morrow and
brown the day after. The old obstacles were removed
from the path of the inquirer, and he saw with indifference
that the blossom faded and that its fragrance departed, or
that the savour of fruit was turned to gall when it began
to rot. Moreover, Zeno's paradox of the grain of millet
lost its point and perplexed no one any more, for all these
qualities of things were divested of their objective validity,
and were expelled from the realm of reality. Here, we
may remark in parenthesis, we perceive a clue to the
possibility that Leucippus had received from Zeno the
impulse that led to his solution of the problem of matter.
But be that as it may, a true, solid, unchangeable object
of cognition in the corporeal world had at last been
gained, and persistent matter stood out as the genuine
reality in opposition to the volatile and variable qualities
of sensation which we call secondary, and which are not
properly the attributes of objects. The individual bodies,
as the constituent parts of such matter, were distinguished from one another by their sizes and shapes alone,
inclusive of their degree of capacity, determined by the
size and shape, to exert an effect on other bodies by impact
and pressure.

These fundamental differences of bodies have been expressed more clearly by Democritus with respect, too, to their
reciprocal relations. He drew the following distinctions,
which he stamped with particular technical terms. Thus

there were (1) the shape, including size, we may add ; (2) the arrangement ; and (3) the position of bodies. When Aristotle took up the theme, he visualized these three conceptions by examples which he borrowed from the shapes of the letters in the Greek alphabet. The difference of shape he illustrated by the opposition of A and N ; that of arrangement, which Democritus called "contact," by the double symbol of AN and NA; and that of position, which Democritus called "turning," by the conversion of N to Z. It must be remarked, however, that Democritus was not considering the great material structures which rise into the sphere of visibility and were spoken of by him as "apparent to the eye ; " he had in view rather the minutest constituent parts of those structures, which were no longer perceptible, but were merely to be inferred under the names of "atoms," or "indivisibles." It may be asked how he and Leucippus reached their assumption of atoms and their peculiar employment of the conception of a vacuum ; nor can this question be answered without reminding the reader of some part of their former knowledge. For here, as elsewhere, their theory was the sum of the labours of their predecessors. Atomism, we may state with all possible emphasis, was the ripe fruit on the tree of the old doctrine of matter which had been tended by the Ionian physiologists.

We revert, then, to the Ionian schools. When Anaximenes explained the changes in the form of his primary matter by condensation and rarefaction, when he taught that its fundamental form proceeded intact from each successive variation, the thought must plainly have dawned on him that minute imperceptible particles were there at work, now coming closer together and now departing from one another.* Again, when Heraclitus proclaimed his doctrine of the ceaseless transformation of things, and declared the uninjured existence of an individual object to be a mere delusion brought about by the constant accession of fresh particles in the place of those that had been severed, he was obviously assuming the presence of

* Bk. I. Ch. I. § 4.

invisible parts of matter as well as of their invisible movements.* And finally, when Anaxagoras complained of the
"weakness" of our senses, when he combined in every
corporeal structure an infinite number of "seeds" or of the
minutest primary particles, and made the appearance of the
structure depend on the predominance of one sort of those
particles,† he was stating in unambiguous words the very
doctrine which inference alone enables us to attribute to his
two predecessors. Nor, indeed, do we feel the remotest
surprise at the early appearance of beliefs which must have
been induced every day and all day by common observation. Take, for instance, the example of a piece of linen or
cloth which has been soaked by the rain and dried by the
returning sun ; the watery particles with which it was
drenched have taken their departure, though no eye saw
them departing. Or take the example of a scent-bottle
which has perfumed the room in which it is kept, though no
one has seen the particles that convey the fragrance distribu-
ting themselves through the room, while its contents have
nevertheless been gradually diminished. These experiences
and others of equally frequent occurrence secured the admission of invisible ways or paths besides the invisible particles
and movements, breaking through the apparently uninterrupted consistency of bodies. We would further remind
our readers that the kindred conception of vacant spaces
emptied of matter, which was probably due to the Pythagoreans, had already been known to Parmenides, and had
formed an objective of his energetic attack.‡

These two agents, invisible moving particles and
invisible vacant interstices, comprised, as it were, the raw
material for the atomistic theory. It derived its form
and shape from two ideal factors. We refer to the twin
postulates of matter which we have already discussed to
satiety, and which we may claim with equal right as the
contribution of the philosophers of Ionia. Parmenides was
indeed the first to have moulded them to a definite
shape, but the postulate of quantitative constancy was

* Bk. I. Ch. I. § 5.   † Bk. II. Ch. IV. § 2.
‡ Bk. II. Ch. II. § 4, and cp. § 5 below.

the key to the whole doctrine of primary matter, and had originated and controlled all the attempts at moulding this doctrine from Thales downwards. With regard to the second postulate of qualitative constancy, we have already discovered its earliest traces in Anaximenes; next, we saw it developed to its full extent in Anaxagoras, who agreed with the Eleatics in no other point, and was diametrically opposed to them on every important question, whereas Empedocles, who was demonstrably a disciple of the school of Parmenides, laid far less stress on that postulate, and employed it in a far less perfect form. When we reach Leucippus we find that he clung with the utmost rigour to both these postulates, the fulfilment of which was correctly conceived as the indispensable condition of the steady process of nature in the kingdom of corporeal existence. Still, the rigour displayed by Leucippus did not mislead him either to deny nature like Parmenides or to do violence to her like Anaxagoras. We may reserve our opinion as to whether or not he was aware that even these most important postulates are at bottom nothing but questions addressed to nature by the inquirer ; nor are we certain that he supported the new doctrine merely by sound conclusions drawn from empiric facts. For we cannot neglect the temptation that besets many great discoverers. They are not content to build their most splendid achievements on the only trustworthy foundation of knowledge—experience ; they prefer to try to increase their certainty by resting them on pretended necessities of thought. Something of this kind might not unreasonably be expected from the pupil of Zeno the metaphysician. But be that as it may—and we shall revert to it later—the one decisive factor is still lacking to complete our account of the origin of the atomic theory. We have marked the conceptions of the indestructibility and unchangeableness of matter contained in its twin postulates, and we have now to add a physical insight of the utmost value. We refer to the recognition of the impenetrability of matter. Experiments of the kind, one of which we saw attempted by Anaxagoras,* must have led to the promotion

* Bk. II. Ch. IV. § 1 *fin.*

of this quality as a universal attribute of substances. The resistance offered to every attempt at compression by the air contained in the inflated bag selected as an example by Anaxagoras must have led to the perception of a palpable and rapidly increasing resistance. And with that perception a fresh difficulty arose. It was a difficulty which could not have arisen as long as the homogeneous character of the material world, so far from being known, was obscured and disguised by the difference of the states of aggregation. When the air is at rest, or nearly so, no obstacle worth mentioning, certainly no impassable obstacle, opposes the movement of our body. But then came experiments of the kind tried by Anaxagoras, to which may be added the test applied by Empedocles to confirm the pressure of the atmosphere and the theories of matter resting doubtless on kindred observations, especially that of Anaximenes, which deprived the difference in the states of aggregation of its fundamental significance. With these facts and doctrines that difficulty could no longer be overlooked. It was no longer feasible to doubt that one was dealing with impenetrable matter, whether air, or water, or solid bodies, and the question necessarily arose—How was movement within that region possible at all? Other questions suggested themselves as the corollaries of this problem. Whence came, it was asked, the remarkable differences of resistance offered to one and the same movement in different media? How did it happen that a flying arrow met with no noticeable opposition from the air, but was impassably resisted by a rock? At this point the theory of a vacuum, which, as we have seen, was not wholly new, afforded a welcome outlet to the bewilderment of thought. The material world, it was argued, was not continuous ; rather it consisted of separate impenetrable nuclei divided from one another by empty penetrable interstices. Inasmuch and in so far as one impenetrable nucleus could give way to another, therefore, and to that extent, motion was possible. And such motion would take place with case or difficulty or not at all, according as the constitution and the distances of such nuclei rendered it easy, difficult, or impossible for one to give way to another. Those atoms or units of matter were actually inseparable, though not ideally indivisible or unextended in space. Their minuteness caused them to escape observation, and it was their indestructibility, unchangeableness, and impenetrability which really invested matter with those qualities. The complex was the aggregate of its simple parts, and the shape and size of the primary particles gave the key to the attributes of the composite body.

3. Words fail us to express the value and importance of this great doctrine. We must begin by speaking of the services which the theory was calculated to render, and which it actually has rendered, to the cause of modern science. It will then be time enough to consider the imperfections of its oldest form and of its earliest employment. It explains spatial movement of every kind. It makes it compatible with the impenetrability of matter, and it unravels the processes of motion in every sort and degree, whether they are enacted in universal space or in a drop of water. Its clear light is shed on the differences of the three states of aggregation. The same groups of atoms or molecules of a fluid are contracted under the influence of cold, and coalesce in a solid body; they are segregated under the influence of heat and volatilized in a gas. Nothing but the external and superficial appearance contradicts any more the indestructibility of matter. The growth of an apparently new material structure is revealed as the union of a hitherto distributed complexus of atoms, its decay as the separation of a complexus hitherto united. We advance from the mechanics of masses —the relations of movement and equilibrium in comprehensive groups of atoms—to the mechanics of atoms and of the groups immediately superior to them, the minutest atomic combinations, or the molecules with which chemistry deals. The proportions of weight and volume in such a combination of several substances would often be numerous, but would never show arbitrary variations, and this fact of their fixed recurrence is explained by modern science by the theory of equivalents, or atomic

weights, which meant that a fixed number of atoms of one kind entered in combination with a fixed number of atoms of another kind or of several other kinds. The qualities of sense in a body, and in part its physical attributes, are necessarily dependent on the relations of position and the conditions of movement in its minutest parts. Nothing, then, would be more natural than a change of colour, for instance, in the same collection of similar atoms according to the disposition of the atomic groups or molecules. Thus by allotropy common phosphorus is yellow and amorphous phosphorus is red. The same observation holds good of chemical combinations. By the law of isomery the qualities vary according to the structure of the compound though the same atoms be mixed in precisely the same proportions. "According to the manner in which the atoms are disposed," we may add, in the words of Fechner, "the object will assume different qualities in different directions (differences of expansion, foliation, hardness, and so forth)." But the atomic theory applied to chemistry is not as simple as it sounds. The relation of the qualities of a compound to those of its constituent parts can never be quite perspicuous. Deep-going changes take place at the entry of substances into a chemical combination. They are condensed, for instance, or their latent heat is released, or some other result is effected with all the consequences it entails. We have no right, therefore, to expect that the qualities of the compound will be the sum of those of its ingredients, and neither more nor less. John Stuart Mill, for example, was not the only great thinker who has been startled into questioning the perfectibility of chemistry by such facts as that the qualities of water are not merely the total of those of oxygen and hydrogen, nor the colour of blue sulphate of copper a mere mixture of the colours of sulphuric acid and copper. These facts, however, as we have just shown reason to believe, by no means contradict the view that the atoms in a compound remain precisely the same as they were before they entered it, and as they will be after they emerge from it. Even now direct proof can be offered of the continuous unchanged condition of some of their

qualities, and recent science has begun to smooth the way
for the accumulation of fresh evidence of that kind, as well
as for the more comprehensive illustration of the causal
dependence of the qualities of a compound on those of
their constituents. Thus the specific heat of elements
persists in their combinations, the power of carbon to
refract light is maintained in carbon compounds, and other
proofs of the connection between the qualities of a compound
and those of its parts are constantly coming to light. We
should add that it is occasionally possible to foretell the
qualities of a compound not yet experimentally produced.
Without multiplying this evidence, enough will have been
said to show that chemistry, resting as it does wholly on
the atomic theory, approximates more and more closely to
that stage of perfection in which deduction or inference
replaces the crude method of empiricism. Quite recently,
indeed, it has succeeded in deriving physical qualities of
elements, such as their extensibility, fusibility, and volatility,
from the weight and volume of the respective atoms ; and
even in rivalling the astounding feats of astronomy, by
foretelling the existence and the nature of elements, and
in subsequently confirming its predictions by actual discovery. Here, then, we pause. We have seen enough of
the record of the atomic theory to appreciate Cournot's
dictum to the full measure of its truth : " None of the ideas
that antiquity has bequeathed to us has had a greater or
even a similar success." Nor is the modern atomic theory
a mere sister-doctrine to that of Leucippus and Democritus :
it is rather its direct descendant, flesh of its flesh and
bone of its bone. It is difficult to determine how far
Galilei, the founder of modern natural science,* who was
certainly acquainted with the teachings of Democritus, was
influenced by them, and how far he thought out anew for
himself some of their fundamental principles. But we
know that René Descartes† was obliged to meet the reproach
that that portion of his theory was nothing but a "patchwork of tags from Democritus," and Pierre Gassendi,‡ the
French dean and prebendary, who finally introduced the

---

* Born 1564. † Born 1596. ‡ Born 1592.

atomic theory in modern physics, was directly inspired by the study of the teachings, writings, and the life of Epicurus, who walked in the footsteps of Leucippus and Democritus, and contributed very materially to their better understanding and appreciation.

The atomic theory looks back on a long and eventful history, which has lately been narrated in a manner as pleasant as it is thoughtful, though, unfortunately, the narrative does not take account of the rudiments of the doctrine. It is not our intention to discuss its changes and transformations, nor yet the objections that have been levelled at it by the so-called dynamic philosophers. We shall confine our attention to a few of the chief differences between ancient and modern atomism. Contemporary physics no longer admit the conception of a vacuum. Ether has taken its place, and the assumption has shown itself of far greater service in the explanation of natural processes. But in the decisive point before us both conceptions are found completely to coincide. Ether, no less than the vacuum, is absolutely penetrable, since absolute elasticity is ascribed to it ; the impenetrable substances are imbedded in it, as it were ; it surrounds them and encloses them. A second distinction with still more important consequences is the following. The chemistry of our day does its work with seventy-odd elements, and modern chemists believe—especially since the discovery of "the natural series" of the elements—that their number will be considerably diminished in the future, and that the whole collection will in all probability ultimately be reduced to a single primary element. Leucippus, on the contrary, had felt himself compelled to assume an infinite variety of the atoms in respect to their size and shape, though in no other relation. His hypothesis accordingly proved more serviceable than it appeared in the conception of its author, and this is not his least title to renown. The number of qualitative differences due merely to variations in the number and disposition of the atoms combined on each occasion in one structure was proved incalculably larger than was dreamed of by Leucippus and Democritus.

Alcohol and sugar, for example, are so distinct in appearance and effect that no one could ever have conjectured that both are compounded out of the same three kinds of atoms merely in different proportions. Muscarine, again, is a deadly poison, and neurine is a substance to be found in all animal and vegetable cells, and yet the one differs from the other merely by a single atom's weight of oxygen. These and similar facts were as foreign to them as that the inexhaustible multiplicity of organic structures is for the most part to be referred to four different kinds of atoms in their various proportions and dispositions. The question leaps to the lips, why, in that case, those atomists were not satisfied with a more modest hypothesis ; and it is reasonable to reply that their exaggeration was a kind of reaction against the popular and unscientific conception of the material world, and, further, in the instance of Democritus, against the doctrine of matter associated with the name of Anaxagoras. "There is no need," cried the authors of the new theory to their opponents, "there is no need of your assumption of innumerable qualitative differences ; not a single such difference need really be assumed. Differences in the size and shape of the primary substance are in themselves completely adequate to explain the inexhaustible multitude of the differences of phenomena." With this declaration an immense step was taken towards simplifying fundamental hypotheses. At a single blow the lavishness of nature had been checked on the qualitative side. Was she also to be impelled to thrift on the quantitative side ? At first there was no necessity for this measure. The whole object of the founders of the doctrine was to adapt the new hypothesis to the most ambitious and even to exaggerated demands, and it was surely not too much to expect that nature would display in this important instance the same wealth and lavishness which she showed in other respects. Measure and limit would only be imposed by the gradual growth of positive knowledge. Moreover, though the theory of Democritus recognized isolated instances of double atoms, yet in general it excluded the conception of groups of atoms or molecules.

The atom itself had to fulfil the task that is performed in modern science by the molecule, and its richer variety was an obvious condition. We do not dispute that this part of the hypothetical structure may have been equipped with too generous a hand, but we would urge that at least the wealth was not squandered, but was applied in the most lucrative manner possible. All physical differences of simple substances were referred without any exception to those differences of size and shape. Democritus felt himself on sure enough ground to dispense with any other assumption of distinctions. It is true that we are insufficiently informed on some points important to this inquiry. But we are acquainted with his explanation of specific gravity, which he derived entirely from the greater or less density of the material structure. If of two bodies with the same volume one were lighter than the other, the one would contain a larger vacuum than the other. Here, however, a difficulty arose. According to the premise the hardness of the body would likewise have to increase and decrease with its density, and with its density alone. And some explanation was required for instances where the hardness and the specific gravity did not go together. Thus iron, for instance, is harder than lead, but lead is heavier than iron. A further ingenious expedient here came to the philosopher's aid. He accounted for this contradiction by fixing the responsibility on a difference in the distribution of the vacuum. A piece of lead, Democritus contended, contained more body and less vacuum than a piece of iron of the same size, otherwise its weight could not be greater. But the distribution of the vacuum in the lead must, he argued, be more equable, the solid matter must be interrupted by more numerous though by smaller empty interstices, otherwise its hardness could not be less.

4. We have no exact information as to which bodies in the theory of Democritus were simple and which were complex. The rays of enlightenment break through at two points only of what we may term his physiology of the senses. In the light of those rays, we may assert with confidence at least one negative conclusion. The infinite

multiplicity which he recognized in the sizes and shapes of atoms did not arise from his incompetence to perceive or to conjecture a complex in an apparently simple body. Thus his eminently noteworthy theory of colours, which, parenthetically remarked, is in dire need of fresh expert treatment, started from the assumption of four primary colours—white, black, red, and green. These, with the exception of green, which had taken the place of yellow, were likewise the primary colours in the scheme of Empedocles. All other colours were designated as mixed, and we see that all the numerous bodies which were not equipped with one of the four primary colours must have been of a composite nature. That is to say, they must have included other than merely homogeneous elementary particles. Passing to Democritus' attempt to explain the difference in the impressions of taste, we find that it was based in principle on the differences in the shape, and secondarily on those of the size of the atoms contained in the respective substances. Pungency he derived from sharp or pointed particles of matter, sweetness from the rounded form of moderately big particular atoms, and the same doctrine was applied to tartness, saltness, bitterness, and all other impressions of the palate. First, let us advert to these explanatory attempts, based on mere vague resemblances between impressions of taste and touch. That they were fallacious is beyond dispute, and their clumsiness may excite our surprise. But our readers may be inclined to temper their justice with mercy if they recollect that practically the same theories of the differences of taste as depending on the differences in the shapes of particular atoms were current in the eighteenth century, and enjoyed a well-nigh unchallenged authority, as we learn from Alexander von Humboldt's "Essay on the stimulated nervous and muscular fibre." The point on which our interest is concentrated, however, is rather the relation of those theories to the doctrine of simple and complex substances. The statements about the atomic forms underlying the several tastes give rise at first to the impression that each of the countless "juices" or materials of taste is composed of homogeneous atoms possessing the size and shape required for the purpose. But this, we plainly perceive, was not the opinion of Democritus. His own view of the mixed colours cries against it. The homogeneity of the atoms was admissible in the case of white salt, but it was not admissible in that of yellow-gold honey or of brownish-yellow human bile. It is true that he must have referred the sweetness of the one and the bitterness of the other to the presence of the atomic forms by which those impressions were produced. But yellow and brown were mixed colours in his theory, and he must accordingly have inferred that honey and bile alike contained atoms of other forms as well. The true meaning of those statements should therefore be expressed as follows: In all substances of mixed colours at least the kind of atoms which lends them their specific taste is merely the predominant and preponderant kind, and without wasting more words on this subject, Theophrastus, who is our best authority for Democritus' theory of sensation, relates that this doctrine was expressly taught by him.

We pass from individual atoms to atomic groups. These were regarded by Democritus as combinations or concatenations, in the literal sense of that word. Their contact in his eyes was the result of their being linked or "hooked" together, and the infinite variety of shapes which the atoms possessed in the theory of Democritus helped him to account for such processes. He drew instructive distinctions between the gregarious capacities of his atoms. Some were unsociable particles, affording no handle for combination except by enclosing them in a shell; others were supplied with hooks and eyes, with balls and sockets, with involuted edges, with mortice and dovetail, or with some other of the countless means of rendering them attachable, some at one and others at two points. This last distinction, with certain similar differences, was presumably intended to account for the greater or less degree of mobility in the particular atoms, their faster or looser combination, and for the corresponding nature of the complex body in each instance. The last echo of this mode of explaining chemical combinations was heard in Descartes and Huyghens, and since then its voice has grown unfamiliar. But at the same time we should remember that the conceptions of chemical affinity which have partially replaced this crude mechanical view are equally inadequate to their task ; that they enjoy their existence as mere conveniences of expression, as plausible fictions, or, to quote a modern chemical philosopher, as phrases " in the room of a clear conception." We may further remark that contemporary science is more and more under the sway of the doctrine of contact—albeit through the medium of ether—instead of that of attraction, to explain the union of particles, a revolution of thought which may be traced to Huyghens' important " Discourse on the Cause of Gravity " (1690). But, despite these considerations, we might still apostrophize Democritus in Pascal's dictum anent the Cartesian theory of matter: " Roughly we may say that this happens through shape and motion, but to presume these and to set the machine at work . . . that is uncertain, useless, and idle trouble."

Let us now see how out of the infinitesimally small arose the infinitely great. The atoms fit for combination flit about in empty space and occasionally meet one another. They are woven to larger wholes till they gradually form a shell which encloses and imprisons the hosts of free, errant atoms, and thus, severing themselves from the infinite vacuum, they finally become a separate world or cosmos, of which there are infinitely many. These are constructed where all the conditions favourable to their growth are found, and they are destroyed and revert to their constituent parts as soon as the conditions cease to be favourable. But for a cosmos such as that familiar to our experience the presence of enormous atomic groups and their combination on the largest scale do not suffice ; the discrimination of the substances on an equal scale is also requisite. No mere conglomeration of vagabond atoms, but a collection of groups of matter few in number but wholly or nearly homogeneous, is the spectacle that meets our eyes—heaven and earth, and the wide expanse of ocean. The old riddle was set to the atomists, and they found a new, though not a completely new, answer. Empedocles had constructed the universe by the attraction of like to like, and his solution was now revived, though in a somewhat altered form. For Democritus also recognized a regulative principle in the universe in the endeavour of like substances to consort with like. But he did not dismiss it as inaccessible to explanation or as an ultimate fact requiring none. He sought to understand it and to discover its cause ; and, seeing that the problem was material, he looked for a physical or a mechanical cause. He saw homogeneous substances collected together in groups ; one particle of earth lay next to another, one drop of water found a sister-drop, and these observations ranged themselves in his mind with the fact that the atoms or atomic groups which determined the qualities of earth, water, and so forth, had once been united and agglomerated in immense masses. Thus he found himself confronted with a problem which he was at pains to solve. His solution may be expressed in axiomatic language as follows : Particles of equal size and shape have an equal power of reaction, and particles of different sizes and shapes have a relatively different power of reaction. Reflecting on the great processes which have lent our world its present appearance, Democritus recalled the effects produced by the winnowing-fan or by the tide breaking on the seashore. The heterogeneous grains swung to and fro by the farmer with the winnowing-fan in his hand would be sifted and separated owing, in the opinion of Democritus, to the consequent current of air. "Lentils lie next to lentils, barley to barley, and wheat to wheat." And a similar effect was to be remarked on the seashore, where "the movement of the waves flung long stones next to long stones, and round pebbles next to round pebbles."

The vortex of atoms played in cosmic processes the part of the winnowing-fan and the tide. The sidewise contact of moving chains of atoms in any part of space produced a rotatory or whirling movement which affected the two chains in the first instance, and next extended itself to the neighbouring tissues of atoms till it finally sifted and severed all the agglomerated masses. The axiom mentioned above governed this process of separation in so far that atoms of similar size and shape reacted in a similar manner on the impulse they received, the resistance increasing and diminishing according to the size of the primary particles. Nor was it only the attraction of like substances — watery particles situated next to watery, particles of air next to particles of air, and so forth—that was traced to this cause. It accounted further for the order of the masses thus agglomerated, inasmuch as their resistance to the motory impulse would be weaker or stronger according as the particles were smaller in size and more mobile in shape, or larger in size and less mobile in shape. Therefore the mass of earth, composed of the atoms which were larger and less mobile, formed the central point, and the ether, consisting of the smaller and rounded particles of fire, formed the exterior shell of the cosmos that was thus composed. It is about ten years since this cosmogonic doctrine was correctly interpreted by two independent investigators, each of whom succeeded in clearing away the accumulated parasites of centuries of error, and in restoring the thoughts of Leucippus and Democritus in their pristine purity. But the admirable services of these two writers were defective at one point. Neither of them noted that the use of the vortex as the vehicle of cosmic order was by no means an innovation on the part of the atomists. We have met with similar assumptions in Anaxagoras as well as in Empedocles, and we can name the common source from which all these speculations were derived with at least a high degree of probability. We refer to Anaximander of Miletus, the patriarch of cosmogonic speculation. His were the assumptions based on experiments with the slingstone which we mentioned in the first chapter of this work, and the Anaximandrian parentage of this theory is vouched for in a passage from Aristotle. But important as these signs of agreement are, the differences that meet us in the employment of this aid to cosmogony are no less remarkable. Anaxagoras traced the first impulse of the rotatory movement to an immaterial or at least a half-material principle. The masses which had hitherto been huddled together in wild confusion were extricated by that principle, relieved of their internal friction, and enabled to follow the bias of their specific gravity and to sort themselves in due order. We cannot determine at what point Empedocles discovered the first impulse in his process of motion, which likewise produced a vortex and caused the separation of the material mass conglomerated hitherto in the one "divine ball." Certain it is, however, that his mechanical process served the purpose of Discord—one of his two powers not inherent in matter. But no trace of this dependence was preserved by the atomists. The cosmogonic process was the means to no preconceived end whatsoever ; it did not spring from the intention of a Nous forming the universe, nor was it the emanation of any other power regulating and controlling phenomena. It was due wholly and solely to natural forces, in the strictest sense of the word, which were immanent in matter itself. It was an assumption purely due to the need of scientific explanation, and its only object was to supply without reservation or prejudice a satisfactory answer to the question, how could it happen that here and there in the infinite expanse of empty space, and at this and that point in the extent of infinite time, there should have occurred that severance and disposition of material masses of which the world that surrounds us is obviously no isolated instance ? We must pause here to illustrate the misunderstandings that accrued at an early date to a portion of the atomists' answer.

In our opening remarks in this context we spoke of atoms flitting about in the vacuum. We related how, in the theories of Leucippus and Democritus, hosts of such atoms would meet together, how those suited for combination would then be combined, and how those not so suited would partly at least be kept together by a shell of atomic tissues, and thus preserved from total dispersion. Finally, we have considered the mobile complexes of atoms whose sidewise impact on one another produced the cosmogonic vortex. Two questions here arise, one of detail and the other of principle. The first relates to the vortex and to the effects ascribed to it. For these effects were the precise contrary of what they should have been by the laws of physics. The centrifugal force which is released by a rotatory movement is doubtless admirably adapted to sift an agglomerated mass of matter. But, as every centrifugal machine would show, it is the heaviest substances which are hurled to the greatest distance. Anaximander, whose theory we have just mentioned, would appear to have been aware of this, and the essentially deductive bias of his genius drew direct inferences from his observations of everyday centrifugal movements to the effects of similar forces which he conceived to be at work in the formation of the world. The successors of Anaximander would appear to have been alarmed at the audacity of thought which connected the immensely great with the minutely small. So in adopting the hypothesis of rotation they looked for more exact parallels in their earthly experience to the cosmogonic vortex. Such a parallel they discovered in the region of meteorological phenomena, and they were promptly misled by their discovery. An eddy of comparative strength, like that not unfrequently produced in Greece by the summer north winds, would carry away lighter objects, though it was too weak to lift heavier ones as well. Further, the motion of every whirlwind takes an inward direction as it approaches the ground in consequence of the friction there ensuing, so that a heap of matter is actually deposited at its centre which remains unmoved. Thus the erroneous belief might arise that such consequences were inherent to a vortex-like movement as such, and that they must have accompanied the motion of the supposed cosmic vortex as well.

Of far greater importance is the question of the causes of all these movements and inhibitions of movements. It was a question which perplexed thought at an early date, and gave rise to the most notable protests with which the atomic theory has had to contend. To a certain, indeed to a very great, extent, a direct. satisfactory, and luminous answer was available. The factors borrowed from experience and conceived as efficacious in those cosmical processes were impact, pressure, counter-shock, and resistance, increasing with the mass. It may be fatal to the atomic theory in its customary form that it implies the resilience of atom from atom, and thus assumes the elasticity of absolutely hard bodies. But this has nothing to do with the question of principle here concerned. Those factors further proved themselves more amply adapted to explain the earlier phases of the cosmic process than a superficial view might lead us to suppose. For even the atoms flitting in the vacuum might have met other atoms in the infinite extent of time past, and thus have been set in motion by the blows they received. This expedient, however, could by no means be regarded as final. It supposed that A was struck by B, B by C, C by D, and so forth, and that these shocks set them in motion. But when philosophy began to trace the process backwards, it was inevitably brought to the question of the starting-point of the series, however numerous its members may have been. The reply offered by Democritus to these interrogatories displeased many succeeding thinkers, and we may now inquire into the justice of their displeasure. His explanation was that such atomic motion was original, eternal, and without beginning, and that it would be a wild-goose chase to seek for the beginning or the cause of a process that never began. Hereupon he was told that his explanation was at variance with the principle of universal causation so emphatically proclaimed by him and his master, that he was exalting causelessness and accident to a controlling rank in the universe, that he was placing chance at the head of the universal process, and so forth, and so forth. The recriminations have been sustained from the time of Aristotle till our own day, and in order to decide fairly between the combatants we must first get a clear idea of what we mean by "cause." If we take its German equivalent *Ursache*, we shall see at a glance how its ambiguity may have arisen and have produced this

ancient conflict.* For *Ursache* may mean a *Sache*—a thing
in the widest sense of the term, a being or substance of
any kind—which was present before a phenomenon and
called it into existence. Democritus was evidently fully
entitled to decline to search for such a cause of an
aboriginal process. For if he regarded the atoms as
existing from all eternity, he was certainly not obliged by
his belief in causation to send something yet more aboriginal
in advance of that aboriginal thing. But the word
Ursache has a second meaning which is the predominant
meaning in scientific usage to-day. Briefly stated, we
understand by the word "cause" the totality of conditions
by which an event is produced. It is irrelevant whether the
conditions are partially at least exterior to the object which
forms the scene of the event, or whether they are exclusively
forces or qualities immanent in it and determining the kind
of its action. In this second meaning of the word the
question of the cause even of an aboriginal event is admissible to research. In the present instance such a question
would lead us to a definition of the quality of the atoms
which enables them to move previously to any impulse
from without and independently of it. And if the answer
were to satisfy more rigid demands, it would have to
include the regulative law as well as the quality ; in other
words, the strength and direction of that aboriginal motion.
Democritus fulfilled the first but not the second part of
this demand. He declared the original or natural condition
of atoms to be a state of motion, but he stopped short at
the problem of the direction and strength with which
they moved. Nor indeed could he have done otherwise,
inasmuch as no material of observation was placed at his
disposal. In his world as in ours matter had long since
emerged from its aboriginal period in which the desired
law of motion could alone have been studied. The
philosophy of Democritus, moreover, was especially hostile
to such study, in consequence of the vortex from which
he dated the beginning of the world as it exists. And,
these considerations apart, where was he to look for a

* Or cp. the derivation of Fr. *chose* and Ital. *cosa* from Lat. *causa.*

particle of matter which in the course of the ages had never yet collided with other particles, nor suffered any impact or pressure? Nay, even if he had found it, and if it had proved amenable to observation, and fit in itself to yield up that law of aboriginal motion, how, we may ask, could Democritus have prosecuted the inquiry, ignorant as he was of its past history in mechanics or of its lack of such a past? Thus his rejection of that demand as superfluous and vain was not merely pardonable but inevitable. He was content with declaring that the atoms had been in motion since all eternity, and no one who is conversant or duly familiarized with the foundation and the course of his philosophy will doubt the legitimacy of that declaration. Leucippus and his disciple were concerned with the present phenomena of the universe, and their especial attention was given to the preliminary condition of those phenomena, and to attempts to explain the composition and origin of a cosmos such as ours and the separation and disposition of its constituent material parts. As genuine scientific thinkers, working from the known to the unknown, they were at pains to construct the minimum basis of assumption on which, together with the qualities of matter discovered by empirical methods, they might construct the universe and devise a reasonable theory of the activity of its component parts. It was one of these assumptions that the primary particles of matter had originally existed in a state of motion and not in a state of rest. By this means they could meet one another, by this means they could combine with one another, by this means the aggregates of atoms which had met in a specific way could and must produce a vortex, and so forth. But there was no cause whatever to make statements or to form conjectures as to the character of that motion. It was not necessary to the nature of the problem, nor could it be justified on any other ground. This refusal to meet his opponents on their own terms, in the midst of so many instances of temerity, does credit to the scientific moderation and self-restraint of the philosophers of Abdera.

At this point, however, our progress is obstructed by

various pretended metaphysical difficulties which are really the rooted prejudices of metaphysics. Their roots strike so deep that we should be tempted to call them ineradicable in the face of the fact that a famous natural philosopher of recent times has once more spoken of the problem of a bond between matter and motion as one of the insoluble " riddles of the universe." And that, we may add, is the least pretentious disguise in which our apparent difficulty has clothed itseif. For all ultimate facts of creation are at bottom riddles of the universe in as far as they are inaccessible to what we call explanation. The existence of matter itself is as great a riddle as its motion. But when we come to the idea that the " conception " of matter contains something that makes it particularly difficult— not to say, with most metaphysicians, impossible—to associate it with primordial movement, then, we venture to assert, we are presented with one of the most remarkable of the illusions to which the credulous mind of man has ever fallen prone. In this, as in other similar difficulties or impossibilities of thought, we see nothing but an effect of habit. The unique feature to be remarked in this habit of thought which usurps the dignity of a principle of thought is the fact that we can point to its source with absolute definiteness in the extremely narrow limits of our faculties of perception. So far as we are acquainted with the universe, matter in motion, and not matter at rest, is the practically unexceptional rule. The whole treasury of science does not contain a single genuine instance of more than relative rest. The luminary which we inhabit and those revealed to our sight are involved in ceaseless velocity. They are as exempt from rest as the atoms and molecules of which every bodily substance is composed. But by an accident of vision we are not directly aware of the circumgyration by which we and our planet and all that it contains are borne through space. And another accident of vision withdraws from our limited senses the unceasing circulation of the particles of matter. Thus, by this combination of accidents, our eyes are almost exclusively accustomed to substances of a moderate size, and such a substance, it is to be noted, when we cease to regard it as a part of its whole or as the whole of its parts, will frequently produce the impression of a permanent peace, though there is merely a temporary truce to its motory forces.   Here and here alone, we presume, is the root of that remarkable opinion which grew to dogmatic strength, and which presumed that a state of rest was more natural to matter than a state of motion, or even that it was absurd to consider motion as a part of the primordial endowment of matter.

From the dawn of modern times a little band of chosen spirits set themselves to oppose this dogma. Giordano Bruno and Francis Bacon were united in this purpose, and Leibniz and Spinoza repudiated the authority of Descartes as emphatically as eminent philosophers of the nineteenth century. One of these, John Tyndall, coined a beautiful phrase : " If Matter starts as a ' beggar,' it is because the Jacobs of theology have deprived it of its birthright." We would correct but a single word in this dictum.   Instead of theology we should blame metaphysics, which has so frequently fanned and flattered the prejudices of mankind. For it better accords with the omnipotence and the omniscience ascribed by the theologians to the Deity that He should have given movement to matter at the outset than that He should have added it as a kind of afterthought. Democritus, at any rate, was not troubled by such questions. He flourished before the times when matter was regarded as " an inert mass " or " a quiescent load " obedient to exterior impulses alone. The future still guarded " that invention of the human intellect," to speak in the words of Bacon, " spoliated and passive matter." It was unknown to the hylozoists, and it seems proper to point out that the Atomists too, though they were disposed to regard the universe as a mechanism, were yet fortunately preserved from this fallacious generalization founded on the mechanics of earthly masses.   In this instance as in others they were the heirs of their great forefathers, the physiologists of Ionia.

5. It is more common, we admit, to dwell on the debt of gratitude which the authors of Atomism owed to the

Eleatic philosophers. Our readers will already be in a position to decide with approximate accuracy for themselves the extent and the nature of the obligation, but we need not hesitate to quote the view expressed on the subject by Theophrastus, the most important of ancient authorities.

" Leucippus," he wrote, " who was a native of Elea or Miletus, was familiar with the doctrine of Parmenides, but did not follow in his footsteps nor in those of Xenophanes, but, methinks, pursued the opposite road. For while they represented the universe as uniform, moveless, changeless, and limited, and turned aside from the bare question of non-being [*i.e.* the vacuum], Leucippus presumes an infinite number of primary bodies, the atoms, involved in ceaseless movement. He declares their forms to be infinite in number, because "—not to mention other reasons—" he perceived in the objects incessant birth and incessant change. Further, he did not regard being as more real than non-being, and he recognizes in both equally the cause of every process."

Without reading into the introductory words the statement, which we believe to be untrue, that Leucippus was a pupil of Parmenides, we may remark that he would have proved as unsatisfactory a disciple to that sage as Voltaire must have been to his Jesuit fathers. But the passage is more instructive in displaying the error of those who account the second postulate of matter as the creation of Parmenides. The fundamental contradictions so justly and emphatically mentioned by Theophrastus do not prevent them from assuming the far-reaching dependence of the atomistic on the Eleatic doctrine. We should exhaust the patience of our readers if we were to recapitulate the grounds on which we have recognized both postulates of matter as the product and property of the Ionian school. Still, we are anxious to give Parmenides the full credit of having formulated them strictly—a credit, indeed, which is not inconsiderably diminished by the vain attempt to support them by *à priori* arguments. It was not entirely to no purpose that the Eleatic metaphysicians exercised their intellect in great efforts of abstraction. The acceptance of the second postulate of the qualitative constancy of matter left the alternative between two ways of thought, and two only, which may briefly be designated as the road of Anaxagoras and the road of Leucippus. The one theory of matter presumed as many primary substances as there were actual combinations of the qualities of sense, and the other presumed one primary matter, possessing all the common fundamental qualities of bodies, but excluding the diverging qualities of sense. The ground preliminary to this last-named view was prepared by Parmenides, who likewise drew a line of demarcation between qualities characteristic of bodily substances as such and those that we may call the accidents of bodily substance. The "Being" of Parmenides, by which space was filled, possessed bare eternity and unchangeableness. Motion was inconceivable to him, and was therefore deemed impossible, and the mechanical qualities of substance, by which all motion is caused and controlled, were therefore also meaningless in his eyes. This doctrine was silent about impact and pressure, and all the modifications of those processes. Thus the hard and fast line which he drew between true Being and mere delusive appearance did not coincide with the distinction drawn by Leucippus between the objective and merely subjective reality, between the primary and secondary attributes of things. On the contrary, it relegated motion, the centre and pivot of the atomistic theory of the universe, to the realm of appearance. Still, it was something that he drew such a distinction at all, that he recognized a difference between the essential attributes of his Being and other non-essential attributes, and that he kept them firmly apart ; and, inasmuch as he did this, he may be said to have promoted that theory of the universe almost in his own despite. The paths of intellectual progress cross one another so wonderfully that the very man who denied all movement, all change, and all process, and who therefore robbed natural research of its contents, advanced the cause of natural research. Unconsciously and unwillingly he served the cause of the science which recognized change and process, which reduced them to mechanical motion and which was solely concerned with such problems. Full justice has thus been done to the contribution of the Eleatics in the advancement of positive knowledge. And more than this, perhaps. For who shall say if Leucippus, face to face with that alternative, would not have espoused the right side, and have entered the lists against Anaxagoras even without being prompted by Parmenides? It is idle to discuss what might have been, but it would be wrong to conclude from the points of contact of both doctrines that the one was dependent on the other. Contradiction is contact, and to that extent it is fair to say that these two theories were related. The Eleatics argued as follows:—

> "Without a vacuum there is no motion.
> There is no vacuum.
> ∴ There is no motion."

The Atomists argued on the contrary:—

> "Without a vacuum there is no motion.
> There is motion.
> ∴ There is a vacuum."

The conclusions are plainly in striking contrast, but it is legitimate to ask if the Atomist did not owe the Eleatic the major premise common to both, and thus the corner-stone, as it were, of at least that portion of his philosophy. An affirmative answer has frequently been returned to this question, but we venture to regard it as wholly erroneous. The Eleatics could not have been the authors of this common premise. Melissus had already treated of empty space in a manner which does not lead us to believe that he set up the hypothesis in order to knock it down, and the tone in which Parmenides himself refuted the assumption of the vacuum or non-being makes it impossible to doubt that he found the doctrine ready-made as an aid to the explanation of nature. No, it was not Parmenides who influenced Leucippus in this instance. That influence must be traced to older anonymous thinkers anterior to both—probably, as we have twice had occasion to remark, to Pythagoreans.* We venture to go one step further.

* Bk. II. Ch. II. § 4; and cp. § 2 above.

These nameless philosophers did not only invent the vacuum, but they bequeathed to their successors an analogue to the atoms. Parmenides speaks of something in which nothing but vacuum can be seen, but which, according to the assumptions of teachers whom he bitterly opposed, occupied in part a continuous space and in part was "regularly distributed throughout space." In other words, he was acquainted with the doctrine which assumed not merely continuous space empty of all matter, but also empty interstices traversing the whole material world. The islets of matter, as we may call them, surrounded by these interstices as though by a network of canals, approximate very closely in their object and intention to the atoms of Leucippus. Moreover, the conception of a material mass regularly and unexceptionally interrupted can hardly have been due to any other demand than the need of explaining a universal fact. Finally, the fact requiring explanation can hardly have been other than the fact of motion. These conclusions we believe to be true—not the less true, indeed, because they have never been drawn before. Here once more the attentive reader will remark the organic growth of ideas and that progressive development which enhances the value of scientific achievements without seriously detracting from the merits of their authors.

6. We are now at liberty to ask what was the chief contribution made by Leucippus to science, and what part of his doctrine bore most conspicuously the impress of his original genius. He did not introduce the conception of the vacuum, nor did he do more than to refine and to raise to the dignity of a self-contained system the atomic theory which existed before him, though in a rough, rudimentary, and imperfect shape. Whether the labours of Parmenides were indispensable or not, Parmenides at least preceded Leucippus, and prepared the way for the distinction of essential and unessential attributes, or, to speak with John Locke, of the primary and secondary qualities of objects. But Leucippus entered a virgin field in his attempt to relate the world of substances with the world of phenomena,

instead of following the Eleatics in rejecting the world of phenomena as a phantasm and delusion to be expelled from the fane of science. He tried to build a bridge between two worlds which had once been combined without distinction, and which, when they had afterwards been distinguished, were utterly sundered from each other; and this grand undertaking, this endeavour to prove that the totality of the sensible qualities is, mathematically speaking, a function of their corporeal qualities, of their size, shape, position, situation, nearness, and distance, and thus to approach the universe as a whole, not as a sceptic, not as an iconoclast, but in the humble spirit of explanation, this is the crown and apex of the intellectual work of Leucippus. The most original part of his achievement was also the most permanent: yea, we may call it indestructible. Atomism may be superseded; the theory of cognition in its progress has already weakened the distinction between primary and secondary qualities; but the attempt to correlate all qualitative differences with differences of size, and shape, and situation, and movement, is destined to survive all changes of opinion and thought. The exact knowledge of nature rests entirely on this attempt to reduce qualities to quantities, or, to speak more precisely, to establish fixed relations between the two. Mathematical physics were contained there as in a germ, and modern research took its starting-point thence. Galilei, Descartes, Huyghens,—they all followed the same path. "I do not believe," declared Galilei, "that anything else is required than magnitudes, shapes, quantities, and slow movements or swift, to produce in us tastes, smells, sounds." Huyghens presupposed bodies formed of homogeneous matter, "in which no qualities were distinguished, but only different magnitudes, shapes, and movements;" and this was likewise the point of view which was maintained before him by Descartes. These philosophers led the van of the natural science of to-day, and they were united, as they expressly testify, in their acquaintance with the doctrine which they describe as Democritean, though its true author was Leucippus. And here we shall do well to remark that the links thus discerned in the chain of natural phenomena, and the dominion over nature which such discernment implies, are wholly independent of all systems of philosophy, whether that which we ourselves prefer, or that which our descendants may adopt. The electric lamp loses none of its brightness for the agnostic, dark as he may deem the innermost essence of nature. The laws of optics are the same for the champion of the mechanics of the universe as for him who derives the essence of the world's process from something other than material substance and its movements. Whatever answer the future may return to these fundamental problems of human knowledge, there is one fact that can never be shaken : Corporeal movements, as an element that can be quantitatively determined, are the " Open, Sesame," that has unlocked countless secrets in the system of nature, and that will unlock countless more. Here, if anywhere, it is legitimate to speak of finality. And that Leucippus by his theory put this key in the hand of mankind—this is his highest title to honour, this his imperishable renown.

It detracts very little from his merit that his own attempts to prove the great doctrine with which he endowed the world frequently bore the stamp of that *à priori* reasoning which he probably learnt from Zeno. Thus he was not content to found his supreme hypothesis on those facts of experience which really underlie it, on a reference to the facts of spatial movement, rarefaction and condensation, compression and other changes of volume, which thus were accounted for, and of which the growth of organic beings is an important special instance. He was also at pains to equip his arguments with the compelling force which should deprive an adversary of every outlet, and refute him by an *ad absurdum*, or reduce him to a self-contradiction when he contradicted the new theory. One of his ratiocinations, for example, is said to have begun as follows : " The full cannot take in anything." Certainly not, we may add, since fulness in the strict sense of the word, and incapacity to take in anything, are but synonymous expressions. When we have poured water into a vessel till it cannot nold any more we call it full, and if we are told that a vessel is full we invariably understand that it cannot take in anything more. We shall presently see if Leucippus employed this tautology merely as an innocent device to expound the conception of fulness. He is said to have continued as follows :—

" But if the full were to take in anything more, and if in that way two bodies [of equal magnitude] were to find room where hitherto there was only room for one, then there would be no end to the number of bodies which could be located in the same place, and the smallest could contain the greatest."

In making this last statement, Leucippus had played his trump card. It concealed an ambiguity, however, in which the fate of the whole argument was involved. No anti-atomist was really committed to the belief that the smallest could contain the greatest, as such, in the sense that a nutshell could hold an elephant. But that a substance with the size of an elephant can be so far compressed as to enter a nutshell or eggshell, though actually untrue, is neither an absurd nor a self-contradictory proposition. It would only become so if the incompressibility of matter had already been granted ; if, that is to say, the thing to be proved were already taken as proven. But the opening words of the argument served to beg that question. There the conception of fulness, which was first employed in a purely empirical sense compatible with either theory, was transferred into the conception of impenetrability or incompressibility by the pseudo-explanatory phrase about "taking nothing in." The second meaning replaced the first, and it was only when this transference was effected that the desired conclusion could be drawn from the premises. Otherwise the process of inference would have been invalid. We may here note another demonstration of a still less innocent kind which belonged to the same category. From Leucippus downwards the atomists were at pains to prove the infinite number of different forms of atoms. " There is no reason why the atoms should possess this form rather than that," and therefore, it was argued,

they represented all conceivable forms. To a certain extent
this simply expressed the expectation that the exuberant
wealth of forms displayed by nature in other respects
would be repeated in the present instance, and so far—as
we have remarked before—it contained an inference by
analogy, to which it is impossible to deny some small
measure of justification as a presumption or provisional
opinion. But any claim advanced by the argument to the
force of dogmatic truth is evidently null and void. It
attempted to trespass the eternal barriers of human knowledge by prying into the resources of nature, and by
forming a judgment on their limited or unlimited range.
Its method recalls Anaximander's sham proof that the
earth is at rest, as well as the kindred attempts at
demonstration which we have mentioned above on the part
of metaphysical mechanicians to found the law of inertia on
à priori considerations instead of an empirical basis.* But
the likeness has at least one point of difference. Those
other speculations supplied an untenable proof to a veritable
fact of nature, but in the present instance the fact which
awaited demonstration, apart from its erroneous proof, was
itself a dubious fact. When we reach the following direct
attempt to prove the existence of a vacuum, we are probably correct in ascribing it to Democritus with his marked
bias to empiricism. He stated it in this form : A vessel
filled with ashes will take in as much water—by which
he probably meant "nearly as much water"—as if there
were no ashes there ; the condition that renders this
possible is that the ashes contain a very large amount of
vacuum. We need hardly point out to our readers that
the interpretation of the fact was erroneous. Porous
bodies, such as ashes, contain great quantities of air,
and these are expelled by the water poured into the
ash-pail. It is true that Democritus, if he had been
informed of this, might have retorted by the question :
Whither can the air escape, when it makes room for the
water, if the whole space be already occupied by impenetrable matter ? And, in this modified form, the argument

* Bk. I. Ch. I. § 3.

would have implied neither more nor less than any other reference to a progressive movement in space which demands the assumption of vacua as soon as the impenetrability of matter is already taken as proved.

7. Such were some of the mistakes committed by these giants of thought, and neither separately nor collectively are they calculated to detract seriously from their renown. Still, we are bound to mention them, as well on other grounds as because they help to show, what is true beyond a doubt, that the atomic theory has never properly been proved either in ancient or in modern times. It was, it is, and it remains, not a theory in the strict sense of the word, but merely an hypothesis, though an hypothesis, it is true, of unparalleled vitality and endurance, which has yielded a splendid harvest to physical and chemical research down to our own day. By its aid old facts have ever been satisfactorily explained and new facts have been discovered, so that it must fairly be conceded a large degree of objective truth, or, more precisely expressed, it must follow for a long way a road parallel to the real objective condition of things. Still, as has been said, it is an hypothesis, and its assumption of facts that lie far beyond the limits of human perception deprives it for all time of direct verification. Now, the indirect proof of an hypothesis can only become a complete proof if it be shown not merely that it provides a most satisfactory explanation of the phenomena, but that no other possible hypothesis would do equally well or better. In the present instance, where the phenomena concerned are the most secret processes of nature and those furthest removed from our sense-perception, the more than approximate proof of this kind will hardly ever, nay, will certainly never be attainable. The most cautious thinkers of to-day, accordingly, while paying every honour to the atomic hypothesis, do not affect to regard it as more than a conjecture which comes sufficiently close to the finality of truth to be used with considerable advantage and success, but which yet should never be employed without the silent reservation that it is perhaps not an ultimate truth, nor even the ultimate truth at our disposal.

And when we change our point of view and look at the theory of cognition instead of the facts of nature, we find ourselves impelled to another and a deeper reservation. The student of that theory is doubtful whether in the last resort he can learn anything about the exterior world, or at least can learn anything else, except what is taught him by the existence of series of sensations connected by laws of uniformity. The difference between primary and secondary qualities, which plays so prominent a part in the foreground of cognition, loses its fundamental importance in his eyes. His mature self-consciousness obliges him to refer back to sensations not merely smells, tastes, colours, and sounds, but also all the essential characteristics of material substance, and to acknowledge that the conception of matter itself is robbed of its contents when the perceiving and feeling subject of sensation is abstracted. But the atomic theory is not valueless even in the eyes of thinkers who take the above point of view. They recognize in it "a mathematical model for the statement of facts," and they ascribe to it "a function in physics similar" to that possessed by "certain auxiliary mathematical conceptions." To this, as we have stated before, we shall have occasion to return. We have merely considered it in this place, hastily and cursorily though it may have been, in order to add the remark that the authors of atomism took no account whatsoever of the dubiety that marked a later phase in the development of speculation. And in general we may say it works for the salvation of science that its pioneers in their respective periods are not distracted from the direct and limited task set before them by the confusion and bewilderment of higher and more distant views.

Atomism and Materialism—the question now arises, how far these two are identical. These early Atomists were content to be confined to the bodily world, nor was their complacency disturbed by the ghost of a scruple arising from the theory of cognition; and the name of Idealism having been given to the reverse of this naïve philosophy, Leucippus and Democritus may fairly be called materialists. They were materialists, too, in as far as they did not assume the continued existence of the psyche or breath-soul, but rather outdid Parmenides and Empedocles, in whose systems the conception played a sorry part wholly irrelevant to the explanation of actual facts, by rejecting it altogether and replacing it by soul-atoms. But they were not materialists if by that term we mean thinkers who deny or dispute the existence of spiritual substances; for the simple reason that the transference of the conception of substance from the material world, its original home, had not yet taken place. And, in common with the rest of their predecessors and contemporaries in natural philosophy, with the sole exception of Anaxagoras, they were materialists in as much as they looked for the only causes or conditions of the states and qualities of consciousness in the material world alone. Nor did they differ essentially from the great majority of their precursors in their relation to the divine. Like these, they acknowledged no divine creator of the world, and they were as loth as Empedocles to admit immortal individual gods. Democritus derived the belief in such deities and their might from the terror with which thunder and lightning, solar and lunar eclipses, and similar marvels had impressed the imagination of primitive man. At the same time, he is said to have admitted the divinity of the stars, doubtless on account of their fiery nature, in accordance, that is to say, with his doctrine that they were composed of soul-atoms, and he shared the belief of Empedocles in supernatural Beings of long though not of unlimited life. On the whole, he was inclined to regard the course of the universe as unaffected by the gods, and his assumption accordingly lacked a true scientific pretext. But he was still unable to make up his mind to dismiss to the limbo of fiction all that had been told of the gods and their influence on mankind. The combination and concatenation of his innumerable and multiform atoms afforded a teeming material for such constructions, and doubtless he used these resources to account for the origin of Beings surpassing all human standards in size and in beauty. They were designed to move in aërial space. The images emanating from them were to enter in our bodies and in their most diverse organs. Thus by indirect means and by direct impressions on our senses—by appearing to us in dreams and speaking to us—they were to exercise in all kinds of ways their beneficial and malignant influences.

8. The reader will have been able to gather some acquaintance with the psychology of Democritus and his master, and especially of their perceptive theories, from some of the preceding extracts. That portion of their teaching was not particularly fertile, though Epicurus and his disciples did not hesitate to incorporate it in their system of philosophy. For both those reasons, therefore, we shall deal with it here as briefly as possible, leaving its further significance to be discussed in the history of Epicurism, which possesses the additional advantage that far ampler evidence is there at our disposal than the destructive criticism of antagonists such as that which Theophrastus levelled at isolated points in the Democritean theory of cognition. The vehicles of psychic functions in the system of Democritus were the most mobile of the atoms—a fact which was partly due to the apparent need of such a vehicle for the proverbial swiftness of thought,* and partly to the picture of ceaseless change presented by the process of life, which was also regarded as a product of the soul in its identity with vital force. On this account the atoms actually employed for the functions of the soul were conceived as small, round, and smooth. It was obvious that their great mobility would keep them constantly endeavouring to escape from the body, and respiration was accordingly entrusted with the task of counteracting such attempts. It worked in two ways: first, by holding the atoms back by a current of air; and secondly, by continually renewing them. Meanwhile the extinction of this process would bring about their final dissipation. Another consideration suggests itself here. These soul-atoms being derived from the external world, it is quite comprehensible that Democritus, following in the footsteps of Parmenides and Empedocles, should have drawn no sharp line of demarcation between the animate and the inanimate creation, but should have distinguished the two

---

* Cp. Homer, "Swift as a wing or as thought."

merely by a difference of degree. And lastly, we may remark his identification of the soul-atoms with the atoms of fire, thus again reminding us of Heraclitus— a conclusion to which he was led as much by the vital heat of the higher organisms as by the ceaseless vibration of the atoms resembling the movement of a flame. Our philosopher took account of all the processes of perception, but his closest attention was given to the visual function. The wonderful fact that distant objects affect our organs of sight was held by Democritus to be inexplicable without the assumption of an intervening agent. Even to-day, when use and wont have blunted the edge of the wonder, it strikes us with ever fresh surprise, and, where modern physics speaks of the medium of ether, Democritus believed that the explanation was to be found in air. The air was supposed to receive impressions from the objects of sight and to transfer them to our organs of vision, such impressions being literally impressed like the mark of the signet on wax. He represented the objects themselves as incessantly shedding thin husks or membranes, which entered the eye that happened to be in their immediate neighbourhood, and there became visible as the picture in the pupil; when the eye was at a distance, he conceived this effect to be produced by the intermediary action of the air. Air, then, was indispensable for this purpose, but yet it was not regarded as a wholly favourable agent in visual perception. The disturbing influence of the medium was held to account for the darkening and final disappearance of the most distant objects of sight. Except for such disturbance, according to Democritus, we should be able to perceive an ant crawling on the vault of heaven. The reader will be able to gather even from this hasty sketch that the great thinker was still wholly unacquainted with even the elements of optics; nor will it escape him that Democritus was misled in this instance by his attempt, partially successful in other respects, to derive every effect of one object on another from direct contact, and from its immediate mechanical manifestations in pressure and impact. It must further be acknowledged that this feature in

the fundamental doctrine of Democritus made his speculations on optics suffer in comparison with those of Alcmæon
and Empedocles. They represent a cruder and a more
primitive stage of thought, nor are we in a position to say
how he himself dealt with the difficulties that arose out of
his own hypothesis. Two possibilities suggest themselves.
Either he must have failed to notice that this incessant
shedding of thin atomic layers or membranes (called by
him "idols" or images) must in course of time have
brought about a considerable diminution in the substantial
bulk of bodies, or else he must have met this objection by
a reference to the perishableness of all objects of sense.
One point only in this strange theory is deserving of praise.
So far as it traced hallucinations and so-called subjective
sensations of all kinds to these "images" introduced from
outside, it agreed with modern science in not destroying
every link of community between the sensations produced
by the most diverse kinds of stimulus, and in that point
alone. But, instead of emphasizing the common subjective
factor, it rather did the reverse ; instead of recognizing and
asserting, as we now do, the specific energy of the nerves of
sense, and thus assimilating perception to hallucination, it
rather assimilated hallucination to perception. In all this
we have no right to be surprised. We have only to recall
the foundation of the doctrine on the unshaken and unreasoning belief in matter as the sole and only reality, a
belief undisturbed by any scepticism or any trace of
refined and matured self-consciousness, in order to extend
it our free pardon.

We have spoken of the mind of Democritus as exempt
from scepticism, and we repeat this claim, though there
are several utterances in the sparse fragments of his
works which may produce the opposite appearance. But
it is merely apparent and nothing more. Three groups
of sentiment may be distinguished which have not been
kept apart with sufficient care. Democritus, like Faust,
was "consumed at heart" because, despite the thought and
trouble and research of a long life devoted to science, his
sum of knowledge was so small that he could only cast a

few fitful and furtive glances into the secrets of nature. "Truth dwelleth in the deep;" "reality is shut out from human ken;"—these and similar sighs of a labouring spirit are still preserved in the fragments of his work entitled "Corroborations," which pursued mainly an inductive or empirical method, in deliberate opposition, perhaps, to the *à priori* tendencies of Leucippus. In a further passage of the same treatise we read the following plaintive protest: "We perceive in fact nothing certain, but such things only as change with the state of our body, and of that which enters it, and which resists it." The attempt might be made to infer from this passage that Democritus was a victim, though merely for a time, to the principles of scepticism. But in drawing such a conclusion we should err with the ancient sceptic, to whom we owe the quotation, and who forced it to subserve his own teaching, in overlooking one point which is really sufficiently obvious. The protest in question was founded on the very nature of the body about which the philosopher, when he penned those words, was no more dubious than at any other time. "In truth there are atoms and vacuum"—this was the fundamental theory of Democritus, and no shadow of a doubt ever approached him as to its unconditional validity. We may assert this the more definitely because Sextus himself, the ancient sceptic who would have greeted the great Atomist as a brother, and who searched through his writings to this end with tireless industry and persistency, was yet wholly unable to discover the evidence that he looked for.

We pause at the challenge of Colotes. He quotes a remark from Democritus which utterly destroyed all certainty of knowledge, and which, in the words of this favourite pupil of Epicurus, "brought life itself into confusion." But the challenge has long since been met. The seemingly incriminating remark is not a proof of the loose hold which his principles possessed over the mind of Democritus; it affords, on the contrary, direct evidence of the unshaken confidence with which he clung to his fundamental view and to the consequences it entailed. The sentence in question ran as follows: "An object is not naturally constituted in one way any more than in another," but the context in which it occurs makes it irrefutably clear that it refers expressly to those qualities of objects which modern science terms "secondary," and to which, as our readers already know, Democritus denied objective reality. And the remark proscribed by Colotes was admirably suited to point this distinction in the most emphatic way possible. The sweet taste of honey to a man in good health, its bitter taste to the jaundiced palate,—these and similar facts were commonly known and acknowledged; but, as generally stated, they were at variance not merely with that important distinction, but even with ordinary common sense. The expressions used were as loose and inexact as they are on the lips of most cultivated people to-day. "Honey," they said, as they still say, "*is* sweet; but to those patients it *seems* bitter." To this Democritus demurred. Truth and untruth, he contended, were not to be determined by a plebiscite. In such a case, if many men had jaundice and only a few were free from it, the standard of truth would be altered. It was not a difference of fact and semblance, but merely of majority and minority. The one sensation, he maintained, was just as subjective, just as relative, just as exterior to the object, as the other. Normal sweetness was no more an objective quality of honey than its abnormal bitterness. Honey was not sweet "any more than" it was bitter. What honey was in his theory was a complex of atoms of such and such a shape, size, and position, and containing such and such a proportion of vacuum. The rest was nothing but the effect exercised by it on other bodies, and among them on the human organs of taste. That effect, again, must partly depend on those organs and on their permanent or temporary, common or individual qualities. Democritus was never assailed by any scruple whatsoever as to the objective existence of bodies and their attributes. He was rather animated by the desire to sever as sharply and as definitely as possible the unchangeableness of these causes from the changeableness of the effects which they exerted in combination with the varying subjective factor, and thus to prevent the spread of the scepticism aroused by those changes into the domain of the unchangeable. On this account alone Democritus said what he did say.

The third and last of the groups in which these fragments of Democritus fall contains the celebrated passage in which a distinction was drawn between genuine and obscure knowledge. His *chef d'œuvre* was a work in three books on reasoning, entitled "The Canon," which presumably founded and discussed a system of inductive logic. Somewhere in this work the following sentences occurred. "There are two kinds of insight, the genuine and the obscure. To the obscure belong all these: sight, hearing, smell, taste, touch; but the genuine, which is severed from it——" But here the haste of Sextus, our authority, has robbed us of the end of the extract. Still, enough has been preserved to lend a show of correctness to those critics who would call the physicist of Abdera a metaphysician or ontologist. It may well be argued that he made a clean sweep of the evidence of the senses, and that nothing was left to him, accordingly, save to take refuge on the heights of pure Being. But cavalierly as Sextus dealt with his author, the extract can nevertheless be used to rectify this first erroneous impression. After a brief interlude he resumed the dropped thread of his disquisition, and added a second sentence to the first. Unfortunately, it is likewise a mutilated, probably a decapitated, sentence. Genuine cognition begins, so Democritus wrote, "where the obscure is no longer (adequate), where it cannot perceive the minutely small either by sight or hearing, or smell or taste or touch, but the object becomes too fine for that purpose." In a word, Democritus was longing for a microscope of ideal power. Had he possessed such an instrument, he would have subtracted colour from what it showed him as a subjective accretion, and would have accepted what was left as the highest attainable objective truth. The reproach that he levelled at the senses collectively was that their evidence did not extend far enough; that they deserted us at the point where the minutest bodies and the most delicate processes were to be got at, from which the material masses and the processes obtaining in them are composed. Corporeal things and material processes were likewise in his view the objects of the genuine or undisturbed knowledge which transcended the limits of obscure or disturbed cognition. Lacking the ideal instruments of precision, which we still do not possess, the aids to knowledge which Democritus obtained were naturally nothing but inferences, though they were inferences of a kind intended for no other purpose than . to lighten the darkness of the material world, and resting on no other foundation than the evidence of the senses, inadequate and untrustworthy indeed, but not wholly to be rejected, and capable of considerable use by their mutual powers of self-correction and control. These inferences of his were obviously based on analogy, or rather, in as far as they were more strictly formulated, they were inductive inferences which started from perceptible facts, and, premising that the forces or qualities thus obtained were valid beyond the limits of perception, attempted to overstep those limits both in space and time. We are now in a position to resume in a few words the facts bearing on the scepticism of Democritus. Beyond its pale may be placed not merely his belief in the corporeal world, but also his fundamental hypotheses anent the composition of bodies out of atoms and vacuum as well as the primary qualities of matter. This region of the highest knowledge was situated on the heights above scepticism, whereas another region was situated below it. That second region was occupied by those secondary or subjective phenomena which, strictly speaking, are neither true nor false, but simply the effects of natural causes, at once inevitable and undeniable. It was the middle region between the two, that of the detailed explanation of nature, which formed the play-ground of the doubts and scruples by which Democritus was tormented and confused. He was constantly engaged in trying to reconcile the two spheres of thought. He was constantly asking himself what real processes, remote from direct perception, were to be presumed behind the phenomena that were revealed to the senses; and what bodily movements were to be pre-supposed in order to harmonize these phenomena with the known forces of nature or qualities of things. The mind of Democritus dwelt by choice on the details of investigation, and it was problems of this kind that drove him again and again to question the adequacy of his internal and external auxiliaries, and that drew from his heart the bitter reiterated complaint which affords such striking evidence of his insatiable thirst for knowledge and his unappeasable criticism of self.

9. The rules of investigation contained in the "Canon" of Democritus have long since been lost and forgotten. We can only deduce them to-day from his practice, or rather from the criticism which that practice entailed. His chief critic was Aristotle, who deserves our best thanks in that respect, though we cannot always subscribe to his views. One reproach, indeed, directed by Aristotle at the method of Democritus is changed in our eyes into a title to the highest honour. He blamed the philosopher of Abdera for proposing in the ultimate resort no other solution of the problems of natural processes than "it is so or it happens so always," or "it has happened heretofore likewise." In other words, Democritus recognized experience as the ultimate source of our knowledge of nature. The chain of our deductions might be infinitely long and its links might be as many as possible, but at last, he argued, we must reach a point where elucidation stops short, and where nothing is left to us but to admit a fact capable of no further deduction. Every deductive process rests in the last resort on inductions—this is a fundamental truth which Aristotle himself never actually disputed. But in individual instances his desire for explanation would frequently not rest satisfied with the admission of ultimate facts based solely on experience and entirely impervious to human insight. Too often his theory of nature introduced a pseudo-explanation where it ought actually to have abandoned all further search for knowledge. Democritus had no such disposition to substitute sham explanations derived for the most part from an insidious prejudice. As he had rejected the arbitrary

assumption, which we have already discussed to satiety, that matter must have received its first motive impulse from without, so he stood aloof from the Platonic-Aristotelian theory of "natural places"—the tendency of fiery matter upwards, of earthy matter downwards, and so forth. Accordingly, when Aristotle accuses Democritus and Leucippus of "carelessly neglecting to investigate the origin of motion," modern science adopts unreservedly the cause of the defendants and not of the plaintiff. There is a marked resemblance between the criticism directed by Aristotle at the treatment of these questions by the Atomists, and the reproaches aimed against Galilei and his method of natural research in the correspondence of Descartes with Mersenne. In the one case as in the other we see the spirit of metaphysics incapable of appreciating the work of the less pretentious but more fruitful empirical methods.

When we come to the problem of design and its treatment, it is more difficult to frame a fair judgment on the rights and wrongs of this controversy. The Atomists left the conception of design altogether on one side in their view of the origin and arrangement of the world, or rather of the worlds. They confined their efforts to following and tracing back as far as possible the road of the mechanical explanation of nature. Nay, even when they reached the processes of organic life, they did not attempt to strike out a new path of elucidation. On both charges alike they incurred the reproach of Aristotle. In his eyes the assumption that the order and beauty of the universe were of spontaneous growth was just as inadequate as the second assumption, that the adaptation of means to ends in the structure of animals and plants had occurred without the control of an immanent principle of purpose, or, to use the word coined by Karl Ernst von Baer and precisely corresponding to Aristotle's meaning, had been developed without *Zielstrebigkeit* or "spontaneous teleology." In his eyes, again, their proceeding in this respect was just as silly as to argue that in tapping a dropsical patient the cause of the process was the lancet of the surgeon, and not the desired purpose of curing the subject by the operation.

Here we enter the field of a controversy which is still raging to-day, and we know so little of the details of the Atomistic doctrines that it would be difficult to adjudicate between the disputants even if the points at issue had been settled at least in principle. Let us put the question in a concrete form. In popular handbooks of Materialism we frequently meet a solution which may be stated compendiously as follows: Stags have long legs not in order that they may run swiftly, but they run swiftly because they have long legs. True, cause and effect are likely enough to be confused with means and end, and this confusion plays a conspicuous part in the history of human thought. It is not the less true that the teleological method can frequently be successfully refuted by the argument that only such forms as are fit to endure can acquire consistency and permanence, and that unfit forms, though they may often arise, must sooner or later be destroyed, and must especially succumb in the struggle for existence. But neither of these views would suffice for a complete settlement of the problem of design, unless two fundamental facts in the region of organic life which seem to point to different explanations could first be got rid of. These facts are: (1) the reciprocity and co-operation of several and sometimes very numerous organs and parts of organs in one common function; (2) the structure of the organs, and especially of the organs of sense in animal life, with their wonderful suitability to the influence of outward agents. Science, invincible science, has not yet despaired of finding the key to these great riddles, though the expectations which attended the birth of Darwin's attempt at solution in the middle of the nineteenth century have been somewhat disappointed in the progress of research, till the most advanced thinkers of to-day recognize in his "spontaneous variation" and "survival of the fittest" only one of the factors required instead of their totality. But, be this as it may, the Atomists' experiment in the mechanical explanation of nature proved eminently fertile—far more so, in point of fact, than the opposite theories which paused at an earlier stage on the path of research, and set a premature goal to the pursuit of knowledge, whether by the assumption of supernatural intervention or by the introduction of equivocal forces defying all exact demarcation, such as the "vital force" of the earlier vitalists.

10. In the doctrine of Democritus there were no immovable barriers between the several departments of terrestrial phenomena, and the philosopher at the same time withheld his assent from the plausible division of the universe into essentially different regions. He recognized no contrast between the sublunary world of change and the changeless steadiness of the divine stars, important and fatal though that difference became in the Aristotelian system. At this point Democritus was once more fully in agreement not merely with the opinions of great men like Galilei, who released modern science from the fetters of Aristotelianism, but even with the actual results of the investigations of the last three centuries. It is almost miraculous to observe how the mere dropping of the scales from his eyes gave Democritus a glimpse of the revelation which we owe to the telescope and to spectrum analysis. In listening to Democritus, with his accounts of an infinitely large number of worlds different in size, some of them attended by a quantity of moons, others without sun or moon, some of them waxing and others waning after a collision, others again devoid of every trace of fluid, we seem to hear the voice of a modern astronomer who has seen the moons of Jupiter, has recognized the lack of moisture in the neighbourhood of the moon, and has observed the nebulæ and obscured stars which the wonderful instruments that have now been invented have made visible to his eyes. Yet this consentaneity rested on scarcely anything else than the absence of a powerful prejudice concealing the real state of things, and on a bold but not an over-bold assumption that in the infinitude of time and space the most diverse possibilities have been realized and fulfilled. So far as the endless multiformity of the atoms is concerned, that assumption has not won the favour of modern science, but it has been completely vindicated in respect to cosmic processes and transformations. It may legitimately be

said that the Democritean theory of the universe deposed in principle the geocentric point of view. Nor would it be unfair to suppose that Democritus smoothed the way for its actual deposition at the hands of Aristarchus of Samos. We shall return to this subject in a subsequent chapter, where we shall have to show the partially hidden threads by which Democritus is bound no less to the Copernicus of antiquity than to the great physicists of Alexandria and their disciple Archimedes, and by which Archimedes in his turn is connected with Galilei and other pioneers of modern science.

To-day, as two thousand years ago, the question is asked whether our earth is the only home of living beings, and our experience is still without data on which to base a reply. But Democritus and those who thought with him are not necessarily to be charged with temerity because they refused to make an exception in that respect in favour of the one star of which our knowledge is exact. Democritus contended that only a few worlds were without animals and plants because the requisite fluid was lacking which should supply them with nourishment. And this dictum of the sage is especially remarkable, inasmuch as it was obviously based on the assumption of the uniformity of the universe in the substances composing it and in the laws controlling it which the sidereal physics of our own day has proved beyond dispute. He evinced the same spirit which animated Metrodorus of Chios, himself a Democritean, in his brilliant parable : "a single ear of corn on a wide-spreading champaign would not be more wonderful than a single cosmos in the infinitude of space."

The genius of Democritus did not stop at anticipating modern cosmology, but inherent in those speculations was his yet more striking view of life. How petty must man appear ; how worthless his aims, pursued by most of us with such breathless haste ; how great his modesty and humility, how small his arrogance and pride, if the world he lives in is deprived of every prerogative, if it loses all claim to unique distinction, and becomes in his eyes a grain of sand on the shore of the infinite! Here, we venture to believe, is the key to the ethics of Democritus. Posterity has characterized the sage as "the laughing philosopher," because he saw the disproportion of the business of man with his actual place and meaning. Unfortunately, the sources from which we are accustomed and, to some extent, constrained to draw for the details of his moral philosophy, are mostly troubled and untrustworthy, but we know enough of one of his chief ethical treatises to sketch in outline at least a portion of its tenour. It treated of the tranquillity of the soul, of its εὐθυμία, or "cheerfulness," and it was remarkable for the modesty of the goal which it set before human endeavour. Not bliss, not happiness, was the end to be attained, but a state of bare "well-being," of a soul's peace undistracted alike by superstitious fears as by overmastering passions, of a "composure" or equanimity similar to the "smooth mirror" of the stormless sea. The treatise opened with a description of the miserable condition of the majority of mankind, ever unquiet, ever impelled on a vain search for happiness, now seizing one thing and now another, without obtaining permanent satisfaction. The immoderateness of human desires, the neglect of the narrow limits by which mortal happiness is confined, the disturbances wrought by superstition on man's peace of mind,—these, it would seem, were the chief sources of unhappiness, as characterized by Democritus. Our authorities deny us the pleasure of reconstructing these fundamental ideas in all their brilliant detail. In the large quantity of the so-called utterances of Democritus in the field of moral philosophy there is much that is demonstrably false, and in the rest of the fragments the critics have not yet succeeded in sifting the false from the true. Still, there are many statements with a distinctive individuality of inspiration and style which one would fain claim as the genuine property of the sage. Foremost among these is the brilliant fragment, unluckily very much mutilated, but yet capable of restoration with practical certainty, in which the worst evil of democratic institutions is assailed. It attacks the dependence of the authorities on the judgment of the populace—on the very persons, accordingly, whom it is their bounden duty to hold in check. This significant fragment must have run more or less as follows :—

" In the existing order of the State it is not possible that the rulers should never do wrong, even though they be the very best. As things are, it is like delivering the (royal) eagle into the power of the reptiles. But some means ought to be devised to ensure that, however severely he may punish the evildoers, yet he should not be given over into their power. Rather some law or other institution ought to guarantee complete protection to him who dispenses judgment."

The genuineness, perhaps, of no one of these fragments can be warranted beyond all possibility of doubt ; their totality, however, paradoxical as it may sound, is none the less characteristic of the ethics of Democritus. For let us conceive how great a recoil from his exclusively mechanical view of nature was made by heathen no less than by Christian orthodoxy. And yet, despite that recoil, Christian and heathen writers of antiquity vied with one another in their eagerness to fill the mouth of the founder of Atomism with a series of utterances, each and all of which were stamped with the seal of sublime sentiment, and were designed to lead human life on a path of noble aspiration. Whence, then, it may fairly be asked, could this impression have been derived, save from the genuine works of Democritus? They must have borne the stamp of a personality exciting, or, rather, irresistibly compelling men's admiration and awe; they can have contained no word that could have given even the weakest handle to the misinterpretation or depreciation of prejudice or partisanship. Even at this day a widespread prejudice exists, to the effect that there is a necessary connection between scientific materialism and what may be called ethical materialism. But nothing is better calculated to dispel that obstinate prejudice than the picture of the sage of Abdera as it was known to antiquity and as tradition has preserved it unimpaired.

CHAPTER III.

THE ECLECTIC PHILOSOPHERS OF NATURE.

1. WITH the promulgation of the Atomic theory, a halt was called to the endeavours of more than one century at solving the problem of matter. It might be thought that an hypothesis which has maintained itself for over two thousand years would succeed in satisfying contemporary thought and in providing a starting-point for the immediate further progress of knowledge. But there were many obstacles in the way. The art of experimentation and the mathematical sciences were still imperfect, and the fruitful germ that was contained in atomism did not fall on a fortunate soil. A second circumstance which hindered the supremacy of the new doctrine was the traditional respect enjoyed by its older rivals. The shifting shapes successively assumed by material monism were calculated, as we have already seen reason to believe,* to cancel one another in turn, to destroy the exclusive validity of every one of the old theories of matter, and even to arouse a scepticism which affected the evidence of the senses themselves and shook the common basis of the doctrine. But here a second effect followed inevitably from these causes. Purely negative or merely sceptical results rarely satisfy more than a small part of the minds that are athirst for knowledge. Moreover, the contrast between the distinctive individual doctrines of a Thales, an Anaximenes, a Heraclitus, and so forth was counterbalanced by the underlying harmony of their fundamental assumptions. Meantime, too, other important

* Bk. II. Ch. II. § 3, *init.*

doctrines, promulgated by important men, had arrived on the scene. Nothing, then, was more natural than the attempt to reconcile these authorities one with another, to put prominently forward the elements they contained in common, and to touch up and transform those teachings by which they were kept apart. This attempt was considerably facilitated by the following circumstance. All the ways open, or at least those open in the existing state of knowledge, to a solution of the problems of the universe had already been trodden. Compromise and eclecticism, these are the redeeming words. Under their sign stood a series of new systems, which now come into view, and which form the real conclusion of the era of research, at the several stages of which we have made so long a pause. In a previous chapter we have made the acquaintance of Hippasus of Metapontum,* an eclectic philosopher of this kind, who sought to reconcile the teaching of Heraclitus with that of Pythagoras, and we shall presently have to consider other representatives of that movement. Its most distinguished member was Diogenes of Apollonia. He was a native of Crete, an island prominent in Greek history in the dawn of the fine arts, but without significance in her literary development, and it was perhaps the fame of Anaxagoras which attracted him from those distant shores to the learned capital of Athens, where his attitude as a freethinker involved him in a perilous experience similar to that which attended the great philosopher of Clazomenæ. A comprehensive anatomical fragment of his treatise "On the Nature of Man" gives evidence of his familiarity with the medical knowledge of his age, and supports the conjecture that he was himself a professional physician. The object at which he aimed was to harmonize Anaxagoras with Anaximenes, or, more exactly said, to harmonize the Nous-theory of the one with the other's theory of matter. In a less degree he stood under the influence of Leucippus from whom he had borrowed the doctrine of the cosmogonic vortex, and echoes of whose expressions he reproduces, as,

* Cp. Bk. I. Ch. V. § 4, *fin.*

for instance, in his favourite word "necessity." Nor can we doubt, from the ridicule that was poured on him by the comic writers, and from the references to his doctrine in the dramas of Euripides no less than in professional treatises on medicine, that Diogenes of Apollonia was one of the foremost figures in the age of Pericles.

We are not dependent, however, on merely indirect testimony for the contents of the system of Diogenes, which, it must be conceded, was conspicuously wanting in originality and consistency. We possess comparatively extensive fragments of his masterwork "On Nature," and these thoroughly justify, by their elevated yet simple style and unambiguous clarity, the claims to literary distinction which he advanced in the preface to his book. Thus they provide us with a remarkably clear insight into the motive and methods of his inquiry, and they frequently tell us in express language what, in the instance of his predecessors, we could only ascertain inferentially. Nor does this apply least of all to the fundamental motive of the monistic theory of matter itself. Its truth was established by Diogenes to his own satisfaction in the following words :—

"If that which is now in this world, earth and water and whatever else plainly existeth in this world, if one of these were different from the rest, if it were different by its own nature, and not rather the same, though frequently changed and altered, then neither would objects be able to mingle with one another, nor could one object affect another, prejudicially or beneficially ; then, too, no plant could grow out of the earth, no animal or anything else be born, if it were not the same according to its composition. Nay, but all this proceedeth from the same, becometh by alteration some other thing at some other time, and returneth to the same again."

Diogenes was further strongly influenced by the teleological argument of Anaxagoras.

"For it is impossible," he wrote, "that everything should thus be distributed without intelligence [more exactly, without the intervention of a Nous], that summer and winter, night and day, rain, wind, sunshine, and all else, should be regulated by measure. And he who reflecteth over this and the rest, will find that it is arranged as beautifully as possible."

We see, however, that Diogenes was not satisfied with the Nous-theory of Anaxagoras. He felt himself constrained to supplement it by the older air-theory of Anaximenes, and two causes may have induced him to take this step. The theory of matter promulgated by Anaxagoras may well have appeared to him as absurd and unjustified as it actually is. We venture to infer this from the fact that he simply dropped it. On the other hand, he was obviously anxious to relate the Nous, or the principle of order in the universe, with one or other of the forms of matter with which we are acquainted. In that way alone did its government, its universal diffusion and efficacy, seem to him comprehensible and explicable. He tells us this himself in the following unequivocal words:—

"And that which possesseth the intelligence seemeth to me to be what men call air, and this it is in my opinion that governeth and controlleth all things. For from air, meseemeth, doth Nous proceed, and"—by means of this vehicle—"penetrateth universally, ordereth all things, and existeth in all. And there is no single object that is without its share, but none hath the same share as another. There are rather many varieties of air, as of intelligence itself. For it is of many kinds, now colder and now warmer, now drier and now moister, now quieter and now more violently moving, and it displayeth countless other differences in respect to smell and colour. Moreover, the soul of all living things is the same, namely air, which is warmer than the external air surrounding us, though much colder than the air about the sun. But, comparatively speaking, this heat is not the same in any two animals or in any two men. The difference is not considerable: it is sufficient to exclude complete equality, though not to exclude similarity. But of all things liable to change, no one thing can become any other thing before it hath become the same."

In other words, the necessary condition and intermediate step for the issue of one particular form of matter from another is its preliminary transition through the primary form of matter.

" Since the alteration is of many kinds," continued **Diogenes**, " so too are living beings, and in consequence of the great number of alterations they resemble one another neither in appearance, nor in mode of life, nor in intelligence. Nevertheless that by which all of them live, and see, and hear is one and the same, and the rest of their intelligence cometh to them all from the same, namely, from air."

The conclusion of a second fragment, from which we have already quoted, supplies the evidence for the last of these statements.

" Moreover," it runs, " this too is a powerful proof. Man and the rest of the animals live by the air they breathe. This is their soul as well as their intelligence, and when it departeth from them they die, and their intelligence leaveth them."

Diogenes further entitled that primary being "an eternal and immortal body," or substance ; at another time he called it "a great, mighty, eternal, immortal, and multiscient being," and occasionally, too, he spoke of it as the "deity."

It is hardly necessary to discuss in detail all the teachings of Diogenes as they were expounded in his "Theory of Heaven" as well as in the two treatises we have mentioned. He was an encyclopædist whose mobile genius traversed all the fields of knowledge which the science of his age had discovered. He derived his impulses from every side, he learned from all masters, and, though he never completely reconciled either for himself or for his readers all their various teachings, yet he impressed on them the common seal of his own mind. All the roads of investigation which his predecessors had trodden led him to his principle of air, and the secret of the success he attained lay in his combination of versatility and one-sidedness, of indiscriminate eclecticism united with an obstinate consistency. There were many mansions in the house of his eclectic system. It contained the mechanical theory of the universe, the teleological view of nature, material monism, and the rule of an intelligent principle in matter. It did not abandon the doctrine of a

single primary substance, which had been familiar to
Greek learning for several generations. It did not reject
the assumption of a directing principle which adapted
means to ends, indispensable in the recent opinion of
many thinkers. The origin of cosmos in the blind
government of Necessity had been admirably argued and
widely adopted, and this doctrine too was an ingredient in
the new philosophic cauldron. The vortex of Leucippus
found a place side by side with the Nous of Anaxagoras,
and the Nous had to make up its mind to live at peace
with the air-god of Anaximenes. Nor was there anything
in the new-fangled science to shock the beliefs of the
orthodox. Homer, declared Diogenes, was not the
author of myths or fairy tales ; he merely used such aids
as a vehicle for telling the truth. His Zeus was air and
nothing but air. In other words, Diogenes was the first
to break fresh ground in introducing the allegorical
method in national poetry and religion. In this he was
the forerunner of the Stoics, who owed to him likewise,
through the intervention of the Cynics, several of their
doctrines in physics.

And now for the reverse of the medal, where we reach
the extreme one-sidedness of Diogenes, who affected to
recognize in all phenomena, physical, cosmological, physiological, and even psychical, the operation of a single principle of matter. Air, in his opinion, was the vehicle of
all sense-perception. In imitation doubtless of Leucippus,
he explained visual perception as an impression made by
the object perceived on the pupil of the eye through the
medium of air, but he added the original complementary
explanation that the pupil communicated the impression
to the brain through the same medium once more. We
may remark, by way of parenthesis, that he probably learnt
from Alcmæon to regard the brain as the sensorium proper.
Further, Diogenes was acquainted with the inflammation
of the nerve of sight and with the blindness that results
from it. a process which he explained in the following
manner. The nerve he regarded as a vein, and he believed
that the vein, when inflamed, hindered the entrance of the

air into the brain, and thus prevented the visual perception, though the picture might appear on the pupil of the eye. Man's higher intelligence, in the opinion of this thinker, was the boon of his upright gait. He breathed a purer air than the four-legged animals who walked with their heads bowed earthwards ; and this view, that they inhaled an air tainted by the moistures of the soil, was applied by Diogenes in a less degree to children also with their smaller stature. Air and its influence on the blood were likewise invoked to explain the passions as well. When the nature of the air was unsuited to mingle with the blood, which became accordingly less mobile and more coagulated, a feeling of pain was produced ; and, in the contrary instance, when the movement of the blood was accelerated by air, the result was a sensation of pleasure. Here, however, we may fitly pause. Though this theory, owing to the reasons we have mentioned above, did not fail to exercise a powerful influence on its author's contemporaries, yet its omissions incurred the biting criticism of posterity, and its absurdities were the butt of the ridicule of the comic Muse. Thus Theophrastus, in his brilliant critical review of the psychology of Diogenes, exclaimed that the birds should surpass us in understanding, if it be true that the purity of the air we breathe is the measure of the excellence and refinement of our reason. Why, he asked, should not our whole thought be changed with every change of residence according as we breathe the air of the mountains or the marshes ? The erudite pupil of Aristotle found himself for once in striking agreement with "the undisciplined favourite of the Graces," for Aristophanes in his "Clouds," produced in the year 423 B.C., lashed with his biting satire the most diverse manifestations of the era of enlightenment, and did not spare, as has long since been remarked, the doctrines of the sage of Apollonia. We hear this in the blasphemous cry, "Long live King Vortex, who has dethroned Zeus ;" we see it in the spectacle of Socrates swinging in his basket above the earth in order to inhale the purest intelligence through an atmosphere undefiled by the moisture of the soil ; we mark it again in

the goddess "Respiration" to whom the Socratic disciples
lift up their hands in prayer ; and we discern it finally in
the Chorus of the Cloud-women, who were provided with
enormous noses in order to take in as much of the spirit
of the air as possible. Each and all of these examples of
the wit of Aristophanes were aimed at the philosophy of
Diogenes, and were doubtless received in the theatre at
Athens with storms of laughter and applause.

2. The derision of the philosophy of the age was not
confined to Aristophanes. An older comic writer, the
bibulous poet Cratinus, devoted one of his dramas to that
theme. It was called "The Omniscients" (πανόπται), a
title properly applied only to Zeus himself and to Argus,
the thousand-eyed guardian of Io, but here extended to
characterize with bitter satire the adepts of philosophy who
affected to hear the grass grow. The "Omniscients" who
formed the Chorus of the play were recognizable at once
by their masks composed of two heads and countless eyes.
The butt of the satire in this instance was not Diogenes,
but Hippo—Hippo the atheist, either alone or with others,
who had come to Athens from Lower Italy, if not from
Samos. We are but imperfectly acquainted with the
life and work of this thinker, of whose writings there survives but a single brief fragment, and whom Aristotle
reckoned as one of the "coarser" minds, hardly deserving
the name of philosopher, on account of "the tenuity of his
thought." We range him here with the eclectics because
he was obviously at pains to weld the teachings of Parmenides with those of Thales. Thus the van of his cosmic
process was led by "the moist," from which "the cold"
and "the warm" (water and fire) proceeded, with fire as
the active cosmogonic principle, and water as the passive
matter.

Nearer to Diogenes than Hippo was Archelaus, a native
of Athens or Miletus. He was known as a disciple of
Anaxagoras, though he transformed his master's teaching
so considerably that he may almost be said to have reformed
it on older models. His cosmogony in especial bore the
traces of these differences. He did not admit the application

of Nous to matter from outside in order to organize it and to mould it to a cosmos. Archelaus, if we have understood the evidence aright, was rather of opinion that Nous was originally inherent to matter, and in that respect he approached more closely to the older representatives of the philosophy of nature, and likewise, it is legitimate to add, to the spirit of the old Greek view of the world. Taking these facts in connection with his craving to discern something divine in substance—a craving that was not satisfied by the dispersion of matter whether into infinitesimally small "seeds" or into the atoms of Leucippus—it was but natural that Archelaus employed himself similarly to Diogenes of Apollonia in building a serviceable bridge between the doctrines of Anaxagoras and Anaximenes. He did not reject the countless elements which the sage of Clazomenæ had entitled "seeds" or ὁμοιομέρειαι; but the great material forms which had played the chief part in the theory of the "physiologists" were again brought into prominence. The primary form of those "seeds," and at the same time the seat of Nous, the intellectual principle which first regulated cosmos, was represented by air, as the most immaterial, so to say, of material substances. Out of this intermediate stage fire and water, the vehicles of motion and rest, were produced by rarefaction and condensation, or by the disjunction and conjunction of the "seeds." It is hardly necessary to remind the reader that Archelaus was influenced at this point, not merely by the philosophy of Anaximenes, but by that of Parmenides, if not of Anaximander himself. A higher degree of originality would appear to attach to his attempt to describe the rudiments of human society and the fundamental conceptions of Ethics and Politics. To this, however, we shall have to return in another connection.

3. Another pupil of Anaxagoras was Metrodorus of Lampsacus. He displayed the same desire to reconcile the old with the new, to harmonize, in the present instance, the new science with the old faith. Unfortunately, our first impression of his allegorical key to Homer is one of disgust at its grotesque extravagance. We cannot conceive what induced him to identify Agamemnon with ether, Achilles

with the sun, Hector with the moon, Paris and Helen with the air and the earth, or to establish a parallel between portions of the animal body, the liver, the spleen, and the bile, on the one part, and Demeter, Dionysus, and Apollo on the other. We are reminded by these experiments of the worst excesses of the interpreters of the myths in our own day, not to speak of kindred fantastic exercises of other epochs, in all of which the desire is manifest to discover in sacred writings, the literal truth of which can no longer be upheld, the mere husk of completely different beliefs. We may recall, for instance, the Greek Jew, Philo of Alexandria, with his religious philosophy, who perceived in the garden of Eden the symbol of the divine wisdom, in the four streams that issued from it the four cardinal virtues, in the altar and tabernacle the "intelligible" or ideal objects of cognition, and so forth. Rightly, indeed, did Ernest Renan remark about Philo's allegorizing interpretation of the scriptures, that the root of his method, which was fraught with such important consequences, alien though it be to the true spirit of science, is founded in piety, and not in arbitrary wantonness. "Before one determines," he wrote, "to reject the teachings of a cherished faith" (or the authority of highly-esteemed writings) "one has recourse to every kind of identification, even to the most untenable ;" one has recourse, that is to say, to explanations which create a sense of wild absurdity outside the charmed circle of believers. In the present instance Metrodorus was entering and courageously pursuing a path which had been opened long before his day. Already in the sixth century Theagenes of Rhegium had applied the panacea of allegory to the authority of Homer which Xenophanes had assailed so bitterly. The battle of the gods in the twentieth book of the Iliad had given considerable offence. The sound reason, not to speak of the sound morality, of mankind had naturally been scandalized by the sight of the heavenly powers, who had come to be regarded more and more as the types of a uniform order in nature as in conduct, joined in actual hand-to-hand combat. The scandal had to be explained away, and an expedient was found in the sense that the Homeric deities represented partly inimical elements, partly contrary qualities of human nature. A kind of handle was afforded for the first of these categories of explanation by the fact that Hephæstus the god of fire, and Poseidon the lord of the sea, the twins Apollo and Artemis, who, if not originally identical with the sun and the moon, were at least frequently identified with those divinities, and lastly Xanthus the river-god, were all participants in the fight. Another considerable aid was the inexhaustible stores of etymology which the ancients found so malleable, and all kinds of moralizing reflections were added, among which may be mentioned the happy thought, worthy of an Elihu Burritt, that Ares the war-god was the personification of un-reason, and was thus the antagonist of reason incarnate in Athene. In this connection we first meet the name of Theagenes as the earliest "apologist" for the Homeric poems. Even Democritus and Anaxagoras did not disdain to contribute their mite to the allegorical interpretation of the national poetry ; Diogenes of Apollonia has already been mentioned in the same context ; and in Antisthenes, the disciple of Socrates, we shall meet yet another representative of the movement, which passed from the keeping of his followers, the Cynics, into that of the Stoic school, where it attained its highest development.

CHAPTER IV.

THE BEGINNINGS OF MENTAL AND MORAL SCIENCE.

1. THE constant increase in the attempts to effect a compromise between the old and the new in the national view of the universe and human life helps us to measure the gulf which had opened between the two. Our readers are already acquainted with the chief manifestations of this cleavage. They have learnt of the silent growth of the empirical knowledge of nature. They have seen the spirit of criticism seeking its springs of nourishment in the deepened speculation of philosophers, in the wider intellectual horizon, revealed by geographers and ethnologists, in the schools of disputatious physicians, and in the larger faith in sense-perception, as opposed to arbitrary assumptions of all kinds, which resulted from that cause. Here, then, we must go back in order to go forward. We must inquire into the changes undergone by Greek politics and society since the age of the tyrants,* in order to extend our survey of the progress of Hellenic civilization. In Athens, which is henceforward to be considered as the seat and centre of the Greek mind, the social struggle, as elsewhere, had ended with the victory of the middle classes. The privileges of the nobles had been more and more curtailed, and a corresponding impulse had been given, at the expense of the landed interest, to the influence of the mobile wealth derived from industry and trade. The population of the city had been increased by rural and foreign immigrants, and the new residents, who included many emancipated slaves,

* Cf. Bk. I., Intro., § 2.

were added in larger numbers to the civic lists. The
reforms of Clisthenes (509 B.C.), which followed swiftly
on the downfall of the Pisistratidæ, had been expressly
designed to bring about the inner reconciliation of these
diverse elements in Athens, and a chief factor in this movement, which finally ended in a fully developed democracy,
was supplied by the Persian wars. The nation was threatened by an enemy in overwhelming force, who could only
be met with any prospect of success by a rally of all the
powers at its disposal. At an earlier date, as we saw, the
rise of the heavy-armed middle-class infantry and the decline
of the mounted nobles produced far-reaching effects, and
this experience was now repeated in the employment of
the masses for service at sea. Universal conscription was
followed in a score or so of years by universal suffrage.
Athens, resting on her sea-power, became the head of a
confederacy which gradually transformed the conditions of
economic as well as of political life. She enjoyed lucrative
commercial monopolies ; she derived a rich income from
the tolls, and from the tributes and judiciary fees of the
confederates ; and, finally, the confiscated lands of a rene-
gade ally would fall to her from time to time for repartition.
By these means she was enabled to meet the cost of a
numerous civil population. The democracy built on this
foundation became the model for the states dependent
on Athens, and was imitated by various communities
outside of the federation. And whether the sceptre
wielded by the democrats was moderate or unlimited, the
chief instrument of government in practically the whole of
Greece was the power of the tongue. More than this. It
was not merely in the council-chamber and the popular
assembly that the efficacy of speech was supreme. In the
law courts too, where hundreds of jurymen would sometimes be sitting together, words were the universal weapons,
the clever manipulation of which was more than half the
battle. The gift and faculty of speech were the sole road
to honour and power. And speech, too, was the sole protection against injustice of every kind. Without that weapon
a man was exposed to the dangers of hostile attack, in his

own city and in times of peace, as hopelessly and defence-
lessly as a warrior without sword or shield on the battle-
field. It is not to be wondered at, therefore, that the
art of speech should have been cultivated for the first
time in the democratic communities of that age as
a profession, and that it should have assumed a prominent if not actually the first place in the education of
the young. But the art of rhetoric is double-faced ; it
is half dialectic, and half style or grammar. Its would-
be masters were required to attain to an infallible certainty
of expression, in addition to complying with the demands
on their quickness of thought and on their control
of the manifold principles regulating public life in all
its various departments. Nor was the tendency of the
times exhausted by the increased variety and earnestness
in the ideals of formal culture. Thought and research
were supplied with new riches and resources by the problems of political life which sprang from the transformation
of society and State, and which were grasped and attacked
with passionate devotion. Every one was interested in the
results of the discussion, and the conflict of opinions and
sentiments took as lively a course as the struggle of interests
itself. And the science of politics, like that of its formal
handmaiden, rhetoric, quickened the intellectual movement
on several sides at once. The question of right and wrong
in certain particular circumstances led by a very slight transition to the second and wider question of political justice in
general. Nor did the awakened curiosity pause at the confines of politics. It was inevitable that it should extend its
barriers to embrace all spheres of human activity and
business. In other words, the study of politics led to the
study of economics, of education, of the arts, and especially
of ethics. Moreover, when the inquiry had been widened to
include the rules of human action, it gave rise to a further
investigation into the sources of those rules and into the
origin of State and of society. To complete our picture of
the factors at work in that age we must recollect its intellectual conditions. The critical spirit, with its hostile attitude
towards authority, was already in full vigour, and the social

and political life of the fifth century must obviously have reinforced its powers. The foundation of all criticism is comparative observation, and in this respect the Greeks were fortunate in their contact with foreign populations, though it occurred by way of conflict during the Persian wars. Even more significant, perhaps, was the development of commercial and personal intercourse within the pale of the Attic naval confederacy. Considerable portions of the wide and scattered dominions of Hellas were now included in a common league. A constant stream of travellers was passing between the capital and the outlying members of the confederation, familiarizing reciprocally the Greeks of Athens with those of Asia Minor and the islands. The crowding of the cities—largely by immigration from other parts of Greece and from abroad—must have assisted that exchange of information and opinion which has been aptly defined as the friction of intellects. Finally, we must recollect the introduction of foreign cults which ensued on the Persian wars, and which led to a notable growth of religious sects in Athens. Burghers, metics, and visitors were united on the same spot ; the autocracy of the established faith was broken down, and thus, indirectly at least, a considerable step was taken towards the emancipation of thought.

2. These, then, so far as we can judge, were the conditions and circumstances obtaining in Greece at the time of her great intellectual progress, and of its contribution to the history of the world. Moral or mental philosophy took its place by the side of the natural philosophy that had preceded it, and its scope was at once the fullest possible, though its powers were somewhat limited. For, having sprung from practical needs, it was unable to repudiate its connection with the soil of practice. Hence, indeed, were derived its freshness and its warmth of pulsating life, but hence, too, in many cases, its marked defect in logical rigour and systematic completeness. Moreover, its flight was hampered by another restraining fetter, which, consisting as it did of the search for artistic diction, might be called a chain of flowers. Apart, perhaps, from the

professional rhetoricians, there was no expert public in any of these fields of learning. The art of rhetoric was supplied with dry and dreary, but methodical, text-books, but in other departments of knowledge the professors had to appeal to the cultured classes in general, whose pampered taste had to be tempted by all kinds of artifices of style. It is only on the heights of learning that a permanent union can be effected between beauty and truth. In laying the foundations of a science, and particularly of a science the fundamental conceptions of which require above all a clearness of outline and a sharpness of demarcation, the popularizing method is almost incompatible with success. In the age with which we are dealing, several excellent men were concerned in the attempt to overcome this difficulty. There was Prodicus, whose reputation rests on his studies in the differences of synonyms, and chief of all there was Socrates, the son of Sophroniscus, whose labours were at once the least pretentious and the most fruitful of results. His unadorned dialogues rose from the homeliest to the highest themes. He paused at every step to interrupt the flow of thought in order to test its depth and purity. Each fresh conception had to deliver its passport in the course of cross-examination ; every slumbering doubt was awakened ; every hidden contradiction was exposed ; and thus a splendid contribution was made to that sifting and purifying of fundamental ideas of which this early age stood in the greatest need.

In a later volume of the present work we shall be occupied with the name of Socrates, but here we may remark that if he surpassed the majority of his contemporaries at this point, he was fully in agreement with them at another. We refer to that heightened respect for reason and reflection as the supreme arbiters of human affairs which may perhaps be termed Intellectualism. This intellectualism was by far the most characteristic feature of the age. On the soil of Italy and Sicily, in particular, the new confidence which was produced by the reign of criticism and by the revolt from authority, went hand-in-hand with the growth of refinement of thought. Our readers will recollect the subtle and pointed arguments of Zeno of Elea, and, about fifty years earlier, Charondas, the legislator at Catania, had filled his office in a manner which won from Aristotle the praise that "by his sharpness and subtlety he has surpassed even the lawgivers of to-day." One example may stand as a type. The law of Charondas relating to the guardianship of orphans distributed their care between the relatives on the father's and on the mother's side, giving the first-named the charge of their fortune, and the second the charge of their person. Thus the administration of their fortune was committed to the hands of their presumptive heirs, who would have the greatest interest in increasing it, and the life and health of the orphans were entrusted to those of their relatives who would have no sinister motive to injure them. Meantime the conscious art of life, which aimed at reducing practice to fixed and reasonable laws, had made uninterrupted progress. The time had come when undisciplined empiricism had more and more to give way to the conscious rule of art. There was hardly any department of life which remained unaffected by that tendency. What was not reformed was codified, and both processes went almost hand-in-hand. Professional authorship took its rise on all sides; a profusion of text-books was poured forth ; all the business of mankind, from cooking a dinner to painting a picture, from going a walk to waging a war, was guided by rules and, where possible, reduced to principles. A few examples will help to make this clearer. Mithæcus discussed the art of cooking ; Democritus the philosopher wrote on tactics and warfare ; Herodicus of Selymbria made a systematic study of diet as a branch of science separate from medicine ; and even the treatment of horses was professionally described by Simo. All departments of the fine arts were theoretically elaborated. Lasus of Hermione, who, as early as the sixth century B.C., had added to the means of musical expression and supplied them with a basis of theory, now found several followers, among whom may be mentioned Damon, a personal friend of Pericles, and Hippias of Elis, who lectured on rhythm and harmony. Sophocles, too, following in the steps of an otherwise unknown Agatharchus, did not consider it beneath him to write a technical treatise on the stage ; and the great sculptor Polycletus reduced in his "Canon" the proportions of human anatomy to numerical equivalents. Democritus discussed the theory of painting, and both he and Anaxagoras were authors of treatises on the perspective of the stage. Agriculture, too, which was first raised to the dignity of literature by Hesiod in his peasants' calendar, the "Works and Days," was likewise treated by Democritus as a subject of philosophic discussion. Nor did the practitioners of prophecy or soothsaying lack their handbooks. Nothing was to be left any more to the mercy of chance or caprice. Urban architecture was reformed by Hippodamus of Miletus, a man of marked originality, who displayed his love of innovation even in his clothing and headdress, and we may perhaps regard the rectilineal and rectangular system of streets which Hippodamus introduced as a symbol of the increasing demand for the universal rule of reason.

3. An age of eager and restless innovation will spontaneously ask itself whence are derived right, law, and custom. What is the source of their sanction, and what are the supreme standards by which to direct the universal endeavours at reform? Now, every such inquiry beginning with "whence?" must go back to the origin of mankind. Mythology and didactic poetry had long ago painted in brilliant hues the raptures of a golden age. Hesiod is our earliest authority for this tendency of sentiment and thought to throw a halo on the distant past. It was a tendency which expressed the bias to gloom and pessimism by which he and his readers were affected. For the genius of the Greeks, like that of other peoples, escaped to the Elysian fields of past or future bliss in reaction from the stress and sorrow of their everyday life.* But in a critical epoch triumphing in its own culture and looking forward to further progress in that unlimited sphere, the picture of the primordial past takes a different complexion. An era which believes itself

* Bk. I. Ch. II. § 1.

superior to its ancestry, which views its own enlightenment not without pride, perhaps not without arrogance, is unlikely to seek its ideals in the dim spaces of past or future time, looking forward to the one with admiration, or back to the other with repining. This tendency of sentiment was accompanied by some facts of correct perception. It became a common conviction, we might almost say a self-evident commonplace, that the prehistoric ages were barbaric. The progress of humankind through the rising stages of civilization was a slow and gradual ascent from the depths of animal savagery. "Slow and gradual" by the evidence of scientific thought which had abandoned its belief in supernatural and miraculous intervention, and which, in the sphere of natural research, had obtained an insight into the method by which the minutest processes were gradually consummated to great results. We recollect in this connection the rudiments of the theory of descent which we found in Anaximander,* and the anticatastrophic geology of Xenophanes,† with his complementary view of the anticatastrophic course of civilization. We recollect, too, the medical writer ‡ who distinguished the men of his day from their less civilized ancestors and from the animal world in the matter of the culinary art.

The age of the Troglodytes was no more. They, with their ignorance of the plough and of iron instruments of all kinds, with their deeds of violence that did not shrink from cannibalism, had made way for civilized men who sowed the field and planted the vineyard, built their homesteads, fortified their cities, and finally had learnt to pay funeral honours to the dead. Thus Moschion, the tragic poet, who properly belongs to the fourth rather than the fifth century B.C., described the origin of civilization, leaving it doubtful, however, whether we owed it to the philanthropy of the Titan Prometheus, or to the force of necessity, or to "long practice" and gradual habituation in which "Nature played the part of schoolmistress." Nor had the leading men of the fifth century been free from

* Bk. I. Ch. I. § 2. † Bk. II. Ch. I. § 3.
‡ Bk. III. Ch. I. § 5.

similar reflections. Take, for instance, the opening verses of the tragedy "Sisyphus" by the Athenian statesman Critias, or take the title of a lost book by Protagoras of Abdera "On the Aboriginal State of Mankind," to which Moschion was presumably referring in the first words of the fragment we have mentioned, "Let man's first form be to your eyes revealed." The dominant conception of progress in that fragment of Moschion may be defined as organic, for though, as we have seen, it touched incidentally on the legend of Prometheus, yet the weight of its attention was given to the effects brought about by Nature, by Necessity, by Habit, and above all by "Time, that produceth all things and nourisheth all things." The idea of development was supreme ; its fruit was the order of society. Similarly, in the work of Critias, "the starry radiance of heaven" was spoken of as the "handiwork of the wise artist, Time." Now, Protagoras had treated these problems from a slightly different point of view. We might fairly speak of a mechanical—or, in the sense we have explained, of an intellectualistic—view of progress, as distinct from the organic. Design, Deliberation, and Invention fill the room of Nature, Habit, and unconscious Instinct. So much at least we may infer with approximate certainty from Plato's reproduction of that description. The account doubtless is partly a travesty, but its exaggeration of the details to be caricatured makes the features of the original more recognizable. Primeval man, so we read, could not gain the victory in his conflict with the wild animals, because they did not as yet possess the "art of government, of which the art of war is a part." Again, their want of the art of government permitted them to injure one another. The theft of fire, which the legend ascribed to Prometheus, was here explained as the theft of the wisdom of art from the chamber where Athene and Hephæstus presided over it. The fact that he stole the fire as well and gave it to mankind was merely because the "wisdom of art" would have availed them very little without that aid. Further, when Zeus sent "Justice" and "Reverence" on earth, Hermes, who was charged to distribute the boon, asked if the precious gift should be distributed to all men equally, or should be given in the proportion of the arts, with many laymen, that is to say, to one master or expert. By "art," too, men began to articulate their sounds and to invent language. By "art," "wisdom," or "virtue"—the words are deliberately used as equivalents, and are frequently put one for the other—they built houses, governed the State, and fulfilled the moral law. Art and its masters, in the sense that we should rather speak to-day of handicraft and artisans, formed a permanent contrast with nature and chance. Through all the Platonic caricature there shines that conception of life which our study of the conditions of this age has fully prepared us to encounter. We think we discern a pedantic note in these utterances, a hint of the schoolmaster's exaggerated reverence for what is founded on reflection, reduced to rule, and teachable by precept. Such a view of life was eminently suited to the childhood of the mental and moral sciences, and in no instance out of many, as we shall have occasion to remark, was it more strongly or more clearly developed than in the person of Socrates.

4. We need hardly say that this projection into the misty past of the achievements of an age of ripe reason is an unhistorical method. The genius and inventiveness of individual minds were of course at all times indispensable. Many of the greatest works of progress in which adult humanity acquiesces as self-evident were doubtless wrought by anonymous heroes of civilization, and we gladly join in the eulogistic pæan which George Forster raises in honour of the great Unknown who first subdued the horse and pressed him into the service of mankind. But progress depends on something more than the work of individual great men. Account must also be taken of the slow and imperceptible achievements of the moderately gifted multitude, climbing, as it were, the rungs of a ladder provided by Nature herself. It would be wholly incorrect, and at variance with historical facts, if the first stage instead of the last stage of evolution were taken as marking the

possession of a system or network of rules, which is what we mean by a practical art, and it is precisely this mistake in historical perspective which commonly characterizes the great epochs of intellectual emancipation. Unwittingly they shape the past according to their own image, and they are fain to adorn the childhood of the race with the features of precocious wisdom. Thus in such epochs we frequently meet the doctrine of the Social Contract. Minds that have repudiated the yoke of tradition, that have virtually outgrown the discipline of supernatural authority, and that perceive in the institutions of State and society nothing but means to human ends, are far too prone to ignore the different ages of mankind, and to ascribe to their remotest ancestors modes of thought and action corresponding exactly to their own. The fact is that the individual as such was originally of no account whatever. He was merely a member of his family, his tribe, or his clan. His adherence to the group of which he formed a part was conditioned by his birth, or imposed on him by force ; his obedience was given blindly, and no play at all was permitted to his powers of free-will or self-determination. These were the facts, which the apostles of enlightenment promptly proceeded to neglect, and to distort into an opposite significance. Moreover, that natural tendency was often considerably strengthened by the demands of practical politics. We begin to doubt the evidence of our own eyes when we see what views were expressed by John Locke * in his two treatises "On Civil Government." This acute and profound thinker maintained in all seriousness that the political community rested in all instances on voluntary combination and on the free choice of the rulers and of the forms of government ; and we watch with astonishment his eager but idle efforts to press the facts of history and ethnology into the service of this fallacious theory. Our astonishment abates, however, on homœopathic principles, when we glance at Locke's opponents, the theoretical defenders of absolutism. Those champions of the divine right of kings contended that the Creator

* A. D. 1632–1704.

had endowed Adam with the plenitude of governing powers, and that from Adam they had descended on all the monarchs of the earth. And the question was discussed throughout as if there were no alternative offered to contemporary thought except between these two doctrines thus at variance with history and reason. It is true that gleams of correct judgment flashed across the mind of Locke. He was aware that "an argument from what has been to what should of right be, has no great force." But the light of this perception did not prevent him from considering the cause of political freedom through hundreds of pages, as if it were bound to stand or fall with the triumph or defeat of his pseudo-historical theory. Reverting from Locke to the dawn of modern philosophy at the opening of the fourteenth century, and passing over the many intermediate links in that great chain of development, we are met by similar tendencies of thought. Marsilius of Padua, for example, the older contemporary of Petrarch, and the friend of William of Occam, the bold Minorite friar, was the author of a treatise, "The Defender of Peace," inscribed to Lewis of Bavaria, in which he asserted the doctrine of the Social Contract. He too, as we find, was filled with the belief that the war against priestly pretensions could only hope to end in the complete triumph of monarchical rule limited only by semi-constitutional or democratic checks, if it were waged under the standard of the sovereignty of the people and of this pseudo-historical fact on which it rested. In the earlier Middle Ages similar effects had been produced by a precisely contrary tendency. The wish to exalt ecclesiastical authority at the expense of the secular power had fostered the spread of the opinion that the State had sprung from the anarchy which ensued on the fall of man ; that it was not created by divine dispensation, but owed its origin to the disasters of mankind and to the Social Contract erected as a barrier against them.

If some one were to forbid us to walk upright unless we could prove that we had never crawled on all-fours in infancy, we should be hardly less surprised than at the prohibition imposed on modern men to exercise a free choice in political affairs unless their ancestors had exercised it in remote antiquity. We have just now alluded to the manner in which this mode of thought, which rests on a great over-estimate rather than on any under-estimate of the value of positive law, has re-arisen in more recent times, and every one is acquainted with the manner in which it reached its summit in Rousseau, the precursor of the French Revolution. Though this argument in favour of the theory of the Social Contract was not known to the ancients, yet the theory itself was familiar to them. We have already struck its psychological root. Reduced to its elements, the theory can be expressed in the form of a question and an answer, in which the answer will appear as wholly unprejudiced and impartial, but imbued with an error derived from the total lack of historical understanding. The question was, "How did our ancestors happen to resign their apparent individual self-independence, and to consent to those limitations of it which the State laid on them?" The answer was, "They accepted this disadvantage for the sake of a greater advantage. They resigned to a certain degree their own liberty in order to be protected from the abuse of liberty by other people —in order to protect life and property, their own as well as that of their dependents, from outside violence." In the light of common sense, this will be seen to be nothing but a special instance of a far-reaching tendency to error. Anything that fulfils a purpose may readily be regarded, by virtue of a false generalization, as necessarily owing its existence to a deliberate dispensation expressly directed to that end. Plato was acquainted with that doctrine, and at the beginning of the second book of the "Republic" he put it in the mouth of Glaucon, in the words:

"And when men have done and suffered [injustice] and had experience of both, not being able to avoid the one and obtain the other, they think that they had better agree with one another to have neither."

Here, then, was the beginning of laws and covenants;

hence the ordinances of the law were entitled right and just, and this was the nature and the origin of justice. Epicurus adopted that theory ; and his heavy debt to Democritus suggests that in this instance too he was following in the steps of his great predecessor—a conjecture, however, which cannot yet be asserted with more than a moderate degree of probability.

5. The probability is supported by the fact that in an allied sphere of learning the mind of Democritus took a similar bent. In the question of the origin of language, antiquity was divided into two hostile camps. Their conflict of opinions was a striking illustration of what John Stuart Mill has somewhere called the bandying of half-truths. One party asserted that language had a natural origin, the other party that it was based on convention. In the theory of the natural origin of language, two different contentions were involved. First, that the formation of language does not arise from deliberate design, but from a spontaneous impulse of instinct ; and, secondly, that the primordial natural connection between sound and meaning may still be recognized and proved in existing forms of language—that is to say, in the words of the Greek tongue. Now, contemporary philologers are convinced that the first of these contentions is true, but the second totally false. We know how ill we succeed in obtaining absolute certainty as to genuine original types of speech. Comparative analysis has disclosed many roots of the aboriginal Indo-Germanic language, but even there we are scarcely ever certain of standing in the presence of words without a past,—of true examples of the primordial impulse to language, free from all previous history. And yet we are far better equipped for that purpose than were the ancient Greek grammarians who hardly ever knew any other language than their own, and who lacked the means for all deeper analysis equally with the means for comparison. Philosophers approached the problem of the origin of language, which has never yet been completely solved, with the same helplessness and the same confidence with which they attacked the problem of the origin of organic

life. In both instances alike they succumbed to the temptation of mistaking the highly complicated as simple, and the last link in a long chain of development as aboriginal. The result was obviously an etymological scrimmage. An overwhelming subjective factor of error in the habitual mental association between the word and its meaning contributed to the breakdown in consequence of the difficulties of the facts. We are reminded of the Frenchman who maintained that his mother-tongue was constructed more naturally than English, because in English *pain* is called "bread," whereas in French it is called *pain* and it is *pain*. And even when attempts were made to treat the subject more rationally, to analyze the words and compare them with the impressions they produced, fresh delusions defeated the experiment, which failed to attain a single tenable result. Even in cases where the endeavours of the etymologists possessed a certain plausibility, their speculations, which Plato ridiculed in his dialogue "Cratylus," suffered the same fate as the lay philologers of our day who affect to perceive in the verb "to roll" a consonance with the sound of rolling thunder or of rolling wheels. They do not know that the word is derived from the Low Latin *rotula*, a diminutive of *rota* ("a wheel"), and that *rota*, like the German *Rad*, springs from the same root as *rash*,[*] so that the consonance is completely accidental. Heraclitus was the first to maintain this doctrine with its curious mixture of falsehood and truth. Or, rather, it is probably more correct to say that he tacitly assumed the theory than that he expressly promulgated and supported it. Undoubtedly he discerned in the consonance of words a reference to the affinities of the ideas to which they corresponded, as indeed may be gathered from some of his untranslatable sentences.[†] Similarly, he was evidently pleased at finding his doctrine of the coexistence of contraries foreshadowed in the Greek language, in the sense that one and the same word (βίος and βιός) meant at one time "life" and at another time an instrument of death, namely,

[*] N.B.—The German *rasch* = "swift."
[†] Bk. I. Ch I. § 5.

"the bow." It is at least questionable, however, if Heraclitus discussed the origin of linguistic formations and expressed his views on that subject. But, considering that he regarded all human activity as the image and emanation of the divine, he must have been very far from believing that the vocal incorporation of the processes of the mind was something merely artificial, and he would probably have rejected the assumption, even if, as is hardly credible, it had found a champion among his own contemporaries.

The name of Democritus is mentioned as the author, or at least as the earliest champion, of this counter-theory. At the same time we are made acquainted with the outline of the arguments which he marshalled against the doctrine of the natural origin of language. The sage of Abdera referred to the plurality of meanings borne by certain words (homonymy), and to the plurality of words used to designate certain objects (polyonymy). Further, he was struck by the occasional phenomenon of a change of appellations, and lastly by the "anonymity" of certain objects or ideas. The point of the first two of these arguments is quite clear. If, as had been assumed, it were true that an inner and necessary relation exists between an object and its name, cases could not arise as in the instances of "bill," or "gin," or "seal," in which the same complex of sounds denotes objects of different kinds. Similarly, the assumption was incompatible with the fact that one object could be called by more than one name. Thus the same locality is now a "room," now a "chamber;" the same piece of furniture is now a "chair," and now a "seat;" the same animal now a "dog," now a "hound." The third argument is little more than a variant of the first. For it makes but little difference whether an object is called by several names simultaneously, or whether these appellations are given to it in temporal succession. Thus "placket" was the seventeenth-century word for the petticoat of to-day, and we speak of "sherry" to-day in the place of Falstaff's "sack." The fourth and last argument, however, seems to transgress these bounds of reasoning, for it is hardly a proof against the existence of an inner connection between the names of things and the things named that certain objects or ideas are without appellations. Here, we fancy, Democritus must have been trying to express something of a different and more comprehensive kind. He would appear to have argued to this effect: If language were a divine gift or a product of nature, we should recognize in its manifestations a higher degree of adaptation than is actually apparent. But the alternating picture of excess and defect, of change and inconstancy, and finally of a total lack of the requisite means to an end, though familiar enough in the imperfect types of human invention, should not appertain to creations which we ascribe to the government of nature or to the control of divine agencies. And, rendering this reflection of Democritus into the language of modern thought, we may interpret him as follows: Language is not an organism, for experience teaches us that organisms contain a far higher degree of perfection than is contained in language—a concession to experience with which Democritus may fairly be credited despite his strong anti-teleological bias.

The incisive criticism thus directed at the theory of a natural origin of language affected it merely in its rudest and most incomplete form. Democritus succeeded in proving that men have not been constrained as if by an invincible necessity to describe objects by the names appertaining to them and by no other names. But this result might have been reached by a mere reference to the fact that there exist more languages than one. Democritus, it must be added, was as guilty as any of his opponents of the fundamental crime of that theory. He too confused what is original with what is the result of development, and he too neglected all the facts pointing to what we call the growth and evolution of language. In order to evade the difficulties which threatened the theory of his adversaries, he was compelled to adopt an hypothesis which brought no less serious difficulties in its train. Language, according to this hypothesis, was to be entirely conventional in origin ; primeval men were to have agreed together to call the objects by such-and-such names in order that they might keep as a permanent possession this important aid to instruction and communication. The objections to that view are obvious. The critics of antiquity, led by Epicurus, were quick to ask the awkward question, How could such agreement have been reached in an age when language itself, the most important means of communication, did not yet exist? Thus the Epicurean author of a book written on stone which has only lately been discovered, asked if the "name-giver" was to be represented as a kind of schoolmaster, who showed his pupils at one time a stone and at another time a flower, and insisted on their learning the proper names. If so, he wondered, what would bind them to use those names and no others when the schoolmaster's eye was removed; and what would preserve those names for the information of posterity, or even for the use of remote quarters of the country? or were we to suppose that this remarkable lesson was imparted at one time to great masses of men, and if so, did it take place by written communications, which could certainly not precede the invention of language, or by the concourse in one spot of scattered multitudes of men in an age which was deficient in all perfected means of locomotion? This was the kind of ridicule which was poured on the exposition of Democritus, and we are unable to say at this date how far he really deserved it. It is quite possible that he refrained from elaborating his central thought in detail, and that he was content to set up the theory of convention as the sole solution of the problem adequate to replace the old theory of nature which, as a whole, he could not but condemn. Be that as it may, it was left to Epicurus to dispel a portion of the darkness which surrounded this theme, and by the assumption of a natural as well as of a conventional element in language to untie the knot as efficiently as his inadequate resources permitted. At that point, if not earlier, in the present history, we shall have to come to closer contact with the problem, and to examine Epicurus's attempt at a solution, correct in principle as it was, in relation to the subsequent teachings of comparative philology.

A single example will suffice to help us to realize the conceptions of the natural and the conventional element in speech. The original Indo-European language possessed a root *pu*, which carried with it the meaning of "to cleanse." Presuming, as is extremely probable, that this is a genuine original root and not derivative, we may be permitted to speculate on the manner in which this little syllable reached its fundamental significance. If we employ the mouth itself, the organ of speech, to perform an act of cleansing, this is done by blowing away the particles of dust, straw, etc., which cover and pollute any superficial plane. If we do this energetically by a determined narrowing of our protruded lips, we produce sounds like *p*, *pf*, or *pu*. In this way the last-named sound might at least have obtained its primitive significance. Presuming our conjecture to be correct, a definite position and movement of the organs of speech formed in this instance, as doubtless in countless others, the bond between sound and meaning. In our opinion, too, this imitation of movements was by far the most fertile source in the formation of language—far more fertile, indeed, than the imitation of sounds merely at second hand and not self-produced, such as the name "cuckoo" or the verb "to mew." Opinions of course may differ on this point, but both instances may fairly be claimed as cases of what, without any taint of mysticism, we may call the natural element in language. When we come to look at the various offshoots of that root, however, in the separate Indo-European languages, we are confronted at once with the arbitrary forces of selection and preference—in other words, with the element of convention. For side by side with this one appellation of the cleansing process, numerous others are found to describe precisely the same operation, though with different shades of meaning. There was nothing to compel the Roman to use the adjective *purus* ("clean"), which sprang from that root, nor to compel the Roman and Greek to employ the substantives *pœna* and *poiné* ("punishment"), springing from the same root. We can only say that several uses of those words, especially their combination with expressions signifying soul, disposition or sentiment, such as " mens pura," "pureté d'âme," "purity of mind," and so forth, corresponded fairly exactly to the fundamental meaning of the root, and formed a kind of reflection of its primitive significance. Further, the conception of punishment as a religious atonement or purification would be more appropriately expressed by the derivatives of *pu* than by descendants of other roots, such as sweeping, scouring, washing, etc., which import an additional conception of coarse material violence into their expression of the same operation. There was, of course, no compulsion to use this or that word in any given context. We can only speak of tendencies which were as liable to be defeated by the accidents of use and wont as they were likely to profit by favourable circumstances. As we descend more deeply into the history of a language, to reach at last the new formations of later epochs or of the present, we perceive more and more the importance of the alternating fortunes of the long historical process, and we watch the gradual disappearance of the tendency originally appertaining to the natural element as it yields to the caprice of the speaker or the writer. For a word which popular parlance or authors of decisive authority have used for a definite conception becomes dedicated, as it were, to that purpose. Thus words become more and more mere signs of conventional agreement, mere coins that have passed from hand to hand till their original impress can only be read or renewed by the inventive genius of the artist of speech, and, above all, of the poet. In other instances a breath of their vanished perfume still haunts these withered flowers of thought, and teaches even the coarser senses of the multitude how to use them aright. And now to revert to *pu* and its offspring. If one of the new forms of dentifrice was advertised as " Puritas," this was solely due to the preference of one man, its inventor ; but even in the French word *peine*, and transcendently in *à peine*, meaning "scarcely," in the German *Pein*, or the English *pain*, there is no trace whatsoever of their original meaning. The Puritans received their party-name on account of their endeavour to restore the ecclesiastical institutions in their original shape, free (or

pure) from later accretions. But the shade of meaning in
the root of the word had hardly any marked effect on the
choice of the name, though it may indeed have operated
tacitly and unconsciously in the fact that the appellation
was presently transferred to the ethical sphere, in which the
term " moral Puritanism " became a familiar phrase.

The same example will serve to show that the argument
derived by Democritus from homonymy admits of refutation even in such cases as exhibit the vocal identity of
original, not of derivative forms of speech. If we blow
something away, we are not always moved by the intention of cleansing the object ; we may also do it from a
desire, or, if instinctively, with the effect, of removing from
ourselves something ugly or repugnant. In this way,
as Darwin tells us, numerous nations of the earth use this
gesture to express repugnance and contempt, and the
spoken equivalent of the gesture, such as the German
pfui, or the English *pooh*, which is likewise used by the
Australian aborigines, serves to express those emotions.
Similarly, Greek and Latin words denoting foul smells and
the like, were derived from the same root, as we may
still see in suppuration, putrescence, pyemy. The course of
language-formation flows nowadays with but a sluggish
stream, but it never entirely runs dry, and English in recent
times has come to employ the exclamation we are speaking
of as a verb, so that an Englishman, wishing to cast doubts
on the honesty of another man's purpose in an emphatic
form, may combine both fundamental meanings of that
phonetic gesture in the sentence, " I pooh-pooh the purity
of your intentions."

6. The fascination of this great controversy over the
origin of language is second in importance, however, to the
contrast it involves between nature on the one part and
convention on the other. We are already familiar with
the distinction. We met it in the theory of sense-perception formulated by Leucippus and Democritus, in which
we learned to recognize convention as the type of change,
subjectiveness, and relativity, in opposition to the changeless constancy of the objective world. But the true home

of this contrast was not the sphere of sense-perception, nor was it the domain of language ; it was rather to be found in political and social phenomena. Archelaus, the pupil of Anaxagoras, is mentioned as the first representative in literature of this fundamental antithesis, but little more than this fact is known to us. His works have been lost, and we can only say with certainty that he discussed "Beauty, Justice, and the Laws" in the sense of that distinction, that he considered in this connection the "severance" of mankind from the rest of animal life, and that he treated of the rudiments of the social state. The antithesis between law and nature was foreign to all epochs in which the spirit of criticism was still in a rudimentary stage. Wherever authority and tradition reigned in undisputed supremacy, the extant rules of life were accepted as the only natural laws, or, more exactly stated, their relation to nature was outside the region of doubt or even of discussion. This is the attitude of the Mohammedan of to-day, who walks among us like a living fossil, clothed in the impassivity of that early era of thought, and invoking the revelation of Allah, as manifested in the Koran, as the supreme authority beyond the reach of appeal in all questions of religion, law, ethics, and politics. To revert to the distinction, however, between nature and convention, we see that its recognition entails two great series of consequences. On the one part, it supplies the weapons for the incisive and destructive criticism of all extant and valid laws ; on the other part, it provides a new and paramount standard for the reform which is presently inaugurated in the most diverse fields. But the ambiguity in the word "nature," which was clearly recognized in later antiquity, rendered that standard extremely vacillating and uncertain —a fact that seems to have increased the readiness of mankind to use it, inasmuch as the vagueness of the formula made it easier for them to include the most various aims and desires. Thus the poet Euripides, when he exclaimed, "This Nature does, who no convention knows," was thinking of the power of natural impulse which laughs at law and locksmiths ; but when he said of a bastard, " His name's his fault, no difference Nature knows," the dramatist was thinking of the actual individual nature of men and of its independence of the artificial distinctions of society. In a similar, though not in completely the same sense, Alcidamas the rhetorician * exclaimed in his " Messenian Speech," "the Deity made all men free : Nature has enslaved no man." The speaker was here dominated by the conception of an imaginary primeval state in which universal equality was the rule ; or else he was thinking of a natural law, founded on this or on some other basis, which took precedence of all human institutions.

A distinction of this kind was bound to serve as a means of criticism and negative attack. History and ethnology had widened the study of the moral and political conditions of various tribes, nations, and epochs, and hence was derived a keener perception of the Protean multiformity of human customs and laws. People began to busy themselves with applying the comparative method to the most glaring contrasts. A new literature sprang up about this subject, which reached its summit in antiquity in the treatise " On Fate," by Bardesanes, the Syrian Gnostic,† and which reaped a rich harvest in the age of the Encyclopædists. Herodotus himself took pride in parading antitheses of this kind. A notable instance occurs in one of his stories about Darius. He relates that the monarch sent for the Greeks at his court to ask them their price for devouring the corpses of their ancestors. They replied that no price would be high enough. Thereupon the Persian king summoned the representatives of an Indian tribe which habitually practised the custom from which the Greeks shrank, and asked them through the interpreter, in the presence of the Greeks, at what price they would burn the corpses of their ancestors. The Indians cried aloud and besought the king not even to mention such a horror. From these circumstances the historian drew the following notable moral for human guidance : If all existing customs could somewhere be set before all men in order that they might select the most beautiful for themselves, every nation would choose

* Fourth century B.C. ; cp. Ch. VII. § 4, *infra.*　† Born *circ.* 200 A.D.

out, after the most searching scrutiny, the customs they had already practised. And he ends his tale by giving Pindar right in his remark, " Convention is the king of all men." The same thought is developed at greater length and with even more point in a treatise which may probably also be referred to this age. There we find the opinion expressed that " if all men were to gather in a heap the customs which they hold to be good and noble, and if they were next to select from it the customs which they hold to be base and vile, nothing would be left over, but all would be distributed among all." We can hardly conceive a more direct and definite expression of the belief that no act or institution is so bad or ugly as not to be held in high honour by some portion of humanity. This relativist point of view has an enlightening and emancipating effect on which we may pause for a moment. We see it most clearly in the dramas of Euripides, the great poet and prophet of free thought. We marked just now his indifference to the stain of illegitimacy, and we would add here that he made no more account of the brand on the forehead of the slave. In his opinion it was the convention and the name, not nature, that imposed slavery:

> " The name alone is shameful to the slave ;
> In all things else an honest man enslaved
> Falls not below the nature of the free."

He was equally explicit, too, on the question of the difference between noble and humble birth :

> " The honest man is Nature's nobleman.
> Who keeps not justice, though the son of Zeus,
> Or sprung more highly, count I but as mean."

We see that little was wanting to break down the barriers of nationality and to make room for the cosmopolitan ideal which we shall meet in full splendour in the Cynics. That ideal was anticipated by Hippias of Elis, in whose mouth Plato put the words—

" All of you who are here present I reckon to be kinsmen and friends and fellow-citizens, by nature and not by law; for by nature like is akin to like, whereas law is the tyrant of mankind, and often compels us to do many things which are against nature."

7. While Nature meant here the social instinct, the real or probable original equality of mankind, it is obvious that the opposite opinion would not go begging for champions. The victory of the stronger over the weaker and the superiority of talent to mediocrity were bound to attract attention and to be regarded as an emanation of Nature, especially in a society founded on conquest and slavery. We may recall the glorification of war by Heraclitus as "the father and king" * of all things, which had differentiated free and slaves as well as gods and men. The sage of Ephesus was the first to recognize and exalt the significance of war or the application of force in the foundation of State and society. When we come to Aristotle we shall meet a kindred point of view, though somewhat less comprehensive and marred by a national prejudice. Aristotle undertook to discover a natural basis for slavery. He justified it in the interests of the barbaric slaves themselves, who were unfit for self-government, and he combated the view that slavery was merely the work of arbitrary convention. Whether or not the literature of the age of enlightenment contributed to this tendency is uncertain, but the probability is on the negative side. Plato at least, who rejected it, selected as its champion among the contemporaries of Socrates, not an author or a teacher of youth, but one of their bitterest foes, a practical politician, who plumed himself on his extreme practicality, and who is otherwise unknown to us. It is in the dialogue called "Gorgias" that this Callicles made a passionate plea for the right of might. He there refers to the dominion which the strong exercises over the weak as a fact founded in nature, and to be characterized accordingly as a "natural law." The natural law changed forthwith on his lips to a "natural right" or to a dispensation of "natural justice." The bridge between the recognition of a natural fact and the approval of the conduct corresponding to it was built with considerable ease,

* Bk. I. Ch. I. § 5 (p. 72).

and the operation was assisted by the fact that there was one domain at least in which antiquity could perceive hardly any difference between the two. In international relations it was deemed at once natural and right that the strong states should overthrow and absorb the weak. This explanation, however, is not exhaustive in the present instance. For, though Callicles appeals to the right of conquest as well as to the example of the whole animal creation, yet he differs in two essential points both from Heraclitus and from Aristotle. He aims at the subjection, not of a portion, but of the whole of mankind, and his sympathies, if not exclusively, are yet mainly on the side of the strong and the clever rather than of the weak and dull. He takes the part of the man of genius, the "hero" as we should say to-day, against the multitude which tried at once to enslave his soul and to reduce him to the level of their own mediocrity. Callicles rejoiced to think that the man of genius, like a young half-tamed lion, would rise in the fulness of his strength—

" will shake off and break through and escape from all this ; he will trample under foot all our formulas and spells and charms, and all our laws sinning against nature : the slave will rise in rebellion and be lord over us, and the light of natural justice will shine forth."

Such remarks as these express the æsthetic delight in the untamed force of a strong human nature. They represent, moreover, the feeling expressed by a modern champion of absolutism in the words, "the rule of the mightier is the eternal ordinance of God." A little later on, Callicles in Plato is made to defend a tenet which was less bitterly at variance with the spirit of popular institutions. The better and more intelligent man in his view was to exercise supremacy, and, as we do not live in an ideal world, he was not to be robbed of the right of personal profit. In other words, the fittest and most competent men were to exert the strongest influence and to draw the richest rewards in political life. But the character of Callicles underwent a strange transformation in the further course of the dialogue. The champion of a Carlylean hero-worship, of Haller's political theories, and of the principle of uncorrupted aristocracies, was suddenly turned to the evangelist of the gospel of an unbridled lust for pleasure. It is clear that this view had not found a spokesman in that age, from the ingenuous remark of Plato himself, " For what you say is what the rest of the world think, but are unwilling to say." We may confidently assert that the philosopher-poet combined this theory with the others so alien to it, in order to increase the odium which he desired to attach to them. But what was undoubtedly genuine and heartfelt was Plato's indignation at the yoke of average mediocrity and the frequent blunders of democratic institutions. It formed an intelligible protest against the existing order of the State with its shifting lights and shades. The ideal Athens varied according to the critic's mood. Some were disposed to hero-worship, with Alcibiades at that moment as their idol. Others were inclined to revive the institutions of aristocracy either in whole or in part. Finally, Plato himself, who was a thorough hater of democracy, preached the Utopian doctrine of the philosophic kings. Thus "nature" and "natural law" were on one side the chosen shibboleth of the growing love of equality with its steady advance to cosmopolitanism, and on the other side they served the aristocrats and the worshippers of a strong personality. One ambition was common to both tendencies. They were moved alike by the desire to break loose from the bonds in which tradition and authority had fettered the mind of mankind.

8. We are met here by a double question. How far did the diminishment of authority extend, and what were the effects that accompanied it? We are not in a position to give even an approximately exact answer to either of these questions. But one thing at least is quite clear—that no domain of life or faith was exempt from the attacks of criticism. The inquisitorial scepticism of the age did not pause even at the gates of heaven. Diagoras

of Melos, a dithyrambic versifier, whose sparse poetical remains are steeped in awe of the gods, fell a victim to some unavenged injury, and became in consequence a sceptic as to the divine justice. He gave expression to this change of view in a volume of "Crushing Speeches," a title which affords a glimpse into the blasphemous disposition of the orthodox poet now turned revolutionary. In a later chapter we shall have to deal with the religious doubts of Protagoras, clothed in far more moderate garb, as well as with the theory of Prodicus on the origin of religion. The abandoned throne of authority was usurped on all sides by reason and reflection. Every question of human conduct was treated by way of ratiocination, and one and all were submitted to the verdict of Reason. Nor was this innovation confined to philosophy and rhetoric. The poets and the historians, too, surprise us by the subtlety of their arguments. The dialogue of the dramatists, which even as early as Sophocles showed traces of the influence of the new tendency, became in the pliant hands of Euripides the playground of intellectual tournaments. Not old Herodotus himself, with his patriarchal modes of thought, escaped the spirit of his age and the temptation to discuss the great problems of human existence from a philosophizing moralist's point of view. Both he and Euripides started a discussion on human happiness and brought similar methods to bear on it. Herodotus, in his conversation between Solon and Crœsus, set up two abstract types, the first of the man who had lost every claim to happiness except his bare title to wealth, and the second of the poor man favoured in all other respects by good fortune. In the same way, in a fragment of the "Bellerophon" of Euripides, we find three rivals competing for the palm of happiness. Unlike the artificial creations of Herodotus, these types are taken from real life. They are (1) the low-born but rich man, (2) the high-born but poor man, and (3) the man without great riches or good birth, to whom by a paradoxical argument the meed of victory was awarded. In the passage where Herodotus introduced three Persian nobles disputing about

the best form of government, he equipped the champion
of his own favourite, democracy, with the strongest show
of reason, but at the same time he displayed considerable
dialectic skill by providing the defenders of monarchy
and oligarchy with no mean arguments for their cases.
In the times of which we are speaking, the problem of
education occupied the foreground of interest. Questions
were constantly asked, and the most diverse answers were
returned, whether instruction or natural disposition was
the more important factor, and whether theoretical teaching or practical habituation was to be preferred. Euripides,
with his usual adaptability, laid equal emphasis on the
teachable quality of "manly virtue," and on the necessity
of familiarizing youth at a tender age with good examples.
In this connection we may quote the following exclamation
of one of his tragic characters :—

> " Nature is all in all ; in vain men try
> To teach the evil to be changed to good."

The parallel between the cultivation of the intellect and
the sowing of a field with fruits became a commonplace
of the age. Talent was compared with the constitution of
the soil ; instruction with the planting of the seed ; the
industry of the learner with the labour of the husbandman,
and so on throughout the resources of the metaphor. In
this simile, to the features of which we shall probably
have occasion to return, we see that the doctrines of
education, which were originally kept rigidly apart, have
already been merged in one thesis.

The same epoch was remarkable for its fertility in
schemes of reform. Thus Phaleas of Chalcedon, in the
second half of the fifth century, expressed himself in
favour of the equalization of wealth, and formulated
proposals to that end, which, so far as we are aware,
however, would have affected real property alone. Another
item in his programme was the state control of all
industrial labour, its organization, that is to say, by a
system of state slaves. Hippodamus of Miletus, again,
whose acquaintance our readers have already made, and

who was slightly senior to Phaleas, recommended a complete transformation of the internal constitution of states as well as of the external arrangement of cities. His ideal polity comprised three classes, in the respective spheres of industry, agriculture, and war. Of his three divisions of the land one-third only was to be private property; another third was to be devoted to the purposes of divine worship, and the remainder to military supply. All the public officials were to be elected by the suffrages of the total community of 10,000 men. The magic number three was also efficacious in Hippodamus' division of the criminal code into three sections, applied respectively to offences against life, honour, and property. The administrative work of government similarly fell in three categories, dealing respectively with the citizens, the orphans, and the foreigners. It is in this scheme that the thought was first expressed of the duty of the State to honour with special marks of distinction the authors of useful inventions. Moreover, the creation of a supreme court of appeal, and the acquittal of defendants *ab instantia*, were innovations first recommended by Hippodamus, and, except for the counter-testimony of Aristotle, we should add to the list of his original projects the principle of educating at the expense of the State the children of the victims of war. But it was the disciples of Socrates who first soared to the summits of boldness; the doubts that still gnaw at the foundations of social order took their rise in that select band.

But apart altogether from the extreme consequences first drawn by Plato and the Cynics from the sovereignty of reason, the spectacle is vivid enough to recall the radicalism of the French Revolution. The two epochs are divided, however, by one deep line of cleavage. The age of Greek emancipation was innocent of any serious attempt to transfer its theories into the practice of social and political life. A single parallel may be taken as typical in this connection. In Paris the "goddess Reason" enjoyed a real though ephemeral worship, and the Athens of the epoch we are discussing was also acquainted with that goddess. Her shrine, however, was on the stage of comedy, and her priests were the buffoons of Aristophanes, who put in the mouth of Euripides the prayer, "Hear me, O Reason, and ye olfactory organs!" Nor did the other Radical doctrines of that age try to escape from the shadows of literature and the schools into the light of reality. At the same time it would be completely erroneous to conclude that ancient Radicalism was deficient on the side of intensity. The history of Cynicism will show us that there was no lack of persons ready to push their break with tradition to the extreme length of their serious convictions. Moreover, the indirect influence of philosophic radicalism on the culture of the succeeding centuries will loom before us in huge proportions. Still, generally speaking, philosophy may be said to have been a powerful intellectual fermentation without directly becoming a factor in practical life. And the cause of this suspense in its development is probably to be sought in the following circumstances. The economic condition of those times, which afforded a pointed contrast with that obtaining in Sparta in the third century B.C., was at least not intolerable to the masses. Violent collisions were indeed not unfrequent, but they did not differ essentially from the conflicts of the classes in former generations. Their acuteness in the course of the Peloponnesian War was due to the influence of transient political constellations. The Greek religion was pliant enough to follow the immense changes in philosophic thought; and, finally, the national character of the Greeks, and pre-eminently of the Athenians, was instinctively averse from all suddenness and precipitancy, and was marked by a sense of measure and tact favourable to a gradual progress in all fields of development. So much, perhaps, by way of provisional reply to the questions asked at the beginning of this section. Before we go further we must pass in review some of the rhetoricians, teachers, poets, and historians, who formed the chief figures in this great intellectual movement.

CHAPTER V.

THE SOPHISTS.

1. FERTILE though the fifth century had been in literary productions, it was far from earning the character of "an age of scribblers." The Greek still preferred to take his knowledge through the ear instead of the eye. The old-time rhapsodist was gradually vanishing, but his place in the public life of Hellas was being filled by a new figure. The "sophist" at Olympia and elsewhere wore the same purple raiment, attended the same great festivals, and delivered original harangues and panegyrics, instead of the old heroic poems, before the assembled holiday-makers. Moreover, elaborate lectures on the various questions of learning and life had become familiar in smaller social circles.* And thus we are able to measure the revolution which had taken place in the education of youth shortly before the last third of the century. The higher demands of political life, and the claims of an increased intellectual activity, were no longer satisfied with the old scanty instruction in the elements of reading, writing, and arithmetic, which, to-gether with music, gymnastics, and ultimately draw-ing, had formed the complete curriculum of instruction. There had been no provision, either from the public or from private sources, for the kind of education which is imparted in our public schools and in our non-professional universities, but the time came when men of original talents voluntarily undertook to fill up these gaps in

* Cp. Bk. II. Ch. II. § 1.

education. Itinerant teachers began to wander from
city to city, gathering young men round them and
giving them lessons. Their instruction comprised the
elements of the positive sciences, the doctrines of the
nature-philosophers, the interpretation and criticism of
poetry, the distinctions of the newly-founded rudiments of
grammar, and the subtleties of metaphysics. But the
central point of the education consisted, as was proper, of
a preparation for practical, and especially for public, life.
Thus Protagoras of Abdera, whom we hear of as the
earliest and most renowned of these itinerant teachers,
formulated his educational ideal, according to Plato, in the
following words :—

" And this is prudence in affairs private as well as public ; he
will learn to order his own house in the best manner, and he
will be best able to speak and act in affairs of the state."

The essence of the instruction, in a word, was contained
in the moral and political sciences, or in such rudiments
thereof as were constructed or in course of construction.
The art of eloquence, however, the high significance and
constant care of which we have already had occasion to
discuss,* was the soul of practical politics. These self-
styled sophists, these masters or teachers of wisdom, would
obviously not confine their activity to the education of the
young. They brought to the altars of rhetoric and literature
the same gifts and resources which served them in their teaching capacity. In a certain sense, too, it was a necessity of
their position that they should be restlessly engaged in
these different pursuits, for they were entirely without subsidy
from the State, they relied absolutely on their own efforts,
they resided more frequently abroad than at home, and
thus handicapped, they were compelled to enter on a
keen competition among themselves. Modern life contains
no exact parallel to the sophists. They were like the
German professor of to-day, but were distinguished from
him by the lack of all relationship to the State, whether

* Bk. III. Ch. IV. § 1.

useful or hurtful to their calling, as well as by the absence of all facultative narrowness and specialist limitations. Their standard of attainments for the most part was well-nigh encyclopædic, and they resembled the journalists and men of letters of to-day in their constant readiness for the war of words. Half professor and half journalist—this is the best formula that we can devise to characterize the sophist of the fifth century B.C. They earned a rich meed of applause no less than of material success, and the enthusiasm that their foremost representatives aroused in the youth of Greece, with its keen worship of beauty of form and intellectual culture, was almost immeasurable.

The sophists, as Plato expresses it, were borne on the shoulders of their disciples, and the appearance of one of these heroes was the signal for an outburst of excitement in wide circles of the young men of Athens. We are told—in a passage of Plato from which we borrow the following account—how even before daybreak the house and bedchamber of Socrates were stormed by a high-born pupil, who woke the master with the cry, " Hast heard the great news ? " and how the sage answered in alarm, " For heaven's sake, what evil tidings dost thou bring ? " " God forbid," replied the pupil, " 'tis the best of all. He has come." " Who ? " " The great sophist of Abdera." The youth then besought Socrates to put in a good word for him with the renowned Protagoras, that he might be admitted in the band of his disciples. In the morning, they went together to the house of the wealthy Callias, where the guest from Abdera was lodging. There they found the liveliest excitement. Protagoras was walking to and fro in the vestibule, with three distinguished friends on either side of him, including his host and the two sons of Pericles, and followed by a troop of secondary worshippers.

" And nothing," adds the Platonic Socrates in his satiric vein— " nothing amused me so much as to see how the young men took pains to give precedence to the master, and how, as soon as the van of the procession reached one end of the hall, the train parted itself asunder, in order to close up again in due order behind the great man and his companions."

In various apartments of the interior of the house other sophists were holding their court, each surrounded by a bevy of admirers like the belle of a ball. And now Socrates preferred his request in an ordinary conversational tone, and the rhetorician replied in measured language, with a long set speech delivered with impressive ceremony. A philosophic discussion sprang up between the two, and the rest of the company, hurriedly collecting all the benches and seats in the house, sat down to the feast of ear and mind. Protagoras left it to the audience to decide whether he should answer Socrates in a concise or discursive manner, whether by a speech or by the narration of a myth. The listeners, as soon as he began to speak, hung with eager expectation on his lips, and broke, when the discourse was ended, into storms of long-pent applause : the imperishable charm of Plato's style has made the whole story familiar, and though it contains a strong element of caricature, yet its realistic features are still clearly perceptible.

2. We may be asked, What was the genuine common factor in the several sophists? and to that question we can but reply that it consisted merely of their teaching profession and the conditions of its practice imposed by the age in which they lived. For the rest, they were united, as other people were united too, by the part they took in the intellectual movements of their times. It is illegitimate, if not absurd, to speak of a sophistic mind, sophistic morality, sophistic scepticism, and so forth. It would have been miraculous if the sophists, the paid teachers of youth, whether they were found in the Thracian colony of Abdera, or in the Peloponnesian province of Elis, in Central Greece, or in Sicily, had stood nearer to one another in sentiment and thought than to the other representatives of contemporary thought. The most that we can say is, that the majority of popular writers and teachers of every age have been on the side which made for victory, and have not backed the losing or retrograde cause. And this was true of the sophists as of the rest. Dependent as they were on their public, they necessarily became the mouthpiece of ideas which, if not dominant, were at least rising into

predominance. It is, therefore, not wholly inadmissible to regard the members of this profession in general as the vehicles of emancipation, though not all sophists were the leaders of emancipated thought, nor—far less—all emancipators sophists. Furthermore, we shall see that the majority of them, possibly on account of that very dependence, maintained in the main a moderate attitude, and that no one of them was so advanced a Radical in social or political thought as Plato and the Cynics.

But before we go further, if our readers are not to be misled by false associations of ideas, we must acquaint them with the history of the words "sophist," "sophistical," "sophistry." The name σοφιστής, or "sophist," is derived from the adjective σοφός ("wise"), and directly from the verb σοφίζομαι ("to think out," or "to devise"). Thus it originally means more or less any man who has attained to eminent success in some faculty or other. The name was applied to great poets, important philosophers, famous musicians, and to the seven wise men whose sententious maxims made them renowned in public and private life. At an early time the word seems to have acquired a tinge of disfavour, but at first at least the tinge must have been very slight, for otherwise Protagoras and his successors would never have selected the title for themselves. It was a disfavour which was destined to increase, however, and it flowed from various sources. In the first place, it is to be noted that any attempt to penetrate the secrets of nature aroused the mistrust of pious men. Theologians looked on the natural philosophers with suspicion, and even other words, originally neutral in their significance, acquired an unfavourable bye-taste. Thus in the popular decree introduced by Diopeithes and directed at Anaxagoras the science of the heavens, or meteorology, was associated with a disbelief in the gods, and a flavour of suspicion attached to the word "meteorologist." It was hardly to be wondered that the new speculation about problems of knowledge, and questions of morality and right, should likewise have brought on their authors the charge of an indiscreet curiosity. And to this fear, whether genuine or pretended, of the pursuit of knowledge in general, there was added now a dislike from a fresh and fertile spring for the new professional class devoted to the practice and spread of science. The Greek view of life was at all times aristocratic. Their respect for wage-earning stood even lower than in other slave-owning communities. Herodotus, in asking if the Greeks had learnt their contempt of industry from the Egyptians, tells us that "the Corinthians despise manual labour least and the Lacedæmonians most." In Thebes there was a law that no one should be eligible to public office who had not absented himself from the markets for the space of ten years ; and even Plato and Aristotle were of opinion that artisans and traders should be excluded from full civic rights. Only a very few wage-earning professions, such as that of the physician, were not wholly incompatible with social respect. An especial reproach attached to the employment of intellectual labour for the benefit of some one else who paid for it ; this was regarded as a degradation, as a yoke of servitude that was voluntarily assumed. When the development of the law courts engendered the calling of the orator or advocate, his profession was ridiculed by the comic writers no less than that of the sophist. Past members of the profession did their best to wipe out the recollection, as may be seen in the instance of Isocrates ; and he, too, when reduced to founding a school of rhetoric, is said to have wept tears of shame on receiving his first fee. We are reminded of the embarrassment felt by Lord Byron, as well as by the aristocratic founders of the *Edinburgh Review,* on accepting their earliest honorarium as authors. A third cause for the disfavour which attached to the calling of a sophist was discovered in the feeling of those persons who were unable to pay for such instruction, and who were accordingly placed at a disadvantage, in their own opinion at least, in public affairs no less than in private quarrels, in comparison with their opponents or rivals who had enjoyed a training of that kind. In this respect the position of the sophists has been aptly compared with that of professors of fencing in a community where the duel is an established institution—a parallel particularly applicable to the litigious community of Athens, the city of law-suits. Lastly, these tacit and spontaneous factors which operated to discredit the sophist were reinforced by the deliberate purpose of a powerful personality whose hand wielded the engine of a magnificent literary style. Plato contemned the whole existing order of society. Its greatest statesmen seemed to him as despicable as its poets and other intellectual leaders. He was anxious, above all, to separate by fosse and wall, so to speak, his own teaching and his own school, in which he saw the sole chance of salvation, from everything which could possibly be confused with them, or which might even distantly resemble them. As a man of brilliant parts and of noble birth, he might have contended for honour and glory in the open day of public life. Instead of so doing, he chose to live in the shadow of a school, where he wove his words and spun his ideas "conversing in low tones with two or three admiring youths." For this he was severely censured, and certainly by no one more severely than by his nearest friends. Accordingly, he was earnestly at pains to distinguish as sharply as possible his own methods, aimed, as he believed, at the regeneration of mankind, from those which seemed to be directed at less exalted goals. Socrates, his master, in contemporary opinion had been ranked more or less as a sophist, and had even served as the type of that order; but in a later passage we shall see how thoroughly Plato succeeded, though not altogether without violence, in consecrating to the honour of his master a particular niche in the memory of posterity.

No resources of satire were foreign to the art of Plato. He would as lief be coarse as delicate, and his attacks on the sophists were even more remarkable for their extent than for their intensity. Every member of that order, as he trod the boards of the Platonic dialogue, was received with terms of contempt or at the best with marks of ridicule. But no: this rule has one exception. In an unguarded moment, as we must suppose, Plato let slip an expression of unqualified appreciation in respect to one of the sophists. In the dialogue "Lysis" he spoke of Miccus in one breath as "a friend and eulogist of Socrates" and "a clever man and an excellent sophist." Miccus is otherwise completely unknown to us, and perhaps we may add that his insignificance saved him from attack. For otherwise Plato gave his malice full rein. Even in instances where the doctrines of the sophist revealed not the slightest blemish even to his jealous eye, still a comic effect would be produced by bringing him in at an awkward moment and in an obtrusive way. This was the fate of Prodicus and Hippias, who were further ridiculed respectively for their weak health and their fussy versatility. It is true that Protagoras was accorded the full tribute of respect due to his exalted personality and honour, but the old-fashioned and obsolete texture of his rhetoric was submitted with perfect mimicry to the ridicule of the reader, while every real or supposed error in his argument was remorselessly dragged into the light. But Plato's most emphatic language was reserved for the features at which the aristocratic sense of his countrymen, and especially of his peers, took particular umbrage. He delighted in jeering at the professional element in sophistry, which he considered vulgar and *banal*, with especial reference to the system of fees. If the reward were small, he affected to regard it as a proof of the worthlessness of the service performed, and if it were large, he represented it as entirely disproportionate and undeserved. Modesty, as we know, was not a virtue of that age,* and Plato himself, by the way, was no exception. It is extremely probable, therefore, that the sophists, whose business it was to advertise themselves in difficult circumstances, displayed a degree of over-confidence in the manner of their appearance. Nor would the members of that class fail to display the petty jealousies and rivalries which are inevitable to all competitive professions. But this should by no means be taken as implying that the picture of the profession was complete when its share in our common human weakness had been described. It would be as unfair to draw that conclusion as to apply the same method to the modern successors of the sophists—teachers, and popular authors— or to the members of any other class, such as barristers or

* Cp. Bk. III. Ch. II. § I.

members of Parliament. Plato's contempt of the sophists stands on the same plane of thought as Schopenhauer's scoffs at the "philosophy professors" or Comte's assault on the "Academicians."

In one instance, however, Plato's criticism hit the mark. We see his sophists measuring themselves with Socrates in dialectic bouts and suffering complete defeat. The dialogues as such were pure fiction, but this particular feature may be taken as an historical fact, for Socrates' championship in dialectic forms an undisputed title to fame and is one of the secrets of his influence on posterity. In this connection, however, a curious point is to be noted. When Plato abandons the rapier-thrusts of ridicule in order to attack the sophists with the heavy artillery of serious argument, the names of Protagoras, Hippias, and Prodicus disappear, and sophistry itself wears a different face. Those genuine old sophists had shown themselves incapable of adopting the Socratic method of cross-examination. They had no champion to enter for the contest of short questions and answers ; but when Plato became serious, the sophists whom he introduced were precisely the men for that work. The key to this riddle has long ago been found. It is to be discovered in the fact that Plato's literary activity embraced more than half a century. We are not, accordingly, surprised that between his youth and his old age a new race of sophists should have arisen. Indeed, at the time when Plato first took up the pen, the old generation was dying out. Thus the composition of three at least of the comedies which made a butt of the activity of the sophists and of their pedagogic innovations fell in the same decade in which Plato was born. The "Epulones" of Aristophanes was produced in the winter of 427 B.C., a few months before the birth of Plato, who was four years old when the "Clouds" was produced, and six at the time of the "Flatterers" of Eupolis. It is entirely natural, therefore, that the Athenian thinker in the evening of his long life should have thought much less of these sophists than of other philosophers whom he hated, and whom he delighted to call by ill names. In a word, the sophists

who were assailed with such bitter mockery in the
Platonic "Sophistes" itself, and in other similar dialogues
composed at about the same date, were the disciples of
Socrates and the disciples of his disciples, above all
Antisthenes and his crew—the deadliest enemy of Plato.
It must be conceded that the art of Plato sought to
weave threads of connection between these sophists and
those others to whom the name properly belonged, but
the artificiality of such attempts can escape no intelligent
reader of the "Euthydemus" and "Sophistes." Aristotle,
as may readily be conceived, inherited this convention of
language. In not a single passage of his numerous writings
was the expression "sophist" ever used to designate a
member of that profession in the older generation, while
once at least, in speaking of the system of fees, the name
of Protagoras was honourably mentioned by him in sharp
contrast with the sophists. Aristotle used the word in three
senses: First, in the old simple, blameless significance,
in which he too described the seven sages as sophists ;
secondly, to describe a few philosophers personally in little
sympathy with himself, such as Aristippus, a disciple of
Socrates ; and, thirdly and chiefly, the term was employed
as a title for the "Eristics," for the dialecticians, that is to
say, with whom Aristotle was engaged in a life-long feud,
and who emerged, spoiling for a fight, from the schools of
Antisthenes and Euclides, the Socratic resident in Megara.
Now, as the wits of these philosophers were engaged in
contriving puzzles and fallacies, the result was that the
words "sophism" and "sophistical" were added to
"sophist" and "sophistry" in the vocabulary of the polemic
waged by Plato in his old age and by Aristotle against
the Eristics, and the meaning which has since become
dominant was won and established at that time. The use
of the term "sophist," as employed by Aristotle, was
preserved till the end of antiquity. Even then it was
still occasionally used in its originally neutral if not
precisely honourable sense. At times, indeed, such as that
of the later sophistry of the Roman Empire, this became
once more the predominant usage, but it has been far

more frequently employed as a more or less scornful term of reproach. Nor did Plato himself escape this contemptuous appellation. He was rebuked as a sophist in that sense by his contemporary adversaries and rivals, the rhetoricians Lysias and Isocrates ; Aristotle incurred the same fate by the verdict of the historian Timæus ; his cousin Callisthenes by that of Alexander the Great ; Anaxarchus the Democritean by that of Hermippus the Aristotelian ; Eubulides the Socratic by that of Epicurus ; Carneades the Academician by that of Posidonius the Stoic, and so on with scarcely an exception through the whole catalogue of the philosophers and their opponents, till we reach the name of the Founder of Christianity, whom Lucian designated a sophist.

3. The history of this change of meaning is not related here for the first time. Still, it is well to pause on it, to dwell ever more fondly on its details, and to impress its significance on the reluctant senses even of the experts in this branch of learning. For many who cannot but admit the correctness of these statements are too apt to forget or to neglect them. They begin with a handsome acknowledgment of the ambiguity of the word " sophist," and of the injustice done to the bearers of that name in the fifth century B.C. by the ugly sense in which the term came to be used, and they admit that restitution is due. But the debt is forgotten before it is paid ; the debtor reverts to the old familiar usage, and speaks of the sophists once more as if they were really mere intellectual acrobats, unscrupulous tormentors of language, or the authors of pernicious teachings. The spirit may be willing, but the reason is helpless against the force of inveterate habits of thought. Verily the sophists were born under an evil star. Their one short hour of triumphant success was paid for by centuries of obloquy. Two invincible foes were banded together against them—the caprice of language, and the genius of a great writer, if not the greatest writer of all times. Little indeed did he imagine, when he played upon them with the lightnings of his wit and irony, that the airy creations of his fertile invention and of his exuberant youthfulness

would one day be called to the bar of serious historical investigation. He made game of the living, and not of the dead, and it was the third and most fatal calamity which befell the sophists that their vitality departed, and that they became a part of the dead past. The restless itinerant teachers founded no schools. No faithful bands of disciples watched over their writings and kept their memory green. After the lapse of a few centuries, of all their literary productions but a few sorry fragments were preserved, and merely fragments of those fragments are at our disposal to-day. We are almost totally deprived of first-hand witnesses to their work.

We shall presently turn to the individual sophists, and endeavour to gain acquaintance with their personality and their teachings. But first we are bound to mention a literary monument, which, though it does not bear the name of a sophist on its title-page, is yet admirably adapted to help us to realize the character of at least a portion of what is called sophistic literature. The Hippocratic collection comprises, our readers will remember, a great variety of contents. Among them is a treatise which may confidently be ascribed to the age and the circle that we are discussing, apart altogether from any attempt to identify its author. It is entitled "On the Art," and, treating of the art of medicine, it undertakes to defend it against the attacks which it encountered from an early date. This "apology for medicine" displays all the features which we should expect to find in the intellectual work of a sophist of that age. It is not so much a set treatise as an address designed for oral delivery, carefully constructed for that purpose, and polished with consummate mastery. These facts alone would go far to exclude the theory of its authorship by a physician, even if other circumstances did not remove the last possibility of doubt. At the close of the work, for instance, the writer contrasted his own discourse with the "evidence of facts from professional medical men," thus, so to say, taking a courteous leave of the physicians and claiming the dues of mutual respect for himself and his brothers of the pen. Further, he referred

to another speech which he hoped to compose in the future
in respect to the remaining arts ; and a discussion of the
theory of knowledge, in which, parenthetically remarked,
he was clearly an opponent of Melissus, led him to mention
a longer disquisition on the same theme which may
almost certainly be ascribed to no other author but himself. He was so habituated to polemics that it had
become his second nature to rig up an adversary before
his eyes and meet his arguments with counter-arguments.
His learning was encyclopædic. He jumped at every
opportunity of trespassing the narrow limits of the matter
before him, now for the sake of a brief allusion, and again
for longer excursions in which to display his familiarity
with ideas of the widest range. Thus in the course of
a very few pages he touched on the problems of causality
and of the origin of language, on the element of chance in
human action, on the relation of perception to objective
reality, of natural disposition to the means of culture, of
the industrial arts to the raw material, and so forth. He
may fairly be entitled half rhetorician and half philosopher ;
nor can we fail to mark the unmistakable trait of the
schoolmaster. He betrayed his pedagogic habit by his
dogmatic tone of complacent self-confidence as well as by
his anxiety to subdivide and to define when new ideas
were introduced. The deliberate though successful attempt
to attain to a rhythmic euphony of style reminds us that
the ornate diction had but lately been released from the
fetters of verse. At the same time the scrupulously
regular structure of the sentences, the timid separation of
the whole into small sections, and the prominent relief
given to emphatic words and thoughts likewise testify to
the infancy of the art of prose. The treatise, with its
wealth of ideas and its ambitious eloquence, serves us as
a test by which to measure the enthusiasm which was
aroused by the new kind of style, and we realize the
powerful influence it exerted on contemporary minds. Nor
can we fail to perceive the weaknesses and shadows it
displayed, thus affording so many weapons to the enemy.
No refined ear could endure the emphatic tone of the

rhetorician, and the blatant self-consciousness with which he displayed his own wisdom and learning, just as Xenophanes the rhapsodist had plumed himself on his wisdom in his own day.* The unbridled sweep of language over the shallows of thought was little calculated to guarantee trustworthiness and consistency of argument. Nor would a taste for surprises and a preference for the terminology of polemics escape the suspicion of a striving after effect. In general it may be said that the rhetorical style, with its somewhat rigid forms, its stiff regularity, and its glaring colour-effects, was a reminiscence of archaic sculpture, and as such it was foredoomed to decay. It could not but create the impression of a coldness and pettiness, in comparison with the richer and more harmonious language, with the freer gait and more plastic power of the prose of Plato and, to some extent, of Isocrates.

4. Here, however, a warning is required. Among the features referred to in the foregoing description there is certainly more than one which is purely individual, and we should fall into the error of undue generalization if we were to regard the treatise " On the Art " as throughout a type of its kind. The generalization would be yet more illicit if we were to extend it to the important thoughts, to which we shall have occasion to revert, which the treatise contains. For the sophists were so distinct in the details and in the spirit of their teaching that it is rather from habit than from conviction that we are induced to discuss them together. We would certainly guard against the false impression that they formed a separate class or school in the history of Greek philosophy.

Prodicus of Ceos was sent as his countrymen's ambassador to Athens, where he obtained considerable influence. A distinct position is frequently created for him under the title of "the precursor of Socrates," with whom he was certainly bound in ties of personal friendship. Plato, however, tarred him with the same brush as the rest of his professional brethren. The "all-wise" Prodicus was

* Cp. Bk. II. Ch. I. § 1.

the constant butt of the searching and somewhat coarse satire in which the early Dialogues delighted, nor was he exempt from attack on the part of the comic writers. In the " Broilers " of Aristophanes, for example, the following distich occurred :—

> " Though he escaped corruption by a book,
> 'Twas done by Prodicus, the babbling brook."

In the same way Æschines the Socratic, in his dialogue "Callias," joined the two " sophists Anaxagoras and Prodicus"—a remarkable combination—in a common indictment, and Prodicus was reproached with having educated Theramenes the opportunist, who, though frequently charged with being unprincipled, was regarded by Aristotle, as we have lately learnt, as a highly reputable politician. We cannot help being startled at these remarks of Æschines, so striking is the parallel with the experience of Socrates. He too was charged with the corruption of youth, by the comic writers in the first instance, and he too was confronted with the living results of his education, Alcibiades and Critias. But neither the parallel with Socrates, nor the mention of the great name of Anaxagoras in the same breath, availed to save the memory of Prodicus. His salvation was rather due to the notable circumstance that other and impartial witnesses were ranged in his defence, and that their testimony conflicted with that of the philosopher and the playwright, who paid, by the way, in another passage a marked compliment to the wisdom of the sophist.

Prodicus was a man of very earnest character, who has exercised a very considerable influence on posterity, mainly through the intervention of Cynics. We are no longer able to measure his achievements in nature-philosophy. The titles only of two books have come down to us on that side of his scientific labours—" On Nature " and " On the Nature of Man " respectively. The little we know of another branch of learning to which his activities were directed is derived almost entirely from some satirical references in Plato. From these we learn that he attempted

to deal with synonymy—to collect and to compare, that is
to say, words of kindred meaning and to distinguish their
shades of signification. But when we ask what motive led
him to that work or what degree of success he attained,
no answer can be given. He may have wished to create
an aid to the art of style, by which, as a matter of fact,
Thucydides is said to have profited, or he may have desired
to advance the cause of science by a sharper demarcation
of the limits of ideas, or he may have aimed at both these
ends at once. One fact only can be positively asserted—
that in undertaking this work he was supplying a real
demand. The speculations on language had followed the
cosmic theories to the tablelands of science, where they
were confronted by problems which were practically
insoluble, at least for the age we are dealing with. It
was a wholly meritorious achievement to bring them down
from the heights and to substitute an inquiry into the
material and forms of contemporary speech for the investigation of the origin of language. We shall find that Protagoras was busy with an analysis of the forms of speech, while
Prodicus was the first to submit its material to the methods
of scientific study. In this connection it is a matter of
indifference whether or not his labours contributed to the
artistic use of language : they must at least have helped
to perfect it as an instrument of thought. We may even
sincerely regret that his example was not more assiduously
followed. Our consideration of the Eleatic doctrines has
already served to show us how rich a source of error was
contained in the ambiguity of words, and in the absence of
clear definitions of the ideas expressed by them. If the road
opened by Prodicus had been followed by more numerous
successors, many of the mistakes from which the Platonic
writings themselves are by no means wholly exempt might
well have been avoided, and the harvest of *à priori* pseudo-
demonstrations and of eristic fallacies would certainly have
been far less abundant.

We are much more accurately informed about the
views of Prodicus on moral philosophy. His melancholy
view of life may fairly entitle him to the description of

the earliest of the pessimists. Euripides, speaking of the man who made the evils of life turn the scale of its blessings, had Prodicus in his mind. We cannot determine at this date how far his weakly constitution was answerable for his gloom, nor how far it was due to the inherited character of his countrymen, the inhabitants of Ceos—an island where suicide was of more frequent occurrence than in any other part of Greece. But whatever the cause may have been, the effect was always the same. A profound emotion shook the ranks of his audience when they heard his deep voice, that came with so strange a sound from the frail body that contained it. Now he would describe the hardships of human existence ; now he would recount all the ages of man, beginning with the new-born child, who greets his new home with wailing, and tracing his course to the second childhood and the grey hairs of old age. Again he would rail at death as a stony-hearted creditor, wringing his pledges one by one from his tardy debtor, first his hearing, then his sight, and next the free movement of his limbs. At another time, anticipating Epicurus, he sought to arm his disciples against the horrors of death by explaining that death concerned neither the living nor the dead. As long as we live, death does not exist ; as soon as we die, we ourselves exist no longer. Nor were occasions wanting for enheartening reminders of this kind. For the pessimistic wisdom of Prodicus did not find its goal in a mere mute resignation, nor in an ascetic retreat from the world ; still less was it satisfied with the advice to gather from the troubled waters of human life as many pearls of pleasure as possible. Higher than pleasure Prodicus exalted work, and his practice agreed with his theory. He was famous in antiquity among the few who, despite their physical infirmities, had completely fulfilled their civic duties. He was frequently sent on ambassadorial missions on behalf of his native island. His hero and model was Hercules, the type of manly strength and wholesome activity, and the fact that he took as his patron-saint the ancestor of the Lacedæmonian kings may have contributed to the honourable welcome which he received in Sparta, where foreigners, and, above all, foreign teachers of wisdom, were otherwise so severely discouraged. Every one is acquainted with the fable of " Hercules at the parting of the ways." It is a masterpiece of admonitory eloquence in imitation of the Sophoclean fable of the strife between Athene and Aphrodite in the " Judgment of Paris," and it became in its turn an example for all antiquity. Its influence continued till early Christian times, when its echoes may be heard in literature in the " Shepherd of Hermas " and elsewhere. The work to which this fable of Hercules belonged was entitled " The Seasons." The rest of its contents is unfortunately unknown to us. Perhaps it contained the pessimistic utterances we have mentioned just now ; perhaps, too, as a counterpart to these, it sang the praises of the wholesome pleasures least open to abuse, such as the joy in nature and her works which our philosopher could hardly have omitted in the eulogy of agriculture that is ascribed to him. Thus, then, we have been able to construct no uncertain outline of the views of Prodicus and of his ideal of life. He had drained the dregs of human bitterness, and he resisted the effects of that draught by exalting the virtue of manly valour. It was to expect but little from passive enjoyment, but was rather to look for satisfaction to the exercise of its own strong powers, combined with a preference for simple manners and plain living. Nor was Prodicus merely the eloquent preacher of a partially new ideal. The subtle intellect betrayed in his disquisitions "On Correct Language " was not wanting in his ethical studies. He introduced a conception in moral philosophy which played an important part in the school of the Cynics, and in that of the Stoics, their successors. It was the conception of objects indifferent in themselves, on which a value was impressed only by the right use to which they were put if the dictates of reason were obeyed. In this class of objects he reckoned riches, and most of what we call external goods. We shall presently have occasion to remark how nearly he approached in this connection to the teachings of Socrates. Meantime, we have still to consider one doctrine of the sage of Ceos—his speculation on the origin of the belief in gods. He conjectured that those natural objects which exercise the most lasting and beneficent influence on human life were the first to be paid divine honours. Among these he counted the sun, the moon, the rivers (reminding his readers at that point of the Egyptian worship of the Nile), and he added to the list the fruits of the field, at which point he might have mentioned certain Babylonian customs. Next to these natural objects he reckoned the heroes of civilization who were deified by mankind in grateful recognition of their important and beneficial inventions. On this theory Dionysus would at one time have been a man, an argument which tallies with the phrase of John Henry Voss in our own century * about "the deified inventor of wine." It is to be noted that Prodicus, though by no means completely on the right road, succeeded at least in exposing the fetishistic among the roots of religious conceptions. And if it be asked whether he assumed that a real objective basis was at the back of those conceptions, or that the reality of the Divine was to be repudiated once for all, we may safely reply that the first supposition is correct. Otherwise it would be inexplicable that a man of such orthodox tendencies as Xenophon should have spoken of Prodicus with unfailing honour and respect, and that Persæus, a famous representative of the Stoics and the favourite pupil of Zeno, the founder of that rigidly Pantheistic school, should have expressed his approval of these tenets of Prodicus, in his book "On the Gods." We are accordingly impelled to the opinion that the edge of the polemic in that explanatory attempt was aimed at the gods of popular belief, and was not intended to divest the universe of all that it contained of divinity.

5. We have seen that Prodicus was occupied with studies in nature and language, with problems of moral philosophy, and with the history of religion. When we

* 1834.

reach the name of Hippias, however, we find that Prodicus
was greatly surpassed in versatility of talents and employ-
ments. The kaleidoscopic genius of Hippias was applied to
all the arts in turn. He was astronomer, geometer, arithme-
tician; he wrote on phonetics, rhythm, and music; he
discussed the theories of sculpture and painting; he was
at once mythologist and ethnologist, and a student of
chronology and mnemonics. Moreover, he was the author
of moral admonitions, and he had acted in the capacity of
ambassador on behalf of his native city, Elis, in the
Peloponnesus. Nor does this exhaust the sum of his
achievements. Poetical works of the most diverse kinds
—epics, tragedies, epigrams, and dithyrambs—flowed continuously from his pen. Finally, he had mastered most
of the industrial arts. On one occasion he appeared
at the Olympic gathering in garments every part of
which, from the sandals on his feet to the plaited girdle
round his waist, and the very rings on his fingers, had
been manufactured by his own hand. We children of
this generation, who have carried the principle of the
division of labour to extremes, are hardly able to take in
serious account a Jack-of-all-trades of this kind. But
previous ages have felt and judged differently. There
have been times when the man counted for much more
than his work, when the necessary dissipation of forces
entailed did not seem too heavy a price to pay for giving
full play to personality, for the complete development
of our slumbering powers, the consciousness of being
equal to almost any task, and of being helpless before no
difficulty, and for the ambition and ability to master
every kind of employment. Thus men thought in the
age of Pericles, and thus too in the Italian Renaissance.
In the last-named era, indeed, we meet an exact counterpart to Hippias. Leone Battista Alberti of Venice, who
lived from 1404 to 1472, was equally brilliant as architect,
painter, musician, prose-writer, and poet, in the Italian as
well as in the Latin tongue. He discussed the theory of
domestic economy in the intervals of his studies on the
plastic arts; he was renowned among the wits of his age.

and he bore himself like a master among the gymnasts. Finally, he had acquainted himself with "all the industries of the world" by questioning "craftsmen of every kind, even down to the shoemaker, on their secrets and experiences."

It is obvious that the value of these various achievements could not possibly be uniformly excellent. The poems of Hippias have disappeared without a trace, not altogether, we may presume, to the loss of the poet. He made no mean contributions to the progress of geometry. His system of mnemonics, in which the poet Simonides was his sole precursor, is said to have produced remarkable results. By its aid he was enabled, even as an old man, to repeat fifty proper names which he had heard for the first time without omitting or misplacing a single one. His chronological work was a "List of the Olympic Victors," which undoubtedly supplied an urgent demand of the age, with its deficient historiographical resources, and which was supplemented by kindred attempts, such as the history of Hellanicus, with its divisions corresponding to the succession of the priestesses of Hera at Argos. Plutarch, we are bound to add, disputed the trustworthiness of the lists compiled by Hippias, and we are unable to determine how far, if at all, the criticism was deserved. Except for an insignificant fragment, we possess no remains of his "Collection" of memorable events, save only the brief preface, which affords us pleasing evidence of the grace of his style, and by no means justifies the reproach of a pompous self-conceit which has been levelled at Hippias in consequence of Plato's satire. The Hippias of that prologue is a wholly unpretentious compiler, whose aim it was to select the most important information from the narratives of poets and prosewriters, whether Greek or barbarian, and to arrange them in homogeneous groups, without advancing any other claim whatsoever to originality or versatility as an historian. His work, destined as it was for entertainment rather than for instruction, afforded but a slight handle for critical acumen. Yet many valuable remarks were scattered through its pages,

Accident, for instance, has preserved for us the philological memorandum that the word "tyrant" (τύραννος) occurred for the first time in the poems of Archilochus. Of the work of Hippias "On National Names" we know extremely little, but the little itself would suffice to show that this versatile and busy sophist did not shrink from labour of a dry-as-dust kind. We may conjecture that his studies of the habits and traditions of the most diverse peoples may have caused Hippias to attribute such considerable importance to the distinction between nature and convention which we have already had occasion to discuss.* Further, we may remark as a proof of the above-mentioned leanings to cosmopolitanism, that Hippias the sophist employed non-Hellenic sources of history and devoted himself to the annals of barbarian tribes with equal impartiality. His life's ideal, which he shared with the Cynics whom he had influenced, was "self-sufficiency" (αὐτάρκεια). Unluckily, we possess no remains of his ethical discourses. His *chef d'œuvre* in this field was a duologue, the scene of which was fallen Troy, and the persons of which were Nestor, the old man eloquent, and Neoptolemus, the son of Achilles. In this "Trojan Dialogue," as it is called, probably the earliest instance of its kind, the venerable greybeard prince imparted a wealth of wise and noble counsel to the youthful, ambitious heir of the bravest of the Greeks, and sketched out for him a rule of life. Another of the moralist's themes was a comparison between Achilles and Ulysses, in which the palm was bestowed on the first-named on account of his greater love for truth, a virtue which the Greeks did not commonly prize too highly. These and similar pieces, which were composed by Hippias in a choice but flowing and natural style, won their author very considerable success when he recited them at the great games and in all quarters through the length and breadth of Hellas. He was made a free-man of a large number of cities, and the material rewards that accrued to him were by no means on a small scale. With Hippias, as with Prodicus, it is a significant feature

* Bk. III. Ch. IV. § 6.

that he was held in high esteem by the Spartans, with their old-fashioned and home-keeping ideas, whom he seems to have delighted by his lectures on history and ethics.

6. It is hardly legitimate to count Hippias of Elis as a product of the age of emancipation, and in the instance of the sophist Antiphon, such a view would be wholly inadmissible. Though he is reckoned among the less important members of his order, yet at one and the same time he was not merely moralist and metaphysician, physicist and geometer, but also a soothsayer and an interpreter of dreams. He was the author of a work "On Truth," consisting of two books, in the fragmentary remains of the second of which we encounter physical teachings with a strong reminiscence of older doctrines of the kind. The first book treated more generally of metaphysics or the theory of knowledge. It was the occasion for a polemic against the hypostasy or "objectification" of ideas. We no longer know at whom its point was directed, nor would it be easy to determine it to-day. When Antiphon speaks of time as "a conception or a measure, not a substance," it is just conceivable that he was thinking of those mythical or half-mythical representations in which Chronos or the time-principle appeared as a primary being.* This expedient, however, it must be acknowledged, is incompatible with another fragment, in which we read as follows: "He who recognizes any long objects neither sees length with his eyes nor can perceive it with his mind." The idea of length apparently had a typical meaning in that instance. The true point at issue was undoubtedly the substantial existence of general ideas, and Antiphon might fairly be called the earliest of the nominalists. We hear of very similar utterances in Antisthenes and Theopompus, who disputed the Platonic theory of ideas, but that theory was not in existence at the time that Antiphon, the contemporary of Socrates, was wielding his pen. We must accordingly abandon the

* Cp. Bk. I. Ch. II. §2.

search for the actual adversary with whom Antiphon was fighting. It is enough to recollect that the language which expresses abstractions by substantives, thus lending them the semblance of objectivity, has always paved the way for a naïve and rudimentary realism,* in the philosophical sense of the word, traces of which, indeed, are not wanting in the age we are considering. Among the other lost works of Antiphon antiquity possessed his " Art of Consolations," from which we trace the beginning of a new and fertile branch of letters. But the chief of all his writings was a treatise "On Concord." It was renowned in antiquity for its rich style, for the even flow of its diction, and for the extraordinary wealth of its ideas—virtues which can still be traced in its few fragmentary remains. It was a work of practical philosophy, in which self-seeking, and weak will, and the sluggishness which looks on life as though it were a game of chess that could be renewed after a defeat, and anarchy—"the worst of human evils "—were mercilessly flagellated, while the self-control that is produced by a thorough knowledge of the appetites, and, above all, the power of education, were warmly praised and brilliantly delineated.

The fragments of this treatise have lately received a considerable addition through a discovery as ingenious as it is certain, and its new pieces will be found to teem with passages of fruitful instruction. They reveal, for instance, a fine sense of human nature, as may be seen from the following extract : " Men never wish to render honour to another, for they believe that thereby they derogate from their own respect." But it is more important to note that in these long connected fragments we possess our earliest example of the kind of moral instruction which was imparted by the sophists. We gain at last authoritative evidence for a fact long ago perceived and expressed by the more thoughtful historians, though never credited except by isolated readers. Thus Grote, about half a century ago, wrote that the sophists "were the regular teachers of Greek morality, neither above nor below the standard of

* Bk. II. Ch. III. § 3 *init.*

the age." It is possible that this generalization went a
little too far and taxed the originality of individual sophists
too heavily, but on one point at least there should
never have been any doubt. It was a sheer impossibility
for the sophists, dependent as they were on wide orders
of the public, to promulgate anti-social doctrines. They
were far more liable to the danger of preaching, if we
may so express ourselves, doctrines of a hyper-social
tendency, and of subjecting the individual to the tyranny
of public opinion in perhaps too high a degree, or, not to
exaggerate their influence, of becoming at least the mouthpiece of opinions of that kind.

Such, at any rate, is the impression which we derive
from the new fragments. We recognize there modes of
thought and feeling conceivable only in a democratic community, and realized at the present time hardly anywhere
else than in the Swiss Republic and in the United States
of America. The desire to conciliate the good-will of one's
fellow-citizens, and to take one's place among them as a
man of reputation and esteem, was manifested here with
exceptional intensity. It is not our business to form a
judgment on the advantages and disadvantages of a social
condition of this kind, or of the moral atmosphere which
it is calculated to engender. But it is legitimate to point
out that the wholesome effects it exercises in the repression
of impulses for the common hurt, and in stimulating
enterprises for the common weal, must necessarily be
counterbalanced by a danger of no mean significance. It
is a danger which would affect that domain of life in which
multiformity of development and independence of action are
indispensable to the success of individual life, and tend
therefore indirectly to promote the general prosperity of all.
It may be conceded that individual liberty in the Athens of
the fifth century B.C. was far less exposed to this risk at the
hands of the tyrannous majority than among most other
peoples and in most other times. In evidence of this, we
commend to the attention of every one who has not yet
made acquaintance with it the funeral oration of Pericles,
which Thucydides has preserved, and which forms one of

the most precious monuments to the spirit of genuine freedom in the possession of mankind. Still, the new fragments of Antiphon bear witness to a mode of thought which submitted the individual once for all to the service of the community, or rather, as not a few may have held, which submitted him to the servitude of collective mediocrity. And, this being the case, we are now in a position to understand the protest and reaction of some superior and self-conscious minds. Speeches such as Plato put in the mouth of Callicles, the sworn foe of the sophists and the contemner of the mob, become still more comprehensible to us than they previously were. Nay, in some of the expressions of the resurgent Antiphon, in the bitter polemic, for instance, against the erroneous doctrine that obedience to the laws is cowardice, we seem to be listening to a protest against the opinions sustained by Callicles in the "Gorgias," and incarnated in real life in the persons of a Critias and an Alcibiades.

Education, to come back to that topic, was promoted by Antiphon to the highest rank in human affairs. "According to the seeds," he tells us, "that are sown in the earth, so are the fruits that the reaper may expect. And if a noble disposition be planted in a young mind, it will engender a flower that will endure to the end, and that no rain will destroy, nor will it be withered by drought." This paragraph reminds us of similar reflections expressed in like style by Protagoras, the chief and noblest of the sophists. Our readers are already acquainted with the name of this extraordinary man, and we have now to try to delineate his features as fully and faithfully as our scanty materials permit.

CHAPTER VI.

PROTAGORAS OF ABDERA.

1. PROTAGORAS was a son of Abdera, where he breathed the air of free thought. It is hardly to be doubted that he enjoyed the intercourse of Leucippus, his older fellow-countryman, and of Democritus, his younger contemporary. But the investigation of Nature did not by any means monopolize his interest, which was primarily directed to human affairs. Before his thirtieth year he had adopted the profession, new at that time, of an itinerant teacher or sophist. He had paid repeated visits to Athens, where he was honoured with the intimate friendship of Pericles, and stood in close relationship with Euripides and other eminent men. As a teacher his services were in eager requisition, and his instruction centred, as we have seen, in a preparation for public life. It admitted excursions in every direction : oratory and its auxiliary arts, education, juris-prudence, politics, and ethics, engaged his fertile and re-sourceful mind. He was a man of many-sided endowments, and was equally successful in inventing an apparatus for the use of porters as in performing the task of a legislator. He was employed in the last-named capacity in the spring of 443, when the colony of Thurii was founded by Athens in the heart of a fruitful plain, close to the ruins of Sybaris. The instructions which Protagoras received from Pericles on that occasion were probably to the effect that he should adapt the laws of the "subtle" Charondas, which were current in many parts of Lower Italy, to the peculiar conditions of the new settlement. And Protagoras carried

out his instructions by making those laws yet more subtle than they had been. This political mission was the summit of his life and work. Some of the most illustrious Greeks of that age made their home at Thurii, and others were constantly passing through it, so that Protagoras, wandering through the halls of the beautiful and regular city built on the plans of Hippodamus, might converse one day with Herodotus on questions of ethnology, and on another with Empedocles on problems of natural science. All the Greek tribes were represented in the brilliant life of Thurii, and the division of the citizens into ten provinces was a proof of the Pan-Hellenic principle of its foundation, which, in conjunction with its rapid and peaceful rise, might be taken as a happy omen for the future unity of Hellas. But if Protagoras and his brother sophists, with the rest of the prose-writers and poets who were the true vehicles of the national idea, were buoyed up by hopes of this kind, they were doomed to the bitterest disappointment. Hardly ten years elapsed before the two leading powers, Athens and Sparta, were ranged against one another in a death struggle. All Hellas was split into two hostile camps. Protagoras was in Athens at the time when the fearful ravages of pestilence were added to the horrors of war. He was thus a witness of the heroism displayed by his patron Pericles under the heaviest calamity :

" His sons," wrote Protagoras, after Pericles' too early death, " perished within a week in the beauty of their youth, and he bore it without repining. For he clung to his attitude of serene repose, which permitted him every day to enjoy welfare, tranquillity, and popular fame, for every man who saw him bear his own sorrow with strength would recognize that Pericles was noble and manly and much better than himself, seeing that he would be found wanting in a similar trial."

Thus the closing years of the life of Protagoras were darkened by the shadows of national misfortune, in which Athens was the greatest sufferer, but he was at least spared the burdens of extreme old age. For this he was indebted to one of those sudden impulses of intolerance against which the populace of Athens was never sufficiently proof. Protagoras was almost seventy years of age when, in reliance on his reputation and on the record of an honourable career, he ventured to give undisguised, though at the same time temperate, utterance to somewhat more audacious ideas than usual. It is said to have been in the house of Euripides that he first had his book "On the Gods" recited, thus introducing it to publicity according to ancient usage. A smart cavalry officer, the wealthy Pythodorus, was the self-chosen instrument of the salvation of society. Pythodorus was a political malcontent, who was presently to take part in the conspiracy of the Four Hundred against the existing constitution. In the present instance he was the chief cause of the prosecution of Protagoras for impiety. The book "On the Gods" was condemned. The copies that had already been published were confiscated and burnt. Protagoras himself probably left Athens before his conviction, and betook himself to Sicily, but he suffered shipwreck on the way, and found a watery grave. Euripides, his friend, dedicated, if we are not mistaken, an elegy to him in the two concluding verses of the chorus in the tragedy of "Palamedes," produced in the spring of 415 B.C., "Yea, ye have killed her, the all-wise ; alas for the blameless nightingale of the Muses ! "

Well might the fate of Protagoras, surnamed "Wisdom " itself, recall the memory of Palamedes, Palamedes the inventor, envied for his wisdom, the victim of a hateful charge. But for us, at least, it is difficult to gain a clear conception of the grounds on which the contemporary admiration of Protagoras rested. We seek them in vain in the fragments, barely twenty lines long, the very meaning of which is contested by the commentators. We inquire for them in vain from witnesses whose evidence is largely coloured by prejudice, who have bequeathed to us a chaotic collection of partly unwarranted and partly incomprehensible tidings, preserved by the pen of a positively miserable compiler. We review the description of Plato, the brilliancy of which is dimmed by its plainly polemical tendency, and we compare with that description the contradictory Platonic allusions in which fact and inference, jest and earnest, mingle their diverse hues. For these, and of this kind, are the materials out of which we have to reconstruct the image of the significance of Protagoras.

2. Protagoras, in the first instance, was a successful and a celebrated teacher. In that capacity he had reflected on the problem of education, and his utterances on that subject betoken a calm and impartial mind, wholly free from prepossessions. We read that " Teaching requires natural disposition and exercise, and must be begun in youth," that " Neither theory without practice nor practice without theory avails at all," and, again that " Culture does not flourish in the soul unless one reaches a great deepness." The last of these fragments, selected from the few that have been preserved to us, recalls in a striking degree a weighty maxim in the gospels.* As a teacher Protagoras was the first to introduce grammar in his curriculum, and it is one of the most remarkable facts in the history of Greek thought that before him there was not the remotest attempt to distinguish the forms of expression nor to analyze and reduce them to principles of speech. It is true that a few of the most obvious differences, such as that between a verb and a noun, were known in the uses of language, but even in respect to these elementary notions much had to be done before their boundaries were sharply defined or their names consistently employed. As to what is meant by an adverb or preposition, or the rules of the moods and tenses, neither Pindar nor Æschylus had the faintest conception of those matters. The art of language never passed through its days of apprenticeship. The master was born with full powers before any attempts had been made to define the rules of his craft. This fact obviously contained a useful hint for practice. It suggested that the proper use of language might be largely independent of the conscious knowledge of its rules, and that it might

* Matt. xiii. 5.

be neither necessary nor advantageous to dazzle the brain
of a mere child with the lights of grammatical and logical
abstractions. But we do not propose to discuss these
questions here. The age of Protagoras was marked by a
great awakening of curiosity, by an attempt to co-ordinate
all the material of knowledge, and by a universal search
for causes and rules. Nothing, then, was more natural or
more just than that the chief instrument of thought and
its communication should have been submitted to the
methods of philosophy. So Protagoras wrote his studies
in grammar in the form of a book "On Correct Speech,"
and the title affords some indication of the intention of
the author. The sole really profitable road in the study of
language—the historical—was as foreign to Protagoras as
to the rest of the ancients. Still, the codification of the
rules of speech afforded a rich field for labour; nor could
such an undertaking be attempted in an age which prided
itself on its reason without occasionally being accompanied
by experiments in reform. The recognition of a rule of
language led to the inquiry for its cause, or rather, according to the view obtaining in that epoch, for the
intention of the legislator in the sphere of language. Now
that intention was found to be either incompletely or in-
consistently carried out, and an attempt would accordingly
be made to restore the work of the legislator in its pristine
purity by removing the apparent exceptions, much as a
corrupt manuscript is purged of the mistakes of copyists.
It was probably in this spirit that Protagoras, whom we
have good reason to regard as an adherent of the "conventional" theory of language, approached the problems of
that study. The knowledge of linguistic rules resting on
observation, and the consequent instructions for the correct
use of language, formed probably the chief contents of
his book. There were added to them a few suggestions for
linguistic reforms. Protagoras was the first to distinguish
the several tenses of the verb and the moods of predica-
tion. These last he entitled the "stems" of speech, with
wishes, questions, answers, and commands as their several
branches, and those four kinds of clauses were expressed

in his opinion by the four moods of the verb which we call optative, conjunctive, indicative, and imperative. In one instance—the conjunctive—it must be admitted, however, that the identification was not established without a certain amount of violence. Protagoras seems to have gone chiefly to Homer for his examples of these and other rules of speech, and for the exceptions which he affected to find to them. For we cannot put it down to mere chance that, out of the three excursions· in grammatical criticism which have reached us from the works of Protagoras, two refer to the first two words of the first verse of the Iliad. It may have gratified the critic to add the charge of linguistic inaccuracy to the severe judgment which Xenophanes had passed on the contents of that renowned poem. Thus he argued that the imperative in "Sing, goddess, the wrath," was incorrectly employed, inasmuch as the poet, in addressing the Muse, would not use a command, but merely a wish or a prayer. Further, the Greek word μῆνις ("wrath") should in his opinion have been masculine, and not of the feminine gender. We cannot pretend to dogmatize on the meaning of this last remark. It has probably been correctly taken to convey the opinion that the passion of anger is a manly rather than a womanly characteristic. It would, however, be extravagant to assume that Protagoras was bold enough to undertake the wholesale reform of the genders of substantives through the length and breadth of the Greek language. If he had made so audacious an attempt, we should certainly have heard more about it than an occasional reference in Aristotle to μῆνις and one other word.

The following account is probably more correct. In no domain of language are the traces of its wild growth so clear as in the genders of impersonal substantives. The remarkable fact that several language-groups regard the inanimate to a large extent as animate, and therefore as partly masculine and partly feminine, springs from the same personifying impulse which we have already seen at work in the beginnings of religious conceptions.* The

* Cp. Introd., § 5.

impulse to personification proper was accompanied by a sense of analogy of an extraordinarily refined and sensitive character. The moving, active, nervous, sharp, spare, and hard were regarded as masculine ; the resting, passive, gentle, tender, broad, and soft, as feminine. But opposed to these analogies of sense were secondary analogies of form, and the two influences crossed one another at various points. If a substantival termination had once been appropriated by preference to either sex, a new formation of the same kind would take the same gender, frequently without regard to the meaning of the word. In other instances, and especially in times when the creative force of language was still unbroken, the authority of the meaning would outweigh the authority of the form. These factors help to explain the confusing abundance of exceptions to the rules of gender, built partly on the community of sense and partly on that of form, which are the despair of the modern schoolboy. Now, Protagoras, as a son of the age of free thought, felt no restraint of piety in dealing with the *naïveté* of primitive man ; he had, as we shall find in other instances, a strong sense for rational correctness, and he was accordingly at pains to introduce occasionally something like order in the chaotic condition of language. The second authentic example of the grammatical criticism of Protagoras attached to the word πήληξ, meaning a helmet of war. This word, though feminine in Greek, he wished to see employed as masculine. If we search for his reasons we may probably reject the supposition that he was following a common principle which would make all substantives relating to the manly arts of warfare of the masculine gender. He was probably guided by a less general consideration. The termination -ξ is commonly a sign of the feminine gender, but the rule is by no means without exceptions. And among those exceptions three words are found which designate parts of the accoutrements of war. Protagoras, examining these three words, made that community of meaning responsible for their exception, and he wished accordingly to bring the fourth word under the same exceptional legislation. Further in respect to the word μῆνις mentioned above, his criticism may have been supported by the observation that the termination -ις is very far from being confined to substantives of the feminine gender. We cannot hope to determine whether or not a jest of Aristophanes, which is doubtless justly referred to our sophist's attempts at reform, was founded on an actual fact. But if it was, we see that Protagoras wished to supply a defect in the older Greek language which used the word corresponding to our "cock" for both sexes indifferently. He wished to form a feminine "cockess," much in the same way as we speak of a "lioness" and "tigress" as well as of a "lion" and "tiger."

3. The conception of correctness confronts us again as a leading thought peculiar to Protagoras in other fields of his activity. One of the writings in which he treated of ethics bore the title "On the Incorrect Actions of Mankind." Another of his works on moral philosophy was called "The Imperative Speech"—a title which is consistent with the tone of dogmatic certainty in which Plato's Protagoras speaks in his most characteristic vein. We are not aware how he treated the subject of ethics, though we may presume that he did not make any very original departure from the common Greek type. And we are similarly ignorant of the contents of his treatise "On the State" or "On the Constitution." There he may have discussed the question of criminal law which will shortly engage our attention, and in which he endeavoured to determine who "in accordance with correct opinion" was the truly guilty man. We are reminded at this point of the ridicule poured by Plato on the attempts of Protagoras to reduce all human action and conduct to arts or systems of rules, and we may recall, for the sake of comparison, two sentences from the above-mentioned treatise "On the Art," * which in thought and expression is so closely akin to Protagoras. "But is it not Art," we read, "when the correct and the incorrect both have their limits assigned to them? For I call it non-Art when there is neither

* Cp. Bk. III. Ch. V. § 3.

anything correct nor anything incorrect." Here we see the same powerful craving for rational insight, and the rationalization of all departments of human life, which we have already marked as a characteristic of the whole age, which we shall find in its fullest development in the doctrines of Socrates, and which was extremely active in Protagoras himself. It enabled him to drag the creations of law, not less than those of language, before the judgment-seat of reason. We are but slightly acquainted with what he achieved in that direction, but the little we know is eminently noteworthy.

The gossips of Athens used to amuse themselves by telling of a conversation protracted for many hours between Pericles, the leading statesman, and Protagoras, the foreign sophist. Its theme seemed hardly worthy of the time and interest of at least the first of the interlocutors. One of the participators in the game of throwing the spear had unintentionally killed a bystander, and Pericles and Protagoras were said to have argued a whole day long as to who was the guilty party. Was it the deviser of the game, or the competitor who threw the spear, or, finally, the spear itself? It is this item of the interrogatory which excites our astonishment, and tempts us to regard the whole story, despite its excellent authority, as a sorry jest. But, as a matter of fact, it is precisely this problem of the spear which affords the key to the whole matter. To our thinking the conviction of inanimate objects is just as absurd as the execution of unreasoning animals. But the ancients held a different opinion, which did not expire with the Greeks. Lawsuits against animals were admitted in the Greek and Roman codes, as well as in the old Scandinavian, the old Persian, the Hebraic, and the Slavonic. Mediævalism is full of them, and they extend far across the frontier of modern times. The judicial rolls of France tell us of bulls and swine who ended their life on the gallows in the fifteenth, sixteenth, and even in the beginning of the seventeenth century. The custom still flourishes in the East, and the last traces of it in Western history are found as late as 1793 and 1845 A.D. The first-named date

refers to the very time when Cambacérès was occupied in
elaborating the judicial reform which has found its place in
the *Code Napoléon*. If he had attended the execution of
a sentence passed on a dog by the revolutionary tribunal
on the twenty-seventh of Brumaire in the year II. at the
sign of "The Bull Fight" in Paris, the disgust of this
modern master of jurisprudence could not have been in any
way greater than that of the Greek sophist at Athens,
who saw weapons and other inanimate objects which had
caused the death of a man convicted, purified, and
solemnly banished from the country. It is quite conceivable, then, that the conversation in question may have
grown out of some spectacle of that kind. But it is fair
to believe that it would not have stopped there. It was
a quarrel, as Hegel said, "about the great and important
question of responsibility;" nay, we may add, about the
yet greater and more important question of the purpose of
punishment. Protagoras was just the man to found on
that extreme case of glaring unreason, or "incorrectness,"
as he would have said, familiar to every one from such
proceedings of the tribunal near the Prytaneum, a discussion
which was gradually to lead to an exalted goal, which was
to examine the value and nature of the existing criminal
law, to lay bare its chief bases—the instinct of retaliation,
and the craving for atonement—and thence to proceed to
the question whether it were legitimate for such reasons to
afflict members of human society with grievous suffering,
and, finally, to seek for some more tenable basis on which
to build up a system of criminal law. Nor, when we ask
where he found that basis, are we reduced to mere guesswork. We may listen to Protagoras in the Platonic dialogue of that name raising an emphatic protest against the
mere brutal retaliation of an injury done, and energetically
proclaiming the deterrent theory of punishment; and,
listening thus, we may fancy ourselves once more in
the chamber of Pericles overhearing the earnest and
eager commerce of speech, and better fathoming the
depths of the argument than was vouchsafed to Xanthip-
pus, our authority, the degenerate son of Pericles, or to

Stesimbrotus, the scavenging pamphleteer, to whom he confided the tidings.

4. The question suggests itself, What was the attitude of the powerful and critical mind of Protagoras towards the problems of theology? That early literary *auto-da-fe* which it has been our melancholy duty to report, has robbed us of the accurate answer to this question. One sentence alone has been saved in its entirety from the ruins. It was the sentence which stood at the beginning of the doomed book, and which ran as follows:—

" In respect to the gods, I am unable to know either that they are or that they are not, for there are many obstacles to such knowledge, above all the obscurity of the matter, and the life of man, in that it is so short."

We are overwhelmed here by a flood of questions. What, we ask first, can have been the contents of the book, the opening sentence of which removed the subject it treated from the domain of human knowledge, and thus, as it might seem, settled it out of court? We can do nothing more than take the few words that have been preserved, scrutinize them as closely as possible, and expatiate on them as accurately as we may. And the first point that strikes us is the repetition of the word "know," and the emphasis that it derives from such repetition. For the ancients distinguished the two conceptions of knowledge and belief in the domain of which we are speaking, fully as strictly as we are wont to do ourselves. We need hardly recall the definite distinction drawn by Parmenides, with all the consequences it entailed, between cognition and opinion which engaged our attention in speaking of Parmenides and of his disciples. Even in the Greek vernacular we find that religious convictions, headed by the assumption of the existence of gods, were expressed by a term ($\nu o\mu i\zeta\epsilon\iota\nu$) which had nothing whatsoever in common with scientific cognition. We are accordingly impelled to follow the valuable hint given by Christian August Lobeck, and to contend that the subject of those discussions was not the belief in the gods, but the cognition of the gods. Add to this that there are various other circumstances which make it in the highest degree improbable that Protagoras would have consented to assail such beliefs or even to call them in doubt. In the first place, Plato tells us of the remarkable procedure by which the sophist was accustomed to settle any quarrel about the amount of the honorarium owing to him. If a disciple refused to pay the fee demanded by his teacher after the conclusion of the course, the sophist would invite him to declare on oath in a temple the amount at which he himself estimated the value of the instruction he had received. And, secondly, we may quote the by no means negligible evidence of the manner in which the Platonic Protagoras described the beginnings of human society. For it is at least extremely improbable that a master of characterization like Plato should have put a legend, filled from beginning to end with the gods and their intervention in the fate of mankind, in the mouth of a man who, though only at the end of his life, stood revealed as an opponent of divine worship. The improbability is heightened by the following sentence, to which Protagoras was made to give expression :—

" Now man, having a share of the divine attributes, was at first the only one of the animals who had any gods, because he alone was of their kindred ; and he would raise altars and images of them."

Thus everything leads us to the conclusion that the Protagorean fragment above mentioned did not call in question the theological belief, but the scientific or reasonable knowledge of the existence of the gods. Next we may take the Greek word which we have rendered by " obscurity." In the original it possesses a particular shade of meaning signifying the contrary of " sensibleness." In that connection the reference to the " obscurity " as an obstacle to cognition signified neither more nor less than that the gods were not the objects of direct sense-perception. But in default of perception its place is taken by inference—a generalization not only common to universal human thought, but directly traceable in the literature of the age we are discussing. Thus the warning as to the shortness of the life of man could have been inserted for no other purpose than to remind us that the brief span of time by which our existence is bounded affords no adequate empirical material on which to base the requisite arguments for affirming or denying the existence of gods. Thus far this valuable fragment may be interpreted with certainty. The rest is conjecture. We do not know what contemporary experiments Protagoras had in his mind to prove or disprove the existence of the gods, in order to justify his indictment of their inadequacy, and to recommend in their stead the suspension of judgment as the one safe method of thought; nor, without that knowledge, have we any trustworthy ground for argument. All that we can say is that Protagoras replaced the confidence of Yea and Nay by reminding his readers of the narrow limits of human cognition. Thus his name marks an important chapter in the history of the development of scientific thought. It may well be that he would have assented to the words written down by Ernest Renan shortly before his death in 1892 : " 'We know nothing.' That is all that can be said with certainty on what lies beyond the Finite. Let us affirm nothing, let us deny nothing, let us hope."

5. From theology to metaphysics is only a step. Here again a single sentence has to do duty for a whole book. The work in question was known by three different titles, " On Being," " Truth," and " The 'Throwing' Discourses." The third of these titles, with its metaphor from wrestling, shows us that a considerable portion of this treatise was polemical in character, and we are not wholly unaware of the butt of the attack. According to a late reader of the work in antiquity, the Neo-Platonist Porphyry, who died not long after 300 A.D., Protagoras directed the shafts of his polemic against the Eleatics. The single sentence which has been preserved, and which was again the opening sentence of the book, ran as follows : " Man is the measure of all things, of those which are, that they are, and of those which are not, that they are not." We are struck at once by the resemblance in style between the metaphysical and

the theological fragments, and we are struck no less by their common need of interpretation. The first thing to be done in this instance is to determine what the important and, unfortunately, wholly isolated fragment *cannot* be. It cannot possess an ethical meaning ; it cannot be the shibboleth of any moral subjectivism, to which the sentence has not unfrequently been turned in the hands of popular expositors. Neither the text of the utterance nor its point directed against the Eleatic doctrine of unity offers the slightest handle to any explanation of that kind. One fact may be stated with absolute certainty. The phrase about man as the measure of things—the homo-mensura tenet, as it has been suitably abbreviated—was a contribution to the theory of cognition. Moreover "man," as opposed to the totality of objects, was obviously not the individual, but mankind as a whole. No unprejudiced reader will require to be convinced that this is at least the more natural and the more obvious meaning. Goethe, for example, was a reader of that kind. He made but a cursory reference to the Protagorean phrase, but the intuitive instinct of his genius was a better guide to its meaning than a thousand uninspired commentators :

"We may watch Nature," wrote Goethe, "measure her, reckon her, weigh her, etc., as we will. It is yet but our measure and weight, since man is the measure of things."

We have thus seen reason to favour the non-individual but generic interpretation of "man," and our preference, we believe, can be turned to a certainty by a strictly logical argument. Hitherto the tradition of the experts, which has only recently been seriously shaken, has held fast to the individualistic meaning, the adherents of which, in our opinion, must take one or the other of two roads of thought, both of which we venture to characterize as erroneous. In the one instance the facts may just be brought into harmony with the interpretation, but the grammar breaks down ; in the other instance the grammar is admissible, but the facts are not. Supposing that Protagoras wished to assert that the individual was the measure of all things, he must have been thinking either of the properties or of the existence of the things. The first of these assumptions is the one which we have called admissible on the facts. For the individual differences of sensuous perceptions had already in that age begun to attract the attention of philosophers. But the assumption must surrender unconditionally to the little Greek word ὡς, which, in common with the large majority of philological critics, we have rendered by "that," and not by "how," and which, as numerous parallel passages, among them the fragment about the gods by Protagoras himself, show beyond dispute, cannot possibly be rendered otherwise. And we might further remark, by the way, that by the contrary supposition the negative branch of the sentence—"of those which are not, how they are not"—would be devoid of all reasonable meaning. For no one would ever have been at pains to inquire into the negative properties of that which was devoid of being. Thirdly and lastly, the appearance of this sentence at the opening of the whole book, the comprehensive phrases in which it is clothed, and the importance which its author plainly ascribed to it—all this is hardly compatible with the view that it was the promulgation of a truth not unimportant in itself, but yet of a subordinate and special character, devoted, that is to say, to the individual variation of the sense perceptions, honey tasting bitter to a man suffering from jaundice, and so forth. Coming next to the second species of individualistic meaning, we may refute it by the following simple consideration. We have only to ask what could be meant by setting up the human individual as the criterion or standard for the existence of objects, in order to see that it would involve the complete jettison of the doctrine of objective reality. It would be an expression, and, parenthetically remarked, a somewhat awkward expression, for that aspect of the theory of knowledge which in modern times is known as the phenomenalistic, and which was represented in antiquity by that school of Socratics who derived their name of Cyrenaics from their seat in Cyrene, in Africa. It is the aspect in which there is no room either for "objects" or for the conception of objective being or for existence at all, but solely for subjective "affections." But, so far as the teaching of Protagoras is concerned, there is internal as well as external evidence to show beyond the possibility of dispute that it did not coincide with that of Aristippus and the adherents of his school. Let us summarize the heads of our verdict. The famous and much controverted fragment which opened "The 'Throwing' Discourses" belongs to the theory of cognition. The "man" it speaks of is not this or that specimen of the genus, not any individual Tom, Dick, or Harry, but universal man. The sentence has a generic and not an individual significance. Finally, man in this sense is exalted to the measure, not of the properties, but of the existence of the objects. The evidence of Porphyry in respect to the polemic directed against the Eleatic doctrine affords us additional support in the attitude we have adopted. It is meet, in the first place, to recall Melissus, the nearest contemporary of Protagoras, and we may account it a piece of luck that in the "Thesis of Melissus" we meet the exact counterpart of the Protagorean tenet. The Eleatic repudiation of the testimony of the senses found a clear exponent in Melissus in the words, "wherefore it ensueth that we neither see nor know what *is*" (properly, the beings). This summary denial of the reality of the sensuous world is counterbalanced in Protagoras by its equally summary affirmation: Man or human nature is the standard for the existence of the things. In other words, only what is real can be perceived by us. The unreal cannot supply any object to our perception. So much for the leading thought of Protagoras, the proof of which has not been preserved for us. The emphasis laid on the conception of man was doubtless responsible for his secondary thought that we men cannot break through the limits of our own nature; that the truth attainable by us must lie within those limits; that, if we reject the evidence of our perceptive faculties, we have no right to confide in our remaining faculties ; and, above all, that in such circumstances there would be no material for cognition left over for us. Nay, how should we seek for a criterion of truth, and what significance could we ascribe to the words "true" and "untrue," if we had repudiated root and branch human truth, the sole truth within our reach ?

In the treatise "On the Art," to which we have more than once had occasion to refer, the doctrine of Protagoras assumed a shape in which it was more closely related, and accordingly more sharply contrasted, with the doctrine of Melissus. It was promulgated as follows : "What *is*" (properly, the beings) "may always be seen and known, but what is-not" (properly, the non-beings) "may never be either seen or known." We can imagine the author of the treatise posing Melissus with the questions, How can objects which we perceive be unreal? and, How could the unreal enter in our field of perception? At this point we may go back to the words preceding the above quotation. We read, quite literally, that "if what is-not be equally perceptible with what *is*, I do not know how any one can regard it as non-being, inasmuch as it can be seen with the eye and known by the mind as being. But that will not be the case. Rather what *is*——" and here ensues the passage which we have already cited. It is obvious that we are here confronted with an extremely notable argument. A flash of relativistic or phenomenalistic thought has illuminated the author's mind. He holds fast by the belief that something perceptible, some objective reality, corresponds in each instance to our perception. But even if that expectation happened not to be fulfilled, a man, according to our author, would still have to rest contented with what his faculties of perception set before his vision. If we may venture to complete his argument, he would have said that this was the sole truth attainable by man, that it was the relative or human truth. "But that will not be the case." And here, accordingly, our author turned from the relativistic road, revealed to him in a flash of lightning, back to the old and naïve conception of the world.

This rehabilitation of the evidence of the senses must

have reversed the relations between Protagoras and the natural philosophers on the one part, and Protagoras and Melissus, the " un-natural philosopher," the " stopper-of-the-universe," on the other. And, in point of fact, we find in the treatise " On the Art," not merely, as has just been shown, the homo-mensura tenet, but also the foundations of a strictly empirical method and philosophy. We shall revert later to these features, but one remark will here be in place. There is one scanty piece of testimony for the fact that Protagoras occupied himself with mathematics, on which, indeed, he wrote a book, and that too makes it clear that his mind followed empirical channels. The testimony is found in Aristotle, who wrote (in support of his own remark, " Lines sensibly perceptible are not of the kind which the geometer supposes, for nothing sensibly perceptible is so curved or so straight ") that " Protagoras, in his polemic against the geometers, mentions that the tangent does not touch the circle at one point only." Now, this means neither more nor less than that, to use expressions employed by John Stuart Mill, " There exist no real things exactly conformable to the definitions. There exist no points without magnitude ; no lines without breadth, nor perfectly straight ; no circles with all their radii exactly equal," etc. On this point, however, there never was any conflict of opinion between the adherents of the most diverse schools. The conflict began at a later stage, when the question was asked whether the definitions of geometry were derived from the sensible world, and therefore were only approximately true, as abstractions adapted to serve the ends of science, or whether they were of *à priori* origin and contained absolute truth in themselves. Protagoras, it is hardly to be doubted, subscribed to the first of these opinions. He may even be regarded as its earliest mouthpiece, and thus, as a precursor of the thinkers who, like Sir John Leslie, Sir John Herschel, Mill, and Helmholtz in our own times, have maintained the empirical origin of the tenets of geometry, its axioms as well as its definitions.

We have accordingly established the empirical nature

of the Protagorean method, and our conclusion is corroborated by Plato's view of the homo-mensura tenet. He regarded it as wholly identical with the thesis, " Cognition is sense perception," or all knowledge rests on such perception. And this marks the last legitimate stage in our employment of the testimony of Plato. The reason for our renouncement is simple enough. Henceforward Plato's utterances on this subject are not the evidence of a witness, but attempts to derive from the Protagorean thesis consequences really or ostensibly contained therein. Plato argued somewhat as follows : If the perceptions of sense necessarily contain truth, but the perception of one individual differs frequently from that of another, then it is fair to infer from that tenet that an equal measure of truth belongs even to contradictory perceptions. Moreover, it is probable that Protagoras, like the majority of his contemporaries, failed to distinguish with the requisite strictness between veritable perceptions and the conclusions derived from them, thus opening an avenue for Plato's further deduction from the tenet of Protagoras that even contrary opinions possess the same degree of truth ; in a word, that " what appears to each man to be true, is true for each man." Here, then, we are face to face with the famous so-called Protagorean doctrine, which it would be too high an honour to regard as the expression of extreme subjectivism or scepticism. As a matter of fact, it is hardly distinguishable from blank nonsense. It deals the death-blow to all orderly thought, all merely rational conduct, as well as to all education, all foresight, all science and instruction. And yet this iconoclast, who was supposed to have destroyed objective truth, and with it to have carried away all rules of universal import, laboured for more than forty years in every part of Greece as a teacher highly esteemed and in great request, as a celebrated rhetorician and author ; he was yet a lecturer whose wealth of positive tenets were not merely delivered from the platform, but were pointed and inculcated with extraordinary emphasis, and were promulgated with the force of the pulpit. And it was the same reputed iconoclast who, as we have seen, and as we shall still have occasion to see, assumed the functions of a legislator in the most various departments of life, and whose distinction between the correct and the incorrect, between the right and the wrong, obtained in the circle of his thought too much rather than too little consideration and esteem.

The reader may object at this point that we have heard expressions of scepticism from the very lips of our sophist himself; that he published his doubts as to the existence of the gods in language which amply testifies to his mental disposition. Perfectly true, we reply. And it is precisely from the fragment about the gods that we derive our final and irrefutable argument to prove that the kind of scepticism which Plato read into the homo-mensura tenet was completely alien to the thought of its author. For Protagoras based his suspension of judgment in that single instance on grounds of fact, the roots of which were deeply embedded in the nature of the special problem itself. Hitherto, we may conceive him to say, no one has seen gods; but human life is too short, and the field of our observation too restricted, to affirm or to deny with certainty the traces of their activity in the world of nature and man. Accordingly he withheld his verdict; in respect to that question, he framed no definite answer either in the positive or in the negative. But if the maxim that "every man's truth is the truth which appears to him" had really been the lodestar of his mind, his answer, we take it, would have been different. In that case we conceive he must necessarily have expressed himself to this effect: Gods exist for those who believe in them; they do not exist for those who do not believe in them.

Nor are we reduced to the sophist's own sparse authentic utterances in order to refute this misconception. Plato himself bore witness against it. In the dialogue entitled "Protagoras" he drew a picture of the man, the main features of which are obviously genuine, though the colours are in places too glaring, and though we could dispense with some of the less amiable detail. But, as it stands, it has

nothing whatsoever in common with the sham portrait in
the "Theætetus." The same thinker appears in both
dialogues, but he is characterized in the "Protagoras" by
an excess rather than a defect of definiteness and dogmatism, though he is represented in the "Theætetus" as
denying every distinction between truth and error. It is
significant, too, that in the earlier of the two dialogues
Protagoras is introduced as a living man, while in the
second and much later study he is mentioned as one long
since dead. In the one the biographer is working on the
memory of things seen, in the other fancy is playing with
a shadow or a phantom. The one is a person, the other a
formula ; in the one case the author is governed by intuition, in the other by inference. In a word, the "Protagoras"
shows us a lifelike and finished portrait ; the "Theætetus"
is composed of superfine and thin-spun ratiocinations. No
true student of Plato, whose attention has been called to
this contrast, will hesitate at all where to look for historical
truth, nor will doubt where Plato himself intended that
search to be successful.

When we come to discuss the "Theætetus" at length,
we shall do our best to illustrate the particular object
which its author had in view, but for the purpose of the
present discussion a few preliminary remarks will not be
out of place. The conversational style which Plato
affected landed him in a difficulty of a quite exceptional
kind. He exalted his master Socrates to the chief *rôle*
in his dialogues. Nevertheless he could not and would
not renounce altogether the controversial discussion of
post-Socratic doctrines. We do not pretend that Plato
was particularly at pains to avoid anachronisms. One
thing, however, was plainly inadmissible. Socrates could
not be armed for the fray against the champions of tenets
which had arisen subsequently to his death. Now, in
order to circumvent this difficulty, the ingenuity of the
poet-philosopher had to cast around for artificial ex-
pedients. At one time, for instance, his Socrates learnt
of the existence of a doctrine "in a dream." There was
no other reason for this proceeding except that, inasmuch

as the doctrine was due to his own pupil Antisthenes, he could hardly have heard of it through the orthodox channels of information. Now let us take the "Theætetus" with its notable divergences from the "Protagoras." In the "Theætetus" Socrates is represented as expounding and combating the theory of cognition which is described as a "secret doctrine" of Protagoras, and as very different from that which the sophist published to "the great multitude." An ardent admirer of Protagoras who took part in the conversation, and who was at the same time intimately acquainted with his chief metaphysical treatise, is plainly taken aback by the revelations of Socrates. In other words, Plato tells his readers, as clearly as the conventions of his self-imposed style permit, that he is making use of a fiction. His real object was to establish his position with regard to the theory of knowledge promulgated by Aristippus. This object has long since been recognized, though it has not yet been universally acknowledged. Now, of Plato, the prince of artists, it may legitimately be said *nil molitur inepte*. If this particular fiction had not suited him, he might readily have selected another. Accordingly we may conclude that Plato was anxious to establish an inner relationship between the doctrines of Aristippus and Protagoras. In this light we are now able to see that the indispensable preliminary step to the whole transparent mystification was precisely that exposition of the homo-mensura tenet which engaged our attention above. It was Plato's deliberate intention to enter the lists of the problem of cognition, and to encounter its difficulties in his own person. The introduction, for controversial purposes, of the doctrine of Aristippus under a shallow disguise was but a single step on this long road of thought. The mention of Protagoras was merely an artistic necessity of the fictitious treatment of the whole theme, and nothing was further from the original aim of Plato than to write an appreciative memoir of the historical personage to whom that name appertained. These, then, being the circumstances of the case, Plato, so far from being hindered, was actually encouraged to dissociate, as it were, the Protagorean tenet from its author and its environment. He was not required to ask what it signified to its author, nor how its author employed it. On the contrary, he was completely at liberty to read into the formula whatever meaning its wording would warrant. It would be unfair to speak of the violation of historical truth in an instance where the whole attitude of the writer is directed towards the emancipation of his readers' minds from the trammels of history.

But we have now to reckon with a factor which we did not anticipate. The "godlike" Plato was wholly innocent in intention, but in this particular instance, as well as in respect to the so-called sophists in general, he perverted history despite himself by the authority of his mighty name. All antiquity accepted Plato's interpretation of the doctrine as naked truth ; nor have modern times been able to escape from his guidance till the most recent past. Here and there in the references of isolated authors of antiquity there are feeble traces of dissent, but the great majority of them never once took the trouble seriously to examine the text of the tiny fragment. Our surprise at this omission is lessened by the fact that Timon, who was born just before the dawn of the third century B.C., did not give himself the pains, as his comic verses plainly show, to gain even a correct grammatical acquaintance with the fragment of Protagoras about the gods. We have seen that the influence of Plato was responsible for a negative source of error in the depreciation and neglect of the literature of the sophists, and in this particular instance a positive factor was added by the interpretation put by Plato on the fragment. To these causes it was due that no one till very recently had the curiosity to ask how the gulf was to be filled up that yawned before the eyes of every one between the expositions in the " Protagoras " and in the " Theætetus." It was nobody's business to determine how the sacred fragment and the other sparse remains were compatible with the universal scepticism which was ascribed to their author. The suggestion leaps to the lips—Surely Aristotle was not guilty of the widespread misconception. We have to answer both Yes and No. In two passages of his "Metaphysics" he mentions the homo-mensura tenet in such a manner as to suggest that Plato in the "Theætetus," and again almost literally in the "Cratylus," was writing with historical authority. But, in a third passage, Aristotle grapples with the same subject again and comes to quite a different conclusion. There the "man" is not the individual, but is equipped with the qualities of his kind. The individualistic interpretation passes into the generic. And the Protagorean tenet, which is elsewhere regarded by Aristotle as a dangerous paradox fatal to all intelligible argument, is here dismissed as a pretentious triviality :

"But if Protagoras says," we read, "that man is the measure of all things, that means that the Knowing or the sensibly Perceiving is the measure, inasmuch as the one possesses the sensible perception, and the other the knowledge, which we describe as the measure of their objects. Thus though the doctrine of Protagoras really says nothing at all, it seems to say goodness knows what."

The foregoing attempt at an explanation may not merely incur the reproach of breaking with the tradition of nearly all antiquity ; it may also be censured as incomplete. Nor, we are fain to confess, would the rebuke be wholly unmerited. There is still much that might be said more or less hypothetically about the attitude of Protagoras towards the problems of cognition. But we cannot think it advisable to discuss questions of secondary import while the dispute on the leading question is still unsettled. A superstructure of hypothesis should only be reared on a basis of certainty. Still, we shall not deny ourselves the expression of just one conjecture. Many circumstances make it probable that Protagoras, in his feud against the Eleatics and their repudiation of the testimony of the senses, pointed to subjective truth and to the infallibility, or rather the inevitableness, of every sensation. It is further probable that in this connection he failed to distinguish with the requisite degree of accuracy between sensation, perception, perceptive judgment, and judgment in general. On these accounts the reproach which he incurred of maintaining an equal degree of truth in all ideas and opinions may have been, if not deserved, at least provoked by his own attitude. The reproach may then have contributed to the false interpretation of the homo-mensura tenet. But, be this as it may, however little we know of the Protagorean theory of cognition, one fact stands like a rock. Protagoras may or may not have been carried away by the zest of polemic ; he may or may not have been misled by the incomplete psychological vocabulary of his times into uttering at some place or on some occasion something that gave a handle to the charge of scepticism ; but the Protagorean fragments that have come down to us, few and sparse though they are, are in themselves fully sufficient to support the belief that the universal scepticism ascribed to him was never a guiding star of his own thought.

6. "On every question there are two speeches, which stand in opposition to one another." This precious fragment has likewise been pressed into the service of the theory against which we have been arguing so long. Those who have turned it to this use, however, have overlooked the simple fact that if it really possessed the meaning ascribed to it, and were a corollary of the assertion that every opinion is equally true, it would have had to refer, not to two speeches only, but to an infinite number. Now, the genuine meaning of the fragment may be illustrated from its reproduction by Euripides, the friend of Protagoras, as well as by the context in which it recurs in Isocrates. Amphion, in the "Antiope" of Euripides, employs almost the same turn of expression :

> " In every matter can the speaker's art
> Awaken conflict by a double tongue."

And Isocrates the rhetorician numbers among the useless and absurd paradoxes in which a former generation delighted, the contrary proposition, that "it is impossible to make two opposite speeches on the same subject." Accordingly, it is idle to look for a sceptical bias in the statement of Protagoras. It contains nothing more than the expression of a truism, familiar enough to modern times, which Diderot once formulated as follows : "In all questions, with the single exception of mathematics, there are a *pro* and a *con*." Many pages might be filled with the salutary applications of this dictum. Thus the central thought of the first half of Mill's " Liberty " has been correctly defined as "the necessity of taking account of the *negative* to every positive affirmation ; of laying down, side by side with every proposition, the *counter-proposition*." And to come down to practical questions, every intelligent reader of Parliamentary debates and newspaper articles will be aware of the futility and delusiveness of a discussion which is confined to the illustration of one side only, whether it be the advantages or the disadvantages of a measure or institution. He will be aware that no prospect of a salutary decision can be opened to the feeble judgment of men unless both sides are treated with impartial completeness and are weighed the one against the other. The decisive factor, in practice as well as in theory, is not, to refer to Mill once more—

"what can be said for an opinion, but whether more can be said for it than against it. There is no knowledge, and no assurance of right belief, but with him who can both confute the opposite opinion, and successfully defend his own against confutation."

The principle described in this passage as "the principal lesson of Plato's writings" was foreshadowed in the dictum of Protagoras with which we are now engaged. The great sophist himself, in promulgating his doctrine, was probably chiefly impressed by its educational value. He would have shared the sentiment of Goethe, who eulogized the Mohammedans for beginning—

"their course of philosophy with the lesson that nothing exists of which the contrary cannot be affirmed. Thus," Goethe continues, "they exercise the mind of youth by setting them the task of discovering and defining the contrary to every proposition in their ken, whence there is bound to proceed a high degree of versatility in thinking and speaking."

Doubt is awakened by these means, and from doubt, as Goethe put it, the mind was led to nearer scrutiny and proof, with certainty as its ultimate goal:

" You see," he says, at the close of his conversation with the faithful Eckermann, " that nothing is wanting to this teaching, and that we with all our systems have not arrived any further."

And when Goethe warmly assented to the remark of his friend, that he was "thereby reminded of the Greeks, whose method of philosophic instruction must have been similar," we may add that it was precisely the Protagorean " Antilogies " which headed the list of auxiliaries to this course of instruction.

Unfortunately, of the two books of the celebrated work we possess not a single line save the short sentence quoted above, which probably stood at the beginning. Nor are we in better plight when we come to indirect sources of information. The most important testimony we possess is an incomplete report of Aristoxenus, a philosophic writer on music, from which we can infer, with a moderate degree of confidence, that Plato based the brilliant dialectic discussion of the conception of justice in the first book of the "Republic" to some extent on this work. And even though the report be rejected as untrue, it is not wholly without value. For Aristoxenus, a disciple of Aristotle, and a younger contemporary of Plato, could not have made himself its mouthpiece if the contents of the " antilogies," which had not yet passed into oblivion, were not in agreement at various points with the Platonic masterpiece. The inference may be stated in the following positive form : The " antilogies " discussed problems of ethics and politics in a dialectic fashion. In other words, Protagoras was in this respect a precursor of Socrates, and a successor of Zeno, " the inventor of dialectic." Furthermore, the "cunning wrestler," as Timon entitles him, is associated by anecdote and tradition with " the Palamedes of the Eleatics." Thus the argument of the grain of millet, which our readers will recollect, has been preserved in the form of a game of question and answer between Zeno and Protagoras. Protagoras defends, and Zeno disputes in a series of captious questions, the evidence of the senses. The Eleatic accordingly is the active partner in the dialogue, and the Abderite the passive, and this distribution of parts tallies admirably with the dialectic impotence of Protagoras, despite his renown as an acute sophist, when exposed in Plato to the cross-examinations of Socrates. It further tallies with the fact that the whole rich tradition of apophthegms does not credit Protagoras with a single sophism or fallacy.

At this point we may sum up the dialectic art of Protagoras with comparative certainty in its general outline. He was evidently unpractised in the interchange of question and answer which was founded by Zeno, and developed by Socrates, and of which the chief exponents were the Socratics of Megara. His own favourite dialectic was obviously of a more rhetorical kind. He did not try to confuse his antagonist nor to goad him to contradiction by the method of curt interrogation. The chief weapon in his armoury was that of long speeches delivered successively to refute one another. The prototype of these rhetorical tournaments was found in the contest of speeches which was fought in bitter earnest in the law courts and on the platform, and they helped in turn to train the muscles of the intellectual athletes in the arena of public life.

It is impossible to doubt that dramatic writers like Euripides derived part of their strength from the same sources. The distich from the "Antiope," which we quoted just now, may well have been a token of gratitude from the disciple to his master. But there is another Greek writer in whose work we find the greatest variety of points of view, and who possessed an unrivalled art of sounding the contrasts of interests and arguments hidden in any situation, and of displaying them before our eyes in all their immeasurable abundance ; and it would have been nothing less than miraculous if Thucydides, the writer in question, had escaped this influence. Nor was it only that philosopher among the historians whose strength was steeled and tempered at this well-spring of inspiration. Plato himself went down to its waters to drink, nor is it any argument to the contrary that one of his latest dialogues, the "Sophistes," is a thorough-going invective against every kind of "antilogy." Plato in his old age grew averse from all dialectic. In the "Laws," the last product of his pen, he actually turned his back on it, and filled its vacant place, at the head of his curriculum of education, with mathematics and astronomy. Now, supposing the "Sophistes" were lost, we might reconstruct this portion of its contents by a kind of *à priori* method. For before the anti-dialectic tendency of Plato's mind attained its last and highest triumph, it must necessarily have won its victories where it met with less resistance. Before abandoning his own dialectic, which had served the cause of his theory of ideas, he must first have dismissed those variations of it which he had less immediately at heart. He was waging war in that instance with Antisthenes, but his feud against the Antisthenic handling of the dialectic method was aggravated by his excursions into the past to search for the origins of "antilogic." Here again we meet with the name of Protagoras in a context which merits our serious attention.

7. The sophist, according to the passage we are speaking of, makes all who come in contact with him, in whatever department of life, argumentative and litigious—in divine affairs as well as in earthly, in respect to development and existence as well as to the laws and the totality of civil institutions. " Further," the speaker continues, " in respect to all the arts and to each separate art, the seeker will find abundance of material in these writings for attacks on every craftsman." "You refer," runs the answer, "to the Protagorean discussions on the art of wrestling, and on the other arts ? " "Yes, my friend ; his writings, and those of many others as well." This, then, is all that we know about that branch of Protagoras' work as an author. We see that he had written treatises or controversial speeches on the art of wrestling, and probably on other special arts, apart from his book on the arts as a whole. The tendency of those writings cannot

be gathered from the cursory reference to them in the present place. The hasty manner in which Plato touched on the theme merely to leave it again at once leads us to suppose that he regarded it as but a weak aid to the argument he was sustaining. It is more important to remark, however, that the treatise "On the Art," which we have had repeated occasion to mention, affords a specimen of that kind of literary production which is here being spoken of. That treatise, as our readers are aware, is an apology for the art of medicine written by a pugnacious sophist. It contains several gross inaccuracies and occasional instances of exaggeration, but it is composed with an extraordinary degree of dialectic acuteness and rhetorical cleverness; and, as a defence of medicine, it succeeds in making the difficulties of the art, and the incompetence of many of its practitioners, rather than the art itself, responsible for its mistakes. Thus we are told, for example, that

"Those who blame the physicians for not treating sufferers from incurable diseases require them to do what is unsuitable as well as what is suitable, and in so far as they make this demand they are admired by the nominal physicians, but are laughed at by the genuine members of the profession. For its masters do not stand in need of such foolish praise or blame, but they want critics who will tell them when their work attains its goal and when it falls short, and whether in such cases its deficiencies are to be ascribed to the artists [literally, the craftsmen] themselves, or to the objects of their care."

And at the close of the next paragraph we read—

"It [namely, the treatment of diseases open to view] has not been discovered for those who want to practise it, but for those of their number who can practise it; but those only can whose nature is not repugnant, and who have not lacked the means of training."

Here too, then, we perceive that there is no lack of censorious references to the "craftsmen," and that, to this extent at least, the one characteristic of those

controversial orations which is emphasized in the passage
in the "Sophistes" tallies more or less with the surviving example. But there is another and a more important
point. Reverting to the passage first quoted from the
close of a chapter in the treatise, we find that the
ensuing sentence runs as follows : "Now what concerns
the other arts, that shall be taught at another time and in
another discourse." Thus the author held out a promise
of a treatise to be devoted to the remaining arts, in words
which precisely correspond to the language employed by
Plato in the "Sophistes" in mentioning the existence of
such a treatise by Protagoras. This consentaneity,
combined with numerous other circumstances, has induced
us to ascribe the authorship of the pseudo-Hippocratic
little work "On the Art" to no other than to Protagoras,
the sophist of Abdera. Our readers are already aware
that the chief metaphysical tenet of Protagoras is
repeated in that treatise, which further contains a
reference to "other discourses," perhaps "The 'Throwing'
Discourses," with which we have made acquaintance, which
were to illustrate it more accurately. The conjectural
identity which we have thus ventured to establish is
rendered highly probable by the fact that the dialect,
style, and tone of the treatise recall the very epoch,
surroundings, and personality of Protagoras himself,
down to countless notable echoes of his peculiar mode
of speaking, as imitated in Plato. Additional evidence
is afforded by the following consideration : According to
this very passage in the "Sophistes," the separate arts
possessed an abundant literature of their own, and, so
far at least, there would be little to support the identity.
But in both these cases, besides the treatment of the
individual arts, there is in the one instance a mention,
and in the other a promise, of a general discussion.
Now, we may well be startled at this coincidence. If it
were an opponent of Protagoras who was competing with
him in this field as well, we should have less ground for
surprise ; but the similarity of the metaphysical principles
rules that hypothesis out of court. Thus, if we refuse to

adopt the theory of identic authorship, we are placed on the horns of a remarkable dilemma. We must either suppose that Protagoras, who was far from lacking in originality, had adventured on this occasion on an outworn track, or else that a sophist, who was closely allied to him in many respects, including questions of principle, and was thus presumably his disciple, had undertaken to beat him out of the field. We do not know how Protagoras treated the separate arts, but we may fairly conjecture that he adapted his treatment to their differences. Thus the art of medicine required that its suspect reality should be justified and vindicated, but this was by no means the case with the manual arts. It had often been denied that the art of the physician created health, but it had never been denied that the art of the weaver made woven fabrics, or the art of the shoemaker shoes. Accordingly, certain portions of a composite work of that kind would possess a critical character, and others an apologetic. But in both instances alike there was ample opportunity for inveighing against the performances of the "craftsmen." The release of an art from the reproaches levelled against it meant more frequently than not the transference of the charge on its practitioners. And finally, even if such reproaches were followed by a refutation, still they had been uttered, and Plato accordingly could use them in the sense mentioned above.

We have lingered on this subject at greater length because the treatise "On the Art" contributes much, and much that is of importance, to the picture of the activity of the sophists in the fifth century, and, if its Protagorean authorship be conceded, to the picture of the earliest and the noblest of the sophists. We cannot discuss all the details here, but we may fairly say that the spirit of positive science, nay, of modern positive science, speaks to us from no other literary monument of that age with equal vigour or clearness. The evidence of the senses, and the inferences derived from it, are the author's sole source of medical and other knowledge. Reluctant Nature is put on the rack and compelled to bear witness—a

Baconian simile which, though so familiar to modern times, was otherwise, so far as we are aware, unknown to antiquity. Where observation, experimentation, and the conclusions thus derived proved inadequate, there the impassable barriers of human cognition were erected. Universal causation was recognized and promulgated as the unexceptional law of all occurrences, with a rigour and strictness unparalleled in that age, save only in the theory of the Atomists. The relation between cause and effect was the foundation of all foresight, and foresight the foundation of all deliberate action. Objects possessed fixed qualities with definite bounds. To produce different effects, different causes had to be brought in play ; what was serviceable in one case would be hurtful in a very different or in an opposite case ; what proved beneficial by rightful use would prove pernicious by wrongful use. The limitation of human powers was clearly recognized and emphatically expressed. The author was not disposed to extravagant demands in respect to man's dominion over nature, nor yet to the exercise of an arbitrary fancy in the interpretation of natural phenomena. It is astonishing, in our opinion, that the treatise which gives so clear and forcible an expression to the gospel of the inductive spirit should have hitherto wholly escaped the attention of historians and philosophers. But our statement is too sweeping. There is one exception at least to that indifference which surprises us. Pierre Jean Georges Cabanis, a brilliant representative of the last great era of enlightenment, in his work "On the Degree of Certainty in Medicine," rendered to the treatise "On the Art," which he supposed to be the work of Hippocrates, the full homage that is due to it. At every turn of his argument Mirabeau's physician did not merely display the closeness of his contact with the doctrines of that treatise, he was never tired of making long excerpts from it. And at the close of his own work, when he was resuming his conclusions, he practically reproduced in a very slightly altered shape the fundamental thoughts of the treatise with which he was so well acquainted.

8. And here we might take leave of Protagoras, if his practice of rhetoric did not call for a few remarks. We have to reckon with the disrepute which clung to him on that account. The Greeks, according to the testimony of Aristotle, were justly incensed with Protagoras for boasting that he could turn the weaker speech or cause into the stronger one. At this point an explanation is due. Aristotle's words were consonant with the standing reproach that was levelled at philosophers as well as at rhetoricians. It is mentioned by Socrates in the Platonic "Apology" among the "ready-made charges which are used against all philosophers." It occurs again in a similar context in a speech of Isocrates, who was likewise accused by his adversaries of perverting justice and corrupting the young. Now, it imposes a somewhat severe strain on our credence to imagine that Protagoras, who, in Timon's words, "always carefully avoided what was unseemly," would have boasted of precisely that talent which not many years later was reckoned as so shameful a reproach. Two alternatives are possible with regard to the testimony of Aristotle. He may have been able to quote text and verse for his statement, or he may have been misled by a fallacious tradition, but in either case we are bound to discriminate between the formula and its contents. The formula was unpopular and offensive because it seemed to imply that the rhetorician, in supporting the weaker cause, was supporting the worse cause too—in other words, that he was supporting injustice. But the question on its merits was entirely independent of morality and justice. The common aim of the rhetoricians of antiquity was to turn the weaker cause into the stronger, that is to say, to help arguments weaker in themselves to gain the victory over the stronger. This fact may be stated without exception. It applies to Aristotle, whose text-book of rhetoric lies before us, as well as to any of the orators. Nor was there any difference of opinion among the ancients as to the liability of this dialectic talent to abuse, nor of the evil to which it might be turned in the hands of malicious adepts. On these and on other grounds Plato repudiated rhetoric in the "Gorgias." It is

to be noted, however, that he built it up again on new
foundations in the "Phædrus," and it is further to be noted
that Aristotle himself protested against its rejection with
the greatest possible emphasis. He argued as incisively
as he could that the art of eloquence was governed by the
same laws as other useful things. Nearly all of them were
liable to abuse and

"the most useful of them to the worst abuse. This was the case
with bodily strength, health, riches, and the art of generalship, all
of which, justly employed, were capable of the utmost service,
but, unjustly employed, of the utmost disservice."

Accordingly, it was not the capacity which deserved to be
censured, but the disposition to pervert it to evil uses. In
general Aristotle gives us to understand that it was just
as disgraceful, if not actually more so, for a man to be
unable to defend himself with his tongue as with his fists.

In this context we meet the comparison between the
art of rhetoric and a weapon, which was first introduced
by Plato in the "Gorgias" itself, and was afterwards
repeated, occasionally merely in order to refute it, by the
representatives of every other school, Stoics, Epicureans,
Sceptics, and so forth. Eloquence was a weapon which
was to serve just and not unjust ends; it was not to be
condemned simply for the sake of the facilities it offered to
abuse. "The athlete," according to one of these authors,
"who maltreats his father, does not act thus by reason of
his athletic skill, but by reason of his moral perversity."
When we reach the "Rhetoric" of Aristotle, we find that
he too was at pains to extract the strongest possible
effects from the existing store of evidence. He does not
withhold his hints on the arts of "magnifying" and "mini-
mizing," of inflating an insignificant object, that is to say,
and of detracting from the significance of an important
one. He follows the example of Gorgias in teaching that
the perfect rhetorician must keep two ends in view: he
must be ready to weaken the heavy artillery of his opponent
by a skirmish of wit, and he must receive his opponent's
shafts on the impenetrable shield of his own serious

arguments. Aristotle was opposed in principle to no trick of barrister's eloquence. It was doubtless the necessities of ancient life * which induced him to go considerably further in this direction than modern practice would approve. And even to-day we account it in the better interests of justice that the accusation and defence be conducted with every resource of the pleader's art and power. We are anxious to see the most trivial argument developed to its fullest extent, even at the risk of disturbing the judgment of the court and of misleading its verdict in cases where a too clever advocate is confronted with an inferior opponent. Aristotle at least was always guided by the presumption that no one of these artifices would be employed with disloyal intention ; nor have we any ground to doubt that the same reservation held equally good in the instance of Protagoras. His personal integrity is vouched for by his attitude in the matter of his pupils' fees, which is mentioned by Plato and eulogized by Aristotle, no less than by the whole of the Platonic description of his personality. Whenever Protagoras, in the dialogue of that name, has to choose between a lower or a higher standard of ethics, Plato invariably represents him as preferring the higher point of view ; and in one instance at least his choice is accompanied by the express justification that he took it "having regard not only to" his "present answer, but also to the rest of" his "life." Finally, to show that the ethical treatises of Protagoras, among which we have still to mention those " On the Virtues " and " On Ambition," displayed at least as high a standard of morality as was characteristic of his age, we may quote, not merely the statements of Plato, but also the significant silence of his opponents in other fields.

Protagoras never forgot his principle of education, that practical exercise was fully as valuable as theoretical preparation. Accordingly he devised many methods to develop the faculties of his pupils and to strengthen their powers. As a teacher of rhetoric, he invented themes on which his pupils were to argue the *pros* and *cons*. Such

* Cp. Bk. III. Ch. IV. § 1.

themes were questions of a general kind, isolated or insulated, as it were, from the complications of reality, and thus affording a suitable preliminary to the treatment of the more difficult and more involved problems which life itself would propose. We are reminded of the advice offered by Aristotle to would-be and to actual poets, who were to reduce the complex contents of an epic or dramatic poem to its briefest possible expression before attempting to clothe it with individualizing circumstances. Another branch of this mental training was the production of what the ancients called commonplaces. Instead of discovering and arranging the arguments for or against a theme, the task in this instance was to divert the stream of eloquence into a particular channel, where nothing would interrupt its free current. The subjects of such exercises were speeches of praise or blame which admitted no countervailing circumstances, virtues and vices, or their human prototypes, states of existence, modes of conduct, and so forth. The aim of the themes was to train the pupils' keenness and dexterity in argument; that of the commonplaces was to develop their force, clearness, and fertility of expression, and at the same time to equip them with a stock of thoughts and phrases to be kept in constant readiness for use. Thus, in Quintilian's language, the members were given, out of which the future orator was to create his statue.

These aids in rhetorical training have descended directly to our own times in the form of the "English Essay," which is found in the curriculum of many public schools. Complaints have not unreasonably been made against the dead weight of an unsound formalism, and the habit thus developed of glibly reproducing other people's thoughts and sentiments at second hand. But the blame, so far as it is deserved, recoils on ourselves. It is our own fault entirely if we fail to get rid of an outworn tradition, and no blame attaches to the eminent men who more than two thousand years ago invented for the Greeks those forms of education which were appropriate to the circumstances of their times. We need not trouble to apologize for Protagoras. The advance that is marked by his name in the forensic branch of eloquence corresponds in a second great department of the art to the work of his contemporary and brother orator to whose brilliant achievements we have now to turn our attention.

CHAPTER VII.

GORGIAS OF LEONTINI.

1. ON a late summer morning in the year 427, the hill of the Pnyx, which descends in rocky terraces to the west of the Athenian Acropolis, was the scene of unwonted commotion. A deputation from Sicilian cities had arrived there to petition for protection and assistance against the aggression of Syracuse. After the envoys had introduced their mission to the Council of the Five Hundred, they were brought from the council chamber to the popular assembly on the Pnyx in order to plead their cause. Gorgias, son of Charmadas, was their chief spokesman on that occasion. He was the ambassador of Leontini his native city, then a flourishing community, but now the degenerate hamlet of Lentini, situated on the railway line which joins Catania and Syracuse. The Athenians of that date were no longer wholly unacquainted with the professional art of eloquence. Only a few months earlier the famous rhetorician Thrasymachus of Chalcedon had been ridiculed by Aristophanes in his "Epulones." His vehement and high-handed personality was reserved for the scathing satire of Plato, who was now lying in his cradle ; but neither he nor Pericles the Olympian, who had died but two years before, with his powerful gift of naturalism, had ever tempted the jaded sense of the Athenians with so exquisite a feast of ear and mind as was now provided by the Ionian from Sicily, whose voice was heard by them for the first time as the envoy of his fellow-townsmen on the Pnyx. On one other occasion at

least Gorgias returned to Athens. There, as elsewhere in Greece, at the great festivals of Delphi and Olympia especially, he achieved triumphant successes. Princes, such as Jason the ruler of Pheræ in Thessalia, vied with the populace in rendering him honour, and when he closed his career, upwards of a hundred years old, his natural force was not abated. "Already is sleep beginning to transfer his charge of me to his brother"—with this jest on his lips, he folded his hands to the sleep that knows no earthly waking. His fame was proclaimed to posterity by two statues, a golden one that he himself dedicated to the Delphic god, and another erected at Olympia to the childless old man by his grand-nephew Eumolpus, "as well in love as in gratitude for the instruction received from him." The inscription on the base of the Olympic statue has only recently been discovered, and there we read besides that "none of the mortals invented a finer art to steel the souls of men for works of virtue."

Gorgias was one of the founders of the art of Greek prose. Ancient writers on style distinguish between two great types of eloquence and a third intermediary type. The first, which has chiefly found its way into panegyric orations, was brilliant, exalted, stately, flowery, and full of colour; it soothed the soul by its harmonious euphonies, or it excited the quivering senses by the boldness and grandeur of its imagery. The second, which became the model for forensic oratory, was sharp, cool, clear, and sober; it moved with hasty steps which quickened at times into an impetuous gait, and its effects were produced by reason rather than imagination, on the judgment rather than on the fancy. The development of the last-named type owed its chief impetus to Protagoras, whereas the name of Gorgias is associated mainly with the first. A sparkling wit, a fertile and powerful imagination, were among the gifts which Nature had laid in the cradle of Gorgias, and some brilliant phrases which we can still listen to at his lips justify our admiration of his talents. Take, for instance, his utterance on stage-illusion, in which "the deceived is wiser than the not-deceived;" or take

his indictment of those who turn their back on philosophy
to cultivate special sciences, and whom he compared with
the "suitors of Penelope, dallying with her maidens."
Some of his similes have been censured by the purists
of antiquity on account of their extravagant character ;
thus, not unlike Shakespeare in "Macbeth," he spoke of
vultures as "living tombs," and of Xerxes as "the Persian
Zeus." Nor can we withstand the influence of the changes
of time and taste in reviewing a somewhat longer fragment
in which the artificiality of his style becomes palpable. We
may be permitted to quote in this place a portion of the
most comprehensive extant remains of his "Funeral Oration" delivered in honour of the Athenian victims in war :

"For what was absent in these men," he asked, "which should
be present in men, and what was present of things which should
be absent? Would that I could say what I wish and wish what
I should, evading divine displeasure and eluding human jealousy.
For the virtue of these men was a divine possession; their
mortality was human. Frequently they preferred the clemency of
equity to the harshness of law ; frequently, too, the righteousness
of reason to the rigidity of codes. For this they held to be the
most godlike and most universal code : in the right place to do
aright and to speak aright, to keep silence aright, and to bear
aright."

We must remember that in epochs of great reforms in
style the artificial commonly precedes the artistic. The ·
prose of Gorgias and the faults for which it has been
blamed in ancient and modern times find parallels of an
extraordinary closeness in the productions of the Renaissance. How admirably, for instance, the following description applies to the oratory of Gorgias with its—

"Predilection for an equal number of words in collateral or
antithetical sentences, well balanced often to the number of
syllables, the corresponding words being pointed out by alliteration, consonance or rhyme, [combined with] an exaggerated
hyperbolical style or quaint metaphorical diction."

Yet we have taken it from a criticism of the *alto estilo*
borrowed by John Lyly in England from Guevara the

Spaniard, whose "Golden Book of Marcus Aurelius" appeared in 1529. Lyly's "Euphues" was published just less than fifty years later, and the Euphuistic style, to which it gave a name, did not escape the occasional ridicule of Shakespeare. The turns of expression in which it was parodied by the great Elizabethan playwright recall precisely the excrescences of the style of Gorgias. We may quote, for example, Falstaff's speech to the Prince, "For, Harry, now I do not speak to thee in drink but in tears, not in pleasure but in passion, not in words only, but in woes also." We may well speak of excrescences in this connection, for the history of every new method of style—and the phenomenon is not confined to the arts of speech—may be traced through three stages. It begins with its vigorous employment by those who invented it or who reintroduced it; but in that stage the vigour is not excessive, and, moreover, it is mitigated by the fertility of the thoughts to be expressed. Next comes its exaggerated abuse on the part of imitators, in whose clumsier hands the manner becomes a mannerism. Finally, the circle of available methods of art is widened to receive the new aid, which is now employed in due proportion and in appropriate circumstances. In modern times, according to the judgment of experts, the names of Guevara and Lyly stand for the first two of these stages; in antiquity they were represented by Gorgias and by the author or authors of the two declamations by pseudo-Gorgias ("The Praise of Helen" and "Palamedes"), and, finally, partly by Isocrates. But so far as Shakespeare is concerned, Euphuism was not merely a butt for his satire. One feature which is common to Guevara and Gorgias is common likewise to Shakespeare and Calderon, and has become flesh of their flesh. We refer to the "tennis with *concetti*" and to that teeming wealth of gorgeous images which no longer serve the purpose of interpreting or vivifying the thought, which are no longer means to an end, but to a certain extent an end in themselves. The characteristic features of the language of Gorgias and of its counterpart in the Renaissance may be referred to two fundamental causes. The first is the natural desire at the beginning of a great literary epoch to strike out new modes of expression, the novelty of which is at first taken as the measure of their value. The second is the streaming and unbridled vitality of an age in which the young blood leaps with a wayward pulse, and the mind's activity is in excess of the matter at its disposal. To-day, too, we occasionally meet men whose wit is enlarged beyond the capacity of their control, and who cannot express even the commonest ideas except by uncommon phrases. Thought disdains, so to speak, the ready-made garb of the vernacular ; on every occasion it fashions, as it were, new raiment of its own.

Five only of the speeches of Gorgias are known to us, through the usual sources of brief information or fragmentary remnants. There are the Olympic and the Pythian speeches, there are eulogies of Achilles and the Eleans, and there is the funeral oration which we have mentioned above. The first and the last in this order were distinguished by their Pan-Hellenic tendency. We have once before had occasion to remark * that the itinerant teachers, who found themselves at home in every corner of Greece, equalled or surpassed the poets in Greek universal patriotism, and naturally came to carry the idea of national unity through the sundered cities of Hellas. We may quote at this point two passages from Gorgias which confirm our remarks. In the Olympian oration the sophist urged the Greeks who were engaged in an intestine struggle "to make, not their own cities, but the land of the barbarians the prey of their spear." And in the Athenian funeral oration he commemorated the great deeds wrought in common in the struggle against the Persians, and he delivered himself of the final warning that "victories won over barbarians call for pæans of triumph ; victories wrung from the Greeks call for dirges of lament."

· 2. We pass from Gorgias the reformer of Greek style, from Gorgias the rhetorician and patriot, to his third phase, which concerns us most particularly, as a Greek thinker.

* Cp. Bk. III. Ch. VI. § 1.

He was occupied with natural philosophy, with ethics, and last, but not least, with dialectics. Unfortunately, time has robbed us of all accurate information of his work in the first two of these departments. We only know that as a natural philosopher he followed in the footsteps of Empedocles his master in his study of the problems of optics, and undertook from that point of view to explain the use of burning-reflectors. He never made an appearance as a teacher of virtue, and on this account, if it were possible to draw a strict distinction between rhetoricians and sophists, the name of Gorgias would fall in the first category only. Yet, in the extended meaning of the term "sophist," Gorgias, who was half a rhetorician and half a philosopher, may properly claim the title. He never taught virtue, but he was occupied with it from its literary aspect. As an author he did not aim at simplifying the conception of virtue, nor at reducing its various ramifications to a common root; he was rather at pains to display and discuss in their native multiformity the several special virtues, distinguishing, among other points, their variation according to the difference of sex. As a dialectician he pushed the self-destruction of the Eleatic doctrine of being, which we met with in Zeno, to still further conclusions, which brought him at last to an absolute negation of the conception of Ens. Here, too, we have to deplore the loss of his book "On Nature or Not-Being," the first part of which would doubtless have informed us of the arguments on which his theory was based, while the second part was probably devoted to physics. As it is, our chief authority is a little work which used to be ascribed to Aristotle, but which must really be regarded as a late product of his school. This treatise further discusses the doctrines of Xenophanes and Melissus in a manner, as is universally acknowledged, which is not wholly trustworthy. On the other hand, its evidence for the teachings of Gorgias is commonly accepted as fully credible, but it should not be forgotten that our greater confidence in that instance corresponds to a total absence of original fragments, and to a well-nigh equal lack of verificatory or complementary reports.

Gorgias undertook to prove a threefold case: First, that a Being does not exist; secondly, that if it existed it would not be cognizable; and, thirdly, that if it were cognizable, the cognition would not be communicable.

Two proofs are advanced for the first of these three theses. The following is given as "the first proof, and that peculiar to Gorgias." An insignificant and seemingly innocent little sentence is set up in the words, "Not-Being is Not-Being." From this small beginning the most far-reaching conclusions were derived. It was argued that even if Not-Being is nothing but Not-Being, still it is something; it is; existence can be predicated of it. Thus the distinction between Being and Not-Being was removed, and Being lost its superiority over Not-Being. Further, if, as was just shown, Not-Being is or exists; it followed that Being, as its opposite, is, or exists, not. We are accordingly placed in this dilemma: either the difference between Being and Not-Being must be taken as annulled, according to the first part of the argument, in which case nothing exists; for Not-Being does not exist, and, therefore, Being, its equivalent, cannot exist. Or the distinction is not to be regarded as annulled, in which case, according to the second part of the argument, Being once more does not exist, precisely on account of its opposition to the Not-Being of which existence has been predicated.

The critic follows hot-foot on the trail of the exponent of this doctrine. It is almost superfluous to direct attention to the fact that "Being" and "Not-Being" are here used indiscriminately as equivalent to "to be" and "not to be," a confusion which may be due either to Gorgias himself or to our second-hand authority. Nor need we trouble to point out that Not-Being ceases to be Not-Being as soon as Being is predicated of it. But the author of this series of arguments operates in a really remarkable manner. He takes alternately the negative and the pseudo-affirmative sides of the conception and plays them off against one another. And now, when we come to the little clause of identity itself from which the argument started, we cannot but regard it as inadmissible —nay, if we look at it more closely, as devoid of sense. The sentence, "white is white," conveys in our opinion no self-evident proposition nor even an intelligible meaning. The idea of the subject is simply repeated as the idea of the predicate, whereas it is the function of a judgment or proposition to combine the two conceptions or terms of subject and predicate with one another, and thereby to impart information about connections actually existing in nature. But this is not the place to discuss these matters at length, and we may the more readily transfer our attention to a weightier and less contentious topic. The identic clause with which we are dealing is made to yield conclusions by the ambiguous meaning inherent in the word "is." In the sentence "Not-Being is Not-Being," the verb is simply a copula, though it is afterwards interpreted as if it signified existence—outward, objective existence. By a similar method of reasoning, the sentence, "a centaur is an image of the fancy," might be used to prove, not merely its legitimate conclusion, that the conception of a centaur must pre-exist in our mind before we can discuss it, but also that the centaur possesses external and objective existence. Add to this that in the second part of the argument there is an illicit logical conversion. For even if it were proper to admit that "Not-Being is," no ground would therefore be afforded for the inference that "Being is not." Otherwise it would be permissible to turn the proposition, "Not-white exists," into the converse proposition, "White exists not." But serious though these errors may be, they are by no means peculiar to Gorgias. The abuse of identic propositions, the abuse of the copula, and illicit logical conversions, will all frequently recur in our narrative—most frequently in Plato himself, where they were not confined to the display of dialectic fireworks which is known as the "Parmenides."

We stand on different ground when we reach the second argument that was advanced for the first thesis of Gorgias. The sophist started from the contradictory assertions promulgated by his predecessors, and balanced them against each other. Being must either be one or many, it must either have been generated or not. Now, each of these assumptions had been severally and equally refuted on sufficient—or sufficiently plausible—grounds partly by Zeno, partly by Melissus, and partly, we must add, by Zeno and Melissus combined. But, if the Being is neither one nor many, neither generated nor ungenerated, it cannot exist at all. When all its conceivable predicates had dropped away from it one by one, its very reality disappeared. At a later stage of our history we shall come to recognize and discuss this logical expedient as the principle of the excluded middle. It is the less necessary to dwell on it here because it is at least reasonable to doubt whether Gorgias ascribed more than a conditional value to this second argument of his. Perhaps he meant by it no more than this : The contradictory arguments of the philosophers, and especially the doubts thrown by Melissus and Zeno on the plurality, the unity, and other attributes of Being, would, if granted full power, lead inevitably to the conclusion not drawn by either of those thinkers that that alleged Being does not exist at all. Our chief authority at least seems to hint at this interpretation by speaking of the first proof as "his own," but of the second as "the sum of what other people have said."

We pass to the second thesis of Gorgias, the incognizability of Being even in the case where its existence must be admitted. We may be allowed to render the proof in a somewhat looser form. If Being is to be known, there must somewhere be a warrant of the correctness of the alleged knowledge, but when we come to look for that warrant, we find ourselves disappointed. It is not to be discovered in sense-perception, the infallibility of which has been so vehemently disputed, nor yet in our thought or imagination, for otherwise we should not be able to imagine what is known to be false—a chariot-race on the sea, for example. And if the concordance of many witnesses affords no valid proof of the correctness of our sense-perceptions, their evidence must also be rejected in the sphere of thought and imagination. It might be valid if we lost our faculty of imagining the unreal, but the instance that has just been given completely demonstrates the contrary.

At this point we have two remarks to make, the first of a more general, the second of a more special character. The special remark is due to the philosophic tendencies of that age, and of Parmenides in especial. Our readers will recollect his words, "the Not-Being is unspeakable and unthinkable ;"* and again, "thinking and being are the same."† Expressions of this kind might really have been thought to imply the proposition that the untrue was also unimaginable. Further, if we recollect that the express champion of the fallibility of the senses was no other than Melissus, we may reasonably conjecture that Gorgias aimed this shaft also at the Eleatics. His argument would thus have amounted in intention to the following statement : Melissus taught the unreality of sensuous objects, and directed our desire for knowledge to the "Being" latent behind them. The next thing is to discover a foundation for this knowledge of ours. It can but rest on thought or imagination, according to the verdict of Parmenides that this makes for reality alone. But then we are confronted with the example given of our power to imagine the unreal as well. We come now to the more general remark to which we adverted above. It is at once true and untrue that our imagination cannot make for mere phantoms of the brain. It is true in so far as it refers to the elements of our ideas, it is untrue as it applies to the combinations of those elements. A chariot-race on the open sea is an arbitrary combination of ideas foreign to the nature of things ; it belongs to the same category as a centaur or a winged lion. But the several ingredients out of which the complex is composed must previously have entered our consciousness through the channel of experience. Accordingly, they may claim at least the possession of empiric truth ; and, whether or not we chose to identify

* Bk. II. Ch. II. § 2 *fin.*
† Bk. II. Ch. II. § 4 *fin.*

it with absolute truth, the distinction that has just been drawn between the elements and the combinations of the ideas is at least a distinction of deep import which is wholly neglected in the ratiocination of Gorgias. Once more we must warn our readers that the mistake was not confined to Gorgias, but must be laid to the common charge of his epoch. The thinkers of that age and the next found a serious difficulty in the question, Is it possible, and how can it be possible, to imagine what is false? Plato in the "Theætetus," as we shall see, grappled vigorously with this question, and came off not altogether without success.

The third thesis ran as follows. The knowledge of the Being, even if it existed and were cognizable, would not be communicable. The proof of this was to the effect that, the means of communication being language, it was impossible to convey through words anything else but words. Language and other symbols, not being of the same nature as the thing they symbolize, can only communicate symbols. How, for instance, can the sense of colour be communicated? "The ear is as incapable of perceiving colours as the sight of knowing sounds." And if the person wishing to communicate a colour were to show another person the object which aroused the colour-impression in himself, he would still have no solid ground for assuming that the second impression would precisely resemble his own. Far less, then—thus we may reconstruct the lost conclusion of the argument—can language, a part of our nature, be suited to communicate to others information about external Being foreign to our subjective selves, even if we had knowledge of it. In the proof of this thesis it is to be noted that a really valuable thought is expressed and demonstrated in a manner that admits no contradiction. It is the thought that we can never be certain of the complete identity of our elementary sensations with those of other people. More than one fallacy current in those times was embodied in the argument. Twice at least the confusion was preserved between the identity of species and the identity of number. Thus we read that "in two subjects the same idea cannot exist, for then the one would likewise be two;" and again, "even granted this, still the one could always appear different from both, since they are not completely similar; for if they were completely similar they would be not two, but one." But we quote these passages without pretending that they affect the value of the thought itself.

3. The logical value of this sequence of theses is not so difficult to determine as the problem of its purpose. No one doubts that it was modelled on the polemical pamphlet of Zeno, and it is at least legitimate to ask if it was not dominated by a parallel leading motive. Zeno, as our readers are aware, was retaliating the attacks suffered by Parmenides his master,* and it is quite conceivable that Gorgias was animated by some similar motive. Gorgias was a disciple of Empedocles, and there is certainly a wide gulf between the comparatively naïve belief in the evidence of the senses, to which Empedocles subscribed, and its repudiation at the hands of the Eleatics. The Empedoclean theory of nature was bound to wither at the rise of the new luminaries in the intellectual firmament. It could not but provoke the ridicule and contempt of a Zeno and a Melissus. Indeed, Zeno composed a "critical discussion" of the doctrines of Empedocles, which was extant in antiquity. Now the shafts of Gorgias, as we have seen, were preferentially, if not exclusively, aimed at the Eleatics. Above all, he delighted in setting the two younger representatives of the doctrine of Ens to fight it out with one another. This was his attitude in a portion of the second argument appertaining to the first of his theses, to which we must now revert. Taking it in closer consideration, we see that Melissus had deduced the spatial infinity of the world from the old physical doctrine of its temporal infinity, or its eternity. Now, Gorgias exerted himself to prove to a hair's breadth that such an infinite could not exist. He looked in vain for the place of its existence. If it existed in itself, there would be two infinites, the one containing and the other contained; if it existed in another, it would not be infinite, and both

* Cp. Bk. II. Ch. III. § 2.

objections were fatal to the proposition. Moreover, our authority is quite clear on the point that Gorgias was here supporting himself on Zeno's reasoning about space. It was a source of keen delight to him to confute one of the younger Eleatics by the other, and it is legitimate to conjecture that his delight was at least not wholly impersonal.

When we reach the question whether the so-called nihilism of Gorgias was in truth intended or suited to overthrow the foundations of all knowledge, we can make a more definite reply. Here too no one but George Grote has had the courage to deny this almost universal opinion. Grote believed that Gorgias wanted to demolish, not the phenomenal world, but the "ultra-phenomenal or Noumenon." But this belief has provoked the remark that "our reports do not contain the faintest hint of any such limitation." The remark is valid as far as it goes, but where the facts themselves speak with unequivocal certainty it becomes unnecessary to listen for outspoken or whispered statements. Grote expressed himself in a way which was rather too modern to be quite pertinent. Nevertheless, the relation between the sensible world and the "Being" of Parmenides and Melissus is completely analogous to that which obtains between the phenomenon and the Noumenon or "thing in itself" of Kant. In making this admission, however, we must be careful to note that the "Being" had not yet lost every trace of its empiric origin, that it was still chiefly conceived as extended in space. It is true that the surviving fragments of Gorgias and of his authorities will be searched in vain for a single expression bringing this contrast into sharp relief. But we may fairly ask if any one seriously believes that Gorgias, in renouncing the "Being," was prepared thereby to renounce all acquaintance with the nature of things ; that he was content to deny every regularity in the processes of nature ; that he was opposed to his brother philosophers in neither expecting nor assuming the rise of the morrow's sun, the burgeoning of the spring next year, the repetition of similar processes in similar circumstances—in a word, stability of qualities itself. We need not accept this belief. We need not load the subtle genius of Gorgias with the crudest and grossest inconsistency. But we must assume that this line of demarcation was present to his mind, whether or not he had nailed it down to a fixed terminology. And it will perhaps not be inadmissible to look for the missing word in the sole place where Gorgias speaks to us out of his own mouth, in the title, that is to say, of his work "on Nature or the Not-Being." Quite recently that title has been dismissed as a "grotesque farce," and has been quoted as evidence that Gorgias set up his theses merely by way of a jest. We beg to differ from that view. We venture to quote the example of Xeniades, a Corinthian philosopher and contemporary of Democritus, who maintained that everything proceeded "from the Not-Being," and sank back "to the Not-Being again." And we would add that Plato's doctrine of matter will introduce us to a form of the conception of Not-Being which was intended to be taken quite seriously.

It is when we reach the second of the theses, however, that, if all the indications do not mislead us, we meet the real and fundamental motive of the polemics of Gorgias. There we learn that the point of his quarrel with the Eleatic school was one with which the impartial reader of to-day must likewise gravely quarrel. With all due respect to the doctrines of Parmenides and Melissus, we feel bound to give expression to one important protest. We are tempted to ask both those thinkers how they could have dismissed to the limbo of delusion so considerable a part of all human knowledge with such confident certainty, and yet, with equal confidence, have treated the rest of it as truth unassailable. Where, we ask, was their warrant for assuming that a part of their faculties caused them utterly to err, while another part led them to unerring insight? And where, we wonder, did they discover the bridge which should translate them from the world of subjective appearance, in which they themselves were completely submerged, to the region of pure objective Being? The doctrine of Parmenides was plainly open to this reproach—the more so, indeed, because he based the psychical processes wholly and solely on the physical. This fact is expressed in his "Words of Opinion"* alone, but it is nowhere contradicted in his "Words of Truth." He and his adherents could not avail themselves of the saving device by which the body was held to be encompassed by error, while our immortal soul brought us tidings from the world of pure truth. For by no single word are we given to believe—and all inner probability is against it—that Parmenides ascribed to "psyche" any share in the life of the waking intellect, and thus in the process of knowledge, though he agreed with the Pythagoreans and Orphics in letting it survive the body and experience various destinies.† We shall hardly be wrong, then, in marking as the strongest motive in the polemic of Gorgias against the Eleatics and the theory of Being which they upheld, his amazement at the confident dogmatism which they themselves had been at pains to deprive of its basis.

4. At this point we may revert to the allied features of the age. In surveying the change effected by Hippocrates and his disciples in the domain of medicine, we saw that its chief monument was to be found in the growth of modesty, and in the reaction from the self-satisfied dogmatism of older schools. This trait was naturally connected with a tendency to Relativism, the first traces of which we perceived as early as Heraclitus. The far-sighted author of the treatise "On Old Medicine" described as the modest but hardly attainable goal of research, not what man is in himself, but what he is in relation to what he eats and drinks, and to the rest of the business of his life.‡ He contrasted the comparatively meagre certainties due to experiment and observation with the pretentious fictions which he expelled from the domain of his art; and now, if we revert to the sole surviving literary monument of the movement known as sophistry—the work "On the Art"—we meet the same contraction of formerly high-flown ambitions, and the same spirit of Relativism. And

---

* Bk. II. Ch. II. § 5 *fin.*　　　† Bk. II. Ch. V. § 7.
‡ Bk. III. Ch. I. § 5 *fin.*

whether or not we may call Protagoras its author, we have still seen reason to recognize there the chief metaphysical tenet of that sophist in a form that is likewise an obvious reflection of the Relativistic spirit. Nor need we dwell on the fact that the thinker who pushed "man" so decisively into the foreground of the problem of cognition, must have been more or less conscious of the limitation of all knowledge by the bounds of human faculties.

Modesty and Relativism—the teachings of Socrates, the next great chapter of our inquiry, will be true to these kindred points. And we shall there be confronted with a third token of the increased stringency of the claims of science in the endeavour sharply to define conceptions. An early milestone on this road was marked by the attempt of Prodicus, surviving unfortunately but in the barest outline, exactly to distinguish synonymous words. Further, the speeches put by Plato in the mouth of Protagoras show a respect for the precise value of words ; nor does Plato's satirical aim prevent us from recognizing that advance. Thus, when the Platonic Protagoras remarks of the culinary use of oil, that it is intended merely "to correct the discomfort which is a concomitant of the sensations conveyed to us through the nose at eating meats and sauces," the humour lies in the disproportion between the subtlety of the expression and the trivial, not to say the repulsive, character of the subject. But this artifice of the incomparable caricaturist cannot destroy our perception of the great gain to philosophy in the strict and novel distinction drawn between the sensible impression and its object on the one part, and the sensation itself and its concomitant pleasure or pain on the other. The earliest experiment in definition proper occurs in the treatise "On the Art," where we read—

"and first of all I shall lay down what I regard as the essence [or end] of the art of healing, namely, the complete removal of the suffering from the patients, and the mitigation of its severity, and "—he adds with intentional paradox—" the not-daring-at-all to meddle with cases where the patients are already overcome by disease."

Democritus, again, began a definition which he speedily let fall, in the little sentence "Man is—what we all know," and Aristotle was acquainted with his definitions of the conceptions of hot and cold, though they have not been preserved. It was natural enough that mathematics should have been the home of these experiments. There was first a definition of number commonly ascribed to Thales, and apart from that we are acquainted with the polemic of Protagoras against the definition of tangential lines, as well as with the definitions with which Autolycus opened his two elementary treatises, "On the Moving Sphere" and "On the Rise and Setting of the Stars." For though these writings belong to the close of the fourth century, yet they plainly testify to a long series of precursors. It was obviously not due to chance that the Pythagoreans, the cultivators of mathematics, had, as Aristotle tells us, already begun to define a few ethical ideas. Finally, we are acquainted with two definitions of Gorgias. One, with which we need not concern ourselves at present, dealt with the conception of rhetoric, and the other with that of colour. The definition of colour was stated in a solemn form of speech which excited the ridicule of Plato when he mentioned it for the first time. Its contents, however, were incorporated in a work of Plato's maturity, and the respect which he paid throughout to the person of Gorgias was extended, in a work of his old age, to the ethical doctrines of that sophist. The definition in question was based on the Empedoclean doctrine of "pores" and "effluvia," according to which colours could only be perceived when the two were in conformity, and it ran as follows: "Colour is an effluvium which proceeds from a form extended in space, which corresponds to sight, and which is liable to perception." According to the "Meno" of Plato, the youth of that name had heard this definition at the lips of Gorgias himself during his residence in Thessaly in the last years of his life.

An important consequence follows on this fact. Plato, who never committed mere arbitrary anachronisms, may be quoted to show that Gorgias, even in his ripe old age, and a considerable time after the publication of his dialectic theses, was engaged in the discussion of physical problems. This view is supported by the observation that most of the pupils of Gorgias, though their interest gravitated to rhetoric and politics, were still by no means without traces of the discipline of the natural sciences. Our readers are already acquainted with the name of Alcidamas * as the champion of the law of nature, and we still possess from his pen an admirable oration praising the art of ready improvisation, and declaring its productions to be far more valuable than elaborate written discourses. But what is to be noted in this connection is that he was likewise the author of a work on physics composed perhaps in the form of a dialogue. Another and less important pupil of Gorgias was Polus the rhetorician, whom Plato also mentions as a student of nature. And, finally, though Isocrates renounced physics no less than dialectic, yet he immortalized his teacher Gorgias, as, above all, his teacher in the natural sciences. On the richly carved monument which marked the tomb of Isocrates, Gorgias was represented directing his attention to a globe. And, as a master does not readily survive in the memory of his disciples as the representative of an earlier phase of activity since abandoned by himself, this circumstance likewise refutes the assumption that the paradoxes of Gorgias formed a kind of break in his career, sundering it into two completely dissimilar halves. We are quite unable to say whether he thereafter clothed his physical doctrines, after the manner of Parmenides, with a cloak of reservation ; whether, in disputing the conception of Ens, he kept its strict Eleatic form with rigid exclusiveness before his eyes ; or whether he advanced to a purely phenomenalistic view and like his pupil Lycophron, avoided the use of the verb "to be" altogether, even as a copula. And our ignorance on these points is the less surprising since we cannot even solve the primary contradiction between the two statements in our chief authority, which asserts that Gorgias maintained that

* Cp. Bk. III. Ch. IV. § 6.

"nothing exists," and that he disputed the conception of Non-Ens as vehemently as that of Ens.

The so-called nihilism of Gorgias has given rise to the opinion that he had abandoned thenceforward every true search for knowledge, and had devoted himself exclusively to the art of persuasion, or rather, that this, in despite of the facts, would have been his more logical proceeding. But the curious thing is that, in a case where the circumstances are virtually repeated, no one has tried to draw the same conclusion. The Xenophontic Socrates exposes the contradictions of his predecessors in philosophy in a way not dissimilar to the procedure of Gorgias. Some maintained that the Being was single, others that it was infinite in number. Some had taught the doctrine of incessant motion, others of total immobility: some had maintained the birth and decay of all things, others had repudiated those processes *in toto*. On these grounds Socrates inferred the vanity and fruitlessness of those kinds of investigations which, in his opinion, exceeded the bounds of human capacity. But he did not go even so far as to draw the conclusion that all endeavours to understand nature are vain. ·Rather he desired that his disciples should acquire a degree of natural science adequate for their practical purpose, that the young steersman, for example, should have the requisite astronomy at his disposal. He never conceived the idea that the mere conflict of opinions excluded, as long as it lasted, the possibility of scientific instruction. Nay, so inconceivable was it to him, that we rather identify his name with the opening out of a fresh region for investigation, inasmuch as Socrates was at pains to exalt "human affairs" to an object of more thorough insight than had as yet been attained in any department of knowledge. And his prospect of success in that fresh field of inquiry was not marred by the scepticism arising from his exposure of the contradictions we have mentioned.

Socrates, it is true, unlike Gorgias, never attacked in a spirit of critical destructiveness the conception of "Being." At the same time it would be idle to pretend that the conception played even the smallest part in his intellectual life. He was as indisposed as Gorgias to ascribe to it with confidence any predicates whatsoever. The one certain fact is that he left the old and beaten track of investigation because it seemed to lead to no prosperous goal. And here we reach a point which is of the utmost importance to our study of the civilization of the age. We have marked in many isolated phenomena the indications of an intellectual revolution, and we are now in a position to characterize as one of the factors in that change the difference as to the assumed solubility of problems with which former generations had grappled with strenuous eagerness. Cosmology, in the widest sense of that term, was superseded more and more by Anthropology in an equally comprehensive sense. Other factors, some of which we have already tried to appreciate,* worked in combination with this one. But we have still to mention the factor which was at once the least obtrusive and perhaps the most efficacious, namely, the simple lapse of time. Many years were required before man regarded himself as a worthy subject of scientific treatment. And with the many years went the growth of self-respect consequent on the improved dominion of man over nature, on the gradual perfection of civil and social order, and, not least, on the steady increase of the treasures and resources of the intellect. At first the rising spirit of curiosity had been directed almost exclusively to external nature. Man did not wholly forget himself, but at most he regarded himself as a kind of fragile mirror, in which the external world was seen through a glass darkly. But the moment came when his maturer self-consciousness reminded him that his own faculties were the limit and condition of all knowledge, when he was discouraged by the series of vain attempts to solve the riddle of the universe at one guess, and when he had gradually reached a higher degree of self-respect. Then it was that the attention of the inquirer was directed to man as "the proper study of mankind." And when

* Cp. Bk. III, Ch. IV. § 1.

the change had been effected, one of its foremost tokens was the deeper seriousness and intensity with which the field of history was cultivated. The leading minds which fifty years before would have reinforced the ranks of the nature-philosophers now obeyed the invitation of Socrates, their contemporary, and turned to the study of "human affairs." He it was who formulated this demand most clearly, and who realized it most vigorously. But before we open a new book with the name of the Athenian thinker, whom we have mentioned so frequently, it will be appropriate to glance at the changes in historiography which may be traced to the tendencies we have been describing.

CHAPTER VIII.

THE ADVANCE OF HISTORICAL SCIENCE.

1. THE study of history in this age had reached enormous dimensions. Side by side with the great compilations of legendary matter, such as the work of Pherecydes contained, went descriptions of the living present. The historian's pen turned from Uranus and Cronos to Pericles and Cimon. His sceptre stretched from the pellucid tranquillity of Olympus to the turbid scandal of his own day. It happened sometimes that the same mind made itself equally at home on the heights and in the depths of its art. Thus Stesimbrotus of Thasos, who, in his work " On the Mysteries," was a diligent student of the echoes of forgotten myths, proved at the same time a no less industrious scavenger in the mire of the contemporary gossip with which he sullied the figures of the great statesmen of Athens. Moreover, he found leisure to expatiate in a special study on the life of Homer and on the interpretation of his poems. Nor did the history of art and literature suffer otherwise from lack of cultivation. Damastes and Glaucus of Rhegium are mentioned as the two earliest labourers in that field. Damastes was the compiler of a treatise " On Poets and Sophists," in which the " sophists " obviously meant nothing else than philosophers, if for no other reason than because of their association with poets. And Glaucus, a contemporary of Democritus, had written on ancient poets and musicians. The prince of encyclopædists, Democritus himself, who had discussed the beginnings of poetry in his works on the composition and language

of Homer, was occupied in other treatises with the beginnings of music, and he was the first to utter the thought, elaborated at a later date by Plato and Aristotle, that leisure and a certain amount of material prosperity are the most favourable soil for the productions of art and science. A list of poets and musicians, chronologically arranged, preserved in Sicyon, and consulted by Heraclides of Pontus, may have been older than the works we have just mentioned. Nor was chronology any longer the mere handmaid of historical research, as in this special catalogue and in the lists of Hellanicus and Hippias.* It was a subject of independent study. Cleostratus worked at it in verse as early as the sixth century, and his labours were continued in the fifth by Harpalus and others, among whom may be named Œnopides and Meton, the great reformers of the calendar. About this time, too, the Greeks began to write the history of other nations besides their own. Histories of Persia were composed by Charon of Lampsacus and Dionysius of Miletus; and Xanthus the Lydian, in narrating the history of his own people, set a precedent to other foreigners at a later date in availing himself of the vehicle of the Greek language. History was constantly being provided with fresh material by the reports of explorers such as Scylax of Carianda and Euthymenes of Massalia, as well as by the growing literature of memoirs. To this class belonged the "Pilgrimage" of Ion the poet, of which but a few delightful fragments survive.

So much, perhaps, for the extension of the horizon of history. The inward change through which it passed is of far greater importance. Political wisdom presently attained a height from which the historians looked down on the Herodotean view of politics as the mature and supple intellect of the grown man looks down on the limitations of his childhood. The earliest traces of this change are found in the sole surviving remnant of the rich literature of pamphlets which distinguished the close of the fifth century.

* Bk. III. Ch. V. § 5 *fin.*

2. The treatise "On the Constitution of Athens" is one of the most remarkable literary productions of all ages. It bears the marks of a strong political passion, but that passion is tempered by so notable a tendency to scientific method that we recognize at once the powerful brain and the embittered heart which went together to its composition. The author might be compared to an officer sent to reconnoitre a hostile fortress in order to spy out its weaknesses and to devise the best means of attack. But the officer, to press the simile home, must be conceived as struck with surprise at the perfect plan of the fortress, and at the intelligent manner in which all its parts are suited to one another and to the common purpose they are intended to fulfil. Hence we must suppose him not merely to deprecate any hasty assault, but even to give unreserved expression to his admiration of the architectural design, and thus to become the eulogist, as it were, of his deeply hated foe. Hatred it was, at least, which put a fine edge on the keenness of the vision of this oligarch, and opened his eyes to many a political principle hitherto undisclosed. The harmony of political institutions with the conditions of society, and the agreement between the outward forms and the inner contents of a community, were here discovered for the first time. This treatise took account of the sea-power of Athens, and of the commercial supremacy which rested thereon. It discussed Athenian modes of warfare, and the relation between the army and the fleet. It subjected the democratic constitution to a searching criticism, in the course of which many recognized and deplorable evils, such as the judiciary compulsion of confederates, the delays of the law, the arrogant and undisciplined character of the metics and slaves, were shown to be no mere accidental abuses, but to be inherent to democracy. Superficial views were discarded throughout; links of connection and common causes were looked for, and the whole treatise was informed with so strong a logical light that, despite its unpretentious character, it has earned its significant title

to the rank of the earliest model of the deductive method as applied to society and politics.

Yet this title cannot be conceded by us without making some deductions. We fully appreciate the endeavour by which the author of the treatise was moved to reduce the abundance of isolated phenomena to a few great common principles. Nor would we detract from the value of the sense of causation which that endeavour brought into play. Still, the fact remains that the deductive method is but poorly adapted to account for the results of historical development and to illustrate its processes. Our author may fairly claim to have commanded an exceptional wealth of fine observations and penetrating inferences. In some of his isolated passages he has not unjustly been called a worthy predecessor of Burke, Machiavelli, and Paolo Sarpi. But it is an exaggeration to speak of his work as the " earliest contribution to the knowledge of the natural laws governing political institutions." The starting-point of all his researches was the inner bond of connection between sea-power and democracy. But, although we may grant that this connection was a specific product of Athenian evolution, we need but glance at the stories of Carthage, Venice, Holland, and England herself, to prove that it was not governed by any "law of nature." Nor can the author invariably be acquitted of the charge of straining his conclusions. The thesis which he undertook to prove was announced at the opening of his treatise in the following words :—

" I praise the Athenians not because they preferred this kind of political constitution, for therein they preferred the welfare of the evil to the welfare of the good. But I praise them because, having made their decision, they knew how to preserve the constitution they chose, and because in other respects likewise, where the rest of the Greeks think them wrong, they attain what they aim at. This, then, is what I shall prove."

And near the end of the treatise we read again—

" Much might be devised to improve the constitution, but

nothing could readily be discovered to preserve the democracy and yet to effect any serious improvement. Such a work could only be done in an insignificant degree by adding something in one place and taking something away in another."

Thus we see that our author regarded the Athenian democracy as a finished work of art. If it was to fulfil its aim of satisfying the masses, its essentials must remain unchanged. At the same time there is no attempt to disguise the fact that "baseness and ignorance" were rampant, and that "madmen" played the chief parts in the council and in the popular assembly. This opinion was rather over-emphasized than otherwise, but the readers were given to suppose that the populace was right in prosecuting its own interests, and was better served by the "ignorance, baseness, and good-will" of its present authorities than by the "virtue, wisdom, and ill-will" of the "good" or "noble." All the same, the best constitution would not be obtained by such conduct, though it afforded the best guarantee for the preservation of the democracy.

"For the people do not want," wrote our author, "in a lawfully administered state, to be the bond-slaves of their rulers, but they claim freedom and supremacy. Out of the very circumstances which thou regardest as the travesty of law and order the people derive the sources of their strength and freedom."

We need hardly point out that, despite the apparent objectivity and actuality of these political arguments, they are yet largely the reasoning of an embittered doctrinaire, or rather of a man cloaking his bitterness in a doctrinal disguise. How would it have been, for example, if the ignorance, the baseness, and the madness of the rulers had endangered the power of the state, and had led to the loss of the fleet, the tributes, and of the empire itself? How would it then have been with the advantage of the populace, which was supposed to be so well protected? The truth is that, though our oligarch hit the bull's-eye in many single instances, yet he wrote with a biassed mind. His reason was subservient throughout to his passion as a partisan, the subtlety of his mind was the instrument of his gall. The Athenian democracy in every respect and in every sense of the word was to be incapable of improvement. Its worst evils, and those which pressed most heavily on members of the author's class and party, were to be exposed without exception as the inevitable consequences of the ruling principle of the state. It was his pleasure to condemn the Athenian constitution root and branch, to strike at the very pulse of its existence. Reading between the lines of his treatise, we can conceive him warning his friends to put no faith in reform, and to expect nothing from compromise. He would have told them that what in their view were occasional mistakes, accidental evils, and temporary signs of decay, were really manifestations of the one fatal principle of the commonwealth. With that principle the prosperity of the multitude must stand or fall, and therefore the multitude would support it at all times and at every cost. Hence he would have urged them to avoid all half-measures and to attempt nothing precipitate ; above all, to beware of striking at the wrong time and with inadequate forces. If the great blow were ever to be struck, it would have to be final and decisive, and to get rid once for all of what the factious language of the times described as the "accursed Demos." So he would have bid them close their ranks and arm their persons and provide themselves with sturdy allies, "for"—and here we may quote the *ipsissima verba* of our author—"for no few are wanted to make an end once for all of the Athenian popular supremacy."

3. This extraordinary product of political passion and political reason was first published in 424 B.C. The date has another significance. It was the year in which leisure for the completion of his lifework descended on a man whose nature contained practically the same elements, though they were developed to a far greater splendour and mingled in far more wholesome proportions. The leisure, it must be added, was not voluntary. Thucydides, son of Olorus, was a man of considerable wealth, and of noble origin, in whose veins Thracian blood flowed as well as

Greek. At the time of the siege of Amphipolis he was in command of a naval division stationed at the island of Thasos, and he failed to bring his ships quickly enough to the relief of the beleaguered city. His failure was punished by a twenty years' exile, which he employed partly in preliminary travel, and partly in completing, at his country-house on the Thracian coast, the work which possesses an indisputable and seldom disputed claim to rank as the greatest historical monument of antiquity. It is our intention to glance as rapidly as we can at the spirit of Thucydides as an historian, at his methods of historical research, and at other points of capital interest to the purpose of our studies. And if we should make a somewhat longer pause than is absolutely necessary at the name of the great Athenian and his immortal legacy, our readers may account it to us for righteousness. For here we have reached a veritable peak of intellectual development. We are standing on the table-lands of earnest truth, on the summits of richly dowered thought, and on the heights of artistic power.

There is hardly any pair of contemporaries who offer a more glaring contrast than Herodotus and Thucydides. Barely a score of years divided their works from one another, but a gulf of centuries seems to yawn between their temper and inspiration. Herodotus creates throughout an entirely old-fashioned impression ; Thucydides is a modern of the moderns. He made a clean sweep of the poetical and religious bias, the legendary and novelistic sympathies, and the primitive beliefs, rarely mitigated by the light of criticism, which marked the elder historian. The gaze of Thucydides was primarily fixed on the political factors, on the actual relations of forces, on the natural foundation, so to speak, of historical phenomena. He looked for their springs, not in the dispensations of supernatural beings, nor yet, except in a moderate degree, in the caprices and passions of individual men. Behind those he always sought for the universal forces that animated them, for the conditions of the peoples, and the interests of the states. Thus he prefaced his discussion of all the points of difference which led to the Peloponnesian war by the pregnant observation—

> "The real though unavowed cause (of the war) I believe to have been the growth of the Athenian power, which terrified the Lacedæmonians and forced them into war." *

His biographer states that he was a pupil of Anaxagoras, the mechanical physicist, and the report, whether true or not, is fully in harmony with his view of the world as well as with his treatment of history. It was his constant endeavour to describe the course of human affairs as though it were a process of nature informed by the light of inexorable causality. His pursuit of strict objectivity was so keen that long passages of his work may be read without obtaining a hint to which side his favour inclined, and to which side his disfavour. Yet his power of dispassionate narration is no proof of the absence of passion. No one can doubt this who knows that complete devotion to human affairs, and their faithful reproduction, can only successfully be founded on an intense and absorbing personal interest. Moreover, it is not in isolated instances alone that the objective tranquillity which Thucydides so carefully preserved was interrupted by a sudden outcry of emotion ; his description of the fatal Sicilian expedition affects us with the pathos of tragedy.

Herodotus wrote history "in order," in his own words, "that the actions of men may not be effaced by time, nor the great and wondrous deeds . . . deprived of renown." † Nor is there any doubt that Thucydides, in his inmost soul, was moved by similar impulses. But in the foreground of his narrative, as though in self-justification, he wrote—

> "But if he who desires to have before his eyes a true picture of the events which have happened, and of the like events which may be expected to happen hereafter in the order of human things, shall pronounce what I have written to be useful, then I shall be satisfied." ‡

---

* Thuc., i. 23 : trans. Jowett.   † Herod., i. 1 : trans. Cary.
‡ Thuc., i. 22 : trans. Jowett.

In this sense, and because he was conscious that the rejection of all legendary issues had made his work less "fascinating," he spoke of it with strong but just self-respect as "an everlasting possession, not a prize composition which is heard and forgotten." * The strict sobriety in the demarcation of his purpose was reproduced by Thucydides when he came to choose the means to his end. Surprise has recently been expressed that he preferred to deal with a short span of contemporary history rather than to fill his canvas with pictures of universal historical interest. But the historian has returned his own reply to such expressions of surprise. Again and again he bitterly complained of the difficulty of attaining complete accuracy about the events even of his own day :—

"Of the events of the war I have not ventured to speak from any chance information, nor according to any notion of my own.† I have described nothing," he continued, "but what I either saw myself, or learned from others of whom I made the most careful and particular inquiry. The task was a laborious one, because eye-witnesses of the same occurrences gave different accounts of them, as they remembered or were interested in the actions of one side or the other." *

Bitter indeed is the complaint : "So little trouble do men take in the search after truth ; so readily do they accept whatever comes first to hand" (recalling Bacon's *ex iis quæ præsto sunt*). With that delight in criticism which the Greeks seemed to imbibe with their mothers' milk, and the influence of which Herodotus himself, good-humoured though he was, did not escape in respect to his predecessor Hecatæus, Thucydides likewise was infected. He sought out errors which Herodotus had committed with special reference to Spartan institutions, and accompanied them with the remark that "there are many other matters, not obscured by time, but contemporary, about which the other Hellenes are equally mistaken." ‡

* Thuc., i. 22 : trans. Jowett.
† Cp. the Preface of Hecatæus, Bk. II. Ch. VI. § 1.
‡ Thuc., i. 20: trans. Jowett.

Nevertheless, Thucydides could not or would not altogether avoid the claims of the history of dim antiquity. On such occasions, his method was marked by certain peculiarities, which require to be characterized. Two essential points may be mentioned. Thucydides was the first historian to employ the method of inverse deduction. When trustworthy authority failed him, he would argue back from the conditions and institutions —even the names—of the present to those of times past. Thus, in seeking to establish the fact that the room occupied by the Acropolis at Athens had once contained the whole city, he reminded his readers of the vernacular usage by which the word "city," or Polis, signified Acropolis, or "the city on a height." And a similar purpose inspired the second fact quoted by him in this connection, namely, that the most important shrines of the gods were partly included in that district and partly found in its immediate neighbourhood, and that certain religious rites were associated with a spring situated in that spot. The same method may be observed in Aristotle's constitutional treatise, which has been discovered in quite recent times. The second point to be noted is the use made by Thucydides—and by him first of all—of the present conditions of less highly developed peoples to illustrate the earlier stages of civilization of more advanced communities. The historians of morality, religion, and law in our own day employ them to the full extent of their capacity, and have brought the study of ethnology into close connection with that of prehistoric man. In Central Brazil, for instance, there is still an actual "Stone Age," and the pile-work in the New Guinea of to-day recalls the similar buildings in prehistoric Europe. At this point we may give an instance of the comparative method of Thucydides. Nestor in the Odyssey, in questioning Telemachus, on his arrival at Pylos, about the objects of his voyage, mentions piracy in the same breath as the business of commerce, and with no trace of moral disapproval. The courtly *savants* of Alexandria and the dry-as-dust scholars of the nineteenth century have vied with one another in their painful astonishment at the state of Nestor's conscience, and in their attempts to explain it away. The first had lost their sympathy with the naïve primitiveness of the ancients, and the second had not yet regained it. In this respect Thucydides stood on a pinnacle above them both. He had no intention or desire to force the Homeric verses into a Procrustean bed of meaning. He was rather at pains to shed a brilliant light on the rude minds of Homeric heroes by comparing them with the modes of life and sentiment among backward Greek tribes of his own day. For here, as in other passages, he was true to his principle of vivifying and enriching his picture of antiquity by appropriate parallels.

No doubt can subsist as to the legitimacy of this use of the evidence of Homer. If popular poems can tell us nothing else with certainty, at least they afford trustworthy evidence of the sentiment of those for whom they were intended. But Thucydides went further. He summoned the Homeric poems to the bar of history in his attempt to reconstruct the early annals of Greece. And if we measure that attempt by modern canons of criticism, we are constrained to arraign Thucydides, with Herodotus, on the charge of adopting the semi-historical method. But at least he erred in good company. To the names of Hecatæus and Herodotus must be added that of Aristotle and those of almost all the thinkers and authors of antiquity. We may accordingly try to fix more precisely the point of view from which Thucydides surveyed his theme. He believed on the whole in the historical reality of the human personages and of their deeds mentioned in the epic poems; and to a certain extent in legend generally. Hellen, the ancestor of the Hellenic race, was as good an historical personage for Thucydides as Ion, the ancestor of the Ionians, was for Aristotle. So far, then, the issues are quite clear. We are justified of our scepticism, and even the most critical of the Greeks were the victims of their own credulity. But when we come to the race of the Atridæ, to Agamemnon, and to the Trojan War, we cannot speak with equal certainty. Scholarship at least has not yet said its last word on these matters. It is the habit of heroic legends in the great majority of instances to go to reality for their central figures and their chief events, however freely they may subsequently deal with them. The mediæval epicists in France, for example, turned the ages upside down and made Charlemagne participate in the Crusades. But despite this violence to chronology, they cannot be said to have invented either Charlemagne or the Crusades, nor yet to have borrowed them from the storehouse of mythology. And when we revert to the method of Thucydides, we find that his faithfulness to tradition was limited to the principal features displayed by the narratives of the poets. Again and again he expressed in emphatic language his distrust of the details of their stories, and he never lent the least favour to the method of historical patchwork so much beloved by his predecessors. It was not his purpose to transform, nor to harmonize, but rather to supplement the materials with which he dealt. He was clearly convinced that he had no means at his disposal which would enable him to extract anything like a trustworthy picture of the distant past from the embellishments, exaggerations, and disfigurements of the poets. Accordingly he struck out a wholly new path of investigation, and pursued it in a manner which testifies at once to the depth of his insight and the breadth of his mental horizon. The great instrument which the historian employed, without fear, but without temerity, was the deductive method, in the sole form in which it is adapted to unravel the problems of history, namely, as inverse deduction. This, then, was the equipment of Thucydides. He was, further, gifted with a faculty of vision, to which nothing was too great or too small, and he was free from every bias and limitation of national conceit or flattering predilection. Dowered with these advantages, and employing the handful of data which he considered trustworthy, he succeeded in producing a sketch of the earliest stages of Greek evolution, which in its outline is certainly correct. We may briefly summarize its chief features. It showed that the Greeks were late in evolving the consciousness of national unity; that in an earlier phase of their civilization they were hardly distinguishable from the Barbarians or non-Greeks; that pillage and piracy by land and by sea afforded them a chief means of subsistence; and that their advance was retarded for a long time by the difficulties of intercourse and by the sparseness and poverty of the population. Moreover, the evidence was adduced, and skilfully employed, of the changes effected in course of time in the situation of cities, of the gradual progress in the art of shipbuilding, of the fashion in clothing and headgear, and of the alterations in the garb of the competitors at the Olympic games. Nor did Thucydides omit to mention the sterility of the soil of Attica, the security thus guaranteed from foreign attack,* and the stability which was thus afforded—a stability favourable in turn to the immigration of foreign families, with its natural consequence in the more rapid increase of population, and the eventual colonization of Ionia. Similarly, he noted the diminished sedentary habit and the increased love of wandering among Greek tribes, due to the lack of regular agriculture; he was aware of the change of proprietors which fell most frequently on the most fertile regions; and he remarked how the increase of wealth assisted the transformation of the patriarchal monarchy into the so-called tyranny. With the foregoing examples we may fitly illustrate the deductive method as employed by Thucydides, and the conclusions to which it led him.

4. The attitude of our historian towards the poets in their accounts of human events and natural contingencies may be described as one of cool scepticism. In respect to their tales of gods and miracles, however, his distrust rose to absolute repudiation. Moreover, it is apparent that he belonged to a circle of thoughtful minds within which this disbelief passed as something self-evident and not requiring any special mention or justification. There is no trace, for example, of the boisterous tone in which

* Cp. Introd., § 1.

Herodotus contested the truth of some of the tales which he considered incredible. Thucydides obviously never conceived the possibility that he could be suspected of giving credence to an interruption of the course of nature. Accordingly he treated the oracles and soothsayers with chilling contempt, sometimes diversified by biting satire. Moreover, he was thoroughly aware of the weaknesses of the mind which foster such superstitions, and he characterized them in places with a brilliant word. Thus when the outbreak of the plague at Athens increased the sufferings of war, some people remembered an alleged ancient oracle which ran: "A Dorian war will come, and a plague with it." This saying led, according to the historian's account, to a conflict of opinions, some people maintaining that the verse referred to *limos* ("a famine") and not to *loimos* ("a plague") :—

" Nevertheless, as might have been expected, for men's memories reflected their sufferings, the argument in favour of *loimos* prevailed at the time. But if ever in future years another Dorian war arises which happens to be accompanied by a famine, they will probably repeat the verse in the other form." *

Nor was the destructive satire of Thucydides confined to a piece of anonymous vaticination. He expressed himself with equal emphasis about an oracle of the Pythian god. When the people streamed into Athens from the country-side devastated by the Peloponnesians, the so-called Pelasgic or Pelargic field to the north-west of the Acropolis was also invaded by the fugitives, despite an ancient oracle prohibiting such occupation. Necessity took no account of the divine prohibition, but its violation was presently burdened with a part of the guilt for the heavy calamities with which Athens was afflicted :—

" And to my mind the oracle came true in a sense exactly contrary to the popular expectation ; for the unlawful occupation to which men were driven was not the cause of the calamities which befel the city, but the war was the cause of the occupation ; and the oracle without mentioning the war foresaw that the place would be inhabited some day for no good." †

* Thuc., ii. 54: trans. Jowett.
† Thuc., ii. 17: trans. Jowett.

And Thucydides denounced not merely as baseless, but as positively hurtful, the superstitious

"error of which so many are guilty, who, although they might still be saved if they would take the natural means, when visible grounds of confidence forsake them, have recourse to the invisible, to prophecies and oracles and the like, which ruin men by the hopes which they inspire in them." *

Bearing these and kindred utterances in mind, we may fairly assume that the historian's mention of the sole piece of prophecy which he knew has been fulfilled—that, namely, which stated that the Peloponnesian war "would last thrice nine years"—was merely intended to point to a noteworthy coincidence. Much the same explanation applies to the catalogue of natural occurrences partly ominous and threatening in character, and partly destructive, which accompanied the course of the great war and enhanced its terrors. At that point of his exordium Thucydides stood on the threshold of the mighty drama on which the curtain was to be raised. He was ready to turn the limelight on the majesty and greatness of the period to which he had consecrated his pen, and it would have been wholly inappropriate in that place to introduce a recommendation to caution. At another time he did not withhold it. When he was telling his readers of the prophecies of the sooth-sayers and of the earthquake at Delos, which, as was "generally believed," presaged the outbreak of war, Thucydides did not omit to utter the pregnant hint, "and everything of the sort which occurred was curiously noted." †

It is perfectly obvious by this time that the great Athenian had been thoroughly alienated from the faith of his countrymen. The word "mythical" on his lips carried the same derogatory sense as on the lips of Epicurus. It would be interesting to know, however, not what he denied, but what he affirmed; above all, what attitude he took towards the great problems of universal origin and government. There is no word in his works from which his views

---

* Thuc., v. 103 : trans. Jowett.
ᴸ Thuc., ii. 8 : trans. Jowett.

on those subjects may be gathered. We have already sufficiently shown that he did not subscribe to the belief in supernatural interventions. He was fond of tracing back to their natural causes phenomena which had been regarded as miraculous or at least as significant. In this manner he disposed of eclipses, thunderstorms, floods, and the vortex of Charybdis ; and apart altogether from his campaign against superstition, he was admirably fitted by taste and endowment for the observation and interpretation of nature. In this connection we need but recall his extremely careful discussion of the geographical conditions which brought the group of islands situated near the mouth of the Achelous ever nearer and nearer to the mainland, or, again, his masterly description of the plague at Athens which has been the admiration of experts in every age. In so far, then, we may assume that the sympathies of Thucydides tended to the physicists and the "meteorologists," and we must regard it as an especial boon that he preferred, notwithstanding, historiography to physics. But we can scarcely assume that he was satisfied for any length of time with either of the attempts then hanging in the balance to solve the great riddle of the universe, whether with that of Leucippus or with that of Anaxagoras. His repugnance to both would probably have been due not so much to their divergence from the tenets of popular religion as to their intrinsic boldness and undemonstrableness. Thucydides himself complained that it was impossible to obtain information on the course of a battle from the depositions of soldiers on both sides who had participated in it. Every one, he remarked, could only accurately relate the events in his immediate neighbourhood. And, guided by this attitude, we may fairly assume that he would have withheld his assent from the philosophers who presumed to report on the origin of the universe with the circumstantial precision of an eyewitness. Doubtless Thucydides gave his deep attention to the greatest questions which can occupy the human mind, but we can best characterize the results of his long and earnest thought as a halting suspension of judgment.

Thucydides was absolutely tireless in his search for truth. He shrank in its pursuit from no sacrifice and from no trouble, and this devotion, together with the high standard which he maintained, is perhaps the most prominent feature in the historian's character. He was anxious to preserve the artistic finish of his work, but his anxiety did not prevent him from occasionally breaking its bounds, nor even from destroying the level flow of his language in order to give his readers full authentic information on important documentary evidence. Among such interruptions may be mentioned the report of a general, and some treaty Acts composed partly in the Dorian dialect. A possible objection may be urged at this point. Apart from a few petty mistakes, which merely prove the superfluous point that Thucydides too was a fallible mortal, it may be asked how the high estimate we have formed of the veracity of the historian is compatible with his frequent habit of reporting speeches of historical personages when a faithful reproduction of their words was actually impossible. The answer lies ready to hand. It is supplied by the historian himself in a prominent place in his work, where he explained his attitude in this matter in a way which was designed and suited to prevent all misconception. He aimed, we are there informed, at the utmost conceivable "exactness" in his description of events, but in his reproduction of speeches he renounced that aim as unattainable. In such cases he was content to arrive at an "approximate" objective truth, or even at nothing but an inner verisimilitude corresponding to the respective situation and character of the speaker. Thus he developed his interpolation of speeches into the great artistic instrument by which he was enabled to infuse a soul into the body of history.

5. Nothing is more wonderful than the use which Thucydides made of this artifice, which, though he did not discover it, he was the first to use in the grand style. He employed it for two purposes apart from its dramatic value in animating the narrative. First, it served to characterize the speaker, and, secondly, to communicate the author's thought. It was a very considerable aid to the sharpness

of characterization that the speeches were mostly introduced as portions of a debate, in which opposite tendencies were played off on one another, thus frequently producing a marked effect of contrast. We may instance as a type of this method the speeches delivered by Alcibiades and Nicias in the popular assembly at Athens on the Sicilian Expedition. Every word spoken by Alcibiades bore witness to the fire, the impetuosity, and the high aspirations of that passionate genius, and deepened the effect of the cautious judgment and caustic wit of the experienced old man whose strength in criticism was shortly to be matched by his weakness in action. Sometimes, too, a character is revealed to us as much by its silence as by its speech. It cannot possibly be due to chance that the magnificent funeral oration of Pericles, which inevitably included some concessions to convention in addition to its nobler contents, should have omitted all allusion to the figures of the popular religion. The omission was obviously intentional, and we recognize the historian's wish to characterize the free-thinking pupil of Anaxagoras in his true colours as the champion of philosophic doubt in respect to the whole system of mythology. Finally, it was not merely individuals who were distinguished by the manner of their speech, but Thucydides used the same means to typify classes and nations. Thus the passionate but unintellectual Bœotians were made to deliver speeches appealing to the feelings rather than to the reason of their audience ; and when a Spartan plebeian, such as the Ephor Sthenelaidas, was introduced, he was characterized not merely by his laconic pithiness of expression, but also by the homely and ready mother-wit which was the common heritage of the Dorian race.

We pass from the purpose of characterization aimed at by the introduction of speeches to that of the communication of the author's own thought. And here it is almost impossible to avoid the appearance of exaggeration in any attempt to do justice to the historian's success in creating an inexhaustible storehouse of ideas without unduly obtruding his own personality. For keen observations, penetrating proofs, and maxims of enduring validity are presented in extraordinary profusion. To find a parallel to this treasury of political wisdom we must go to the works of Machiavelli. And even that comparison will be found to be in favour of the Athenian rather than of the Florentine, if we take the circumstance in account that every reflection in Thucydides arose spontaneously out of its historical environment, and was free from all traces of dry and systematic didacticism. And sometimes, too, the occasional speeches in Thucydides open out into philosophic discussions of the most comprehensive kind. In an earlier chapter of this work we have expressed our opinion that Protagoras was the earliest champion of the deterrent theory of punishment. It is appropriate accordingly to remark that Thucydides took a suitable opportunity to combat this doctrine by an incisive oration placed in the mouth of Diodotus the Athenian, and directed perhaps against Protagoras himself. The topic then under discussion was the penalty to be meted out to the Lesbian rebels, and Diodotus drew an incomparable picture of the irresistible force of passion and of its subversive influence on the evildoer's judgment. In other cases Thucydides substituted for a systematic treatment scattered passages of description up and down the pages of his work which the intelligent reader could collect into a complete account. Of such a kind is his description of the character of the Athenian people.

It might be expected that the two objects served by the artifice of historical speeches should occasionally have defeated each other, especially that the exposition of the author's thoughts should have been injurious to the characterization. Thucydides had so much to tell us that it would not be surprising if he should sometimes have chosen an unsuitable mouthpiece. It was difficult, too, if not impossible, to attain complete harmony in that respect, inasmuch as the situations which suggested certain lines of thought and invited their development, and the personages in whose mouths they were placed, were alike circumscribed by actual and given conditions. We do not contend that Thucydides was never beaten by this difficulty, but we do venture to contend that he succumbed to it merely in isolated instances, that the circumstances of his defeat, moreover, have an especial attraction of their own, and are full of the most welcome instruction. For through such flaws in the edifice of his art the personality of the artist shines like a flame. Take, for example, the funeral oration of Pericles. There the philosophy of Athenian politics is reduced to its quintessence. The wonderful chapters read as if the ancient material had been informed by a great modern mind—by the mind of a De Tocqueville, for instance. They form a valuable jewel, perhaps the most valuable jewel, in the treasury of Greek prose. In unequivocal tones they proclaim individual liberty, the unfettered freedom and variety of the private life of the citizens, exempt from the tyranny of the greatest number, as the feature most characteristic of Athenian social life. The historian resumes this theme elsewhere. He puts the praises of this feature, the most precious fruit of Greek civil institutions, in the mouth of Nicias in his last speech just before the decisive battle in the harbour of Syracuse. And we may legitimately urge that the exhortation comes far less appropriately from the lips of that type of narrow orthodoxy and conventional morality than from those of Pericles, the philosophers' friend. We may fairly say that in this instance Thucydides was more concerned to preserve the probabilities of the situation than those of the personages, and that it was his own teeming sentiment which flowed from the mouth of Nicias. Lapses of this kind may occasionally escape our notice because Thucydides is generally our sole authority for the characters, which we cannot accordingly test by comparison with other witnesses. But even taking all this in account, such instances are certainly but rare exceptions. For this is the point at which the incomparable art of the master attained the height of its triumph. Let us take as an example on which to found this judgment the one figure on the historical stage of Thucydides with whom the author was least in sympathy— Cleon the tanner. And yet how wonderfully he succeeds in turning that orator whom he dislikes to the purposes of his narrative when he wants to show the spots on the sun, the shadows on the virtues of the Athenians! Thucydides himself was obviously convinced that his clever countrymen were sometimes too clever, that the refinement of their thought was not unfrequently prejudicial to its wholesomeness and soundness, and that the sons of Attica were often the victims of their own versatility. To this conviction he could give no more effective expression than by the mouth of the coarse demagogue who was not particularly distinguished by the higher qualities of intellect. It was Cleon, therefore, in the pages of Thucydides, who roundly reproached his fellow-countrymen, saying, You are the slaves of paradox, the contemners of what is familiar. You follow debates on the most vital questions of the hour with the same attitude of mind as though you were attending a barren tournament of wits. You look at facts through no medium save that of speech ; you look to speech to disclose the future and to judge the past. Appearance and reality, actuality and its image, have changed their places in your conception.

The name of Cleon recalls us to the path of discussion from which we fear that we have digressed too far. We were speaking of the historian's love of truth, and it is precisely in respect to Cleon that his impartiality has been most strongly, and, we readily admit, most justifiably attacked. We cannot doubt that the demagogue's noisy vehemence, his plebeian conduct, with its manifest contempt for the refinements of life, were as repugnant to Thucydides as to Aristotle in his "Athenian Constitution," and produced a similar blindness to Cleon's solid deserts. But though we hold this opinion, we hold it solely by the favour of the evidence supplied to us without diminishment or malice by Thucydides himself. The occurrences on the island of Sphacteria in especial reveal a striking contradiction between the facts related by the historian and the verdict passed by him on those facts. The most casual reader could not miss it. Cleon had pledged himself to bring the four hundred Spartan hoplites, who were cut off in that islet from every chance of relief, alive or dead within twenty days to Athens. He commanded an over-whelming force; he associated himself with Demosthenes, the best general then at the disposal of the Athenians; and the success of his undertaking completely answered his expectation. Nevertheless the historian, who cannot be said to have been free from a feeling of contempt and even of personal hatred, spoke of Cleon's promise as a "mad" one. Yet it is precisely this instance of gross partiality which supplies us with the strongest argument for the historian's love of truth. How readily might he have narrowed, if he could not wholly have filled in, the gulf that yawned between his account of the facts and his judgment on them. He might at least have referred to some unforeseen pieces of luck which contributed to the fulfilment of Cleon's "mad" undertaking. But there is not a syllable in the whole of his report which contains any hint of this kind. In circumstances where his judgment was actually poisoned by hatred, his narrative was wholly free from every suspicion of deceit; nor was there the remotest attempt to shape or adapt the facts to suit the bias of his prejudice. The same stringency in narrative marked the work of the historian in instances where his judgment was coloured by favour. When Nicias, for example, atoned with his life for the failure of the Sicilian Expedition, which he had conducted with such conspicuous want of skill, Thucydides broke out into a lament which did not merely express his deep sympathy with the tragic fate of the unfortunate general, but bore emphatic witness to the historian's high estimate of his character. Never-theless, there was no attempt to hush up or to whitewash any of the numerous and hardly conceivable mistakes which Nicias committed. Despite his love for the man, he framed an indictment of the general which is an absolutely crush-ing document. For to Thucydides too, intellectual giant though he was, there was given that singleness, that "sim-plicity" of heart, which, to speak in his own words, "is so large an element in a noble nature."

But, reluctant though we may be, we must part from Thucydides for the present. The parting will not be of long duration, for we shall have to use his evidence for the circumstances of moral and political thought, when we seek to sketch in outline at least the conditions under which Socrates began his wonderful career. There we shall meet the first serious attempt at a systematic foundation of ethics. The writings of the poets, and of the tragedians in especial, will supply us for the most part with the evidence we require, but we shall not omit to refer to the testimony of the rhetoricians and historians, of whom Thucydides, as the deepest thinker, will claim our chief consideration

NOTES AND ADDITIONS.

BOOK I.

THE motto of this book is taken from Sir H. S. Maine's *Rede Lecture*, May 22, 1875, p. 38.

Page 4. Cp. Bursian, *Geographie von Griechenland*, i. 5–8; Nissen, *Italische Landeskunde*, i. 216 : "Nowhere else in so restricted an area is so striking a variety of bays, promontories, mountain ranges, valleys, plains, highlands, and islands of all kinds to be found." Cp., too, G. Perrot, *Revue des deux Mondes*, Feb., 1892 : "Le sol et le climat de la Grèce," especially p. 544. For the "poverty . . . her familiar friend," cp. Herodotus, vii. 102 ; and for "the most philosophical historian . . . ," cp. Thuc., i. 2.

Page 6. On the extension of the geographical horizon, cp. further H. Berger, *Geschichte der wissenschaftlichen Erdkunde*, i. 16 *ff.* ; Ed. Meyer, *Geschichte Ægyptens*, 367. Settlers from Samos in the Libyan desert are mentioned by Herodotus, iii. 26.

Page 7, § 2. Cp., for the points of view taken here, B. Erdmannsdörfer, *Preussische Jahrbücher*, 1869 : "Das Zeitalter der Novelle in Hellas."

Page 8, l. 27. On "kettles" and "tripods," cp. Iliad, ix. 264 *f.* ; Odyssey, xiii. 13 *f.* and 217. They were used as units of value in the laws of Crete (Comparetti, in the *Museo Italiano*, iii. *passim*), and were finally represented as an accessory design on Cretan coins. Though the laws may possibly refer to these coins, as Svoronos contends (*Bulletin de Corr. Hell.*, xii. 405), yet the Homeric passages are clear enough in themselves.

Page 10, l. 36. "Masters of choric song :" we are thinking more especially of Stesichorus and his peculiar treatment of the myth of Helen ; cp. K. O. Müller, *History of the Literature of Ancient Greece* (London, 1840), i. 262 and 267.

Page 11, § 3. On Asiatic and Egyptian influences in Mycenean art, cp. Schuchhardt, *Schliemann's Excavations* (London, 1891),

p. 303 ; and Reisch, " Die Mykenische Frage," in the *Verhandlungen der* 42. *Versammlung deutscher Philologen,* p. 104. While the Mycenean style continued to develop in other regions, esp. in Attica and the islands, its development was interrupted in the Peloponnesus, probably in consequence of the Dorian invasion. The influence of Egypt on the origins of Greek sculpture is acknowledged, amongst others, by Collignon (*Histoire de la Sculpture Grecque,* i. 119) and by Lechat (*Bull. de Corr. Hellen.,* xiv. 148 *ff.*).

Page 11, l. 25. " Adventurer : " Greek mercenaries have commemorated their names by inscribing them on the feet of a colossal statue at Abu Simbel, in Nubia ; *Inscript. Græcæ antiquissimæ,* ed. Roehl (Berlin, 1882), pp. 127 *ff.* Psammetich I. and Psammetich II. employed such mercenaries by thousands (cp. Ed. Meyer, *op. cit.,* 360 *ff.*). Antimenidas, brother of the poet Alcæus, lived as a mercenary in Babylon (cp. Strabo, xiii. 617).

Page 14, § 4. The climate of Ionia is described by Herodotus, i. 142.

On the origin of the Ionians, cp. Ed. Meyer, *Philologus, New Series,* ii. 273 ; also von Wilamowitz, in *Hermes,* xxi. 108.

On their versatility and its causes, cp. the excellent remarks of Grote, *History of Greece,* iii. 4 (10 vols. 1888).

On the blessings of a mixture of races, cp. Sprenger, " Versuch einer Kritik von Hamdânis Beschreibung," in vol. xlv. (separate ed.) of the *Zeitschrift der deutschen morgenländischen Gesellschaft,* p. 367 : " We may say that the Moslem civilization, which we commonly call Arabian, has sprung from a cross between the Arab blood and spirit and those of Persia."

Page 15, § 5. The author treated the same questions in a little pamphlet (*Traumdeutung und Zauberei,* Vienna, 1866), and still adheres to the position formulated by David Hume in his *Natural History of Religion:* " There is an universal tendency among mankind to conceive all beings like themselves, and to transfer to every object those qualities with which they are familiarly acquainted, and of which they are intimately conscious " (*Essays and Treatises,* Edinburgh, 1817, ii. 393). The science of religion is at present labouring seriously under the want of a fixed terminology. The eminent investigator who, more than any one else, gave currency to the important term " animism," and whose works we have here freely used, himself owns to employing the term sometimes in a looser and at other times in a stricter sense (Tylor, *Primitive Culture,* ii. 100). It is still worse with the term " fetishism," which is variously used to denote the worship of (1) the great natural objects, (2) certain classes of inanimate objects, (3) insignificant single things, such as an oddly-shaped stone, a gaudy-coloured shell, etc. Here the ambiguity of the word has seriously hindered the progress of knowledge. The legitimate reaction against the assumption that the last-named sort of fetishism was the original form of all religions has, we think, far exceeded its aim, and has led many, notably Herbert Spencer, to underestimate the importance of fetishism in general. The just perception that among the objects of worship called fetishes many are merely secondary religious creations, and that they are often revered solely as the lasting or transient dwelling-places of a spirit or divinity, has been generalized into the sentence, " that fetishism is a sequence of the ghost theory " (H. Spencer, *Principles of Sociology,* i. 345). We think ourselves entitled to use the word in its traditional sense, which, indeed, does not agree with etymology (cp. Réville, *Prolégomènes de l'histoire des religions,* 3rd ed., p. 130), and declare that we are not at all convinced by the illustrious English thinker's attempt to reduce all nature-worship to the worship of ghosts, and especially of ancestral ghosts.

The great plausibility of the hypothesis that all religion was originally the worship of ancestors or ghosts is due to the following circumstance among others. There is a continual after-growth of such gods, *e.g.* in India (cp. Grant Allen, *The Evolution of the Idea of God,* 1897, p. 32 ; Lyall, *Asiatic Studies,* ed. 2, 1–54). The great objects of nature have long ago found their representatives, as have also the chief interests of human life, in old traditional divinities. Now, all *generally* acknowledged gods have a certain tendency to wear out. There arises a craving for ever new special divinities, with whom their own worshippers may enter in a closer relation. For this reason, that part of religious evolution which we see going on under our own eyes is chiefly soul-worship.

The statement in the text about the origins of religion is meant to include all the forces that contribute to its formation, though they may not all have been at work in each single instance. The latest scientific researches have revealed many unsuspected differences in this respect. The long-sought evidence of a tribe living utterly without any religion has at last been given by P. and F. Sarrasin in their work on *Die Weddas auf Ceylon,* Wiesbaden, 1892–3. Karl von den Steinen, in his *Unter den Naturvölkern Central-Brasiliens* (Berlin, 1894), introduces us to communities who exhibit faint traces of sacrifice to the dead only in their funeral rites, when they burn the goods of the deceased and trickle blood over his fleshless bones. But ancestor-worship, or spirit-worship of any kind, is as foreign to them as, at present at least, the cult of natural objects. This last form of worship, according to verbal communications received from Dr. Oscar Baumann, is also unknown—or, at least, is known only in the secondary phase mentioned above—to the Bantu tribes in Africa. Accordingly, when we speak in the text of primitive or primeval man, we wish it to be understood in a typical sense, with the restriction just mentioned.

Page 18, l. 37. " Souls of things " or objects : cp. Tylor, *Primitive Culture,* i. 431. The importance of dream-phenomena for the belief in the existence and immortality of the soul has been set in the clearest light by Tylor, Spencer, and their followers. Oscar Peschel,

Völkerkunde, 271·(Leipsic, 1875), fully acknowledges the justice of this deduction. On the other hand, Siebeck, *Geschichte der Psychologie,* i. 6, opposes it with arguments that strike us as inadequate, while he speaks (*ibid.,* 9) of the circumstances attending the extinction of life, and interprets the same, much in the manner of our own text (p. 20).

Page 19,l. 16. "The Basutos . . . think that if a man walks on the river-bank, a crocodile may seize his shadow in the water and ·draw him in" (Tylor, *op. cit.,* i. 388). We have not scrupled to draw largely on Tylor's statements.

Page 22, l. 26. "It was during an epidemic of small-pox that the Jakutes first beheld a camel, and they declared it to be the hostile deity that had brought the small-pox on them" (Wuttke, *Geschichte des Heidentums,* i. 72).

Here should be mentioned the fear of the uncanny power of the dead, which equals, and perhaps surpasses, the desire for their help. Cp., though his statements are somewhat exaggerated, Ihering, *Vorgeschichte der Indoeuropäer,* 60 (1894).

Page 24, l. 23. "An old theological poet:" Hesiod, *Theogony,* 126 *ff.*

Page 24, l. 31. "By Homer:" *Iliad,* xxi. 356 *ff.*

Page 26, l. 22. Hymn to Aphrodite, 258 *ff.*

Page 26, l. 32. *Iliad,* xx. 8, 9.

Page 27. Cp. Welcker, *Griechische Götterlehre,* i. 38 *ff.*

Page 28, l. 5. Cp. especially Schuchhardt, *Schliemann's Excavations,* chiefly the concluding chapter.

Page 29, l. 16. In the Odyssey the ethical point of view comes far more strongly to the fore. Its conclusion, in particular, in the slaughter of the suitors, appears as a divine chastisement (cp. especially xxii. 413 *ff.*). On top of it, however, there ensue traces of the wildest barbarism (*ibid.,* 475 *ff.*). After the surprisingly fine ethical passage (xix. 109 *ff.*), it is not a little disconcerting to find theft and perjury enumerated among the gifts which Hermes bestowed on his favourite Autolycus (*ibid.,* 395). In the *Iliad,* Zeus appears as the avenger of wrong (xvi. 385 *ff.*) ; penalties in the lower world for perjury (iii. 278).

Page 20, l. 8. Cp. Diels, *Sibyllinische Blätter,* 78, n. 1.

Page 30, l. 26. "Human sacrifices:" cp. Preller, *Griechische Mythologie,* ed. 2, i. 99, 201 *ff.,* 542 ; ii. 310.

For the obsequies of Patroclus, cp. *Iliad,* xxiii. 22 *f.,* 174–177. Here ample use has been made of Erwin Rohde's pioneer-work, *Psyche : Seelenkult und Unsterblichkeitsglaube der Griechen,* especially I. 100 *ff.* ed. 2.

Page 31, § 7. On the funeral sacrifices of the Scythians, cp. Herodotus, iv. 71, 72.

Page 32, ll. 10 *ff.* Cp. Schuchhardt, *op. cit.,* 147 *ff.,* 159, 205, 287, 295.

Page 32, ll. 21 *ff.* Cp. Rohde, *op. cit.,* i. 251, n. 1 ; also the author's *Beiträge zur Kritik und Erklärung griechischer Schriftsteller,* ii. 35.

Page 33, l. 27. These views on the influence of the custom of burning were expressed by Rohde, *op. cit.*, i. 27. But we find "both kinds of burial . . . practised side by side in Vedic antiquity" (Zimmer, *Altindisches Leben*, 401 *ff.*; cp. also 415), without detriment to ancestor-worship.

Pages 33, 34. Cp., *e.g.*, *Iliad*, i. 396 *ff.*, with Hesiod, *Theogony*, 148 *ff.*—the one, the battle of the Titans ; the other, virtually a palace-revolution of the Olympians.

Page 35, l. 4. On the sun and moon, cp. Tylor, *op. cit.*, i. 260–262. On the solar character of Samson, cp. Goldziher, *Der Mythos bei den Hebräern*, 128. The story is one of the most transparent of all nature-myths.

For what follows, cp. A. Kaegi, *Der Rigveda*, ed. 2, 59 *f.*

Cp. Tylor, *op. cit.*, ii. 189 ; also Æschylus, *Prometheus*, 369 *ff.* (Kirchhoff).

Page 36, l. 4. The poetical myth of the Maoris was recorded by Sir George Grey about the middle of the nineteenth century (cp. Tylor, *op. cit.*, i. 290 *ff.*). Another version, in substantial agreement with the first, is given by Bastian, *Allerlei aus Volks- und Menschenkunde*, i. 314. There, after one of the children of Rangi and Papa "has seen the sunlight shine forth from under the armpit of Rangi," *i.e.*, when the yearning for the light hitherto unknown to them has been once awakened, they all cry out together, "We will kill our father, because he imprisoned us in darkness." But they finally follow the advice of one who proposes not to kill their father, but to hoist him aloft. For the parallel Chinese legend, cp. Tylor, *op. cit.*, i. 294. The Phoenician legend is hinted at by Eusebius, *Præp. Evang.*, i. 10, following Philo of Byblos and his authority, Sanchuniathon. Note particularly the words, ὡς καὶ διαστῆναι ἀλλήλων, and ὁ δὲ οὐρανὸς ἀποχωρήσας αὐτῆς κτέ.

Page 36, l. 19. Hesiod, *Theogony*, 154 *ff.*

Page 37, l. 16. "Cherchez la femme :" these words are put by Alexandre Dumas, *père*, in the mouth of an experienced chief of police in *Les Mohicans de Paris*, ii. 16.

For what follows, cp. Hesiod, *Theogony*, 570 *ff.* ; *Works and Days*, 90 *ff.* On the myth of Pandora, cp., too, Buttmann, *Mythologus*, i. 48 *ff.*, who correctly compared it with the legend of Eve, but wrongly identified the two.

Page 38, l. 31. Homer and Hesiod are coupled in this sense by Herodotus, ii. 53.

Page 39, l. 34. Cp. Kaegi, *op. cit.*, 117.

In Homer, too (*Iliad*, xiv. 259 *ff.*), Night is introduced as an exalted goddess whom Zeus himself regards with reverential awe. In the cosmogony of the Maoris the "primeval mother Night" heads the pedigree of all Beings. After her come Morning, Day, Empty Space, etc. (cp. Bastian, *op. cit.*, 307).

Page 40, l. 11. "Eros:" on the Love-god in Hesiod, cp. Schoemann, *Opuscula Academica*, ii. 64–67.

Page 41, ll. 22, 23. On Apsū and Tiāmat, cp. Sayce, *Records of the Past*, 2nd Series, i. 122 *ff.* ; Lenormant-Babelon, *Histoire ancienne de l'Orient*, ed. 9, v. 230 *ff.* ; Halévy, *Mélanges Graux*, 58–60 ; Jensen, *Kosmologie der Babylonier*, 300. Fritz Hommel renders *Apsū* by "heaven's-ocean" and *mummu-tî' āmat* by " chaos," *i.e.* " sea-bottom " (*Deutsche Rundschau*, July, 1891, pp. 110, 111). On the chaos of the Scandinavians, cp. James Darmesteter, *Essais Orientaux*, 177 *ff.* Analogous to chaos is the aboriginal, immense, and desert sea in the cosmogony of the Chippeway Indians (cp. Fritz Schultze, *Der Fetischismus*, 209). There is an old Indian parallel in the Rig-Veda, x. 129, 1–4 (F. Max Müller, *History of Ancient Sanskrit Literature*, 1859, p. 564) :—

> "Nor aught nor naught existed ; yon bright sky
> Was not, nor heaven's broad woof outstretched above.
> What covered all ? What sheltered ? What concealed ?
> Was it the water's fathomless abyss ? "

[The translator is indebted for the use of this version to the courtesy of Mrs. Max Müller.]

Page 42, l. 1. If Schoemann, *op. cit.*, infers from the idea of gaping, contained in the Greek "chaos" (cp. χαίνω and χάσμα), that this chaos was conceived as limited, he attributes, in our opinion, far more precise ideas to those primitive thinkers than it is right to expect of them. (ll. 19 *ff*) : Cp. Hesiod, *Theogony*, 224 *ff.* and 211 *ff.* For a correct judgment on the " progeny of night "—apart from what he says about the " compiler," who may well have been Hesiod himself—see O. Gruppe, *Die griechischen Kulte und Mythen*, i. 571. Much more life-like than these shadows of Hesiod are those figures in Homer which, like Ἄτη (" Infatuation ") and the Λιταί (" Prayers "), may, rather than any others perhaps, be called allegorical (cp. especially *Iliad*, xix. 91 *ff.*, and ix. 502 *ff.*).

BOOK I.—CHAPTER I.

Page 43. Some questions of more general import may here be alluded to. We consider the limits between philosophy and science as fluctuating, and all attempts at sharply defining the scope of philosophy seem to us equally unsuccessful. The usual definitions are either too wide or too narrow. They apply, in fact, either to a portion only of the subject, *e.g.* Herbart's *Elaboration of Conceptions*, or they are not restricted to philosophy alone. For if one speaks of " the science of principles," or of " the investigation of the essence of things and the universal laws of all processes," there is no apparent reason why the fundamental truths of physics and chemistry should lie outside the bounds of such definitions. There surely is a great difference between questions of principle and questions of detail in scientific matters. Yet the claim to detach the former from the complex of the special sciences, and hand them over to an independent branch of knowledge, can be raised and approved only by him who believes that there are other means of knowledge available for solving questions of principle than for solving questions of detail. Every science contains its own philosophy. The philosophy of language, for example, forms but the topmost storey in the science of language, and is not a kind of separate and distinct edifice. Any one applying the terms "philosophy of nature," " philosophy of language" to aught save the highest generalizations of the respective sciences would nowadays hardly be taken in earnest by the devotees of those sciences. Clearness here is only obtained by viewing the subject historically. Philosophy from the first was " universal science," considered, as the ancients did consider it, as a power guiding and determining human conduct. In proportion as the separate branches of knowledge increase in size, especially when they are able to occupy the entire life of an inquirer, they crystallize out of the matrix, so to speak, and become special branches of knowledge. It might seem not unlikely that the fate of the old " universal science " is to suffer, in the course of time, entire disruption into special sciences. Yet this would be asserting too much, for two things will for ever remain : (1) the elements of knowledge common to all studies, *i.e.* the theory of cognition and the theory of methods, in the widest sense ; and (2) the occasional, though rare, attempts of superior minds to gather the highest results of many and, if possible, of all the branches of knowledge—the peaks of all cognition, so to say—and form them into a homogeneous unity whereon to found a view of life and of the world. The nearest approach to this our conception will be found in Wundt's introduction to his *System der Philosophie* (Leipsic, 1889). In the present work the treatment of the subject is restricted within the boundaries prescribed and imposed by the limits of space, as well as of the knowledge possessed by the author, and to be presumed in his readers.

We shall not discuss at length the chronological division of our subject. The different schools and groups of schools will appear in turn upon our field of vision without requiring special introductions. The most appropriate division of the whole of ancient civilization seems to be that proposed by Paul Tannery, *Pour l'Histoire de la Science Hellène* (Paris, 1887), pp. 1–9. He would divide the time between 600 B.C. and 600 A.D. into four periods of about 300 years each, which may shortly be styled the Hellenic, Hellenistic, Græco-Roman, and Early Byzantine periods. The first extends from the beginnings of prose-writing to the age of Alexander the Great, the second reaches to that of Augustus, the third to Constantine, and the fourth to Justinian, or, as Tannery prefers, to Heraclius. The chief recommendation of this division is that the four epochs tally with real turning-points in the history of civilization. Its drawback is that the four periods are of such very unequal value—at least, as far as concerns the historical matter here treated. The contents of the first period alone will, according to the plan of the present work, occupy about two-thirds of our space, while the second and third periods, with only a few glimpses of the fourth, must be compressed within the remaining third.   Another point of view, not unworthy of consideration, was indicated by Laertius Diogenes (iii. 56, modified by i. 18).   The gradual unfolding of philosophy is compared to that of tragedy, which employed first one, then two, and finally three actors.   Thus, to physics, which originally stood alone, dialectic was added by Zeno of Elea, and, finally, ethics by Socrates.   This comparison, which for its ingenuity deserves to be quoted, is neither perfectly apt in itself, nor, for obvious reasons, available as a principle of demarcation.   The mighty figure of Socrates may, indeed, be taken to mark the division between two main epochs, for after his entrance on the scene philosophy moved in a different, though not entirely new, path.   The predominant place of nature-philosophy was henceforth usurped by ethics.

Here, also, we may touch on the question of the aims which the study of the history of Greek philosophy is meant to serve.   They are the aims of all historical investigation in general, modified by the peculiar nature of this particular branch of knowledge.   Historical interest flows from three main sources : a simple curiosity about the past, especially about all its greatness and glory ; a desire to utilize the lessons taught by this knowledge ; and, lastly, the purely scientific and, as it were, disinterested craving after knowledge, which, in matters of history, is directed to an understanding of the laws of historical development.   In our particular case, something might be said on the first and third of these motives ; but on the second there is much more to say.   Considering the immense progress which science has made in the course of these many centuries, we may well feel doubts as to the usefulness of occupying ourselves with the thoughts and doctrines of such distant ages.   To allay these doubts, it may be remarked that progress has been by no means uniform in the various branches of knowledge, and that it has been much slower in moral than in natural science.   Even in natural science there are many fundamental questions awaiting solution ; the most universal and most difficult problems have, indeed, often changed their outward guise, but have intrinsically remained the same.   Still more important is it to remind the reader of an indirect kind of use or application of the highest significance in our instance.   Almost the whole of our intellectual culture is of Greek origin.   A thorough comprehension of those origins is indispensable if we are to escape from the overpowering despotism of their influence.   It is not only highly undesirable, but in this case simply impossible, to ignore the past.   Even those who have no acquaintance with the doctrines and writings of the great masters of antiquity, and who have not even heard the names of Plato and Aristotle, are, nevertheless, under the spell of their authority.   It is not only that their influence is often transmitted to us by their followers, ancient and modern : our whole mode of thinking, the categories in which our ideas move, the forms of language in which we express them, and which therefore govern our ideas,—all these are to no small extent the products of art, in large measure the art of the great thinkers of antiquity. If we are not to mistake a result of development for something aboriginal, and a product of art for a natural product, we must try thoroughly to understand this process of evolution. Auguste Comte said, and with perfect justice, that, where practice is concerned, "on ne détruit que ce qu'on remplace : " so, with respect to theory, we may say, "we refute only what we account for."

A few words as to the chief sources of our knowledge may likewise be inserted at this point. But very little of the works of the great original thinkers of antiquity has come down to us. Of works preserved to us in their full entirety, Plato alone is complete. We possess about half of the works of Aristotle—his didactic writings, that is to say, but not his popular books, which were written exclusively, or almost exclusively, in the form of dialogues. Separated from these by a considerable difference of bulk, we have in their integrity a few of the smaller pieces of Epicurus, and, finally, the Enneades of the Neo-Platonist Plotinus. All the rest are either fragments or the work of disciples, continuators, collectors, commentators, and reporters. The whole pre-Socratic philosophy is one vast field of ruins. The Socratics, of whom only Plato and Xenophon remain, in spite of the many branches of this school, the Middle and New Academy, the Neo-Pythagoreans, the Old and Middle Stoics, and, with the one exception of the didactic poem of Lucretius, the Epicureans,—all these have left mere ruined heaps. In the case of the Epicureans our fragments are very numerous and ample, thanks to the protecting ashes of Herculaneum. Of all the schools, the New Stoics have been best treated by fate. Seneca, Epictetus, and Marcus Aurelius still speak to us as they spoke to their contemporaries. The doctrines and reasonings of the Sceptics have also, to a large extent, been preserved to us in the comprehensive extract made by Sextus (about 200 A.D.), and the religious philosophy of the Alexandrian Jews in the original works of Philo. Further details will be given later on. For the present, enough has been said to show the reader the importance of indirect, as an adjunct to direct, tradition.

Two chief branches of tradition must be distinguished : the doxographic and the biographic, *i.e.* writings which treat respectively of the doctrines and of the lives of philosophers. The former are now, for the most part, collected in the justly esteemed work of Hermann Diels (*Doxographi Græci*, Berlin, 1879). The chief source and root of all the latter doxographers—at least, so far as concerns physics in the ancient and comprehensive sense—has been shown to be an historical work by Theophrastus (Φυσικαὶ δόξαι). This has been utilized by numerous authors, sometimes directly, at other times indirectly; amongst others, by Cicero and by Ætius (between 100 and 130 A.D.), whose work is presented to us in several versions. One such version is the *Placita Philosophorum*, falsely attributed to Plutarch; another, certain pieces in the *Florilegium* of Johannes Stobaeus (about 500 A.D.); and a third version is the work of Theodoret, an ecclesiastical historian in the middle of the fifth century. Similarly, though indirectly, based on the doxography of Theophrastus, is another and very important authority—the *Refutation of All Heresies*, by the presbyter Hippolytus, in the beginning of the third century. Its first book was long known under the title of *Philosophumena*, and was ascribed to Origen, the great Father of the Church. But in 1842 books iv.-x. were discovered, and the authorship of Hippolytus immediately ascertained.

The other traditions, chiefly of a biographical character, have been mostly collected in that veritable reservoir of material, the work of Laertius Diogenes (*not* Diogenes of Laerte). He was himself a writer of very low standing, and his work is characterized by the grossest thoughtlessness. Yet his work, composed, or rather concocted, probably in the first third of the third century A.D., has an immense value for us. His principal immediate authority was, as Diels and Usener discovered, the work of an author of the time of Nero, Nicias of Nicæa, in Bithynia. This writer selected his materials from an extremely copious literature, the ultimate sources of which were the biographies of philosophers, first put in the form of "Diadochies," *i.e.* "successions," or histories of the different schools, by Sotion of Alexandria, about the end of the third century B.C. Two samples of this kind of historical writing, from the pen of Philodemus the Epicurean, have been recovered in recent times. The compilation of Laertius Diogenes contains the residue of the whole literature so richly developed during the four centuries that lie between him and Sotion.

In each separate section we shall enumerate the chief authorities and the more important collections of fragments that refer to our subject, but modern monographs and reports will be quoted only to the extent mentioned in the author's Preface. The most numerous literary references are to be found in Ueberweg-Heinze, *Grundriss der Geschichte der Philosophie des Alterthums;* the most comprehensive and profound discussions of all the problems connected with the subject in Eduard Zeller's masterly work, *Die Philosophie der Griechen;* and a compendious *résumé* of the whole of our great theme in Windelband, *Geschichte der Philosophie.* Of older but not antiquated works on the subject, mention must first be given to Christian Aug. Brandis, *Handbuch der Geschichte der griechisch-römischen Philosophie.* A complete collection of philosophical fragments, or even a tolerably good treatment of a considerable part of them, is still lacking. The want is partly supplied by Ritter and Preller, *Historia Philosophiæ Græcæ*, ed. 7, by Schultess and Wellmann, 1888.

Page 48, l. 9. "Elements of geometry." Our knowledge of Egyptian geometry has lately been increased by the Rhind papyrus, A. Eisenlohr's *Ein mathematisches Handbuch der alten Ägypter*, Leipsic, 1877. Cp. also Bretschneider, *Die Geometrie und die Geometer vor Euklides*, 16–20.

Cp. Herodotus, ii. 109; Aristotle, *Metaphysica*, i. 1; Plato, *Phædrus*, 274 C. Herodotus, *loc. cit.*, is likewise our authority for the fact that the Greeks borrowed the elementary astronomical instruments from the Babylonians. On the prediction of eclipses by the Babylonians, cp. Lenormant, *La Divination chez les Chaldéens*, i. 46, and J. Ménant, *La Bibliotheque de Ninive*, 93 *ff.*

Page 45, l. 17. *Iliad*, vii. 99, ἀλλ' ὑμεῖς μὲν πάντες ὕδωρ καὶ γαῖα γένοισθε; and *Iliad*, xiv. 211, 246. Cp. also Gen. i. 3, 19.

Page 46, l. 24. Justus Liebig wrote to Friedrich Wöhler, April 15, 1857, "It may be foolish even to speak of such a thing, but we must never lose sight of the fact that the metals count as simple substances, not because we know that they are so, but because we do not know that they are not" (*Briefwechsel*, ii. 43). Very similarly Herbert Spencer said, in a paper first published in 1865, "What chemists, for convenience, call elementary substances, are merely substances which they have thus far failed to decompose ; but . . . they do not dare to say that they are absolutely undecomposable" (*Essays*, iii. 234). Cp. L. Barth in the *Almanach der Kaiserlichen Akademie der Wissenschaften* (Vienna, 1880), p. 224 : "In fact, there is hardly any chemist who now deems certain, absolutely and beyond dispute, the existence of the seventy-odd elements as such ; every expert . . . will have admitted the probability, nay, the necessity, of their reduction to smaller numbers." Lothar Meyer, *Die modernen Theorien der Chemie*, ed. 4, p. 133, says, "It is quite conceivable that the atoms of all or of many elements are composed for the most part of smaller elementary particles of a single original material, perhaps hydrogen. . . ." A sketch of the history of this hypothesis, which was originated by Prout in 1815, will be found in the same place.

Pages 46, 47, § 2. Thales. Chief sources : Laert. Diog., i. ch. 1, and *Doxographi Græci*, passim. Herodotus, i. 170, calls him "a Phœnician by origin," τὸ ἀνέκαθεν γένος ἐόντος Φοίνικος. The objections lately brought forward against this, and summed up by E. Meyer (*Philologus*, new series, ii. 268 *ff.*), may be reduced to one, viz. that Herodotus may *possibly* here have made a mistake. But as we are totally in ignorance of the foundations of his assumption, and as it is *à priori* most unlikely that the Greeks would choose to represent their great men as foreigners, we think the above-named possibility extremely remote from any degree of certainty. The mother had a Greek name,

Cleobuline ; the father's name, Examyes, is Carian (cp. Diels, *Archiv für Geschichte der Philosophie*, ii. 169).

For what follows the chief references are : Plato, *Theœtetus*, 174 A ; Herodotus, i. 170 ; (the story in Herodotus, i. 75, very doubtful). Eudemus, the fellow-disciple of Theophrastus, in his highly important history of geometry, tells of Thales in Egypt (cp. L. Spengel, *Eudemi Rhodii quæ supersunt*, 113 *ff*.). Thales' attempts to explain the rise of the Nile (cp. Laert. Diog., i. 37 ; Diodorus, i. 38, etc.). On Thales as a geometrician, cp. Allman, *Greek Geometry from Thales to Euclid*, 7 *ff.*

Page 47, ll. 22, *ff.* Lydia's position as an outpost of Assyrio-Babylonian culture is vouched for by the pedigree of its dynasty, traced back to its god Bel ; many legendary features in its history ; and, above all, the Assyrian protectorate over the kings Gyges and Ardys, established by cuneiform inscriptions. No doubt the inquisitive Ionians who visited the gorgeous capital, Sardis, situated in their immediate neighbourhood (cp. Herodotus, i. 29), there first became acquainted with the elements of Babylonian science (cp. Georges Radet, *La Lydie et le Monde Grec au temps des Mermnades*, Paris, 1893). The eclipse of the sun predicted by Thales is No. 1489 in Th. von Oppolzer's " Canon of Eclipses," *Denkschr. der math.-naturwiss. Klasse der kais. Akademie d. Wissensch.* (Vienna), vol. 52. On Thales as an astronomer, cp. Sartorius, *Die Entwicklung der Astronomie bei den Griechen*, Halle, 1883.

On the shape of the earth : cp. Aristotle, *De Cœlo*, ii. 13 ; *Doxographi Græci*, 380. 21.

Meteorological forecasts, like that mentioned by Aristotle, *Politics*, i. 11, are frequent " dans le grand traité astrologique," according to Lenormant, *op. cit.*

Page 48, l. 1. Even in antiquity the writings ascribed to Thales were declared spurious, according to Laert. Diog., i. 23.

Page 48, l. 2. On Thales' doctrine of primary matter, cp. Aristotle, *Metaphysics*, i. 3. Aristotle, *De Anima*, i. 2, accepts the traditional account (ἐξ ὧν ἀπομνημονεύουσι) which made Thales declare the magnet to possess a soul. If this report is well founded, it may be said that we have here a survival of primeval fetishistic views. The statement which Aristotle (*ibid.*, i. 5) ascribes to Thales (" All is full of gods ") is ascribed to Pythagoras by another authority, in the words, " The air is full of souls, and those are called heroes and demons " (Laert. Diog., viii. 32). This again is a specimen of the simplest primitive conception of nature. In our own day it is found among the Finns, the Khonds of India, and the North American Algonquin Indians (cp. Tylor, *Primitive Culture*, ii. 169–172, 187 *f.* May we conjecture that Thales was here influenced by Babylonian, *i.q.* by Accadian, religious ideas ? In them were included numberless spirits whose affinity to those recognized by the Finns has been traced tentatively by Lenormant, *La Magie chez les Chaldéens* (cp. his index, *s.v.* " Esprits ").

The picture which Thales formed of the world—viz. the earth floating like a flat piece of wood on the water, and the universe filled with his primary matter, and therefore virtually a liquid mass —corresponds nearly to the Egyptian idea of the primeval water *Nun*, and its division into two separate masses (cp. Tannery, *Pour l'histoire de la Science Hellène*, 70 *ff.*). This assumption of an upper and lower ocean is also old Babylonian : cp. Fritz Hommel, *Der babylonische Ursprung der ägyptischen Kultur* (Munich, 1892), p. 8 ; cp. also Gen. i. 7. We are quite in the dark as to the agreement between the fundamental doctrine of Thales and that of the half-Jewish sect of the Sampseans (cp. Hilgenfeld, *Judentum und Juden-christentum*, 98) ; his authority is Ephan. haeres., xix. 1 ; cp. also Plutarch on the Syrians, *Quæst. Conviv.*, viii. 8, 4 (891, 7 *f.*, Dübner). The recent increasing tendency to regard Thales merely as the middleman in the importation of foreign science is refuted by the way in which our best authority, Eudemus, speaks of Thales' geometrical achievements and their relation to Egyptian mathematics.

Page 48, § 3. Anaximander : chief sources, Laert. Diog., ii. ch. 1 (very scanty), and *Doxographi Græci*. One little sentence is preserved by Simplicius, *In Aristotel. Phys.*, xxiv. 13, Diels. (This diligent commentator on Aristotle's works lived in the sixth century A.D., and has preserved for us more fragments of the pre-Socratic philosophical literature than any other writer.) Besides this, a few words are quoted by Aristotle, *Phys.*, iii. 4.

Page 49, l. 30. Egyptian maps : two are preserved, one of a mining district, the other of a region that cannot be identified, cf. Erman, *Life in Ancient Egypt*, 466 (translated by H. M. Tirard, London, 1894).

Page 50, l. 10. The borrowing of the gnomon from Babylon is attested, as we have already mentioned, by Herodotus, ii. 109. Laert. Diog. (*loc. cit.*) knew that a gnomon had been set up at Sparta by Anaximander, while Pliny (*Hist. Nat.*, ii. 76, 187) names Anaximenes. For what follows, cf. Bretschneider, *op. cit.*, 62.

Page 50, l. 15. "Accounts of the size of the heavenly bodies :" cf. *Doxogr.*, 68. On the shape of the earth, cf. Hippolytus, i. 6 ; *Doxogr.*. 559. 22. On its floating state, cf. Aristotle, *De Cælo*, ii. 13.

Page 51, l. 15. "It has been said :" the reference is to J. S. Mill, *Logic*, vol. ii., bk. v. ch. iii. § 5.

Page 52, l. 1. Anaximander called his primary matter "the Infinite" (τὸ ἄπειρον), and declared it to be devoid of any material differentiation ; hence Theophrastus calls it an undefined matter (ἀόριστος φύσις); cf. *Doxogr.*, 476. 18, and 479. 13.

Page 52, l. 22. "Differentiations" of primary matter: according to Theophrastus (*Doxogr.*, 133-4).

Page 52, l. 33. "As 'the tree by its bark:'" Pseudo-Plutarch in Eusebius, *Præp. Evang.*, i. 8 (*Doxogr.*, 579. 15). For the facts adduced in the following, see *Doxogr.*, 133-4, 342, 345, 381, 494-5.

Page 53, l. 8. Retreat of the sea: cf. Philo, *De Æternitate Mundi*, c. 23-4 (according to Theophrastus).

Page 53, *ad fin.* Cf. Teichmüller, *Studien zur Geschichte der Begriffe*, pp. 14-16 ; and *Neue Studien zur Geschichte der Begriffe*, ii. 276 *sqq.* ; also Doxogr., 25.

Page 54, ll. 9 *ff.* The problem of organic creation, cf. *Doxogr.* 135, 430, and 579 ; also Plutarch, *Quæst. Conviv.*, viii. 8. 4, with the excellent emendation by Döhner, γαλεοί instead of παλαιοί. My colleague Eduard Suess has kindly called my attention to the two following points : (1) The opinion of Anaximander—later on typically expressed in the phrase *omne vivum ex aqua*—is more and more considered by palæontologists as ascertained truth. (Still, the theory of the "pelagic origin" of all organic life is emphatically contested by Simroth, *Die Entstehung der Landtiere*, Leipsic, 1892. Yet even this authority comes near to Anaximander's hypothesis [sea-slime], p. 67 : "In the coastal zone the three great promoters of life meet together—water, air, and the solid, with its profusion of nourishment.") (2) Anaximander here may very likely have been influenced by the observation that frogs originally live in water as tadpoles (provided with gills), and only gradually (by the formation of lungs) become fitted for existence on land.

Page 55, l. 4. On the Babylonian fish-man, Oannes, cf. George Smith, *The Chaldean Account of Genesis*, 39 *ff.*

Page 55, l. 28. "Gods of an inferior order:" cf. Cicero, *De Natura Deorum*, i. 10, 25 (where, by-the-by, what he says about Thales straightly contradicts Aristotle's description of the progressive development of philosophy, in *Metaphys.*, i. 1-5, and is therefore wholly untrustworthy) ; also *Doxogr.*, 302, 579, and Simplic. *Phys.*, 1121. 5 *sqq.*, Diels.

Perishable gods as well as perishable worlds are also recognized by Buddhism (*Buddhistischer Katechismus*, Brunswick, 1888, pp. 27, 54).

Page 56, § 4. Anaximenes: Chief sources, Diog., ii. ch. 2 ; Theophrast., *apud* Simplic., *Phys.*, 24, 26, Diels ; Hippolytus, i. 7 (*Doxogr.*, 476 and 560).

Page 56, ll. 8, 9. These words seem to be Anaximenes' own. Cf. Philodemus, *On Piety* (edited by the author of the present work), p. 65, completed by Diels, *Doxogr.*, 532, and Hippolytus, *loc. cit.* (also *Doxogr.*, 560. 14).

Page 56, l. 26. Comparison of the breath of life with the air : *Doxogr.*, 278.

Page 57, *init.* Nothing is more curious than to see how, as late as the eighteenth century, metaphysical arguments were produced against what Anaximenes had recognized with the penetration of a man of genius. In the year 1731 the chemist G. E. Stahl wrote in his *Experimenta, Observationes et Animadversiones,* § 47, as follows. " *Elastica illa expansio aeri ita per essentiam propria est,* ut nunquam ad vere densam aggregationem nec ipse in se nec in ullis mixtionibus coivisse sentiri possit." Four years earlier the plant-physiologist Stephen Hales, in his *Vegetable Staticks,* had taught, again precisely as Anaximenes, "que l'air de l'atmosphère . . . entre dans la composition de la plus grande partie des corps ; qu'il y existe sous forme solide, dépouillé de son élasticité ; . . . que cet air est, en quelque façon, le lien universel de la nature. . . . Aussi M. Hales finit-il par comparer l'air à un véritable Protée," etc. (*Œuvres de Lavoisier,* i. 459–460).

Page 57, l. 30. " Miserably misunderstood experiments : " cf. Plutarch, *De Primo Frigido,* 7, 3 (1160. 12 Dübner).

Page 58, *ad fin.* Cf. Hippolytus, *loc. cit.,* and Aristotle, *Meteor.,* ii. 1 (354 A 28). Remarkable concordance with Egyptian conceptions : " Elle [la barque solaire] continuait sa course, en dehors du ciel dans un plan parallèle à celui de la terre, et courait *vers le Nord,* cachée aux yeux des vivants *par les montagnes,* qui servaient d'appui au firmament " (Maspero, *Bibliothèque Égyptologique,* ii. 335). For the meteorological attempts of Anaximenes, cf. *Doxogr.,* 136–7, according to Theophrastus.

Page 59, § 4, *fin.* Cf. Augustine, *De Civitate Dei,* viii. 2.

Page 59, § 5. Heraclitus. Chief authorities : Laert. Diog., ix. ch. 1, and more than 100 fragments, now collected, with all the literary material connected with them, in *Heracliti Ephesii Reliquiæ* recens. I. Bywater, Oxford, 1887. The so-called Heraclitean letters, dating from various epochs and composed by various writers, now also printed in Bywater's book, may be regarded as an authority of secondary importance.

Page 60, l. 3. Since his " floruit " is placed at the time of the Ionian revolt, we may conjecture that his attitude to that event (perhaps as an antagonist of Hecatæus, whom he upbraids) was the occasion of this reference. The man who, according to tradition, corresponded with King Darius (cf. letters 1–3) may have clearly recognized the hopelessness of such an uprising, and, moreover, have deemed the aristocratic government, which he preferred, better guaranteed under a Persian protectorate. In truth the national liberation in 479 did lead to democracy, the existence of which is presupposed in the fragments of his work.

Page 60, l. 22. " His native city : " the author speaks of Ephesus as an eye witness. Cf. Fragm., 119, 126, 130, 127, 125, 16.

Pages 60, 61. Cf. Fragm., 112, 18, 111, 113.

Page 61, l. 22. " The mob : " Timon the Phliasian, in his satiric poem on the philosophers, calls him ὀχλολοίδορος (*Sillographorum Græcorum Reliquiæ,* ed. C. Wachsmuth, p. 135, Fragm. 29). On what follows, cf. Fragm., 115, 51, 11, 12, 111.

Page 62.   Cf. Fragm. 114, and Pliny, *Hist. Nat.*, xxxiv. 5, 21.
Page 63, l. 6.   Theophrastus: *apud* Laert. Diog., ix. 6.
Page 63, l. 8.   Aristotle : *Rhetor.*, iii. 5.
Page 63, l. 10.   Commentators : among them Cleanthes, the second head of the Stoa (Laert. Diog., vii. 174).   The division into three sections (l. 15) may perhaps be due to the Alexandrine librarians.
Page 64.   Cf. Fragm. 20, 69, 21, 65, 79.
Page 65, *ad fin.*   Cf. Fragm. 32 and Bywater's remarks on it. The theory of the conflagration of the world has been denounced as a Stoic accretion by several modern writers, *e.g.*, by Schleiermacher, who first collected and edited the fragments (*Philos. Werke*, ii. 1–146), by Lassalle (*Die Philosophie Herakleitos des Dunklen*, 1858), and lastly by Burnet (*Early Greek Philosophy*, London, 1892).   Against them, however, cf., above all, the decisive Fragm. 26.
Pages 66, 67.   Cf. Fragm. 41 and 81.
Page 67, l. 16.   Aristotle, *Phys.*, viii. 3.   And cf. Lewes, *Problems of Life and Mind*, ii. 299.   Likewise Grove, *On the Correlation of Physical Forces*, p. 22, " though as a fact we cannot predicate of any portion of matter that it is absolutely at rest."   Also Herbert Spencer, *The Study of Sociology*, ed. 4, p. 118 : " but now when we know that all stars are in motion, and that there are no such things as everlasting hills— now when we find all things throughout the Universe to be in a *ceaseless flux*," etc.
Page 67, l. 21.   Cf. Schuster, *Heraklit von Ephesus*, in the *Acta Societ. Philol. Lips.*, iii. 211.
Page 68, l. 25.   Cf. Fragm. 52.
Page 68, l. 33.   Cf. Fragm. 57.   In what follows we have made ample use of our own treatise, *Zu Heraklits Lehre und den Überresten seines Werkes* (Wiener Sitzungsber., 1886, 997 *ff.*).
Page 71.   " Coexistence of contraries : " cf. Fragm. 45, 47, 104.
Page 71, l. 13.   Cf. Fragm. 43.   Numerous illustrations of what follows in Gomperz, *op. cit.*, 1039–40.
Page 72, l. 1.   Cf. Fragm. 44, 84.
Page 72, l. 17.   " A lucky discovery "—namely, that of the portions of the work of Hippolytus which were lost till 1842.
Page 72, l. 31.   Cf., besides Fragm. 38, the highly important Fragm. 47, and thereon our own treatise, p. 1041.   In this case I cannot agree with E. Rohde (*Psyche*, ed. 2, ii. 150).
Page 73, l. 14.   Callinus, Fragm. 1 in Bergk, *Poetæ Lyrici Græci*, ed. 4, ii. 3.   (ll. 16–18).   Cf. Fragm. 101, 102.
Pages 73, 74.   " Dicta : " Fragm. 29, 91, 2.
Page 75, l. 10.   Schuster (*op. cit.*, 41, n. 1) compares him with Francis Bacon.   For what follows, cf. Fragm. 73 and 74.
Page 76, l. 6.   Aristotle : cf. *Metaphys.*, i. 6 : ὡς τῶν αἰσθητῶν ἀεὶ ῥεόντων καὶ ἐπιστήμης περὶ αὐτῶν οὐκ οὔσης.

Pages 76, 77. Cf. especially Fragm. 24, 36 ; and Laert. Diog., ix. 8. Reference should further be made to Laert. Diog., ix. 7 ; to Fragm. 103, 19, 10 and 116, 7, 48, 118 ; also to 91, 100, 110.

Page 77, l. 32. Hegel: cf. Haym, *Hegel und seine Zeit*, 357 *ff.* ; also Hegel, *Gesammelte Werke*, xiii. 328 and 334.

Page 78, l. 4. Proudhon: on his intellectual affinity with Heraclitus, see Gomperz, *op. cit.*, 1049–1055.

Page 79, Ch. I., *ad fin.* Just a word by way of justifying our order of arrangement, by which we treat Heraclitus before Pythagoras and Xenophanes, while admitting that he was influenced by both. The links in the intellectual development of those centuries may be compared to a row of parallel threads, running lengthwise, and connected by a quantity of cross-threads. Two alternatives are offered—either to pursue the principal threads (represented in our case by the series of development : Thales, Anaximander, Anaximenes, Heraclitus and Pythagoras, Xenophanes, Parmenides, etc.), and to mention the side influences by anticipation, or else constantly to jump to and fro between one principal thread and others, thus rendering the picture intolerably disturbing. Xenophanes and Parmenides belong very closely together. Now, Heraclitus knew Xenophanes, and Parmenides, again, engaged in polemics with Heraclitus. So, to do full justice to all these relationships, one would have to put Heraclitus after Xenophanes and before Parmenides, thus violently tearing asunder what is intimately bound together.

BOOK I.—CHAPTER II.

Page 80, l. 10. " Expiation of murder, worship of souls, sacrifices to the dead : " cf. Lobeck, *Aglaophamus*, i. 300 *ff.* ; and Grote, *History of Greece*, i. 23 (10 vols. 1888), who, however, here overrates foreign influences. Diels has shown (*Sibyllinische Blätter*, 42, 78, and elsewhere) that the primeval in custom and belief was far more probably driven into the background by the civilization mirrored in epic poetry. Cf., likewise, Rohde's epoch-making exposition in *Psyche*, e.g., i. 157 *ff.* and 259 *ff.* (2nd ed.). The growth of the *retribution-theory* out of what Tylor called the *continuance-theory* is admirably described in *Primitive Culture*, ii. 77 *ff.*, and frequently elsewhere.

Page 82, l. 16. " Reward and punishment." The simplest form of punishment is annihilation. The experts are at variance as to whether, in the views of the Vedas, the wicked are considered worthy of continued existence at all. Roth, the late eminent Sanskritist, denied it, whereas Zimmer (*Altindisches Leben*, 416) affirms the thesis, and supports his affirmation by arguments which can scarcely be called decisive. For an epoch succeeding the Rig-Veda, there is, anyhow, undoubted proof of the belief in a place of punishment and in infernal tortures (*Ibid.*, 420–1).

Page 84, § 2. The Orphic poems were last collected by Eugen Abel (*Orphics*, Leipsic and Prague, 1885) ; previously by Gottfried Hermann, Leipsic, 1805.

Page 84, l. 24. "The most recent discoveries : " cf. Kaibel, *Inscriptiones Græcæ Siciliæ et Italiæ*, Nos. 638–642. His omissions may be supplemented by Comparetti, *Notizie degli scavi*, 1880, p. 155 ; and *Journal of Hellenic Studies*, iii. 114 *ff*. The tablets belong partly to the fourth century for certain, partly perhaps to the beginning of the third.

Page 84, l. 29. "Reference in Proclus : " Fragm. 224, Abel : ὁππότε δ' ἄνθρωπος προλίπῃ φάος ἠελίοιο, which is almost identical with No. 642, 1 : ἀλλ' ὁπόταμ ψυχὴ προλίπῃ φάος ἀελίοιο. These and several other coincidences have also been pointed out by O. Kern, *Aus der Anomia* (Berlin, 1890), p. 87.

Page 84, l. 32. Phanes : cf. Diodorus, i. 11, 3.

Page 85, l. 10. "Theologians : " *e.g.* Aristotle, *Metaphys.*, xii. 6, where they are opposed to the Physicists.

Page 85, l. 35. Pherecydes of Syros. The fragments are now collected and combined with allied remains in O. Kern, *De Orphei Epimenidis Pherecydis theogonis quæstiones criticæ*, Berlin, 1888. See also Diels, in the *Archiv für Geschichte der Philos.*, ii. 91, 93–4, 656–7.

Page 86. I am building here on Augustine, *Confessiones*, iii. 11, and on K. von Raumer's commentary on the passage. Others too, as soon as their attention is directed to the point, will probably discern that this Manichæan doctrine goes back to Pherecydes.

"Ogēnos : " Hommel, *Der babylonische Ursprung der ägyptischen Kultur*, p. 9, derives the Greek 'Ωκεανός from the Sumerian *Uginna* = "circle," "totality." It would be more appropriate to derive from it the enigmatic and quite unique Ogenos, of course on the supposition (hereafter to be proved) that Pherecydes took account of foreign traditions. Besides the resemblance of the names, the following circumstance has to be considered. The vanquished in the battle of the gods are hurled into Ogenos. Now, the chief of the defeated, however, is the serpent-god Ophioneus, evidently a Chthonic or terrestrial deity. The permanent home of him and his companions is the nether-world, which, according to the Greek view, is in the depths of the earth, and, according to the Babylonian (cf. Hommel, *op. cit.*, p. 8), under the ocean. May not the Ophioneus of Pherecydes be identical with the Babylonian serpent-like goddess of the Chaos? Cf. Jensen, *Kosmologie der Babylonier*, 302. Such a borrowing from the Phœnician mythology, so closely related to the Babylonian, was assumed by Philon of Byblus at least (*apud* Euseb., *Præp. Evang.*, i. 10, p. 41 = i. 93, Gaisf.). It is no longer possible to follow Zeller (*Philos. d. Gr.*, edit. 5, i. 86), in rejecting Philon's evidence as that of a "forger : " cf. C. Wachsmuth, *Einleitung in das Stud. der alt. Geschichte*, 406, Leipsic, 1895. At this point it is especially noteworthy that Halévy (*Mélanges*

Graux, 55 *ff.*) has proved the essential identity of the Phœnician cosmogony as described by Philon (or in his source Sanchuniathon) with the Babylonian ; cf. also Renan in *Mém. de l'Académie des Inscr.*, xxiii. 251.

Page 89, l. 25. On the relation of Pherecydes to Anaximander, cf. Diels, *Archiv für Geschichte der Philos.*, i. 14–15.

Pages 90, 91. For the four versions of the Orphic theogony, cf. now Kern, *op. cit.*

Page 92, ll. 2, 3. Kern, *op. cit.*, especially, following the precedent set by Lobeck in *Aglaophamus*, has established the much-disputed high antiquity of the rhapsodist theogony, or at least of its essential contents, on grounds that seem to me completely pertinent. Gruppe's would-be proof that Plato was not acquainted with the rhapsodist theogony (*Jahrbücher für Philol., Suppl.* xvii. 689 *ff.*) I regard as wholly unsuccessful, despite the remarkable fact that it won the assent of Rohde: *Psyche*, ii. 416 (ed. 2). Viewed in full light, however, the difference between Rohde and myself shrinks to a minimum. For while Rohde grants that "the agreement of the rhapsodies with old Orphic doctrine and poetry is still" demonstrable at many points, I willingly concede that the huge bulk of that work—twenty-four books—and the clear indications of an interweaving of various versions of the legends compel us to assume that the rhapsodist theogony was somewhat considerably removed from the starting-point of Orphic literature. We lack, at present at least, the requisite means for converting this relative determination of age into an absolute one. This view is also held by Diels, who thinks it "probable" that "the original form of the Orphic rhapsodist theogony belongs to the sixth century," and adds that "the Orphic eschatological mysticism" seems "a good deal older still" (*Archiv*, ii. 91).

Of decisive importance for fixing the age of those Orphic poems in which the god Phanes appears, is the occurrence of that name on the above-mentioned tablets in Lower Italy. How improbable the assertion of Zeller now sounds (*Philos. d. Gr.*, edit. 5, i. 98) : "In Aristotle it is also unmistakable that in the Orphic theogony which he used the figure of Phanes was still lacking." Indeed, the passages adduced by Zeller (pp. 88 n. 5, 90 n. 3) to support his assertion were in themselves scarcely convincing. Because Aristotle (*Metaphys.* xiv. 4) speaks of "old poets" who assume primeval deities "such as Night and Heaven, or Chaos or Oceanus," therefore he must not have known any account wherein Phanes plays a part. Yet in truth Phanes, even according to the rhapsodist theogony, is not properly the primeval Being, as Zeller himself acknowledges (p. 95). Rather, he is preceded by Chronos (Time), who engenders "Æther and the dark unfathomable abyss, or Chaos," and out of both forms the world-egg, from which Phanes issues. I cannot regard as well founded the conclusion drawn by Zeller from this passage of the *Metaphysics*, viz. "that these words . . . presuppose a cosmology, in which Night, alone, or together with other similarly primeval principles, occupied the first place." It is otherwise in *Metaphys.*, xii. 6, where "Theologians" are spoken of "who make everything issue out of night" (οἱ ἐκ Νυκτὸς γεννῶντες). Nor can I follow Zeller in referring both these passages to one and the same Orphic cosmogony, when the mere use of the word οἶον (as) in the first of the passages seems to point to more than one. The plurals ("the old poets" and "the theologians") likewise suggest anything rather than a homogeneous, uniform system. And the least acceptable point in Zeller's treatment of this subject seems to me his assumption that at about the third century one had begun to invest Stoic thought with a completely new mythical garb. Risky as all such general statements are, yet the fact that the power of myth-making was practically extinct in the Hellenistic age may be boldly stated, and much more confidently at least than that pantheistic myths in the sixth or seventh century could not have been created, or produced by the transformation partly of older local, partly of non-Greek traditions.

Page 92, ll. 30, 31. The verses will be found in Abel, *Orphica*, 167.

Page 94, l. 1. The world-egg : in Persia and India, cf. Darmesteter, *Essais Orientaux*, 169, 173, 176; in Phœnicia and Babylon, cf. Halévy, *Mélanges Graux*, 61 ; also Welcker, *Griechische Götterlehre*, i. 195 ; finally, the remarkable statement in Alberuni's *India* (translated by Sachau, i. 222, 223) : " If this our book were not restricted to the ideas of one single nation, we should produce from the belief of the nations who lived in ancient times in and round Babel ideas similar to the egg of Brahman."

Page 94, l. 5. In Egypt : the quotation is from Brugsch, *Religion und Mythologie der alten Ägypter*, 101. The version (l. 16) relating to the god Ptah will be found in Erman, *Life in Ancient Egypt*, trans. by Tirard (London, 1894). Cf. also Dieterich, " Papyrus magica," in *Jahrb. für Philol.*, *Suppl.* xvi. 773. Lepage-Renouf is hitherto unsupported in his judgment which denies the world-egg to Egyptian mythology (*Proceedings of the Soc. of Bibl. Archæology*, xv. 64 and 289 n. 2). We must not omit to mention that we find this myth of the world-egg in places where borrowing is most unlikely or utterly impossible, *e.g.* among the Lettes, in the Sandwich Islands, among the Peruvians (cf. Lukas, *Die Grundbegriffe in den Kosmogonien der alten Völker*, 261 *ff.*), and among the Finns (cf. Comparetti, *The Traditional Poetry of the Finns*, trans. by J. M. Anderton, London, 1898, pp. 159–60). Still, no impartial consideration could well miss the more exact agreement between the forms this myth has assumed among some of the nations mentioned in the text.

Page 94, l. 26. " Epicene godheads" in Babylon : cf. Lenormant-Babelon, *Hist. anc. de l'Orient*, edit. 9, v. 250.

Page 94, l. 28. Testimony of Eudemus : in *Eudemi Fragmenta* coll. Spengel, 172, cf. also 171 ; where the doctrine of the Magi is spoken of, *i.e.* the religion of Zoroaster and the place occupied in it by the Time-principle.

Page 94, l. 31. Zrvan Akarana : cf. Avesta i., trans. by James Darmesteter (*Sacred Books of the East*, iv.), Introduction, p. 82 ; and Fargard, xix. 9, p. 206.

Page 95, l. 28. " Fairy lore : " On the wanderings of fairy tales, cf. Scherer, *Jacob Grimm*, edit. 2, p. 111 *ff.* One vehicle for their dispersion was Islam, which in the tenth century was propagated in India, and thus permitted the collections of tales to spread to Persia and Arabia, where they found a second home. Thus they wandered on the one hand " through the lands of Islam to Byzantium, Italy, and Spain," and on the other hand, by virtue of community in the Buddhistic faith, to China, Thibet, " and to the Mongols, and, through their 200 years of European domination, to Europe once again from that side."

Page 96, l. 29. On the cuneiform archives of Tell-el-Amarna and Lachish, cf. Winkler, in the *Mittheilungen aus den orientalischen Sammlungen der kgl. Museen zu Berlin*, i.–iii. ; Bezold and Budge, *The Tell-el-Amarna Tablets in the Brit. Mus.*, 1892 ; and finally, Flinders Petrie, *Tell-el-Hesy* (Lachish), 1890. Parts of them have been translated by Sayce, *Records of the Past*, New Series, vol. iii. No. 4, 1890.

Page 97, ll. 34, 35. The two verses of Æschylus here quoted are from his drama, " The Daughters of the Sun," in Nauck, *Fragmenta Tragicorum Græcorum*, edit. 2, Fragm. 70, p. 24.

BOOK I.—CHAPTER III.

Page 99, *init.* Pythagoras : Apollodorus (*Laert. Diog.*, viii. 1) fixes his " floruit " in the year 532–1. Diels, *Chronologische Untersuchungen über Apollodors Chronika* (Rheinisches Museum, New Series, 31, pp. 25, 26), should be consulted.

The few contemporary notices of him are mentioned in the text. The next earliest more detailed information about his life, mixed up with many inventions, is furnished by Porphyry (in his *Life of Pythagoras*) and by Iamblichus in his similar treatise (both printed in the appendix to Laert. Diog. in the Firmin-Didot edition, Paris, 1850) ; cf. A. Nauck, *Porphyrii Opuscula Selecta*, ed. 2, Leipsic, 1886, and *Iamblichi De Vita Pythagorica Liber*, ed. Nauck, St. Petersburg, 1884. Cf. Zeller, *Pythagoras und die Pythagorassage*, in *Vorträge und Abhandlungen geschichtlichen Inhalts* (Leipsic, 1865), p. 47.

Page 99, l. 22. " No line from his own pen." This is a correct inference from Laert. Diog., viii. 6. The " Golden Sentences " ascribed to him are as a whole a fabrication probably belonging to the beginning of the fourth century A.D. Still, they contain some isolated old and genuine portions, verses that belong to the age of Pythagoras, and perhaps are actually his own. Cf. Nauck's masterly investigation, in the publications of the Imp. Russian Academy of Sciences (*Mélanges Gréco-Romains*, iii. 546 *ff.*).

Page 100, l. 1. "The pupil of Pherecydes." The doubt as to the trustworthiness of this tradition might have been even more sharply expressed than in the text. Rohde, *Psyche*, ii. 167, n. 1. (ed. 2), is obviously correct in remarking that it was the (as we add, supposed) agreement between their doctrines that "caused later writers to make the old theologian the master of Pythagoras." The report that Pherecydes had actually taught metempsychosis rests solely on the authority of the Byzantine lexicographer Suidas (*s.v.* Φερεκύδης). And even he makes the reservation, τινὲς ἱστοροῦσι, "some people relate," just as he grounds the *status pupillaris* of Pythagoras on a mere λόγος, or "it is said." The instability of the foundation of all this may be judged from the very statement to which Rohde—incorrectly, as we believe—attaches some weight : "In his (*i.e.* Pherecydes') mystic writings one must have found such doctrines hinted at (cp. Porphyry, *Antr. Nymph.* 31)." If Porphyry alleges in this passage that Pherecydes, by his doctrine of the various caverns, doors, and so forth, was hinting darkly (αἰνιττόμενος) at the fate (γενέσεις and ἀπογενέσεις) of the souls, I for my part believe that one conclusion only can be drawn with certainty from the words, viz. that no definite reference to that doctrine, obtained otherwise than by neo-Platonic arts of interpretation, was discovered in the treatise of Pherecydes. Nothing, in fact, remains of Preller's proofs (*Rhein. Mus.*, New series, iv. 388), to which Rohde appeals, save the vague statement of Cicero (*Tusc.*, i. 16. 38), that Pherecydes taught the immortality of the soul—a statement which leaves us in the dark on the essential point as to wherein Pherecydes modified the primeval doctrine of Greek religion about the survival of souls.

Page 100, l. 12. Good grounds for the credibility of the news that Pythagoras visited Egypt are given by Chaignet, *Pythagore et la Phil. Pythag.*, i. 40, 41, and 48.

Page 100, l. 16. On the practices borrowed from the Egyptian priesthood, cp. Herodotus, ii. 81 (and ii. 37, where the Pythagoreans are not mentioned by name, but where the agreement is a striking one in view of the universal knowledge in antiquity of the prohibition against beans. An apt explanation of the denial of this by Aristoxenus is given in Rohde, *op. cit.*, ii. 164, n. 1).

Page 102, l. 27. The quotation is from Röth, *Geschichte unserer abendländischen Philosophie*, ii. 785, 786, whose view and exposition of this fundamental experiment in acoustics I adopt likewise in what follows.

Page 104, l. 26. Aristotle: see *Metaph.*, i. 5 ; iii. 5 ; vii. 2.

Page 105, l. 11. "Analogy between numbers and spatial relations." Precisely similar ideas on this point will be found in Zeller, *Philos. der Griechen*, ed. 5, i. 404.

Pages 105, 106. For the widely scattered evidence in the present context, see Brandis, *Handbuch der Geschichte der griechisch-römischen Philosophie*, i. 469 *ff.*

Page 107, l. 11. Cf. Aristotle, *De Cœlo*, i. 1. For what just precedes about the sacredness of the number three, cf. Usener, *Der heilige Theodosios*, 135 ; and " Ein altes Lehrgebäude der Philologie," *Münchner akad. Sitzungsber.*, 1892, p. 591 *ff.*

Page 107, l. 14. Giordano Bruno: cf. his book, *De Monade Numero et Figura.* Auguste Comte: cf. his *Politique Positive*, vol. i. Preface and " Synthèse subjective."

Page 107, l. 16. Laurence Oken : *Naturphilosophie*, p. 12, and in what follows, cf. Aristotle, *loc. cit.*

Page 107, l. 35. "Table of contraries." The chief passage is Aristotle, *Metaphys.*, i. 5. That it is of Assyrio-Babylonian origin I gather from a remark in Lenormant-Babelon, *Hist. anc. de l'Orient*, ed. 9, v. 181.

Page 108, l. 36. Services of Pythagoras to geometry and arithmetic : The chief testimony is that of Eudemus, 114 (Spengel) ; cf. Cantor, *Vorlesungen über die Gesch. der Mathematik*, i. 124 *ff.*

Page 110, l. 15. The references in Aristotle are to *Metaphys.*, i. 5 and *De Cœlo*, ii. 13 respectively.

Page 110, *ad fin.* On the equilibrium and central position of the earth, and what follows, cf. chiefly Schiaparelli, *I Precursori di Copernico nell' Antichità*, in *Memorie del R. Istituto Lombardo*, xii. 383. This conclusive exposition is borrowed by H. Berger, *Wissenschaftl. Erdkunde der Griechen*, ii. 4 *ff.*, who also offers much excellent matter of his own. Cf. too Rudolf Wolf, *Gesch. der Astronomie*, 5, 26, 28. The question whether the globular shape of the earth was discovered in Greece or abroad is left open by Berger. He might well have decided in favour of Greece, for he had only to refer to Diodorus, ii. 31, whose statement is fully confirmed by the examination of the original authorities, in order to convince himself that such insight was denied to the Babylonians. But when H. Martin, in an essay quoted by Berger (p. 7, n. 3), "credits the Egyptians with a knowledge of the earth-ball," he is contradicted by the conception of the earth's shape which Maspero, a leading authority on these subjects, brings forward and expounds in his *Hist. anc. des Peuples de l'Orient classique*, pp. 16, 17.

Book I.—Chapter IV.

Page 112, l. 1. Voltaire : *Œuvres complètes*, ed. Baudouin, vol. 58, p. 249.

Page 112, l. 3. Sir George Cornewall Lewis : *An Historical Survey of the Astronomy of the Ancients*, p. 189. The material here employed is for the main part collected in the epoch-making treatise of Schiaparelli mentioned above. We are considerably indebted, too, to the rich contents of this and of a second masterly work by the same author, *Le sfere omocentriche, etc.*, Milan, 1876. The first to shed light on this confusion was Boeckh, in his *Philolaos des Pythagoreers Lehren.* In another connection we shall have to deal with the personality of this Pythagorean, and with the other doctrines that may with greater certainty be attributed to him.

Page 112, l. 24. "Simple, steady, and regular :" cf. Geminus, in Simplicius, *Phys.*, 292, 26, 27 D.

Page 114, l. 23. We are of opinion that Schiaparelli errs in disputing the movement of the firmament of fixed stars in the Philolaic system, *I Precursori di Copernico, etc.* (separate edition), p. 7. For then we should have to credit our authorities, above all Aristotle, who speaks of ten heavenly bodies in motion (*Metaphys.*, i. 5), with a hardly conceivable mistake. It is, further, contrary to the strongly marked sense of symmetry shown by the Pythagoreans, that they should ascribe immobility solely to the firmament of the fixed stars. It is true they could no longer believe in the daily movement of this firmament, since it had been superseded by the movement of the earth. "What then remains," asks Böckh, *op. cit.*, 118, "but to assume that the movement of the firmament of the fixed stars is the precession of the equinoxes?" Later, Böckh renounced this opinion (*Manetho und die Hundssternperiode*, 54); still later he returned to it, though with hesitation (*Das Kosmische System des Platon*, 95). In this we unconditionally agree with him, chiefly on account of the following consideration. The precession of the equinoxes is a phenomenon which, as Martin justly remarks (*Études sur le Timée de Platon*, ii. 38), "requires only long and steady observations without any mathematical theory, in order to be recognized." It is in itself hardly credible that a deviation in the position of the luminaries, which in the course of a single year amounts to more than fifty seconds of an arc, could remain unnoticed for long. It becomes quite incredible on the following consideration, to which an expert authority, Dr. Robert Fröbe, of the Vienna Observatory, has directed my attention. The data derived from Philolaus or other early Pythagoreans for the angular velocities of the planetary movements are approximately correct. Only prolonged observations of the stars could have made them so, since there was no other means of eliminating the grossest of the errors then inevitable to observation.

Page 117, l. 6. Cf. Stobæus, *Eclogues*, i. 22 (i. 196 Wachsmuth) = Ætius in *Doxogr.*, 336, 337. It has been conjectured on the best grounds that the torch which the bride's mother waved at the marriage ceremony was "kindled at the parental hearth" (cf. Herman-Blümner, *Griech. Privataltertümer*, 275, n. 1: "Hence ἀφ' ἑστίας ἄγειν γυναῖκα, Iambl., *Vit. Pythagor.*, c. 18, § 84"). It seems an almost unavoidable assumption that the new hearth was kindled with the same torch, especially in view of the similar custom obtaining at the foundation of colonies. For this last ceremony, cf. Herodotus, i. 146 ; Scholiast to Aristides, iii. p. 48, 8 Dindorf ; *Etymol. Magn.*, p. 694, 28 Gaisford.

Page 118, l. 11. Karl Ernst von Baer : *Reden . . . und Kleinere Aufsätzen*, St. Petersburg, 1864, i. 264. On the harmony of the spheres and the reason why it is inaudible, cf. especially Aristotle, *De Cœlo*, ii. 9.

Page 119, l. 9. Aristotle, *Metaphys.*, i. 5.

Page 120, l. 10. "Eclipses of the moon, which occurred so frequently." As a matter of fact, eclipses of the sun are more frequent ; thus in the period of time comprised in Oppolzer's *Canon der Finsternisse* there are 8000 eclipses of the sun against 5200 of the moon. At every single point of the earth, however, very many more of the latter than of the former are visible.

Page 120, l. 20. "Extension of the geographical horizon :" On Hanno's *Periplus* and the influence of that voyage of discovery on the transformation of the doctrine of a central fire, cf. Schiaparelli, *I Precursori, etc.* (separate edition), p. 25, and H. Berger, *Wissenschaftliche Erdkunde*, ii. 387.

Page 121, l. 15. Heraclides : cf. chiefly Laert. Diog., v. ch. 6. The view taken in the text of Heraclides as the immediate precursor of Aristarchus, is based on the account by Geminus, in Simplicius, *Phys.*, 292, 20 *ff.* D.—a passage not without its difficulties. After the most ample consideration, I find myself compelled to dissent from Diels' view of the passage (*Über das physik. System des Straton*, in the *Berliner Sitzungs-Berichte*, 1893, p. 18, n. 1). Either the passage must be emended, precisely or similarly as Bergk proposed (*Fünf Abhandlungen zur Gesch. der griech. Philos. u. Astronomie*, 149), or the words Ἡρακλείδης ὁ Ποντικός must be taken as inserted by a (well-informed) reader. The evidence for the progress of astronomy described in the text, and likewise the explanation of that progress, are given by Schiaparelli, *op. cit.* The doctrine of Aristarchus was mentioned by Copernicus, in a passage which he afterwards suppressed : "Credibile est hisce similibusque causis Philolaum mobilitatem terræ sensisse, quod etiam nonnulli Aristarchum Samium ferunt in eadem fuisse sententia," etc. (*De Revolut. Cælest.*, ed. Thorun., 1873, p. 34 n.).

BOOK I.—CHAPTER V.

Page 124, l. 1. Aristotle : *De Anima*, i. 3 *fin.*

Page 124, l. 4. Xenophanes : *apud* Laert. Diog., viii. 36. The suspicions lately uttered concerning the reference to Pythagoras in these verses seem to me totally groundless—as groundless as the similar doubt that has been expressed as to the testimony of Empedocles (l. 15), cp. Stein, 415 *ff.*

Page 124, l. 20. Gallic Druids: cf. Wilkinson's account in G. Rawlinson, *History of Herodotus*, ed. 3, ii. 196.

The Druses: cf. Benjamin of Tudela (12th century) in Tylor, *Prim. Culture*, ii. 13. The other ethnographical details are also taken from Tylor, *op. cit.*, ch. 12, though his derivation of the belief in metempsychosis from the physical and spiritual resemblance between descendants and ancestors (ii. 14), seems to me quite an inadequate explanation.

Page 126, l. 8. Indirect evidence of the non-Greek origin of metempsychosis is afforded by the vain endeavours of the most bitter antagonists of that origin; Dieterich, for example, in his valuable book *Nekyia*, p. 90, finally contents himself with pointing out mere vague possibilities.

Page 126, l. 28. Herodotus, ii. 123.

Page 126, ll. 35 *ff.* The quotation is from Erman, *Life in Ancient Egypt*, 306 (English trans., London, 1894). What follows is based on Maspero, *Bibliothèque égyptologique*, ii. 467, n. 3, and 466. Maspero, *ibid.*, i. 349, ascribes metempsychosis to the Egyptian belief in the age when the country came into contact with Greece. He considers that in later times these theories fell into discredit or even almost entirely disappeared. In a later treatise (the passage first quoted), Maspero modifies this judgment of his, in the words: " Il ne faut pas oublier que l'assomption de toutes ces formes est purement volontaire et ne marque nullement le passage de l'âme humaine dans un corps de bête."

Page 127, ll. 25 *ff.* On the pre-Buddhistic origin of the Indian belief in metempsychosis, cf. Jacob, *A Manual of Hindu Pantheism*, ed. 2, p. 25. As I have learned from my colleague, Professor Bühler, that belief arose in an age that cannot be fixed quite accurately, though it fell in a very early period of the Brahman religion and literature. The chief work promulgating the new doctrine is regarded, even in the oldest Buddhist writings, as of primeval legendary antiquity. On the lifetime of Buddha (who died not long after 500 B.C.), cf. Oldenberg, *Buddha*, ed. 2, p. 2. On that of Zarathustra, cf. Justi, *Geschichte Persiens*, 67, 68. " In India Cyrus had already subjugated the Gandarians south of the river Kabul" (*ibid.*, 96).

Page 128, § 2. On what follows, cf. especially Rohde (*Psyche*). He seems to me to err only in a tendency to overrate the influence of the Thracians, whom Herodotus justly speaks of as living " wretchedly and in a very uncivilized manner" (iv. 95, trans. Cary), and who in truth were savage and predatory, and to underrate the moral elements of Orphicism. To discuss these questions here would lead us too far. With regard to the second point we may refer to Dieterich's *Nekyia*, 193, 194; with regard to the first, the reader may be briefly reminded that the features most characteristic of Orphicism, such as consciousness of sin, craving for purification and redemption, the penalties of Hades, etc., are absolutely undiscoverable among the Thracians.

Page 130, l. 5. For Crete, cf. Joubin, " Inscription crétoise rélative à l'Orphisme," in the *Bulletin de correspondence hellénique*, xvii. 121–124.

Page 131, l. 7. On the belief in retribution, cp. pp. 81, 82.

Page 131, l. 9. Image of the Erinyes : cf. Rohde, *Psyche*, i. 270, (ed. 2), and more details in *Rhein. Mus.*, L. p. 6.

Page 131, ll. 29 *ff*. On these crude representations of a blissful after-life, cf. Dieterich, *op. cit.*, 79, 80. The numerous parallels adduced by him, to which I might add the wide selection (from various ancient Indian sources) given by Muir, *Sanscrit Texts*, v. 307 *ff.*, make the conclusion that the Orphic dogmas were of Thracian origin appear extremely hazardous.

Page 132, l. 10. " Hypnotic trance : " on the use of hypnotism in the ascetic meditation of the Buddhists, cf. H. Kern, *Der Buddhismus und seine Geschichte in Indien* (trans. into German by Jacobi), i. 502.

For what follows, the reader may be referred to Rohde, *ibid.*, ii. 14 ; Eduard Meyer, *Geschichte Ägyptens*, 87 ; Fr. Lenormant's article, " Eleusis," in Daremberg and Saglio, *Dictionnaire des Antiquités;* and Dieterich, *De hymnis Orphicis capitula quinque*, 38.

Page 133, l. 29. Confession of sin : cf. Maspero, *Bibliothèque Egyptol.*, ii. 469 *ff*.

Page 134, ll. 13–15. I have added two items of the confessional from Brugsch, *Steininschrift und Bibelwort*, 253, 254, a quite justifiable "contaminatio," as experts assure me, since the negative confession of sins displays manifold variants in different texts. Cf. also Maspero, *Hist. ancienne, etc.*, 191.

Page 135, l. 3. " Plato's expression : " *Timæus*, 22 B.

Page 136, l. 10. " Horror of bloodshed : " cf. Aristoph., *Frogs*, 1032, Meineke : Ὀρφεὺς μὲν γὰρ τελετάς θ' ἡμῖν κατέδειξε φόνων τ' ἀπέχεσθαι.

Page 136, l. 13. " Dike and Nomos : " cf. *Orphica, passim*, and especially Fragm. 33 ; 125, 1 ; 126, Abel.

Page 138, l. 19. " Authors of Orphic poems : " cf. Rohde, *Psyche*, ii. 106 (ed. 2).

Page 138, l. 39. " Particles of dust in the sunlight : " according to Aristotle, *De Anima*, i. 2.

Page 139, l. 26. " Leaning to monotheism : " according to Cicero, *De Deorum Natura*, i. 11 (27).

Page 139, l. 27. " Dualism : " according to Ætius, *apud* Stobæum, *Eclogues*, i. 1 = *Doxogr. Gr.*, 302.

Page 139, l. 34. " Exhalation of the world : " Aristotle, *Phys.*, iv. 6, p. 213, B 22, where I read αὐτὸ and cancel πνεύματος (as Chaignet also tentatively proposed).

Page 140, l. 4. " Remark of Eudemus : " pp. 73, 74, Spengel.

Page 142, ll. 23 ff. " The ' world-year ' . . . of the Babylonians :" cf. Lenormant-Babelon, *Histoire de l'Orient*, ed. 9, v. 175. Somewhat differently Berossus, in Syncellus (C. Müller, *Fragm. Hist. Gr.*, ii. 499).

Page 143, l. 7. " Periodical conflagrations and floods : " cf. Seneca, *Quaest. Nat.*, iii. 29, as well as Censorinus, *De Die Nat.*, 18, 11.

Page 143, l. 19. " Double destruction :" cf. *Doxogr. Gr.* 333, 7 ff.

Page 143, l. 24. " We cannot admit," etc. : the opinion here contested is that of Zeller : " When the stars resume their former places, everything else must return to the same condition, and similar persons must likewise be present in the same circumstances as before " (*Philos. der Griechen*, ed. 5, i. 443).

Page 143, l. 31. Theophrastus : cf. Engelbrecht, in *Eranos Vindobonensis*, 129. The Pythagoreans may be credited with the knowledge of isolated tenets of the Babylonian astronomy, just as Heraclitus was acquainted with the fundamental doctrine of their astrology, as shown by Engelbrecht, *ibid.*, 126. But it is too great a jump from this to the assumption that old Greek philosophers—above all, the Pythagoreans, or any considerable section of them—simply followed the lead of the Babylonians on a fundamental question intimately bound up with the whole view of the world, or rather followed their astrological system to its extreme consequences, and developed it further. We may add that Eudemus, who occasionally touches on religious doctrines of the Phœnicians and the (Zoroastrian) Magi (p. 171, Spengel), would then have been just the man to recognize and point out such a connection.

Page 146, l. 28. Hippasus of Metapontum : cf. Aristotle, *Metaphys.* i. 3, and Theophrastus (in *Doxogr. Gr.* 475, 476) ; also Ætius, *ibid.*, 283, 284.

Page 147, § 5. Cf. for the whole of this section, the collection and discussion of the fragments in the supplement appended to the programme of the Gymnasium at Wittenberg : *Alkmæon von Kroton*, by Julius Sander (Wittenberg, 1893). Alcmæon and his significance were to a certain extent rediscovered by Philippson, in his Ὕλη ἀνθρωπίνη (Berlin, 1831). Note, for example, what he says (pp. 20, 21) on a passage of Theophrastus overlooked by all previous scholars.

The proem of his book, *apud* Laert. Diog. viii. 5, 2. In translating the concluding words, I have read ὡς δ' ἄνθρωπον τεκμαίρεσθαι, instead of ὡς δ' ἀνθρώποις τεκμαίρεσθαι, which seems to me impossible. Some such phrase as ἔχει που ὧδε may have followed.

Page 148, l. 9. " The brain as the central organ :" according to Theophr., *De Sensibus*, § 26 = *Doxogr. Gr.*, 507.

Page 148, l. 28. " The . . . belief that the sperma originates in the spinal marrow " is not merely a Greek, but also an Indian and a Persian belief ; cf. Darmesteter, *Zend-Avesta*, i. 164, n. 1 (Sacred Books of the East, vol. iv.).

Page 148, l. 35. " Doctrine concerning sickness and health : " cf. *Doxogr. Gr.*, 442. In that connection, cf. the much-disputed doctrine of contraries, Aristotle, *Metaphys.*, i. 5.

Page 149, l. 8. The echoes in Geber I take from Berthelot's essay in the *Révue des Deux Mondes*, 1893, p. 551 : " Quand il y a équilibre entre leurs natures " (he is speaking of the four elements, and the four fundamental qualities, the hot, the cold, the dry, and the moist), " les choses deviennent inaltérables. . . . Tel est encore le principe de l'art médical, appliqué à la guérison des maladies." Berthelot here recognizes Greek influences, without expressly recalling Alcmæon. Nor, indeed, was Alcmæon alone in proclaiming the four fundamental qualities just mentioned. But even as early as Aristotle they occur exclusively in a connection which clearly reveals the influence of Alcmæon ; cf. Sander, *op. cit.*, 31. Likewise in the treatise of Polybus, *De Natura Hominis* (Littré, *Œuvres d'Hippocrate*, vi. 38). The traces of Alcmæon are most unmistakable in the following passage : πολλὰ γάρ ἐστιν ἐν τῷ σώματι ἐνεόντα, ἃ ὁκόταν ὑπ' ἀλλήλων παρὰ φύσιν θερμαίνηταί τε καὶ ψύχηται καὶ ξηραίνηταί τε καὶ ὑγραίνηται, νούσους τίκτει (*ibid.*, 36). Littré himself (i. 562) clearly recognized that Alcmæon was a precursor of Hippocrates.

Page 149, ll. 14 *ff.* On Alcmæon's doctrines of the several senses, cf. Theophrastus *op. cit. ;* Ætius and Æius Didymus in *Doxogr. Gr.*, 223, 404, 456. To these may be added the pertinent remarks of Diels, " Gorgias und Empedokles," *Berliner Sitzungsberichte*, April, 1884, pp. 11, 12, and *Hermes*, xxviii. 421, n. 2, where, by-the-by, the reference to Aristotle, *De Generat. Animal.*, must be read B 6, 744 A 7 (and not 363 A 7). My colleague, Professor Bühler, has directed my attention to the very remarkable similarity between Alcmæon's theory of vision and the Indian theory, most completely elaborated in the *Nyaya-Vaíseshika*. According to that doctrine the organ of sight consists of " fire ; " this combines with the object and assumes its shape. The impression thus produced is received by the " inner organ," the *manas*, and is transmitted by it to the *âtman*, the soul proper.

Page 150, l. 8. Psychology of Alcmæon : according to Theophrastus, *op. cit.* § 25 = Doxogr. Gr., 506 ; supplemented by Plato, *Phædo*, 96 B, and *Phædrus*, 249 B. On its after effects in Aristotle, cf. Sander, *op. cit.*, 25, 26, following Hirzel's precedent, especially with reference to *Analytica Post.*, ii. 19.

Page 150, l. 16. On the proof of the immortality of the soul, cf. Aristotle, *De Anima*, i. 2.

Page 151, l. 4. Plato : *Phædrus*, 245 c.

Page 151, l. 13. For the proof of " the perishability of the body," cf. Aristotle, *Probl.* 17, 3.

BOOK II.

The motto is from Helmholtz, *Vorträge und Reden*, ii. 189 (" Das Denken in der Medicin ").

BOOK II.—CHAPTER I.

Page 155. The surviving writings of the Eleatics are collected in Mullach, *Aristotelis de Melisso Xenophane et Gorgia Disputationes cum Eleaticorum Philosophorum Fragmentis*, etc., Berlin, 1845. This alleged Aristotelian book is the work of a late and in many respects an ill-informed Peripatetic, as has at last been established after long discussion among scholars. Mullach's collection of fragments (in which Zeno is not represented) has been added to, as far as Xenophanes is concerned, by Ferdinand Dümmler, *Rhein. Mus.*, xlii. 139, 140, and N. Bach, *Jahrb. für wiss. Kritik*, 1831, i. 480. Cf. also the author's " Beiträge zur Kritik u. Erklärung griech. Schriftsteller," iii., *Wiener Sitzungsber.*, 1875, 570 *ff.* The literary remains of Xenophanes, Parmenides, and Empedocles have been collected and interpreted by Karsten, in his work, *Philosophorum Græcorum Veterum . . . Operum Reliquiæ*, Amsterdam, 1830–38.

Xenophanes : chief sources, Laert. Diog., ix. ch. 2 ; also Aristotle, Clement of Alexandria, Sextus Empiricus.

As to the chronology of Xenophanes, we must start from the evidence given by his own fragments, and, in the second instance, from the fact that he mentions Pythagoras, and in his turn is mentioned by Heraclitus. According to Fragm. 24, he left his home at the age of twenty-five ; his emigration may very possibly have been due to the Persian conquest (545 B.C.), especially as Fragm. 17 almost certainly shows that it did not anyhow occur before that date. If this calculation is correct, he was born in 570 ; and since, according to the evidence of Fragm. 24, he reached the age of at least 92 (and of more than 100 according to Censorinus, *De Die Natali*, 15, 3), the statement of the historian Timæus (*apud* Clement of Alexandria, *Stromat.*, i. 353, Pott.) that Xenophanes lived in the time of Hiero I. (478–467) may be defended as correct.

Page 155, l. 12. " The poor rhapsodist : " His penurious condition is vouched for by the apophthegm in *Gnomolog. Paris.*, ed. Sternbach, Cracow, 1895, No. 160, where Xenophanes, questioned by Hiero as to how many slaves he owns, answers, " Two only, and even these I can hardly support." An anecdote like this would never have been circulated if he had been one of the highly paid members of his profession. Cf. also Fragm. 22.

Page 155, ll. 25, 26. The local description is based on the author's personal observation. The " single soaring tower " is called Torre di Velia, and is not of ancient origin.

Page 157, l. 8 to p. 158, l. 4. For the ideas here expressed the author is indebted to a conversation with Hermann Usener at the Philological Congress in Vienna, May, 1893.

Page 158, l. 39. Aristotle : *Metaphys.*, i. 5 ; and Timon (Wachsmuth, *Corpusc. poes. ludib.*, 156).

Page 160. Xenophanes was formerly regarded as the first Greek monotheist. The decisive arguments to the contrary are contained and driven home in Freudenthal's treatise, *Über die Theologie des Xenophanes*, Breslau, 1886, to which our account is much indebted. At the same time, Zeller can justly claim to have exposed some of the weaker links in Freudenthal's chain of evidence (cf. *Deutsche Litteraturzeitung*, 13 Nov., 1886, and *Archiv*, ii. 1 ff.).

Page 160, l. 34. " An imitation in Euripides :" *Hercules Furens*, 1343, compared with Pseudo-Plutarch, *Stromat., apud* Euseb., *Præp. Evang.*, i. 8, 4.

Pages 160, 161. The alleged monotheism of Xenophanes is at once and finally confuted by the single verse, Εἷς θεὸς ἔν τε θεοῖσι καὶ ἀνθρώποισι μέγιστος, Fragm. 1. Its testimony could be weakened only by the interpretation—contrary to the straightforward sense of the line—"compared with" *real* "men and" *imaginary* "gods." Von Wilamowitz, *Euripides Herakles*, ed. 1, ii. 246, with whom I cannot agree in this instance, holds a different opinion. We much prefer to recognize the reference here to a supreme god who is hardly less superior to the lower gods than to mankind. Cf. perhaps Rig Veda, x. 121. 8, " He who by his might looked even over the waters which held power (the germ) and generated the sacrifice (light), he *who alone is God above all gods :*—Who is the God to whom we shall offer sacrifice ? " translated by F. Max Müller, *Vedic Hymns*, part i. p. 2, Oxford, 1891 (Sacred Books of the East, vol. 32).

Page 162, ll. 15, 16. Besides Syracuse and Malta, our authority (Hippolytus, i. 14) likewise mentions Paros ; but my colleague, Prof. Suess, informs me that there are no fossils in Paros. A remark in his letter, to the effect that the impressions of seals, alleged to be discovered there, are a palæontological impossibility, has led me to the conjecture that, by a very slight change, φυκῶν or φυκίων ("of seaweed ") should be read instead of φωκῶν. On this emendation Suess remarks, ' Quite clear and striking impressions of fucoids, which even the layman readily recognizes as such, are found in a light-grey marl-slate, alternating with sandstone, not indeed in the quarries (of Syracuse) themselves, but at no very great distance from them, and in many other parts of Sicily." Cf. Pseudo-Plutarch, *apud* Euseb., *loc. cit.*, Τῷ χρόνῳ καταφερομένην συνεχῶς καὶ κατ' ὀλίγον τὴν γῆν ἐς τὴν θάλασσαν χωρεῖν.

Page 164, l. 5. Aristotle : *Metaphys.*, i. 5, 986 B. 21, Ξενοφάνης δὲ . . . οὐθὲν διεσαφήνισεν.

Page 164, ch. i. *fin.* We may briefly advert at this point to the remarkable parallelism in the development of Greek and Hindoo thought. How surprising it is to observe that (according to Oldenberg, *Buddha*, 45, ed. 2) the "first traces" of the doctrine "of metempsychosis occur in the Vedic texts not long before the first appearance of the doctrine of the eternal One," precisely as the metempsychosis of Pythagoras immediately precedes the Universal-Unity doctrine of Xenophanes! But in other respects likewise the doctrine of *âtman* strikingly reminds us of the Eleatic theory of *Ens.* In spite of this agreement, however, there are very considerable differences that must not be overlooked. The excess of visionary enthusiasm among the Hindoos is an excess of rational reflection among the Greeks. The difference leaps to light when we remember, for instance, the geological speculations of Xenophanes in the domain of natural science, or the attempts of Parmenides, in the second part of his didactic poem, to give a scientific explanation of the cosmic processes. In Hindoo speculation, metaphysics are connected almost exclusively with religion ; in Greek, not merely with religion, but also with science. Thus, though the results of thought display a striking similarity in either instance, I was yet entitled to presume motives of thought in the instance of the Greeks of an essentially different kind.

BOOK II.—CHAPTER II.

The fragments of the poem of Parmenides were re-edited after Mullach, by Heinrich Stein, in the *Symbola Philologorum Bonnensium*, Leipsic, 1867, fascic. post. 765–806.

Page 165, l. 2.   "On the nature of man : " Littré, *Œuvres d'Hippocrate*, vi. 32 ff.

Page 166, l. 16.   "Un-natural philosophers " and " stoppers-of-the-Universe : " cf. Plato, *Theætetus*, 181, A., and Aristotle, *apud* Sext. Emp., *Adv. Mathemat.*, x. 46 (p. 485, 25, Bekker).

Page 166, § 2.   The chief source for the biography of Parmenides is Laert. Diog., ix. ch. 3. As boundary-marks in the chronology of his life, we may mention generally that he was a younger contemporary of Xenophanes, and likewise of Heraclitus (whose doctrines he knew and ridiculed) ; that he was older than M'lissus, and (according to Plato's trustworthy statement, *Parmenides*, 127 B) a quarter of a century older than Zeno. We do not know the foundation for the date of his "floruit" given by Apollodorus ; but it seems to me wholly illegitimate to impute arbitrary calculations to that great and conscientious inquirer in this instance, considering that he relied on none but autobiographical testimony in his chronology of Anaximander and Democritus, and that he discussed the chronology of Empedocles, in verses which we still possess, in the minutest fashion.

Page 167, l. 35.   For the quotation from Melissus, cf. Mullach, *op. cit.*, 82, 83.   I have emended the concluding sentence of the passage by a transposition which the sense requires ; cf. "Apologie der Heil-kunst," 167 (*Wiener Sitzungsber.*, 1891, No. ix.).

Page 169, ll. 22 *ff.* Cf. Mullach, *op. cit.*, 114, vv. 45–51. The reference to Heraclitus was recognized and proved by Bernays, *Rhein. Mus.*, New Series, vii. 114 *ff.*

Page 171. Since the denial of the generation and decay of matter continues to be ascribed to the Eleatics alone, and not to their prede-cessors, it seems necessary to add at this point the express testimony of Aristotle, *Phys.*, i. 4, 187 A 26 : Διὰ τὸ ὑπολαμβάνειν τὴν κοινὴν δόξαν τῶν φυσικῶν . . . , ὡς οὐ γιγνομένου οὐδενὸς ἐκ τοῦ μὴ ὄντος. *Metaphys.*, i. 3, 984 A *fin.* : Τὸ ἐν ἀκίνητόν φασιν εἶναι καὶ τὴν φύσιν ὅλην οὐ μόνον κατὰ γένεσιν καὶ φθορὰν (τοῦτο μὲν γὰρ ἀρχαῖόν τε καὶ πάντες ὡμολόγησαν). *Ibid.*, 984 A 11 : καὶ διὰ τοῦτο οὔτε γίγνεσθαι οὐθὲν οἴονται οὔτε ἀπόλλυσθαι (viz. the old physiolo-gists from Thales downwards). *Metaphys.*, xi. 6, 1062 B 24 : τὸ γὰρ μηδὲν ἐκ μὴ ὄντος γίγνεσθαι πᾶν δ' ἐξ ὄντος σχεδὸν ἁπάντων ἐστὶ κοινὸν δόγμα τῶν περὶ φύσεως.

Page 172, l. 9. "One of Parmenides' expressions : " we refer to Stein, v. 66.

Page 172, l. 32. The "telling fragment" of Anaxagoras was brought to light by Diels (in *Hermes*, xiii. 4) from a scholion to Gregory of Nazianzus, Migne, *Patrol. Gr.*, xxxvi. 901.

Page 175, l. 23. "A distinguished physiologist : " Du Bois-Reymond, in the *Sitzungsberichte der kgl. preuss. Akademie der Wissensch.*, " Begrüssung des Herrn Landolt," Febr. 1882.

Page 177, l. 10. "The existence of a vacuum." It is true that the word "vacuum" (κενεόν) has only found its way into the text (Stein, v. 84) by means of a false conjecture. But the conception on its own account plays an important part in Parmenides. At one time it appears as the contrary of ἔμπλεον, " the full ; " at another, the vacuum (the empty or non-ens) has to be supplied in thought as the subject of the verb ἀποτμήξει, which has been persecuted with vain emendations, in Stein, vv. 38–40, which are to be separated from what precedes and in no wise belong to the proem : οὐ γὰρ ἀποτμήξει τὸ πέλον τοῦ ἐόντος ἔχεσθαι οὔτε σκιδνάμενον πάντη πάντως κατὰ κόσμον οὔτε συνιστάμενον.

Page 177, l. 20. "In the circle of the Pythagoreans." Cf. what Natorp, following Bäumker, has said on this point, *Philosoph. Monats-hefte*, xxvii. 476. This is evident, moreover, from Aristotle, *Phys.*, iv. 6 (213 B 22), where, however, the vacuum appears in another applica-tion. Perhaps it would actually be more appropriate not to inquire about the authors of this doctrine at all, but rather of the opposite one. For, after all, the old mythical view was that originally a vacuum had stretched from the highest height to the lowest depth, the gap now yawning between heaven and earth being the remains thereof. And in common consciousness even the air too, before its pressure and resistance had been ascertained by experiments such as those of Anaxagoras, was regarded as a vacuum, and not as a "something" (cf. Aristotle, *Phys.* iv. 6, 213 A 25). It was through these and similar attempts that the problem of motion first entered the world. It is easy enough indeed to try to disguise the physical problem with a metaphysical cloak, and to discover its essence in the phrase, "the full cannot take in anything" (see p. 350). Such an apory, however, would never have occurred to any one, as long as that medium in which movements are executed almost without any resistance was not recognized as full, or at least as not essentially different from full.

Page 180, l. 10. Aristotle, *Metaphys.*, i. 5, 986 B 31.

Page 181, l. 35. "Orphic influences" have been traced by O. Kern, *De Orphei . . . Theogoniis*, 52, and in the *Archiv*, iii. 173.

Page 182, l. 24. On the world as depicted by Parmenides, cf. H. Berger, *Geschichte der wissenschaftl. Erkunde*, etc., ii. 31 *ff*.

BOOK II.—CHAPTER III.

Melissus. Personal details about him in Laert. Diog., ix. ch. 4. Apollodorus there puts his *floruit* in the 84th Olympiad. It is obvious and has been generally acknowledged that the year Ol. 84, 4 = 441 B.C. is intended, in which Melissus won the naval battle mentioned in the text. Here for once we can lay actual hands on Apollodorus' method of procedure in connecting his personal facts with some historical event whose date he could fix with certainty, while otherwise we are frequently obliged merely to presume it. Remains of Melissus' treatise, "On Nature or Ens," are preserved for us almost solely by Simplicius in his commentaries on Aristotle's *Physics* and *De Cælo*, which we now possess in the greatly improved editions of Diels and Heiberg. Cf. further A. Pabst in his dissertation *De Melissi Samii Fragmentis*, Bonn, 1889. According to this investigation, it can now be accounted as at least highly probable that only a portion of the fragments really deserve that name, while in others the ideas of Melissus are not rendered with literal fidelity.

Page 184, l. 17. Aristotle. He calls Melissus "crude" ($\phi o \rho \tau \iota \kappa \delta s$), *Phys.*, i. 3; Melissus and Xenophanes together "somewhat clumsy" ($\mu \iota \kappa \rho \delta \nu$ ἀγροικότεροι), *Metaphys.*, i. 5.

Page 184, l. 27. "A condition of undisturbed bliss." "Has any one ever reflected on what kinds of states of consciousness Melissus may have attributed to his bare Being? For he did attribute consciousness to it, since he declares it exempt from pain and grief. By this he evidently aims at endowing it with pure undisturbed bliss." These words were written by the author of this work in January, 1880, and he was soon enabled to add the remark, "This has at last been acknowledged by Fr. Kern in his valuable essay, valuable likewise for its appreciation of Parmenides: 'Zur Würdigung des Melissos von Samos,' in the *Festschrift des Stettiner Stadtgymn. zur Begrüssung der* 35. *Versammlung deutscher Philologen*, etc., Stettin, 1880." If

Melissus was satisfied with these negative designations, and forbore to do honour to his blissful universal Being as such, considerations of prudence may have intervened. The man who occupied a prominent position in the public life of his native country was more strongly bound than other philosophers to respect the religious susceptibility of his fellow-citizens. That is plainly why he preferred not to attribute directly to his "All-One" the bliss of the popular divinities (μάκαρες θεοί), but only to hint at it indirectly.

Page 186, l. 10. Aristotle: *Sophist. Elench.*, 5, 167 B 13; and *Phys.*, i. 3, 186 A 10.

Page 191, l. 33. Zeno of Elea: cf. Laert. Diog., ix. ch.'5. Laertius, *i.e.* Apollodorus, here fixes his *floruit* in the 79th Olympiad, and Plato (cf. *supra*, note on p. 166, l. 31) calls him 25 years younger than Parmenides, whose *floruit* is fixed in the 69th Olympiad : both these accounts may very well rest on truth. For according to what we have remarked above in our note on Melissus, and previously, too, anent the procedure of Apollodorus, there is no reason at all to assume that the same, or even approximately the same, differences of age must correspond with those of the *floruit*—the differences at the zenith.

We shall have to speak later on of Zeno's critical discussion of the doctrine of Empedocles (ἐξήγησις Ἐμπεδοκλέους in Suidas, *s.v.* Ζήνων). It has often been doubted, although without any reason, if Zeno, like his master Parmenides, also propounded doctrines of nature-philosophy. The title of a treatise "On Nature " (Suidas, *ibid.*) is in favour of his having done so, and even more so are the tenets attributed to him in *Laert. Diog.*, ix. 29.

The chief sources from which we gather our knowledge of his arguments are : Aristotle, *Phys.*, iv. 1 ; iv. 3 ; vi. 2 ; and especially vi. 9 ; and the commentaries on those passages in Simplicius.

Page 192, l. 10. Plato: in the dialogue *Parmenides*, 128 D. He describes the astounding impression made by his speeches in *Phædrus*, 261 D.

Page 192, l. 24. Pierre Bayle: in his *Dictionnaire historique et critique*, iv. 536, edition of 1730.

Page 192, l. 25. "A grain of millet : " hinted at by Aristotle, *Phys.*, vii. 5, amplified by Simplicius in his note in the form of a dialogue between Zeno and Protagoras.

Page 196, l. 14. On what follows, cf. Friedrich Überweg, *System der Logik*, 409, ed. 3.

Page 196, l. 26. J. S. Mill, *Examination of Sir William Hamilton's Philosophy*, 533, ed. 3, sees in this confusion of infinite divisibility and infinite magnitude the nucleus of the apory. This was precisely the judgment of Aristotle ; cf. *Phys.*, vi. 2, 233 A 21 *ff.*

Page 201. Interesting side-lights on the so-called sophisms of the Eristics, and, among them, on Zeno's "Achilles and the tortoise," are furnished by the subtle intellect of the Chinese. Cf. H. A. Giles,

Chuang Tzu, 453, London, 1889 : " If you take a stick a foot long and every day cut it in half, you will never come to the end of it."
Page 204, l. 14. Plato : in *Parmenides*, 128 C.

BOOK II.—CHAPTER IV.

Page 208. Anaxagoras : cf. chiefly *Anaxagoræ Clazomenii Fragmenta*, coll. Ed. Schaubach, Leipsic, 1827 ; or W. Schorn, *Anaxagoræ Claz. et Diogenis Apolloniatæ Fragmenta*, Bonn, 1829. The almost exclusive quarry for the fragments is the commentary of Simplicius on the *Physics* of Aristotle. A little phrase in Simplicius (on Aristotle, *De Cælo*, 608, 26 Heiberg), has been overlooked by the collectors of the fragments ; another brilliant remark, which has been missed by the collectors, is in Plutarch, *Moral.*, 98 F (*De Fortuna*, c. 3). On the circumstances of his life, see Laert. Diog., ii. ch. 3. Apollodorus places his birth in the 70th Olympiad (500–497 B.C.), his death in the first year of the 88th (428 B.C.). It is reported by Laert. Diog. as an unauthenticated fact (λέγεται), that he was born in 500 B.C., and thus reached the age of seventy-two. On his relations with Pericles, cf. Plato, *Phædr.*, 270 A, and Plutarch, *Life of Pericles*, especially c. 32. The mental composure with which he bore the loss of his only son was admired by all antiquity, cp. Diels, *Seneca und Lucan*, from the *Berl. Akademie-Abhandlungen*, 1885, p. 8 n. In Laert. Diog., ii. 11, we have certainly to complete the reading thus : ἐπὶ ἄρχοντος Λυσ [ιστράτου] = 467 B.C. That his (p. 209, l. 22) was the first book illustrated with diagrams (except geometrical writings destined for a special professional public ?) has recently been correctly inferred by Kothe, in *Fleckeisens Jahrbucher*, 1886, pp. 769, *ff.*, from Clement of Alexandria, *Strom.* i. 364 Pott., and Laert. Diog., *loc. cit.*

Page 212, l. 35. My explanation of Anaxagoras' utterance about the colour of snow, which at first sight seems so hazardous, is founded on the glaring contrast which otherwise would exist between the basis of his whole theory of matter (the unshakable belief in the qualitative truth of sense-perceptions) and the assertion that we are in this case deceived by sight. My exposition also tallies as exactly as possible with the text of Cicero's statement, which earlier interpreters thoroughly misapprehended : " sed sibi quia sciret aquam nigram esse, unde illa concreta esset, *albam ipsam esse ne videri quidem*" (*Acad. Quæst.* iv. 31).

Page 213, § 2. About the cosmogony of Anaxagoras, cf. the instructive discussion by W. Dilthey, *Einleitung in die Geisteswissenschaft*, i. 200 *ff.* I am at one with Zeller (i. 1002 n., ed. 5), however, in being unable to agree with him in assuming that Anaxagoras imagined the structure of the world to be shaped like a cone. He may probably be credited with the idea that the celestial globe, formed as it had been by rotation (περιχώρησις), would increase in circumference in proportion to the ever larger size of the masses of matter that become involved in the rotatory movement. It is useful, perhaps, to remind the reader that Anaxagoras at any rate seems to know nothing of a material celestial globe, or of such a firmament of the fixed stars. Even where it might most be expected (*e.g.* Fragm. 8, Schaub.) there is no hint of such an image.

Pages 215, 216. The constantly renewed attempts to prove the purely spiritual nature of the Nous of Anaxagoras are characterized partly by their contradiction with the unequivocal assertions of the sage of Clazomenæ himself, partly by the subtle artifices to which their defenders feel compelled to resort. Thus the words of Anaxagoras, λεπτότατον πάντων χρημάτων, are interpreted as "the most sagacious" instead of "the finest of all things ;" or the Aristotelian ἀπλοῦν ("simple ") is taken as something other than a reproduction of the predicate ἀμιγές ("unmixed "). The method here followed consists essentially in setting statements of Aristotle, more or less arbitrarily interpreted, against the clear text of the Anaxagorean utterances. Sound arguments against the entire immateriality of the Nous are to be found in Natorp, *Philos. Monatshefte*, xxvii. 477. The expression "thought-element" (p. 215, l. 29) is from Windelband in Iwan Müller's *Handbuch der klass. Altertumswissenschaft*, v. 1, 165.

Page 216, l. 34. The complaints about the insufficient use of the Nous by its inventor are to be found in Plato, *Phædo*, 97, c. *ff.* and in Aristotle, *Metaphys.*, i. 3, 985 B 17.

Page 220, l. 3. "A difficulty which has still to be realized and explained :" cf. Aristotle, *De Cælo*, ii. 13. It was mentioned, as I now discover, but not, in my opinion, solved, by Brieger, *Die Urbewegung der Atome*, etc. (Gymasial-Programm, Halle, 1884), pp. 21 *f.*

That Anaxagoras attributed a flat shape to the earth (l. 6) is proved by the evidence collected in Schaubach, pp. 174, 175. Simplicius is alone in alluding to a tambourine- or cylinder-shape by the word τυμπανοειδής (on Aristotle, *De Cælo*, ii. 13, p. 520, 28 *ff.*, Heiberg). He, however, weakens his own testimony by mentioning Anaximenes as well as Anaxagoras, for it is quite certain that, with respect to the shape of the earth, Anaximenes agreed, not with Anaximander, but with Thales. It is therefore misleading, to say the least, when Zeller, Überweg, and others speak of a "flat cylinder."

Pages 220-222. On the astronomical and meteorological doctrines of the philosopher, cf. Doxogr. Gr. 137, 138.

Page 221, l. 5. On Anaxagoras' explanation of the clusters of stars in the Milky Way, cf. Tannery, *Pour l'Histoire de la science hellène*, 279. On the problem itself, cf. amongst others, Wundt, *Essays*, 79 *ff.*

Page 223, l. 20. Schleiermacher set the fashion of denying the term Homœomeries to Anaxagoras, and of regarding it as an innovation of Aristotle's. The unequivocal evidence of antiquity against this assumption has been collected by Schaubach, p. 89. That the conjecture is untenable is shown as clearly as daylight from the fact that Epicurus, and after him Lucretius, who had no reason whatever for using the Aristotelian terminology, employ the word. Cf. Munro's commentary on Lucretius, i. 834; and the present writer, in the *Zeitschrift für die Östreichischen Gymnasien*, xviii. 212.

Page 225, l. 18. Xenophon's disdainful judgment is from *Memorab.*, iv. 7.

BOOK II.—CHAPTER V.

Page 227, § 1. Empedocles: cf. H. Stein, *Empedoclis Agrigentini Fragmenta*, Bonn, 1852; Diels, "Studia Empedoclea," in *Hermes*, xv. A new fragment of a verse and a half is given by Knatz, in *Schedæ philol.*, Bonn, 1891; Doxogr. Gr. *passim*. He is further treated by Laert. Diog., viii. ch. 2. There is an excellent investigation of the sources by J. Bidez, *La Biographie d'Empédocle*, Ghent, 1894.

The remarks on Girgenti here and in the following pages are based on the author's personal impressions of travel; still, cp. too Renan's essay, "Vingt jours en Sicile," in his *Mélanges de voyages et d'histoire*, 103, *ff*. For the chronology, we have at our disposal in this instance a series of verses from the chronicle of Apollodorus in Laert. Diog., *loc. cit.* The vexed statement in Aristotle, *Metaphys.*, i. 3, that Anaxagoras was older than Empedocles in years, but younger in achievements, neither contains any reference to the dates of the publication of their works, nor yet any judgment as to their value. It merely serves to account for the inverted chronological order which Aristotle favoured on expository grounds. He treated Empedocles before Anaxagoras, because the four elements of Empedocles were far more akin to the material Monism of the older nature-philosophers than were the infinitely numerous primary substances of Anaxagoras. Cf. the little sentence just before: Ἐμπεδοκλῆς δὲ τὰ τέτταρα πρὸς τοῖς εἰρημένοις γῆν προστιθεὶς τέταρτον.

Page 229, l. 10. On the draining of Selinus, and "On the Boring of a Mountain in Acragas by Empedocles," cf. the essay with that title in the *feuilleton* of the *Allgemeine Zeitung*, Augsburg, November 15, 1881. Bidez, *loc. cit.*, p. 34, preceded by Diels, has made it very probable that the story of a woman wakened from a death-like trance (l. 15) is taken from the treatise Περὶ τῆς ἄπνου by Heraclides of Pontus, and based on a legend already current at that time.

Page 230, ll. 20 *ff*. Tannery, *op. cit.*, 319, was probably the first to suggest the view of a connection between Empedocles' medical studies and his anti-monistic theory of matter.

Page 231, l. 33. The four elements are met with in the popular physics, not only of the Greeks, but likewise of the Hindoos; cf. Kern, *Buddhismus*, German edition by H. Jacobi, i. 438; cf. too the Persian theory of the elements in the Vendîdad, translated by

J. Darmesteter, in the *Sacred Books of the East,* iv. 187. The following passage in Kopp's *Entwicklung der Chemie in der neueren Zeit,* p. 110, shows at how late a date this primeval doctrine disappeared: " If, in the time preceding the rise of Lavoisier's system, a question were asked . . . about the elements of bodies, the answer was that earth, water, air, and fire were still, as ever, to be regarded as elements, or at any rate that most people believed in these elements."

Page 233, l. 10. For the comparison of the four elements with the primary colours, cp. Galen, *Commentary on Hippocrates " De Natura Hominis "* (xv. 32, Kühn).

Page 235, l. 2. The dependence of Empedocles on Alcmæon was proved by Diels, *Gorgias und Empedokles,* p. 11.

Page 238, ll. 11 *ff.* The experiment here alluded to (Stein, vv. 294 *ff.,* presupposes the existence of spaces which are at least temporarily empty. Against this it is strange that both Aristotle (*De Cælo,* iv. 2) and Theophrastus (*De Sensibus,* in Doxogr. Gr., 503, 9–12) should declare that Empedocles denied the existence of empty space. True, Theophrastus is careful to add that Empedocles herein was inconsistent, and much the same remark is hinted by Aristotle (*De Generat. et Corrupt.,* i. 8). Here we are led to conjecture that a misunderstanding blocks the way. The verses alleged to contain the denial of empty space are still preserved (Stein, 91 *ff.*), but they seem susceptible of another interpretation. I should freely reproduce their sense as follows : " Nowhere can be said, *Here the All is not;* nowhere, *Here is something other than the All.*" In my opinion the genitive τοῦ παντός must be made to depend on κενεόν (cf. Stein, 111, τούτων . . . κεινώσεται). If κενεόν were used here absolutely, in the sense of "empty space," what would the neighbouring οὐδὲ περισσόν be doing beside it ? Least of all can the verse be quoted to confute the assumption of permanently empty, or even of temporarily emptied, interstices.

It is curious that Aristotle (*loc. cit.* and *Physics,* iv. 6) denies the vacuum-conception to Anaxagoras likewise, remarking that his experiment with the inflated bag (see p. 213, l. 32), as well as the air-pressure experiment—which must have been that of Empedocles mentioned above—do not prove that there is no empty space, but that " air is something." Here, again, we may be permitted to conjecture that Aristotle somewhat misunderstood the object of those old inquirers. Anaxagoras had made such ample use of the Invisible, that he cannot have escaped the reproach of doing business with Non-entities. He then proved to the sceptics that there are invisible bodies, and that where there seems to be Nothing, Something in truth is present. An emptied bag seems at first to contain nothing. But inflate it—this is precisely the experiment of Anaxagoras alluded to by Aristotle—bind up its opening, tie it and pull it fast, and the resistance which it offers to all attempts at compression will very soon teach us that the Invisible inside it is a material Something. We take the liberty of believing that Anaxagoras intended to prove exactly what he actually did prove. As the theory of an empty space did not originate with Leucippus, so it by no means follows from what has been said that Empedocles must have been influenced by him. This supposition, reiterated of late, seems baseless to me, not merely because Aristotle knew nothing of such a connection (cf. *De Generat. et Corrupt.*, i. 8, especially 324 B, 32 *ff.* and 325 B, 36 *ff.*), but chiefly because the doctrines of Empedocles at many points can very readily be viewed as steps preliminary to Atomism, whereas, if such influence had really been exerted, they would be far more difficult to understand as steps backward or downward from a height already attained.

Page 241, § 5. On the cosmology of Empedocles, cf. Karsten, *Empedoclis Reliquiæ*, 416 *ff.*; Gruppe, *Kosmische Systeme der Griechen*, 98–100; Tannery, *Pour l'histoire*, etc., 316 *ff.*; Doxogr. Gr., *passim.*

Page 242, l. 12. On this experiment with goblets, and the inferences drawn from it, cf. Aristotle, *De Cœlo*, ii. 13. The report, meagre enough in all truth, was utterly misunderstood by Gruppe, *op. cit.*, 99.

Page 243, § 6. "Modes for the beginnings of organic being :" Here the experts are frequently at variance, and full certainty seems hardly attainable. Against Dümmler's view of the case (*Akademika*, 218 *ff.*), which I have adopted in the text, objections have been raised by Zeller, i. 795, 796, ed. 5, which I cannot regard as decisive. Zeller's opinion is that Empedocles was not thinking of a progressive transformation of organic beings, but that they "simply disappear from the scene, and for those which supersede them a fresh creation from the beginning is required." Against this view it is to be urged that of the four modes of origin described by Ætius, probably according to Theophrastus (Doxogr., 430, 431), the first and second at any rate do not stand in this relation. For the "grotesque" (εἰδωλοφανεῖς) formations of the second "genesis" are evidently supposed to have been produced by the concretion of the non-combined members of the first (cf. ἀσυμφυέσι . . . τοῖς μορίοις with συμφυομένων τῶν μερῶν). And the grotesqueness of the organisms of the second series obviously arises from the union of the dissimilar parti-formations of the first genesis (cf. *Empedoclis Fragmenta*, 244–261, Stein). Further, the fourth genesis certainly belongs to the first generated, not to the first generating, beings. Its effect is : fourthly, animal beings arose by sexual generation, *not* animal beings arose which engendered others sexually. This hardly requires demonstration. I do not insist on the point, which might, perhaps, be called captious, that the numeration would otherwise be incomplete ; for then those beings called into existence by generation would form a fifth genesis. But the cause therein assigned (τοῖς δὲ . . . ἐμποιησάσης, Doxogr., 431) can only be interpreted as referring to a modification in this instance of already existing beings, which was the actual condition of the generation.

Thus the relation presumed by Zeller does not exist between the third and the fourth geneses either. The third genesis alone is exceptional in its relation to the second, but then it falls out of line also in every other respect as well. Be it noted, however, the text is corrupt. The decisive word ὀλοφυῶν rests on conjecture. This conjecture, it is true, finds support in Empedocles, v. 265—but what a support it is! To all appearance (even if we do not set store by the word πρῶτα), there is no question there of a genesis ensuing on other modes of generation, nor yet of a mode of generation of animal beings in general, but solely of human beings. We must give Zeller right in maintaining that Dümmler's attempt to assign this anthropogony to another world-period than the rest of the zoogonies does not agree with the excerpt in Ætius. But as this part of the excerpt does not fit in with the context in other respects either, Dümmler's hypothesis is still not yet condemned. I at least do not regard the conjecture as too bold, that Ætius was bearing in mind that versified description of the origin of mankind as proceeding directly from the elements ; that he erroneously inserted it in this evolution-series, thereby expelling what we might have expected to find there, viz. those organisms that survived after the elimination of structures unfit for life. He may have regarded as a member of a consecutive series that which belonged properly by its side and which was only outwardly combined with the links of the self-inclusive chain in an enumeration of the various modes of origin. (By the way, in Doxogr., 530 ; 27, 28, should we not read ἐκ τῶν ὁμοστοίχων instead of ἐκ τῶν ὁμοίων ?)

A striking parallel to the doctrine of Empedocles on the origin of animals is to be found, we may add, in Diderot. Cf. John Morley, *Diderot and the Encyclopædists*, I. 111, London, 1878.

Page 244, l. 17. Among the " gleams of inspiration " of Empedocles, we may further count the fact that he was the first to recognize—we do not in the least know on what grounds—that even light requires a certain time for its propagation (Aristotle, *De Sens.*, c. 6, 446 A 25).

Page 245, l. 24. " Hylozoism *in excelsis*." Thus Rohde, too, has lately called the Empedoclean doctrine "a fully developed hylozoistic" one (*Psyche*, ii. 188, ed. 2). I regard as utterly groundless the view maintained by such eminent men as Windelband, for instance, that the introduction of motive forces by Empedocles was an attempt to fulfil the *petita* of Parmenides: "as pure changeless *Ens* the elements cannot move of themselves ; they can only *be moved*" (Iwan Müller's *Handbuch*, v. 1, 161). Is it necessary to remind the reader that Parmenides considered motion in itself as impossible, without respect to whether its impulse came from within or from without? As far as I can see, the Empedoclean assumption of the two non-material Powers was due solely to the impossibility of tracing back to one tendency, immanent in matter as such, and therefore of equable operation, the tendencies dominant in the two alternative world-periods, and thus relieving one another. The dualism of Empedocles is no whit more fundamental than that of Anaxagoras, whose Nous was merely meant to assist the solution of a definite mechanical and teleological problem. As the gravity inherent to matter was kept by Anaxagoras as an independent source of motion side by side with the impulse of Nous, so Empedocles retained the attraction of like by like side by side with the impulses derived from " Friendship" and " Discord." Aristotle himself (*De generat. et corrupt.*, ii. 6) says that Friendship and Discord are the causes of merely "a certain " motion (ἀλλὰ τινὸς κινήσεως ταῦτα αἴτια), thus proving that Empedocles did not regard these two Powers as the only motive forces, and contradicting what might be read into the first chapters of the *Metaphysics*, where Aristotle is just defending a thesis.

Page 246, l. 4. The phrase cited from Aristotle will be found in *De generat. et corrupt.*, ii. 6 (333 B 21). Immediately before occur the words in which the elements are pronounced older than the deity (viz. Σφαῖρος), τὰ φύσει πρότερα τοῦ θεοῦ.

Page 246, l. 35. On Empedocles' " physics of the soul" cf. *Doxogr. Gr.*, 502, besides the Fragments (especially 329–332, Stein).

Page 247, l. 35. In agreement with Dieterich, *Nekyia*, 119, I compute the 30,000 ὧραι of the soul's wandering at 10,000 years, each consisting of three seasons or ὧραι. This reckoning is compatible with the Platonic data on the subject. Rohde, however, regards the Horai as years, and can see in the number 30,000 merely an expression for an unlimited quantity of years (*Psyche*, ii. 179, n. 3, and 187, ed. 2). But Rohde and also Dümmler (*Akademika*, 237) point to the parallelism which will be found noted in our text at p. 252 (§ 8 *init.*).

Page 249, l. 26. Alfred von Kremer, in the *Wiener Sitzungsberichte* (Phil.-hist. Classe 1889, No. iii., *Studien zur vergleichenden Culturgeschichte*), p. 53.

Page 250, l. 4. Pindar, Fragm. 131, Bergk.

Page 250, l. 23. Parmenides : on the partial perception which he ascribed even to corpses, cf. Theophrastus, *De sensibus* (Doxogr., 499). *Ibid.* : καὶ ὅλως δὲ πᾶν τὸ ὂν ἔχειν τινὰ γνῶσιν. His doctrine of the fate of souls is known to us from Simplicius, *Phys.*, p. 39, 19, Diels.

Parallel to the κρᾶσις μελέων of Parmenides (l. 35) is the κρᾶσις καὶ ἁρμονία of Philolaus (cp. Plato, *Phædo*, c. 36, compared with 61 D).

Page 251, l. 35. The " Questions of King Milinda : " *Sacred Books of the East*, xxxv. pp. 40 *ff.* and 71 *ff.*

Page 253, l. 2. The identification of that spiritual divinity with Apollo goes back to Ammonius, who probably read in their original context the verses (347–351, Stein) which he alone communicates in their entirety.

Page 253, l. 26. " The occasional attitude of hostility " to Xenophanes : cf. vv. 146 *ff.*, Stein.

BOOK II.—CHAPTER VI.

Page 255, § 1. For the remains of Hecatæus (l. 22) see C. Müller's *Fragmenta Historicorum Græcorum*, i. 1 *ff.* On his deeds of state-craft (l. 20), cf. Herodotus, v. 36 and 125 *f.*, and Diodorus, x. 25, 2, Dindorf. His adventure at Thebes (p. 257) is related by Herodotus, ii. 143. His rationalizing historical method has been characterized by Grote, *History of Greece*, i. 350 (new edit., 10 vols., 1888), and has lately been illustrated by Diels in *Hermes*, xxii. 411 *ff.* Similar ideas to those in our text will be found in Ed. Meyer, *Philologus*, New Series, ii. 270.

Page 258, § 2. Out of the extensive literature on Herodotus I am glad to give special mention to a little book, as unpretentious as it is valuable, *Sittlich-religiöse Lebensanschauung des Herodotos*, by Hoff-meister, Essen 1832.

Pages 259 to 272. The passages from Herodotus treated in these pages, besides the proem (i. 1 *ff.*), are : ii. 113 *ff.* (Helen) ; ii. 54 *ff.* (Dodona) ; vii. 129 (Poseidon) ; ii. 11 *ff.* (the Nile delta) ; vii. 189 *ff.* (Magi and storm) ; ii. *passim* (identification of Greek and Egyptian divinities) ; ii. 53 (Homer and Hesiod) ; i. 131 (nature-worship of the Persians) ; ii. 45 (forgiveness of the gods and heroes) ; ii. 120 (distrust of the epic poets) ; ii. 3 (equal ignorance about divine things) ; iii. 108 ("Divine Providence") ; vii. 10 and i. 32 (jealousy of the gods) ; vii. 133 *ff.* (Bulis and Sperthies) ; iv. 25 (Polar nights) ; iii. 115 ("Isles of Tin") ; iv. 36 (the rounded earth) ; ii. 33 (Nile and Danube) ; iii. 107 (winged serpents) ; iii. 102 (gold-digging ants) ; iii. 116 (Arimaspians) ; ii. 21 (Ocean and the flood of the Nile). Compare on this subject the author's "Herodoteisc e Studien," ii. 8 [526] *ff.*, in the *Wiener Sitzungsberichte*, 1883.

BOOK III.

Page 273. The first motto is taken from an essay by Berthelot, "La Chimie dans l'antiquité et au moyen-âge," in the *Revue des deux mondes*, September 15, 1893, pp. 316, 317. The second is from Boltz-mann's academic address, "Der zweite Hauptsatz der mechanischen Wärmetheorie," in the *Almanach der Kaiserl. Akademie der Wissen-schaften*, Vienna, 1886, p. 234. The third I once found in a para-phrase of Philodemus in the Herculanean papyri, *Wiener Studien*, ii. 5.

BOOK III.—CHAPTER I.

Pages 277, l. 14. The quotation is from Homer, *Iliad*, xi. 514.

Page 277, l. 27. The Indogermanic "formula of blessing" men-tioned here is due to Ad. Kuhn, *Zeitschrift für vergleich. Sprach-forschung*, xiii. 49. The "Song of a Physician" (l. 31) is translated by R. T. H. Griffith, *The Hymns of the Rigveda* (x. 97), ii. 533, 2nd edit., Benares, 1897. On this and on the oldest Hindoo medicine, cf. Zimmer, *Altindisches Leben*, 375, 394, 396, 398, 399.

Pages 277, 278. The examples of popular medical superstition are taken from the *Pharmacologia* of Dr. Paris, quoted by J. S. Mill, *Logic*, vol. ii. bk. v. ch. 3, § 8 ; Erman, *Life in Ancient Egypt*, trans. by H. M. Tirard, p. 232 ; Fossel, *Volksmedicin und medic. Aberglauben in Steiermark*, quoted in the *Allgemeine Zeitung*, Munich, September 23, 1891.

Page 278, l. 34. On the surgery of savages and their bold operations, cf. Bartels, *Die Medicin der Naturvölker*, Leipsic, 1893, pp. 300 and 305, 306; also Von den Steinen, *Unter den Naturvölkern Centralbrasiliens*, p. 373.

Pages 278, 279. Here, and again at p. 283, l. 28, frequent use has been made of Welcker's essay, "Epoden oder das Besprechen," *Kleineschriften*, iii. 64 *ff.* For what follows (p. 279, l. 12), cf. Odyssey, xix. 457 *f.* and xviii. 383 *ff.* On itinerant Indian physicians (p. 279, l. 19) in the earliest times, cf. Kaegi, *Der Rigveda*, p. 111.

Page 279, l. 33. On Democedes and his adventures, cf. Herodotus, iii. 125 *ff.*

Page 280, l. 9. " The Cypriot physician Onasilus : " cf. the inscription at Edalion, now in Collitz, *Griechische Dialektinschriften*, i. 26 *ff.* In what concerns the date of the inscription I follow O. Hoffman, *Die griechischen Dialekte*, i. 41, in opposition to Larfeld in Bursian's *Jahresberichte*, lxvi. (1892) 36.

Page 280, l. 23. "The Physician's Oath " is in É. Littré, *Œuvres d'Hippocrate*, iv. 628 *ff.* The prohibition of castration (p. 281, l. 2) I discover in the words οὐ τεμέω δὲ οὐδὲ μὴν λιθιῶντας, which can only be translated, " I will not cut, not even those who suffer from stony induration." Now, as a general prohibition of the knife, in an age when " cutting and burning " were the chief features of medical practice, would be an absurdity, no choice is left but to take the word τέμνειν in a special sense, and to understand it as " castrate," as it was used by Hesiod, *Works and Days*, 786 and 790 *f.*, by Pseudo-Phocylides, v. 187, Bergk, and by Lucian, *De Syria Dea*, § 15 (cf. also τομίας = ἐκτομίας). But then we must not take λιθιῶντας to refer to stone in the bladder, but to those stone-like hardenings which can only be relieved by castration ; indeed, the verb in question is employed of indurations of the most diverse kinds. This old conjecture of mine on the meaning of the passage was first communicated and discussed by my medical colleague, Theodor Puschmann, in Virchow-Hirsch's *Jahresberichte über die Fortschritte der gesamten Medicin*, 1883, i. 326, and he has frequently returned to it.

Page 281. "Duties and status:" the passages relating to the conduct and personal appearance of physicians in general are : Littré, iv. 182, 184, 188, 312, 638, 640 ; ix. 14, 204, 210, 254, 258, 266, 268.

Page 282, l. 3.   Aristotle speaks of Hippocrates as a great physician. *Politics*, iv. (vulgo vii.) 4, 1326 A 24.

Page 282, l. 21.   Diels brings the most recent portions of the Hippocratic collection somewhat lower down than I do, ascribing them to the middle of the fourth century B.C.   (This was verbally communicated in his address at the Philological Congress at Cologne, Sept. 1895.)

Page 284, l. 14.   Epidaurus : the description is based on the personal impressions of the author.   The " notes " of cases at Epidaurus mentioned in the text have been collected by Kavvadias, *Les Fouilles d'Epidaure*, i. pp. 23–34.

Page 285, l. 25.   " A recent discovery : " we refer to the London papyrus : *Anonymi Londinensis ex Aristotelis iatricis Menoniis et aliis medicis eclogæ*, ed. H. Diels, Berlin, 1893.   Cf. the discussion of its contents by Diels in *Hermes*, xxviii. (" Über die Excerpte von Menons Iatrika ").   On the writings in the Hippocratic collection which belong to the Cnidian school (p. 286, l. 5), cf. especially Littré, viii. 6 *ff.*, and recently Johannes Ilberg in *Griech. Studien. . . H. Lipsius dargebracht* (Leipsic, 1894), pp. 22 *ff.*

Page 286, § 4.   The books " On Diet " have been practically alone among the Hippocratic writings in attracting the attention of philosophers and philologists.   Cf. Bernays, *Gesammelte Abhandlungen*, i. 1 *ff.* ; Teichmüller, *Neue Studien zur Geschichte der Begriffe*, ii. 3 *ff.* ; Weygoldt, *Jahrbücher für Philologie*, 1882, pp. 161 *ff.* ; and Zeller, *Philosophie der Griechen*, i. 694, ed. 5.   I do not consider Weygoldt and Zeller successful in their attempts to prove the more recent date of this treatise.   The influence on its author of Heraclitus and Empedocles is beyond dispute ; indeed, the way the two systems are employed points to a time when both were still full of life—the doctrine of Empedocles, that is to say, still young, and that of Heraclitus not yet antiquated.   Teichmüller's refutation (pp. 48–50) of the assumption that the writer " On Diet " also made use of Archelaus seems to me wholly pertinent.   If he required any precursor in respect to material dualism, a much more likely name is that of Parmenides, who, according to Aristotle (*Metaphys.*, i. 3), looked on fire, just as our author does, as a kind of moving cause.   Anaxagoras likewise appears to have been not unknown to our author, though by no means to have exercised any permanent influence over him.   In the very chapters whose contents Weygoldt (p. 174) traces to Anaxagoras and Archelaus, there is a sentence which straightly contradicts the fundamental theory of Anaxagoras : ἄτε γὰρ οὔποτε κατὰ τωὑτὸ ἱστάμενα, ἀλλ' αἰεὶ ἀλλοιούμενα ἐπὶ τὰ καὶ ἐπὶ τά (vi. 374, Littr.).   This is directly preceded by a sentence which admittedly reminds one of an Anaxagorean fragment (No. 3 in Schaubach).   It stands there like a notice-board to warn us to regard such similarities as anything rather than decisive proofs.   If the author really had this fragment before his eyes, he only borrowed its verbal form, and not its thought, the term σπέρματα, for instance, being used in an entirely different sense in each. I cannot perceive the reminiscences of Democritus which Zeller finds. His argument founded on the seven vowels is irrelevant, for the distinctive signs for H and Ω, though indeed not officially introduced into Athens till 403 B.C., were yet known to non-official usage long before, not merely in Ionia, where the author almost certainly wrote, but also in Athens itself, where Zeller thinks that he resided.

The passages here adduced from the treatise " On Diet " are to be found in vi. 468, 470 (cf. also 606), and 472.

Page 288, l. 6. The doctrine of organic equilibrium is most distinctly formulated in Littré, vi. 606, and at the end of Book III. p. 636.

Page 288, ll. 14, 17. My statements here about the Cnidians Euryphon and Herodicus are drawn from the above-mentioned Papyrus Londinensis (p. 7), where all the fragments of Euryphon are authenticated in the index.

Page 289. The quotations refer to Book i. " On Diet," vi. 484, 474, 476.

Page 289, l. 39. On the experiment here mentioned, cf. Littré's remark, vi. 527.

Page 290, l. 11. "An exact knowledge " is attributed to the interpreters of dreams, vi. 642 (εἰσὶν, οἳ κρίνουσι περὶ τῶν τοιούτων ἀκριβῆ τέχνην ἔχοντες).

Page 290, l. 22. The little treatise περὶ σαρκῶν (" On Flesh," or " On the Muscles ") is in Littré, vol. vii. There is certainly no need to follow Littré in calling it post-Aristotelian on the ground that the author is aware that two chief veins originate in the heart. The time at which such obvious facts of anatomy became known could not possibly be stated with certainty even in antiquity. The date of the composition of this little book is most clearly illuminated by its eclectic features noticed on p. 293.

Page 293, l. 5. " Aristotle's words : " *Politics*, i. 2 *init.*

Page 294, l. 12. For the treatise " On the Number Seven," see Littré, viii. 634 *ff.* (a better version in ix. 433 *ff.*), and cf. Ilberg, *op. cit.*, and Harder, " Zur pseud-hippokratischen Schrift, περὶ ἑβδομάδων," *Rheinisches Museum*, New Series, xlviii. 433 *ff.*

Page 295, l. 13. The remark at the close of the paragraph on the part played by the number seven in the alchemy of the Arabs is based on an article by Berthelot in the *Revue des deux mondes*, 1 Oct. 1893, p. 557.

Page 297, l. 8. The treatise " On Old Medicine " forms the conclusion of Littré's first volume. Our citations from it (pp. 297 to 299) will be found in Littré, i. 570-606.

Page 300, l. 9. The important 20th chapter of the treatise " On Old Medicine " here treated is in Littré, i. 620-624.

Page 300, l. 31. " The almost verbal resemblance : " *i.e.* of the words in i. 620 to those in vi. 468.

Page 305, l. 21. See Littré, i. 572.

Page 307, ll. 16, 17. Herodotus, ii. 33 ; Euripides, Fragm. 574, Nauck, edit. 2 ; Epicurus, *apud* Laert. Diog., x. 32.

Page 309, l. 16. The quotation is from Bunge's *Lehrbuch der physiol. und pathol. Chemie*, p. 86, edit. 2.

Page 310, l. 28. For the treatise " On the Nature of Women," see Littré, vii. 312. The introduction should be read, and likewise ii. 110–112, the introduction to the *Prognosticon*.

Page 311, l. 3. For the treatise " On Water, Air, and Sites," see Littré, ii. 12 *ff.* For that " On the Sacred Disease " (l. 23), see Littré, vi. 352 *ff.* The maxims (ll. 30 *ff.*) on diseases as at once human and divine, Littré, vi. 394 and 364 and ii. 76.

Page 312. For the polemical expressions quoted, see Littré, vi. 354 to 362.

Pages 314, 315. The quotations made here from Hippocratic physicians will be found in Littré's edition, ii. 302, 328 ; iv. 212, 252, 254. Littré's opinion of the treatise " On the Joints " is taken from iv. 75. I call the author of that work a " pioneer of comparative anatomy " on account of his expressions in Littré, iv. 192 and 198.

BOOK III.—CHAPTER II.

Page 316, l. 10. " A romance in letters : " *Œuvres d'Hippocrate*, ix. 320 *ff.*, especially 350 and 354 L. On Hippocrates' visits to the sick in Abdera, see the undoubtedly genuine third book of the *Epidemics*, iii. 122, 124, 128.

Page 317. On Leucippus, cf. Laert. Diog., ix. ch. 6. It seems most reasonable to consider Miletus as his birthplace (l. 8), because in the two other cases of Elea and Abdera his relations with Zeno and Democritus respectively might be regarded as probable sources of error. The dispute as to his historical reality (l. 19) has most recently been carried on between Rohde (*Verhandlungen der* 34 *Philologen-Versammlung*, 64 *ff.*, and Fleckeisen's *Jahrbücher*, 1881, pp. 741 *ff.*), Natorp (*Rhein. Museum*, xli. 349 *ff.*), and Diels (*Verhandlungen der* 35 *Philol. Versmlg.*, 96 *ff.* ; cf. also *Rheinisches Museum*, xlii. 1 *ff.*). The authority of Aristotle and Theophrastus is decisive against the doubts of Epicurus (*apud* Laert. Diog., x. 13). Though I agree unreservedly with Diels in this view, yet I cannot share his opinion that Theophrastus regarded Leucippus as a disciple of Parmenides. For the words κοινωνήσας Παρμενίδῃ τῆς φιλοσοφίας (Doxogr., 483, 12) need not, *me judice*, express this ; just as little does the verbally identical utterance on the relation of Anaxagoras to the doctrine of Anaximenes—κοινωνήσας τῆς Ἀναξιμένους φιλοσοφίας (Doxogr., 478, 18 *ff.*)—oblige us to credit Theophrastus with the consequent anachronism. Again, it was no other than Theophrastus who attributed (*apud* Laert. Diog., ix. 46) "The Great Order of the Universe" (l. 30) to Leucippus. The only extant fragment, quoted in the text, is from the treatise "On the Mind" (Ætius, in Doxogr., 321 B 10).

Page 318. On Democritus, cf. Laert. Diog., ix. ch. 7. As to the date of his birth, which on autobiographical evidence is placed in the 80th Olympiad (= 460–457 B.C., but probably the first year of the Olympiad is meant), cf. Apollodorus, *apud* Laert. Diog., ix. 41. The fragments are (very imperfectly) collected in Mullach, *Democriti Abderitæ operum fragmenta*, Berlin, 1843. The two fragments quoted (ll. 4 and 30) occur in Clement of Alexandria, *Stromat.*, i. 357 (Potter), and Laert. Diog., ix. 36. The Platonic phrase in l. 26 is from *Republic*, ii. 368 A.

Page 319, ll. 4, 11. The two quotations from Aristotle are from *De Generat. et Corrupt.*, i. 2, 315 A 34 *f.* and 316 A 6 *ff.* Cf. also the significant passages, *ibid.*, i. 8, 324 B 35 *ff.* and 325 A 23 *ff.*

Page 320, l. 3.   Mullach, p. 204.

Page 321, l. 21.   Galilei: the quotation from his treatise, "Il Saggiatore" will be found in the Florentine edition of 1844, iv. 333 *f.*

Page 323, l. 2.   The ensuing account is based on Aristotle, *Metaphys.*, i. 4 *fin.* Diels not unjustly conjectures (in a courteous communication to me on the subject) that the exemplification by N and Z rests on an erroneous tradition, and that those two letters should be replaced by H and ⊔.

Page 328, l. 15.   The quotation is from Fechner's book, *Über die physikalische u. philosophische Atomenlehre*, ed. 2. The whole discussion (pp. 79–81) should be read; it is notable equally by its depth of thought as by its brilliance of expression.

Page 328, l. 28.   John Stuart Mill, *Logic*, vol. i. bk. iii. ch. 6, § 1. For what follows, cf. Lothar Meyer, *Die modernen Theorien der Chemie*, ed. 4, *passim, e.g.* 253, 273, 183.

Page 329, l. 25.   Cournot, *Traité de l'enchaînement des idées fondamentales dans les sciences et dans l'histoire*, i. 245. Descartes (l. 35) writes to Mersenne: "J'admire ceux qui disent que ce que j'ai écrit ne sont que centones Democriti," etc., *Œuvres*, viii. 328, ed. Cousin. Here the great Robert Boyle (1627–1691) ought likewise to be remembered, who said that "possibly there was at the bottom of all bodies one and the same primeval matter, extended, divisible, and impenetrable, and that the differences we discern in them were only the consequence of the unequal size, shape, rest, or movement, and of the respective position of the atoms" (Kopp, *Geschichte der Chemie*, ii. 308).

Page 331, ll. 4, 5.   What is here said about muscarine and neurine I have taken from Bunge, *Lehrbuch der physiol. u. patholog. Chemie*, 80, ed. 2.

Page 332, l. 13. For Democritus' explanation of specific gravity, cf. Mullach, p. 215. The witness is Theophrastus, *De Sensibus*, to whom we are also indebted for the rest of our information on Democritus' theory of the senses (Doxogr. Gr., 516 *ff.*).

Page 333, l. 33. The reference is to *Versuch über die gereizte Nerven- und Muskelfaser* (Berlin, 1797), i. 429. Humboldt, however, does not express these ideas as his own. The most eminent modern exponent of this theory is probably Nic. Lemery, from whose *Cours de Chymie* (1675) Kopp, in his *Geschichte der Chemie*, iii. 84, quotes the following passage : ". . . je ne crois pas qu'on me conteste que l'acide n'ait des pointes . . . ; il ne faut que le gouter pour tomber dans ce sentiment, car il fait des picottements sur la langue," etc.

Page 335, l. 3. Descartes and Huyghens : cf. Lasswitz, *Geschichte der Atomistik*, ii. 91 ; and Huyghens, *Discours de la cause de la pesanteur*, in the appendix to the *Traité de la lumière*, p. 102, Leipsic edition : " des corps faits d'un amas de petites parties *accrochées* ensemble." But similar ideas are also to be found in Lemery (1645– 1715) according to Kopp, *op. cit.*, ii. 308. Descartes, according to Huyghens' terse formulation of his point of view (*op. cit.*, 93), refers everything back to principles, "tels que sont ceux qui dépendent des corps considérez sans qualitez et de leurs mouvements." For what follows (l. 10) cf. L. Meyer, *op. cit.*, 223: " The term 'saturation' is merely a word in the room of an idea, in the room of a clear conception." Cf., too, *ibid.*, p. 387. Pascal's dictum (l. 18) will be found in his *Pensées*, ii. 17 (ii. 249 of the Paris edition, 1823) : " Il faut dire en gros : cela se fait par figure et mouvement, car cela est vrai. Mais de dire quels, et composer la machine, cela est ridicule ; car cela est inutile et incertain et pénible."

Pages 335, 336. The chief evidence for the Democritean cosmogony will be found in Laert. Diog., ix. 31 ; Hippolytus, i. 10 ; Democritus, Fragm. 2 (*Phys.*), p. 207, and Fragm. 6, p. 208, Mullach ; cf. Plato, *Tim.*, 52 E. The whole subject has recently been admirably treated by Brieger, *Die Urbewegung der Atome und die Weltentstehung bei Leukipp und Demokrit* (Gymnasial-Programm, Halle, 1884), and by Hugo Carl Liepmann, *Die Mechanik der leucipp-democrit'schen Atome* (The Doctorate Dissertation, Berlin, 1885).

Page 337, l. 38. "A passage from Aristotle :" *De Cœlo*, ii. 13, where the doctrine of the "vortex" is attributed to "all," *i.e.* as the context shows, to all the older nature-philosophers and originators of cosmogonies (295 A 9 *ff.*). Teichmüller, *Studien zur Geschichte der Begriffe*, p. 83, Berlin, 1874, first noted and demonstrated that Anaximander is almost certainly included amongst these.

Page 339, l. 27. The statements in the text on the actual effect of whirlwinds, and especially of the " Etesiai," or summer north winds in Greece, have been approved by my colleague, Professor Hann, and are partly based on his courteous and instructive communications.

Page 340, l. 5. Aristotle's remarks on this subject are to be found in *De Cœlo*, iii. 2 (300 B 8), and *Metaphys.*, i. 4 (985 B 20).

Page 343, l. 6. "Riddles of the universe:" cf. *Über die Grenzen des Naturerkennens. Die sieben Welträtsel.* Two discourses by Emil du Bois-Reymond, ed. 3, Leipsic, 1891, p. 83.

Page 344, ll. 13–16. A number of Bacon's utterances on this subject are collected in Grote's *Plato*, i. 92 *f.*

Cf. further L. Stein, *Leibniz und Spinoza*, 66 *f.*

Tyndall's phrase is taken from his *Fragments of Science*, 5th ed., 1876, p. 355.

Page 345, l. 5. Theophrastus: Doxogr., 483, 12 *ff.*

Page 348, l. 3. Cf. the reference to Parmenides on p. 177.

Page 349, l. 27. Galilei: cp. *op. cit.*, p. 336: "Ma che ne' corpi esterni, per eccitare in noi i sapori, gli odori e i suoni, si richiegga altro che grandezze, figure, moltitudini e movimenti tardi o veloci, io non lo credo." Similarly, Huyghens, *op. cit.*, 96: "En ne supposant dans la nature que des corps qui soient faits d'une mesme matière, *dans lesquels on ne considère aucune qualité* ni aucune inclination à s'approcher les uns des autres, *mais seulement des differentes grandeurs, figures et mouvements*——" A clear allusion, quoted by Lasswitz, *op. cit.*, ii. 49, shows us that Galilei was well acquainted with the doctrines of Democritus, and Löwenheim, *Der Einfluss Demokrits auf Galilei* (*Archiv*, vii. 230 *ff.*), has recently proved that Galilei applied himself closely to the theories of Democritus.

As to Huyghens, cf. the expression of his astonishment (*op. cit.*, 93) that not only the other philosophers but even Democritus omitted to explain gravity: "On peut le pardonner à ceux qui se contentoient de pareilles solutions en bien de rencontres ; mais non pas si bien à Démocrite et à ceux de sa Secte, qui aiant entrepris de rendre raison de tout par des Atomes en ont excepté la seule Pesanteur."

Pages 350, 351. The evidence for the existence of the vacuum is given in Aristotle, *Physics*, iv. 6 (213 B 5 *ff.*).

Page 351, l. 36. "From Leucippus downwards :" cp. Theophrastus (Doxogr. Gr., 483, 17 *f.*). The sentence, καὶ τῶν ἐν αὐτοῖς σχημάτων ἄπειρον τὸ πλῆθος διὰ τὸ μηδὲν μᾶλλον τοιοῦτον ἢ τοιοῦτον εἶναι, I regard as parenthetical, and I supply in thought τὸ σχῆμα αὐτῶν as the subject to τοιοῦτον. It has become customary to identify this utterance of Leucippus with the Democritean statement on the secondary qualities, οὐ μᾶλλον τοῖον ἢ τοῖον (in Plutarch, *Adv. Colot.*, 4, 1, and Sextus Emp., *Pyrrh. Hyp.*, i. 213 = 48, 13 *ff.*, Bekker). Yet, pardonable though this confusion may be, the context in which the two sentences appear cannot leave us in any doubt as to the difference between them.

There would be no end to the meanings we should have to read into Theophrastus' account in order to make it even half-comprehensible on that supposition. How can that phrase of Democritus, which, as Zeller, too, is ready to admit (i. 920, n. 2, ed. 5), relates " merely to the secondary sensible qualities," help to prove the infinite number of the shapes of the atoms ? The number of subjective variations, of which the typical example, also quoted by Sextus (*ibid.*), is the honey that tastes bitter to a jaundiced man, may perhaps amount to three, four, or even ten ; but, even if there were a hundred or a thousand such variations, this would have nothing to do with the infinite number of the shapes of the atoms. And, what is yet more significant, the existence of this infinite number is one thing : their combination in each single object of sense is a different thing altogether. And how intolerably violent it would be to have to think forward to combination from existence, which is solely the subject in Theophrastus, and which, according to the whole context, can solely be his subject ! Above all, Theophrastus himself (Doxogr., 518, 20 *f.*) speaks merely of the combination of *many* shapes of atoms, and by no means of infinitely many, in a single sensible object. Here, moreover, a special case is in question, and not a general rule. (The passage, by the way, stands in need of critical aid, and may have originally read thus : ἀλλ' ἐν ἑκάστῳ [λείῳ] πολλὰ εἶναι [καὶ τραχέα] καὶ τὸν αὐτον [χυλὸν μετ]έχειν λείου καὶ τραχέος, κ.τ ἑ.)

Page 354, ll. 18–21. The quotations are from Ernst Mach, *Die Principien der Mechanik*, etc. (Internationale wissenschaftliche Bibliothek), 463 *f.*

Page 355, l. 19. On the theological doctrines of Democritus, cf. chiefly Sextus Emp., *Adv. Math.*, ix. 1, p. 394, 28 *ff.*, and 396, 5 *ff.*, Bekker ; also Tertullian, *Ad Nationes*, ii. 2 (connected by Zeller— justly, of course—with Eustathius on Odyssey, xii. 63). A notable feature is his rationalistic explanation of the practice of divination from entrails (Cicero, *De Divinatione*, ii. 13, 30), which has been recently declared to be the one correct explanation by Ihering, *Vorgeschichte der Indoeuropäer*, 448. Though certainly far from being true, yet this elucidatory attempt is precisely characteristic of Democritus. Elsewhere, too, he devotes himself to finding a basis of reality in religious customs and beliefs ; he considered divine apparitions and significant visions of sleep as alike something more than fictions, just as he discerned in the gods of popular belief indications of natural factors and even of moral forces, disfigured, indeed, and misinterpreted by the caprice of poets (cf. Clement of Alexandria, *Protrept.*, ch. vi. p. 59, Potter ; cf., too, the same author's *Stromat.*, v. 14, 709, Potter). To restore the corrupt words consult also Eusebius, *Præp. Evang.*, xiii. 13, § 27, iii. 322, Gaisford ; Laert. Diog., ix. 46. Diels discusses " Demokrits Dämonenglauben" in *Archiv*, vii. 154–157.

Page 356, l. 17. Theophrastus states and criticizes Democritus' theory of cognition in Doxogr., 516 *ff.* On the soul-atoms of Leucippus and Democritus, and the part played by respiration, cf. Aristotle, *De Anima,* i. 2, 403 B, 31 *ff.*

Page 356, l. 36. Parmenides and Empedocles : cf. Doxogr., 390, 19 *ff.* It is important to draw attention to the continuance of the doctrine of universal animation chiefly because most writers assume far too early a date for the disappearance of the hylozoistic mode of thought, fixing it generally as early as Anaxagoras and Empedocles.

Pages 358, 359. These "sighs" are registered by Sext. Emp., *Adv. Math.,* vii. 135 *ff.,* p. 220 *f.,* Bekker ; cf., too, Laert. Diog. ix. 72.

Page 359, l. 22. Cf. above, the note on p. 290, l. 11.

Page 361, l. 12. The maxims about genuine and obscure knowledge are also enumerated by Sextus Emp., *Adv. Math.,* vii. 138 *f.,* p. 121, Bekker.

Page 363, l. 15. Aristotle's critical remarks are contained in *Phys.,* viii. 252 A, B. With this cf. some remarks of Theophrastus on Plato, which for once sound wholly un-Aristotelian, and which Proclus quotes in his commentary on the *Timæus,* p. 176 of the Basle edition (also in Doxogr., 485, 13 *ff.*).

Page 364, l. 6. Aristotle's accusation will be found in *Metaphys.,* i. 4, *fin.* For what follows, cf. Dühring, *Kritische Geschichte der allgemeinen Principien der Mechanik,* 109–112. For "the reproach of Aristotle" (l. 27), cp. *Phys.,* ii. 4, 196 A, 24 *ff.* ; and *De generat. animal.,* v. 789, B 2.

Page 366, l. 20. "In listening to Democritus," etc.: cp., chiefly, Hippolytus, i. 13, which Löwenheim (*Archiv,* vii. 246) has turned to good use with the remark that Democritus had "already deposed in principle the geocentric point of view."

Page 367, l. 27. Metrodorus of Chios : *apud* Stobæum, *Eclogæ,* i. 496 (i. p. 199, i., Wachsmuth).

Pages 367, 368. On the ethical fragments of Democritus, cf. Lortzing's eponymous *Berliner Gymnasial-Programm,* 1873 ; Hirzel, *Demokrits Schrift* περὶ εὐθυμίης (Hermes, xiv. 354 *ff.*) ; Natorp, *Die Ethika des Demokritos,* 1893 (reviewed by Diels in the *Deutsche Litteratur-Zeitung,* 1893, No. 41). Scanty but evidently genuine information on the ethics of Democritus is given by Laert. Diog., ix. 45. The terms "cheerfulness," "well-being," and "composure" represent respectively the Democritean expressions εὐθυμίη, εὐεστώ, and ἀθαμβίη.

Page 368, l. 37. The "brilliant fragment" mentioned in the text, and preserved in Stobæus, *Florilegium,* 46, 48, has been conjecturally restored by the author of this work in his *Beiträge zur Kritik und Erklärung griech. Schriftsteller,* iii. 26 (= 586, Wiener Sitzungsber., 1876).

BOOK III.—CHAPTER III.

Page 371, l. 21. Diogenes of Apollonia : he is treated by Laert. Diog. (ix. ch. 9), who quotes his proëm, but otherwise deals with him very scantily. The fragments are in Schorn (cf. note to p. 208, *supr.*) and in Panzerbieter, *Diogenes Apolloniates*, Leipsic, 1830. Also cf. Chr. Petersen, *Hippocratis nomine quæ circumferuntur scripta*, etc. (Hamburger Gymnasial-Programm, 1839) ; Diels' above-mentioned discourse on Leucippus and Democritus, and his essays on "Leukippos und Diogenes von Apollonia" (*Rheinisches Museum*, xlii. 1 *ff.* ; and "Über die Excerpte von Menons Iatrika" (*Hermes*, xxviii. 427 *ff.*). The chief evidence is that of Theophrastus (Doxogr., 477, 5).

Page 373, l. 21. On the wording of this slightly corrupt passage, cf. my *Beiträge zur Kritik und Erklärung*, etc., i. 39 (= 271, Wiener Sitzungsberichte, 1875).

Page 374, l. 22. The "Theory of Heaven" (μετεωρολογία), and likewise the treatise περὶ ἀνθρώπου φύσεως, were not actually seen by Simplicius, to whom we are once more indebted for nearly all the fragments ; he only found them mentioned in the principal work of Diogenes (*Phys.*, i. 4, p. 151, Diels).

Page 375, l. 13. The remark on Homer is in Philodemus, *On Piety*, p. 70 of my edition. Dümmler (*Akademika*, 113) seeks to show that the Stoics depended on Diogenes "in their theory of perception and also in their . . . embryology." Dümmler (*ibid.* 225), and Weygoldt besides (*Archiv*, i. 161 *ff.*), discuss the relation of Diogenes to certain treatises in the Hippocratic collection.

Page 376, l. 21. For Theophrastus' "critical review of the psychology of Diogenes," see *De Sensibus*, 39 *ff.* (Doxogr., 510 *ff.*). The verse quoted (l. 35) from the *Clouds* of Aristophanes runs : Δῖνος βασιλεύει τὸν Δί' ἐξεληλακώς (828 Meineke, repeated 1472 ; cf., too, 380 *f.*).

Page 377, l. 20. Hippo : the fragments of the Πανόπται in Kock, *Comicorum Atticorum Fragmenta*, i. 60 *ff.* For the single fragment (l. 24), cp. Nicole, *Les scolies Genevoises de l'Iliade*, i. 198 (Geneva, 1891) ; it maintains the opinion, much discussed at that time, that the water of all springs and wells is derived from the sea. On this, cf. Diels, "Über die Genfer Fragmente des Xenophanes und Hippon," in the *Berliner Sitzungsberichte*, 1891, 575 *ff.* Aristotle's remark is from *Metaphys.*, i. 3, and *De Anima*, i. 2. My own views in the text (l. 27) rest on a combination of Aristotle's *Metaphys.*, i. 3, of his commentator Alexander on the passage (p. 21, 17, Bonitz), and of Hippolytus, i. 16 (Doxogr., 566, 20). The valuable information of Hippolytus first permitted us to include Hippo in the eclectic movement of the age, whereas the bald and all too brief statement of Aristotle made him appear as a singularly belated follower of Thales.

Page 377, l. 34. Archelaus : cf. Laert. Diog., ii. ch. 4 ; further,

Theophrastus, in Doxogr., 479 *f.*, Ætius (*ibid.*, 280), Hippolytus, i. 9 (*ibid.*, 563).

Page 378, § 3. I recovered Metrodorus' "allegorical key to Homer" from *Herculanensium Voluminum Collectio Altera*, vii. 90, on the basis of a short note in the lexicographer Hesychius, Ἀγαμέμνων· τὸν αἰθέρα Μητρόδωρος ἀλληγορικῶς. This "find" was first published in the *Academy*, 15 Jan., 1873.

Renan's "remark about Philo's allegorizing interpretation of the scriptures :" *Histoire du peuple d'Israël*, v. 349.

On Theagenes and his followers, cf. Bergk, *Griechische Litteratur-Geschichte*, i. 264, 891. The apology of Theagenes is mentioned in a scholion to *Iliad*, xx. 67. His "floruit" (or birth, γεγονώς ?) is fixed by Tatian (*Adv. Græc.*, cap. 48), in the reign of Cambyses, *i.e.* between 529 and 522, so that he was a neighbour of Xenophanes in a temporal no less than in a local sense. We have already mentioned Democritus' share in the allegorical interpretation ; the share of Anaxagoras is warranted by a tradition, which has been quite needlessly suspected, in Laert. Diog., ii. 11.

BOOK III.—CHAPTER IV.

Page 381. Here, and also in the following chapter, I have to some extent drawn on my old essay, "The Greek Sophists" (*Deutsche Jahrbücher für Politik und Litteratur*, April, 1863), in part verbally, and in part with sundry additions and corrections.

Page 384, l. 18. "Introduction of foreign cults :" cf. M. Clerc, *Les métèques Athéniens*, 118 *ff.*, Paris, 1893. (For the Athenians' love of strangers as extended even to the gods, see Strabo, x. 3, 18, p. 471.) Cf. Foucart, *Les associations réligieuses chez les Grecs*, 57, Paris, 1873.

Page 386, l. 2. Charondas : The question as to the period of his activity has been treated most recently by Busolt, *Griech. Geschichte*, i. 279, n. 1, but unfortunately still without finality. Aristotle (l. 3) on Charondas, *Politics*, ii. 12. For his "law relating to the guardianship of orphans" (l. 6), see Diodorus, xii. 15.

Pages 386, 387. "Professional authorship :" the art of cooking, by Mithæcus, see Plato, *Gorgias*, 518 C. Athenæus, i. p. 5 B, preserves a little of a versified work of this kind by Philoxenus the Leucadian. The books of Democritus on tactics and warfare appear in the catalogue of his writings, Laert. Diog., ix. 48. His treatises on painting and agriculture are also mentioned there. (The doubts as to the authenticity of the last-named work expressed by Gemoll, *Untersuchungen über die Quellen . . . der Geoponica*, 125, Berlin, 1883, seem to me utterly unfounded.) The *Dietetics* of Herodicus of Selymbria are several times mentioned by Plato, in the Hippocratic writings, in Galen, etc., and finally in the London

Papyrus. Xenophon in his little treatise περὶ ἱππικῆς names Simon as his predecessor. Lasus of Hermione, who lived at the court of the Pisistratidæ, is called by Suidas the oldest theorist in music. There seems to me no doubt, especially after the quotations in Philodemus (cf. my treatise, *Zu Philodems Büchern von der Musik*, 10, Vienna, 1885), that Damon, whose personality and importance are well known, likewise discussed music. Bücheler's reserve (*Rheinisches Museum*, xl. 309 *ff.*) can hardly hold out against these passages. Of Hippias we shall speak later. On the painter Agatharchus, who wrote on scenic decoration, cf. Vitruvius, pref. to Book VII. (also on Anaxagoras, *ibid.*). Sophocles perfected the technique of the stage, and certainly wrote on the Chorus (Suidas, *s.v.*). On the " Canon " of Polycletus, cf. Galen, *De Hippocrat. et Plat. Placitis*, v. 448, Kühn ; the sole fragment, a small one, is in Philo, *Mechanic. Syntaxis*, ed. Schöne, iv. 50, 5 *ff.* A library on the art of soothsaying, apparently not altogether insignificant, is mentioned by the orator Isocrates, *Orat.* 19, 5. Hippodamus of Miletus is treated by Aristotle, *Pol.*, ii. 8. To the category of professional authorship, too, belong the mathematical, astronomical, and rhetorical manuals, which we have not expressly mentioned here.

Page 388, l. 30. Moschion : see Fragm. 6 in Nauck's *Tragicorum Græcorum Fragmenta*, p. 812, ed. 2.

Page 389, l. 2. For the great fragment of the *Sisyphus* of Critias, *ibid.* 771. The treatise by Protagoras " On the Aboriginal State " of mankind (l. 4) is mentioned by Laert. Diog., ix. 55. Plato's reproduction of it (l. 24) is in the dialogue *Protagoras*, 320 C *ff.*

Page 390, l. 30. George Forster : see the introduction to the German translation of *Cook's Third Voyage*, v. 67 *ff.*, in the edition of Gervinus.

Pages 391, 392. Locke's treatises " On Civil Government " are in the fifth vol. of his collected works (10 vols., London, 1823). Chief passages, 398, 400, 405. On p. 398 (§ 103 of the second treatise) is the curious saying about the argument from what has been to what should be.

Page 392, l. 18. Marsilius of Padua : his *Defensor Pacis* was published in manuscript in 1346 ; but the book had been completed before 11 July, 1324 : cf. O. Lorenz, *Deutschlands Geschichtsquellen im Mittelalter*, ii. 349, ed. 3. A noteworthy sentence is the following in c. xii. : " Convenerunt enim homines ad civilem communicationem propter commodum et vitæ sufficientiam consequendam et opposita declinandum." And another : " Quia . . . nemo sibi scienter nocet aut vult iniustum, ideoque volunt omnes aut plurimi legem convenientem communi civium conferenti " (in the sense of the Greek συμφέρον = advantage).

On the earlier medieval forms of the doctrine of the social contract (l. 28), cf. H. von Eicken, *Geschichte und System der mittelalterlichen*

Weltanschauung, 356 *ff.* Friedrich von Gentz did indeed state in so many words that "the social contract is the basis of general political science " (cf. John Austin, *The Province of Jurisprudence*, i. 310, ed. 2) ; but still he added the counter-statement : " The original contract . . . was . . . nowhere actually concluded" (Biester's *Berliner Monatsschrift*, 1793, p. 537). Karl Welcker (died 1869) may be taken as the last representative of the original-contract theory, though, admittedly, in a strongly modified sense ; cf. Bluntschli, *Geschichte des allgemeinen Staatsrechts*, p. 538.

Page 393, l. 31. Plato, *Republic*, ii. 358 E ; the authors of the theory are not mentioned.

Page 394, l. 3. Epicurus : *apud* Laert. Diog., x. 150, and Lucretius, v. 1017 *ff.*, 1141 *ff.*

Page 394, § 5. John Stuart Mill : *Essays on Some Unsettled Questions of Political Economy*, p. 157 (London, 1844) : " But while the philosopher and the practical man bandy half-truths with one another, we may seek far without finding one who, placed on a higher eminence of thought, comprehends as a whole what they see only in separate parts."

Page 395, l. 36. Heraclitus on βίος and βιός, Fragm. 66, Bywater.

Page 396, l. 14. The arguments of Democritus are quoted by Proclus in his commentary on Plato's *Cratylus*, p. 6 of Boissonade's edition.

Page 398, l. 4. Epicurus : the principal passage is in Laert. Diog., x. 75 *f.* Besides Lucretius, v. 1026 *ff.* (Bernays), and Origen, *Contra Celsum*, pp. 18 *ff.* (Spencer), the Oenoanda stone must now be specially consulted ; cp. *Bulletin de correspondance hellénique*, 1892, pp. 43 *ff.* (discussed by myself in the gazette of the Imperial Academy of Sciences, Vienna, 6 July, 1892 ; at greater length, and in many respects better, by Usener, *Rheinisches Museum*, xlvii. 440 *ff.*).

Page 401, l. 15. Darwin, *The Expression of the Emotions*, 270, and 272, 273, 2nd ed., London, 1890.

Page 402, l. 3. Archelaus : besides Laert. Diog., ii. ch. 4, cf. Hippolytus, i. 9 (Doxogr. Gr., 564, 6 *ff.*). Euripides (l. 36) : Fragm. 920 and 168.

Page 403, l. 5. Alcidamas : *Oratores Attici* (Zurich edition), ii. 154. Bardesanes (l. 21) : Excerpts in Eusebius, *Præp. Evang.*, vi. 10 ; the Syriac text in Cureton's *Spicilegium Syriacum*. To this category belongs also the fragment in *The Flinders Petrie Papyri*, i., No. 9, Dublin, 1891. Herodotus (l. 22): iii. 38 ; note also the intentness with which he traces the contrast between Egyptian and Greek usages down to the smallest details, ii. 35. An allied tendency which came to marked expression dominates the narrative of the medieval traveller, Sir John Mandeville.

Page 404, l. 3. The fragment of Pindar quoted by Herodotus is in Bergk, *Poetæ Lyrici Græci*, i. 439, ed. 4. The next quotation (l. 7) is taken from the so-called Διαλέξεις, written in the Doric dialect (*Opuscula moralia*, coll. Orelli, ii. 216 = Mullach, *Fragm. Philos. Gr.*, i. 546 B). On this, cf. Rohde in the *Göttingen University Gazette*, 1884, p. 30 ; Dümmler, *Akademika*, 250 ; and my remarks in the *Deutsche Litteratur-Zeitung*, 1889, col. 1340. Euripides (l. 17), *Ion*, 854 *ff.*, and *Fragm.* 336. Hippias (l. 34), in Plato, *Protagoras*, 337 C.

Page 405. Our remarks on the affinity between the doctrine voiced by Callicles and Heraclitean thought agree very well with the very words in *Gorgias*, 490 A : πολλάκις ἄρα εἶς φρονῶν μυρίων μὴ φρονούντων κρείττων ἐστί, and again : εἰ δ εἶς τῶν μυρίων κρείττων, chiming exactly with Heraclitus, Fragm. 113 : εἶς ἐμοὶ μύριοι, ἐὰν ἄριστος ᾖ, a harmony which did not remain unnoticed even in antiquity ; cf. *Olympiodori Scholia in Plat. Gorg.*, p. 267, ed. Jahn, in *Jahrb. für Philol.*, xiv., suppl. vol. (Leipsic, 1848). Bergk's conjecture (*Griech. Litteratur-Geschichte*, iv. 447) that Callicles was but a transparent mask for Charicles, a well-known oligarch of that age, can hardly be correct. The slight change in the form of the name would have been to no purpose, inasmuch as a number of details are introduced about the personality of the man (cf. especially 487 C), which would have been silly if they did not apply to the original, and, if they did, would have frustrated Plato's intention. Callicles appears as a hater of sophists in *Gorgias*, 520 A, where to the question οὐκοῦν ἀκούεις τοιαῦτα λεγόντων τῶν φασκόντων παιδεύειν ἀνθρώπους εἰς ἀρετήν ; he answers, ἔγωγε · ἀλλὰ τί ἂν λέγοις ἀνθρώπων πέρι οὐδενὸς ἀξίων ;

Page 406. The quotations from the *Gorgias* refer to 483 E and 492 D. The phrase occurring between the two about " the rule of the mightier " is a quotation from Haller, against whom Hegel, *Rechtsphilosophie* (Gesam. Werke, viii.), 317, directs a polemic, as spirited as it is clever.

Page 407, § 8. Diagoras of Melos. Of this writer we possess five verses from two different poems (Philodemus, *On Piety*, p. 85, ed. Gomperz), besides the title (*ibid.*) of a third poem. These verses breathe a thoroughly religious spirit, and lend complete credibility to the report that his faith in the gods or in providence was shattered by some unrequited injury of which he was the victim. Cp. the Scholion to Aristophanes, *Clouds*, 830, Meineke; Sext. Emp., 402, 17 *ff.*, Bekker ; and Suidas, *s.v.* Of his prose writings we are acquainted with two titles, the ἀποπυργίζοντες and the Φρύγιοι λόγοι (Suidas ; Tatian, *Or. ad Gr.*, c. 27), both probably designating the same work, in which he seems to have satirized the belief in mysteries, and to have employed that semi-historical method of treating the gods which was later known as the Euhemeristic (cf. Lobeck, *Aglaoph.*, 370 *f.*). A precise date is afforded only by the statement in Diodorus, xiii. 6, that the Athenians had put a price on the head of Diagoras in the year 415-4, during the sensational days of the Mutilation of the Hermæ and kindred occurrences. This is not contradicted by the reference in the speech of Pseudo-Lysias against Andocides, which, according to Jebb, *Attic Orators*, i. 277, ed. 2, was composed in the year 399. It is more difficult to reconcile with it the allusion in the *Clouds* of Aristophanes, 830 (Meineke), according to which the irreligious spirit of the poet must have been notorious as early as 423. Thoroughly confusing are the *data* in Suidas, who places his "floruit" in the 78th Olympiad, and at the same time makes Democritus (who was yet unborn !) emancipate him from slavery. Nor does Eusebius furnish any help, for he at one time reckons Diagoras among the nature-philosophers and at another connects him with the lyric poet Bacchylides, and sets his "floruit," first in the 75th, and secondly in the 78th Olympiad (*Chronicon*, ii. 102 *f.*, Schöne). We may mention in passing the anecdote in Cicero, *De Natura Deorum*, iii. 37, and in Laert. Diog., vi. 59, which wavers between Diagoras and Diogenes the Cynic, nor should we forget in so doing the ludicrous contradictions in which Cicero involves himself (*De N. D.*, ibid. ; and cp. i. 1 and 42).

Page 408, l. 21. Herodotus, i. 32. Euripides (l. 25), *Fragm.* 285. Then Herodotus, iii. 80 *ff.* ; Euripides, *Fragm.* 810 ; *Suppliants*, 911 *ff.* (Nauck) ; and *Fragm.* 1027.

Page 409, l. 19. "The parallel between the cultivation of the intellect and the sowing of a field :" cp. pseudo-Hippocrates, Νόμος (iv. 640, Littré), and *Antiphontis Soph. Fragm.*, 134 (Blass). Natural disposition, education, knowledge, exercise—these ideas appear as early as Thucydides (i. 121, 3), like the worn coinage of currency. We shall have to consider later on what Protagoras has to say on the same subject. "Culture" and "natural disposition" are likewise combined by the author of the pseudo-Hippocratic treatise, "On the Art" (vi. 16, Littré). Cf., further, Democritus (?), *Fragm. mor.*, 130 and 133 (Mullach), which may again be compared with Nauck, *Fragmenta Græcorum Tragicorum*, ed. 2, "Adespota," 516, and Critias, *Fragm.* 6 (Bergk). Echoes of all these discussions in Isocrates, *Orat.* 13, 17 *f.*, and in Plato, *Phædrus*, 269 D.

Page 409, l. 30. Phaleas of Chalcedon : cf. Aristotle, *Politics*, ii. 7. His date may be fixed with approximate certainty by the fact that he was younger than Hippodamus (who πρῶτος τῶν μὴ πολιτευομένων ἐνεχείρησέ τι περὶ πολιτείας εἰπεῖν τῆς ἀρίστης, *ibid.*, 8), and yet evidently older than Plato. In Aristotle's account of the political ideal of Hippodamus, the words ᾤετο δ' εἴδη καὶ τῶν νόμων εἶναι τρία μόνον · περὶ ὧν γὰρ αἱ δίκαι γίνονται, τρία ταῦτ' εἶναι τὸν ἀριθμόν, ὕβριν βλάβην θάνατον can only refer, in my opinion, to penal laws. This is not merely because αἱ δίκαι points to that interpretation, nor because the three given categories can only form the basis of a classification of the penal code, but also because Hippodamus, so far from repealing or limiting legislation for the public welfare, was far rather concerned to extend and enlarge its conventional boundaries. And, apart from this, what room would otherwise be left for constitutional law, for the administrative code, for civil justice? Aristotle uses the word νόμοι in the same restricted sense when he calls Pittacus, and again Draco (with but a slight change of diction), 'an author of νόμων ἀλλ' οὐ πολιτείας (*Pol.*, ii. 12). What the μόνον in the citation is meant to exclude we do not know ; perhaps those portions of criminal law in which the injured—or likewise the injuring—parties are other than human beings?

Page 411, l. 2. For the Aristophanic buffoonery, cp. *Frogs*, 892 *f.* (Meineke): αἰθὴρ ἐμὸν βόσκημα καὶ γλώττης στρόφιγξ καὶ ξύνεσι καὶ μυκτῆρες ὀσφραντήριοι.

BOOK III.—CHAPTER V.

Page 412, l. 8. Ælian, *Var. Hist.*, xii. 32, relates that Gorgias and Hippias wore purple raiment on holiday occasions. On the similar appearance of the rhapsodists, cf. Plato, *Ion*, 530 B. More details, though with but a paltry explanation, are given by Eustathius on *Iliad*, i. *init.* For the description of a richly decked rhapsodist, relating indeed to the very earliest times, cf. Nicolaus Damasc., Fragm. 62 (*Fragm. Hist. Græc.*, iii. 395). The first impulse towards the teaching of drawing (l. 20) was given by the painter Pamphilus of Sicyon, who is mentioned in the *Plutus* of Aristophanes (produced B.C. 388) ; cf. v. 385, Meineke. Cf. Hermann-Blümner, *Privat-Altertümer*, 324 and 473).

Page 413, l. 10. Protagoras of Abdera : in the Platonic dialogue of that name, 318 E. Cf. with this the very similar object pursued by the orator Isocrates in his instruction, *Or.* 15, §§ 304 *f.* (*Oratores Attici*, i. 289 A), and also the way in which Xenophon at least regarded the intercourse of Socrates with young men (*Memor.*, i. 2, 64).

Pages 414, 415. This account is freely adapted to Plato's in the dialogue just alluded to.

Page 416, l. 10. Valuable evidence on the use of the word " sophist " had already been collected in antiquity by the orator Aristides (ii. 407, Dindorf). Æschylus and Sophocles employ the term of clever musicians (cf. the lexicons of those authors for proofs) ; Æschylus, moreover, calls Prometheus a sophist (vv. 62 and 943, Kirchhoff: in the latter passage not without a certain bitterness). Pindar speaks so of musicians and poets, *Isthm.*, 5, 28. The comic poet Cratinus comprises under that designation all the poets, Homer and Hesiod included, σοφιστῶν σμῆνος, *Atticorum Comicorum Fragmenta*, i. 12, Fragm. 2, Kock. The historian Androtion applied the name sophist to the seven sages (Aristides, *loc. cit.*). Herodotus, implicitly at least, calls Solon a sophist (i. 29), and Pythagoras likewise (iv. 95). Diogenes of Apollonia called his predecessors by that name according to Simplic., *Physics*, 151, 26, Diels. In Isocrates

(*Helena*, 9) the sophist is the antithesis of the layman or everyday man ; cf. also *Ad Nicocl.*, 13, and *Ad Demonic.*, 51 (the latter indeed of doubtful authenticity). In a no less honourable sense the word is used by Alcidamas in the exordium of his speech " On the Sophists." The popular decree introduced by Diopeithes (l. 31) is in Plutarch, *Life of Pericles*, ch. 32.

Page 417, l. 5. On the contempt of manual labour, cf. Herodotus, ii. 167. On the Theban law of exclusion (l. 9), cf. Aristotle, *Politics*, iii. 5 (1278 A 25). Later we shall have to treat of Plato's and Aristotle's contempt of industrial activity (l. 11) ; here a couple of examples will suffice : τοὺς φαύλους τε καὶ χειροτέχνας, Plato, *Republic*, iii. 405 A ; ἡ δὲ βελτίστη πόλις οὐ ποιήσει βάναυσον πολίτην, Aristotle, *Politics*, iii. 5, 1278 A 8. For the contempt felt for the orator or writer of speeches (l. 20), cp. the account of the gibes at Antiphon by the comic poet Platon in pseudo-Plutarch, *Vit. X. Orator.*, p. 833 C (= ii. 1015, Dübner), and Philostratus, who is vaguer, *Vit. Sophist.*, i. 15 (= ii. 16, Kayser). On Isocrates, cf. Blass, *Attische Beredsamkeit*, ii. 14, ed. 2, and pseudo-Plutarch, *op. cit.*, 837 B (= 1020, 20, Dübner), to which Blass refers (*ibid.*, 21). Note, too, the satisfaction with which Theopompus, the disciple of Isocrates, in the *Bibliotheca* of Photius, cod. 176, p. 120, Bekker, plumes himself on his own independent means, which saved him from the necessity of writing speeches for pay, or giving lessons as a sophist.

On Lord Byron (l. 27), who sneered at Sir Walter Scott because he wrote for money and " worked for his patrons," cf. Brandes, *Hauptströmungen der Litteratur*, etc., iv. 190. My remarks on the founders of the *Edinburgh Review* are based on Cockburn's *Life of Lord Jeffrey*, i. 133, 136, ii. 70 (Edinburgh, 1852). J. J. Rousseau's antipathy to writing for a livelihood is well known ; cf. his *Confessions*, book 9. Scherer, *Poetik*, 122, says, " In the sixteenth century the payment of authors was not firmly established ; it was still doubtful if it was honourable to accept remuneration."

To look at the thing from the standard of antiquity, the words attributed to Isocrates (*loc. cit.*), ὅτε καὶ ἰδὼν τὸν μισθὸν ἀριθμούμενον, εἶπε δακρύσας ὡς " ἐπέγνων ἐμαυτὸν νῦν τούτοις πεπραμένον," should be compared with those of Xenophon (*Memor.*, i. 2, 6), τοὺς δὲ λαμβάνοντας τῆς ὁμιλίας μισθὸν ἀνδραποδιστὰς ἑαυτῶν ἀπεκάλει. No less striking is the agreement between the utterance of Plato (*Republic*, ix. 590 C), βαναυσία τε καὶ χειροτεχνία διὰ τί, οἴει, ὄνειδος φέρει ; and that of Xenophon (*Cyneg.*, 13, 8), ἀρκεῖ ἑκάστῳ σοφιστὴν κληθῆναι, ὅ ἐστιν ὄνειδος παρά γε τοῖς εὖ φρονοῦσιν. From this point of view we may get to understand Xenophon (*Memor.*, i. 6, 13) expressing his contempt of the sophists in the crude words, καὶ τὴν σοφίαν ὡσαύτως τοὺς μὲν ἀργυρίου τῷ βουλομένῳ πωλοῦντας (remember the πεπραμένον of Isocrates) σοφιστὰς ὥσπερ πόρνους ἀποκαλοῦσιν, though, indeed, the same Xenophon at other times means by "sophists" simply "philosophers : " cf. *Memor.*, i. 1, 11, ὁ καλούμενος ὑπὸ τῶν σοφιστῶν κόσμος; and iv. 2, 1, γράμματα πολλὰ συνειλεγμένον **ποιητῶν** τε καὶ σοφιστῶν τῶν εὐδοκιμωτάτων. And it signifies but little else when Plato (*Protagoras*, 312 A) makes young Hippocrates, "the son of a great and rich family," whose heart is so set on the instruction of Protagoras, answer with a decided "No" and a blush the question if he meant to become a sophist himself. In order not to be misled at this point, let the reader now open his Plutarch at the life of Pericles, ch. 2: "There was never any young gentleman nobly born, that seeing the image of Jupiter (which is in the city of Pisa) desired to become Phidas ; nor Polyclitus, from seeing of Juno, in the city of Argos; nor that desired to be Anacreon, or Philemon, or Archilochus, for that they took pleasure sometime to read their works " (North).

Page 418, l. 16. Cf. (Jowett) Plato, *Gorgias*, 485 D : μετὰ μειρακίων ἐν γωνίᾳ τριῶν ἢ τεττάρων ψιθυρίζοντα. The words are addressed to Socrates, but, as was remarked long ago, they apply better to Plato than to Socrates.

Page 418, l. 38. John Stuart Mill, *Dissertations and Discussions*, iii. 295 (1867), being a reprint of his review of Grote's *Plato*, refers to this passage (*Lysis*, 204 A), which had previously been neglected in the discussion of the present question. In the *Meno*, 85 B, the geometers are called sophists.

Page 419, l. 22. Plato sneers at the trifling fees paid to the sophists, *Apology*, 20 B, C, and *Cratylus*, 384 B ; he reproaches them for their high charges, *ibid.*, 391 B, C, and elsewhere.

Pages 420, 421. The late Professor Henry Sidgwick (*Journal of Philology*, iv. 288 *ff.*) was the first, and, so far, we believe the only, writer to draw attention to the change which the use of the word "sophist" underwent in Plato's own day. This valuable essay ("The Sophists") constitutes, indeed, the most important supplement yet furnished to Grote's treatment of this subject, which Sidgwick justly calls "a historical discovery of the highest order," though it has gained more renown than serious consideration.

Page 421, l. 10. The Aristotelian use of the word "sophist" can be found by any one in Bonitz's excellent Index.

Pages 421, 422. The authorities for the statements here advanced are Isocrates, *Philipp.*, 84 ; Aristides, *op. cit.*; Polybius, xii. 8 ; Plutarch, *Life of Alexander*, chs. 53, 55 ; *Neue Bruchstücke Epikurs*, published by the author of the present work in the *Wiener Sitzungsberichte*, 1876, pp. 91 *f.* (7 *f.* of the separate reprint) ; Galen, iv. 449, Kühn ; Lucian, *De Morte Peregrini*, § 13.

On the use of the word "sophist" in the time of the Roman Empire, see a valuable note in Edwin Hatch, *The Influence of Greek Ideas and Usages upon the Christian Church* (The Hibbert Lectures, 1888), p. 101, n. 2, London, 1890. Just as Plato sneers at the large fees paid to the sophists, so ecclesiastical writers, especially Justin and Tatian, sneer at those paid to the heathen philosophers and rhetoricians of their time (cf. Renan, *Origines du Christianisme*, vi. 483 *ff.*).

Page 423, l. 24. The author has devoted a comprehensive dissertation to the treatise " On the Art," of which frequent use is made in this and the next section (" Die Apologie der Heilkunst," *Wiener Sitzungsberichte*, 1890, No. ix.).

Page 425, § 4. Prodicus : cf. chiefly Welcker's treatise, " Prodikos von Keos, Vorgänger des Socrates " (*Rhein. Museum für Philol.*, i., and reprinted in his *Kleine Schriften*, ii. 393 *ff.*), a treatise eminently distinguished alike by its richness of contents and impartiality of view. Next, see Cougny's valuable little work, *De Prodico Ceio, Socratis Magistro et Antecessore*, Paris, 1857. We possess no actual fragments of Prodicus, for the three sentences in Stobæus (*Florilegium*, i. 236, and ii. 391, Meineke) and in Plutarch (*De Sanit. præc.*, ch. 8 = 151, 4 *f.*, Dübner) can hardly be regarded as such. The personal friendship (l. 36) between Prodicus and Socrates is vouched for by Xenophon (*Conviv.*, iv. 26) and Plato (*Theætetus*, 151 B, *Meno*, 381 D, etc.), who are for once in striking agreement, though Plato, as is his wont, cannot mention the evidently established fact without a tinge of irony.

On the satire of Aristophanes (page 426, l. 4) in the Ταγηνισταί, see Kock, *Atticorum Comicorum Fragmenta*, i. 490. Yet Aristophanes mentions him with special esteem in *Clouds*, 361 (Meineke). The allusion to him in the *Birds*, 692 (Meineke), admits no certain deductions. The quotation in the text (l. 8) from the *Callias* of Æschines has been handed down to us by Athenæus, v. 220 B. The historian Diodorus, as well as Æschines, calls Anaxagoras a sophist, in a passage, too, quite free from animosity : 'Αναξαγόραν τὸν σοφιστήν, διδάσκαλον ὄντα Περικλέους, ὡς ἀσεβοῦντα εἰς τοὺς θεοὺς ἐσυκοφάντουν.

On the influence of Prodicus on the Cynics (l. 29), cf. especially, besides Welcker, Dümmler, *Akademika, passim*. His two books on nature-philosophy are mentioned, with a scanty and not even verbal transcript from them, by Galen, i. 187 ; ii. 130 ; xv. 325, Kühn. Cicero, *De Oratore*, iii. 32, 128, ascribes an active interest in the *natura rerum* to him in conjunction with Protagoras and the orator Thrasymachus.

Antyllus, quoted by Marcellinus, *Vit. Thuc.*, § 36 (in Krüger's edit., ii. 197 ; cf. also Spengel, *Artium Scriptores*, 53 *f.*), credits the influence of Prodicus on Thucydides (page 427, l. 7).

Page 428, l. 1. Euripides : *Suppliants*, 196 *ff.*, ἔλεξε γάρ τις, ὡς τὰ χείρονα πλείω βροτοῖσίν ἐστι τῶν ἀμεινόνων. The deep voice of Prodicus (l. 11) is mentioned by Plato, *Protagoras*, 316 A, where there is also an allusion to his weakly constitution. Plato, *ibid.*, 341 E, hints at the inherited gloom of the inhabitants of Ceos (l. 6) ; cp. Welcker, p. 614. The description of life's evils, and the simile tacked on to it (l. 13 *ff.*), occurs in the pseudo-Platonic *Axiochus*, 360 D, *ff.* For what follows, cf. *ibid.*, 369 B. For the similar remark by Epicurus (l. 21), see Laert. Diog., x. 125.

Here, however, a reservation must be made. The quotations in the last dozen lines are transmitted to us in the pseudo-Platonic *Axiochus.* This is a comparatively late literary production, and its language is all too leniently criticized by K. F. Hermann (*Geschichte und System der platonischen Philosophie*, p. 583), when he calls it, non-Platonic indeed, but for the most part pure Attic. It is far more likely that the little treatise dates from post-Alexandrian times, as seems to be clearly proved by the occurrence of non-Platonic and non-Attic word-forms and constructions in absolute profusion. Now, since the ideas attributed therein to Prodicus partly reappear in later writers (*e.g.* in Crates the Cynic, in Epicurus, and apparently, at least, also in Bion of Borysthenes), one may begin by hazarding the conjecture that the author of the *Axiochus* and these writers did not really draw from a common source, but that he far more probably drew from them. Early and late, many scholars have been found to vote for this view, H. Feddersen's recent discussion being the most confident and searching (*Über den pseudo-platonischen Dialog Axiochos*, Realschul-Programm, Cuxhaven, 1895). After the maturest reflection I cannot subscribe to this judgment. We cannot, indeed, absolutely exclude the possibility that the author of the *Axiochus* may here and there have attributed a thought or a shred of a thought to the old sophist without due right. But he who will carefully read the chief passages—the review of the various stages of life and the simile of death as a creditor—first in the *Axiochus*, and then in its alleged "sources," and will weigh them against one another, he will not be able to resist the impression that the style of the pseudo-Platonic dialogue bears the stamp of complete originality. In it, for example, the successive extinction of the vital functions, the partial death of single organs preceding the total death of the organism, is aptly compared with a series of distraints, with the part-payments, that is to say, wrung by the impatient creditor to compensate him for the postponement of the payment in full. Outwardly like, but essentially quite different, is the simile in Bion, who compares the burdens of old age to the contrivances hit upon by a landlord to relieve his house from the occupancy of a tenant in arrears ; such as, *e.g.*, removing the doors and cutting off the water. Here it is sought to affect the *will* of the tenant. His further stay in the house is to be made unbearable. And as the inconsiderate behaviour of the landlord corresponds to the cruelty of nature, so *quitting* the house in the one case must correspond to *quitting* life in the other. And so it actually is. In the passage concerned, Bion is discussing suicide : in cases of such grave affliction he recommends suicide (in Teles, *apud* Stobæ., *Florilegium*, v. 67 = iii. 46, Wachsmuth-Hense). Now, the more poorly we think of the author of the *Axiochus*—and we have not the least reason to think highly of him—the less likely we are to believe that Bion's simile, brilliant in its way, was transformed by him so cleverly, and was made to serve an essentially different purpose. We must refrain here from entering into further details. Yet, since the composition of the dialogue, however late we may date it, almost certainly does not belong to a time when the writings of Prodicus, especially the *Seasons*, with which we are most concerned, were already forgotten, we can at least hardly doubt that what is put in the mouth of Prodicus is in harmony with the main character of his view of life; indeed, it tallies well with the conception we have formed of him from the fable of Hercules, from some statements in Plato, and from the unassailable testimony of the dialogue *Eryxias*, which, to judge by its language, is more ancient than the *Axiochus*. (I am gratified to find myself in agreement on this subject with Zeller, *Philosophie der Griechen*, i. 1124, n. 2, ed. 5.)

Page 429, l. 4. " Hercules at the parting of the ways : " the fable is told by Xenophon, *Memorabilia*, ii. 1, 21. On the Sophoclean model, already recognized as such by Athenæus (xii. *init.*), cf. Nauck, *Fragm. Trag. Gr.*, p. 209, ed. 2. The subsequent influence of the apologue is very thoroughly treated by Cougny, *op. cit.*, 79 *ff.*; some fresh contributions to the subject are added by Dieterich, *Nekyia*, 191. Cougny (*ibid.*, 38) with some probability interprets " The Seasons " (l. 13) as the various ages of man.

" Eulogy of agriculture" (l. 19). It is legitimate to infer such a purpose from a reference in Themistius (τὰ καλὰ τῆς γεωργίας, *Or.* xxx. p. 349, Dindorf). The "conception of objects indifferent in themselves" (l. 34) is thoroughly discussed, and assigned to Prodicus, in the pseudo-Platonic *Eryxias*, with which cf. Plato, *Euthydemus*, 279 *ff.*

Page 430, l. 3. " Origin of the belief in gods." On this the chief passages are Philodemus, *On Piety*, 71 and 75 *f.* of my edition (my restoration of the text now completed by Diels, *Hermes*, xiii. 1) ; a short sentence from the same in Cicero, *De Natura Deorum*, i. 42, 118 ; and Sextus Emp., *Adv. Math.*, ix. 18, with 39 ; 52 (394, 22 ; 399, 39, and 402, 15, Bekker). J. H. Voss (l. 16), *Mythologische Forschungen*, i. 62 ; and on Persæus (l. 27), cf. Philodemus, *loc. cit.*

Page 431, l. 3. Hippias : cf. the collective account in C. Müller, *Fragm. Hist. Gr.*, ii. 59–63. Only No. 6 therein deserves the name of a fragment ; it was handed down by Clement of Alexandria, *Strom.*, vi. 745 (Pott.), and most recently treated in my *Beiträge zur Kritik und Erklärung*, iv. 13 *f.* (*Wiener Sitzungsberichte*, 1890, 4th treatise). His personality is described in Plato's *Hippias Minor*, and in the *Hippias Major* (perhaps pseudo-Platonic). Cf. also Plato, *Protagoras*, *passim;* and Philostratus, *Vit. Sophist.*, 11 = ii. 13 *f.*, Kayser. On his achievements as a geometer, Tannery, *Pour l'histoire de la science Hellène*, 246, pronounces that " Hippias d'Elis fut un mathématicien remarquable." More on the subject in Allman, *Greek Geometry*, 191.

L. B. Alberti (l. 34) : cf. Burckhardt, *Cultur der Renaissance,* i. 152, ed. 4.

Page 432, l. 21. Plutarch's doubts as to the trustworthiness of the "List of the Olympic Victors" occur in his *Numa* (ch. i.), and have lately won the assent of Mahaffy, *Problems in Greek History,* 68 and 225 *ff.*

Many valuable remarks on the positive contents and the far-reaching influence of Hippias' doctrines are afforded by Dümmler in the *Akademika.*

Page 434, § 6. Antiphon : cf. chiefly H. Sauppe, *De Antiphonte Sophista* (Göttinger Universitäts-Programm, 1867) ; next, the collections of the fragments in the *Oratores Attici,* ii. (Zurich edition) ; in the appendix to Blass, *Antiphontis Orationes,* 130 *ff.,* ed. 2. Cf., also, Croiset in the *Annuaire de l'association pour l'encouragement des études Grecques,* 1883, 143 *ff.*

Page 435, l. 5. On the traces of a naïve realism, cf. the author's *Apologie der Heilkunst,* p. 24; and on the "Art of Consolations" (l. 8), cf. Buresch, *Consolat. Hist. Crit.,* 72 *ff.* On the style and contents of the treatise "On Concord" (l. 11), cf. Philostratus, *Vit. Sophist.,* 15 (ii. 17, Kayser) ; on the literary characteristics of Antiphon generally, cf. Hermogenes, *Rhet. Gr.,* ii. 415 (Spengel).

Page 435, l. 24. We owe the increase in new fragments of Antiphon to Blass, who, in the "Kieler Festprogramm" *De Antiphonte Sophista Jamblichi Auctore,* 1889, has, I think, adduced convincing proofs of the fact that the *Protrepticus* of Jamblichus (ed. Pistelli, 95 *ff.*) contains great pieces from a book of Antiphon, and indeed, as he might have ventured to say without misgiving, from the book περὶ ὁμονοίας. "Thus Grote" (l. 36): not exactly Grote himself, but a reviewer of him (the late Sir William Smith ; originally in the *Quarterly Review,* clxxv. 53), whose "terse and perspicuous" rendering of his own point of view Grote himself quotes with approval, *History of Greece,* vii. 80, 81 n., new ed., 10 vols., 1888. Cf. *The Personal Life of George Grote,* 231.

To what Sauppe (*op. cit.* 9 *ff.*) has said of the influence on Antiphon of the nature-philosophers who preceded him, we may add that Fragm. 94 (Blass) seems reminiscent of Empedoclean doctrines. The effect of it is as follows : Antiphon designates the present order of the universe as "the now ruling διάστασις," and this tallies exactly with the result of a closer investigation of the remaining fragments of Empedocles, viz. that the present state of the universe, in which the elements are for the most part separated from one another, stands under the sign, not of "Friendship," but of waxing "Discord." Cf. also Fragm. 105 (Blass), where the sea is called an exudation, with the Empedoclean γῆς ἱδρῶτα θάλασσαν (Stein, v. 165). Sauppe (*op. cit.*) had already treated with well-founded suspicion the casual remark of Origen that the author of the Ἀλήθειαν had "deposed Providence"

(*Adversus Celsum,* iv. ch. 25). We entirely agree with Sauppe's opinion that Origen read that meaning into Antiphon's treatise, "interpretando et concludendo." In any case, as Sauppe again observed with perfect correctness, not only Fragm. 108, but also 80 (Blass), point to the acknowledgment of a Deity. That two such dissimilar characters— the soothsayer and the aggressive freethinker—should here have been united in one person is so highly improbable, if not utterly impossible, that the report in question, in order to gain credibility, would have to be much better vouched for. An ecclesiastical writer might see a deposing of Providence in any nature-philosopher's attempt to explain the universe—especially in one which tries, after the manner of Empedocles, to trace the arrangement of organic life, and the purpose it fulfils, back to natural causes.

BOOK III.—CHAPTER VI.

Page 438, l. 1. Protagoras : cf. Laert. Diog., ix. ch. 8. The few surviving fragments of his works, as well as all the other information we have about him, are collected and amply discussed in Johannes Frei, *Quæstiones Protagoreæ,* Bonn, 1845, and in A. J. Vitringa, *Disquisitio de Protagoræ vita et philosophia,* Gröningen, 1852.

Of Protagoras' studies in natural science faint but, in my opinion, not uncertain traces are preserved. Cf. Cicero, *De Oratore,* iii. 32 (128) ; Dionys. on Isocrates, i. (p. 536, Reiske) ; Eupolis in the *Flatterers,* Fragm. 146, 147 (i. 297, Kock).

The catalogue of his works in Laert. Diog., ix. 55, is not even a complete list of the "extant" writings (σωζόμενα βιβλία) ; his metaphysical *chef-d'œuvre,* read as recently as by Porphyry, is wanting there.

Heraclides of Pontus (*apud* Diog. Laert., *loc. cit.*) records that he gave laws to the Thurians (l. 21). My conjectural account in the text of the nature of that legislation was more fully advanced in my contribution to the *Beiträge zur Geschichte des griechischen und römischen Rechts,* 93 *ff.,* by Professor Franz Hoffmann, my colleague for jurisprudence (Vienna, 1870). I am now aware that I was anticipated in this by M. H. E. Meier, *Opuscula,* i. 222.

Page 439, l. 5. There is no tradition that Protagoras actually visited Thurii, but it may be taken as extremely probable. On the architecture of the city, cf. Diodorus, xii. 10 ; on Hippodamus there are proofs in Schiller, *De Rebus Thuriorum,* 4. Apollodorus, in extant verses of his Chronicle (Laert. Diog., viii. 52), relates that Empedocles (l. 9) stayed at Thurii soon after its foundation. Herodotus, whom Aristotle (*Rhet.,* iii. 9) calls a Thurian, is generally known to have resided there.

On "the division of the citizens into ten provinces" (l. 11), cf. Diodorus, xii. 11.

The fragment on Pericles (l. 26) is in Plutarch, *Consol. ad Apollon.*, 33.

Page 440, l. 10. An equestrian statue discovered at Eleusis has been identified, with a high degree of probability, as that of the accuser of Protagoras (cf. Brückner, in *Athen. Mitt.*, xiv. 398 *ff.* ; to the contrary, Kaibel, *Stil und Text der* πολιτεία 'Αθηναίων, 186). In the statement that this Pythodorus was one of the Four Hundred (Laert. Diog., ix. 54), I, in common with some others, recognize merely a more exact designation of the person of the accuser, not of the date of the accusation. For it is scarcely probable that in this brief oligarchic interregnum (411 B.C.) the law-courts would have been at work and 500 Heliasts have been convoked—this, as shown by the trial of Socrates, being the number required in a charge of ἀσέβεια. But far weightier reasons remain to contradict that assumption. Plato, in his dialogue *Protagoras*, 317 C, puts these words into the sophist's mouth : " There is no one here present of whom I might not be the father " (Jowett). Here Plato, who on this occasion had no reason whatever to confuse chronology, must first of all have thought of Socrates. Now Socrates, who died in 399 B.C., can hardly have been born later than 471 (for the reading πλείω ἑβδομήκοντα in the *Apology*, 17 D, may be taken as unassailable), but likewise not, indeed, much earlier ; otherwise the round number of 70 years would be inadmissible in the *Crito*, 52 E. Thus we arrive at the year 485, or still more probably, at 486 or 487, for the birth of Protagoras. This date also accords with that of the Thurian legislation (443), which could not well have been entrusted to Protagoras until he had established by long practice a considerable reputation as a sophist, and we know that he was about 30 when he took up the profession (cf. Laert. Diog., ix. 56 ; Plato, *Meno*, 91 E). Now, since Apollodorus represents him as living to the age of 70 (" about 70," says Plato, *Meno*, 91 E), it is necessary to place his death, which is said to have followed immediately on the accusation, a few years— say, five or six—before 411. Hence, then, it becomes possible for us to apply to Protagoras those verses from the *Palamedes* of Euripides (Fragm. 588, Nauck, ed. 2) in which even in antiquity an allusion was correctly perceived (Laert. Diog., ii. 44), but was incorrectly applied to the death of Socrates, who was executed 16 years after the production of the play. Another dialectician, Zeno, was also compared with Palamedes (Plato, *Phædrus*, 261 D), for, says the scholiast, he was πανεπιστήμων. And the words of Xenophon (*Memor.*, iv. 2, 33) show how closely in this respect he recalled that mythical personage : τοῦτον γὰρ δὴ πάντες ὑμνοῦσιν ὡς διὰ σοφίαν φθονηθεὶς . . . ἀπώλετο. It remains a moot question whether or not the poet also alluded to his dead friend in his *Ixion* (Philochorus *apud* Laert. Diog., ix. 55).

Page 441, § 2. Of the fragments relating to education, the first two are to be found in Stobæus, *Florilegium*, 29, 80 (iii. 652, Hense), and Cramer, *Anecd. Par.*, i. 174. The third was recovered lately

(Bücheler and Gildemeister in the *Rhein. Museum*, xxvii. 526 *ff.*) from the Syriac translation of pseudo-Plutarch's treatise, περὶ ἀσκήσεως, published by Lagarde in 1858. As I was writing this [1894] I was informed by the kind offices of Diels of a new alleged fragment of Protagoras relating to education, published in Sachau's *Inedita Syriaca*, præf., v. The empty verbiage of this oration hardly admits the thought of genuineness, the less so since a similar fragment which is preserved there, and which flaunts the name of Anaxagoras, looks even more unlike the work of the sage of Clazomenæ than this of the sage of Abdera.

Page 442, l. 11. On the linguistic studies of Protagoras, cf. Laert. Diog., ix. 52, 53 ; Aristotle, *Poetics*, ch. 19 ; *Rhetoric*, iii. 5 ; *Sophist. Elench.*, ch. 14 ; and the gibes in Aristophanes, *Clouds*, 658 *ff.* (Meineke). On Protagoras as an adherent of the "conventional" theory of language (l. 29), cf. my *Apologie der Heilkunst*, 111 *ff.*

Page 444, l. 36. The three words are θώραξ, πόρπαξ, and στύραξ.

Pages 445–448, § 3. Cf. the list of writings in Laert. Diog., ix. 55.

For the following story, cp. Plutarch, *Life of Pericles*, ch. 36 (Stesimbrotus is named as the authority in the next sentence).

On lawsuits against animals, cf. chiefly Karl von Amira, *Tierstrafen und Tierprocesse*, in the Proceedings of the Institut für östreichische Geschichts-Forschung, xii. 545 *ff.* ; also the newspaper *Ausland*, 1869, 477 *ff.* ; Miklosich, *Die Blutrache bei den Slaven*, p. 7 (from the Wiener Denkschriften, 1887) ; Tylor, *Primitive Culture*, i. 259 ; Zend-Avesta, i. (*Sacred Books of the East*, iv.) 159 ; *Rhein. Museum*, xli. 130 *f.* ; finally, Sorel, *Procès contre les animaux*, etc., 16 (Compiègne, 1877). Hegel's remark is in his *Geschichte der Philosophie*, ii. 27, ed. 2 (*Werke*, xiv.). The passage from Plato is in the *Protagoras*, 324 B.

Pages 448–450, § 4. The first sentence of Protagoras' book on the gods is in Laert. Diog., ix. 51.

Lobeck's hint : Protagoras was "accused of Atheism because he denied the cognizability of God through the reason" (A. Lehnerdt, *Auswahl aus Lobecks akademischen Reden*, 189).

On his mode of settling his honorarium, cf. Plato, *Protagoras*, 328 B.C., and Aristotle, *Nicom. Ethics*, ix. 1 (where, however, the oath is not mentioned).

On ἀδηλότης (obscurity, want of perceptibility), cf. Gomperz, *Apologie der Heilkunst*, 143 ; also the use of ἀφανές as practically equivalent to ἄδηλον.

Renan's words are taken from his *Feuilles Détachées*, pp. xvi. *f.*

Page 450, l. 25. The three titles of the chief work of Protagoras occur in Porphyry (*apud* Euseb., *Præp. Evang.*, x. 3 = ii. 463, Gaisford) ; in Plato, *Theætetus*, 161 C ; and in Sextus Emp., *Adv. Math.*, vii. 560 = 202, 27, Bekker. The chief passage is quoted in the *Theætetus*, 152 A, and in Laert. Diog., ix. 51.

Page 451, l. 23. Goethe : in Riemer, *Briefe von und an Goethe* ("Aphorisms"), p. 316.

The author has discussed the meaning of the phrase exhaustively in his *Apologie\ der Heilkunst*, pp. 26 *ff.* His predecessors in preferring the generic interpretation of "man" are : Peipers, *Die Erkenntnisstheorie Platos*, 44 *ff.*; Laas, *Neuere Untersuchungen über Protagoras* (in the Vierteljahrschrift für wissenschaftliche Philosophie, viii. 479 ff.) ; and Halbfass, *Die Berichte des Platon und Aristoteles über Protagoras . . . kritisch untersucht* (in Fleckeisen's *Jahrbucher*, Suppl., xiii. 1882). The author's arguments were partly strengthened and partly modified by W. Jerusalem, *Zur Deutung des Homo- Mensura- Satzes* ("Eranos Vindobonensis," 153 *ff.*) ; he is, however, mistaken in attributing the generic interpretation to Grote likewise. So far was Grote from this, that he even incorporated the individualistic interpretation in his translation of the tenet : "As things appear to me, so they are to me : as they appear to you, so they are to you" (Grote, *Plato*, ii. 323).

Page 455, l. 13. Aristotle, *Metaphys.*, iii. 997 B 35 to 998 A 4. The quotation from Mill (l. 20) refers to his *Logic*, vol. i. bk. ii. ch. 5, §§ 1, 6. Cf. Sir John Herschel, *Essays*, p. 216 ; Helmholtz, in the *Academy*, i. 128 *ff.* (12 Feb., 1870), and *Populäre Aufsätze*, 3rd series, p. 26.

Page 458, l. 38. "In a dream :" *Theætetus*, 201 D. Out of the voluminous Theætetus-literature the following may be specially selected : Schleiermacher's *Einleitung;* Bonitz, *Platonische Studien*, 2nd ed., with special reference to pp. 46–53 ; Dümmler, *Antisthenica*, pp. 56 *ff.*, and *Akademica*, pp. 174 *ff.*

Page 460, l. 22. Timon : Fragm. 48 (*Corp. poes. ep. Gr. ludibundæ*, ii. 163). Aristotle (l. 38), *Metaph.*, 1007 B, 22 *ff.* ; 1009 A, 6 *ff.* ; 1053 A 35.

Page 461, l. 4. Plato, *Cratylus*, 386 A. Judged by the standard of language, the *Cratylus* is not later, but—however little—earlier, than the *Theætetus* (cp. Dittenberger, *Hermes*, xvi. 321 *ff.*, and Schanz, *ibid.*, xxi. 442 to 449). This circumstance will in all likelihood be urged against the view of the *Theætetus* advanced on pp. 458, 459 of our text. But, apart from the fact that the—probably inconsiderable— distance of time between the two dialogues does not exclude the possibility that Plato was already busy with the *Theætetus* when he published the *Cratylus;* apart from this, and other like possibilities, I have in no wise maintained that the scheme of the *Theætetus* stood alone in permitting its author to expound the homo-mensura tenet in the individualistic form which he there preferred. It was the most suitable place for it, because that exposition helped to smooth the way for the extensive account of the fictitious Protagorean theory of cognition. Still, there was nothing to prevent him from introducing and casually mentioning it, as he actually does in the *Cratylus*, in any other place ;

in none, however, does the historical figure of Protagoras appear in as strong a light as in the dialogue that bears his name. I have already willingly admitted that this interpretation can be drawn as a deduction from the statement, directly contained in the words of Protagoras, that every perception has an objective reality as its basis. And I shall be equally willing to admit that the subjective theory is directly contained in that statement, and that the intention of the sophist was directed thereto, as soon as any one has confuted my arguments against the traditional acceptation of the tenet. This, however, no one of my critics has as yet even attempted to do. For the rest, cp. to the close of § 5, my *Apologie der Heilkunst*, 173–178. It is highly deplorable that we depend for our information anent the polemic of Democritus against Protagoras solely on an isolated notice in Sextus Emp., *Adv. Mathem.*, vii. 389 (p. 275, Bekker). On this, cp. *Apologie der Heilkunst*, 176. We may add that Plato (*Euthydemus*, 286 C), in referring the doctrine (of Antisthenes) that there is no ἀντιλέγειν back to Protagoras "and others yet more ancient," can hardly have been thinking of the homo-mensura tenet, which is, on the contrary, always represented as striking astonishment by its novelty. In conclusion, we may point to the paraphrase by Hermias, *Irrisio Gent. Philos.*, c. 9 (Doxogr. Gr., 653), which agrees almost exactly with the view we have taken : Πρωταγόρας . . . φάσκων· ὅρος καὶ κρίσις τῶν πραγμάτων ὁ ἄνθρωπος, καὶ τὰ μὲν ὑποπίπτοντα ταῖς αἰσθήσεσιν ἔστιν πράγματα, τὰ δὲ μὴ ὑποπίπτοντα οὐκ ἔστιν ἐν τοῖς εἴδεσι τῆς οὐσίας. On this also, cp. *Apologie der Heilkunst*, 174.

Page 462, § 6. "Two Speeches:" cf. Laert. Diog., ix. 51; Euripides, Fragm. 189, Nauck, ed. 2; Isocrates, *Orat.* 10, *init.* Seneca (*Epist. Moral.*, 88, 43 = iii. 254, Haase) is alone in having understood the sentence as if the two λόγοι were of equal value. This, however, as already perceived by Bernays (*Rhein. Mus.*, vii. 467), is by no means implied in the text of the utterance. The doctrine, we may add, belongs to Arcesilaus (cf. Euseb., *Præp. Evang.*, 14, 4 = iii. 430, Gaisford).

Page 463. The four quotations on this page will be found in Diderot, *Œuvres Complètes* (ed. Assézat), ii. 120; Alexander Bain, *John Stuart Mill: a Criticism* (1882), p. 104; Mill's own *Dissertations and Discussions* (1867), iii. 331; and Goethe, *Gespräche mit Eckermann* (3rd ed.), i. 241.

Page 464, l. 18. Aristoxenus: cf. Laert. Diog., iii. 37; discussed more exhaustively in my *Apologie der Heilkunst*, 184 *f.* Timon (l. 33): Fragm. 10 (*op. cit.*, p. 109).

Though Laert. Diog., ix. 55, ascribes to Protagoras a τέχνη ἐριστικῶν, and, in § 51, adds to the sentence about the δύο λόγοι the remark οἷς κα. συνηρώτα, yet neither the one statement nor the other can yield us a conception of the Protagorean dialectic different from that which the Platonic dialogue supplies. Nobody ever called himself an Eristic;

the term remained at all times one of disparagement (cf. Isocrates, *Orat.* 10, *init.*, οἱ περὶ τὰς ἔριδας διατρίβοντες) ; so that the above-mentioned title of his book cannot have been of Protagoras' own choosing. But if the book—doubtless his τέχνη, or text-book of Rhetoric—showed a great dexterity in argument, and gave instruction in the art of making speeches for and against a thesis, this was ground enough for our compiler, or rather for his authorities, to bestow that designation upon it.

Page 466, l. 2. In calling the *Sophistes* of Plato "one of his latest dialogues," I find myself in agreement with the great majority of modern Platonic scholars. Yet, since so great an authority as Zeller opposes this conclusion, I should certainly not omit to establish it here, were it not that a later volume of this work will be infinitely better suited for that purpose. Accordingly, at this point I shall merely express my conviction that in the whole range of Platonic inquiry nothing has been more triumphantly established than the chronology of the writings classed as ii. *b* by Dittenberger (*Hermes*, xvi. 326) ; cf. now especially Prof. Lewis Campbell, *Plato's Republic*, ii. 46 *ff.* (Oxford, 1894).

Page 466, § 7. The passage herein discussed of the Platonic *Sophistes* (232 D) was differently taken and rendered by me in the *Apologie der Heilkunst,* 181 *f.* Since then I have been happy to avail myself of the learning of my reviewers, and of several private correspondents, and to admit that my then interpretation, which agreed with Campbell's and Jowett's, was wrong. The context forces us to the conviction that we must make the best of the somewhat harsh hyperbaton (in the position of αὐτόν). This is the sole point on which I have considered myself obliged to modify the statements contained in that book of mine which has been so frequently mentioned. It is likewise my firm conviction that the removal of this sorry prop has not in any way damaged the structure of argument which is therein built up. As to the other contents of this paragraph, I must again refer to the *Apol. der Heilkunst*, where the present hints are more fully developed.

Page 471, § 8. Aristotle: *Rhetoric,* ii. 24 *fin.*

For what follows, cf. Plato, *Apology*, 23 D ; and Isocrates, *Orat.* 15, §§ 16 and 32. Cf. also the excellent remarks of Grote, *History of Greece*, vii. 46 *n.* (10 vols., 1888), where he decisively condemns the use commonly made of the Aristophanic burlesque, in which the δίκαιος and the ἄδικος λόγος are introduced as speakers : "If Aristophanês is a witness against any one, he is a witness against Sokratês, who is the person singled out for attack in the 'Clouds.' But these authors [Ritter and Brandis are named in the text], not admitting Aristophanês as an evidence against Sokratês whom he *does* attack, nevertheless quote him as an evidence against men like Protagoras and Gorgias whom he *does not* attack."

On what follows, cf. especially Aristotle, *Rhetoric,* i. 1 (1355 A, B) ; Plato, *Gorgias,* 456 D ; Sextus Emp., *Adv. Math.,* ii. 44 (683, 22 *ff.,* Bekker) ; Philodemus, in his rhetorical writings, *passim* (the passages are discussed by the author of this work in the *Zeitschrift für die Oestr. Gymnasien,* 1866, p. 698) ; Chrysippus, in Plutarch, *De Stoic. Repugn.,* c. 10, 15 (= *Moralia,* 268, 37 *ff.,* Dübner) ; finally, Aristotle, *Rhetoric,* ii. 26 *init. ;* iii. 18 *fin.*

Page 473, l. 12.   Aristotle : *Rhetoric,* i. 1 *fin.* ; further, cp. above, notes to pp. 448–450 ; and Plato, *Protagoras,* 351 D.   On Protagoras as " a teacher of rhetoric " (l. 37), cp. the evidence in Frei, *Quæst. Protag.,* pp. 150 *ff.*

Page 474, l. 24.   Quintilian : *Inst. Orat.,* ii. 1, 12.

BOOK III.—CHAPTER VII.

Page 476, § 1.   The life of Gorgias had been treated by Hermippus and Clearchus in their biographies (Athenæus, xi. 505 D, and xii. 548 D).   Trustworthy data are now lacking concerning his birth and death.   We may believe Apollodorus (*apud* Laert. Diog., viii. 58) that he lived to be 109 years old.   He survived Socrates (Plato, *Apology,* 19 E), and spent his last years in Thessaly, where (according to Pausanias, vi. 17, 9) he enjoyed the favour of Jason of Pheræ, who ascended the throne *circ.* 380.   By far the greatest part of his long life, however, evidently falls in the fifth century, so that at the time of his appearance as an envoy in Athens (Diodorus, xii. 53) he was already approaching old age.   Diels, in his *Gorgias und Empedocles,* p. 3, holds " firmly to Frei's delimitation, 483–375 " (*Rhein. Museum,* New Series, vii. 527 *ff.*).   Von Wilamowitz not improbably fixes his Olympic oration in the summer of 408 (*Aristoteles und Athen,* i. 172).   He is treated most fully, though not without an admixture of anachronisms (cf. *Apologie der Heilkunst,* 171 *f.*), by Philostratus, *Vitæ Sophist.,* c. 9 ; and, in modern times, by Blass, *Attische Beredsamkeit,* i. 47 *ff.,* ed. 2.   The fragments are collected in *Oratores Attici,* ii. 129 *ff.* Bernays (*Rhein. Museum,* New Series, viii. 432) has added the fragment of the Olympic oration preserved by Clement of Alexandria, *Strom.* i. ch. 11 (346, Potter).

On the ridicule of Thrasymachus (l. 17) in the Δαιταλεῖς of Aristophanes, see Kock, *Atticorum Comicorum Fragmenta,* i. 439.

Page 477, l. 7.   The last words of Gorgias are in Ælian, *Var. Hist.,* ii. 35.   The inscription on the base of the Olympic statue (l. 15) is in Kaibel, *Epigr. Gr.,* p. 534.

Page 478, l. 6.   Shakespeare, *Macbeth,* iii. 4 : " Our monuments shall be the maws of kites."   The two similes of Gorgias were censured by Longinus, περὶ ὕψους, iii. 2 (p. 5, Jahn-Vahlen).

The characteristics of the *alto estilo* (l. 37) are taken from

Landmann's essay, *Shakspere and Euphuism,* in the Transactions of the New Shakspere Society, Series I., 1880–86, p. 250.

Page 479, l. 8. "Falstaff's speech:" *Henry IV., Pt. I.,* ii. 4. This passage, which we follow Brandes (*William Shakespeare, A Critical Study,* i. 53) in selecting as characteristic, is likewise quoted by Landmann (*ibid.*). The reader will note the alliteration with *d*rink, *t*ears, *p*leasure, *p*assion, *w*ords, *w*oes.

Page 479, l. 27. In rejecting the two declamations that have come down under the name of Gorgias, I follow Leonhard Spengel's demonstration (*Artium Scriptores,* 73 *ff.*), which has been frequently ignored but never confuted; cp. my *Apologie der Heilkunst,* 165 *f.,* and Von Wilamowitz, *Aristoteles und Athen.,* i. 172.

Page 481, l. 5. On the relation of Gorgias to Empedocles, cp. Satyrus, *apud* Laert. Diog., viii. 58, and Diels' illuminating discussion in his *Gorgias und Empedocles,* to which such frequent reference has been made.

The "little work which used to be ascribed to Aristotle" (l. 30) has been best and most recently edited by Apelt in the collection *Aristotelis quæ feruntur de plantis,* etc., Leipsic, 1888. Our note on page 155, *supra,* should be consulted at this point. It is absolutely out of the question to regard this treatise as the work even of Theophrastus, to whom the Vatican MS. ascribes it, and to whom Simplicius—elsewhere so well informed—seems likewise to have attributed it (*Phys.,* 22, 26, Diels); especially, we may add, on account of the notices it contains about Anaximander (975 B 12; cp., too, the wrong φασί τινες, *ibid.,* l. 7). A complement to the account in this *libellus* is furnished by Sextus, *Adv. Math.,* vii. 65 *ff.* = 203 *ff.,* Bekker.

Page 483, l. 36. A most modern parallel to the second argument for the first thesis of Gorgias is offered by Mansel's ratiocination, noted in Mill's *Examination of Sir William Hamilton's Philosophy,* p. 114, 3rd edit.

Page 487, l. 23. A "critical discussion" of the Empedoclean doctrine formed the contents of the ἐξήγησις Ἐμπεδοκλέους, mentioned by Suidas, *s.v.* Ζήνων—as Diels, *Gorgias und Empedokles,* 17 [359], has shown to be in the highest degree probable.

Page 488, l. 10. George Grote: *Plato,* i. 107 *f.,* and *History of Greece,* vii. 51 (10 vols., 1888). The "remark" (l. 14) in contradiction therewith is in Zeller, *Philos. der Griechen,* i. 1104, 5th edit.

Page 489, l. 9. Cp. Windelband, *Geschichte der Philosophie,* 69. Our sole authority on Xeniades (l. 12) is Sextus, *Adv. Math.,* vii. 53 = 201, 9 *ff.,* Bekker. A notable parallel occurs in the Rig Veda, x. 72, 3 : "Existence, in the earliest age of Gods, from Non-existence sprang" [Griffith, *Hymns of the Rig Veda,* ii. 486, Benares, 2nd edit., 1897. The translator is indebted for this reference to Mrs. Max Müller].

Page 491, l. 21. The quotation is from Plato, *Protag.,* 334 C.

The "earliest experiment in definition proper " (l. 32) is from [Hippo-crates] *De Arte*, § 3 (Littré, vi. 4).

Page 492, l. 1.   Democritus : cp. Mullach, 209 (from Sextus, *Adv. Math.*, vii. 265 = 248, 25, Bekker) : ἄνθρωπος ἐστιν ὃ πάντις ἴδμεν. Very similarly Pascal (*Pensées*, i. 2, Paris edit., 1823, p. 28) : "Quelle nécessité y a-t-il d'expliquer ce qu'on entend par le mot *homme ?* Ne sait-on pas assez quelle est la chose qu'on veut désigner par ce terme ?" Genuine attempts at definition by Democritus and the Pythagoreans are mentioned by Aristotle, *Metaph.*, xiii. 4 (1078 B 19, *ff*.).   Autolycus (l. 10) : cp. *Autolyci de Sphæra*, etc., edit. Hultsch, Leipsic, 1885, pp. 2 and 48.   Cp., too, the definition of Number attributed to Thales in *Iamblichi in Nicomachi Arithm. Introduct. Liber* (Pistelli, p. 10) with the remarks of Hultsch, *Berliner Philologische Wochenschrift*, 15 June, 1895, column 775.   The invaluable fragment of Eudemus (*Fragmenta coll. Spengel*, 113 *ff*.) instructs us on the earliest phases of the study of geometry, as likewise the oldest surviving geometrical demonstration (by Hippocrates of Chios, middle of the fifth century) *apud* Simplic., *Phys.*, 60 *ff*., Diels.   Gorgias' definition of rhetoric (l. 20) : *Oratores Attici*, ii. 130 B 18.   The definition of colour is in Plato, *Meno*, 76 D (where I should defend σχημάτων against Diels, *Gorgias und Empedokles*, 8, who otherwise has materially furthered the comprehension of the definition).

On what follows, cp. Plato, *Timæus*, 67 C, and *Philebus*, 58 A *ff*. (see Hirzel, *Hermes*, x. 254, and Dümmler, *Akademika*, 33).

Page 493, l. 7.   The oration of Alcidamas " On the Sophists " is now in the appendix to Blass, *Antiphontis Orationes*, edit. 2, Leipsic, 1881.   His Φυσικός is mentioned by Laert. Diog., viii. 56.

On Polus (l. 15) as a student of nature, cp. Plato, Gorgias, 465 D.,

On the tomb of Isocrates (l. 20), cp. Pseudo-Plutarch, *Vit. x. Orat.*, iv. 26 (1021, 43, Dübner).

On Lycophron's avoidance of the copula (l. 34), cp. Aristotle, *Phys.*, i. 2 (185 B 27).

Page 494, l. 10.   " The Xenophontic Socrates " : *Memor.*, i. 1, 14, and iv. 7, 2 *ff*.

BOOK III.—CHAPTER VIII.

Pages 497, 498.   The fragments of the historians here mentioned are to be found in C. Müller's *Fragmenta Historicorum Græcorum*.

On Stesimbrotus, cf. Heuer's *Münsterer Dissertation* (1863), supple-mented now by fresh fragments in Philodemus, *On Piety*, pp. 22, 41 *f*., 45 of my edition.

On the oldest historical writings on literature and music, cf. Hiller, *Rheinisches Museum*, xli. 401.

Page 498, l. 2.   The " thought " uttered by Democritus is from

Philodemus, *De Musica*, col. 36 (Kemke, p. 108), with which cf. Plato, *Critias*, 110 A, and Aristotle, *Metaphys.*, 981 B, 20.

On the earliest chronological publications, cf. Unger, in Iwan Müller's *Handbuch der Klassischen Altertumswissensch.*, i. 573.

Page 499. Here we would especially refer to the brilliant and thoughtful University Festival Oration by the late Rudolf Schöll, whom learning lost too soon : *Die Anfänge einer politischen Litteratur bei den Griechen* (Munich, 1890). Yet I have not been able to assent to Schöll's view of the "Constitution of Athens," and I contest it on page 500.

Page 502, l. 24. The "accursed Demos" is mentioned in the epitaph on Critias, in the scholia to Æschines, *Adv. Timarch.*, 39 (*Oratores Attici*, ii. 15).

Page 502, § 3. The year 424 B.C. was fixed as the date of publication of the treatise " On the Constitution of Athens," by Kirchhoff, *Die Abfassungszeit der Schrift vom Staate der Athener* (Akademie-Abhandlung), Berlin, 1878. Xenophon's claim to the'Aθηναίων πολιτεία, formerly included in his works, is now very properly disallowed, but no other known author has as yet been allowed to have even a presumptive claim to it.

Page 503, l. 12. Schöll, *op. cit.*, has some excellent remarks on Thucydides' methods of historical research ; likewise Köhler, " Ueber die Archäologie des Thukydides," in *Commentationes Mommsenianæ*, 370 *ff.* There is a brilliantly correct utterance, too, in Scherer, *Poetik*, p. 67.

Page 504, l. 6. "A pupil of Anaxagoras." To this notice of Marcellinus, § 22 (Krüger's edition, ii. 194), K. O. Müller adds the pertinent remark : " We may justly regard him as the Anaxagoras of history " (*History of the Literature of Ancient Greece*, continued by J. W. Donaldson, London, 1858, ii. 132).

The quotation immediately preceding, and those following on pages 504 *ff.*, are from Thucydides, i. 23 ; Herodotus, i. 1 ; Thucydides, i. 22 ; i. 20 ; ii. 15 (very similar with respect to method is Aristotle's discussion, *Constitution of Athens*, c. 3); i. 5, 6.

Page 506, l. 34. Cf. *Odyssey*, iii. 73, and Aristarchus in the scholia.

Page 507, l. 34. For Hellen, the ancestor of the Hellenic race, see Thucydides, i. 3 ; Ion as an historical personage, Aristotle, *Constitution of Athens*, c. 3. On what follows, cf. Thucydides, i. 1–19.

Pages 510, 511. Cf. Thucydides, ii. 54 (oracle about the plague) ; ii. 17 (Pelasgic field) ; v. 103 (superstition denounced) ; v. 26 (duration of the war) ; i. 23 (ominous natural occurrences) ; ii. 8 (earthquake at Delos) ; i. 21 (the word " mythical ").

Pages 512, 513. Cf. Thucydides, ii. 28 (eclipse of the sun) ; vii. 50 (eclipse of the moon) ; vii. 79 (thunderstorm) ; iii. 89 (flood) ; iv. 24 (Charybdis) ; ii. 102 (Achelous) ; ii. 47 *ff.* (description of the plague) ;

vii. 44 (the course of a battle) ; iv. 118 *f.*, v. 18 *f.*, 23 *f.*, 47, 77, 79 (documentary evidence of treaties, apart from those contained in the probably unfinished book, viii. ; of these, v. 47 has been re-discovered as an inscription ; v. 77 and 79 are in the Doric dialect; cf. now Kirchhoff, *Thukydides und sein Urkundenmaterial*, Berlin, 1895); vii. 11 (report of a general, viz. Nicias) ; i. 22 (characterization of the speeches).

Pages 514, 515. Cf. Thucydides, vi. 8 *ff.* (speeches of Nicias and Alcibiades) ; ii. 35 *ff.* (funeral oration of Pericles) ; i. 86 (speech of Sthenelaidas) ; iii. 45 (Diodotus against the deterrent theory).

Pages 516, 517. Cf. Thucydides, vii. 69 (speech of Nicias before the decisive battle) ; iii. 38 (Cleon's censorious speech).

Page 518. Cf. Thucydides, iv. 40 (Cleon's " mad " promise) ; vii. 86 (lament on the death of Nicias) ; iii. 83 (" simplicity " of heart: τὸ εὔηθες οὗ τὸ γενναῖον πλεῖστον μετέχει).

INDEX.

Ecphantus, 120
Edinburgh Review, 417
Education, metaphor from the field,
409, 578; curriculum extended,
412; activity of the sophists, 413;
views of Antiphon, 437; of Protagoras, 441
" Effluvia," 236, 492
Egypt, influence on Greek religion,
96 *f.*; visited by Pythagoras, 100;
visited by Hecatæus, 257 *f.*;
influence on popular medicine,
283; on Mycenean art, 521;
Egyptian geometry, 531
El-Amarna, cuneiform archives, 96
Eleatic school reviewed, 205 *ff.*;
relation with Empedocles, 253;
with the Atomists, 345 *ff.*; polemic
of Protagoras, 450; of Gorgias,
485; authorities, 550
Embryo, Hippocratic views, 291
Empedocles of Acragas (Bk. II. Ch.
V.), 91, 130, 140; and Parmenides,
183; his native city, 227; ambition,
228; versatility, 229; speculative
chemist, 230; doctrine of four
elements, 231 *ff.*; theory of vision,
235; allied physiological doctrines, 236 *ff.*; twin forces of
" Friendship" and " Discord," 239
f.; details of his cosmology, 241 *f.*;
theory of organic being, 243 *f.*;
endows matter with soul, 245; his
dualistic psychology, 246 ff.; self-
contradiction, 251; his harmonious
theology, 252; relation with
Eleatics, 253; summary, 254;
and *corpus Hippocrat.,* 282; as
physician, 285; and Democritus,
336, 355; and Gorgias, 481, 487;
sources, 558
" Empty " hypotheses, 305 *f.*
" English Essay," 474
Epaminondas, 101
Ephesus in the time of Heraclitus, 62
Epicharmes, 313
Epictetus, 77
Epicurus, 330, 356, 394; on lan-
guage, 398
Epidaurus as health-resort, 284
Epilepsy, 312
Epimenides, 91
Equivalents in chemistry, 328
Eristic, 590 *f.*
Ether in contemporary physics, 330
Euclides, 421
Eudemus, 90 *f.*, 94, 140, 144
Eudoxus, 121
Eumolpus, 477

Euphuism, ancient and modern, 480 *f.*
Eupolis, 420
Euripides, 160, 372; on nature and
convention, 404; on happiness,
408; on Prodicus, 428; and Prota-
goras, 440, 462
Euryphon, 288
Εὐθυμία, Democritean, 368
Euthymenes, 498
Exact science, 299
Existence of elements, 45

F

Fairy tales, their migration, 541
" Fall of the soul by sin," 128
" Fate," treatise on, 403
Fechner, 182, 328
Fees, Protagorean mode of settle-
ment, 449, 473
Fetishism, 18 *ff.*; yields to polytheism,
27; exposed by Prodicus, 430;
origin and authorities, 522 *f.*
Fichte, 145
Fine arts, professional studies, 386 *f.*
Fire, in doctrine of Heraclitus, 64
ff.; of Philolaus, 117; of Hippo-
cratic treatise " On Diet," 287; in
atomic hypothesis, 357; in the
legend of Prometheus, 389
Fish-men, 53
Flux in the doctrine of Heraclitus,
68 *ff.*; influence on Parmenides,
167
Forster, George, 390
Franklin, Benjamin, 219
French Revolution, 393, 410
" Friendship " and " Discord," 239 *f.*
" Funeral Oration," of Gorgias,
478; of Pericles, 436, 516

G

Galilei, 321, 329, 349; criticized by
Descartes and Mersenne, 364; and
Aristotelianism, 366; and Archi-
medes, 367
Games of Olympia, 12
Gassendi, 329
Geber, 149
Gender of substantives, 443 *ff.*
" Genealogies," by Hecatæus, 255
" Genesis," 560 *f.*
Geographical exploration, 7 *f.*
Girgenti, 227
Glaucus of Rhegium, 497
Gnomon, 50, 532

END OF VOL. I.

PRINTED IN GREAT BRITAIN BY WILLIAM CLOWES AND SONS, LIMITED, LONDON AND BECCLES.